50,000 Baby Names

C000318903

from Around the World

Published in 2002
by Hinkler Books Pty. Ltd
17–23 Redwood Drive
Dingley, Victoria 3172 Australia

www.hinklerbooks.com

In association with Meadowbrook Press

Printed 2002. Reprinted 2002 (twice), 2003 (twice), 2004

Editor: Liya Lev Oertel
Production Manager: Joe Gagne
Cover Photo: Elena Ungar

© 1999 by Bruce Lansky

All rights reserved. No part of this book may be reproduced or
transmitted in any form or by any means, electronic or mechanical,
including photocopying, recording, or using any information storage and
retrieval system, without written permission from the publisher, except in
the case of brief quotations embodied in critical articles and reviews.

ISBN: 1865157201

Printed and bound in Australia by McPherson's Printing Group

Contents

15 things to consider
when naming your baby

1 NAMESAKES
Exact reproductions of a person's name, even if it is followed by Jr. or II, are often confusing to everyone involved. Parents frequently vary the middle name of a son who carries his father's first and last names, and then call the son by his middle name to distinguish him from his father; but the potential for confusion still exists. What's worse, the child never gets the satisfaction of having a name and a clear identity of his own.

Namesakes can also lead to unfortunate name choices. Somehow the name Mildred just doesn't seem to fit a little girl comfortably, even though it fits eighty-year-old Aunt Mildred perfectly. Generally, make sure that a namesake's name is one you'd choose on its own merits, quite apart from the good feelings you have for the person you're complimenting this way.

2 NATIONALITY
If you choose a 'foreign-sounding' name, be sure it's not unpronounceable or unspellable, or the name will be a burden to your child. Combinations of names from different countries, like Francois Finklebaum or Marco Mazarowski, may provoke smiles. So if you want to combine names with different ethnic roots, try them out on lots of people before making a final decision.

3 RELIGION
To some parents it is important to follow religious traditions in naming a baby. Roman Catholics have

traditionally chosen saints' names, sometimes using Mary as a first name for each daughter and pairing it with different middle names: Mary Rose, Mary Margaret, and so on. Jews traditionally choose Old Testament names, often the name of a deceased relative, while Protestants choose both Old and New Testament names. Muslims turn to the Koran and the names of Mohammed and his family as traditional sources of names.

4 GENDER
There are two opposing lines of thought on names that can be given to boys and girls alike, whether they are changeable ones like Carol/Carroll, Leslie/Lesley, and Claire/Clair or the truly unisex names like Robin, Chris, and Terry. Some parents feel that a unisex name allows them to pick a name with certainty before the baby's sex is known and that such names 'type' children in sexual roles and expectations less than traditional boy-girl names do. Others argue that it's unfair and psychologically harmful to require a child to explain which sex he or she is (remember the song 'A Boy Named Sue'?). Finally, boys feel more threatened or insulted when they are presumed to be girls than girls do when they're taken to be boys.

5 NUMBER OF NAMES
No law requires a person to have three names, though most forms provide spaces for a first name, middle initial or name, and surname. When choosing a name for your child, you have several

options: a first and last name; a first and last name and only a middle initial (Harry S Truman's S is just an S); initials for both first and middle names; or several middle names. Keep your child's lifelong use of the name in mind when you do something unusual—four middle names are going to cause space problems for your child every time he or she fills out a form!

6 SOUNDS
The combination of letters in a person's name can make saying the name easier or harder. Alliteration, as in Tina Turner or Pat Paulsen, is fine, but such rhymes as Tyrone Cohn or Alice Palace invite teasing. Joke names, punning names, and other displays of your wit may sound funny, but living with such a name is no laughing matter.

7 RHYTHMS
Most naming specialists agree that unequal numbers of syllables create pleasing rhythms. Such names as Dwight David Eisenhower or Molly Melinda Grooms fit this pattern. When first and last names have equal numbers of syllables, a middle name with a different number creates a nice effect, as in Albert Anthony Cleveland or Gail Canova Pons. Single-syllable names can be especially forceful if each name has a rather long sound, as in Mark Twain or Charles Rath.

8 PRONUNCIATION
Nobody likes having their name constantly mispronounced. If you pick an unusual name, such as Jésus or Genviève (Hay-soos and Zhan-vee-ev), don't expect people to pronounce them correctly. Other names with high mispronunciation potential are names that have more than one common pronunciation, as in Alicia (does the second syllable rhyme with fish or leash?) or Shana (does the name rhyme with Anna or Dana?). And if you choose a unique pronunciation of

a name (for example, pronouncing Nina like Dinah), don't expect many people to get it right.

9 SPELLING
In his poem Don Juan, Byron writes, 'Thrice happy he whose name has been well spelt,' and it's true that you feel a special kind of irritation when your name gets misspelled.

Ordinary spellings have the force of common sense behind them. On the other hand, a new or unusual spelling can revitalize an old name. If the name Ethel only reminds you of Ethel Mertz in the old I Love Lucy show, but your mate is crazy about having a daughter with that name, perhaps Ethelle will be a happy substitute. However, some people think it's silly to vary from 'traditional' spelling of names and are prejudiced against any Thom, Dik, or Hari.

10 POPULARITY
Some names are so popular you shouldn't be surprised to find more than one child with that name in your child's classroom. A child with a very popular name may feel that he or she must 'share' it with others, while a child with a very uncommon name is likely to feel that it is uniquely his or hers. However, a child with a popular name may be accepted by peers more easily than a child with a very uncommon name, which may be perceived as weird.

11 UNIQUENESS
Did you ever try to look in the phone book for the telephone number of someone called John Smith? You wouldn't be able to find it without also knowing the address. To avoid confusion many people with common last names choose distinctive first and/or middle names for their children. However, a highly unusual name, such as Teague or Hestia, could be an even greater disservice to your child than Michael or Emily.

12 STEREOTYPES

Most names call to mind physical or personality traits that often stem from a well-known namesake, real or fictional. Some names—Adolph and Judas, for instance—may never outlive the terrible associations they receive from a single person who bore them. Because the image of a name will affect its owner's self-image, as well as the way he or she is perceived by others, consider what associations come to mind as you make your selections.

13 INITIALS

Folk wisdom has it that a person whose initials spell a word—any word—is destined to be successful in life. But it can be irksome, even embarrassing, to have DUD or HAG stamped on your suitcases and jewelry. So be sure your child's initials spell 'happy' words—or none at all—to avoid these problems.

14 NICKNAMES

Most names have shortened or familiar forms that are used during childhood or at different stages of life. For example, Michael might be called Mikey as a child, Mike as a teenager, and Michael on his college application. So, if you don't want your daughter to be called Sam, don't name her Samantha.

If you are thinking of giving your child a nickname as a legal name, remember that Trisha may grow weary of explaining that her full name is not Patricia. And consider the fact that names that sound cute for a child, as in Missy and Timmy, could prove embarrassing later in life. Can you picture Grandma Missy and Grandpa Timmy?

15 MEANINGS

Most people don't know the meanings of their names—first, middle, or last. But most names do have meanings, and you should at least find out what your favorite choices mean before giving them to your child. A name that means something funny or embarrassing probably won't overshadow your child's life, but if you have to choose between two names that are equally attractive to you, meanings may help tip the balance.

The 100 most popular Girls' Names in 1998

1. Emily	26. Jasmine	51. Kimberly	76. Caitlin
2. Hannah	27. Stephanie	52. Vanessa	77. Breanna
3. Samantha	28. Alexandra	53. Sierra	78. Briana
4. Ashley	29. Sydney	54. Kelsey	79. Miranda
5. Sarah	30. Rebecca	55. Michelle	80. Alexandria
6. Alexis	31. Julia	56. Erin	81. Autumn
7. Taylor	32. Anna	57. Grace	82. Diana
8. Jessica	33. Katherine	58. Melissa	83. Mikayla
9. Madison	34. Allison	59. Katelyn	84. Cassandra
10. Elizabeth	35. Amber	60. Bailey	85. Kaylee
11. Alyssa	36. Kaitlyn	61. Andrea	86. Kelly
12. Megan	37. Haley	62. Mariah	87. Chloe
13. Kayla	38. Destiny	63. Paige	88. Isabella
14. Lauren	39. Courtney	64. Jenna	89. Katie
15. Rachel	40. Danielle	65. Mackenzie	90. Kathryn
16. Victoria	41. Natalie	66. Marissa	91. Erica
17. Brianna	42. Jordan	67. Sabrina	92. Alexa
18. Amanda	43. Maria	68. Tiffany	93. Claire
19. Abigail	44. Brooke	69. Hailey	94. Chelsea
20. Jennifer	45. Savannah	70. Christina	95. Lindsey
21. Emma	46. Mary	71. Laura	96. Amy
22. Olivia	47. Gabrielle	72. Makayla	97. Monica
23. Morgan	48. Sara	73. Caroline	98. Jacqueline
24. Nicole	49. Madeline	74. Sophia	99. Alicia
25. Brittany	50. Shelby	75. Cheyenne	100. Michaela

The 100 most popular Boys' Names in 1998

1. Michael	26. Dylan	51. Sean	76. Luke
2. Jacob	27. Jordan	52. Juan	77. Jesus
3. Matthew	28. Samuel	53. Jared	78. Cole
4. Joshua	29. Jose	54. Gabriel	79. Stephen
5. Christopher	30. Kevin	55. Alex	80. Antonio
6. Nicholas	31. Noah	56. Richard	81. Garrett
7. Brandon	32. Benjamin	57. Patrick	82. Tanner
8. Tyler	33. Thomas	58. Trevor	83. Blake
9. Andrew	34. Nathan	59. Nathaniel	84. Kenneth
10. Austin	35. Hunter	60. Isaiah	85. Spencer
11. Daniel	36. Cameron	61. Jack	86. Mason
12. Joseph	37. Aaron	62. Carlos	87. Miguel
13. William	38. Ethan	63. Devin	88. Dalton
14. Zachary	39. Eric	64. Evan	89. Seth
15. John	40. Jason	65. Bryan	90. Paul
16. David	41. Brian	66. Mark	91. Victor
17. Ryan	42. Caleb	67. Isaac	92. Tristan
18. Anthony	43. Cody	68. Jeremy	93. Jeffrey
19. James	44. Logan	69. Chase	94. Alejandro
20. Justin	45. Luis	70. Angel	95. Bryce
21. Jonathan	46. Adam	71. Elijah	96. Lucas
22. Alexander	47. Steven	72. Ian	97. Brendan
23. Kyle	48. Connor	73. Adrian	98. Travis
24. Robert	49. Timothy	74. Jesse	99. Marcus
25. Christian	50. Charles	75. Dakota	100. Jake

Most popular names from 1880 to 1990

1880

Boys	Girls
John	Mary
William	Anna
Charles	Elizabeth
George	Margaret
James	Minnie
Joseph	Emma
Frank	Martha
Henry	Alice
Thomas	Marie
Harry	Annie, Sarah (tie)

1890

Boys	Girls
John	Mary
William	Anna
James	Elizabeth
George	Emma
Charles	Margaret
Joseph	Rose
Frank	Ethel
Harry	Florence
Henry	Ida
Edward	Bertha, Helen (tie)

1900

Boys	Girls
John	Mary
William	Helen
James	Anna
George	Margaret
Charles	Ruth
Joseph	Elizabeth
Frank	Marie
Henry	Rose
Robert	Florence
Harry	Bertha

1910

Boys	Girls
John	Mary
William	Helen
James	Margaret
Robert	Dorothy
Joseph	Ruth
Charles	Anna
George	Mildred
Edward	Elizabeth
Frank	Alice
Henry	Ethel

1920

Boys	Girls
John	Mary
William	Dorothy
James	Helen
Robert	Margaret
Joseph	Ruth
Charles	Virginia
George	Elizabeth
Edward	Anna
Thomas	Mildred
Frank	Betty

1930

Boys	Girls
Robert	Mary
James	Betty
John	Dorothy
William	Helen
Richard	Barbara
Charles	Margaret
Donald	Maria
George	Patricia
Joseph	Doris
Edward	Joan, Ruth (tie)

1940

Boys	Girls
James	Mary
Robert	Barbara
John	Patricia
William	Carol
Richard	Judith
Charles	Betty
David	Nancy
Thomas	Maria
Donald	Margaret
Ronald	Linda

1950

Boys	Girls
John	Linda
James	Mary
Robert	Patricia
William	Barbara
Michael	Susan
David	Maria
Richard	Sandra
Thomas	Nancy
Charles	Deborah
Gary	Kathleen

1960

Boys	Girls
David	Mary
Michael	Susan
John	Maria
James	Karen
Robert	Lisa
Mark	Linda
William	Donna
Richard	Patricia
Thomas	Debra
Steven	Deborah

1970

Boys	Girls
Michael	Jennifer
David	Lisa
John	Kimberly
James	Michelle
Robert	Angela
Christopher	Maria
William	Amy
Mark	Melissa
Richard	Mary
Brian	Tracy

1980

Boys	Girls
Michael	Jennifer
Jason	Jessica
Christopher	Amanda
David	Melissa
James	Sarah
Matthew	Nicole
John	Heather
Joshua	Amy
Robert	Mishelle
Daniel	Elizabeth

1990

Boys	Girls
Michael	Jessica
Christopher	Ashley
Joshua	Brittany
Matthew	Amanda
David	Stephanie
Daniel	Jennifer
Andrew	Samantha
Joseph	Sarah
Justin	Megan
James	Lauren

Gender-neutral names

In the past few years, the naming trends have been heading in less traditional directions. One of such trends is using gender-neutral names for both boys and girls. Below is a list of such popular cross-gender names. While **all** the names below are given to both boys and girls, some names are used **equally** by both genders, some are used **more for girls**, and some are used **more for boys**.

Kim
Leigh
Leslie
Lindsay
Lindsey
Lynn
Mackenzie
Madison
Michele
Morgan
Nicola

Paris
Robin
Sandy
Shannon
Shelby
Stacey
Stacy
Stevie
Tracy
Whitney

USED EQUALLY

Avery
Britt
Brook
Carey
Casey
Channing
Gurpreet
Harpreet
Jean

Kayle
Kendal
Kerry
Kirby
Kristian
Loren
Mandeep
Regan
Sandeep

MORE FOR BOYS

Aaron
Adrian
Alex
Austin
Blair
Bobby
Cameron
Charlie
Christian
Corey
Cory
Dakota
Dale
Dallas
Daniel
Darcy
Daryl
Devan
Devin
Devon
Drew
Dusty
Evan

Francis
Frankie
Jan
Jesse
Joel
Jordan
Kendal
Kyle
Lee
Logan
Micah
Michael
Noel
Quinn
Randall
Riley
Ryan
Shawn
Shea
Taylor
Terry
Tory
Tory

MORE FOR GIRLS

Alexis
Ali
Amandeep
Andrea
Angel
Ariel
Ashley
Ashton
Aubrey
Carmen
Courtney
Dana
Dominique

Elisha
Erin
Jackie
Jaime
Jamie
Jayme
Jessie
Jody
Justine
Kacey
Kasey
Kelly
Kelsey

In addition, various spellings of the same name influence how that name is perceived. Below are some examples of how a slightly different spelling determines whether that name is used for girls or boys.

GIRLS	BOYS
Adrienne	Adrien
Billie	Billy
Bobbie, Bobbi	Bobby
Carlyn	Carlin
Casie, Casy	Casey
Codi, Cody	Codey
Cori, Corie, Corrie	Corey, Cory
Dani	Danny
Darci, Darcie	Darcy
Dionne	Dion
Frances	Francis
Gabriell, Gabrielle	Gabriel

GIRLS	BOYS
Geri	Gerry
Jacey	Jace
Jerri	Jerry
Jo	Joe
Juliann	Julian
Kalyn	Kalin
Kellyn	Kellen
Kori	Korey, Kory
Lani	Lanny
Loni	Lonni
Michell, Michelle	Michel
Randi	Randy
Ricki, Rikki	Rickey, Rickie, Ricky
Toni	Tony
Terri	Terry
Tori, Torrie	Torrey

Birthstones and flowers

JANUARY
Birthstone: garnet
Flower: carnation

FEBRUARY
Birthstone: amethyst
Flower: violet

MARCH
Birthstone: aquamarine
Flower: jonquil

APRIL
Birthstone: diamond
Flower: sweet pea

MAY
Birthstone: emerald
Flower: lily of the valley

JUNE
Birthstone: pearl
Flower: rose

JULY
Birthstone: ruby
Flower: larkspur

AUGUST
Birthstone: peridot
Flower: gladiolus

SEPTEMBER
Birthstone: sapphire
Flower: aster

OCTOBER
Birthstone: opal
Flower: calendula

NOVEMBER
Birthstone: topaz
Flower: chrysanthemum

DECEMBER
Birthstone: turquoise
Flower: narcissus

How to create a unique name

Many parents believe that if they give their baby a unique name, their child will grow into a unique person. Of course, every child is born unique, but I don't doubt that a unique name can make a child feel special and proud of his or her name; or special and unhappy with his or her name.

As long as you understand that a unique name can have positive and negative consequences for the child, let's review some ways to create one:

1 SPELL A TRADITIONAL NAME IN A UNIQUE WAY, BUT RETAIN THE PRONUNCIATION. For example you might want to use a phonetic spelling:

Britnee or Britni instead of Brittany
Dwain or Dwane instead of Dwayne
Jesica or Jessika instead of Jessica
Mikul or Mikl instead of Michael

2 ADD A PREFIX, such as Da, De, Ja, Je, La, Le, Na, Ne, Sha, She, Ta, Ti, Tra, Tri, or Wa, to the beginning of a name. For example:

Leron instead of Ron
Deandre instead of Andre
Shakara instead of Kara
Shalena instead of Lena
Taleah instead of Leah
Wanita instead of Nita

3 CHANGE THE LAST SYLLABLE OF THE NAME OR ADD A SYLLABLE TO THE END, such as al, do, el, elle, ika, ique, ita, etta, kita, on, na, nita, rita, shay, von, vonna, vonne, or yell. For example:

Davon instead Dave
Donaldo or Donyell instead of Donald
Erique instead of Erik
Sharika or Sharita instead of Shari
Wondetta or Wondelle instead of Wanda

4 CHANGE THE FIRST LETTER OR LETTERS OF A NAME. For example:

Devin instead of Kevin
Jarryl instead of Darryl
Maura or Naura instead of Laura
Nolly instead of Molly or Polly
Shavonne instead of Yvonne

5 CHOOSE A WORD THAT DESCRIBES A PERSONAL CHARACTERISTIC OR TRAIT YOU ADMIRE. For example:

Faith	Pride
Hope	Tuff

6 CHOOSE A RIVER, MOUNTAIN, CITY, STATE, OR COUNTRY YOU LIKE AS A NAME. For example:

Capri	Montana
China	Nevada
Dakota	Rio

7 CHOOSE AN OCCUPATION OR HOBBY AS A NAME.
For example:

Chantal	Rider
Fisher	Skipper
Hunter	Solo

8 CHOOSE A WEATHER TERM AS A NAME.

For example:

Aurora	Starr
Breezy	Stormi
Dawn	Sunny
Rainy	Windy

9 CHOOSE SOME ASPECT OF NATURE AS A NAME.

For example:

Fawn	Buck
Forest	Robin
Brooke	Skye

10 CHOOSE THE NAME—FIRST OR LAST—OF AN AUTHOR, ARTIST, MUSICIAN, POLITICIAN, OR CHARACTER IN A BOOK, PLAY, OR MOVIE YOU ADMIRE.

For example:

Celine	Prince
Kennedy	Ringo
Matisse	Shania
Monet	Sting

11 CHOOSE THE NAME OF A PRODUCT YOU LIKE:

Chanel	Nike
Cheer	Starbuck
Hershey	Tide

12 COMBINE THE NAMES OF THE TWO PARENTS INTO A NAME.

For example:

Jamal or Jamali is a combination of James and Ali

Mardon is a combination of Mary and Don

Ronell is a combination of Ron and Ellen

After you've had your fun creating a unique name for your child, think again about the fact that your child will have to live with this name for a lifetime. And during that lifetime, tens of thousands of people will form an opinion about your child after seeing the name in print or hearing it. Think carefully about whether this name will give off positive or negative vibes—whether it will be a help or nuisance to your child when he or she is introduced to classmates on the first day of kindergarten or when he or she applies to college or for a job.

Remember, names don't make children unique; biology, parenting, and life experience do. So, pick a name that will present your child to the world in the best possible way.

Countries/languages represented in this book

AFRICAN			
Abaluhya	Lomwe	Tanzanian	Chippewa
Afrikaans	Luganda	Tiv	Choctaw
Akan	Lunyole	Tswana	Comanche
Ashanti	Luo	Twi	Coos
Ateso	Muganda	Ugandan	Dakota
Bambara	Musoga	Umbundu	Dene
Benin	Mwera	Uset	Eskimo
Dutooro	Ngoni	Xhosa	Fox
Egyptian	Nigerian	Yao	Hopi
Ethiopian (Amharic, Tigrinya)	North African	Yoruba	Iroquois
	Nyakusa	Zimbabwean	Kiowa
	Ochi	Zulu	Lakota
Ewe	Rhodesian		Lenape
Fante	Rukigo	**NATIVE AMERICAN**	Mahona
Ga	Runyankore	Algonquin	Mohawk
Ghanian	Runyoro	Apache	Moquelumnan
Hausa	Rutooro	Arapaho	Navajo
Ibo	Shona	Blackfoot	Omaha
Kakwa	Somali	Carrier	Osage
Kikuyu	South African	Cherokee	Pawnee
Kiswahili	Swahili	Cheyenne	Pomo

Ponca

Quiché

Sauk

Shoshone

Sioux

Taos

Tupi-Guarani

Ute

Watamare

Winnebago

Zuni

EAST ASIAN & PACIFIC

Australian

Burmese

Cambodian

Chinese

Filipino

Fijian

Hawaiian

Japanese

Korean

Malayan

Maori

Polynesian

Samoan

Tai

Tibetan

Vietnamese

West Australian
    Aboriginal

EASTERN EUROPEAN & NORTHERN ASIAN

Armenian

Basque

Bulgarian

Czech

Estonian

Hungarian

Latvian

Lithuanian

Mongolian

Polish

Romanian

Russian

Slavic

Turkish

Ukranian

Western
    European

Cornish

Danish

Dutch

English

Finnish

French

German

Gypsy

Icelandic

Irish

Italian

Norwegian

Portugese

Scandinavian

Scottish

Spanish

Swedish

Swiss

Welsh

Yiddish

MIDDLE & NEAR EASTERN

Afghani

Arabic

Hebrew

Hindi

Pakistani

Pashto

Persian

Punjabi

Tamil

Todas

Urdu

SOUTH & NORTH AMERICAN

American

Peruvian

HISTORICAL LANGUAGES

Aramaic

Assyrian

Babylonian

Greek

Latin

Phoenician

Sanskrit

Syrian

Teutonic

Name index by country/language

ABALUHYA	AFRICAN	Kosey	Gyasi
BOYS	**GIRLS**	Liu	Kojo
Jimiyu	Afi	Moswen	Kontar
Nangila	Ama	Ohin	Kwabena
	Baba	Paki	Kwako
AFGHANI	Halla	Senwe	Kwame
GIRLS	Imena	Ulan	Kwasi
Seema	Kia	Zareb	Minkah
Shahla	Pita		Msrah
Yashira	Poni	**AFRIKAANS**	Nsoah
	Reta	**BOYS**	Sono
BOYS	Sharik	Bron	Yawo
Iskander	Siko	Kerel	Yoofi
Matteen	Tawia	**AKAN**	**ALGONQUIN**
Mirwais	Thema	**GIRLS**	**GIRLS**
Nadir	Winna	Morowa	Odina
Yasir	Zina	**BOYS**	**AMERICAN**
Zalmai	**BOYS**	Adom	**GIRLS**
Zelgai	Afram	Bodua	Abelina
Zemar	Bello	Donkor	Abianne

Abinaya	Becky	Camberly	Crisbell
Adaya	Betsy	Camisha	Crystalin
Adriyanna	Bettina	Camri	Daelynn
Ajanae	Beverlyann	Camryn	Daeshawna
Akayla	Billie-Jean	Candi	Dafny
Akeisha	Billie-Jo	Carlisa	Daisha
Akeria	Blinda	Carlissa	Dakayla
Akia	Blondie	Carolane	Dakira
Akira	Bobbette	Caylee	Dalisha
Alaysha	Bobbi	Chalonna	Damonica
Albreanna	Bobbi-Ann	Chanise	Danalyn
Alexanne	Bobbi-Jo	Charnette	Danella
Alora	Bobbi-Lee	Charnika	Danesha
Amberly	Bonnie-Bell	Charyanna	Danessa
Amberlyn	Braelyn	Chavonne	Danessia
Ambria	Brandy-Lynn	Chesarey	Danette
Andee	Brenda-Lee	Chessa	Danice
Anetra	Brieana	Cheyla	Danille
Annjanette	Brooklyn	Cheyna	Danyel
Areli	Brylie	Cissy	Darilynn
Arlynn	Buffy	Corabelle	Darnesha
Babe	Caeley	Coralee	Dashawna
Babs	Caelin	Coralie	Dashonda
Baby	Cailin	Cordasha	Davalinda
Barbie	Caleigh	Coriann	Davalynda
Barbra	Camara	Corianne	Davalynn

(American girls continued)

Davisha

Dawnisha

Daysha

Deandra

Debra

Dedra

Dedriana

Deena

Delacy

Denisha

Deshawna

Dolly

Dondi

Doneshia

Doniella

Doretta

Dori

Dyshawna

Eddy

Elnora

Elodie

Elora

Emilyann

Emmalee

Emmalynn

Emmylou

Fannie

Flo

Frankie

Geena

Genell

Genice

Genita

Gennifer

Geralyn

Geri

Glennesha

Glorianne

Ideashia

Iesha

Isha

Jacalyn

Jacelyn

Jackalyn

Jackeline

Jacki

Jacklyn

Jaclyn

Jacqulin

Jadelyn

Jaelyn

Jailyn

Jakelin

Jakki

Jaleesa

Jalena

Jalesa

Jalia

Jalisa

Jalyn

Jalysa

Jamani

Jamaria

Jamesha

Jammie

Jamonica

Jamylin

Janae

Janai

Janalynn

Janesha

Janessa

Janita

Jaquana

Jaquelen

Jarian

Jas

Jasmarie

Jatara

Jaycee

Jaydee

Jayla

Jalene

Jaylin

Jaylyn

Jazlyn

Jelisa

Jenelle

Jenessa

Jenilee

Jenisa

Jennilee

Jennilyn

Jeri

Jerica

Jerilyn

Jerrica

Jessa

Jessalyn

Jesslyn

Jetta

Jevette

Jimi	Judyann	Karelle	Keneisha
Jimisha	Jumaris	Kariane	Kenisha
Jin	Kacey	Karilynn	Kenyatta
Jinny	Kaci	Karlee	Keosha
Jizelle	Kadedra	Karlene	Kesha
Jo	Kadelyn	Karley	Keshia
Jocacia	Kadesha	Karli	Keyana
Jodi	Kadisha	Karlotte	Keyona
Jodiann	Kaelee	Karolane	Keysha
Johnna	Kaelin	Karolyn	Khrissa
Johnnessa	Kaelyn	Karri	Kiana
Jolisa	Kailee	Karyn	Kianna
Jolynn	Kailyn	Kasey	Kineisha
Jonelle	Kaishawn	Kashawna	Kinsley
Jonesha	Kalee	Kassi	Kiyana
Joni	Kalisa	Kassidy	Kizzy
Jonika	Kalisha	Kaycee	Klaudia
Jonni	Kalyn	Kaydee	Kloe
Jontel	Kameron	Kaylee	Kodi
Joriann	Kamri	Kayleigh	Kolby
Jorja	Kamryn	Kayley	Koral
Josee	Kandace	Kaylin	Kori
Josiane	Kandi	Kaylyn	Kourtney
Joyanne	Kandra	Keandra	Kris
Joycelyn	Kaneisha	Keesha	Krissy
Joylyn	Kapri	Keisha	Kristy

(American girls continued)

Krystal
Krystalee
Krystalynn
Krystle
Kyana
Lachandra
Ladasha
Ladeidra
Ladonna
Lajuana
Lakayla
Lakeisha
Laken
Lakendra
Lakenya
Lakesha
Laketa
Lakresha
Lamesha
Lamonica
Laneisha
Laporsha
Laqueena
Laquinta

Laquisha
Laquita
Lashae
Lashana
Lashanda
Lashawna
Lashonda
Latanya
Latara
Latasha
Latavia
Latesha
Latia
Latisha
Latonya
Latoria
Latosha
Latoya
Latrice
Latricia
Lavonna
Lawanda
Layce
Lekasha
Leneisha
Lindsi

Lissie
Liza
Lizzy
Loni
Lora
Lorelle
Loren
Lori
Lorin
Lou
Luann
Lynda
Lyndsay
Lyndsey
Lynsey
Lysanne
Macayla
Mackenna
Mahalia
Maitlyn
Makaela
Makayla
Makell
Makenna
Malley
Mamie

Marciann
Marcilynn
Marieve
Marilee
Marilou
Markayla
Marquisha
Marybeth
Maryellen
Maryjane
Marykate
Marylou
Maylyn
Mckayla
Mckell
Mckenna
Mekayla
Melly
Melonie
Micki
Mikayla
Mikhaela
Minnie
Moesha
Monisha
Myesha

Mykaela	Qwanisha	Shaday	Shanice
Myriam	Raeann	Shadrika	Shanida
Nakeisha	Raelene	Shajuana	Shanika
Nakeita	Raelyn	Shakarah	Shaniqua
Nakita	Rashawna	Shakeena	Shanise
Nashawna	Rashel	Shakeita	Shanita
Nekeisha	Rayanne	Shakia	Shantal
Nichelle	Raylene	Shalana	Shantana
Niesha	Reanna	Shaleah	Shantara
Nikayla	Reanne	Shaleisha	Shanteca
Nikki	Reshawna	Shalena	Shantel
Nisha	Rexanne	Shalisa	Shanteria
Nitasha	Rickelle	Shalita	Shantesa
Nyesha	Ricki	Shalona	Shantia
Onesha	Ricquel	Shalonda	Shantille
Quadeisha	Roanna	Shalyn	Shantina
Quaneisha	Rodneisha	Shameka	Shantora
Quanesha	Rohana	Shamika	Shantrice
Quanika	Roneisha	Shamiya	Shaquanda
Quanisha	Ronisha	Shanda	Shaqueita
Queisha	Ronni	Shandra	Shaquila
Quenisha	Roshawna	Shaneisha	Shaquira
Quiana	Ruthann	Shaneka	Sharissa
Quinesha	Sadella	Shanel	Sharita
Quinshawna	Saralyn	Shaneta	Sharlotte
Quintrell	Satara	Shania	Sharma

(American girls
continued)

Sharmaine

Shatara

Shatoria

Shavon

Shavonne

Shawanna

Shelsea

Sherylyn

Shevonne

Shiquita

Shug

Sienna

Sindy

Sissy

Sueann

Sueanna

Sugar

Sumaya

Susie

Sylvianne

Taesha

Takayla

Takeisha

Takenya

Takeria

Takila

Takira

Taleah

Taleisha

Talena

Talesha

Talina

Tamesha

Tamila

Taneisha

Tangia

Taniel

Tanika

Tanisha

Tanissa

Tanita

Tarissa

Tashana

Tashara

Tashawna

Tasheena

Tashelle

Tawanna

Tawnya

Teanna

Telisha

Tenesha

Tennille

Teralyn

Terriann

Terrianna

Terrica

Terry-Lynn

Tichina

Tina

Tinesha

Tinisha

Tiona

Tocarra

Tonesha

Tonisha

Tranesha

Trashawn

Trixie

Tyanna

Tyeisha

Tyesha

Tyfany

Tykeisha

Tykera

Tynesha

Tynisha

Tyshanna

Unika

Vantrice

Veanna

Vianey

Vianna

Voneisha

Vontricia

Wakeisha

Waynesha

Yaletha

Yamary

Yamelia

Yaneli

Yanet

Yareli

Yaritza

Yomara

Ysanne

Zabrina

BOYS

Adarius

Ajay

Akshay

Bubba	Dawan	Devaughn	Jailen
Buddy	Daylon	Devayne	Jajuan
Buster	Dayquan	Devonta	Jakari
Butch	Dayshawn	Devonte	Jakeem
Caden	Dayvon	Dewayne	Jalan
Cayden	Dejuan	Dionte	Jalen
Cazzie	Delon	Diquan	Jalin
Ceejay	Delshawn	Dontae	Jalon
Chuck	Demarcus	Dontrell	Jam
Daequan	Demarius	Draven	Jamar
Daeshawn	Demarquis	Dreshawn	Jamarcus
Daevon	Demichael	Drevon	Jamari
Daiquan	Demorris	Dushawn	Jamario
Daivon	Deontae	Dwaun	Jamarquis
Dajuan	Deonte	Gabby	Jamond
Damarcus	Deontre	Gabino	Jamor
Damario	Dequan	Hank	Janeil
Dannon	Deron	J	Jaquan
Dantrell	Desean	Jacari	Jaquarius
Daquan	Deshane	Jace	Jaquavius
Dashawn	Deshaun	Jack	Jaquon
Davante	Deshawn	Jackie	Jareth
Davaris	Deshea	Jacorey	Jashawn
Davion	Deshon	Jadrien	Javante
Davon	Destry	Jaelen	Javonte
Davonte	Devante	Jahmar	Jawaun

(American boys continued)

Jayce

Jayde

Jayden

Jaylee

Jaylin

Jaylon

Jayquan

Jayvon

Jazz

Jequan

Jerrick

Jevonte

Jimbo

Jock

Jomar

Jontay

Jorell

Juwan

Kacey

Kadarius

Kaiven

Kashawn

KC

Keandre

Kendarius

Kenyatta

Keonte

Keshawn

Keyshawn

Kishan

Kyven

Labaron

Ladarian

Ladarius

Ladarrius

Laderrick

Lanny

Laquan

Laquintin

Larnell

Lashawn

Lashon

Lathan

Latravis

Latrell

Lavaughan

Lavon

Ledarius

Lequinton

Leron

Leshawn

Levon

Lucky

Marquan

Marquel

Marquice

Marquon

Marshawn

Maverick

Montel

Mychal

Mykal

Naquan

OJ

Okie

Philly

Pinky

Quadarius

Quamaine

Quandre

Quantavius

Quashawn

Quindarius

Quintavius

Raekwon

Raequan

Raeshawn

Raishawn

Rangle

Raquan

Rashaan

Rashard

Rashaun

Rashawn

Rashean

Rashon

Rayshawn

Rayshod

Rayvon

Rebel

Red

Reno

Reshad

Reshawn

Reshean

Rishad

Rishawn

Rocky

Ronel

Ronté

Roshad

Roshean

Ryker	Tequan	Tyquan	Adra
Sambo	Terrick	Tyran	Afra
Sanjay	Terron	Tyrees	Aiesha
Saquan	Teshawn	Tyrel	Aisha
Savon	Tevan	Tyrick	Akilah
Shaheem	Tevin	Tyrin	Alea
Shaquan	Tevon	Tyron	Alima
Shaquell	Tex	Tyshawn	Aliye
Shaquon	Tiger	Tyvon	Alma
Shavon	Tiquan	Vashawn	Almeda
Shawnta	Tishawn	Woody	Almira
Shiquan	TJ	Wrangle	Amal
Shon	Traquan	Zaquan	Aman
Tadarius	Trashawn	Zeshawn	Amina
Taishawn	Traven	Ziggy	Amira
Tajuan	Travion		Anisa
Taquan	Travon	## APACHE	Ara
Taren	Trayvon	### BOYS	Arin
Taron	Treavon	Cochise	Asha
Taryn	Trequan	Nantan	Ashia
Tashawn	Treshawn	## ARABIC	Aza
Tavon	Trevaughn	### GIRLS	Bibi
Tayshawn	Trevin	Abia	Cala
Tayvon	Trevion	Abida	Callie
Tedrick	Trevon	Adara	Cantara
Telvin	Treyvon	Adila	Elmira

(Arabic girls
  continued)

Emani

Faizah

Fatima

Ghada

Guadalupe

Habiba

Halimah

Hana

Hayfa

Iman

Imani

Jalila

Jamila

Janan

Janna

Jarita

Jena

Jenna

Jesenia

Kadejah

Kadijah

Kaela

Kala

Kalila

Karida

Karimah

Kayla

Kaylah

Keila

Khadijah

Khalida

Laela

Laila

Lakia

Lamis

Lamya

Lateefah

Layla

Leila

Lila

Lilith

Lily

Lina

Lisha

Lucine

Lulu

Lydia

Mahala

Maja

Majidah

Manar

Maritza

Mariyan

Martiza

Marya

May

Maysa

Medina

Mina

Mocha

Mouna

Mumtaz

Muriel

Muslimah

Nabila

Nadda

Nadira

Naila

Najam

Najila

Nakia

Natara

Nekia

Nima

Nisa

Oma

Omaira

Polla

Qadira

Qamra

Qitarah

Qubilah

Rabi

Radeyah

Radwa

Rafa

Ráidah

Raja

Rana

Raniyah

Rasha

Rashieka

Rayya

Rida

Rihana

Rima

Rukan

Saarah

Saba

Sabi

Sabiya

Sadira

Sadiya	Tabina	Zarifa	Alam
Safiya	Tahira	Zaynah	Alem
Sahara	Takia	Zia	Ali
Saida	Talitha	Zita	Alim
Salima	Tara	Zuleika	Altair
Sameh	Thana	Zulima	Amal
Sami	Ulima	Zurafa	Amani
Samira	Vega		Amar
Sana	Wadd	**BOYS**	Amin
Saree	Waheeda	Aaron	Amir
Selma	Walad	Abbud	Amit
Shahar	Xaviera	Abdirahman	Antwan
Shahina	Yamila	Abdul	Antwon
Shakayla	Yaminah	Abdulaziz	Anwar
Shakera	Yashira	Abdullah	Arif
Shakila	Yecenia	Abdulrahman	Asád
Shakira	Yemena	Aden	Asadel
Shakyra	Yesenia	Adham	Aswad
Shamara	Yessenia	Adil	Atif
Shardae	Yiesha	Adnan	Azeem
Shatara	Zada	Ahmad	Azim
Sherika	Zafina	Ahsan	Aziz
Shula	Zafirah	Akbar	Bahir
Skye	Zahra	Akil	Basam
Sommer	Zakia	Akmal	Bilal
Syreeta	Zakiya	Aladdin	Borak

(Arabic boys
continued)

Boutros

Cairo

Caleb

Cemal

Coman

Dabir

Daoud

Dekel

Fadi

Fadil

Fahd

Faisal

Fakhir

Fakih

Farid

Faris

Faruq

Fath

Fatin

Ferran

Firas

Gadi

Gamal

Ghazi

Gilad

Guadalupe

Habib

Haddad

Hadi

Haidar

Hakeem

Hakim

Halim

Hamal

Hamid

Hamza

Hanbal

Hanif

Harb

Harith

Haroun

Hasan

Hashim

Hassan

Hatim

Hibah

Hilel

Hud

Husam

Hussain

Hussein

Hussien

Ibrahim

Imad

Imran

Isa

Isam

Ishaq

Ismael

Ismail

Jabir

Jabril

Jamaal

Jamaine

Jamal

Jamel

Jamil

Japheth

Jawhar

Jemal

Jemel

Jericho

Jermal

Jibril

Jimell

Jumah

Kadar

Kadeem

Kaden

Kadin

Kadir

Kaeden

Kahlil

Kairo

Kale

Kalen

Kali

Kalil

Kaliq

Kamal

Kamil

Kardal

Kareem

Karif

Karim

Kaseem

Kasib

Kasim

Kasimir

Kateb

Kayden

Kayle

Khaldun	Marwan	Nadim	Rafiq
Khälid	Masud	Nadir	Raghib
Khalíl	Mazin	Naeem	Rahul
Khaliq	Mohamad	Nailah	Raíd
Khayru	Mohamed	Najee	Rakim
Khoury	Mohamet	Naji	Rakin
Labib	Mohammad	Najib	Ramadan
Lais	Mohammed	Nakia	Rashaad
Lateef	Mohamud	Nasser	Rashad
Lukman	Mouhamed	Nazih	Rashaud
Lutfi	Mousa	Nibal	Rasheed
Mahammed	Muhammad	Nizam	Rashid
Mahdi	Muhannad	Numa	Rashod
Mahir	Muhsin	Numair	Rayhan
Mahmoud	Muhtadi	Nuri	Reda
Mahmúd	Mujahid	Nuriel	Reyhan
Mahomet	Mukhtar	Nusair	Rida
Maimun	Munir	Omar	Rigel
Majid	Musád	Omer	Riyad
Makin	Mustafa	Qabil	Saddam
Malcolm	Mustapha	Qadim	Sa'id
Malek	Muti	Qadir	Salam
Málik	Nabiha	Qamar	Sálih
Mansür	Nabil	Qasim	Salím
Marid	Nada	Qudamah	Sameer
Marr	Nadidah	Rabi	Samír

(Arabic boys continued)

Samman

Saqr

Sariyah

Sayyid

Seif

Shadi

Shahid

Shakeel

Shakir

Shakur

Shaquille

Sharíf

Shihab

Shunnar

Siraj

Sofian

Subhi

Sued

Suhail

Sulaiman

Syed

Tabari

Tahír

Talib

Tamir

Tarek

Tarif

Tarik

Táriq

Taz

Thabit

Timin

Tut

Ubadah

Umar

Usamah

Uthman

Wahid

Waleed

Wali

Wasim

Wazir

Witha

Xavier

Yahya

Yardan

Yasin

Yasir

Yazid

Yusuf

Zafir

Zahid

Zahir

Zaid

Zaim

Zakariyya

Zaki

Zavier

Zero

Zimraan

Ziyad

Zuhayr

ARAMAIC

GIRLS

Beth

Bethani

Bethany

Mardi

Maren

Marit

Martha

Noor

Nura

Nuria

Razi

Samantha

Shera

Tabatha

Tabetha

Tabitha

Tabytha

Tameka

Tara

BOYS

Barnabas

Og

Razi

Talmai

Talman

Tavares

Tavaris

Tavi

Tavor

Thomas

ARAPAHO

GIRLS

Natane

BOYS

Hosa

Nakos

ARMENIAN

GIRLS

Nairi

Seda

BOYS

Dickran

Jirair

Kaloosh

Khachig

Krikor

Magar

Nishan

Shabouh

Vartan

Yervant

Zeroun

ASHANTI

GIRLS

Kessie

BOYS

Kesse

ASSYRIAN

BOYS

Abel

ATESO

BOYS

Ejau

Opio

AUSTRALIAN

GIRLS

Narelle

AZTEC

GIRLS

Xochitl

BABYLONIAN

GIRLS

Eden

BOYS

Shadrach

Shedrick

BAMBARA

GIRLS

Pemba

BASQUE

GIRLS

Floria

Julene

Kalare

Kesare

Landa

Leire

Lide

Lore

Lucine

Mendi

Molara

Ula

Xaviera

Yera

Yordana

Yulene

Zelizi

Zuri

BOYS

Balasi

Dabi

Dunixi

Edorta

Edur

Errando

Erroman

Estebe

Exavier

Gilamu

Gilen

Iban

Ibon

Iker

Ilan

Ilari

Illan

Inigo

Jakome

Jerolin

Jokin

Kasen

Kelmen

Kemen

Kerbasi

Kerman

Kindin

Kuiril

Lander

Luken

Luki

Maren

Matai

Mikel

Ortzi

(Basque boys continued)

Palben

Patxi

Pelí

Pello

Sabin

Sein

Todor

Txomin

Ugutz

Unai

Urtzi

Xabat

Xaiver

Xarles

Xavier

Xzavier

Yuli

Zadornin

Zigor

Zorion

BENIN

GIRLS

Isoka

Oseye

BOYS

Ode

Odion

Omolara

Osahar

Osayaba

Osaze

BLACKFOOT

GIRLS

Peta

BULGARIAN

BOYS

Andrei

Foma

Gedeon

Grigori

Ioan

Iustin

Kir

Matai

Mihail

Petr

Piotr

Veniamin

BURMESE

GIRLS

Chun

Meit

Mima

Mya

Nu

Yon

BOYS

Lin

Min

Myo

On

Saw

Tan

Than

CAMBODIAN

GIRLS

Chan

Chantrea

Kalliyan

Kannitha

Tevy

Vanna

BOYS

Arun

Bourey

Chankrisna

Dara

Kiri

Munny

Nhean

Phirun

Rangsey

Rithisak

Sovann

Veasna

Win

Yo

CARRIER

GIRLS

Peni

Sadzi

BOYS

Kuzih

Tadzi

Yakez

CHEROKEE

GIRLS

Ayita

Salali

Sequoia

BOYS

Adahy

Cherokee

Tennessee

Tooantuh

CHEYENNE

GIRLS

Cheyanne

Cheyenne

Chyanne

Shaianne

Sheyenne

Shianne

Shyann

BOYS

Cheyenne

Hiamovi

Shayan

Viho

CHINESE

GIRLS

An

Bo

China

Chu Hua

Chyna

Ciana

Hua

Jun

Lee

Lian

Lien

Lin

Ling

Mani

Marrim

Mei

Meiying

Nuwa

Ping

Shina

Shu

Syà

Sying

Tao

Tu

Ushi

Xiang

Xiu Mei

Yáng

Yen

Yín

Zhen

BOYS

An

Chen

Cheung

Chi

Chun

Chung

De

Délì

Déshì

Dewei

Dingbang

Fai

Gan

Guotin

Ho

Hop

Howin

Hu

Jin

Jing-Quo

Joss

Jun

Kanoa

Keung

Kong

Kueng

Lei

Lí

Liang

Liko

Lok

Long

Manchu

On

Park

Po Sin

Quon

Shaiming

Shen

Shìlín

Shing

(Chinese boys continued)

Sying

Taiwan

Tywan

Wang

Wei-Quo

Wing

Yong

Yu

Zhìxin

Zhuàng

CHIPPEWA

BOYS

Namid

Ogima

Waban

CHOCTAW

GIRLS

Nita

Opa

Poloma

Tallulah

BOYS

Koi

Nashoba

COMANCHE

BOYS

Quan

Quanah

COOS

GIRLS

Yoomee

CORNISH

GIRLS

Kerensa

BOYS

Denzel

Denzil

Donzell

CZECH

GIRLS

Anezka

Anica

Anna

Bela

Fiala

Gizela

Jenka

Jirina

Juliana

Katarina

Krista

Krystin

Magda

Markita

Milada

Milka

Ondrea

Otilie

Pavla

Reza

Rusalka

Ruza

Ryba

Teodora

Trava

Tyna

Vondra

Zusa

BOYS

Adamec

Arno

Bela

Bobek

Brandeis

Cestmir

Dano

Durko

Edo

Eman

Erich

Ezven

Frantisek

Hanus

Holic

Honza

Ianos

Imrich

Izak

Janco

Jaroslav

Jindra

Jiri

Josef

Jur

Karel

Karol

Klement

Kuba

Ladislav

Lukas

Matus

Maxi

Milko

Miloslav

Miroslav

Noe

Ondro

Ota

Pepa

Rostislav

Rubert

Ruda

Salman

Samo

Slane

Tonda

Tynek

Vaclav

Viliam

Waltr

Zdenek

Zenda

Zlatan

DAKOTA

GIRLS

Kenda

Lakota

Macawi

Nahimana

Nokomis

Wakanda

Weeko

BOYS

Ciqala

Dakoda

Dakota

Dakotah

Dekota

Hinto

Lakota

Tasunke

Tokala

Wicasa

DANISH

GIRLS

Caryn

Helsa

Kara

Karah

Kari

Ovia

BOYS

Anker

Aren

Argus

Espen

Gert

Ib

Jens

Jorgen

Kaj

Loritz

Lucas

Mette

Niels

Perben

Poul

Rasmus

Sakeri

Sören

Steen

Stetson

Tage

Torquil

DENE

BOYS

Enli

Nalren

Yakecen

DUTCH

GIRLS

Aleena

Aleene

Brandee

Brandi

Brandy

Hester

Lia

Loris

Mariel

Mariela

Marika

Mena

Sanne

Schyler

Skye

(Dutch girls
continued)

Skylar

Skyler

Trudel

Tryne

BOYS

Brandy

Deman

Dutch

Gerrit

Govert

Haven

Hendrick

Henrick

Jaap

Jan

Jilt

Joop

Joost

Joris

Jurrien

Kees

Kerstan

Kleef

Kort

Laurens

Loris

Lucas

Marten

Mogens

Narve

Pieter

Ramone

Rip

Roosevelt

Schuyler

Schyler

Skelton

Skye

Skylar

Skyler

Skylor

Van

Vandyke

Zeeman

DUTOORO

BOYS

Kiho

Kugonza

EGYPTIAN

GIRLS

Icess

Isis

Nenet

BOYS

Ammon

Keb

Moses

Nen

Pinchas

Sef

Shen

ENGLISH

GIRLS

Ada

Addison

Adela

Adele

Adelina

Adeline

Adelle

Adilene

Adison

Adria

Adriane

Adrien

Adrina

Afton

Agate

Aida

Airiana

Alden

Alfie

Alfreda

Alicia

Alina

Alisha

Alishia

Alison

Allysha

Allyson

Alonza

Alvina

Alycia

Anabel

Analisa

Anamaria

Anice

Anissa

Anka

Annabel	Audey	Bliss	Caralyn
Annabelle	Audreanne	Blossom	Carla
Annalisa	Audree	Blythe	Carlee
Annamarie	Audrey	Bonnie	Carleen
Annelisa	Audriana	Bradley	Carli
Annie	Avery	Braeden	Carly
Anona	Bailee	Branden	Carol
Anyssa	Baileigh	Braxton	Carole
Arden	Bailey	Bree	Carolyn
Arianne	Baylee	Brenda	Carrie
Arleigh	Bayley	Brennan	Carson
Arlette	Berkley	Brita	Carter
Artis	Berlynn	Britaney	Catherine
Ashely	Bernadine	Britani	Chancey
Ashlee	Berni	Britany	Chanel
Ashleigh	Berti	Britin	Chanell
Ashley	Bertina	Britney	Charla
Ashlin	Bethann	Britni	Charlaine
Ashlyn	Betty	Briton	Charlee
Ashten	Bev	Britteny	Charlene
Ashton	Beverly	Brittini	Charlie
Ashtyn	Billi	Brittnee	Chelci
Asia	Binney	Brook	Chelsea
Aspen	Birdie	Bryttani	Chelsee
Aster	Blake	Bunny	Chelsey
Aubriana	Blakely	Cady	Chelsie

(English girls
  continued)

Chenelle

Cher

Cherilyn

Cherish

Chrissy

Christine

Christy

Chrys

Cicely

Cinderella

Clare

Codi

Colby

Corliss

Cortney

Courtenay

Courtnee

Courtney

Cristy

Dae

Daisy

Dale

Dana

Daniella

Darla

Darnelle

Daryl

Davonna

Dawn

Dawna

Dayle

Daysi

Dayton

Deana

Deisy

Delaney

Delicia

Della

Delsie

Dena

Deonna

Devon

Devonna

Dixie

Domino

Dona

Doralynn

Dusti

Dustine

Earlene

Eartha

Easter

Eda

Edeline

Edie

Edith

Edwina

Effie

Elberta

Elisa

Elise

Elissa

Elizaveta

Ella

Ellen

Ellice

Ellie

Elva

Elvina

Emilee

Eppie

Erica

Erna

Ernestine

Essie

Estee

Ethel

Etta

Evelin

Evelyn

Evline

Faith

Fancy

Farah

Faren

Faye

Felicity

Fern

Flair

Florie

Floris

Flossie

Frannie

Freddi

Gail

Gardenia

Garnet

Garyn

Gayle

Gayna

Genna

Georgeanna

Georgeanne	Hali	Hope	Jill
Georgene	Halley	Hunter	Joana
Georgianna	Halsey	Ida	Joanne
Georgie	Happy	Idalina	Jobeth
Georgina	Harlee	Idalis	Joby
Gerardo	Harley	Ilisa	Joleen
Gilda	Harleyann	Iolanthe	Jolene
Ginette	Harriet	Ivy	Jonquil
Ginnifer	Hattie	Jamey	Juliann
Ginny	Haven	Jami	Julie
Giorgianna	Hayden	Jamia	Kadie
Golda	Haylee	Jamilynn	Kady
Goldie	Hayley	Jan	Kaltha
Graceanne	Hazel	Janet	Karalynn
Gracie	Heather	Janeth	Karsen
Grant	Heaven	Janice	Kate
Grayson	Henna	Janie	Katee
Gypsy	Henrietta	Janis	Kathi
Hadley	Hertha	Jannie	Kathryn
Haeley	Hetta	Jayme	Katie
Haiden	Holley	Jaymee	Katy
Hailee	Hollis	Jayne	Kelsey
Hailey	Holly	Jaynie	Kenda
Haili	Hollyann	Jemma	Kendal
Halee	Hollyn	Jeraldine	Kendall
Haleigh	Honey	Jetta	Kendra

Kenenza

Kennice

Kim

Kimber

Kimberlee

Kimberlyn

Kinsey

Kirby

Kortney

Kymberly

Kyndal

Lallie

Landon

Lane

Laney

Lark

Lauren

Laurianna

Laurie

Laury

Lauryn

Lean

Leanna

Leanore

Lee

Leeann

Leeza

Leigh

Letty

Liana

Liane

Lilibeth

Lillyann

Lin

Lindsay

Linsey

Lisa

Lisbeth

Lisette

Liz

Lizabeth

Lizbeth

Lolly

Lona

London

Lorena

Loretta

Louisa

Love

Lucetta

Lucille

Luella

Lulu

Luvena

Lyla

Lyndell

Lyndsey

Lynelle

Lynette

Lynn

Lynnell

Mada

Madaline

Maddie

Maddison

Madelina

Madeline

Madisen

Madison

Madisyn

Madyson

Mae

Maggie

Maggy

Maia

Maida

Malina

Malva

Marabel

Marcelen

Marci

Marcy

Maretta

Marge

Margery

Margie

Marian

Mariane

Maribel

Maridel

Marigold

Markeisha

Marla

Marlana

Marlee

Marley

Marlis

Marlo

Marsha

Marta

Marti

Maryann

Mattie	Olivia	Quintana	Robyn
Maud	Ollie	Rae	Rodnae
Maxie	Ona	Raeven	Romy
May	Ora	Ragine	Ros
Meg	Orva	Raina	Rosalie
Mercia	Osma	Rainbow	Rosanna
Mercy	Paige	Ramsey	Rosanne
Merilyn	Paiton	Randall	Rosemarie
Merry	Parker	Randi	Rosemary
Mildred	Patia	Raven	Rosie
Millicent	Patience	Ravin	Rosina
Millie	Patty	Ravyn	Rowan
Minta	Payge	Rayna	Rowena
Missy	Peace	Rayven	Royale
Misty	Pierce	Reanna	Royanna
Myla	Piper	Reggie	Rue
Nan	Pippa	Regina	Rula
Nanci	Pollyanna	Remington	Rusti
Nancy	Presley	Rennie	Sable
Nara	Primrose	Reyna	Sabreena
Natie	Princess	Rhona	Sabrina
Nedda	Purity	Rina	Sabryna
Nellie	Queen	Robbi	Sada
Neva	Queenie	Roberta	Saffron
Nollie	Quenna	Robin	Sage
Odella	Quinn	Robinette	Saige

(English girls
continued)

Salliann

Sally

Saundra

Sawyer

Scarlett

Sebrina

Seelia

Sela

Shandi

Sharee

Shelbi

Shelby

Sheldon

Shelee

Shelley

Sherleen

Shirlene

Shirley

Shyla

Sibley

Sigourney

Sommer

Spencer

Spring

Stacia

Starla

Starleen

Starley

Starling

Starr

Sterling

Stockard

Stormie

Stormy

Summer

Sunny

Sunshine

Suzanne

Sybella

Tabby

Tacey

Taci

Taelor

Tailor

Taite

Talisa

Tallis

Tammi

Tammy

Tandy

Tanner

Tate

Tatum

Tauri

Tawni

Tawny

Taya

Tayla

Taylar

Tayler

Taylor

Teal

Tetty

Teylor

Timi

Timothea

Tinble

Topsy

Tori

Toria

Toriana

Torie

Torilyn

Torri

Tory

Tottie

Trilby

Tuesday

Twyla

Tyler

Tyne

Udele

Unice

Unity

Vail

Vanetta

Vanity

Velvet

Vina

Walker

Wallis

Wanetta

Waverly

Waynette

Wendelle

Weslee

Whitley

Whitney

Whitnie

Whittney

Whoopi

Wilda

Wileen	Aldair	Arthur	Barclay
Willette	Alden	Artie	Barker
Willie	Alder	Arundel	Barlow
Willow	Aldred	Ascot	Barnaby
Wilona	Aldrich	Ashford	Barnard
Windy	Aldwin	Ashley	Barnes
Winnie	Alfie	Ashton	Barnett
Winter	Alford	Aspen	Barney
Wren	Alfred	Aston	Barnum
Wynter	Alger	Atherton	Baron
Yetta	Algernon	Atley	Barric
Yudelle	Algie	Atwater	Barrington
Zanna	Alistair	Atwell	Bartlet
Zelene	Allard	Atwood	Barton
Zeta	Alston	Atworth	Bartram
Zina	Alton	Auden	Bassett
	Alvar	Audie	Bat
BOYS	Amicus	Audrey	Baxter
Ackerley	Archer	Audric	Bay
Acton	Archie	Averill	Bayard
Addison	Arledge	Avery	Beacher
Adney	Arley	Ayers	Beaman
Afton	Arlo	Aylmer	Beamer
Ahearn	Armstrong	Baker	Beasley
Aiken	Arnette	Bancroft	Beaver
Alcott	Art	Banner	Beck

(English boys
continued)

Bede

Belden

Bell

Benoit

Bentley

Benton

Ber

Berkeley

Berry

Bert

Bertie

Berton

Bertram

Berwyn

Beverly

Bickford

Binky

Birch

Birkey

Birkitt

Birley

Birney

Birtle

Bishop

Blade

Blaine

Blake

Blakely

Blaze

Bliss

Blythe

Bo

Bob

Bobby

Bond

Booker

Booth

Borden

Bosley

Bourne

Brad

Bradburn

Braden

Bradford

Bradlee

Bradley

Bradly

Bradon

Bradshaw

Brady

Bradyn

Braeden

Braedon

Brainard

Bramwell

Brand

Branden

Brandon

Brandt

Brandyn

Branson

Brant

Brantley

Brawley

Braxton

Brayden

Braydon

Brendan

Brendon

Brennan

Brent

Brenton

Brewster

Brick

Bridger

Brigham

Brighton

Brock

Brod

Brodrick

Bromley

Bronson

Brook

Brooks

Brown

Bryon

Bryton

Buck

Buckley

Buckminster

Bud

Buell

Buford

Burgess

Burke

Burl

Burleigh

Burne

Burney

Burr

Burris

Burt

Burton	Chadwick	Clint	Crawford
Butcher	Chance	Clinton	Creighton
Byford	Chancellor	Clive	Cromwell
Byram	Chandler	Codey	Crosley
Byrd	Channing	Codi	Crowther
Byrne	Chanse	Cody	Culver
Byron	Chapman	Colbert	Cuthbert
Cable	Charles	Colby	Cutler
Cadby	Charlie	Cole	Daegel
Calder	Charlton	Coleman	Daelen
Caldwell	Chauncey	Colley	Dagwood
Calvert	Chaz	Collier	Dalbert
Carl	Chester	Colson	Dale
Carlisle	Chet	Colt	Dalen
Carlton	Chick	Colten	Daley
Carnell	Chilton	Colter	Dallan
Carson	Chip	Colton	Dallin
Carter	Churchill	Connie	Dalston
Cartwright	Clay	Cook	Dalton
Carvell	Clayborne	Cooper	Dalvin
Carver	Clayton	Cornwallis	Dane
Case	Cleavon	Corwin	Danforth
Cater	Cleveland	Courtland	Darby
Cedric	Cliff	Courtney	Darell
Cedrick	Clifford	Coy	Darnell
Chad	Clifton	Crandall	Darren

(English boys
continued)

Darton

Darwin

Daulton

Dawson

Dax

Dayton

Dean

Dearborn

Deems

Del

Delbert

Dell

Delton

Delvin

Delwin

Dempster

Denham

Denley

Denman

Dennison

Denton

Denver

Dermot

Derward

Derwin

Deverell

Dexter

Diamond

Dickson

Dixon

Doane

Dob

Drake

Draper

Drew

Dru

Dryden

Dudd

Dudley

Dunley

Dunstan

Dunton

Durell

Durward

Durwin

Dustin

Dusty

Dustyn

Dwight

Dyer

Dyke

Dyson

Ean

Earl

Earnest

Easton

Eaton

Ebner

Ed

Edbert

Eddie

Eddy

Edgar

Edison

Edmond

Edmund

Edric

Edsel

Edson

Edward

Edwin

Egbert

Egerton

Elbert

Elden

Elder

Eldon

Eldred

Eldridge

Eldwin

Elgin

Elian

Ellery

Elliot

Ellis

Ellison

Ellsworth

Elmer

Elmo

Elmore

Elsdon

Elston

Elsworth

Elton

Elvin

Elvy

Elwell

Elwood

Emerson

Emmett

Emmitt

Eric

Erick	Farr	Franklyn	Garwood
Erickson	Farrow	Fraser	Gary
Erland	Felton	Frayne	Geary
Erling	Fenton	Freeborn	Geffrey
Ernest	Field	Freeman	Gent
Ernie	Fielding	Frewin	Genty
Errol	Filbert	Frey	Geoff
Erskine	Filmore	Frick	Geoffery
Ervin	Firth	Fridolf	Geoffrey
Ervine	Fiske	Fuller	Geraint
Esmond	Fitch	Fulton	Gerard
Evan	Fitz	Galton	Germain
Evelyn	Fitzgerald	Gar	Gerome
Everett	Fitzhugh	Gardner	Gerry
Everley	Fitzpatrick	Garen	Gerson
Everton	Fleming	Garfield	Gib
Ewert	Fletcher	Garland	Gibson
Ewing	Flint	Garman	Gifford
Fairfax	Floyd	Garnett	Gig
Falkner	Flurry	Garrad	Gil
Fane	Ford	Garrick	Gilbert
Farley	Forester	Garren	Gilmer
Farnell	Fowler	Garroway	Gipsy
Farnham	Frank	Garry	Gladwin
Farnley	Frankie	Garson	Glanville
Farold	Franklin	Garvin	Glentworth

(English boys continued)

Godwin

Goldwin

Gomer

Gordon

Gordy

Gore

Graham

Grant

Grantland

Gray

Grayden

Graydon

Grayson

Greeley

Greenwood

Gresham

Greyson

Grimshaw

Grover

Guilford

Hadden

Haden

Hadley

Hadwin

Hagley

Haiden

Haig

Hal

Halbert

Hale

Halford

Hall

Hallam

Hallan

Halley

Halliwell

Hallward

Halsey

Halstead

Halton

Hamill

Hamilton

Hammet

Hammond

Hampton

Handel

Hanford

Hanley

Harden

Harding

Hardwin

Harford

Hargrove

Harlan

Harland

Harley

Harlow

Harman

Harper

Harris

Harrison

Harry

Hart

Hartley

Hartwell

Hartwood

Haslett

Hassel

Haven

Hawk

Hawley

Hawthorne

Hayden

Hayes

Hayward

Haywood

Hearn

Heath

Heathcliff

Heaton

Hedley

Henderson

Henley

Hewson

Hilton

Hobson

Hodgson

Holbrook

Holden

Hollis

Holmes

Holt

Horton

Houghton

Houston

Howard

Howie

Howland

Hubie

Hudson

Huey

Hugh

Hunt	Jamie	Jimmie	Kester
Hunter	Jamison	Jimmy	Kestrel
Huntington	Jarett	Johnson	Key
Huntley	Jarrell	Judson	Kidd
Hurst	Jarrett	Kane	Kim
Hutchinson	Jasper	Karson	Kimball
Hutton	Javaris	Keane	King
Huxley	Jaxon	Keaton	Kingsley
Hyatt	Jay	Kedrick	Kingston
Hyde	Jayme	Keene	Kingswell
Hyder	Jaymes	Kelton	Kinsey
Hyman	Jeff	Kelvin	Kipp
Ingram	Jefferson	Kemp	Kirby
Iram	Jeffery	Kempton	Kirkland
Irv	Jefford	Kendal	Kirkley
Irvin	Jeffrey	Kendall	Kirklin
Irving	Jeffry	Kendell	Kirkwell
Irwin	Jem	Kenley	Kirkwood
Isham	Jerald	Kenneth	Kirton
Ives	Jerall	Kenrick	Klay
Jackson	Jerel	Kent	Knight
Jacobson	Jeremy	Kenton	Knowles
Jagger	Jermey	Kentrell	Knox
Jago	Jeron	Kenward	Kodi
James	Jervis	Kerrick	Kody
Jameson	Jim	Kerwin	Kolby

(English boys
continued)

Kole

Koleman

Kolin

Kolton

Korbin

Kordell

Kortney

Kourtland

Kyler

Kyndall

Kyne

Ladd

Laine

Lake

Landen

Lander

Landon

Landry

Lane

Langdon

Langford

Langley

Langston

Latham

Lathrop

Latimer

Laurie

Lave

Lawford

Lawson

Lawton

Layne

Layton

Lee

Leigh

Leighton

Leland

Leonel

Les

Lester

Lew

Lewin

Lewis

Lex

Lin

Linc

Lincoln

Lindell

Linden

Lindley

Lindon

Lindsay

Lindsey

Linford

Linley

Linton

Linwood

Lister

Litton

Livingston

Locke

London

Lord

Lorry

Louvain

Lovell

Loyal

Ludlow

Lyman

Lyndal

Lyndon

Lynn

Mace

Macon

Maddox

Madison

Maitland

Malden

Malin

Malvin

Manford

Manfred

Manley

Manning

Mansel

Mansfield

Manton

Manville

March

Markham

Marland

Marley

Marlin

Marlow

Marsden

Marsh

Marston

Martell

Marv

Marvin

Marwood

Massey

Mather	Milton	Newland	Ollie
Maxfield	Miner	Newman	Onslow
Maxwell	Mister	Newton	Ormond
Maxy	Mitch	Nichols	Orrick
Mayes	Mitchel	Nick	Orrin
Mayhew	Mitchell	Niles	Orton
Maynard	Moe	Nixon	Orval
Mayo	Montgomery	Norris	Orvin
Mead	Monty	Northcliff	Osbert
Mel	Moreland	Northrop	Osborn
Melbourne	Moris	Norton	Osgood
Meldon	Morley	Norville	Osman
Melvin	Morse	Norvin	Osmar
Mendel	Mort	Norward	Osmond
Mercer	Morton	Norwood	Osric
Merlin	Moss	Nowles	Oswald
Merrick	Myer	Nye	Oswin
Merton	Nat	Nyle	Oxford
Mick	Nayland	Oakes	Ozzie
Mickael	Ned	Oakley	Pace
Milborough	Nellie	Obed	Paden
Miles	Nelson	Obie	Padget
Milford	Nesbit	Ode	Paige
Miller	Nevin	Odell	Palmer
Mills	Newbold	Ogden	Park
Milt	Newell	Olin	Parker

Parkin	Phineas	Rafe	Rayce
Parr	Pickford	Raine	Raymon
Parrish	Pickworth	Raleigh	Raymond
Pat	Pierce	Ralph	Rayne
Patton	Piers	Ralphie	Read
Payden	Pierson	Ralston	Reading
Payton	Pitney	Ram	Redford
Pearce	Pitt	Ramsden	Redley
Pearson	Pollock	Ramsey	Redpath
Peers	Powell	Rance	Reed
Peirce	Prentice	Rand	Reeve
Pelham	Prescott	Randal	Reg
Pell	Presley	Randall	Reggie
Pelton	Preston	Randolph	Reginal
Pembroke	Princeton	Randy	Reginald
Penley	Purvis	Rankin	Reid
Penn	Putnam	Ransford	Remington
Perkin	Quentin	Ransley	Renfred
Perry	Race	Ransom	Renshaw
Pete	Rad	Raven	Renton
Peterson	Radbert	Ravenel	Rexford
Peyton	Radburn	Ravon	Rexton
Phelps	Radcliff	Rawdon	Reyes
Philbert	Radford	Rawleigh	Reymond
	Radley	Ray	Reynold
	Radnor	Rayburn	Rice

Rich	Rob	Rover	Ryland
Richard	Robbie	Rowan	Ryle
Richie	Robby	Rowell	Ryman
Richman	Robert	Rowland	Sadler
Ricker	Roberts	Rowley	Safford
Rickey	Robin	Rowson	Sage
Rickie	Robinson	Roxbury	Salton
Rickward	Robyn	Royce	Sanborn
Ricky	Rochester	Royden	Sander
Rider	Rock	Rudd	Sanders
Ridge	Rockford	Rudy	Sandy
Ridgeley	Rockland	Rudyard	Sanford
Ridgeway	Rockledge	Ruford	Santon
Ridley	Rockley	Rugby	Sawyer
Rigby	Rockwell	Rumford	Sax
Rigg	Rod	Rush	Saxon
Ring	Roddy	Rushford	Scott
Ringo	Roden	Rutherford	Scottie
Rip	Rodney	Rutledge	Scotty
Ripley	Roe	Rutley	Seabert
Risley	Rollie	Rycroft	Seabrook
Riston	Rollin	Ryder	Searle
Ritchard	Rollo	Rye	Seaton
Ritchie	Roper	Ryerson	Sedgely
River	Rosswell	Ryese	Seeley
Roan	Roswald	Rylan	Sefton

(English boys
continued)

Seger

Seibert

Selby

Seldon

Selwyn

Severn

Seward

Sexton

Shadwell

Shandy

Shap

Shattuck

Shaw

Sheffield

Shel

Shelby

Sheldon

Shelley

Shelton

Shem

Shep

Shepherd

Shepley

Sherborn

Sherill

Sherlock

Sherman

Sherrod

Sherwin

Sherwood

Shipton

Siddel

Sidwell

Sinjon

Skeeter

Slade

Slater

Smedley

Smith

Snowden

Somerset

Somerville

Son

Sonny

Southwell

Spalding

Spark

Spear

Spence

Spencer

Spenser

Spike

Spoor

Sproule

Spurgeon

Squire

Stacey

Stafford

Stamford

Stan

Stanbury

Stancliff

Standish

Stanfield

Stanford

Stanley

Stanmore

Stannard

Stanton

Stanway

Stanwick

Stanwood

Starbuck

Starling

Starr

Steadman

Steel

Steph

Sterling

Sterne

Stevie

Stewart

Stillman

Sting

Stockman

Stockton

Stockwell

Stoddard

Stoker

Stone

Storm

Stover

Stowe

Stratford

Strong

Stroud

Stu

Stuart

Studs

Styles

Suffield

Sugden

Sully	Tannin	Thompson	Torrey
Summit	Tanny	Thorgood	Townley
Sumner	Tanton	Thorley	Townsend
Sunny	Tarleton	Thorndike	Trader
Sutcliff	Tarver	Thorne	Trae
Sutton	Tate	Thornley	Travell
Swaggart	Tatum	Thornton	Travis
Swain	Tayler	Thorpe	Tray
Swaley	Taylor	Thurlow	Trayton
Swinbourne	Tearle	Thurmond	Tredway
Swindel	Teasdale	Tieler	Trevelyan
Swinfen	Ted	Tige	Trevis
Swinton	Teddy	Tilden	Trey
Symington	Tedmund	Tilford	Trip
Tab	Teller	Tilton	Trot
Taffy	Telmo	Tinsley	Trowbridge
Taft	Templeton	Todd	Troy
Talcott	Tennant	Toft	True
Talen	Tennyson	Toland	Truesdale
Talmadge	Terry	Tolbert	Truitt
Talon	Thane	Toller	Truman
Talor	Thatcher	Tom	Trumble
Tam	Thaw	Tomlin	Trustin
Tammy	Thel	Tony	Tucker
Taner	Theo	Topper	Tupper
Tanner	Thom	Torr	Turk

(English boys continued)

Twain

Twitchell

Twyford

Ty

Tyger

Tylar

Tyler

Tylor

Tymothy

Tyrus

Udell

Udolf

Ulmer

Unwin

Upshaw

Upton

Upwood

Urbane

Vail

Vance

Vian

Vince

Vinny

Vinson

Wade

Wadley

Wadsworth

Wain

Wainwright

Waite

Wakefield

Wakely

Wakeman

Walcott

Walden

Waldron

Wales

Walford

Walker

Wallace

Waller

Wally

Walsh

Walt

Walter

Walton

Walworth

Walwyn

Warburton

Ward

Wardell

Wardley

Ware

Warfield

Warford

Warley

Warton

Warwick

Washburn

Washington

Watford

Watkins

Watson

Waverly

Wayland

Waylon

Wayman

Wayne

Webb

Webley

Webster

Weddel

Welborne

Weldon

Welford

Wells

Welsh

Welton

Wendell

Wenford

Wentworth

Werner

Wes

Wesley

West

Westbrook

Westby

Westcott

Westley

Weston

Wetherby

Wetherell

Wetherly

Weylin

Whalley

Wharton

Wheatley

Wheaton

Wheeler

Whistler

Whit

Whitby

Whitcomb	Wilton	Worcester	**ESKIMO**
Whitelaw	Win	Wordsworth	**GIRLS**
Whitey	Winchell	Worth	Hiti
Whitfield	Windsor	Worton	Kirima
Whitford	Winfield	Wray	Sedna
Whitley	Wingate	Wren	
Whitman	Winslow	Wright	**ESTONIAN**
Whitmore	Winston	Wrisley	**GIRLS**
Whitney	Winter	Wriston	Kati
Whittaker	Winthrop	Wybert	Leena
Wickham	Winton	Wycliff	Reet
Wickley	Winward	Wylie	**BOYS**
Wid	Wit	Wyman	Jaan
Wilbur	Witter	Wymer	Juku
Wilder	Witton	Wyn	Leks
Wildon	Wolcott	Wythe	Nikolai
Wiley	Wolf	Yale	Peeter
Wilford	Wolfe	Yardley	Riki
Wilkie	Wood	Yates	Toomas
Wilkins	Woodfield	Yeoman	
Wilkinson	Woodford	York	**ETHIOPIAN (AMHARIC, TIGRINYA)**
Will	Woodrow	Young	
William	Woodruff	Yudell	**GIRLS**
Willoughby	Woodson	Yule	Desta
Wills	Woodward	Zain	Louam
Wilson	Woodville	Zane	
Wilt	Woolsey	Zayne	

(Ethiopian
(Amharic,
Tigrinya) girls
continued)

Maharene

Melesse

Seble

Selam

Zena

BOYS

Beniam

Dawit

Hagos

Hakim

Kelile

Lebna

Mengesha

Ogbay

Semer

Tefere

Tekle

EWE

GIRLS

Quaashie

BOYS

Coffie

Lumo

Mawuli

Mensah

Quaashie

Tse

Yao

FANTE

GIRLS

Panyin

BOYS

Ata

Ebo

Fifi

Jojo

Kesse

Lado

Osei

Sisi

Twia

Yooku

Yorkoo

FIJIAN

GIRLS

Levani

FILIPINO

GIRLS

Mahal

Malaya

Rosario

BOYS

Bienvenido

Honesto

Lauro

Matalino

Pacifico

Rosito

FINNISH

GIRLS

Aili

Annalie

Kalle

Lusa

Maija

Marja

Meri

Mielikki

Valma

BOYS

Antti

Eikki

Hannes

Janne

Juhana

Kalevi

Kelevi

Kosti

Lasse

Mikko

Nilo

Paavo

Reku

Risto

Taaveti

Taneli

Tapani

Tauno

Timo

Viljo

Yrjo

FLEMISH

BOYS

DeWitt

Jenkin

FOX

BOYS

Nashashuk

FRENCH

GIRLS

Abrial

Abrielle

Abril

Aimee

Alair

Alberta

Ambar

Amber

Ami

Angelique

Annette

Antionette

Antoinette

Ariane

Arielle

Armine

Auberte

Aubree

Aubrey

Aubrie

Audra

Avril

Babette

Belle

Bernadette

Berneta

Bertille

Bette

Billie

Blaise

Blanche

Blondelle

Briar

Brie

Brielle

Brienne

Brigette

Brigitte

Burgundy

Cachet

Cami

Camille

Camylle

Cantrelle

Caressa

Carol

Caroline

Cera

Cerise

Chablis

Chadee

Chalice

Chambray

Chandelle

Chantal

Chante

Chantel

Chantilly

Chantrice

Chardae

Chardonnay

Charla

Charlotte

Charmaine

Chauntel

Cher

Cherelle

Cheri

Cherise

Cherry

Cheryl

Christabel

Christelle

Christine

Cidney

Cinderella

Claire

Claudette

Colette

Cosette

Cydney

Daeja

Daija

Daja

Damica

Danielle

Danielle

Darcelle

Darci

Darielle

Darlene

Darselle

Daryl

Déja

Dejanae

Dejon

Demi

Denise

(French girls
continued)

Denisse

Desarae

Deserae

Desi

Desiree

Dessa

Desta

Destany

Destinee

Destiney

Destiny

Destynee

Dezarae

Dior

Dixie

Dominique

Doreen

Elaina

Elaine

Elayna

Elise

Elita

Eloise

Ember

Emerald

Emmaline

Esmé

Estelle

Estrella

Étoile

Evaline

Eve

Evette

Evonne

Fancy

Fawn

Faye

Femi

Fifi

Fleur

Fontanna

Francine

Françoise

Frederique

Gabriel

Gabrielle

Gaby

Garland

Gay

Gena

Geneva

Genevieve

Genevra

Genovieve

Georgette

Germaine

Gervaise

Gigi

Guinevere

Harriet

Helene

Heloise

Isabeau

Isabelle

Ivette

Ivonne

Jackquel

Jacquelin

Jacqueline

Jacquelyn

Jacqui

Jae

Jaime

Jaimee

Jaimie

Jamee

Janel

Janelle

Janette

Janine

Jaquelin

Jaquelyn

Jardena

Jeanette

Jermaine

Jessamine

Jewel

Jolie

Josephine

Josette

Juliet

Karessa

Laine

Lainey

Laverne

Leala

Liana

Linette

Lisette

Lizet

Lori

Lorraine

Lourdes	Mérane	Nikole	Raquel
Lucie	Merle	Ninon	Raula
Lyla	Michelle	Noelle	Rayna
Madelaine	Miette	Nycole	Remi
Madeleine	Mignon	Odelia	Renae
Mallorie	Mimi	Odetta	Renata
Mallory	Minette	Oralia	Renée
Manette	Monet	Orva	Renita
Manka	Monique	Padget	Richelle
Manon	Moriah	Page	Riva
Mardi	Moselle	Pansy	River
Margaux	Musetta	Paris	Rochelle
Margo	Nadette	Parris	Romaine
Marguerite	Nadia	Pascale	Romy
Maribel	Nadine	Patrice	Rondelle
Marie	Naeva	Pernella	Rosabel
Marion	Nanette	Perri	Rubi
Marjolaine	Natalle	Pier	Ruby
Marquise	Nettie	Pippi	Rue
Marvella	Nichole	Pleasance	Russhell
Maureen	Nicki	Precious	Salena
Maurelle	Nickole	Questa	Salina
Maurise	Nicole	Quiterie	Sarotte
Mauve	Nicolette	Rachelle	Satin
Mavis	Nicoline	Racquel	Sebastiane
Melisande	Nicolle	Raphaelle	Shanta

(French girls
continued)

Shari

Sharice

Sharita

Sharla

Sharlene

Shelley

Sheree

Sherelle

Sheri

Sherice

Sherissa

Sherita

Sherleen

Sherry

Sheryl

Sidney

Sidonie

Simone

Sinclaire

Solange

Solenne

Sorrel

Stella

Susammi

Susette

Suzette

Sydnee

Sydney

Sydni

Talia

Talley

Tallis

Tempest

Toinette

Turquoise

Vedette

Verna

Veronique

Vi

Vilette

Violet

Violeta

Virginie

Vonna

Vonny

Yvette

Yvonne

BOYS

Adrien

Aimon

Alain

Alaire

Albert

Alexandre

Amando

Amato

Ames

Andre

Ansel

Antione

Antoine

Aramis

Arnaud

Aubrey

Audon

Avent

Averill

Aymon

Bailey

Bay

Bayley

Beale

Beau

Beaufort

Beaumont

Beauregard

Belden

Bell

Bellamy

Benoit

Berger

Bevis

Blaise

Boden

Boone

Borden

Bourne

Boyce

Briar

Brigham

Bruce

Byron

Cable

Camille

Campbell

Canaan

Cannon

Carvell

Cassius

Chace

Chaise

Chaney	Deandre	Forrest	Griswold
Channing	Delano	Fortune	Grosvener
Chante	Delroy	Franchot	Guillaume
Chase	Demont	François	Guy
Chayse	Deondre	Fraser	Hackett
Chevalier	Derrell	Frayne	Hackman
Chevy	Derryl	Frederique	Hamlet
Christophe	Destin	Gage	Hamlin
Clark	Didier	Gaige	Harbin
Claude	Dominique	Garland	Harcourt
Coco	Donatien	Garner	Henri
Colar	Dondre	Garrison	Hervé
Cordell	Drury	Gaspar	Hewitt
Cornell	Duke	Gaston	Holland
Cory	Duval	Gautier	Hyacinthe
Coty	Edouard	Gaylord	Jacque
Coyne	Elroy	Gedeon	Jacques
Crepin	Émile	Georges	Jacquez
Curtis	Étienne	Géraud	Jasper
Dandré	Fabron	Germain	Jay
Darcy	Fermin	Gervaise	Jean
Darrell	Ferrand	Ghislain	Jehan
Darryl	Firman	Giles	Jemond
Daryl	Florent	Gillett	Jerard
Dax	Fontaine	Granger	Jermaine
Dean	Forest	Granville	Jocquez

Jontae	Lourdes	Mathieu	Parnell
Jules	Lowell	Maxime	Pascal
Justis	Luc	Melville	Patrice
Kristophe	Lucien	Merle	Pembroke
Kurt	Lyle	Merrill	Percival
Kurtis	Mace	Merville	Percy
Lafayette	Macy	Michel	Pernell
Lamar	Mallory	Montague	Peverell
Lamond	Manger	Montre	Philippe
Lancelot	Manville	Montreal	Pierre
Landry	Marc	Montrell	Pierre-Luc
Laramie	Marcel	Moore	Platt
Laron	Marin	Morel	Pomeroy
Larrimore	Marion	Morell	Prewitt
LaSalle	Markese	Mort	Purvis
Laurent	Markis	Mortimer	Quennell
LaValle	Marlon	Narcisse	Quincy
Lavell	Marmion	Neville	Ranger
Leggett	Marquis	Noe	Raoul
Lemar	Marsh	Noël	Rapier
Leron	Marshal	Norman	Raul
Leroy	Marshall	Norris	Rawlins
Leverett	Martial	Norville	Ray
Lionel	Martin	Olivier	Raynard
	Maslin	Orville	Remi
	Mason	Page	Remy

Renard	Sebastien	Travers	Adelle
Renaud	Senior	Trent	Alberta
René	Sennett	Troy	Alda
Renny	Séverin	Tyson	Alice
Reynard	Seymour	Urson	Alisha
Roi	Shantae	Vachel	Aloisa
Romain	Sid	Vallis	Amalia
Rondel	Sidney	Vardon	Amalie
Ross	Simeon	Vere	Amelia
Roy	Sinclair	Verney	Amelie
Royal	Sorrel	Verrill	Amilia
Ruff	Stéphane	Victoir	Amorie
Rush	Sully	Warner	Anna
Ruskin	Sydney	Wyatt	Aria
Russ	Sylvain	Yves	Armine
Russel	Talbot	Yvon	Arnelle
Russell	Talon		Aubrey
Rusty	Tanguy	**GA**	Audris
Saber	Telford	**BOYS**	Axelle
Salaun	Tempest	Oko	Babette
Sargent	Teppo		Barrett
Satchel	Thayer	**GERMAN**	Berit
Satordi	Thibault	**GIRLS**	Bernadine
Saville	Thierry	Ada	Bertha
Scoville	Tiennot	Adalia	Berti
Searlas	Travaris	Addie	Billie
		Adelaide	

(German girls
continued)

Birdie

Bruna

Brunhilda

Carla

Carol

Catarina

Charlee

Charlie

Christa

Clotilda

Dagmar

Delana

Delia

Derika

Dustine

Edda

Elfrida

Elga

Elke

Elsa

Elsbeth

Elsie

Elvira

Emery

Emily

Emma

Emmy

Etta

Everett

Fern

Fernanda

Freda

Frederica

Frederike

Fritzi

Genevieve

Geraldine

Gerda

Gertie

Gertrude

Gilberte

Gill

Gisela

Giselle

Gissel

Greta

Gretchen

Gricelda

Grisel

Griselda

Hedda

Hedy

Heidi

Helga

Helma

Hermina

Hetta

Hettie

Hilda

Hildegarde

Hydi

Ida

Ilise

Ilse

Ima

Imelda

Johana

Karla

Katrina

Keana

Klarise

Klarissa

Lamia

Landra

Lene

Lenia

Lenore

Leona

Leonie

Liese

Liesel

Lise

Lois

Lona

Lorelei

Lotte

Louise

Lovisa

Luann

Luanna

Ludovica

Luella

Lulu

Lurleen

Mallory

Malorie

Marelda

Margret

Mariel

Mariela

Marilla

Marlena

Mathilde

Matilda

Melia

Mena

Meryl

Meta

Mileta

Milia

Mina

Minna

Mitzi

Monika

Nan

Nixie

Odetta

Oma

Orlanda

Ormanda

Porscha

Quinn

Radella

Raena

Raina

Raymonde

Reanna

Resi

Reynalda

Richelle

Rilla

Roderica

Rolanda

Rolene

Rosamond

Rudee

Rue

Selda

Selma

Sigreda

Sigmunda

Stina

Tilda

Tillie

Trudy

Ulla

Ulrica

Ulva

Unna

Uta

Vala

Valda

Vanda

Velda

Velma

Vilhelmina

Vilma

Walda

Wanda

Wandie

Warda

Wilda

Wilhelmina

Willa

Wilma

Win

Winifred

Winola

Yseult

Zelda

Zelma

BOYS

Abel

Abelard

Addy

Adelard

Adler

Adolf

Adolph

Aimery

Alaric

Albern

Albert

Aldair

Alder

Aldous

Aleric

Alger

Algis

Alois

Aloysius

Alphonse

Altman

Alvan

Alvin

Alwin

Amory

Anno

Anselm

Anson

Archibald

Archie

Aric

Arlo

Armand

(German boys continued)

Arne

Arnie

Arno

Arnold

Arnulfo

Arvin

Auberon

Aubrey

Audie

Aurick

Axel

Baden

Baldemar

Baldric

Baldwin

Ballard

Bardolf

Barnum

Baron

Barrett

Bastien

Benedikt

Berg

Bergen

Berl

Berlyn

Bern

Bernal

Bernard

Bernie

Bert

Berthold

Bertram

Bertrand

Bill

Billy

Bing

Bogart

Bruno

Bryon

Buck

Buell

Burke

Burl

Carl

Carroll

Casper

Chadrick

Charles

Charlie

Claus

Clovis

Conrad

Cort

Darick

Dedrick

Dereck

Derek

Deric

Derrek

Derrick

Detrick

Dick

Diedrich

Dietbald

Dieter

Dino

Dirk

Dolf

Dustin

Eberhard

Edel

Eginhard

Egon

Ehren

Elger

Ellard

Elman

Emerson

Emery

Emil

Emmett

Emmitt

Emory

Emrick

Engelbert

Erbert

Erhard

Eric

Erich

Ernst

Eugen

Everardo

Ewald

Faber

Faxon

Ferdinand

Finn

Folke

Fonso

Fonzie

Franz

Fred	Hamlet	Horst	Kiefer
Freddie	Hamlin	Howe	Klaus
Freddy	Handel	Hubbard	Konrad
Frederic	Hanno	Hubert	Konstantin
Frederick	Harbin	Hulbert	Korb
Frederik	Hardy	Humbert	Kort
Fredrick	Hartman	Humphrey	Krischan
Fremont	Hartwig	Ingelbert	Kurt
Friedrich	Harvey	Ivo	Lamar
Fritz	Hassel	Jaegar	Lambert
Fulbright	Heinrich	Jarman	Lance
Gary	Heinz	Jarvis	Len
Gerald	Helmer	Jerry	Lenard
Gerhard	Helmut	Johan	Lenny
Gert	Henning	Johannes	Leo
Gilen	Henry	Jupp	Leon
Goddard	Herb	Kai	Leonard
Godfrey	Herbert	Kaiser	Leonhard
Gottfried	Herman	Karl	Leopold
Gotzon	Hernan	Kasper	Lindberg
Griswold	Herrick	Kass	Linfred
Guthrie	Hewitt	Kay	Lonnie
Guy	Hildebrand	Keane	Lonzo
Hackett	Hilliard	Keene	Loring
Hackman	Hobart	Keiffer	Lothar
Hagan	Hobert	Kelby	Lou

Loudon

Louie

Louis

Lucas

Ludovic

Ludwig

Luther

Macon

Mallory

Mandel

Manheim

Mann

Manny

Mathe

Matheu

Mathias

Mauritz

Medgar

Medwin

Meinhard

Meinrad

Menz

Meyer

Miles

Milko

Milo

Moritz

Myles

Nando

Nardo

Oberon

Obert

Odolf

Onofrio

Orlando

Orman

Othman

Otis

Otto

Ottokar

Paulin

Penn

Penrod

Pepin

Philipp

Pippin

Poldi

Pollard

Raimund

Rainer

Rainey

Redmond

Reinhart

Richart

Richmond

Rick

Rigoberto

Ritter

Roderich

Roderick

Rodger

Rodman

Rodrick

Rodrik

Roger

Roland

Rolf

Rory

Roth

Rowland

Rudolf

Rudolph

Ruland

Rune

Rupert

Ruprecht

Schafer

Schmidt

Schneider

Schön

Seifert

Selig

Sepp

Shon

Siegfried

Sig

Sigifredo

Siggy

Sigmund

Sigurd

Sigwald

Spangler

Stark

Steen

Stefan

Stein

Stern

Stoffel

Strom

Tab

Talbert

Tarell

Terell	Viktor	Willie	**GREEK**
Terrell	Vilhelm	Willis	**GIRLS**
Terrill	Volker	Wilmer	Aalisha
Tewdor	Volney	Winfried	Acacia
Theobald	Von	Wolf	Adair
Theodoric	Wagner	Wolfgang	Adara
Thoma	Waldemar	Wouter	Addie
Till	Waldo	Yale	Adrienne
Tomas	Walfred	Yoan	Afrodite
Toni	Wallach	Yohan	Agatha
Traugott	Waller	Zacharias	Agathe
Udo	Walmond	Zamiel	Aggie
Ulbrecht	Walter		Agnes
Ulf	Walther	**GHANIAN**	Alcina
Ulfred	Warner	**GIRLS**	Aleasha
Ulger	Warren	Effia	Alecia
Ullock	Weber		Aleisha
Ulmo	Welby	**BOYS**	Aleksandra
Ulric	Wendell	Fynn	Alesia
Ulrich	Wies	Manu	Alessa
Uwe	Wilbert	Odom	Aleta
Varick	Wilfred	Tano	Alethea
Vasyl	Wilhelm	Tuaco	Alex
Vernados	Willard	**GOTHIC**	Alexa
Verner	Willem	**BOYS**	Alexandra
Verrill	Williams	Attila	

Alexandrea

Alexandria

Alexandrine

Alexas

Alexi

Alexia

Alexis

Alexius

Alexsandra

Alexzandra

Alexsis

Alexys

Ali

Alice

Alie

Aliesha

Alisa

Alise

Alisha

Alix

Alixandra

Alli

Allise

Allissa

Allysa

Alpha

Althea

Alysa

Alysha

Alyssa

Alysse

Alyx

Alyxandra

Amairani

Amara

Amari

Amaryllis

Anastacia

Anastasia

Anatola

Andrea

Andreana

Andreane

Andria

Andriana

Aneesa

Anessa

Angel

Angela

Angelia

Angelica

Angie

Anjelica

Anthea

Antonia

Aretha

Ariadne

Ariana

Arista

Asia

Astra

Atalanta

Athena

Aundrea

Aura

Ava

Belen

Berenice

Bernice

Beryl

Bunny

Calandra

Cali

Callie

Callista

Calypso

Candace

Candice

Carina

Carisa

Carissa

Casandra

Casey

Cass

Cassandra

Cassaundra

Cassia

Cassie

Cassiopeia

Cassondra

Catharine

Catherine

Cathi

Cathrine

Cathryn

Celena

Celene

Celina

Celine

Charis

Charissa

Cherese

Chloe	Cora	Delphine	Eleanor
Chloris	Coretta	Delta	Eleanora
Chris	Corey	Demetria	Electra
Chrissa	Corina	Demi	Elena
Christain	Corinne	Dessa	Eleni
Christen	Corissa	Diantha	Elexis
Christena	Corrina	Dionna	Elexus
Christi	Cristina	Dionne	Elisha
Christian	Crystina	Dodie	Elissa
Christin	Cybele	Dora	Ella
Christina	Cyndi	Doreen	Esmeralda
Christophe	Cynthia	Doria	Eudora
Christyn	Cyrilla	Dorian	Eugenia
Cindy	Dacey	Doris	Eugenie
Cinthia	Damaris	Dorothea	Eulalia
Clairissa	Damiana	Dorothy	Eunice
Clarisa	Danae	Dorrit	Euphemia
Clarissa	Daphne	Dottie	Eurydice
Clea	Daphnee	Drew	Eustacia
Cleo	Daria	Ebone	Eva
Cleone	Darian	Eboni	Evangelina
Cleopatra	Darien	Ebony	Evania
Cleta	Daryn	Echo	Fantasia
Clio	Deitra	Edrianna	Feodora
Cloe	Delfina	Effie	Gaea
Colette	Delia	Elana	Galen

(Greek girls continued)

Galena

Gemini

Georgia

Hadriane

Haidee

Hedy

Helen

Helena

Hera

Hermia

Hermione

Hilary

Hyacinth

Ianthe

Ilena

Iliana

Iola

Iona

Iphigenia

Irene

Iris

Jacey

Jaci

Jacinda

Jolanda

Kacia

Kaia

Kairos

Kalli

Kalliope

Kallista

Kalyca

Kandace

Kara

Karah

Karen

Kari

Karis

Karissa

Kasandra

Kassandra

Kate

Katharine

Katherine

Kathrine

Katlyn

Kay

Kearsten

Kineta

Kirsten

Kirstyn

Kitty

Kora

Korina

Korine

Kosma

Kristan

Kristen

Kristian

Kristina

Kristyn

Krysten

Krystian

Krystina

Kynthia

Kyra

Lacey

Lalita

Lara

Larina

Larisa

Larissa

Leanore

Leda

Lelia

Lena

Leonore

Leora

Leta

Lexandra

Lexi

Lexia

Lexis

Lexus

Lia

Licia

Lida

Lidia

Lina

Lissa

Loris

Lotus

Lycoris

Lyda

Lydia

Lyra

Lysandra

Madalyn

Madeline

Madelyn

Madge

Madilyn

Madolyn	Melba	Nereida	Pandora
Magan	Melina	Nerine	Pansy
Magdalen	Melinda	Nerissa	Panthea
Magdalena	Melisa	Nessa	Parthenia
Maggie	Melissa	Nike	Pasha
Maia	Melita	Nitsa	Patra
Maida	Melody	Nora	Peggy
Maiya	Melyssa	Nyssa	Pelagia
Mala	Mena	Obelia	Penelope
Malinda	Milena	Oceana	Penny
Malissa	Milissa	Odele	Peony
Mara	Millicent	Odelia	Peri
Margaret	Mindy	Odessa	Pernella
Margarit	Mona	Ofelia	Perri
Maris	Monica	Ola	Persephone
Marjorie	Mylene	Olesia	Petra
Marlene	Myrtle	Olinda	Petronella
Marmara	Naida	Olympia	Phaedra
Maya	Naiya	Omega	Phebe
Mead	Nani	Ophelia	Pheodora
Medea	Nara	Ora	Philana
Medora	Narcissa	Orea	Philantha
Megan	Nastasia	Oretha	Philippa
Megara	Nelle	Orsa	Philomena
Melanie	Neola	Pallas	Phoebe
Melantha	Neona	Pamela	Phylicia

Phyllida

Phyllis

Psyche

Pyralis

Rasia

Rea

Reena

Rene

Reyna

Rhea

Rheanna

Rhoda

Rissa

Rita

Ritsa

Riza

Ronaele

Saba

Sandi

Sandra

Sandrea

Sandrica

Sandrine

Sandy

Sapphire

Sebastiane

Seema

Selena

Selene

Selina

Serilda

Sibley

Sirena

Sofia

Sondra

Sonya

Sophia

Sophie

Sophronia

Stacey

Staci

Stasya

Stefani

Stefanie

Stefany

Steffi

Stephani

Stephanie

Stephany

Stephene

Stephenie

Stephney

Stevie

Sula

Sybil

Symphony

Tabatha

Tabetha

Tabitha

Tabytha

Tahlia

Talia

Taliyah

Tansy

Tasha

Tassos

Tecla

Teddi

Tedra

Teona

Teresa

Terese

Teri

Terrelle

Terri

Terry

Tess

Tessa

Tessie

Thaddea

Thalassa

Thalia

Thea

Thelma

Theodora

Theone

Theophania

Theophila

Theresa

Therese

Theta

Thetis

Tia

Tiana

Tiauna

Tiffany

Tita

Titania

Titiana

Tiyana

Toni

Tracey

Tracy	Yolie	Alexandro	Aries
Tresha	Zandra	Alexi	Arion
Tressa	Zanthe	Alexis	Aristides
Triana	Zena	Alic	Arsenio
Trice	Zenaide	Alisander	Artemus
Trina	Zenobia	Alixander	Athan
Trini	Zephania	Altair	Atlas
Tryna	Zephyr	Ambrose	Aundre
Tytiana	Zina	Anastasius	Avel
Urania	Zoe	Anatole	Aymil
Ursa	Zoey	Andonios	Baltazar
Ursula	Zondra	Andrea	Balthasar
Vanesa		Andreas	Barnabas
Vanessa	**BOYS**	Andrew	Basil
Vanna	Achilles	Andy	Belen
Vannesa	Adon	Anfernee	Binkentios
Vorsila	Adonis	Angel	Bishop
Xandra	Adrian	Annas	Cadmus
Xanthe	Aeneas	Antares	Carey
Xanthippe	Agamemnon	Anthany	Cornelius
Xena	Alcandor	Anthonie	Carsten
Xenia	Alec	Anthony	Castor
Xylia	Aleksandar	Apollo	Cerek
Yalanda	Alekzander	Aretino	Chris
Yalena	Alex	Ari	Christain
Yolanda	Alexander	Arian	Christian

Christien

Christofer

Christopher

Christophoros

Christos

Cleon

Cletus

Cole

Colin

Collins

Colson

Cornelius

Corydon

Cosmo

Costa

Cristian

Cristobal

Cristopher

Cyrano

Cyril

Daemon

Daimian

Daimon

Dametrius

Damian

Damien

Damion

Damon

Darius

Darrick

Darrius

Daymian

Deacon

Deion

Demetri

Demetris

Demetrius

Demos

Denis

Dennis

Denny

Deon

Dimitrios

Dimitrius

Dinos

Diogenes

Dion

Dionysus

Doran

Dorian

Elias

Elmo

Eneas

Ennis

Enrikos

Erasmus

Erastus

Euclid

Eugene

Eustace

Evagelos

Feoras

Filip

Gale

Galen

Gaylen

Gene

George

Georgios

Georgy

Geronimo

Gil

Gino

Giorgos

Hali

Hector

Hercules

Hermes

Hesperos

Hieremias

Hieronymos

Hippolyte

Homer

Iakobos

Ilias

Iorgos

Iosif

Isidore

Isidro

Jacen

Jaison

Jason

Jasson

Jayson

Jörg

Jörn

Josef

Julian

Julius

Karey

Karsten

Kay

Khristian	Maximos	Nikola	Pirro
Khristopher	Mette	Nikolas	Plato
Khristos	Mihail	Nikolaus	Pollux
Kimball	Mikhail	Nikolos	Polo
Kit	Mikolas	Odell	Porfirio
Korudon	Miles	Odysseus	Prokopios
Kosmo	Milos	Orestes	Quant
Kostas	Mimis	Orion	Rasmus
Kris	Mitsos	Otis	Rhodes
Kristian	Morey	Panayiotis	Rodas
Kristo	Moris	Panos	Romanos
Kristoff	Myron	Paris	Sabastian
Kristopher	Napoleon	Parthenios	Sandro
Kyros	Narcissus	Pello	Sebastian
Lazarus	Nectarios	Perben	Sebastion
Leander	Nemo	Pericles	Semon
Leon	Nestor	Petar	Socrates
Leonidas	Nicholas	Peter	Solon
Leopold	Nicholaus	Petros	Soterios
Lexus	Nickalus	Phil	Spiro
Lidio	Nicklaus	Philander	Spyros
Linus	Nickolas	Philemon	Stamos
Lukas	Nicky	Philip	Stavros
Lysander	Nico	Phillip	Steeve
Makarios	Nicodemus	Phillipos	Steeven
Makis	Nike	Philo	Stefanos

Stephan

Stephen

Stephon

Stevan

Steve

Steven

Stevens

Stevin

Strephon

Strom

Symon

Tad

Taddeus

Takis

Tanek

Telly

Thad

Thaddeus

Thanos

Theodore

Theophilus

Theron

Thomas

Tim

Timmothy

Timmy

Timon

Timothy

Tino

Titus

Toni

Tony

Topher

Tracy

Tyrone

Urian

Vasilis

Venedictos

Xan

Xander

Xenophon

Xenos

Xylon

Yanni

Yoni

Yorgos

Ysidro

Zale

Zander

Zeno

Zephyr

Zeus

Zorba

Zotikos

GYPSY

GIRLS

Chavi

Miri

Patia

Rawnie

Tasarla

Tawny

BOYS

Baul

Bavol

Bersh

Cam

Cappi

Chal

Chik

Danior

Dukker

Durriken

Durril

Fordel

Jal

Jibben

Kerey

Kistur

Lash

Lel

Lennor

Lutherum

Mander

Nav

Nicabar

Patrin

Pattin

Pias

Pov

Rye

Stiggur

Tas

Tawno

Tem

Tobar

Wen

Wesh

Yarb

HAUSA

GIRLS

Tashi

BOYS

Danladi

Daren

Ibrahim

Rago

Taliki

Yohance

Zaki

HAWAIIAN

GIRLS

Ailani

Akela

Alamea

Alana

Alani

Aleka

Alika

Aloha

Amaui

Ana

Anela

Ani

Anouhea

Aolani

'Aulani

Halia

Ikia

Ilima

Inoa

Iolana

Kai

Kalama

Kalani

Kalea

Kalei

Kalena

Kali

Kalia

Kalina

Kamea

Kamiya

Kanani

Kani

Kanoa

Kapua

Kaulana

Kawena

Keala

Keiki

Keilani

Kekona

Kiele

Kina

Kini

Kona

Lahela

Laka

Lana

Lani

Lea

Lei

Leilani

Luann

Makala

Makana

Makani

Malana

Malia

Mamo

Mana

Mei

Mele

Miliani

Mililani

Moana

Mohala

Nalani

Nana

Nani

Noelani

Noma

Okalani

Olina

Peke

Pua

Pualani

Rapa

Roselani

Suke

Sukey

Suse

Ululani

Wainani

Wanika

Wilikinia

BOYS

Aukai

Bane

Ekewaka

Hawaiian boys
  continued)

Elika

Hanale

Haoa

Havika

Hiu

Iokepa

Ionakana

Iukini

Ka'eo

Kahale

Kaholo

Kai

Kaili

Kainoa

Kaipo

Kala

Kalama

Kalani

Kale

Kali

Kamaka

Kamakani

Kamuela

Kanaiela

Kane

Kanoa

Kapono

Kawika

Keahi

Keaka

Kealoha

Keawe

Kekapa

Kekipi

Kekoa

Kele

Keli

Keli'i

Keoki

Keola

Keoni

Kiele

Kika

Kimo

Kimokeo

Kini

Koi

Koka

Kona

Konane

Koukalaka

Laban

Lani

Lei

Lekeke

Liban

Likeke

Liko

Lio

Loe

Lokela

Lono

Lopaka

Lui

Lukela

Lulani

Mahi'ai

Makaio

Makani

Maleko

Mamo

Mano

Manu

Mauli

Meka

Mikáele

Mililani

Nahele

Namaka

Nohea

Oke

Oliwa

Onaona

Pakelika

Palaina

Palani

Paulo

Pekelo

Peleke

Peniamina

Pilipo

Uku

Wene

Wikoli

Wile

Wiliama

HEBREW

GIRLS

Aaleyah

Aaliah

Aaliyah

Abagail	Aleya	Ayla	Danit
Abbagail	Alia	Basia	Danna
Abbey	Aliya	Bathsheba	Dannielle
Abbygail	Aliza	Becca	Dara
Abegail	Alizabeth	Bess	Davida
Abigail	Allia	Beth	Debbie
Abira	Alliyah	Betty	Deborah
Abra	Alyah	Betula	Delilah
Abria	Amaris	Bina	Dena
Abygail	Amira	Boacha	Denae
Adah	Amissa	Branda	Devora
Adama	Amita	Carmela	Dina
Adena	Anais	Cayla	Dinah
Adina	Aphra	Chai	Diza
Adira	Ardi	Chana	Dodie
Adleigh	Ardice	Chava	Dorrit
Adrielle	Ardith	Chavon	Eden
Aerial	Arella	Chavonne	Edna
Afra	Ari	Chaya	Eleora
Ahava	Ariel	Dalia	Elia
Ahliya	Arin	Daneil	Eliana
Ailya	Aryn	Danelle	Eliane
Airiél	Atara	Dani	Elicia
Aldine	Atira	Dania	Elisabeth
Aleeya	Aviva	Danica	Elisha
Aleeza	Aya	Danielle	Eliza

(Hebrew girls continued)	Hannah	Jesica	Jordyn
Elizabet	Hanni	Jesse	Jori
Elizabeth	Hava	Jesseca	Josey
Elsa	Haviva	Jessica	Joshlyn
Emanuelle	Hinda	Jessie	Jourdan
Emmanuelle	Ian	Jessika	Jozie
Ethana	Ikia	Jessyca	Judith
Eva	Ilana	Jésusa	Judy
Eve	Ileana	Jezebel	Kaela
Ezri	Ilisha	Jimi	Kaila
Gada	Itamar	Joan	Karmel
Gail	Ivria	Joanie	Katriel
Gali	Iyana	Joanny	Kayla
Ganya	Jacobi	Joaquina	Kaylah
Gavriella	Jael	Joby	Kaylan
Geela	Jaffa	Joelle	Kayleen
Geva	Jami	Johanie	Keila
Gilana	Jane	Johnnie	Kelila
Gisa	Janice	Jolene	Kenia
Gurit	Janna	Jonatha	Kenya
Hadara	Jardena	Jonina	Keren
Hadassah	Jayna	Jonita	Keziah
Hagar	Jem	Jora	Kitra
Hania	Jemima	Jordan	Laela
Hanna	Jemma	Jordana	Lateefah
Hanna	Jerusha	Jorden	Layla

Leah	Maika	Micayla	Nizana
Leeza	Malha	Michaela	Noemi
Leila	Malina	Michala	Noemie
Lena	Mangena	Mika	Noemy
Leora	Maraya	Mikaela	Noga
Levana	Maria	Mikala	Nurita
Levia	Mariah	Milena	Nyomi
Levona	Mariam	Mireille	Odeda
Lewana	Marilla	Mireya	Odelia
Lia	Marily	Miriam	Odera
Liana	Marlyn	Moriah	Ofira
Liane	Marni	Moselle	Ofra
Libby	Marnie	Nagida	Ohanna
Liora	Marnina	Naomi	Oma
Lirit	Mary	Naomie	Oprah
Liron	Maryam	Nasya	Oralee
Lisa	Matana	Natania	Orinda
Lisha	Mathena	Nava	Orli
Livana	Mattea	Neta	Ornice
Livia	Mazel	Nili	Orpah
Liviya	Mehira	Nima	Oz
Livona	Mehitabel	Nina	Ozara
Luann	Meira	Nirel	Pazia
Machaela	Meka	Nissa	Peninah
Magali	Micaela	Nita	Perah
Mahira	Micah	Nitza	Pora

Rabecca

Rachael

Racheal

Rachel

Rae

Raechel

Rafaela

Rama

Rani

Ranita

Raphaela

Raya

Raychel

Reba

Rebeca

Rebecca

Rebekah

Rebi

Rena

Reubena

Reva

Rimona

Rinah

Rishona

Riva

Rivka

Rochelle

Ronli

Rubena

Ruth

Ruthie

Sabra

Sabrina

Sade

Sadie

Saida

Saira

Salome

Samala

Samantha

Samatha

Sameh

Sami

Samone

Samuela

Samuelle

Sanne

Sapphira

Sara

Sarah

Sarai

Saree

Sariah

Sarina

Sarrah

Sayde

Sayra

Selima

Serafina

Shamira

Shana

Shara

Sharai

Sharna

Sharon

Sharonda

Sharrona

Shauna

Shawna

Shayna

Sheba

Sheena

Shifra

Shilo

Shira

Shoshana

Shulamith

Shyra

Sidonia

Simcha

Simone

Sue

Sula

Susan

Susana

Suzanna

Symone

Tahlia

Takenya

Talia

Tamar

Tamara

Tamassa

Tamera

Tamira

Tammy

Tamra

Temira

Thirza

Thomasina

Tirza

Tivona

Tobi	Zahar	Abisha	Amin
Tommie	Zahavah	Abner	Amir
Tovah	Zaira	Abraham	Amon
Urit	Zakira	Abrahan	Amos
Varda	Zara	Abram	Amram
Vida	Zayit	Absalom	Ardon
Vina	Zemirah	Adam	Ari
Yachne	Zera	Adamson	Ariel
Yadira	Zilla	Adar	Armani
Yael	Zilpah	Addy	Armon
Yaffa	Zimra	Adin	Arnon
Yahaira	Zipporah	Adir	Aron
Yajaira	Ziva	Adiv	Arran
Yakira	Zohar	Adlai	Arvid
Yarkona	Zohra	Admon	Aryeh
Yehudit		Adon	Asa
Yeira	**BOYS**	Adriel	Ash
Yesica	Aaron	Ahab	Ashby
Yessica	Abbey	Akeem	Asher
Yoanna	Abbott	Akiva	Asiel
Yonina	Abe	Almon	Avi
Yonita	Abel	Alon	Aviv
Yosepha	Abiah	Alva	Avner
Yovela	Abie	Amal	Avram
Zacharie	Abiel	Ameer	Avshalom
Zachary	Abir	Amiel	Azriel

Azuriah	Chaim	Dovev	Ely
Barak	Chanan	Dur	Emanuel
Barnabas	Chiram	Eb	Emmanuel
Bart	Chuco	Eben	Enoch
Bartholomew	Coby	Ebenezer	Enos
Baruch	Dagan	Eden	Ephraim
Ben	Dan	Eder	Esau
Ben-ami	Danial	Efrain	Esequiel
Benjamen	Daniel	Efrat	Eshkol
Benjamin	Daniele	Efrem	Ethan
Benjiman	Danno	Efren	Ezekiel
Benny	Danny	Eitan	Ezequiel
Beno	Danyel	Elam	Ezer
Benoni	Dar	Elan	Ezra
Benson	Dave	Elchanan	Gabe
Benzi	Davey	Eleazar	Gabrial
Ben Zion	David	Eli	Gabriel
Binah	Dekel	Eliazar	Gavriel
Boaz	Dermot	Elie	Geremia
Bram	Deron	Elihu	Gershom
Cain	Deror	Elijah	Gibor
Cale	Didi	Eliseo	Gideon
Caleb	Dor	Elisha	Gidon
Carmel	Doran	Eliyahu	Gil
	Dotan	Elkan	Gilon
	Dov	Elrad	Givon

Goel	Iman	Jaivon	Jediah
Goliath	Immanuel	Jake	Jedidiah
Gomer	Ira	Jakob	Jehu
Gozol	Isaac	James	Jerad
Gurion	Isaak	Jamin	Jerahmy
Guy	Isaiah	Jamon	Jeramie
Hadar	Isaias	Japheth	Jere
Ham	Ishmael	Jarad	Jered
Hanan	Israel	Jarah	Jereme
Harel	Isreal	Jardan	Jeremiah
Harrod	Issac	Jareb	Jeremie
Haskel	Issiah	Jared	Jeriah
Heber	Itzak	Jaren	Jermiah
Heman	Izzy	Jarod	Jerod
Herschel	Jabez	Jaron	Jerrett
Hersh	Jabin	Jarred	Jeshua
Hershel	Jacan	Jarren	Jess
Hezekiah	Jacob	Jarrod	Jesse
Hillel	Jacobi	Jarryd	Jessy
Hiram	Jacobo	Jaryn	Jesus
Hod	Jaden	Javan	Jethro
Honi	Jadon	Javon	Jett
Hosea	Jadyn	Jaycob	Jevan
Ichabod	Jael	Jeb	Jevon
Ike	Jahvon	Jebediah	Jim
Ilan	Jaiden	Jed	Jo

(Hebrew boys
continued)

Joab

Joachim

Job

Joby

Jodan

Jody

Joe

Joel

Joeseph

Joey

John

Johnathan

Johnathon

Johnnie

Johnny

Jon

Jonah

Jonas

Jonatan

Jonathan

Jonathon

Jonny

Jora

Joram

Jordan

Jorden

Jordon

Jordy

Jordyn

Jory

Joseph

Josh

Joshua

Josiah

Josue

Jotham

Jourdan

Jubal

Judah

Judd

Kaeleb

Kaleb

Kaniel

Karmel

Kayle

Kayleb

Kayne

Kedem

Kenaz

Kenya

Kiva

Lapidos

Lavan

Lavi

Lemuel

Leor

Lev

Levi

Levin

Liron

Lot

Lyron

Magen

Mahir

Malachi

Manuel

Marnin

Mathew

Matson

Matt

Matthew

Matty

Mayer

Mehetabel

Meir

Melchior

Menachem

Menassah

Mered

Meshach

Meyer

Micah

Micha

Michael

Mika

Mikal

Mike

Misael

Mordecai

Mose

Moses

Moshe

Naaman

Nachman

Nadav

Naftali

Nagid

Namir

Natanael

Nate

Nathan

Nathanael

Nathanial	Pinchas	Sean	Tal
Nathanie	Raanan	Seraphim	Tam
Nathaniel	Racham	Seth	Tamar
Nathen	Rafi	Shai	Telem
Nazareth	Rani	Shalom	Teman
Nehemiah	Raphael	Shamar	Teva
Nemo	Rapheal	Shamir	Thaniel
Nethaniel	Ravid	Sharron	Timur
Nimrod	Raviv	Shavar	Tivon
Nissan	Rayi	Shayne	Tobias
Noach	Reuben	Shem	Tobin
Noah	Reuven	Shiloh	Tommie
Noam	Ron	Shimon	Tommy
Noé	Roni	Shimshon	Tovi
Nuri	Ruben	Shlomo	Tuvya
Nuriel	Ruby	Shmuel	Tzadok
Obadiah	Rueben	Si	Tzion
Oded	Salomon	Simcha	Tzuriel
Ofer	Sam	Simms	Tzvi
Ophir	Sami	Simmy	Uri
Oren	Sammy	Simon	Uriah
Ori	Samson	Simpson	Uriel
Oved	Samual	Sivan	Uzi
Oz	Samuel	Sol	Uziel
Palti	Sasson	Solly	Vered
Pesach	Saul	Solomon	Yadid

Yadon

Yael

Yagil

Yair

Yanton

Yaphet

Yarden

Yarom

Yaron

Yavin

Yechiel

Yedidya

Yehoshua

Yehoyakem

Yehudi

Yeshaya

Yeshurun

Yigal

Yirmaya

Yishai

Yisrael

Yitro

Yitzchak

Yoav

Yochanan

Yoel

Yonah

Yonatan

Yoram

Yosef

Yoshiyahu

Yosu

Yoyi

Yuri

Yuval

Zac

Zacary

Zaccary

Zaccheus

Zach

Zachari

Zacharia

Zachariah

Zacharie

Zachary

Zachery

Zachry

Zack

Zackary

Zackery

Zackory

Zadok

Zaide

Zakaria

Zakary

Zakery

Zakkary

Zamir

Zanvil

Zared

Zayit

Zeb

Zebediah

Zebedee

Zebulon

Zechariah

Zed

Zedekiah

Zedidiah

Zeév

Zephaniah

Zev

Zevi

Zia

Zimra

Zion

Ziv

Zohar

Zollie

Zubin

Zuriel

HINDI

GIRLS

Aditi

Adya

Aiyanna

Aja

Ajia

Amlika

Amma

Anala

Ananda

Anila

Artha

Ayanna

Baka

Bakula

Bel

Chandler

Channa

Daru

Deva	Lila	Ratri	Trina
Devi	Mahesa	Rekha	Tula
Ganesa	Makara	Risha	Tulsi
Hara	Malini	Rohana	Uma
India	Mandara	Rohini	Usha
Indira	Matrika	Ruana	Vina
Jaya	Maya	Ruchi	Yamuna
Jayne	Medora	Rudra	

BOYS

Jibon	Mehadi	Sadhana	Aakash
Kalinda	Mela	Sagara	Adri
Kamala	Mesha	Sakari	Agni
Kanya	Mina	Sakti	Akash
Karma	Minda	Sala	Amin
Karuna	Mitra	Saura	Amol
Kasi	Narmada	Shaka	Anand
Kaveri	Natesa	Shakti	Anil
Kavindra	Nirveli	Sharan	Arjun
Kerani	Nitara	Shatara	Arun
Kiran	Opal	Shivani	Ashwani
Kirsi	Padma	Sita	Ashwin
Kona	Pandita	Soma	Balin
Kusa	Pausha	Sumati	Balraj
Lajila	Pinga	Syreeta	Bhagwandas
Lakya	Pollyam	Taja	Braham
Lalasa	Priya	Tira	Chander
Latika	Rama	Tirtha	

Daksh

Dandin

Darshan

Deven

Hansh

Hara

Hari

Hasin

Hastin

Inay

Inder

Indiana

Ishan

Jahlil

Jaleel

Jalil

Jatinra

Jivin

Josha

Kabir

Kakar

Kala

Kalkin

Kamal

Kami

Kannan

Kantu

Kapila

Karu

Kavi

Kedar

Kesin

Kinton

Kiritan

Kistna

Krishna

Lal

Linu

Lusila

Madhar

Mahesa

Manu

Marut

Mayon

Mohan

Murali

Nadisu

Nandin

Narain

Natesh

Navin

Nehru

Nila

Onkar

Palash

Paramesh

Pavit

Pramad

Prem

Purdy

Qimat

Rajah

Rajak

Rajan

Raktim

Ram

Ramanan

Ranjan

Ravi

Rishi

Rohan

Rohin

Rohit

Sahir

Sajag

Salmalin

Sanat

Sani

Sanjiv

Sankar

Santosh

Sarad

Sarngin

Sarojin

Shalya

Shiva

Siddhartha

Singh

Siva

Sunreep

Tayib

Thaman

Ultman

Vadin

Valin

Varun

Vasin

Venkat

Vidur

Vijay

Vikas

Vikram

Vikrant	Mansi	Klara	Bela
Vimal	Nova	Lenci	Csaba
Vinay	Sunki	Mali	Domokos
Vinod	Takala	Malika	Elek
Vipul	Talasi	Margit	Endre
Viraj	Toski	Neci	Erno
Virat	Totsi	Nusi	Ferenc
Vishal	Una	Onella	Gábor
Vishnu	Yamka	Réz	Gellert
Vivek	Yoki	Sarolta	Gyula
Yash	Zihna	Sasa	Imre
Yashwant		Shari	Ince
Yatin	**BOYS**	Teca	István
Yogesh	Makyah	Tsigana	János
		Vianca	Jenö
HISPANIC	**HUNGARIAN**	Zigana	Kelemen
BOYS	**GIRLS**	Zizi	Lajos
Chavez	Anci	Zsa Zsa	László
Jesús	Bela	Zsofia	Loránd
Julio	Evie	Zsuzsanna	Lóránt
Hopi	Franci		Maco
	Ila	**BOYS**	Maks
GIRLS	Ilka	Andor	Marcilka
Hola	Ilona	András	Maxi
Kai	Juci	Antal	Micu
Kasa	Juliana	Bandi	Miksa
Kaya			

(Hungarian boys continued)

Miska

Natan

Niki

Nikko

Ödön

Orbán

Pál

Pista

Rendor

Réz

Sándor

Szygfrid

Tabor

Tass

Tibor

Tomi

Vencel

Vidor

Viktor

Vili

Vinci

Zako

Zoltán

Zsigmond

IBO

GIRLS

Adamma

Chinue

Olisa

BOYS

Agu

Chike

Chinua

Chioke

Chuma

Dumaka

Ilom

Iniko

Jaja

Madu

Mazi

Ngozi

N'nambi

Ogbonna

Okechuku

Okeke

Okorie

Okpara

Orji

Uche

Worie

Yafeu

ICELANDIC

GIRLS

Artis

Falda

Sula

BOYS

Arthur

Erikur

INDONESIAN

BOYS

Kersen

INDO-PAKISTANI

BOYS

Adri

IRISH

GIRLS

Africa

Afrika

Aileen

Ailis

Aislinn

Alaina

Alana

Alanna

Allana

Allena

Alonna

Arlene

Artis

Ashlyn

Barrie

Bedelia

Berget

Biddy

Blaine

Brady

Brea

Breana

Breann

Breauna

Breck

Bree

Breeana

Breena

Breiana

Brenda

Brenna	Carra	Darnee	Fionnula
Breona	Casey	Daron	Flannery
Brett	Casidy	Daryn	Gitta
Breyana	Casie	Deidra	Gladis
Breyona	Cassady	Deirdre	Gladys
Briana	Cassidy	Delainey	Glenna
Brianne	Catelyn	Delaney	Ilene
Bridey	Cathleen	Delanie	Ina
Bridget	Ceara	Derry	Ita
Bridgett	Ceira	Devan	Jilleen
Brienna	Ciara	Devin	Kacey
Brina	Ciera	Devyn	Kaetlyn
Briona	Colleen	Diedra	Kaitlin
Brita	Collina	Dillan	Kaitlyn
Briyana	Connor	Doreen	Karah
Brodie	Corey	Earlene	Kasey
Bryana	Cori	Eda	Kassidy
Bryna	Cristen	Edana	Katalina
Bryona	Curran	Eileen	Katelin
Caitlan	Cyerra	Ena	Katelyn
Caitlin	Dacey	Erin	Kathleen
Caitlyn	Dacia	Erinn	Katilyn
Cara	Dallas	Eryn	Katlin
Caralee	Darby	Evania	Katlyn
Carlin	Darci	Fallon	Kaytlin
Carlyn	Darion	Fiona	Keaira

Keana

Keara

Keeley

Keelyn

Keena

Keiana

Keira

Kelley

Kelli

Kelly

Kellyanne

Kellyn

Kenna

Kennedy

Kenzie

Keona

Keri

Kerry

Kevyn

Keyara

Kiara

Kiera

Kiley

Kyara

Kyla

Kyle

Kylee

Kyleigh

Kylene

Kylie

Lana

Lee

Logan

Mab

Mackenzie

Maegan

Maeve

Maira

Makenzie

Mare

Maura

Maureen

Maygan

Mckinley

Mckinzie

Meagan

Meara

Megan

Megane

Melvina

Meri

Meriel

Meryl

Moira

Mollie

Mona

Morena

Muriel

Myrna

Nayely

Neala

Neely

Neila

Nessie

Nevina

Nia

Nila

Niya

Nokomis

Nola

Noreen

Nuala

Nya

Nyla

Ona

Oona

Oriana

Orinda

Orla

Ornice

Payton

Peyton

Phallon

Quincy

Raegan

Ragan

Raleigh

Ranait

Reagan

Regan

Reganne

Reilly

Riana

Richael

Rilee

Riley

Riona

Rori

Ryan

Rylee

Ryleigh

Ryley

Sass	Sheena	Ula	Blaine
Seana	Sheila	Una	Blair
Seirra	Shena	Yseult	Blane
Selma	Sheridan		Blayne
Shae	Shona	**BOYS**	Bogart
Shaelee	Shonda	Adan	Bowie
Shaelyn	Shonta	Aden	Brady
Shana	Shunta	Aiden	Brannon
Shanae	Siara	Aimon	Brayan
Shane	Sianna	Aindrea	Breck
Shanley	Siera	Al	Brendan
Shanna	Sierra	Alan	Brenden
Shannen	Sina	Allan	Brennan
Shannon	Sinead	Allen	Breyon
Shauna	Siobhan	Alpin	Brian
Shaunda	Sloane	Ardal	Brion
Shaunta	Tara	Arlen	Brodie
Shawna	Tari	Arthur	Brody
Shawnda	Tarra	Bain	Bryan
Shawnee	Taryn	Bainbridge	Bryant
Shawnta	Tierney	Baird	Caley
Shay	Tipper	Banning	Calhoun
Shayla	Trevina	Bard	Callahan
Shaylee	Trevona	Barry	Callum
Shaylyn	Troya	Beacan	Car
Shea	Tullia	Beagan	Carlin

(Irish boys
    continued)

Carney

Carrick

Carroll

Case

Casey

Cass

Cassidy

Cassie

Cavan

Cian

Clancy

Cleary

Cluny

Colin

Collins

Coman

Conall

Conan

Conary

Conlan

Conner

Connie

Connor

Conor

Conroy

Conway

Corcoran

Corey

Cormac

Corrigan

Corrin

Cosgrove

Cowan

Coyle

Craig

Crofton

Cullen

Culley

Cunningham

Curran

Cyle

Dacey

Daley

Daran

Darby

Darcy

Daren

Darian

Darien

Darin

Darion

Daron

Darren

Darrin

Darrion

Darron

Declan

Delaney

Delano

Demond

Dempsey

Dermot

Derren

Derry

Desmond

Devan

Deven

Devin

Devine

Devlin

Devon

Devyn

Dewayne

Dezmon

Digby

Dillan

Dillon

Dinsmore

Doherty

Dolan

Donahue

Donal

Donavan

Donnell

Donnelly

Donnie

Donovan

Dooley

Dow

Doyle

Duane

Dugan

Dwayne

Ea

Eachan

Eagan

Eamon

Earl

Egan

Eion

Erin

Eron

Evan	Garvey	Irv	Keaven
Evin	Gaynor	Irvin	Keefe
Fagan	Genty	Irving	Keegan
Farrell	Ghilchrist	Kacey	Keelan
Fergus	Gilby	Kaelan	Keeley
Ferrell	Gilchrist	Kaenan	Keenan
Ferris	Gillean	Kagan	Keenen
Fineas	Gillespie	Kailen	Keevon
Finian	Gilmore	Kain	Kegan
Finlay	Gilroy	Kalan	Keigan
Finn	Girvin	Kallen	Keivan
Finnegan	Glen	Kalon	Kellan
Fitzroy	Glenn	Kane	Kellen
Flann	Glenville	Karney	Keller
Flynn	Godfrey	Kasey	Kelly
Forbes	Gorman	Kassidy	Kelvin
Gair	Grady	Kavan	Kenan
Galbraith	Guthrie	Kavin	Kendrick
Galen	Hagen	Kaylen	Kennard
Gallagher	Hailey	Keagan	Kennedy
Galloway	Haley	Keanan	Kenneth
Galvin	Harkin	Keane	Kenyon
Gannon	Hogan	Keanu	Keon
Garett	Hoyt	Kearn	Kermit
Garret	Hurley	Kearney	Kern
Garrett	Innis	Keary	Kerry

(Irish boys
continued)

Kerwin

Kevan

Keven

Kevin

Kevon

Kevyn

Keyon

Kiel

Kieran

Kiernan

Kile

Killian

Kinnard

Kion

Konner

Konnor

Korey

Korrigan

Kory

Kraig

Kyele

Kylan

Kyle

Larkin

Laughlin

Lawler

Lennon

Liam

Lochlain

Logan

Lomán

Lorcan

Lucas

Lunn

Lynch

Macallister

Macarthur

Maccoy

Maccrea

Mackenzie

Mackinnley

Macklain

Maclean

Macmahon

Macmurray

Magee

Maguire

Mahon

Mairtin

Maitias

Maitiú

Makenzie

Mal

Malachy

Maloney

Malvin

Mannix

Mayo

McKenzie

Mckinley

Mel

Melrone

Melvin

Merrill

Merritt

Merv

Mervin

Micheal

Mickenzie

Mickey

Mikeal

Monahan

Monroe

Moss

Mundy

Murphy

Murtagh

Neal

Neil

Nevan

Nevin

Niall

Nolan

Nyle

Ode

Odell

Odran

Oistin

O'neil

Oran

Oren

O'Shea

Owen

Owney

Paddy

Padraic

Parth

Parthalán

Patterson

Phelan

Phinean

Piran

Quigley	Ryne	Strahan	Troy
Quillan	Ryon	Struthers	Tully
Quinlan	Scanlon	Sullivan	Tynan
Quinn	Scully	Sully	Tyrone
Rafer	Seamus	Sweeney	Uaine
Rafferty	Sean	Taggart	Uilliam
Raghnall	Searlas	Teagan	Uinseann
Rayan	Sedric	Teague	Uistean
Reagan	Shaine	Tegan	

IROQUOIS

GIRLS

Onatah

Orenda

Seneca

ITALIAN

GIRLS

Regan	Shamus	Thady	
Reilly	Shan	Tiernan	
Renny	Shanahan	Tierney	
Rhyan	Shane	Tomás	
Rian	Shanley	Tomey	
Riddock	Shannon	Torian	
Riley	Shaun	Torin	Abriana
Riordan	Shawn	Tormey	Adriana
Roarke	Shay	Torn	Adrienna
Rogan	Shea	Torrance	Alessandra
Ronán	Sheehan	Torren	Anna
Rooney	Sheridan	Torrence	Aryana
Rory	Sierra	Trace	Bambi
Ryan	Siseal	Tracey	Bianca
Ryen	Skelly	Tracy	Bianka
Rylee	Slevin	Trev	Bionca
Ryley	Sloan	Trevor	

(Italian girls continued)

Blanca

Camellia

Camila

Capri

Caprice

Carina

Carine

Carlotta

Carolina

Chiara

Ciana

Clarice

Clarissa

Concetta

Crista

Daniela

Deangela

Dona

Doña

Donna

Elena

Elisa

Emilia

Filippa

Filomena

Francesca

Franchesca

Francisca

Gabriela

Gaetana

Gema

Gessica

Ghita

Gianna

Gina

Giordana

Giovanna

Giulia

Isabella

Italia

Jianna

Jina

Jovanna

Jovannie

Justina

Kami

Karah

Klarissa

Lia

Lucia

Lucrezia

Margarita

Maria

Marice

Marietta

Marsala

Mia

Michele

Mila

Milana

Nicola

Ortensia

Paola

Pia

Primavera

Rosa

Rosetta

Ruffina

Speranza

Vedette

Venecia

Zola

BOYS

Adriano

Aldo

Alessandro

Alfonso

Alfredo

Alphonso

Amadeo

Angelo

Antonio

Aretino

Arrigo

Arturo

Benito

Beppe

Bonaro

Bonaventure

Braulio

Bruno

Carlo

Carmine

Cirillo

Claudio

Clemente

Cola

Corrado

Cristoforo

Deangelo

Deanthony

Demarco	Fonso	Giovanni	Luigi
Demario	Fortino	Giovanny	Marcelino
Dino	Francesco	Giuliano	Marcelo
Domenico	Gabrielli	Giulio	Marciano
Donato	Gaetan	Giuseppe	Marco
Drago	Geno	Giustino	Mariano
Edoardo	Genovese	Gregorio	Marino
Elmo	Georgio	Gualtiero	Mario
Emiliano	Geovanni	Guglielmo	Markanthony
Emilio	Geraldo	Guido	Marsalis
Enrico	Geremia	Gustavo	Martino
Ercole	Geremiah	Innocenzio	Masaccio
Eriberto	Geronimo	Jeovanni	Massimo
Ermanno	Giacomo	Jiovanni	Maurizio
Este	Gian	Lanz	Maximiliano
Ettore	Giancarlo	Larenzo	Michelangelo
Fabiano	Gianluca	Lave	Michele
Fabrizio	Gianni	Lazaro	Milan
Falito	Gianpaolo	Leobardo	Napoleon
Faustino	Gino	Leonardo	Nicola
Fausto	Giona	Leopoldo	Nicolas
Federico	Giordano	Lorenzo	Nicolo
Felippo	Giorgio	Loretto	Nuncio
Fiorello	Giosia	Luca	Olindo
Flavio	Giotto	Luciano	Orsino
Florencio	Giovani	Lucio	Otello

(Italian boys
continued)

Paco

Paolo

Pasquale

Peppe

Piero

Pietro

Pino

Primo

Rafaele

Raimondo

Ranieri

Renardo

Renato

Ric

Rico

Rinaldo

Rocco

Rodrigo

Romario

Romello

Romeo

Romy

Rudolpho

Ruggerio

Ruperto

Sal

Salvatore

Samuele

Sandro

Santo

Saverio

Sergio

Severiano

Silvano

Silvestro

Silvio

Stefano

Taddeo

Tazio

Teobaldo

Teodoro

Tiberio

Tino

Tito

Tomasso

Tonio

Tristano

Tulio

Uberto

Ugo

Umberto

Urbano

Valentino

Vicenzo

Vincenzo

Vinci

Vittorio

Zan

JAPANESE

GIRLS

Aiko

Aki

Akiko

Akina

Amaya

Aneko

Asa

Chika

Chiyo

Dai

Gen

Gin

Hachi

Hama

Hana

Hanako

Haru

Hisa

Hoshi

Ima

Ishi

Jin

Kaedé

Kagami

Kaiya

Kameko

Kami

Kane

Kaya

Kei

Keiko

Kiaria

Kiku

Kimi

Kioko

Kishi

Kita

Kiwa

Koko

Koto

Kuma

Kumiko	Nami	Sawa	Tomi
Kuniko	Nara	Sayo	Tomo
Kuri	Nari	Seki	Tora
Kyoko	Nishi	Sen	Tori
Leiko	Nori	Shika	Toshi
Machiko	Nyoko	Shina	Umeko
Maeko	Oki	Shino	Uta
Mai	Orino	Shizu	Wakana
Mari	Osen	Sugi	Washi
Mariko	Raeden	Suki	Wattan
Masago	Raku	Sumi	Yasu
Matsuko	Ran	Suzu	Yei
Michi	Rei	Suzuki	Yoi
Midori	Ren	Taka	Yoko
Mieko	Rin	Takara	Yoné
Mika	Rui	Taki	Yori
Miki	Ruri	Tama	Yoshi
Mina	Ryo	Tamaka	Yuki
Miné	Sachi	Tamika	Yuri
Mio	Sada	Tamiko	
Miwa	Sai	Tani	**BOYS**
Miya	Sakaë	Taree	Akemi
Miyo	Saki	Tazu	Akira
Miyuki	Sakura	Tera	Benjiro
Morie	Sasa	Tetsu	Botan
Mura	Sato	Toki	Chiko

(Japanese boys
continued)

Dai

Danno

Goro

Hideaki

Hiromasa

Hiroshi

Hisoka

Isas

Jiro

Jo

Joben

Joji

Jomei

Jun

Juro

Kado

Kaemon

Kana

Kane

Kaori

Kazuo

Keitaro

Ken

Kentaro

Kin

Kioshi

Kiyoshi

Makoto

Manzo

Mareo

Maro

Masahiro

Masao

Masato

Michio

Miki

Minoru

Montaro

Morio

Naoko

Raiden

Rayden

Rei

Renjiro

Ringo

Saburo

Samuru

Sen

Shiro

Takeo

Tani

Taro

Tomi

Toshi-Shita

Udo

Yasashiku

Yasuo

Yóshi

Yuki

Zen

Zinan

KAKWA

BOYS

Tombe

KIKUYU

BOYS

Barasa

Kamau

KIOWA

BOYS

Apiatan

Gomda

Täpko

Zotom

KISWAHILI

BOYS

Rehema

KOREAN

GIRLS

Cho

Eun

Hye

Ki

Sook

Sun

Sun-Hi

U

Yeo

Yon

BOYS

Chul

Gi

Hyun-Ki

Hyun-Shik

Ja

Jae-Hwa

Kwan

Man-Shik

Man-Young

Mun-Hee

Myung-Dae

Suck Chin

Yon-Sun

Young-Jae

Young-Soo

LAKOTA

GIRLS

Chumani

Winona

Wynonna

BOYS

Chayton

Hotah

Kange

Kohana

Lootah

Mahkah

Mahpee

Matoskah

Napayshni

Odakota

Ogaleesha

Ohanzee

Ohitekah

Otaktay

Paytah

Skah

Takoda

Teetonka

Wahkan

Wahkoowah

Wamblee

Wanikiya

Yahto

LATIN

GIRLS

Adora

Adreana

Adrienne

Aida

Aidan

Aimee

Alba

Alette

Alida

Alivia

Allegra

Alma

Aloma

Alta

Alva

Amabel

Amanada

Amanda

Amelia

Amilia

Amity

Amy

Andrea

Antonia

Antonice

April

Apryl

Arabella

Araceli

Ardelle

Armine

Augusta

Augustine

Aura

Aurelia

Aurelie

Aurora

Austin

Autumn

Avalon

Avis

Axelle

Babe

Baptista

Barbara

Beata

Beatrice

Beatriz

Bella

Belva

Benecia

Benedicta

Benedicte

Bennett

Benni

Bente

Bibi

Bibiana

Bina

Brina

Britt

Bryn

Bryna

Cadence

Calvina

(Latin girls continued)

Cambria

Cameo

Candida

Candra

Cara

Carita

Carla

Carlin

Carmen

Caryl

Cecelia

Cecilia

Cecily

Ceil

Celeste

Celia

Cerella

Cesilia

Charity

Chasidy

Chasity

Chastity

Cherry

Christabel

Christal

Chrystal

Cindy

Clara

Clarabelle

Clarie

Claudia

Claudie

Clementine

Concordia

Connie

Constance

Coral

Corbin

Cordelia

Cornelia

Cristal

Crystal

Dayana

Deana

Deanna

Deanne

Dextra

Di

Dia

Diamond

Diana

Diane

Dianna

Divinia

Dominica

Donata

Drew

Drusi

Drusilla

Dulce

Dyamond

Dyana

Dynasty

Elida

Elita

Elvira

Elyse

Elysia

Elyssa

Emalee

Emelia

Emely

Emily

Erma

Ermine

Essence

Eustacia

Fabia

Fabiana

Fabiola

Faline

Felecia

Felice

Felicia

Felisha

Fidelia

Fidelity

Flavia

Flavie

Flora

Florence

Fonda

Fortuna

Fran

Frances

Francis

Gema

Genesis

Gill

Gillian

Ginger

Ginia

Gladys	Jocelyne	Kesare	Lenita
Gloria	Joi	Kira	Leontine
Glory	Jonquil	Konstance	Leta
Grace	Josalyn	Kornelia	Leticia
Grazia	Joscelin	Kosta	Levana
Grecia	Joselin	Kristal	Levina
Gusta	Joselyn	Krystel	Lian
Hadriane	Joshlyn	Laci	Liana
Harmony	Josilin	Lacrecia	Liberty
Hermina	Jossalin	Lana	Lida
Honey	Josselyn	Lara	Lide
Honora	Jovana	Laraine	Lilian
Hortense	Jovanna	Latisha	Lillian
Ignacia	Jovita	Latona	Lily
Imogene	Joy	Latonya	Lillyann
Indigo	Joyce	Laura	Lina
Irma	Julia	Laurel	Lita
Isadora	Julisa	Laurence	Liv
Ivory	June	Laveda	Lona
Jae	Juno	Lavelle	Lora
Jasleen	Justice	Lavena	Lore
Jaye	Justine	Laverne	Lorenza
Jillaine	Kalare	Lavina	Lori
Jillian	Kambria	Leandra	Loris
Jocelin	Karley	Lecia	Lorna
Jocelyn	Karmen	Lena	Lorraine

(Latin girls
continued)

Lucerne

Lucero

Lucinda

Lucretia

Lucy

Luna

Lupe

Lupita

Luvena

Mabel

Madonna

Magnolia

Manda

Mandy

Maranda

Marcela

Marcella

Marcena

Marcia

Maren

Maresa

Maricela

Marina

Maris

Marisa

Marisela

Marissa

Martina

Maryssa

Maxine

May

Maya

Maybeline

Medea

Melba

Melina

Meliora

Meranda

Mercedes

Merissa

Merle

Minerva

Mira

Mirabel

Miracle

Miranda

Mireille

Modesty

Monica

Morrisa

Myra

Myranda

Nata

Natalee

Natalie

Nataline

Nataly

Nathalie

Nelia

Nidia

Nige

Nila

Noel

Nohely

Nokomis

Nola

Noleta

Nona

Noreen

Norma

Nova

Novella

Nunciata

Nydia

Octavia

Oksana

Olethea

Olinda

Olive

Olivia

Olyvia

Ona

Ondine

Onora

Oona

Ora

Orabella

Orela

Oriana

Oriole

Ormanda

Orsa

Osanna

Ovia

Palma

Passion

Pat

Patia

Patra

Patricia

Patsy

Paula

Paulette	Procopia	Samara	Tera
Pauline	Promise	Sebastiane	Terrene
Paxton	Pru	Secilia	Tertia
Pearl	Prudence	Secunda	Thaddea
Pepper	Prudy	Selia	Tiara
Perdita	Prunella	Septima	Tiarra
Perla	Quartilla	Serena	Tiberia
Perlie	Quinella	Serenity	Tiera
Pernella	Quinetta	Serina	Tiff
Perri	Quintana	Shaila	Tiffani
Persis	Quintessa	Sheila	Tiffany
Petra	Quiterie	Sidra	Tiffy
Petronella	Raine	Signe	Tiphanie
Petula	Regina	Silvia	Tish
Philicia	Regine	Stella	Tisha
Phylicia	Reva	Sulia	Toni
Placidia	Réz	Sylvana	Tonia
Polly	Risa	Sylvia	Topaz
Pomona	River	Sylvie	Tory
Poppy	Roma	Tacita	Tracey
Porcha	Rosalba	Taesha	Traci
Porsha	Rose	Talia	Tracy
Portia	Rula	Tansy	Tralena
Prima	Sabina	Taura	Treasure
Priscilla	Sabrina	Tavia	Triana
Prissy	Salvia	Teaira	Tricia

(Latin girls
    continued)

Trinity

Trish

Trisha

Trissa

Trista

Tristan

Tristen

Tristin

Triston

Trycia

Ulla

Ultima

Una

Undine

Unique

Urbana

Ursa

Val

Valerie

Valene

Valentina

Valeria

Valerie

Valery

Valli

Valonia

Valora

Valorie

Varvara

Venessa

Venus

Vera

Verbena

Verda

Verena

Verenice

Verity

Verlene

Verna

Vernice

Veronica

Veronika

Vespera

Vesta

Vi

Vicki

Vicky

Victoria

Vienna

Viktoria

Vincentia

Viola

Virgilia

Virginia

Viridiana

Viridis

Virtue

Vita

Viv

Viva

Viveca

Vivian

Viviana

Yocelin

Yoselin

Zea

Zerlina

Zia

Zinnia

Zona

BOYS

Ace

Adrian

Agustin

Alban

Albin

Albion

Aleron

Alvern

Alvin

Amadeus

Amicus

Angel

Anthany

Anthonie

Anthony

Antony

Aquila

Ardell

Arden

Armand

Auburn

Augie

August

Augustine

Augustus

Aurelio

Aurelius

Austen

Austin

Axel

Balbo	Cephas	Deante	Felix
Barnabas	Cicero	Decimus	Fidel
Basil	Clare	Delfino	Flavian
Beattie	Clarence	Delmar	Florian
Benedict	Claude	Devine	Foster
Bennett	Clem	Dexter	Fran
Blaze	Clement	Dom	Francis
Boniface	Cole	Domenic	Franco
Boone	Coleman	Dominic	Gaius
Bourne	Columba	Dominick	Garnett
Branch	Constant	Dominik	Genaro
Caesar	Constantine	Durand	Greg
Cal	Corbett	Durant	Greggory
Calvin	Corbin	Eloy	Gregory
Camilo	Cornelius	Elvern	Griffin
Campbell	Corry	Emil	Hadrian
Candide	Cory	Emilien	Hastings
Canute	Creed	Errol	Herman
Carmine	Crispin	Eulises	Hilary
Cornelius	Curt	Eustace	Honoré
Cash	Curtis	Fabian	Horace
Cassius	Cyprian	Fabio	Horacio
Castle	Dacey	Falco	Horatio
Cato	Daimon	Faroh	Hugo
Ceasar	Damon	Faust	Iggy
Cecil	Dante	Favian	Ignacio

Ignatius

Illan

Janus

Jarlath

Jerolin

Jerome

Jeromy

Jovan

Jovani

Jovanny

Jr

Judas

Jude

Julian

Julien

Julius

Junior

Justen

Justice

Justin

Justyn

Juvenal

Kalvin

Kornel

Kornelius

Krispin

Kurt

Kurtis

Larry

Laurence

Lawerence

Lawrence

Leo

Lester

Lombard

Loren

Lorimer

Loritz

Lorne

Lucian

Lucius

Luke

Magnus

Major

Marcellus

Marcus

Marius

Mark

Markel

Marko

Markus

Mars

Martin

Martinus

Marty

Maurice

Maurizio

Maury

Max

Maximilian

Maximillian

Mayer

Merritt

Miles

Millard

Minor

Modesto

Mordred

Morey

Morrie

Morris

Myles

Mynor

Neci

Nelius

Neptune

Nero

Nigel

Noble

Nollie

Octavio

Octavious

Oliver

Oral

Oratio

Ordell

Orien

Orleans

Orono

Orris

Orry

Orson

Ostin

Pastor

Patric

Patrick

Patryk

Paul

Pauli

Pax

Paxton

Payne

Pelí

Penn	Renzo	Taddeus	Trinity
Peregrine	Rex	Tatius	Tullis
Perine	Roman	Taurean	Tully
Pervis	Romel	Taurus	Turner
Peter	Romero	Tavey	Ulises
Pharaoh	Romulus	Tavian	Ulyses
Phelix	Ross	Tearance	Ulysses
Phoenix	Rufus	Temple	Unique
Pio	Sanchez	Terance	Urban
Porter	Sancho	Terence	Val
Prince	Scorpio	Terran	Valentin
Proctor	Seasar	Terrance	Valerian
Prosper	Sebastian	Terrence	Varian
Pryor	Septimus	Terrin	Vedie
Quade	Sereno	Terris	Vere
Quenten	Sextus	Tertius	Vergil
Quentin	Silas	Thad	Vernon
Quenton	Silvan	Thaddeus	Vic
Quinten	Silvester	Titus	Victor
Quintin	Stan	Tony	Vin
Quinton	Stanislaus	Torrence	Vincent
Quitin	Sy	Tracy	Virgil
Ransom	Sylas	Trent	Vitas
Regis	Sylvester	Trenton	Vito
Remus	Tad	Trini	Xanthus

LATVIAN

GIRLS

Lizina

BOYS

Ansis

Brencis

Janis

Karlen

Martins

Mikelis

Mychajlo

Niklas

Oleg

Zanis

Zigfrid

LENAPE

BOYS

Talli

LITHUANIAN

GIRLS

Rasa

BOYS

Antavas

Jonas

Jurgis

Moze

Petras

Raulas

Raulo

Valter

Vanda

LOMWE

BOYS

Unika

LUGANDA

GIRLS

Masani

Nafuna

Sanyu

BOYS

Dembe

Kamoga

Kamya

Kibuuka

Kizza

Lutalo

Madongo

Magomu

Mayonga

Mpoza

Mukasa

Mwaka

Mwanje

Sanyu

Semanda

Sempala

Setimba

Zesiro

Zilaba

LUO

BOYS

Kifeda

Ocan

Okuth

Otem

MAHONA

GIRLS

Kamali

MALAYAN

GIRLS

Javana

Javona

MAORI

GIRLS

Nyree

MONGOLIAN

BOYS

Yul

MOQUELUM-NAN

GIRLS

Hateya

Hausa

Heltu

Kaliska

Kamata

Litonya

Lusela

Luyu

Mituna

Oya

Pakuna

Papina

Pati

Sanuye

Sawa

Sibeta

Suki

Suletu

Taipa

Takenya

Wauna

Winema

BOYS

Elki

Helki

Hesutu

Honon

Howi

Kono

Kosumi

Lanu

Leyati

Lise

Liwanu

Lokni

Luyu

Metikla

Misu

Molimo

Momuso

Muata

Notaku

Oya

Patakusu

Sewati

Sipatu

Telutci

Tiimu

Tiktu

Tuketu

Tukuli

Tumu

Tupi

Utatci

Uzumati

Wilanu

Wilu

Wuyi

Yelutci

Yoskolo

Yotimo

Yutu

MUGANDA

BOYS

Najji

MUSOGA

GIRLS

Wesisa

BOYS

Mulogo

MWERA

GIRLS

Kanika

BOYS

Beno

Makalani

Nangwaya

Tumaini

Tuwile

NATIVE AMERICAN

GIRLS

Aiyana

Anaba

Angeni

Aquene

Bena

Chenoa

Cherokee

Cholena

Dakota

Dena

Dyana

Halona

Helki

Heta

Imala

Izusa

Kachina

Kahsha

Kanda

Kiona

Leotie

Lomasi

Lulu

Magena

Mahala

Malina

Mausi

Mika

Minal

Minowa

Nashota

Nata

Netis

Nina

Nituna

Nuna

Ogin

(Native American girls continued)	BOYS	Igashu	Nibaw
	Ahanu	Inteus	Nigan
Olathe	Ahdik	Isekemu	Nikiti
Onawa	Akule	Istu	Nitis
Oneida	Anoki	Iye	Nodin
Petunia	Awan	Jolon	Nokonyu
Rozene	Bly	Kaga	Ohanko
Sakuna	Chesmu	Kijika	Otadan
Satinka	Delsin	Knoton	Otu
Shada	Demothi	Langundo	Paco
Shappa	Dyami	Lenno	Palladin
Sihu	Elan	Lonato	Pat
Sisika	Elsu	Manipi	Patamon
Sora	Enyeto	Maska	Patwin
Soso	Etu	Masou	Payat
Taima	Eyota	Mato	Pillan
Tala	Gosheven	Melvern	Powa
Tiponya	Guyapi	Milap	Sahale
Utina	Hahnee	Mingan	Sahil
Waneta	Hakan	Mojag	Sakima
Wyanet	Helaku	Motega	Siwili
Wyoming	Hinun	Muraco	Son
Yenene	Honovi	Nahma	Songan
Yepa	Hototo	Nawat	Tadan
Yoluta	Huslu	Nayati	Taima
Zaltana	Hute	Neka	Tate

Tohon

Tyee

Wakiza

Wapi

Wemilat

Wemilo

Wenutu

Wichado

Wilny

Wingi

Wuliton

Wunand

Wynono

Yana

Yancy

Yottoko

Yuma

NAVAJO

GIRLS

Kai

Mai

Yanaba

BOYS

Nantai

Sani

NGONI

BOYS

Dulani

Funsoni

Kafele

Kamuzu

Kasiya

Kwacha

Kwayera

Kwende

Mpasa

Mtima

Ndale

Sabola

Tsalani

Zikomo

NIGERIAN

GIRLS

Adanna

Fayola

Femi

BOYS

Azi

Ekon

Kayin

Nwa

Nwake

Ogun

Ottah

Uzoma

NORTH AFRICAN

GIRLS

Kami

Kamilah

NORWEGIAN

GIRLS

Elga

Gala

Gunda

Haldana

Lena

Runa

Unn

BOYS

Aksel

Arkin

Arve

Arvid

Birger

Bodil

Dreng

Dyre

Egil

Eskil

Faste

Finn

Frode

Galt

Gaute

Halvor

Hauk

Havelock

Kare

Kleng

Magnar

Mikkel

Morten

Nicolai

Odd

Odo

Ottar

Oystein

Petter

Ragnar

Reidar

(Norwegian boys continued)

Roald

Roar

Skule

Stefen

Steinar

Stian

Storr

Tor

Trygve

Vegard

Vidar

NYAKUSA

BOYS

Ipyana

Mposi

Mwamba

Watende

OCHI

BOYS

Essien

OMAHA

GIRLS

Migina

Nida

Tadita

Urika

BOYS

Mikasi

Tadi

OSAGE

GIRLS

Minya

Niabi

PAKISTANI

GIRLS

Surata

Surya

BOYS

Sharad

Sharod

PASHTO

GIRLS

Mallalai

PAWNEE

BOYS

Kuruk

Lesharo

Sakuruta

Skiriki

PERSIAN

GIRLS

Alea

Anahita

Armani

Ayesha

Esther

Hestia

Jasmain

Jasmin

Jasmine

Jasmyn

Jazmin

Jazmyn

Jazzmin

Kira

Laleh

Lila

Lilia

Marjan

Mehri

Mina

Mitra

Nahid

Pari

Parveneh

Peri

Roxana

Roxann

Roxy

Sadira

Soraya

Souzan

Taraneh

Vashti

Yasmeen

Yasmin

Yazmin

Zena

Zenda

Zohreh

BOYS

Aban

Arman

Arsha

Bahram

Bijan

Casper

Cass

Cy

Cyrus

Dareh

Feroz

Jamsheed

Jasmin

Kasper

Kaveh

Mehrdad

Nard

Nasim

Shah

Sohrab

Soroush

Tabor

Xerxes

PERUVIAN

BOYS

Manco

PHOENICIAN

GIRLS

Adama

Tanith

BOYS

Adam

Anibal

Hannibal

Ib

POLISH

GIRLS

Ania

Anka

Bryga

Ela

Elizaveta

Elka

Gita

Jasia

Jula

Kasia

Krysta

Macey

Macia

Magda

Manka

Marjan

Mela

Minka

Morela

Nata

Pela

Tawia

Tola

Tosha

Waleria

Wera

Weronika

Wicktoria

Wira

Wisia

Zocha

Zusa

Zytka

BOYS

Andros

Atek

Aurek

Bronislaw

Cerek

Crystek

Danek

Dobry

Fil

Garek

Genek

Gerek

Gerik

Gwidon

Heniek

Holleb

Honok

Iwan

Janek

Jas

Jedrek

Jerzy

Karol

Kazio

Koby

Krystian

Liuz

Lubomir

Luboslaw

Machas

Maksym

Mandek

Marcin

Marian

Marke

(Polish boys continued)

Mateusz

Matyas

Michal

Mikolaj

Milek

Miron

Moshe

Natan

Nelek

Olés

Onufry

Otek

Patek

Paulin

Pawel

Radoslaw

Rafal

Rufin

Slawek

Stasio

Stefan

Stefon

Szczepan

Szymon

Tadzio

Tedorik

Telek

Tymon

Tytus

Walerian

Wicent

Wiktor

Wincent

Wit

Witek

Wladislav

Zarek

Zygmunt

POLYNESIAN

GIRLS

Lulani

Oliana

Palila

Ulani

BOYS

Kannon

Pomo

Boys

Dasan

PONCA

GIRLS

Pazi

BOYS

Mika

PORTUGUESE

GIRLS

Mel

Vidonia

Xuxa

Zetta

BOYS

Belmiro

Cruz

Duarte

Francisco

Giacinto

Gregorio

Guilherme

Henrique

Humberto

Jacinto

Jaco

João

Joaquim

Josef

Lando

Laudalino

Liberio

Lidio

Markes

Marques

Marquez

Martinho

Miguel

Moises

Paulo

Raimundo

Ramiro

Ricardo

Roberto

Rogerio

Rolando

Ronaldo

Rosario

Serafino

Simão

Timoteo

Tonio

Zacarias

Zeusef

PUNJABI

GIRLS

Amandeep

Bandi

Chardae

Gurpreet

Harpreet

Jaspreet

Mandeep

Manpreet

Raheem

Sandeep

Shardae

Sherika

Thanh

Tosha

BOYS

Ajay

Amandeep

Amar

Amir

Amit

Gurpreet

Hardeep

Harpreet

Jaspal

Maalik

Málik

Mandeep

Raheem

Rakeem

Sandeep

Shad

Sundeep

QUICHÉ

GIRLS

Xela

RHODESIAN

BOYS

Kaseko

Matope

Mundan

ROMANIAN

GIRLS

Ioana

Jenica

BOYS

Andrei

Enric

Ioan

Iosua

Mihail

Petru

Toma

RUKIGO

BOYS

Ruhakana

RUNYANKORE

BOYS

Kabonero

Kamuhanda

Kamukama

Kariisa

Karutunda

Kato

Katungi

Kayonga

Nkunda

RUNYORO

BOYS

Kaikara

Mugamba

RUSSIAN

GIRLS

Alena

Angelina

Annik

Anya

Breasha

Dasha

Duscha

Ekaterina

Galina

Gasha

Gelya

Halina

Irina

Jelena

Jereni

Karina

Karine

Katia

Khristina

Kisa

Lada

Lelya

Lenore

(Russian girls continued)

Lera

Liolya

Lizabeta

Lubov

Magda

Manka

Manya

Marisha

Masha

Melana

Mika

Milena

Misha

Nata

Natacha

Natalia

Natasha

Natosha

Neva

Nika

Niki

Nikita

Nyusha

Olena

Orina

Orlenda

Panya

Pavla

Pheodora

Raisa

Rusalka

Sacha

Sasha

Shura

Sonia

Sonya

Stasya

Stepania

Svetlana

Tamar

Taneya

Tania

Tanya

Tasha

Tata

Tosha

Valera

Vania

Yalena

Yekaterina

Yelena

Yelisabeta

Yudita

Yulia

Zasha

Zilya

BOYS

Adrik

Aizik

Aleksei

Andrei

Arkady

Baran

Beredei

Bladimir

Borka

Christoff

Dima

Dimitri

Dmitri

Egor

Evgeny

Feliks

Fillipp

Filya

Foma

Fyodor

Gavril

Gena

Grisha

Gyorgy

Helge

Igor

Ilya

Ioakim

Iosif

Iustin

Ivan

Jasha

Karlen

Kenya

Kesar

Khaim

Kharald

Kolya

Konstantin

Labrentsis

Lavrenti

Leonid

Lev

Maksim

Matvey	Tano	Youri	Kama
Maxim	Timofey	Yov	Kashmir
Michail	Tisha	Yuri	Kumuda
Mika	Todor	Yusif	Lalita
Mikhail	Ustin	Yustyn	Lilac
Misha	Valerii	Zhek	Mahila
Natan	Vanya	Zhora	Nata
Nicolai	Vasily	Zigfrid	Rana
Nikita	Venya		Rani
Nikolai	Viktor	**RUTOORO**	Rita
Nil	Vitya	**BOYS**	Roshan
Oleg	Vladimir	Gonza	Rupinder
Oleksandr	Vlas	Irumba	Sanya
Osip	Vova	Kabiito	Veda
Osya	Vyacheslav	Kabonesa	Vida
Panas	Wanya	Karwana	Zudora
Pasha	Wasili	Mugisa	
Pavel	Yakov	Sabiti	**BOYS**
Pyotr	Yan		Ajit
Sacha	Yanick	**SANSKRIT**	Akshat
Sachar	Yanka	**GIRLS**	Alok
Sasha	Yasha	Amrit	Ambar
Sergei	Yegor	Chaka	Amish
Slava	Yeremey	Chakra	Amrit
Stasik	Yeska	Chanda	Bal
Stepan	Yevgenyi	Chandra	Chan
		Kali	

(Sanskrit boys
continued)

Dalal

Ja'far

Javas

Kiran

Kumar

Kyran

Malajitm

Manoj

Mehtar

Mukul

Poshita

Pumeet

Shaman

Tanmay

Tapan

Tarak

Taran

Tarun

Tej

Tejas

Tungar

Uday

Udit

Uja

Umang

Uttam

Vasant

Vasu

Ved

Veer

SAUK

BOYS

Nashashuk

SCANDI-NAVIAN

GIRLS

Arica

Astrid

Dagny

Dahlia

Darby

Dayna

Erica

Ericka

Freja

Gudrun

Haley

Hallie

Helga

Inga

Ingrid

Karena

Karin

Kelsey

Kerstin

Khristina

Kiersten

Kirby

Kirsta

Kirsten

Kirstin

Kirstie

Kristen

Kristi

Kristin

Kristina

Kristine

Linnea

Lurleen

Nessa

Niesha

Nissa

Norell

Ola

Oletha

Olga

Quenby

Quinby

Ragnild

Ran

Rane

Rayna

Rona

Selma

Signe

Sigrid

Sonja

Thora

Tyra

Ula

Yvonne

BOYS

Alvis

Asgard

Ashby

Audun

Balder

Beck

Bengt

Bergen

Bergren	Georg	Josef	Oskar
Bjorn	Gilby	Kalle	Peder
Boden	Gunnar	Karr	Quenby
Bodie	Gunther	Kell	Quimby
Booth	Gus	Kelsey	Raynor
Borg	Gustave	Kerr	Rikard
Bragi	Hakon	Kirby	Roscoe
Brede	Halden	Kirk	Rothwell
Canute	Hamar	Knute	Rutger
Carr	Hammet	Lamont	Rutland
Cort	Hans	Lang	Skee
Crosby	Hansel	Lars	Skerry
Dag	Hansen	Latham	Skip
Dana	Hanson	Leif	Skipper
Davin	Harald	Matteus	Sutherland
Dayne	Harold	Nels	Sven
Delling	Ing	Nollie	Tait
Denby	Inger	Norbert	Tamson
Einar	Ingmar	Odin	Tate
Elvis	Ingvar	Olaf	Thor
Erek	Ivar	Olav	Thorald
Eric	Ivor	Ole	Thorbert
Erik	Janson	Oliver	Thorbjorn
Frey	Jantzen	Orman	Thorleif
Gamble	Jarell	Osborn	Thorwald
Garth	Jarl	Oscar	Thurston

Trigg

Tug

Turpin

Wray

Wyborn

Wyck

SCOTTISH

GIRLS

Aileen

Aili

Ailsa

Ainsley

Alina

Aline

Ansley

Artis

Berkley

Blair

Blaire

Bonnie

Cameron

Christal

Connor

Davina

Davonna

Elspeth

Geneen

Greer

Ilisa

Isela

Isla

Jean

Jeana

Jeanie

Jeanine

Jinny

Keita

Kelcey

Kelsea

Kelsey

Kelsi

Kenzie

Lesley

Leslie

Lesly

Maisie

Malvina

Marjie

Marjorie

Mckenzie

Mhairie

Paisley

Rhona

Roslyn

Rossalyn

Scotti

Tavie

BOYS

Adair

Ahearn

Ainsley

Alastair

Angus

Annan

Ansley

Arran

Arthur

Balfour

Banner

Barclay

Blackburn

Boyd

Brayan

Bret

Breyon

Brian

Brion

Brit

Britton

Busby

Buzz

Caelan

Calen

Calhoun

Cam

Camaron

Camden

Cameron

Campbell

Camron

Carmichael

Carney

Caylan

Chalmers

Clyde

Collin

Conan

Connor

Craig

Dallas

Dalziel	Glendon	Les	Nairn
Denholm	Graeme	Leslie	Parlan
Don	Gregor	Lochlain	Perth
Donald	Hamish	Lundy	Pony
Dorrell	Hearn	Lyall	Ronald
Doug	Henderson	Mac	Ronnie
Dougal	Iain	Macadam	Ronny
Douglas	Ian	Macaulay	Ronson
Drummond	Kade	Macbride	Ross
Duer	Kamden	Macdonald	Seumas
Duff	Kameron	Macdougal	Stratton
Duncan	Kamran	Macgregor	Tavish
Dunham	Keddy	Mack	Tearlach
Dunlop	Keith	Macnair	Tevis
Dunmore	Kendrew	Malcolm	Tormod
Dunn	Kendrick	Malcom	Tramaine
Durell	Kenn	Manius	Tremaine
Edan	Kennan	McGeorge	Tyree
Ennis	Kenny	Mckade	Wyndham
Erskine	Kenzie	Mckay	
Ewan	Kincaid	Morgan	SHONA
Farquhar	Kraig	Morven	BOYS
Fife	Lachlan	Muir	Dakarai
Fyfe	Laird	Mungo	Hondo
Geordan	Leith	Murdock	Jabulani
Geordie	Lennox	Murray	Kokayi

(Shona boys continued)

Mashama

Petiri

Rudo

Runako

Sekaye

Tichawanna

Zuka

SHOSHONE

GIRLS

Kimana

SIKH

GIRLS

Gagandeep

Gurleen

Ramandeep

Simran

Sukhdeep

BOYS

Gurvir

Harjot

Harvir

Jaskaran

Navdeep

Pardeep

SIOUX

BOYS

Akecheta

Chaska

Enapay

SLAVIC

GIRLS

Alina

Catrina

Chesna

Danica

Denica

Hana

Iva

Ivana

Jana

Janika

Kalina

Kallan

Kamila

Karla

Karolina

Karoll

Katerina

Lala

Lida

Ludmilla

Mara

Marika

Marlene

Mila

Mrena

Nadia

Nadine

Neda

Neza

Paulina

Radinka

Radmilla

Reveca

Roza

Sonia

Sonya

Tana

Taneya

Tani

Tania

Tanis

Tanya

Tashi

Tasia

Tatiana

Tatianna

Tatiyana

Tatyana

Tonia

Tonya

Valeska

Velika

Vera

Veta

Wava

Yana

Yarina

Yarmilla

Yvanna

Zhana

Zofia

Zora

Zorina

Zoya

BOYS

Anton

Benedikt

Boris

Cash

Casimir	Yoakim	Amada	Consuelo
Cezar	Yovani	Amaranta	Corazon
Damek	Zelimir	Amparo	Damita
Danick	Ziven	Ana	Danielan
Danilo	Zorya	Anita	Delores
Feodor		Bebe	Dita
Jan	SOMALI	Belicia	Dolores
Jarek	**GIRLS**	Belinda	Dorinda
Jerney	Deka	Benita	Drinka
Jovan	Kalifa	Bibi	Dulcinea
Kasimir		Bonita	Eldora
Kiril	SPANISH	Bonnie	Elisa
Lomán	**GIRLS**	Brisa	Elmira
Marek	Adalene	Cailida	Elvira
Milos	Adalia	Calida	Enrica
Rad	Adana	Camden	Esmeralda
Radman	Adonia	Catalina	Esperanza
Radomil	Alameda	Chalina	Estefani
Stane	Alandra	Charo	Estephanie
Stanislav	Alanza	Chavella	Evita
Taman	Alegria	Chiquita	Felica
Tavo	Alejandra	Cira	Florida
Toni	Alida	Clarita	Fonda
Vasyl	Alita	Coco	Gitana
Vladislav	Almira	Conchita	Gracia
Wenceslaus	Alondra	Constanza	Guillerma
	Alva		

Hermosa

Ines

Isabel

Isobel

Issie

Itzel

Izabella

Jacinda

Jacinthe

Jacynthe

Jada

Jade

Jaden

Jadyn

Jaida

Jaiden

Jaira

Jamaica

Jamecia

Jameika

Jamica

Jardena

Javiera

Jayda

Jayde

Jayden

Josefina

Juana

Juandalyn

Juanita

Juliana

Julita

Kiki

Lali

Landra

Leya

Linda

Lindy

Lola

Lolita

Lorinda

Lucia

Lucita

Luisa

Lupe

Luz

Lynda

Lyndi

Madrona

Mahogony

Maita

Malia

Manda

Manuela

Margarita

Mari

Maria

Mariana

Marisol

Marita

Marquita

Maruca

Matusha

Mel

Melita

Melosa

Mercedes

Miguela

Milagros

Mira

Montana

Mora

Necha

Neena

Nelia

Neva

Nevada

Nina

Nita

Novia

Nuela

Oleda

Olinda

Ora

Orquidea

Paca

Palmira

Paloma

Pancha

Paquita

Patia

Paz

Pepita

Perfecta

Pilar

Primavera

Querida

Queta

Raman

Ramona

Reina

Remedios

Reseda	Solana	Zelia	Carlito
Ria	Soledad	Zerlina	Carlos
Rica	Suela	Zita	Cesar
Ricarda	Tequila		Chago
Rocio	Tia	**BOYS**	Chan
Rosa	Tijuana	Adolfo	Charro
Rosalind	Tina	Alejándro	Ché
Rosalinda	Tita	Alfonso	Checha
Rosalyn	Toya	Alfredo	Cheche
Rosario	Trella	Aloisio	Chencho
Roselyn	Ula	Alonso	Chepe
Rosita	Valencia	Alroy	Chico
Ruperta	Verdad	Alvaro	Chilo
Salvadora	Vianca	Andres	Chuminga
Salvia	Vina	Antjuan	Chumo
Sancia	Viñita	Aquila	Cid
Santana	Vitoria	Araldo	Cisco
Santina	Xandra	Armando	Clemente
Savana	Ynez	Arrio	Cordaro
Savanah	Ysabel	Barto	Cordero
Savannah	Yuana	Bebe	Cortez
Senalda	Yuliana	Bernardo	Currito
Sevilla	Zaneta	Bertín	Dario
Shaba	Zanna	Berto	Decarlos
Sierra	Zarita	Blanco	Desiderio
Socorro	Zaviera	Bonaro	Diego

(Spanish boys continued)

Domingo

Edgardo

Edmundo

Eduardo

Elonzo

Elvio

Emilio

Enrick

Enrique

Ermano

Ernesto

Estéban

Estevan

Estevao

Eugenio

Farruco

Federico

Felipe

Fermin

Fernando

Fico

Filberto

Flaminio

Flip

Francisco

Frederico

Fredo

Frisco

Galeno

Garcia

Geraldo

Gerardo

Giacinto

Gilberto

Gitano

Gonzalo

Gualberto

Guillermo

Gustavo

Gutierre

Heraldo

Heriberto

Hernando

Hilario

Honorato

Huberto

Iago

Jacinto

Jade

Jaguar

Jaime

Jairo

Jando

Javier

Joaquín

Jobo

Joquin

Jorge

Jorrín

José

Joseluis

Juan

Juancarlos

Juaquin

Kiki

Kruz

Lando

Lao

Larenzo

Laurencio

Leandro

Lencho

Lobo

Lon

Lonnie

Lonzo

Lorenzo

Luis

Macario

Mango

Manny

Mano

Marcos

Marr

Martez

Marti

Martinez

Mateo

Matías

Mauricio

Maxi

Máximo

Menico

Miguel

Miquelangel

Mincho

Minel

Mingo

Mique

Moises

Montana

Monte

Montez	Pancho	Raymundo	Rusk
Mundo	Paquito	Raynaldo	Ruy
Naldo	Pascual	Reinaldo	Salamon
Napier	Patricio	Renaldo	Salvador
Nardo	Paulino	Rey	Sansón
Natal	Paz	Reymundo	Santana
Natan	Pedro	Reynaldo	Santiago
Navarro	Pepe	Ric	Santino
Nelo	Perico	Ricardo	Santo
Nemesio	Peyo	Rico	Santonio
Nero	Phelipe	Riel	Santos
Neto	Pilar	Rio	Sarito
Nevada	Pirro	Riqui	Savon
Nicho	Piti	Roberto	Segundo
Niño	Pitin	Rodas	Senon
Noé	Placido	Rodolfo	Servando
Norberto	Ponce	Rodrigo	Sidonio
Oalo	Porifirio	Rodriguez	Sierra
Olo	Quico	Rodriquez	Stancio
Orlando	Quiqui	Rogelio	Tabo
Oro	Quito	Rogerio	Tadzio
Osvaldo	Rafael	Roja	Tajo
Oswaldo	Raimundo	Rolando	Tano
Othello	Rami	Rolon	Teb
Pablo	Ramiro	Rosalio	Teobaldo
Paco	Ramón	Rudi	Teodoro

(Spanish girls
continued)

Terencio

Tiago

Ticho

Timoteo

Tino

Tobal

Tomás

Topo

Tulio

Turi

Tutu

Vicente

Victorio

Vidal

Vincente

Virgilio

Waterio

Wilfredo

Ximenes

Yago

Zacarias

SWAHILI

GIRLS

Adia

Aiesha

Aisha

Aleela

Alika

Asha

Ashanti

Asia

Aziza

Batini

Bina

Chiku

Chinira

Dalila

Dashiki

Dinka

Eshe

Goma

Hadiya

Hasana

Hasina

Jaha

Jina

Jokla

Kalere

Kaluwa

Kamaria

Kameke

Kanene

Kapuki

Kesi

Koffi

Kolina

Kudio

Kwashi

Kwau

Leta

Malena

Marini

Mashika

Mosi

Neema

Nuru

Paka

Panya

Pasua

Penda

Ramla

Rashida

Raziya

Rika

Sanura

Shafira

Shani

Shany

Siti

Tabia

Tisa

Winda

Yiesha

Zahra

Zakia

Zalika

Zawati

Zuri

Zuwena

BOYS

Abasi

Ahmed

Ali

Annan

Ashanti

Ashon

Ashur

Azizi

Bakari

Chane

Chui

Dauid	Mbwana	Vuai	Kristofer
Enzi	Mhina	Yusuf	Lauris
Faraji	Mosi	Zahur	Lennart
Haji	Musa	Zakia	Lukas
Hamisi	Mwinyi	Zuberi	Lunt
Hasani	Mwita		Mathias
Idi	Mzuzi	**SWEDISH**	Mats
Issa	Nuru	**GIRLS**	Mikael
Jaali	Okapi	Anna	Nansen
Jabari	Omari	Anneka	Niklas
Jahi	Pili	Birgitte	Nils
Jelani	Rajabu	Carina	Pal
Jimoh	Rashida	Ulla	Paulo
Joshi	Rashidi	**BOYS**	Per
Jumaane	Sadiki	Adrian	Pol
Jumah	Safari	Alvar	Reinhold
Kanu	Saka	Anders	Rickard
Khalfani	Salim	Anderson	Rolle
Khamisi	Sefu	Burr	Rune
Kito	Simba	Frans	Stefan
Kitwana	Siwatu	Gustaf	Steffan
Kondo	Sudi	Hadrian	Stig
Kwasi	Suhuba	Halen	Torkel
Mansa	Sultan	Hilmar	Valborg
Masud	Tambo	Kjell	Valdemar
Mbita	Tembo	Krister	Valfrid

(Swedish boys
continued)

Valter

Ville

Yngve

SWISS

GIRLS

Leli

Sefa

SYRIAN

BOYS

Adar

Aram

TAI

GIRLS

Jai

Kanya

Lawan

Mali

Mayoree

Mayra

Ratana

Solada

Suchin

Sumalee

Sunee

Tida

BOYS

Aran

Aroon

Atid

Decha

Jai

Kasem

Kiet

Kovit

Lek

Niran

Pravat

Pricha

Runrot

Sum

Virote

TAMIL

GIRLS

Leya

TANZANIAN

GIRLS

Akili

TAOS

BOYS

Anchali

TEUTONIC

GIRLS

America

Kay

Xiomara

BOYS

Amerigo

Bardrick

Patxi

Wilmot

TIBETAN

BOYS

Polo

TIV

GIRLS

Iverem

Limber

BOYS

Bem

Boseda

Gowon

Teremun

Tor

TODAS

GIRLS

Suri

BOYS

Kers

TSWANA

GIRLS

Moswen

BOYS

Montsho

Tale

Tau

TUPI-
GUARANI

BOYS

Jacy

Piñon

Raini

TURKISH

GIRLS

Elma

Neylan

Rashida

Reyhan

Sarila

Sema

Umay

Zerdali

Zerrin

BOYS

Abi

Acar

Adli

Ahir

Akar

Anka

Asker

Aydin

Azad

Baris

Basir

Berk

Cahil

Duman

Emre

Enver

Erol

Halil

Hasad

Husamettin

Ihsan

Kabil

Kahil

Kahraman

Kemal

Kerem

Khan

Kiral

Mesut

Murat

Ohannes

Onan

Onur

Osman

Ottmar

Ozturk

Sener

Sevilen

Sukru

Tabib

Umit

Uner

Yunus

Yurcel

Zeki

TWI

GIRLS

Kunto

BOYS

Kofi

UGANDAN

GIRLS

Kissa

UKRAINIAN

GIRLS

Yeva

BOYS

Bohdan

Burian

Fadey

Osip

Yuri

UMBUNDU

GIRLS

Kasinda

URDU

BOYS

Taj

USET

BOYS

Kibo

UTE

BOYS

Ouray

VIETNAMESE

GIRLS

Am

Bian

Cai

Cam

Hoa

Hong

Huong

Kim

Lan

Le

Mai

Nu

Ping

(Vietnamese girls continued)

Tam

Thanh

Thao

Thi

Thuy

Tuyen

Tuyet

Xuan

BOYS

An

Anh

Antoan

Bay

Binh

Cadao

Cham

Chim

Dinh

Dong

Duc

Gia

Hai

Hieu

Hoang

Hoc

Hung

Huy

Hy

Lap

Long

Minh

Nam

Ngai

Nghia

Ngu

Nien

Phuok

Pin

Son

Tai

Tam

Tan

Teo

Thai

Thang

Thanh

Thian

Thuc

Tin

Tong

Tu

Tuan

Tung

Tuyen

WATAMARE

BOYS

Marar

WELSH

GIRLS

Bevanne

Blodwyn

Bronnie

Bronwyn

Bryce

Bryn

Carey

Cari

Caron

Carys

Cordelia

Cordi

Dee

Delia

Deryn

Dilys

Dylan

Dyllis

Enid

Genevra

Ginnifer

Gladys

Glenda

Glynnis

Guinevere

Gwen

Gwenda

Gwendolyn

Gwyn

Gwyneth

Idelle

Iola

Isolde

Jenifer

Jenna

Jenni

Jennifer

Jenny

Jennyfer

Linette

Lynette

Mab

Meaghan

Meghan

Meredith

Morgan

Morghan

Olwen

Owena

Perri

Rhian

Rhiannon

Rhonda

Ronda

Ronelle

Ronette

Rowan

Rowena

Sulwen

Taffy

Teagan

Tegan

Trevina

Vanora

Wenda

Wendi

Wendy

Winifred

Wynne

Yenifer

Yseult

BOYS

Aneurin

Arvel

Barry

Bevan

Blair

Bogart

Bowen

Brice

Broderick

Brodrick

Bryce

Bryson

Caddock

Cade

Cadell

Cai

Cairn

Calder

Carey

Carrington

Cary

Cerdic

Clyde

Colwyn

Craddock

Cruz

Dafydd

Davis

Dewey

Dilwyn

Drew

Dylan

Dylon

Emlyn

Eoin

Gareth

Garnock

Garth

Gavin

Gawain

Gerwin

Gethin

Glendower

Glyn

Gower

Griffith

Gwayne

Gwilym

Gwyn

Hew

Howell

Iago

Idris

Iestyn

Inek

Iolo

Irv

Irvin

Irving

Ithel

Jestin

Jones

Kai

Kain

Kane

Keith

Kent

Kynan

Lewis

Llewellyn

Lloyd

Maddock

Maddox

(Welsh boys
 continued)

Malvern

Meredith

Merion

Meurig

Newlin

Parry

Pembroke

Price

Reece

Reese

Renfrew

Rhett

Rhys

Rice

Romney

Sayer

Taffy

Taliesin

Tarrant

Trahern

Treston

Trev

Trevor

Tristan

Tristen

Tristin

Triston

Tristram

Tristyn

Trystan

Tudor

Vaughn

Wren

Wyn

Yestin

WEST AUSTRALIAN ABORIGINAL

GIRLS

Kylie

WINNEBAGO

BOYS

Maona

Nawkaw

XHOSA

GIRLS

Mandisa

YAO

BOYS

Ligongo

Lisimba

Mandala

Mapira

Masamba

Simba

Thenga

Umi

Useni

Usi

YIDDISH

GIRLS

Blum

Chava

Gita

Kyla

Raizel

Rayna

Selda

Shaina

Zelda

BOYS

Ber

Feivel

Fischel

Gershom

Henoch

Hertz

Kuper

Leben

Leib

Moishe

Shneur

Tevel

Velvel

Welfel

Yousef

Youssel

Zalman

Zelig

Zindel

Ziskind

YORUBA

GIRLS

Bayo

Fola

Iyabo

Monifa

Oba

Oni

Shardae

BOYS

Ade

Ajala

Akins

Asa

Ayinde

Ayo

Dada

Foluke

Iyapo

Jibade

Jumoke

Kayin

Kayode

Kehind

Kunle

Mongo

Nika

Oba

Obadele

Ojo

Oko

Ola

Olajuwon

Olamina

Olatunji

Olubayo

Olufemi

Olujimi

Olushola

Orunjan

Segun

Shangobunni

Soja

Sowande

Taiwo

Tobi

ZIMBAB-WEAN

GIRLS

Jendaya

ZULU

BOYS

Ganya

Shaka

Sipho

ZUNI

GIRLS

Kwanita

Lolly

Malia

Pelipa

Suni

Taci

Tiwa

Tusa

BOYS

Elia

Halian

Kwam

Lonan

Lusio

Girls names

AALEYAH (Hebrew) an alternate form of Aliya.
Aalayah, Aalayaha, Aalea, Aaleah, Aaleaha, Aaleeyah, Aaleyiah, Aaleyyah

AALIAH (Hebrew) an alternate form of Aliya.
Aaliaya, Aaliayah

AALISHA (Greek) an alternate form of Alisha.
Aaleasha, Aaliesha

AALIYAH (Hebrew) an alternate form of Aliya.
Aahliyah, Aailiyah, Aailyah, Aalaiya Aaleah, Aalia, Aalieyha, Aaliya, Aaliyaha, Aaliyha, Aalliah, Aalliyah, Aalyah, Aalyiah

ABAGAIL (Hebrew) an alternate form of Abigale.
Abagael, Abagaile, Abagale, Abagayle, Abageal, Abagil, Abaigael, Abaigeal

ABBAGAIL (Hebrew) an alternate form of Abigale.
Abbagale, Abbagayle, Abbegail, Abbegale, Abbegayle

ABBEY, Abbie, Abby (Hebrew) familiar forms of Abigail.
Aabbee, Abbe, Abbea, Abbeigh, Abbi, Abbye, Abeey, Abey, Abi, Abia, Abie, Aby

ABBYGAIL (Hebrew) an alternate form of Abigale.
Abbeygale, Abbygale, Abbygayl, Abbygayle

ABEGAIL (Hebrew) an alternate form of Abigale.
Abegale, Abegaile, Abegayle

ABELINA (American) a combination of Abbey + Lina.
Abilana, Abilene

ABIA (Arabic) great.
Abbia, Abbiah, Abiah, Abya

ABIANNE (American) a combination of Abbie + Anne.
Abena, Abeni, Abian, Abinaya

ABIDA (Arabic) worshiper.
Abedah, Abidah

ABIGAIL (Hebrew) father's joy. Bible: one of the wives of King David. See also Gail.
Abagail, Abbagail, Abbey, Abbiegail, Abbiegayle, Abbigael, Abbigail, Abbigal, Abbigale, Abbigayl, Abbigayle, Abbygail, Abegail, Abgail, Abgale, Abgayle, Abigael, Abigaile, Abigaill, Abigal, Abigale, Abigayil, Abigayl, Abigayle, Abigel, Abigial, Abugail, Abygail, Avigail

ABINAYA (American) an alternate form of Abianne.
Abenaa, Abenaya, Abinaa, Abinaiya, Abinayan

ABIRA (Hebrew) my strength.
Abbira, Abeer, Abeerah, Abeir, Abera, Aberah, Abhira, Abiir, Abir

ABRA (Hebrew) mother of many nations. A feminine form of Abraham.
Abree, Abri, Abria

ABRIA (Hebrew) an alternate form of Abra.
Abréa, Abrea, Abreia, Abriah, Abriéa, Abrya

ABRIAL (French) open; secure, protected.
Abrail, Abreal, Abreale, Abriale, Abrielle

ABRIANA (Italian) a form of Abra.
Abbrienna, Abbryana, Abreana, Abreanna, Abreanne, Abreeana, Abreona, Abreonia, Abriann, Abrianna, Abriannah, Abrieana, Abrien, Abrienna, Abrienne, Abrietta, Abrion, Abrionée, Abrionne, Abriunna, Abryann, Abryanna, Abryona

ABRIELLE (French) an alternate form of Abrial.
Aabriella, Abriel, Abriell, Abryell

ABRIL (French) an alternate form of Abrial.
Abrilla, Abrille

ABYGAIL (Hebrew) an alternate form of Abigail.
Abygael, Abygale, Abygayle

ACACIA (Greek) thorny. Mythology: the acacia tree symbolizes immortality and resurrection. See also Casey.
Acasha, Acatia, Accassia, Acey, Acie, Akacia, Cacia, Casia, Kasia

ADA (German) a short form of Adelaide. (English) prosperous; happy.
Adabelle, Adah, Adan, Adaya, Adda, Auda

ADAH (Hebrew) ornament.
Ada, Addah

ADAIR (Greek) an alternate form of Adara.
Adaire

ADALENE (Spanish) an alternate form of Adalia.

Adalane, Adalena, Adalin, Adalina, Adaline, Adalinn, Adalyn, Adalynn, Adalynne, Addalyn, Addalynn

ADALIA (German, Spanish) noble.
Adal, Adala, Adalea, Adaleah, Adalee, Adalene, Adali, Adalie, Adaly, Addal, Addala, Addaly

ADAMA (Phoenician) woman, humankind. (Hebrew) earth; a woman of the red earth. A feminine form of Adam.

ADAMMA (Ibo) child of beauty.

ADANA (Spanish) a form of Adama.

ADANNA (Nigerian) her father's daughter.
Adanya

ADARA (Greek) beauty. (Arabic) virgin.
Adair, Adaira, Adaora, Adar, Adarah, Adare, Adaria, Adarra, Adasha, Adauré, Adra

ADAYA (American) a form of Ada.
Adaija, Adaijah, Adaja, Adajah, Adayja, Adayjah, Adejah

ADDIE (Greek, German) a familiar form of Adelaide, Adrienne.
Aday, Adde, Addee, Addey, Addi, Addia, Addy, Ade, Adee, Adei, Adey, Adeye, Adi, Adie, Ady, Atti, Attie, Atty

ADDISON, Addyson (English) daughter of Adam.
Addis, Addisen, Addisson, Adison

ADELA (English) a short form of Adelaide.
Adelae, Adelia, Adelista, Adella

ADELAIDE (German) noble and serene. See also Ada, Adela, Adeline, Adelle, Ailis, Delia, Della, Ela, Elke, Heidi.
Adelade, Adelaid, Adelaida, Adelei, Adelheid, Adeliade, Adelka, Aley, Laidey, Laidy

ADELE (English) an alternate form of Adelle.
Adel, Adelie, Adile

ADELINA (English) an alternate form of Adeline.
Adalina, Adeleana, Adelena, Adellyna, Adeliana, Adellena, Adileena, Adlena

ADELINE (English) a form of Adelaide.
Adaline, Adelaine, Adelin, Adelina, Adelind, Adelita, Adeliya, Adelle, Adelyn, Adelynn, Adelynne, Adilene, Adlin, Adline, Adlyn, Adlynn, Aline

ADELLE (German, English) a short form of Adelaide, Adeline.
Adele, Adell

ADENA (Hebrew) noble; adorned.
Adeana, Adeen, Adeena, Aden, Adene, Adenia, Adenna, Adina

ADIA (Swahili) gift.
Addia, Adéa, Adea, Adiah

ADILA (Arabic) equal.
Adeala, Adeela, Adela, Adelah, Adeola, Adilah, Adileh, Adilia, Adyla

ADILENE (English) an alternate form of Adeline.
Adilen, Adileni, Adilenne, Adlen, Adlene

ADINA (Hebrew) an alternate form of Adena. See also Dina.
Adeana, Adiana, Adiena, Adinah, Adine, Adinna, Adyna

ADIRA (Hebrew) strong.
Ader, Adera, Aderah, Aderra, Adhira, Adirah, Adirana

ADISON, Adyson (English) alternate forms of Addison, Addyson.
Adis, Adisa, Adisen, Adisynne, Adysen

ADITI (Hindi) unbound. Religion: the mother of the Hindu gods.
Adithi, Aditti

ADLEIGH (Hebrew) my ornament. A feminine form of Adlai.
Adla, Adleni

ADONIA (Spanish) beautiful. A feminine form of Adonis.
Adonica, Adonis, Adonna, Adonnica, Adonya

ADORA (Latin) beloved. See also Dora.
Adore, Adoree, Adoria

ADRA (Arabic) virgin.
Adara

ADREANA, Adreanna (Latin) alternate forms of Adrienne.
Adrean, Adreanne, Adreauna, Adreeanna, Adreen, Adreena, Adreeyana, Adrena, Adrene, Adrenea, Adréona, Adreonia, Adreonna

ADRIA (English) a short form of Adriana, Adriene.
Adrea, Adriani, Adrya

ADRIANA, Adrianna (Italian) forms of Adrienne.
Addrianna, Addriyanna, Adreiana, Adreinna, Adria, Adriannea, Adriannia, Adrionna

ADRIANE, Adrianne (English) forms of Adrienne.
Addrian, Adranne, Adria, Adrian, Adreinne, Adriann, Adriayon, Adrion

ADRIELLE (Hebrew) member of God's flock.
Adriel, Adrielli, Adryelle

ADRIEN, Adriene (English) alternate forms of Adrienne.

ADRIENNA (Italian) a form of Adrienne. See also Edrianna.
Adreana, Adrieanna, Adrieaunna, Adriena, Adrienia, Adriennah, Adrieunna

ADRIENNE (Greek) rich. (Latin) dark. A feminine form of Adrian. See also Hadriane.

Adrienne (cont.)
Addie, Adrien, Adriana, Adriane,
Adrianna, Adrianne, Adrie, Adrieanne,
Adrien, Adrienna, Adriyanna

ADRINA (English) a short form of
Adriana, Adrianna.
Adrinah, Adrinne

ADRIYANNA (American) a form of
Adrienne.
Adrieyana, Adriyana, Adryan, Adryana,
Adryane, Adryanna, Adryanne

ADYA (Hindi) Sunday.
Adia

AERIAL, Aeriel (Hebrew) alternate
forms of Ariel.
Aeriale, Aeriela, Aerielle, Aeril, Aerile,
Aeryal

AFI (African) born on Friday.
Affi, Afia, Efi, Efia

AFRA (Hebrew) young doe. (Arabic)
earth color. See also Aphra.
Affery, Affrey, Affrie, Afraa

AFRICA (Irish) pleasant. History: a
twelfth-century queen of the Isle of
Man. Geography: one of the seven
continents.
Affrica, Afric, Africah, Africaya, Africia,
Africiana, Afrika, Aifric

AFRIKA (Irish) an alternate form of
Africa.
Afrikah

AFRODITE, Aphrodite (Greek)
Mythology: the goddess of love and
beauty.
Afrodita

AFTON (English) from Afton, England.
Aftan, Aftine, Aftinn, Aftyn

AGATE (English) a semiprecious stone.
Aggie

AGATHA (Greek) good, kind.
Literature: Agatha Christie was a
British writer of more than seventy
detective novels. See also Gasha.
Agace, Agaisha, Agasha, Agata, Agatah,
Agathe, Agathi, Agatka, Agetha, Aggie,
Ágota, Ágotha, Agueda, Atka

AGATHE (Greek) an alternate form of
Agatha.

AGGIE (Greek) a short form of Agatha,
Agnes.
Ag, Aggy, Agi

AGNES (Greek) pure. See also Aneesa,
Anessa, Anice, Anisha, Ina, Inez,
Necha, Nessa, Nessie, Neza, Nyusha,
Una, Ynez.
Aganetha, Aggie, Agna, Agne, Agneis,
Agnelia, Agnella, Agnés, Agnesa, Agnesca,
Agnese, Agnesina, Agness, Agnessa,
Agnesse, Agneta, Agneti, Agnetta, Agnies,
Agnieszka, Agniya, Agnola, Agnus, Aignéis,
Aneska, Anka

AHAVA (Hebrew) beloved.
Ahivia

AHLIYA (Hebrew) an alternate form of
Aliya.
Ahlai, Ahlaia, Ahlaya, Ahleah, Ahleeyah,
Ahley, Ahleya, Ahlia, Ahliah, Ahliyah

AIDA (Latin) helpful. (English) an
alternate form of Ada.
Aidah, Aidan, Aide, Aidee

AIDAN, Aiden (Latin) alternate forms
of Aida.

AIESHA (Swahili, Arabic) an alternate
form of Aisha.
Aeisha, Aeshia, Aieshia, Aieysha, Aiiesha

AIKO (Japanese) beloved.

AILANI (Hawaiian) chief.
Aelani, Ailana

AILEEN (Scottish) light bearer. (Irish) a
form of Helen. See also Eileen.

Ailean, Aileena, Ailen, Ailene, Aili, Ailina,
Ailinn, Aillen

AILI (Scottish) a form of Alice. (Finnish)
a form of Helen.
Aila, Ailee, Ailey, Ailie, Aily

AILIS (Irish) a form of Adelaide.
Ailesh, Ailish, Ailyse, Eilis

AILSA (Scottish) island dweller.
Geography: Ailsa Craig is an island in
Scotland.
Ailsha

AILYA (Hebrew) an alternate form of
Aliya.
Ailiyah

AIMEE (Latin) an alternate form of
Amy. (French) loved.
Aime, Aimée, Aimey, Aimi, Aimia, Aimie,
Aimy

AINSLEY (Scottish) my own meadow.
Ainslee, Ainsleigh, Ainslie, Ainsly, Ansley,
Aynslee, Aynsley, Aynslie

AIRIÉL (Hebrew) an alternate form of
Ariel.
Aieral, Aierel, Aiiryel, Aire, Aireal, Aireale,
Aireel, Airel, Airele, Airelle, Airi, Airial,
Airiale, Airrel

AIRIANA (English) an alternate form
of Ariana, Arianna.
Airana, Airanna, Aireana, Aireanah,
Aireanna, Aireona, Aireonna, Aireyonna,
Airianna, Airianne, Airiona, Airriana,
Airrion, Airryon, Airyana, Airyanna

AISHA (Swahili) life. (Arabic) woman.
See also Asha, Asia, Iesha, Isha,
Keisha, Yiesha.
Aaisha, Aaishah, Aesha, Aeshah, Aheesha,
Aiasha, Aiesha, Aieshah, Aisa, Aischa,
Aish, Aishah, Aisheh, Aishia, Aishiah,
Aiysha, Aiyesha, Ayesha, Aysa, Ayse, Aytza

AISLINN, Aislynn (Irish) alternate
forms of Ashlyn, Ashlynn.

Aishellyn, Aishlinn, Aislee, Aisley, Aislin,
Aisling, Aislyn, Aislynne

AIYANNA (Hindi) an alternate form
of Ayanna.
Aianna, Aiyannah, Aiyonna, Aiyunna

AIYANA (Native American) forever
flowering.
Aiyhana, Aiyona, Aiyonia, Ayana

AJA (Hindi) goat.
Ahjah, Aija, Aijah, Ajá, Ajada, Ajah,
Ajara, Ajaran, Ajare, Ajaree, Ajha, Ajia

AJANAE (American) a combination of
the letter A + Janae.
Ajahnae, Ajahne, Ajana, Ajanaé, Ajane,
Ajané, Ajanee, Ajanique, Ajena, Ajenae,
Ajené

AJIA (Hindi) an alternate form of Aja.
Aijia, Ajhia, Aji, Ajjia

AKAYLA (American) a combination of
the letter A + Kayla.
Akaela, Akaelia, Akaila, Akailah, Akala,
Akaylah, Akaylia

AKEISHA (American) a combination
of the letter A + Keisha.
Akaesha, Akaisha, Akasha, Akasia,
Akeecia, Akeesha, Akeishia, Akeshia,
Akisha

AKELA (Hawaiian) noble.
Ahkayla, Ahkeelah, Akelah, Akelia,
Akeliah, Akeya, Akeyla, Akeylah

AKERIA (American) an alternate form
of Akira.
Akera, Akerah, Akeri, Akerra, Akerra

AKI (Japanese) born in autumn.
Akeeye

AKIA (American) a combination of the
letter A + Kia.
Akaja, Akeia, Akeya, Akiá, Akiah, Akiane,
Akiaya, Akiea, Akiya, Akiyah, Akya,
Akyan, Akyia, Akyiah

AKIKO (Japanese) bright light.

AKILAH (Arabic) intelligent.
Aikiela, Aikilah, Akeela, Akeelah, Akeila, Akeilah, Akeiyla, Akiela, Akielah, Akila, Akilaih, Akilia, Akilka, Akillah, Akkila, Akyla, Akylah

AKILI (Tanzanian) wisdom.

AKINA (Japanese) spring flower.

AKIRA (American) a combination of the letter A + Kira.
Akeria, Akiera, Akierra, Akirah, Akire, Akiria, Akirrah, Akyra

ALAINA, Alayna (Irish) alternate forms of Alana.
Aalaina, Alainah, Alaine, Alainna, Alainnah, Alane, Alaynah, Alayne, Alaynna, Aleine, Alleyna, Alleynah, Alleyne

ALAIR (French) a form of Hilary, Hillary.
Alaira, Ali, Allaire

ALAMEA (Hawaiian) ripe; precious.

ALAMEDA (Spanish) poplar tree.

ALANA (Irish) attractive; peaceful. (Hawaiian) offering. A feminine form of Alan. See also Lana.
Alaana, Alaina, Alanae, Alanah, Alane, Alanea, Alani, Alania, Alanis, Alanna, Alawna, Alayna, Allana, Allanah, Allyn, Alonna

ALANDRA, Alandria (Spanish) forms of Alexandra, Alexandria.
Alandrea, Alantra, Aleandra, Aleandrea

ALANI (Hawaiian) orange tree.
Alaini, Alainie, Alania, Alanie, Alaney, Alannie

ALANNA (Irish) an alternate form of Alana.
Alannah

ALANZA (Spanish) noble and eager. A feminine form of Alphonse.

ALAYSHA, Alaysia (American) forms of Alicia.
Alaysh, Alayshia

ALBA (Latin) from Alba, Italy, a city on a white hill. A feminine form of Alban.
Albana, Albani, Albanie, Albany, Albeni, Albina, Albine, Albinia, Albinka, Elba

ALBERTA (German, French) noble and bright. A feminine form of Albert. See also Auberte, Bertha, Elberta.
Albertina, Albertine, Albertyna, Albertyne, Alverta

ALBREANNA (American) a combination of Alberta + Breanna.
Albré, Albrea, Albreona, Albreonna, Albreyon

ALCINA (Greek) strong minded.
Alceena, Alcine, Alcinia, Alseena, Alsinia, Alsyna, Alzina

ALDA (German) old; elder. A feminine form of Aldo.
Aldina, Aldine

ALDEN (English) old; wise protector.
Aldan, Aldon, Aldyn

ALDINA, Aldine (Hebrew) forms of Alda.
Aldeana, Aldene, Aldona, Aldyna, Aldyne

ALEA, Aleah (Arabic) high, exalted. (Persian) God's being.
Aileah, Aleea, Aleeah, Aleia, Aleiah, Allea, Alleah, Alleea, Alleeah

ALEASHA, Aleesha (Greek) alternate forms of Alisha.
Aleashae, Aleashea, Aleashia, Aleassa, Aleeshia

ALECIA (Greek) a form of Alicia.

Aalecia, Ahlasia, Aleacia, Aleacya, Aleasia,
Alecea, Aleceea, Aleceia, Aleciya, Aleciyah,
Alecy, Alecya, Aleeceia, Aleecia, Aleesia,
Aleesiya, Aleicia, Alesha, Alesia, Allecia,
Alleecia

ALEELA (Swahili) she cries.
Aleelah, Alila, Alile

ALEENA (Dutch) an alternate form of
Aleene.
Ahleena, Aleana, Aleeanna

ALEENE (Dutch) alone.
Aleen, Aleena, Alene, Alleen

ALEEYA (Hebrew) an alternate form
of Aliya.
Alee, Aleea, Aleeyah, Aleiya, Aleiyah

ALEEZA (Hebrew) a form of Aliza.
See also Leeza.
Aleiza

ALEGRIA (Spanish) cheerful.
Aleggra, Alegra, Allegra, Allegria

ALEISHA, Alesha (Greek) alternate
forms of Alecia, Alisha.
Aleasha, Aleashea, Aleasia, Aleesha,
Aleeshah, Aleeshia, Aleeshya, Aleisa, Alesa,
Alesah, Aleisha, Aleshia, Aleshya, Alesia,
Alessia

ALEJANDRA (Spanish) a form of
Alexandra.
Aleiandra, Alejanda, Alejandr, Alejandrea,
Alejandria, Alejandrina, Alejandro

ALEKA (Hawaiian) a form of Alice.
Aleeka, Alekah

ALEKSANDRA (Greek) an alternate
form of Alexandra.
Alecsandra, Aleksasha, Aleksandrija,
Aleksandriya

ALENA (Russian) a form of Helen.
Alenah, Alene, Alenea, Aleni, Alenia,
Alenka, Alenna, Alennah, Alenya, Alyna

ALESIA, Alessia (Greek) alternate
forms of Alice.
Alessea, Alesya, Allesia

ALESSA (Greek) an alternate form
of Alice.
Alessi, Allessa

ALESSANDRA (Italian) a form of
Alexandra.
Alesandra, Alesandrea, Alissandra,
Alissondra, Allesand, Allessandra

ALETA (Greek) a form of Alida.
See also Leta.
Aletta, Alletta

ALETHEA (Greek) truth.
Alathea, Alathia, Aletea, Aletha, Aletheia,
Alethia, Aletia, Alithea, Alithia

ALETTE (Latin) wing.

ALEX (Greek) a short form of
Alexandra.
Aleix, Aleks, Alexe, Alexx, Allex, Allexx

ALEXA (Greek) a short form of
Alexandra.
Aleixa, Alekia, Aleksa, Aleksha, Aleksi,
Alexah, Alexsa, Alexssa, Alexxa, Allexa,
Alyxa

ALEXANDRA (Greek) defender of
mankind. A feminine form of
Alexander. History: the last czarina of
Russia. See also Lexia, Lexie, Olesia,
Ritsa, Sandra, Sandrine, Sasha, Shura,
Sondra, Xandra, Zandra.
Alandra, Alaxandra, Aleczandra,
Alejandra, Aleksandra, Alessandra, Alex,
Alexa, Alexande, Alexandera, Alexandre,
Alexas, Alexi, Alexina, Alexine, Alexis,
Alexsandra, Alexius, Alexsis, Alexus,
Alexxandra, Alexys, Alexzandra, Alix,
Alixandra, Aljexi, Alla, Alyx, Alyxandra,
Lexandra

ALEXANDREA (Greek) an alternate
form of Alexandria.

Alexandrea (cont.)
Alexandreana, Alexandreia, Alexandriea,
Alexandrieah, Alexanndrea

ALEXANDRIA (Greek) an alternate
form of Alexandra. See also Drinka,
Xandra, Zandra.
Alaxandria, Alecsandria, Aleczandria,
Alexanderia, Alexanderine, Alexandrea,
Alexandrena, Alexandrie, Alexandrina,
Alexandrine, Alexanndria, Alexandrya,
Alexendria, Alexendrine, Alexia,
Alixandrea, Alyxandria

ALEXANDRINE (Greek) an alternate
form of Alexandra.
Alexandrina

ALEXANNE (American) a combination
of Alex + Anne.
Alexan, Alexanna, Alexane, Alexann,
Alexanna, Alexian, Alexiana

ALEXAS, Alexes (Greek) short forms
of Alexandra.
Alexess

ALEXI, Alexie (Greek) short forms of
Alexandra.
Aleksey, Aleksi, Alexey, Alexy

ALEXIA (Greek) a short form of
Alexandria. See also Lexia.
Aleksia, Aleska, Alexcia, Alexea, Alexsia,
Alexsiya, Allexia, Alyxia

ALEXIS (Greek) a short form of
Alexandra.
Aalexis, Ahlexis, Alaxis, Alecsis, Alecxis,
Aleexis, Aleksis, Alexcis, Alexias, Alexiou,
Alexiss, Alexiz, Alexxis, Alixis, Allexis,
Elexis, Lexis

ALEXIUS, Alexus (Greek) short forms
of Alexandra.
Aalexus, Aalexxus, Aelexus, Ahlexus,
Alecsus, Alexsus, Alexuss, Alexxus, Alixus,
Allexius, Allexus, Elexus, Lexus

ALEXSANDRA (Greek) an alternate
form of Alexandra.
Alexsandria, Alexsandro, Alixsandra

ALEXSIS, Alexxis (Greek) short forms
of Alexandra.
Alexxiz

ALEXYS (Greek) a short form of
Alexandra.
Alexsys, Alexyes, Alexyis, Alexyss, Allexys

ALEXZANDRA, Alexzandra (Greek)
alternate forms of Alexandra.
Alexzand, Alexzandrea, Alexzandriah,
Alexzandrya, Alixzandria

ALEYA, Aleyah (Hebrew) alternate
forms of Aliya.
Alayah, Aleayah, Aleeya, Aléyah, Aleyia,
Aleyiah

ALFIE (English) a familiar form of
Alfreda.
Alfi, Alfy

ALFREDA (English) elf counselor; wise
counselor. A feminine form of Alfred.
See also Effie, Elfrida, Freda, Frederica.
Alfie, Alfredda, Alfredia, Alfreeda, Alfreida,
Alfrieda

ALI, Aly (Greek) familiar forms of
Alicia, Alisha, Alison.
Allea, Alli, Allie, Ally

ALIA, Aliah (Hebrew) alternate forms
of Aliya. See also Aaliyah, Alea.
Aelia, Allia, Alya

ALICE (Greek) truthful. (German) noble.
See also Aili, Aleka, Alie, Alisa, Alison,
Alli, Alysa, Alyssa, Alysse, Elke.
Adelice, Alecia, Aleece, Alesia, Alicie, Aliece,
Alise, Alix, Alize, Alla, Alleece, Allice, Allis,
Allise, Allix

ALICIA (English) an alternate form of
Alice. See also Elicia, Licia.
Aelicia, Alaysha, Alecea, Alecia, Aleecia,
Ali, Alicea, Alicha, Alichia, Aliciah, Alician,
Alicja, Alicya, Aliecia, Alisha, Allicea,
Allicia, Alycia, Ilysa

ALIDA (Latin) small and winged. (Spanish) noble. See also Aleta, Lida, Oleda.
Aleda, Aleida, Alidia, Alita, Alleda, Allida, Allidah, Alyda, Alydia, Elida, Elidia

ALIE, Allie (Greek) familiar forms of Alice.

ALIESHA (Greek) an alternate form of Alisha.
Alieshai, Alieshia, Alliesha

ALIKA (Hawaiian) truthful. (Swahili) most beautiful.
Aleka, Alica, Alikah, Alike, Alikee, Aliki

ALIMA (Arabic) sea maiden; musical.

ALINA, Alyna (Slavic) bright. (Scottish) fair. (English) a short form of Adeline. See also Alena.
Aliana, Alianna, Alinah, Aline, Alinna, Allyna, Alynna, Alyona

ALINE (Scottish) an alternate form of Alina.
Alianne, Allene, Alline, Allyn, Allyne, Alyne, Alynne

ALISA, Alissa (Greek) an alternate form of Alice. See also Elisa, Ilisa.
Aalissah, Aaliysah, Aleessa, Alisah, Alisea, Alisia, Alisza, Alisza, Aliysa, Allissa, Alyssa

ALISE, Allise (Greek) alternate forms of Alice.
Alics, Aliese, Alis, Aliss, Alisse, Alisse, Alles, Allesse, Allis, Allisse

ALISHA (Greek) truthful. (German) noble. (English) an alternate form of Alicia. See also Elisha, Ilisha, Lisha.
Aalisha, Aleasha, Aleesha, Aleisha, Alesha, Ali, Aliesha, Aliscia, Alishah, Alishay, Alishaye, Alishia, Alishya, Alitsha, Allisha, Allysha, Alysha

ALISHIA, Alisia, Alissia (English) alternate forms of Alisha.
Alishea, Alisheia, Alishiana, Alyssaya, Alisea, Alissya, Alisyia, Allissia

ALISON, Allison (English) forms of Alice. See also Lissie.
Ali, Alicen, Alicyn, Alisan, Alisann, Alisanne, Alisen, Alisenne, Alisin, Alision, Alisonn, Alisson, Alisun, Alles, Allesse, Alleyson, Allie, Allisson, Allisyn, Allix, Allsun

ALITA (Spanish) a form of Alida.
Allita

ALIVIA (Latin) an alternate form of Olivia.
Alivah

ALIX (Greek) a short form of Alexandra, Alice.
Alixe, Alixia, Allix, Alyx

ALIXANDRA, Alixandria (Greek) alternate forms of Alexandra, Alexandria.
Alixandriya, Allixandra, Allixandria, Allixandrya

ALIYA (Hebrew) ascender.
Aaleyah, Aaliyah, Aeliyah, Ahliya, Ailya, Alea, Aleya, Alia, Alieya, Alieyah, Aliyah, Aliyiah, Aliyyah, Allia, Alliyah, Aly, Alyah

ALIYE (Arabic) noble.
Aliyeh

ALIZA (Hebrew) joyful. See also Aleeza, Eliza.
Alieza, Aliezah, Alitza, Aliz, Alizah, Alize, Alizee

ALIZABETH (Hebrew) an alternate form of Elizabeth.
Alyzabeth

ALLANA, Allanah (Irish) alternate forms of Alana.
Allanie, Allanna, Allauna

ALLEGRA (Latin) cheerful.
Legra

ALLENA (Irish) an alternate form of Alana.
Alleen, Alleyna, Alleynah

ALLI, Ally (Greek) familiar forms of Alice.
Ali, Alley

ALLIA, Alliah (Hebrew) alternate forms of Aliya.

ALLISSA (Greek) an alternate form of Alyssa.
Allisa

ALLIYAH (Hebrew) an alternate form of Aliya.
Alliya, Alliyha, Alliyia, Alliyyah, Allya, Allyah

ALLYSA, Allyssa (Greek) an alternate form of Alyssa.
Allissa, Allyisa, Allysa, Allysah, Allyssah

ALLYSHA (English) an alternate form of Alisha.
Alishia, Allysia

ALLYSON, Alyson (English) alternate forms of Alison, Allison.
Allysen, Allyson, Allysonn, Allysson, Allysun, Alyson

ALMA (Arabic) learned. (Latin) soul.
Almah

ALMEDA (Arabic) ambitious.
Allmeda, Allmedah, Allmeta, Allmita, Almea, Almedah, Almeta, Almida, Almita

ALMIRA (Arabic) aristocratic, princess; exalted. (Spanish) from Almeíra, Spain. See also Elmira, Mira.
Allmeera, Allmeria, Allmira, Almeera, Almeeria, Almeira, Almeria, Almire

ALOHA (Hawaiian) loving, kind hearted, charitable.
Alohi

ALOISA (German) famous warrior.
Aloisia, Aloysia

ALOMA (Latin) a short form of Paloma.

ALONDRA (Spanish) a form of Alexandra.
Allandra, Alonda

ALONNA (Irish) an alternate form of Alana.
Alona, Alonnah, Alonya, Alonyah

ALONZA (English) noble and eager. A feminine form of Alonzo.

ALORA (American) a combination of the letter A + Lora.
Alorah, Alorha, Alorie, Aloura, Alouria

ALPHA (Greek) first-born. Linguistics: the first letter of the Greek alphabet.
Alphia

ALTA (Latin) high; tall.
Allta, Altah, Altana, Altanna, Altea, Alto

ALTHEA (Greek) wholesome; healer. History: Althea Gibson was the first African American to win a major tennis title. See also Thea.
Altha, Altheda, Altheya, Althia, Elthea, Eltheya, Elthia

ALVA (Latin, Spanish) white; light skinned. See also Elva.
Alvana, Alvanna, Alvannah

ALVINA (English) friend to all; noble friend; friend to elves. A feminine form of Alvin. See also Elva, Vina.
Alveanea, Alveen, Alveena, Alveenia, Alvenea, Alvie, Alvinae, Alvincia, Alvine, Alvinea, Alvinesha, Alvinia, Alvinna, Alvita, Alvona, Alvyna, Alwin, Alwina, Alwyn

ALYAH, Alyiah (Hebrew) alternate forms of Aliya.
Aly, Alya, Aleah, Alyia

ALYCIA, Alyssia (English) alternate forms of Alicia.
Allyce, Alycea, Alyciah, Alyse, Lycia

ALYSA, Alyse, Alysse (Greek) alternate forms of Alice.
Allys, Allyse, Allyss, Alys, Alyss

ALYSHA, Alysia (Greek) alternate forms of Alisha.
Allysea, Allyscia, Alysea, Alyshia, Alyssha, Alyssia

ALYSSA (Greek) rational. Botany: alyssum is a flowering herb. See also Alice, Elissa.
Ahlyssa, Alissa, Allissa, Allyssa, Alyesa, Alyessa, Alyissa, Alysah, Ilyssa, Lyssa, Lyssah

ALYSSE (Greek) an alternate form of Alice.
Allyce, Allys, Allyse, Allyss, Alys, Alyss

ALYX, Alyxis (Greek) short forms of Alexandra.

ALYXANDRA, Alyxandria (Greek) alternate forms of Alexandra, Alexandria.
Alyxandrea, Alyxzandrya

AM (Vietnamese) lunar; female.

AMA (African) born on Saturday.

AMABEL (Latin) lovable. See also Bel, Mabel.

AMADA (Spanish) beloved.
Amadea, Amadi, Amadia, Amadita

AMAIRANI (Greek) an alternate form of Amara.
Amairaine, Amairane, Amairanie, Amairany

AMAL (Arabic) hopeful.
Amala

AMALIA (German) an alternate form of Amelia.
Ahmalia, Amalea, Amaleah, Amaleta, Amalija, Amalina, Amalisa, Amalita, Amaliya, Amalya, Amalyn

AMALIE (German) an alternate form of Amelia.
Amalee, Amali, Amaly

AMAN, Amani (Arabic) alternate forms of Imani.
Aamani, Ahmani, Amane, Amanee, Amaney, Amanie, Ammanu

AMANADA (Latin) an alternate form of Amanda.

AMANDA (Latin) lovable. See also Manda.
Amada, Amanada, Amandah, Amandalee, Amandalyn, Amandi, Amandie, Amandine, Amandy

AMANDEEP (Punjabi) peaceful light.

AMARA (Greek) eternally beautiful. See also Mara.
Amar, Amaira, Amairani, Amarah, Amari, Amaria, Amariah

AMARANTA (Spanish) a flower that never fades.

AMARI (Greek) an alternate form of Amara.
Amaree, Amarie, Amarii, Amarri

AMARIS (Hebrew) promised by God.
Amarissa, Amarys, Maris

AMARYLLIS (Greek) fresh; flower.
Amarillis, Amarylis

AMAUI (Hawaiian) thrush.

AMAYA (Japanese) night rain.

AMBAR (French) an alternate form of Amber.

AMBER (French) amber.
Aamber, Ahmber, Ambar, Amberia, Amberise, Amberly, Ambria, Ambur, Ambyr, Ambyre, Ammber, Ember

AMBERLY (American) a familiar form of Amber.
Amberle, Amberlea, Amberlee, Amberleigh, Amberley, Amberli, Amberlie, Amberlly, Amberlye

AMBERLYN, Amberlynn (American) combinations of Amber + Lynn.
Amberlin, Amberlina, Amberlyne, Amberlynne

AMBRIA (American) a form of Amber.
Ambrea, Ambra, Ambriah

AMELIA (Latin) an alternate form of Emily. (German) hardworking. History: Amelia Earhart, an American aviator, was the first woman to fly solo across the Atlantic Ocean. See also Ima, Melia, Millie, Nuela, Yamelia.
Aemilia, Aimilia, Amalia, Amalie, Amaliya, Ameila, Ameilia, Amelie, Amelina, Ameline, Amelisa, Amelita, Amella, Amilia, Amilina, Amilisa, Amilita, Amilyn, Amylia

AMELIE (German) a familiar form of Amelia.
Amaley, Amalie, Amelee, Ameleigh, Ameley, Amélie, Amely, Amilie

AMERICA (Teutonic) industrius. A feminine form of Amerigo.
Americana, Amerika

AMI, Amie (French) forms of Amy.
Aami, Amiee, Amii, Amiiee, Ammee, Ammie, Ammiee

AMILIA, Amilie (Latin, German) alternate forms of Amelia.
Amilee, Amili, Amillia, Amily, Amilya

AMINA (Arabic) trustworthy, faithful. History: the mother of the prophet Mohammed.
Aamena, Aamina, Aaminah, Ameena, Ameenah, Aminah, Aminda, Amindah, Aminta, Amintah

AMIRA (Hebrew) speech; utterance. (Arabic) princess. See also Mira.
Ameera, Ameerah, Amirah

AMISSA (Hebrew) truth.
Amissah

AMITA (Hebrew) truth.
Amitha

AMITY (Latin) friendship.
Amitie

AMLIKA (Hindi) mother.
Amlikah

AMMA (Hindi) god, godlike. Religion: another name for the Hindu goddess Shakti.

AMORIE (German) industrious leader. A feminine form of Emory.

AMPARO (Spanish) protected.

AMRIT (Sanskrit) nectar.
Amrita

AMY (Latin) beloved. See also Aimee, Emma, Esmé.
Amata, Ame, Amey, Ami, Amia, Amie, Amio, Ammy, Amye, Amylyn

AN (Chinese) peaceful.

ANA (Hawaiian, Spanish) a form of Hannah.
Anai, Anaia

ANABA (Native American) she returns from battle.

ANABEL,, Anabelle (English) alternate forms of Annabel.
Anabela, Anabele, Anabell, Anabella

ANAHITA (Persian) a river and water goddess.
Anahai, Anahi, Anahit, Anahy

ANAIS (Hebrew) gracious.
Anaise, Anaïse

ANALA (Hindi) fine.

ANALISA, Analise (English) combinations of Ana + Lisa.
Analice, Analicia, Analis, Analisha, Analisia, Analissa

ANAMARIA (English) a combination of Ana + Maria.
Anamarie, Anamary

ANANDA (Hindi) blissful.

ANASTACIA (Greek) an alternate form of Anastasia.
Anastace, Anastacie

ANASTASIA (Greek) resurrection. See also Nastasia, Stacey, Stacia, Stasya.
Anastacia, Anastase, Anastascia, Anastasha, Anastashia, Anastasie, Anastasija, Anastassia, Anastassya, Anastasya, Anastatia, Anastaysia, Anastazia, Anastice, Annastasia, Annastasija, Annastaysia, Annastazia, Annstás

ANATOLA (Greek) from the east.

ANCI (Hungarian) a form of Hannah.
Annus, Annushka

ANDEE, Andi, Andie (American) short forms of Andrea, Fernanda.
Ande, Andea, Andy

ANDREA (Greek) strong; courageous. (Latin) feminine. A feminine form of Andrew. See also Ondrea.
Aindrea, Andee, Andera, Anderea, Andra, Andrah, Andraia, Andraya, Andreah, Andreaka, Andreana, Andreane, Andree, Andrée, Andreea, Andreia, Andreja, Andreka, Andrel, Andrell, Andrelle, Andreo, Andressa, Andrette, Andreya, Andria, Andriana, Andrieka, Andrietta, Andris, Aundrea

ANDREANA, Andreanna (Greek) alternate forms of Andrea.
Ahndrianna, Andreina, Andrena, Andreyana, Andreyonna, Andrina, Andriona, Andrionna

ANDREANE, Andreanne (Greek) alternate forms of Andrea.
Andrean, Andreeanne, Andree Anne, Andrene, Andrian, Andrienne

ANDRIA (Greek) an alternate form of Andrea.
Andri, Andriea

ANDRIANA, Andrianna (Greek) alternate forms of Andrea.

ANEESA, Aneesha (Greek) alternate forms of Agnes.
Ahnesha, Ahnesia, Ahnesshia, Anee, Aneesah, Aneese, Aneeshah, Aneesia, Aneisa, Aneisha, Anessa, Anessia

ANEKO (Japanese) older sister.

ANELA (Hawaiian) angel.
Anel, Anelle

ANESSA (Greek) an alternate form of Agnes.
Anesha, Aneshia, Anesia, Anessia, Annessa

ANETRA (American) a form of Annette.
Anitra

ANEZKA (Czech) a form of Hannah.

ANGEL (Greek) a short form of Angela.
Angele, Angéle, Angell, Angelle, Angil, Anjel

ANGELA (Greek) angel; messenger.
Angala, Anganita, Angel, Angelanell, Angelanette, Angelee, Angeleigh, Angeles, Angeli, Angelia, Angelica, Angelina, Angelique, Angelita, Angella, Angellita, Angie, Anglea, Anjela, Anjelica

ANGELIA (Greek) an alternate form of Angela.
Angelea, Angeleah, Angelie

ANGELICA, Angelika (Greek) alternate forms of Angela.
Angalic, Angelic, Angelici, Angelicia, Angelike, Angeliki, Angellica, Angilica

ANGELINA, Angeline (Russian) forms of Angela.
Angalena, Angalina, Angeleen, Angelena, Angelene, Angeliana, Angeleana, Angellina, Angelyn, Angelyna, Angelyne, Angelynn, Angelynne, Anhelina, Anjelina

ANGELIQUE (French) a form of Angela.
Angeliqua, Angélique, Angilique, Anjelique

ANGENI (Native American) spirit.

ANGIE (Greek) a familiar form of
Angela.
Ange, Angee, Angey, Angi, Angy

ANI (Hawaiian) beautiful.
Aany, Aanye

ANIA (Polish) a form of Hannah.
Ahnia, Anaya, Aniah

ANICA, Anika (Czech) familiar forms
of Anna.
*Aanika, Anaka, Aneeky, Aneka, Anekah,
Anicka, Anik, Anikah, Anike, Anikka,
Anikke, Aniko, Anneka, Annik, Annika,
Anouska, Anuska*

ANICE (English) an alternate form of
Agnes.
*Anesse, Anis, Anise, Annes, Annice, Annis,
Annus*

ANILA (Hindi) Religion: a Hindu wind
god.
Anilla

ANISA, Anisah (Arabic) friendly.
Annissah

ANISSA, Anisha (English) forms of
Agnes, Ann.
*Aanisha, Aeniesha, Anis, Anisa, Anissah,
Anise, Annisa, Annisha, Annissa, Anyssa*

ANITA (Spanish) a form of Ann, Anna.
See also Nita.
*Aneeta, Aneetah, Aneethah, Anetha,
Anitha, Anithah, Anitia, Anitra, Anitte*

ANJELICA (Greek) an alternate form of
Angela.
Anjelika

ANKA (Polish) a familiar form of
Hannah.
Anke

ANN, Anne (English) gracious. Forms
of Hannah.

*Anissa, Anita, Annchen, Annette, Annie,
Annik, Annika, Annze, Anouche*

ANNA (German, Italian, Czech,
Swedish) gracious. A form of Hannah.
Culture: Anna Pavlova was a famous
Russian ballerina. See also Anica,
Anissa, Nina.
*Ahnna, Ana, Anah, Anica, Anita, Annah,
Annina, Annora, Anona, Anya, Anyu,
Aska*

ANNABEL (English) a combination of
Anna + Bel.
Amabel, Anabel, Annabal, Annabelle

ANNABELLE (English) an alternate
form of Annabel.
Anabelle, Annabell, Annabella

ANNALIE (Finnish) a form of Hannah.
*Analee, Annalea, Annaleah, Annalee,
Annaleigh, Annaleigha, Annali, Anneli,
Annelie*

ANNALISA, Annalise (English)
combinations of Anna + Lisa.
*Analisa, Analise, Annaliesa, Annaliese,
Annalissa, Annalisse*

**ANNAMARIE, Annemarie,
Annmarie, Anne-Marie** (English)
combinations of Anne + Marie.
*Annamaria, Anna-Maria, Anna-Marie,
Annmaria*

ANNEKA (Swedish) a form of Hannah.
Annaka, Anneke, Annika, Anniki, Annikki

ANNELISA (English) a combination of
Anne + Lisa.
*Analiese, Anelisa, Anelise, Anneliese,
Annelise*

ANNETTE (French) a form of Ann.
See also Anetra, Nettie.
*Anet, Aneta, Anetra, Anett, Anetta, Anette,
Anneth, Annett, Annetta*

ANNIE (English) a familiar form of Ann.
Anni, Anny

ANNIK, Annika (Russian) forms of Ann.
Aneka, Anekah, Annick, Annicka, Annike, Annikka, Anninna, Anouk

ANNJANETTE (American) a combination of Ann + Janette.
Angen, Angenett, Angenette, Anjane, Anjanetta, Anjani

ANONA (English) pineapple.

ANOUHEA (Hawaiian) cool, soft fragrance.

ANSLEY (Scottish) an alternate form of Ainsley.
Anslea, Anslee, Ansleigh, Anslie

ANTHEA (Greek) flower.
Antha, Anthe, Anthia, Thia

ANTIONETTE (French) a form of Antonia.
Antionet, Antionett, Anntionett

ANTOINETTE (French) a form of Antonia. See also Netti, Toinette, Toni.
Anta, Antanette, Antoinella, Antoinet, Antonella, Antonetta, Antonette, Antonice, Antonieta, Antonietta, Antonique

ANTONIA (Greek) flourishing. (Latin) praiseworthy. A feminine form of Anthony. See also Toni, Tonya, Tosha.
Ansonia, Ansonya, Antania, Antinia, Antionette, Antoinette, Antona, Antoñia, Antonice, Antonie, Antonina, Antonine, Antoniya, Antonnea, Antonnia, Antonya

ANTONICE (Latin) an alternate form of Antonia.
Antanise, Antanisha, Antonesha, Antoneshia, Antonise, Antonisha

ANYA (Russian) a form of Anna.
Aaniyah, Aniya, Aniyah, Anja

ANYSSA (English) an alternate form of Anissa.
Anysa, Anysha

'AOLANI (Hawaiian) heavenly cloud.

APHRA (Hebrew) young doe. See also Afra.

APRIL (Latin) opening. See also Avril.
Aprele, Aprelle, Apriell, Aprielle, Aprila, Aprile, Aprilette, Aprili, Aprill, Apryl

APRYL (Latin) an alternate form of April.
Apryle

AQUENE (Native American) peaceful.

ARA (Arabic) opinionated.
Ahraya, Aira, Arae, Arah, Araya, Arayah

ARABELLA (Latin) beautiful altar. See also Belle, Orabella.
Arabela, Arabele, Arabelle

ARACELI, Aracely (Latin) heavenly altar.
Aracele, Aracelia, Aracelli, Araseli, Arasely, Arcelia, Arceli

ARDELLE (Latin) warm; enthusiastic.
Ardelia, Ardelis, Ardella

ARDEN (English) valley of the eagle. Literature: in Shakespeare, a romantic place of refuge.
Ardeen, Ardeena, Ardena, Ardene, Ardenia, Ardi, Ardin, Ardina, Ardine

ARDI (Hebrew) a short form of Arden, Ardice, Ardith.
Ardie, Arti, Artie

ARDICE (Hebrew) an alternate form of Ardith.
Ardis, Artis, Ardiss, Ardyce, Ardys

ARDITH (Hebrew) flowering field.
Ardath, Ardi, Ardice, Ardyth

ARELI, Arely (American) forms of Oralee.
Areil, Areile, Arelee, Areli, Arelis, Arelli, Arellia, Arelly

ARELLA (Hebrew) angel; messenger.
Arela, Arelle, Orella, Orelle

ARETHA (Greek) virtuous. See also
Oretha.
*Areatha, Areetha, Areta, Aretina, Aretta,
Arette, Arita, Aritha, Retha, Ritha*

ARI, Aria, Arie (Hebrew) short forms
of Ariel.
Ariah, Ariea, Aryia

ARIADNE (Greek) holy. Mythology: the
daughter of King Minos of Crete.

ARIANA, Arianna (Greek) holy.
*Aeriana, Aerianna, Aerionna, Ahreanna,
Ahriana, Ahrianna, Airiana, Arieana,
Ariona, Arionna, Aryonna*

ARIANE (French), Arianne (English)
forms of Ariana, Arianna.
*Aerian, Aeriann, Aerion, Aerionne,
Airiann, Ari, Arianie, Ariann, Ariannie,
Arieann, Arien, Ariene, Arienne, Arieon,
Arionne, Aryane, Aryann, Aryanne*

ARICA (Scandinavian) an alternate
form of Erica.
*Aerica, Aericka, Aeryka, Aricca, Aricka,
Arika, Arike, Arikka*

ARIEL (Hebrew) lioness of God.
*Aerial, Aeriale, Aeriel, Aeriela, Aeryal,
Ahriel, Aire, Aireal, Airial, Ari, Aria, Arial,
Ariale, Arieal, Ariela, Arielle, Arrieal,
Arriel, Aryel, Auriel*

ARIELLE (French) a form of Ariel.
*Aeriell, Ariella, Arriele, Arriell, Arrielle,
Aryelle, Aurielle*

ARIN (Hebrew) enlightened. (Arabic)
messenger. A feminine form of Aaron.
See also Erin.
Aaren, Aerin, Aieron, Aieren, Arinn, Aryn

ARISTA (Greek) best.
Aris, Arissa, Aristana, Aristen

ARLA (German) an alternate form of
Carla.

ARLEIGH (English) an alternate form of
Harley.
Arlea, Arlee, Arley, Arlie, Arly

ARLENE (Irish) pledge. A feminine
form of Arlen. See also Lena, Lina.
*Airlen, Arlana, Arleen, Arleene, Arlen,
Arlena, Arlenis, Arlette, Arleyne, Arliene,
Arlina, Arlinda, Arline, Arlis*

ARLETTE (English) a form of Arlene.
Arleta, Arletta, Arletty

ARLYNN (American) a combination of
Arlene + Lynn.
Arlyn, Arlyne, Arlynne

ARMANI (Persian) desire, goal.
A feminine form of Arman.
Armahni, Arman, Armanee, Armanii

ARMINE (Latin) noble. (German) soldier.
(French) a feminine form of Herman.
Armina

ARNELLE (German) eagle. A feminine
form of Arne.
Arnell, Arnella

ARTHA (Hindi) wealthy, prosperous.
Arthi, Arti, Artie

ARTIS (Irish) noble; lofty hill. (Scottish)
bear. (English) rock. (Icelandic)
follower of Thor. A feminine form of
Arthur.
*Arthea, Arthelia, Arthene, Arthette,
Arthurette, Arthurina, Arthurine, Artina,
Artice*

ARYANA, Aryanna (Italian) forms of
Ariana, Arianna.
Aryan, Aryanah, Aryannah

ARYN (Hebrew) an alternate form of
Arin.
*Aerryn, Aeryn, Airyn, Aryne, Arynn,
Arynne*

ASA (Japanese) born in the morning.

ASHA (Arabic, Swahili) an alternate form of Aisha, Ashia.

ASHANTI (Swahili) from a tribe in West Africa.
Achante, Achanti, Asante, Ashanta, Ashantae, Ashante, Ashanté, Ashantee, Ashantie, Ashaunta, Ashauntae, Ashauntee, Ashaunti, Ashonti, Ashuntae, Ashunti

ASHELY (English) an alternate form of Ashley.
Ashelee, Ashelei, Asheley, Ashelie, Ashelley, Ashelly

ASHIA (Arabic) life.
Asha, Ashya, Ashyah, Ashyia, Ayshia

ASHLEE, Ashli, Ashlie, Ashly (English) alternate forms of Ashley.
Ashle, Ashlea, Ashleah, Ashleeh, Ashliee

ASHLEIGH (English) an alternate form of Ashley.
Ahsleigh, Asheleigh, Ashlei, Ashliegh

ASHLEY (English) ash tree meadow. See also Lee.
Ahslee, Aishlee, Ashala, Ashalee, Ashalei, Ashaley, Ashely, Ashla, Ashlay, Ashleay, Ashlee, Ashleigh, Ashleye, Ashli, Ashlie, Ashly, Ashlye

ASHLIN (English) an alternate form of Ashlyn.
Ashlean, Ashliann, Ashlianne, Ashline

ASHLYN, Ashlynn (English) ash tree pool. (Irish) vision, dream.
Ashlan, Ashleann, Ashleen, Ashleene, Ashlen, Ashlene, Ashlin, Ashling, Ashlyne, Ashlynne

ASHTEN, Ashtin (English) alternate forms of Ashton.
Ashtine

ASHTON (English) ash-tree settlement.
Ashten, Ashtyn

ASHTYN (English) an alternate form of Ashton.
Ashtynne

ASIA (Greek) resurrection. (English) eastern sunrise. (Swahili) an alternate form of Aisha.
Ahsia, Aisia, Aisian, Asiah, Asian, Asianae, Asya, Aysia, Aysiah, Aysian, Ayzia

ASPEN (English) aspen tree.
Aspin, Aspyn

ASTER (English) a form of Astra.
Astera, Asteria, Astyr

ASTRA (Greek) star.
Asta, Astara, Aster, Astraea, Astrea

ASTRID (Scandinavian) divine strength.
Astri, Astrida, Astrik, Astrud, Atti, Estrid

ATALANTA (Greek) mighty huntress. Mythology: an athletic young woman who refused to marry any man who could not outrun her in a footrace. See also Lani.
Atalaya, Atlanta, Atlante, Atlee

ATARA (Hebrew) crown.
Atarah, Ataree

ATHENA (Greek) wise. Mythology: the goddess of wisdom.
Athenea, Athene, Athina, Atina

ATIRA (Hebrew) prayer.

AUBERTE (French) a form of Alberta.
Auberta, Aubertha, Auberthe, Aubine

AUBREE, Aubrie (French) alternate forms of Aubrey.
Auberi, Aubre, Aubrei, Aubreigh, Aubri, Aubrielle

AUBREY (German) noble; bearlike. (French) blond ruler; elf ruler.
Aubary, Aubery, Aubray, Aubrea, Aubreah, Aubree, Aubrette, Aubria, Aubrie, Aubry, Aubury, Avery

AUBRIANA, Aubrianna (English) combinations of Aubrey + Anna.
Aubreyana, Aubreyanna, Aubreyanne, Aubreyena, Aubrianne

AUDEY (English) a familiar form of Audrey.
Aude, Audi, Audie

AUDRA (French) a form of Audrey
Audria, Audriea

AUDREANNE (English) a combination of Audrey + Anne.
Audrea, Audreen, Audrianne, Audrienne

AUDREE, Audrie (English) alternate forms of Audrey.
Audre, Audri

AUDREY (English) noble strength.
Adrey, Audey, Audra, Audray, Audree, Audrie, Audrin, Audriya, Audry, Audrye

AUDRIANA, Audrianna (English) a combination of Audrey + Anna.
Audreanna, Audrienna, Audrina

AUDRIS (German) fortunate, wealthy.
Audrys

AUGUSTA (Latin) a short form of Augustine. See also Gusta.
Agusta, August, Auguste, Augustia, Augustus, Austina

AUGUSTINE (Latin) majestic. Religion: Saint Augustine was the first Archbishop of Canterbury. See also Tina.
Agustina, Augusta, Augustina, Augustyna, Augustyne, Austin

'AULANI (Hawaiian) royal messenger.
Lani, Lanie

AUNDREA (Greek) an alternate form of Andrea.
Aundreah

AURA (Greek) soft breeze. (Latin) golden. See also Ora.

AURELIA (Latin) golden. Mythology: the goddess of dawn. See also Oralia.
Auralea, Auralia, Aurea, Aureal, Aurel, Aurele, Aurelea, Aureliana, Aurelie, Auria, Aurie, Aurilia, Aurita

AURELIE (Latin) an alternate form of Aurelia.
Auralee, Auralei, Aurelee, Aurelei, Aurelle

AURORA (Latin) dawn.
Aurore, Ora, Ori, Orie, Rora

AUSTIN (Latin) a short form of Augustine.
Austen, Austin, Austyn, Austynn

AUTUMN (Latin) autumn.
Autum

AVA (Greek) an alternate form of Eva.
Avada, Avae, Ave, Aveen

AVALON (Latin) island.
Avallon

AVERY (English) a form of Aubrey.
Aivree, Averi, Averie, Avry

AVIS (Latin) bird.
Avais, Avi, Avia, Aviana, Avianca, Aviance, Avianna

AVIVA (Hebrew) springtime. See also Viva.
Aviv, Avivah, Avivi, Avivice, Avni, Avnit, Avri, Avrit, Avy

AVRIL (French) a form of April.
Averil, Averyl, Avra, Avri, Avrilia, Avrill, Avrille, Avrillia, Avy

AXELLE (Latin) axe. (German) small oak tree; source of life. A feminine form of Axel.
Aixa

AYA (Hebrew) bird; fly swiftly.
Aia, Aiah, Aiya, Aiyah

AYANNA (Hindi) innocent.

Ahyana, Aiyanna, Ayan, Ayana, Ayania,
Ayannica, Ayna

AYESHA (Persian) a form of Aisha.
Ayasha, Ayeshah, Ayessa, Ayisha, Ayishah,
Aysha, Ayshah, Ayshe, Ayshea, Aysia

AYITA (Cherokee) first in the dance.

AYLA (Hebrew) oak tree.
Aylana, Aylee, Ayleen, Aylene, Aylie, Aylin

AZA (Arabic) comfort.
Aiza, Aizha, Aizia, Azia

AZIZA (Swahili) precious.
Azize

B

BABA (African) born on Thursday.
Aba

BABE (Latin) a familiar form of Barbara.
(American) an alternate form of Baby.
Babby

BABETTE (French, German) a familiar
form of Barbara.
Babita, Barbette

BABS (American) a familiar form of
Barbara.
Bab

BABY (American) baby.
Babby, Babe, Bebe

BAILEE, Bailie (English) alternate
forms of Bailey.
Baelee, Baeli, Bailea, Bailei, Baillee, Baillie,
Bailli

BAILEIGH, Baleigh (English) alternate
forms of Bailey.
Baeleigh

BAILEY (English) bailiff.

Baeley, Bailee, Baileigh, Bailley, Bailly, Baily,
Bali, Balley, Baylee, Bayley

BAKA (Hindi) crane.

BAKULA (Hindi) flower.

BAMBI (Italian) child.
Bambee, Bambie, Bamby

BANDI (Punjabi) prisoner.
Banda, Bandy

BAPTISTA (Latin) baptizer.
Baptiste, Batista, Battista, Bautista

BARA, Barra (Hebrew) chosen.
Bára, Bari

BARB (Latin) a short form of Barbara.
Barba, Barbe

BARBARA (Latin) stranger, foreigner.
See also Bebe, Varvara, Wava.
Babara, Babb, Babbie, Babe, Babette, Babina,
Babs, Barb, Barbara-Ann, Barbarit,
Barbarita, Barbary, Barbeeleen, Barbera,
Barbie, Barbora, Barborah, Barborka,
Barbra, Barbraann, Barbro, Barùska, Basha,
Bebe, Bobbi, Bobbie

BARBIE (American) a familiar form of
Barbara.
Barbee, Barbey, Barbi, Barby, Baubie

BARBRA (American) a form of
Barbara.
Barbro

BARRETT (German) strong as a bear.

BARRIE (Irish) spear; marks-woman.
A feminine form of Barry.
Bari, Barri, Berri, Berrie, Berry

BASIA (Hebrew) daughter of God.
Basya, Bathia, Batia, Batya, Bitya, Bithia

BATHSHEBA (Hebrew) daughter of
the oath; seventh daughter. Bible: a
wife of King David. See also Sheba.

Bathsheba (cont.)
*Bathshua, Batsheva, Bersaba, Bethsabee,
Bethsheba*

BATINI (Swahili) inner thoughts.

BAYLEE, Bayleigh, Baylie (English)
alternate forms of Bailey.
*Bayla, Bayle, Baylea, Bayleah, Baylei, Bayli,
Bayliee, Bayliegh*

BAYLEY (English) an alternate form of
Bailey.
Bayly

BAYO (Yoruba) joy is found.

BEA, Bee (American) short forms of
Beatrice.

BEATA (Latin) a short form of Beatrice.
Beatta

BEATRICE (Latin) blessed; happy;
bringer of joy. See also Trish, Trixie.
*Bea, Beata, Beatrica, Béatrice, Beatricia,
Beatriks, Beatrisa, Beatrise, Beatrissa,
Beatriz, Beattie, Beatty, Bebe, Bee, Trice*

BEATRIZ (Latin) an alternate form of
Beatrice.
Beatris, Beatriss, Beatrix, Beitris

BEBE (Spanish) a form of Barbara,
Beatrice.
BB, Beebee, Bibi

BECCA (Hebrew) a short form of
Rebecca.
Beca, Becka, Bekah, Bekka

BECKY (American) a familiar form of
Rebecca.
Beckey, Becki, Beckie

BEDELIA (Irish) an alternate form of
Bridget.
Bedeelia, Biddy, Bidelia

BEL (Hindi) sacred wood of apple trees.
A short form of Amabel, Belinda,
Isabel.

BELA (Czech) white. (Hungarian) bright.
Belah, Biela

BELEN (Greek) arrow.
Belina

BELICIA (Spanish) dedicated to God.
Beli, Belia, Belica

BELINDA (Spanish) beautiful.
Literature: a name coined by English
poet Alexander Pope in *The Rape of
the Lock*. See also Blinda, Linda.
Bel, Belindra, Belle, Belynda

BELLA (Latin) beautiful.
Bellah

BELLE (French) beautiful. A short form of
Arabella, Belinda, Isabel. See also Billie.
Belita, Bell, Belli, Bellina

BELVA (Latin) beautiful view.
Belvia

BENA (Native American) pheasant.
See also Bina.
Benea

BENECIA (Latin) a short form of
Benedicta.
*Beneisha, Benicia, Benish, Benisha, Benishia,
Bennicia*

BENEDICTA (Latin) blessed.
A feminine form of Benedict.
*Bendite, Benecia, Benedetta, Benedicte,
Benedikta, Bengta, Benita, Benna, Benni,
Bennicia, Benoîte, Binney*

BENEDICTE (Latin) an alternate form
of Benedicta.

BENITA (Spanish) a form of Benedicta.
Beneta, Benetta, Benitta, Bennita, Neeta

BENNETT (Latin) little blessed one.
Bennet, Bennetta

BENNI (Latin) a familiar form of
Benedicta.
Bennie, Binni, Binnie, Binny

BENTE (Latin) blessed.

BERENICE (Greek) an alternate form of
Bernice.
Berenise, Berenisse, Bereniz, Berenize

BERGET (Irish) an alternate form of
Bridget.
Bergette, Bergit

BERIT (German) glorious.
Beret, Berette, Berta

BERKLEY (Scottish, English) birch tree
meadow. A feminine form of Barclay.
Berkeley, Berkly

BERLYNN (English) a combination of
Bertha + Lynn.
*Berla, Berlin, Berlinda, Berline, Berling,
Berlyn, Berlyne, Berlynne*

BERNADETTE (French) a form of
Bernadine. See also Nadette.
*Bera, Beradette, Berna, Bernadet, Bernadete,
Bernadett, Bernadetta, Bernarda,
Bernardette, Bernedet, Bernedette, Bernessa,
Berneta*

BERNADINE (German) brave as a bear.
(English) a feminine form of Bernard.
*Bernadene, Bernadette, Bernadin,
Bernadina, Bernardina, Bernardine, Berni*

BERNETA (French) a short form of
Bernadette.
Bernatta, Bernetta, Bernette, Bernita

BERNI (English) a familiar form of
Bernadine, Bernice.
Bernie, Berny

BERNICE (Greek) bringer of victory.
See also Bunny, Vernice.
*Berenice, Berenike, Bernessa, Berni, Bernicia,
Bernise, Nixie*

BERTHA (German) bright; illustrious;
brilliant ruler. A short form of
Alberta. A feminine form of Berthold.
See also Birdie, Peke.

*Barta, Bartha, Berta, Berthe, Bertille, Bertita,
Bertrona, Bertus, Birtha*

BERTI (German, English) a familiar form
of Gilberte, Bertina.
Berte, Bertie, Berty

BERTILLE (French) a form of Bertha.

BERTINA (English) bright, shining.
A feminine form of Bert.
Bertine

BERYL (Greek) sea green jewel.
Beryle

BESS, Bessie (Hebrew) familiar forms
of Elizabeth.
Bessi, Bessy

BETH (Hebrew, Aramaic) house of God.
A short form of Bethany, Elizabeth.
Betha, Bethe, Bethia

BETHANI, Bethanie (Aramaic)
alternate forms of Bethany.
*Bethanee, Bethania, Bethannie, Bethni,
Bethnie*

BETHANN (English) a combination of
Beth + Ann.
*Beth-Ann, Bethan, Bethane, Bethanne,
Beth-Anne*

BETHANY (Aramaic) house of figs.
Bible: a village near Jerusalem where
Lazarus lived.
*Beth, Bethaney, Bethani, Bethanney,
Bethanny, Bethena, Betheny, Bethia,
Bethina, Bethney, Bethny, Betthany*

BETSY (American) a familiar form of
Elizabeth.
Betsey, Betsi, Betsie

BETTE (French) a form of Betty.
Beta, Beti, Betka, Bett, Betta

BETTINA (American) a combination of
Beth + Tina.
Betina, Betine, Betti, Bettine

BETTY (Hebrew) consecrated to God. (English) a familiar form of Elizabeth.
Bette, Bettey, Betti, Bettie, Bettye, Bettyjean, Betty-Jean, Bettyjo, Betty-Jo, Bettylou, Betty-Lou, Bety, Boski, Bözsi

BETULA (Hebrew) girl, maiden.

BEULAH (Hebrew) married. Bible: the Land of Beulah is a name for Israel.
Beula, Beulla, Beullah

BEV (English) a short form of Beverly.

BEVANNE (Welsh) daughter of Evan. A feminine form of Bevan.
Bevan, Bevann, Bevany

BEVERLY (English) beaver field. See also Buffy.
Bev, Bevalee, Beverle, Beverlee, Beverley, Beverlie, Beverlly, Bevlyn, Bevlynn, Bevlynne, Bevvy, Verly

BEVERLYANN (American) a combination of Beverly + Ann.
Beverliann, Beverlianne, Beverlyanne

BIAN (Vietnamese) hidden; secretive.

BIANCA (Italian) white. See also Blanca, Vianca.
Biancca, Biancha, Biancia, Bianco, Bianey, Bianica, Bianka, Biannca, Binney, Bionca, Blanca, Blanche, Byanca

BIANKA (Italian) an alternate form of Bianca.
Beyanka, Biannka

BIBI (Latin) a short form of Bibiana. (Arabic) lady. (Spanish) an alternate form of Bebe.

BIBIANA (Latin) lively.
Bibi

BIDDY (Irish) a familiar form of Bedelia.
Biddie

BILLI, Billy (English) alternate forms of Billie.
Billye

BILLIE (German, French) a familiar form of Belle, Wilhelmina. (English) strong willed.
Bilee, Bileigh, Bili, Bilie, Billee, Billi, Billy, Billye

BILLIE-JEAN (American) a combination of Billie + Jean.
Billiejean, Billyjean, Billy-Jean

BILLIE-JO (American) a combination of Billie + Jo.
Billiejo, Billyjo, Billy-Jo

BINA (Hebrew) wise; understanding. (Latin) a short form of Sabina. (Swahili) dancer. See also Bena.
Binah, Binney, Binta, Bintah

BINNEY (English) a familiar form of Benedicta, Bianca, Bina.
Binnee, Binni, Binnie, Binny

BIONCA (Italian) an alternate form of Bianca.
Beonca, Beyonca, Beyonka, Bioncha, Bionica, Bionka, Bionnca

BIRDIE (German) a familiar form of Bertha. (English) bird.
Bird, Birdee, Birdella, Birdena, Birdey, Birdi, Birdy, Byrd, Byrdey, Byrdie, Byrdy

BIRGITTE (Swedish) a form of Bridget.
Birgit, Birgita, Birgitta

BLAINE (Irish) thin.
Blane, Blayne

BLAIR (Scottish) plains dweller.
Blaire

BLAIRE (Scottish) an alternate form of Blair.
Blare, Blayre

BLAISE (French) one who stammers.
Blaize, Blasha, Blasia, Blaza, Blaze, Blazena

BLAKE (English) dark.
Blaque, Blayke

BLAKELY (English) dark meadow.
Blakelea, Blakelee, Blakeleigh, Blakeley, Blakeli, Blakelyn, Blakelynn, Blakesley, Blakley, Blakli

BLANCA (Italian) an alternate form of Bianca.
Bellanca, Blancka, Blanka

BLANCHE (French) a form of Bianca.
Blanch, Blancha, Blinney

BLINDA (American) a short form of Belinda.
Blynda

BLISS (English) blissful, joyful.
Blisse, Blyss, Blysse

BLODWYN (Welsh) flower. See also Wynne.
Blodwen, Blodwynne, Blodyn

BLONDELLE (French) blond, fair haired.
Blondell, Blondie

BLONDIE (American) a familiar form of Blondell.
Blondee, Blondey, Blondy

BLOSSOM (English) flower.

BLUM (Yiddish) flower.
Bluma

BLYTHE (English) happy, cheerful.
Blithe, Blyss, Blyth

BO (Chinese) precious.

BOACHA (Hebrew) blessed. A feminine form of Baruch.

BOBBETTE (American) a familiar form of Roberta.
Bobbet, Bobbetta

BOBBI, Bobbie (American) familiar forms of Barbara, Roberta.

Baubie, Bobbe, Bobbey, Bobbisue, Bobby, Bobbye, Bobi, Bobie, Bobina, Bobbie-Jean, Bobbie-Lynn, Bobbie-Sue

BOBBI-ANN, Bobbie-Ann (American) combinations of Bobbi + Ann, Bobbie + Ann.
Bobbiann, Bobbi-Anne, Bobbianne, Bobbie-Anne, Bobby-Ann, Bobbyann, Bobby-Anne, Bobbyanne

BOBBI-JO (American) a combination of Bobbi + Jo.
Bobbiejo, Bobbie-Jo, Bobbijo, Bobby-Jo, Bobijo

BOBBI-LEE (American) a combination of Bobbi + Lee.
Bobbie-Lee, Bobbilee, Bobbylee, Bobby-Leigh, Bobile

BONITA (Spanish) pretty.
Bonesha, Bonetta, Bonnetta, Bonnie, Bonny

BONNIE, Bonny (English, Scottish) beautiful, pretty. (Spanish) familiar forms of Bonita.
Boni, Bonie, Bonne, Bonnee, Bonnell, Bonney, Bonni, Bonnin

BONNIE-BELL (American) a combination of Bonnie + Belle.
Bonnebell, Bonnebelle, Bonnibell, Bonnibelle, Bonniebell, Bonniebelle, Bonnybell, Bonnybelle

BRADLEY (English) broad meadow.
Bradlee, Bradleigh, Bradlie

BRADY (Irish) spirited.
Bradee, Bradey, Bradi, Bradie, Braedi, Braidee, Braidi, Braidie, Braidey, Braidy, Braydee

BRAEDEN (English) broad hill.
Bradyn, Bradynn, Braedan, Braedean, Braedyn, Braidan, Braiden, Braidyn, Brayden, Braydn, Braydon

BRAELYN (American) a combination of Braeden + Lynn.

Braelyn (cont.)
Braelee, Braeleigh, Braelin, Braelle, Braelon, Braelynn, Braelynne, Brailee, Brailenn, Brailey, Braili, Brailyn, Braylee, Brayley, Braylin, Braylon, Braylyn, Braylynn

BRANDA (Hebrew) blessing.

BRANDEE (Dutch) an alternate form of Brandy.
Brande, Brandea, Brendee

BRANDEN (English) beacon valley.
Brandan, Brandon, Brendan, Brandyn, Brennan

BRANDI, Brandie (Dutch) alternate forms of Brandy.
Brandei, Brandice, Brandiee, Brandii, Brandily, Brandin, Brandis, Brandise, Brani, Branndie, Brendi

BRANDY (Dutch) an after-dinner drink made from distilled wine.
Brand, Brandace, Brandaise, Brandala, Brandee, Brandeli, Brandell, Brandi, Brandye, Brandylee, Brandy-Lee, Brandy-Leigh, Brann, Brantley, Branyell, Brendy

BRANDY-LYNN (American) a combination of Brandy + Lynn.
Brandalyn, Brandalynn, Brandelyn, Brandelynn, Brandelynne, Brandilyn, Brandilynn, Brandilynne, Brandlin, Brandlyn, Brandlynn, Brandlynne, Brandolyn, Brandolynn, Brandolynne, Brandylyn, Brandy-Lyn, Brandylynne, Brandy-Lynne

BRAXTON (English) Brock's town.
Braxten, Braxtyn

BREA, Bria (Irish) short forms of Breana, Briana.
Breah, Breea, Briah, Brya

BREANA, Breanna (Irish) alternate forms of Briana.
Brea, Breanah, Breanda, Bre-Anna, Breannah, Breannea, Breannia, Breasha, Breawna, Breeanna, Breila

BREANN, Breanne (Irish) alternate forms of Briana.
Breane, Bre-Ann, Bre-Anne, Breaunne, Bree, Breean, Breeann, Breeanne, Breelyn, Breeon, Breiann, Breighann, Breyenne, Brieann, Brieon

BREASHA (Russian) a familiar form of Breana.

BREAUNA, Breunna, Briauna (Irish) alternate forms of Briana.
Breaunna, Breeauna, Breuna, Breuna, Briaunna

BRECK (Irish) freckled.
Brecken

BREE (Irish) a short form of Breann. (English) broth. See also Brie.
Breay, Brei, Breigh

BREEANA, Breeanna (Irish) alternate forms of Briana.
Breeanah, Breeannah

BREENA (Irish) fairy palace.
Breenea, Breene, Breina, Brina

BREIANA, Breianna (Irish) alternate forms of Briana.
Breiane, Breiann, Breianne

BRENDA (Irish) little raven. (English) sword. A feminine form of Brendan.
Brendell, Brendelle, Brendette, Brendie, Brendyl, Brenna

BRENDA-LEE (American) a combination of Brenda + Lee.
Brendalee, Brendaleigh, Brendali, Brendaly, Brendalys, Brenlee, Brenley

BRENNA (Irish) an alternate form of Brenda.
Bren, Brenie, Brenin, Brenn, Brennah, Brennaugh, Brenne

BRENNAN (English) an alternate form of Brenden.
Brennea, Brennen, Brennon, Brennyn

BREONA, Breonna (Irish) alternate forms of Briana.
Breeona, Breiona, Breionna, Breonah, Breonia, Breonie, Breonne

BRETT (Irish) a short form of Brittany. See also Brita.
Bret, Brette, Brettin, Bretton

BREYANA, Breyann, Breyanna (Irish) alternate forms of Briana.
Breyan, Breyane, Breyannah, Breyanne

BREYONA, Breyonna (Irish) alternate forms of Briana.
Breyonia

BRIANA, Brianna (Irish) strong; virtuous, honorable. Feminine forms of Brian.
Bhrianna, Brana, Brea, Breana, Breann, Breauna, Breeana, Breiana, Breona, Breyana, Breyona, Bria, Briahna, Brianah, Briand, Brianda, Briannah, Brianne, Brianni, Briannon, Brienna, Brina, Briona, Briyana, Bryanna, Bryona

BRIANNE (Irish) an alternate form of Briana.
Briane, Briann, Brienne, Bryanne

BRIAR (French) heather.
Brear, Brier, Bryar

BRIDEY (Irish) a familiar form of Bridget.
Bridi, Bridie, Brydie

BRIDGET (Irish) strong. See also Bedelia, Bryga, Gitta.
Berget, Birgitte, Bride, Bridey, Bridger, Bridgete, Bridgett, Bridgette, Bridgid, Bridgot, Brietta, Brigada, Briget, Brigid, Brigida, Brigitte, Brita

BRIDGETT, Bridgette (Irish) alternate forms of Bridget.
Bridgitte, Brigette, Bridggett, Briggitte, Bridgitt, Brigitta

BRIE (French) a type of cheese. Geography: a region in France known for its cheese. See also Bree.
Briea, Brielle, Briena, Brieon, Brietta, Briette

BRIEANA, Brieanna (American) combinations of Brie + Anna.
Brieannah

BRIEANN, Brieanne (American) combinations of Brie + Ann. See also Briana.
Brie-Ann, Brie-Anne

BRIELLE (French) a form of Brie.
Briel, Briele, Briell, Briella

BRIENNA, Brienne (Irish) alternate forms of Briana.
Briene, Brieon, Brieona, Brieonna

BRIENNE (French) a form of Briana.
Brienn

BRIGETTE (French) an alternate form of Bridget.
Briget, Brigett, Brigetta, Brigettee, Brigget

BRIGITTE (French) a form of Bridget.
Briggitte, Brigit, Brigita

BRINA (Latin) a short form of Sabrina. (Irish) a familiar form of Briana.
Brin, Brinan, Brinda, Brindi, Brindy, Briney, Brinia, Brinlee, Brinly, Brinn, Brinna, Brinnan, Briona, Bryn, Bryna

BRIONA (Irish) an alternate form of Briana.
Brione, Brionna, Brionne, Briony, Briunna, Bryony

BRISA (Spanish) beloved. Mythology: Briseis was the Greek name of Achilles's beloved.
Breezy, Breza, Brisha, Brishia, Brissa, Bryssa

BRITA (Irish) an alternate form of Bridget. (English) a short form of Brittany.
Bretta, Brieta, Brietta, Brit, Britta

BRITANEY, Brittaney (English) alternate forms of Britany, Brittany.
Britanee, Britanny, Britenee, Briteny, Britianey, British, Britkney, Britley, Britlyn, Britney, Briton

BRITANI, Brittani, Brittanie (English) alternate forms of Britany, Brittany.
Brit, Britania, Britanica, Britanie, Britanii, Britanni, Britannia, Britatani, Britia, Britini, Brittane, Brittanee, Brittanni, Brittannia, Brittannie, Brittenie, Brittiani, Brittianni

BRITANY, Brittany (English) from Britain. See also Brett.
Brita, Britana, Britaney, Britani, Britanna, Britlyn, Britney, Britt, Brittainny, Brittainy, Brittamy, Brittana, Brittaney, Brittani, Brittania, Brittanica, Brittanny, Brittany-Ann, Brittanyne, Brittell, Britteny, Brittiany, Brittini, Brittlin, Brittlynn, Brittnee, Brittony, Bryttany

BRITIN, Brittin (English) from Britain.
Britann, Brittan, Brittin, Brittina, Brittine, Brittini, Brittiny

BRITNEY, Brittney, Brittny (English) alternate forms of Britany, Brittany.
Bittney, Bridnee, Bridney, Britnay, Britne, Britnee, Britnei, Britni, Britny, Britnye, Brittnay, Brittnaye, Brytnea, Brytni

BRITNI, Brittni, Brittnie (English) alternate forms of Britney, Britney.
Britnie

BRITON, Brittin (English) alternate forms of Britin, Brittin.
Britton

BRITT, Britta (Latin) short forms of Britany, Brittany. (Swedish) strong.
Brett, Briet, Brit, Brita, Britte

BRITTENY (English) an alternate form of Britany, Brittany.
Britten, Brittenay, Brittenee, Britteney, Brittenie

BRITTINI, Brittiny (English) alternate forms of Britany, Brittany.
Brittinee, Brittiney, Brittinie, Brittiny

BRITTNEE (English) an alternate form of Britany, Brittany.
Brittne, Brittnea, Brittnei, Brittneigh

BRIYANA, Briyanna (Irish) alternate forms of Briana.

BRODIE (Irish) ditch; canal builder.
Brodee, Brodi, Brody

BRONNIE (Welsh) a familiar form of Bronwyn.
Bron, Bronia, Bronney, Bronny, Bronya

BRONWYN (Welsh) white breasted.
Bronnie, Bronwen, Bronwin, Bronwynn, Bronwynne

BROOK, Brooke (English) brook, stream.
Bhrooke, Brookelle, Brookie, Brooks, Brooky

BROOKLYN, Brooklynn (American) combinations of Brooke + Lynn.
Brookellen, Brookelyn, Brookelyne, Brookelynn, Brooklen, Brooklin, Brooklyne, Brooklynne

BRUNA (German) a short form of Brunhilda.
Brona

BRUNHILDA (German) armored warrior.
Brinhilda, Brinhilde, Bruna, Brunhilde, Brünnhilde, Brynhild, Brynhilda, Brynhilde, Hilda

BRYANA, Bryanna, Bryanne (Irish) alternate forms of Briana.
Bryann, Bryanni

BRYCE (Welsh) alert; ambitious.

BRYGA (Polish) a form of Bridget.
Brygid, Brygida, Brygitka

BRYLIE (American) a combination of the letter B + Riley.
Brylee, Brylei, Bryley, Bryli

BRYN, Brynn (Latin) from the boundary line. (Welsh) mound.
Brinn, Brynee, Brynne

BRYNA (Latin, Irish) an alternate form of Brina.
Brynan, Brynna, Brynnan

BRYONA, Bryonna (Irish) alternate forms of Briana.
Bryonia, Bryony

BRYTTANI, Bryttany, Bryttni (English) an alternate form of Britany, Brittany.
Brytani, Brytanie, Brytanny, Brytany, Brytnee, Brytnie, Bryton, Bryttanee, Bryttanie, Bryttine, Bryttney, Bryttnie, Brytton

BUFFY (American) buffalo; from the plains.
Buffee, Buffey, Buffie, Buffye

BUNNY (Greek) a familiar form of Bernice. (English) little rabbit. See also Bonnie.
Bunni, Bunnie

BURGUNDY (French) Geography: a region of France known for its burgundy wine.
Burgandi, Burgandie, Burgandy, Burgunde

C

CACHET (French) prestigious; desirous.
Cachae, Cache, Cachea, Cachee, Cachée

CADENCE (Latin) rhythm.
Cadena, Cadenza, Kadena

CADY (English) an alternate form of Kady.
Cade, Cadee, Cadey, Cadi, Cadie, Cadine, Cadye

CAELEY, Cailey, Cayley (American) alternate forms of Kaylee, Kelly.
Caela, Caelee, Caeleigh, Caeley, Caeli, Caelie, Caelly, Caely, Cailee, Caileigh, Caili, Cailie, Cailley, Caillie, Caily, Caylee

CAELIN, Caelyn (American) alternate forms of Kaelyn.
Caelan, Caelinn, Caelynn, Cailan, Caylan

CAI (Vietnamese) feminine.
Cae, Cay, Caye

CAILIDA (Spanish) adoring.
Kailida

CAILIN, Cailyn (American) forms of Caitlin.
Caileen, Cailene, Cailine, Cailynn, Cailynne, Calen, Cayleen, Caylen, Caylene, Caylin, Cayline, Caylyn, Caylyne, Caylynne

CAITLAN (Irish) an alternate form of Caitlin.
Caitland, Caitlandt

CAITLIN (Irish) pure. An alternate form of Cathleen. See also Kaitlin, Katalina, Katelin, Katelyn, Kaytlyn.
Caetlin, Cailin, Caitlan, Caitleen, Caitlen, Caitlene, Caitlenn, Caitline, Caitlinn, Caitlon, Caitlyn, Catlee, Catleen, Catleene, Catlin

CAITLYN, Caitlynn (Irish) alternate forms of Caitlin. See also Kaitlyn.
Caitlyne, Caitlynne, Catelyn, Catlyn, Catlynn, Catlynne

CALA (Arabic) castle, fortress. See also Callie, Kala.
Calah, Calan, Calla, Callah

CALANDRA (Greek) lark.
Calan, Calandrea, Calandria, Caleida, Calendra, Calendre, Kalandra, Kalandria

CALEIGH, Caley (American) alternate forms of Caeley.
Caileigh, Caleah

CALI, Calli (Greek) alternate forms of Callie. See also Kali.
Calee

CALIDA (Spanish) warm; ardent.
Calina, Calinda, Callida, Callinda, Kalida

CALLIE (Greek, Arabic) a familiar form of Cala, Callista. See also Kalli.
Cal, Cali, Calie, Callee, Calley, Calli, Cally, Caly

CALLISTA (Greek) most beautiful. See also Kallista.
Calesta, Calista, Callie, Calysta

CALVINA (Latin) bald. A feminine form of Calvin.
Calvine, Calvinetta, Calvinette

CALYPSO (Greek) concealer. Botany: a white orchid with purple or yellow markings. Mythology: the sea nymph who held Odysseus captive for seven years.
Caly, Lypsie, Lypsy

CAM (Vietnamese) sweet citrus.
Kam

CAMARA (American) a form of Cameron.
Camera, Cameri, Cameria, Camira, Camry

CAMBERLY (American) a form of Kimberly.
Camber, Camberlee, Camberleigh

CAMBRIA (Latin) from Wales. See also Kambria.
Camberry, Cambreia, Cambie, Cambrea, Cambree, Cambrie, Cambrina, Cambry, Cambrya, Cami

CAMDEN (Scottish) winding valley.
Camdyn

CAMELLIA (Italian) evergreen tree or shrub.
Camala, Camalia, Camallia, Camela, Camelia, Camelita, Camella, Camellita, Cami, Kamelia, Kamellia

CAMEO (Latin) gem or shell on which a portrait is carved.
Cami, Kameo

CAMERON (Scottish) crooked nose. See also Kameron, Kamryn.
Camara, Cameran, Cameren, Camira, Camiran, Camiron, Camryn

CAMI (French) a short form of Camille. See also Kami.
Camey, Camie, Cammi, Cammie, Cammy, Cammye, Camy

CAMILA, Camilla (Italian) forms of Camille. See also Kamila, Mila.
Camia, Camilia, Camillia, Camilya, Cammilla, Chamelea, Chamelia, Chamika, Chamila, Chamilia

CAMILLE (French) young ceremonial attendant. See also Millie.
Cam, Cami, Camiel, Camielle, Camil, Camila, Camile, Camill, Cammille, Cammillie, Cammilyn, Cammyl, Cammyll, Camylle, Chamelle, Chamille, Kamille

CAMISHA (American) a combination of Cami + Aisha.
Cameasha, Cameesha, Cameisha, Camesa, Camesha, Cameshaa, Cameshia, Camiesha, Camyeshia

CAMRI, Camrie (American) short forms of Camryn. See also Kamri.
Camrea, Camree, Camrey, Camry

CAMRYN (American) a form of Cameron. See also Kamryn.
Camri, Camrin, Camron, Camrynn

CAMYLLE (French) an alternate form of Camille.
Camyle, Camyll

CANDACE (Greek) glittering white; glowing. History: the name and title of the queens of ancient Ethiopia. See also Dacey, Kandace.
Cace, Canace, Canda, Candas, Candece, Candelle, Candi, Candiace, Candice, Candyce

CANDI, Candy (American) familiar forms of Candace, Candice, Candida. See also Kandi.
Candee, Candie

CANDICE, Candis (Greek) alternate forms of Candace.
Candes, Candi, Candias, Candies, Candise, Candiss, Candus

CANDIDA (Latin) bright white.
Candeea, Candi, Candia, Candide, Candita

CANDRA (Latin) glowing. See also Kandra.
Candrea, Candria

CANDYCE (Greek) an alternate form of Candace.
Candys, Candyse, Cyndyss

CANTARA (Arabic) small crossing.
Cantarah

CANTRELLE (French) song.
Cantrella

CAPRI (Italian) a short form of Caprice. Geography: an island off the west coast of Italy. See also Kapri.
Capria, Caprie, Capry

CAPRICE (Italian) fanciful.
Cappi, Caprece, Caprecia, Capresha, Capricia, Capriese, Caprina, Capris, Caprise, Caprisha, Capritta

CARA (Latin) dear. (Irish) friend. See also Karah.
Caira, Caragh, Carah, Caralee, Caranda, Carey, Carra

CARALEE (Irish) an alternate form of Cara.
Caralea, Caraleigh, Caralia, Caralie, Carely

CARALYN (English) a form of Caroline.
Caralin, Caraline, Caralynn, Caralynna, Caralynne

CARESSA (French) a form of Carissa.
Caresa, Carese, Caresse, Carissa, Charessa, Charesse, Karessa

CAREY (Welsh) a familiar form of Cara, Caroline, Karen, Katherine. See also Carrie, Kari.
Caree, Cari, Carrey, Cary

CARI, Carie (Welsh) alternate forms of Carey, Kari.

CARINA (Greek) a familiar form of Cora. (Italian) dear little one. (Swedish) a form of Karen.
Carena, Carinah, Carine, Carinna

CARINE (Italian) an alternate form of Carina.
Carin, Carinn, Carinne

CARISA, Carrisa (Greek) alternate forms of Carissa.
Carise, Carisha, Carisia, Charisa

CARISSA (Greek) beloved. See also Karissa.
Caressa, Carisa, Carrissa, Charissa

CARITA (Latin) charitable.
Caritta, Karita, Karitta

CARLA (Latin) an alternate form of Carol, Caroline. (German) farmer. (English) strong and womanly. See also Karla.
Carila, Carilla, Carleta, Carlia, Carliqua, Carliyle, Carlonda, Carlyjo, Carlyle, Carlysle

CARLEE, Carleigh, Carley (English) alternate forms of Carly. See also Karlee.
Carle, Carlea, Carleah, Carleh

CARLEEN, Carlene (English) forms of Caroline. See also Karlene.
Carlaen, Carlaena, Carleena, Carlen, Carlena, Carlenna, Carline, Carlyn, Carlyne

CARLI, Carlie (English) alternate forms of Carly. See also Karli.

CARLIN (Latin) a short form of Caroline. (Irish) little champion.
Carlan, Carlana, Carlandra, Carlina, Carlinda, Carline, Carling, Carllan, Carlyn, Carllen, Carrlin

CARLISA (American) an alternate form of Carlissa.
Carilis, Carilise, Carilyse, Carleesia, Carlesia, Carletha, Carlethe, Carlicia, Carlis, Carlise, Carlisha, Carlisia, Carlyse

CARLISSA (American) a combination of Carla + Lissa.
Carleeza, Carlisa, Carliss, Carlissah, Carlisse, Carlissia, Carlista

CARLOTTA (Italian) a form of Charlotte.
Carletta, Carlita, Carlota

CARLY (English) a familiar form of Caroline, Charlotte. See also Karli.
Carlee, Carli, Carlie, Carlye

CARLYN, Carlynn (Irish) alternate forms of Carlin.
Carlyna, Carlynne

CARMELA, Carmella (Hebrew) garden; vineyard. Bible: Mount Carmel in Israel is often thought of as paradise. See also Karmel.
Carma, Carmalla, Carmarit, Carmel, Carmeli, Carmelia, Carmelina, Carmelit, Carmelle, Carmellia, Carmellina, Carmesa, Carmesha, Carmi, Carmie, Carmiel, Carmil, Carmila, Carmile, Carmilla, Carmille, Carmisha, Leeta, Lita

CARMELIT (Hebrew) an alternate form of Carmela.
Carmaletta, Carmalit, Carmalita, Carmelita, Carmelitha, Carmelitia, Carmellit, Carmellita, Carmellitha, Carmellitia

CARMEN (Latin) song. Religion: Santa Maria del Carmen—Saint Mary of Mount Carmel—is one of the titles of the Virgin Mary. See also Karmen.
Carma, Carmaine, Carman, Carmelina, Carmencita, Carmene, Carmi, Carmia, Carmin, Carmina, Carmine, Carmita, Carmon, Carmynn, Charmaine

CAROL (German) farmer. (French) song of joy. (English) strong and womanly. A feminine form of Carl, Charles. See also Charlene, Kalle, Karoll.
Carel, Cariel, Caro, Carola, Carole, Carolenia, Carolinda, Caroline, Caroll, Carrie, Carrol, Carroll, Caryl

CAROLANE, Carolann, Carolanne (American) forms of Caroline.
Carolan, Carol Ann, Carole-Anne

CAROLE (English) an alternate form of Carol.
Carolee, Karole, Karrole

CAROLINA (Italian) a form of Caroline. See also Karolina.
Carilena, Carlena, Carlina, Caroleena, Caroleina, Carolena, Carrolena

CAROLINE (French) little and womanly. See also Carla, Carleen, Carlin, Karolina.
Caralin, Caraline, Carileen, Carilene, Carilin, Cariline, Carling, Carly, Caro, Carolann, Caroleen, Carolin, Carolina, Carolyn, Carrie, Carroleen, Carrolene, Carrolin, Carroline, Cary, Charlene

CAROLYN (English) a form of Caroline. See also Karolyn.
Carilyn, Carilynn, Carilynne, Carlyn, Carlynn, Carlynne, Carolyne, Carolynn, Carolynne, Carrolyn, Carrolynn, Carrolynne

CARON (Welsh) loving, kind-hearted, charitable.
Caronne, Carron, Carrone

CARRA (Irish) an alternate form of Cara.
Carrah

CARRIE (English) a familiar form of Carol, Caroline. See also Carey, Kari, Karri.
Carree, Carrey, Carri, Carria, Carry, Cary

CARSON (English) daughter of Carr.
Carsen, Carsyn

CARTER (English) cart driver.

CARYL (Latin) a form of Carol.
Caryle, Caryll, Carylle

CARYN (Danish) a form of Karen.
Caren, Carren, Carrin, Carryn, Caryna, Caryne, Carynn

CARYS (Welsh) love.
Caris, Caryse, Ceris, Cerys

CASANDRA (Greek) an alternate form of Cassandra.
Casandera, Casandre, Casandrea, Casandrey, Casandri, Casandria, Casanndra, Casaundra, Casaundre, Casaundri, Casaundria, Casondra, Casondre, Casondri, Casondria

CASEY (Greek) a familiar form of Acacia. (Irish) brave. See also Kasey.
Cacy, Cascy, Casie, Casse, Cassee, Cassey, Cassye, Casy, Cayce, Cayse, Caysee, Caysy

CASIDY (Irish) an alternate form of Cassidy.
Casidee, Casidi

CASIE (Irish) an alternate form of Casey.
Caci, Caesi, Caisie, Casci, Cascie, Casi, Cayci, Caysi, Caysie, Cazzi

CASS (Greek) a short form of Cassandra.

CASSADY (Irish) an alternate form of Cassidy.
Casadee, Casadi, Casadie, Cassaday, Cassadee, Cassadey, Cassadi, Cassadie, Cassadina

CASSANDRA (Greek) helper of men. Mythology: a prophetess of ancient Greece whose prophesies were not believed. See also Kassandra, Sandra, Sandy, Zandra.
Casandra, Cass, Cassandre, Cassandri, Cassandry, Cassaundra, Cassie, Cassondra

CASSAUNDRA (Greek) an alternate form of Cassandra.
Cassaundre, Cassaundri, Cassundra, Cassundre, Cassundri, Cassundria

CASSIA (Greek) spicy cinnamon. See also Kasia.
Casia, Cass, Casya

CASSIDY (Irish) clever. See also Kassidy.
Casidy, Cassady, Casseday, Cassiddy, Cassidee, Cassidi, Cassidie, Cassity

CASSIE, Cassey, Cassi (Greek) familiar forms of Cassandra, Catherine. See also Kassie.
Cassee, Cassii, Cassy, Casy

CASSIOPEIA (Greek) clever. Mythology: the wife of the Ethiopian king Cepheus; the mother of Andromeda.
Cassio

CASSONDRA (Greek) an alternate form of Cassandra.
Cassondre, Cassondri, Cassondria

CATALINA (Spanish) a form of Catherine. See also Katalina.
Cataleen, Catalena, Catalene, Catalin, Catalyn, Catalyna, Cateline

CATARINA (German) a form of Catherine.
Catarena, Catarin, Catarine, Caterin, Caterina, Caterine

CATELYN (Irish) an alternate form of Caitlin.
Catelin, Cateline, Catelyne, Catelynn

CATHARINE (Greek) an alternate form of Catherine.
Catharen, Catharin, Catharina, Catharyn

CATHERINE (Greek) pure. (English) a form of Katherine.
Cat, Catalina, Catarina, Cate, Cathann, Cathanne, Catharine, Cathenne, Catheren, Catherene, Catheria, Catherin, Catherina, Catheryn, Catheryne, Cathi, Cathleen, Cathrine, Cathryn, Cathy, Catlaina, Catreeka, Catrelle, Catrice, Catricia, Catrika, Catrina

CATHI, Cathy (Greek) familiar forms of Catherine, Cathleen. See also Kathy.
Catha, Cathe, Cathee, Cathey, Cathie

CATHLEEN (Irish) a form of Catherine. See also Caitlin, Kathleen.
Caithlyn, Cathaleen, Cathelin, Cathelina, Cathelyn, Cathi, Cathleana, Cathleene, Cathlene, Cathleyn, Cathlin, Cathline, Cathlyn, Cathlyne, Cathlynn, Cathy

CATHRINE (Greek) an alternate form of Catherine.

CATHRYN (Greek) an alternate form of Catherine.
Cathryne, Cathrynn, Catryn

CATRINA (Slavic) a form of Catherine, Katrina.
Caitriana, Caitriona, Catina, Catreen, Catreena, Catrene, Catrenia, Catrin, Catrine, Catrinia, Catriona, Catroina

CAYLA (Hebrew) an alternate form of Kayla.
Caylea, Caylia

CAYLEE, Caylie (American) alternate forms of Caeley, Cailey, Cayley.
Cayle, Cayleigh, Cayli, Cayly

CEARA (Irish) an alternate form of Ciara.
Ceaira, Ceairah, Ceairra, Cearaa, Cearie, Cearah, Cearra, Cera

CECELIA (Latin) an alternate form of Cecilia. See also Sheila.
Caceli, Cacelia, Cece, Ceceilia, Ceceli, Cecelia, Cecelie, Cecely, Cecelyn, Cecette, Cescelia, Cescelie

CECILIA (Latin) blind. A feminine form of Cecil. See also Cicely, Cissy, Secilia, Selia, Sissy.
Cacilia, Caecilia, Cecelia, Cecil, Cecila, Cecile, Cecilea, Cecilija, Cecilla, Cecille, Cecillia, Cecily, Cecilya, Ceclia, Cecylia, Cee, Ceil, Ceila, Ceilagh, Ceileh, Ceileigh, Ceilena, Celia, Cesilia, Cicelia

CECILY (Latin) an alternate form of Cecilia.
Cacilie, Cecilee, Ceciley, Cecilie, Cescily, Cicely, Cilley

CEIL (Latin) a short form of Cecilia.
Ceel, Ciel

CEIRA, Ceirra (Irish) alternate forms of Ciara.
Ceire

CELENA (Greek) an alternate form of Selena.
Celeena, Celene, Celenia, Celine, Cena

CELENE (Greek) an alternate form of Celena.
Celeen

CELESTE (Latin) celestial, heavenly.
Cele, Celeeste, Celense, Celes, Celesia, Celesley, Celest, Celesta, Celestia, Celestial, Celestin, Celestina, Celestine, Celestinia, Celestyn, Celestyna, Cellest, Celleste, Selestina

CELIA (Latin) a short form of Cecilia.
Ceilia, Celie

CELINA (Greek) an alternate form of Celena. See also Selina.
Caleena, Calena, Calina, Celena, Celinda, Celinka, Celinna, Celka, Cellina

CELINE (Greek) an alternate form of Celena.
Caline, Celeen, Celene, Céline, Cellinn

CERA (French) a short form of Cerise.
Cerea, Ceri, Ceria, Cerra

CERELLA (Latin) springtime.
Cerelisa, Ceres

CERISE (French) cherry; cherry red.
Cera, Cerese, Cerice, Cericia, Cerissa, Cerria, Cerrice, Cerrina, Cerrita, Cerryce, Ceryce, Cherise

CESILIA (Latin) an alternate form of Cecilia.
Cesia, Cesya

CHABLIS (French) a dry, white wine. Geography: a region in France where wine grapes are grown.
Chabeli, Chabelly, Chabely, Chablee, Chabley, Chabli

CHADEE (French) from Chad, a country in north central Africa. See also Sade.
Chaday, Chadday, Chade, Chadea, Chadi

CHAI (Hebrew) life.
Chae, Chaela, Chaeli, Chaella, Chaena, Chaia

CHAKA (Sanskrit) an alternate form of Chakra. See also Shaka.
Chakai, Chakia, Chakka, Chakkah

CHAKRA (Sanskrit) circle of energy.
Chaka, Chakara, Chakaria, Chakena, Chakina, Chakira, Chakrah, Chakria, Chakriya, Chakyra

CHALICE (French) goblet.
Chalace, Chalcie, Chalece, Chalicea, Chalie, Chaliese, Chalis, Chalisa, Chalise, Chalisk, Chalissa, Chalisse, Challa, Challaine, Challis, Challisse, Challysse, Chalsey, Chalyce, Chalyn, Chalyse, Chalyssa, Chalysse

CHALINA (Spanish) a form of Rose.
Chaline, Chalini

CHALONNA (American) a combination of the prefix Cha + Lona.
Chalon, Chalona, Chalonda, Chalonn, Chalonne, Chalonte, Shalon

CHAMBRAY (French) a lightweight fabric.
Chambrae, Chambre, Chambree, Chambrée, Chambrey, Chambria, Chambrie

CHAN (Cambodian) sweet-smelling tree.

CHANA (Hebrew) an alternate form of Hannah.
Chanae, Chanai, Chanay, Chanea, Chanie

CHANCEY (English) chancellor; church official. A feminine form of Chauncey.
Chance, Chancee, Chancie, Chancy

CHANDA (Sanskrit) great goddess. Religion: the name assumed by the Hindu goddess Devi. See also Shanda.
Chandee, Chandey, Chandi, Chandie, Chandin

CHANDELLE (French) candle.
Chandal, Chandel, Shandal, Shandel

CHANDLER (Hindi) moon.
Chandlar, Chandlier, Chandlor, Chandlyr

CHANDRA (Sanskrit) moon. Religion: one of the names of the Hindu goddess Shakti. See also Shandra.
Chandrae, Chandray, Chandre, Chandrea, Chandrelle, Chandria

CHANEL (English) channel. See also Shanel.
Chanal, Chaneel, Chaneil, Chanele, Chanell, Channal, Channel, Chenelle

CHANELL, Chanelle (English) alternate forms of Chanel.
Channell, Shanell

CHANISE (American) an alternate form of Shanice.
Chanisse, Chenice, Chenise

CHANNA (Hindi) chickpea.
Channah

CHANTAL (French) song.
Chandal, Chantaal, Chantael, Chantala,
Chantale, Chantall, Chantalle, Chantara,
Chantarai, Chantasia, Chante, Chanteau,
Chantel, Chantle, Chantoya, Chantrill,
Chauntel

CHANTE (French) a short form of
Chantal.
Chanta, Chantae, Chantai, Chantay,
Chantaye, Chanté, Chantéa, Chantee,
Chanti, Chantia, Chaunte, Chauntea,
Chauntéa, Chauntee

CHANTEL, Chantell, Chantelle
(French) alternate forms of Chantal.
See also Shantel.
Chanteese, Chantela, Chantele, Chantella,
Chanter, Chantey, Chantez, Chantrel,
Chantrell, Chantrelle, Chatell

CHANTILLY (French) fine lace. See also
Shantille.
Chantiel, Chantielle, Chantil, Chantila,
Chantilée, Chantill, Chantille

CHANTREA (Cambodian) moon;
moonbeam.
Chantra, Chantrey, Chantri, Chantria

CHANTRICE (French) singer. See also
Shantrice.
Chantreese, Chantress

CHARDAE, Charde (Punjabi)
charitable. (French) short forms of
Chardonnay. See also Shardae.
Charda, Chardai, Charday, Chardea,
Chardee, Chardée, Chardese, Chardey,
Chardie

CHARDONNAY (French) a dry white
wine. Geography: a wine-making
region in France.
Char, Chardae, Chardnay, Chardney,
Chardon, Chardonae, Chardonai,
Chardonay, Chardonaye, Chardonee,
Chardonna, Chardonnae, Chardonnai,
Chardonnee, Chardonnée, Chardonney,
Shardonay, Shardonnay

CHARIS (Greek) grace; kindness.
Charece, Chareece, Chareeze, Charese,
Chari, Charice, Charie, Charish, Charisse

CHARISSA, Charisse (Greek) forms of
Charity.
Charesa, Charese, Charessa, Charesse,
Charis, Charisa, Charise, Charisha,
Charissee, Charista, Charyssa

CHARITY (Latin) charity, kindness.
Chariety, Charis, Charissa, Charisse,
Charista, Charita, Chariti, Charitie, Sharity

CHARLA (French, English) a short
form of Charlene, Charlotte.
Char, Charlea

CHARLAINE (English) an alternate
form of Charlene.
Charlaina, Charlane, Charlanna,
Charlayna, Charlayne

CHARLEE, Charley (German, English)
alternate forms of Charlie.
Charle, Charleigh

CHARLENE (English) little and
womanly. A form of Caroline. See also
Carol, Karla, Sharlene.
Charla, Charlaine, Charlean, Charleen,
Charleene, Charleesa, Charlena, Charlenae,
Charlesena, Charline, Charlyn, Charlyne,
Charlynn, Charlynne, Charlzina, Charoline

CHARLIE (German, English) strong and
womanly. A feminine form of Charles.
Charlee, Charley, Charli, Charyl, Chatty,
Sharli, Sharlie

CHARLOTTE (French) little and
womanly. A form of Caroline.
Literature: Charlotte Brontë was a
British novelist and poet best known
for her novel *Jane Eyre*. See also
Karlotte, Lotte, Sharlotte, Tottie.
Carlotta, Carly, Chara, Charil, Charl,
Charla, Charlet, Charlett, Charletta,
Charlette, Charlisa, Charlita, Charlott,
Charlotta, Charlottie, Charlotty, Charolet,
Charolette, Charolot, Charolotte

CHARMAINE (French) a form of Carmen. See also Sharmaine.
Charamy, Charma, Charmae, Charmagne, Charmaigne, Charmain, Chamaine, Charmalique, Charman, Charmane, Charmar, Charmara, Charmayane, Charmayne, Charmeen, Charmeine, Charmene, Charmese, Charmian, Charmin, Charmine, Charmion, Charmisa, Charmon, Charmyn, Charmyne, Charmynne

CHARNETTE (American) a combination of Charo + Annette.
Charnetta, Charnita

CHARNIKA (American) a combination of Charo + Nika.
Charneka, Charniqua, Charnique

CHARO (Spanish) a familiar form of Rosa.

CHARYANNA (American) a combination of Charo + Anna.
Charian, Charyian, Cheryn

CHASIDY, Chassidy (Latin) alternate forms of Chastity.
Chasa Dee, Chasadie, Chasady, Chasidee, Chasidey, Chasidie, Chassedi, Chassidi, Chasydi

CHASITY (Latin) an alternate form of Chastity.
Chasiti, Chasitie, Chasitty, Chassey, Chassie, Chassiti, Chassity, Chassy

CHASTITY (Latin) pure.
Chasidy, Chasity, Chasta, Chastady, Chastidy, Chastin, Chastitie, Chastney, Chasty

CHAUNTEL (French) an alternate form of Chantal.
Chaunta, Chauntae, Chauntay, Chaunte, Chauntell, Chauntelle, Chawntel, Chawntell, Chawntelle, Chontelle

CHAVA (Hebrew) life. (Yiddish) bird. Bible: the original name of Eve.
Chabah, Chavae, Chavah, Chavalah, Chavarra, Chavarria, Chave, Chavé, Chavette, Chaviva, Chavvis, Hava, Kaÿa

CHAVELLA (Spanish) an alternate form of Isabel.
Chavel, Chaveli, Chavell, Chavelle, Chevelle, Chavely, Chevie

CHAVI (Gypsy) girl.
Chavali

CHAVON (Hebrew) an alternate form of Jane.
Chavona, Chavonda, Chavonn, Chavonne, Shavon

CHAVONNE (Hebrew) an alternate form of Chavon. (American) a combination of the prefix Cha + Yvonne.
Chavondria, Chavonna, Chevon, Chevonn, Chevonna

CHAYA (Hebrew) life; living.
Chaike, Chaye, Chayka, Chayla, Chaylah, Chaylea, Chaylee, Chaylene, Chayra

CHELCI, Chelcie (English) alternate forms of Chelsea.
Chelce, Chelcee, Chelcey, Chelcy

CHELSEA (English) seaport. See also Kelsi, Shelsea.
Chelci, Chelese, Chelesia, Chelsa, Chelsae, Chelsah, Chelse, Chelseah, Chelsee, Chelsey, Chelsia, Chelsie, Chesea, Cheslee, Chessea

CHELSEE (English) an alternate form of Chelsea.
Chelsei, Chelseigh

CHELSEY, Chelsy (English) alternate forms of Chelsea. See also Kelsey.
Chelcy, Chelsay, Chelssy, Chelssey, Chelsye, Chesley

CHELSIE (English) an alternate form of Chelsea.
Chelli, Chellie, Chellise, Chellsie, Chelsi, Chelssie, Cheslie, Chessie

CHENELLE (English) an alternate form of Chanel.
Chenel, Chenell

CHENOA (Native American) white dove.
Chenee, Chenika, Chenita, Chenna, Chenoah

CHER (French) beloved, dearest. (English) a short form of Cherilyn.
Chere, Cheri, Cherie, Sher

CHERELLE, Cherrelle (French) alternate forms of Cheryl. See also Sherelle.
Charell, Charelle, Cherell, Cherrel, Cherrell

CHERESE (Greek) an alternate form of Cherish.
Chereese, Cheresa, Cheresse, Cherice

CHERI, Cherie (French) familiar forms of Cher.
Cheree, Chérie, Cheriee, Cherri, Cherrie

CHERILYN (English) a combination of Cheryl + Lynn.
Cher, Cheralyn, Chereen, Chereena, Cherilynn, Cherlyn, Cherlynn, Cherralyn, Cherrilyn, Cherrylyn, Cherylene, Cherylin, Cheryline, Cheryl-Lyn, Cheryl-Lynn, Cheryl-Lynne, Cherylyn, Cherylynn, Cherylynne, Sherilyn

CHERISE (French) a form of Cherish. See also Sharice, Sherice.
Charisa, Charise, Cherece, Chereese, Cheresa, Cherice, Cheriss, Cherissa, Cherisse, Cherrise

CHERISH (English) dearly held, precious.
Charish, Charisha, Cheerish, Cherise, Cherishe, Cherrish, Sherish

CHEROKEE (Native American) a tribal name.
Cherika, Cherkita, Cherrokee, Sherokee

CHERRY (Latin) a familiar form of Charity. (French) cherry; cherry red.
Chere, Cheree, Cherey, Cherida, Cherita, Cherrey, Cherrita, Cherry-Ann, Cherry-Anne, Cherrye, Chery, Cherye

CHERYL (French) beloved. See also Sheryl.
Charel, Charil, Charyl, Cherelle, Cherrelle, Cheryl-Ann, Cheryl-Anne, Cheryle, Cherylee, Cheryll, Cherylle, Cheryl-Lee

CHESAREY (American) a form of Desiree.
Chesarae, Chessa

CHESNA (Slavic) peaceful.
Chesnee, Chesney, Chesnie, Chesny

CHESSA (American) a short form of Chesarey.
Chessi, Chessie, Chessy

CHEYANNE (Cheyenne) an alternate form of Cheyenne.
Cheyan, Cheyana, Cheyane, Cheyann, Cheyanna, Cheyeana, Cheyeannna, Cheyeannne

CHEYENNE (Cheyenne) a tribal name. See also Shaianne, Sheyenne, Shianne, Shyann.
Cheyanne, Cheyeene, Cheyena, Cheyene, Cheyenna, Cheyna, Chi, Chi-Anna, Chie, Chyanne

CHEYLA (American) a form of Sheila.
Cheylan, Cheyleigh, Cheylo

CHEYNA (American) a short form of Cheyenne.
Chey, Cheye, Cheyne, Cheynee, Cheyney, Cheynna

CHIARA (Italian) a form of Clara.
Cheara, Chiarra

CHIKA (Japanese) near and dear.
Chikaka, Chikako, Chikara, Chikona

CHIKU (Swahili) chatterer.

CHINA (Chinese) fine porcelain. Geography: a country in eastern Asia. See also Ciana, Shina.
Chinaetta, Chinah, Chinasa, Chinda, Chinea, Chinesia, Chinita, Chinna, Chinwa, Chyna, Chynna

CHINIRA (Swahili) God receives.
Chinara, Chinarah, Chinirah

CHINUE (Ibo) God's own blessing.

CHIQUITA (Spanish) little one. See also Shiquita.
Chaqueta, Chaquita, Chica, Chickie, Chicky, Chikata, Chikita, Chiqueta, Chiquila, Chiquite, Chiquitha, Chiquithe, Chiquitia, Chiquitta

CHIYO (Japanese) eternal.
Chiya

CHLOE (Greek) blooming, verdant. Mythology: the goddess of agriculture.
Chloé, Chlöe, Chloee, Chloie, Cloe, Kloe

CHLORIS (Greek) pale. Mythology: the only daughter of Niobe to escape the vengeful arrows of Apollo and Artemis. See also Loris.
Cloris, Clorissa

CHO (Korean) beautiful.
Choe

CHOLENA (Native American) bird.

CHRIKI (Swahili) blessing.

CHRIS (Greek) a short form of Christina. See also Kris.
Chrys, Cris

CHRISSA (Greek) a short form of Christina. See also Khrissa.
Chrysa, Chryssa, Crissa, Cryssa

CHRISSY (English) a familiar form of Christina.
Chrisie, Chrissee, Chrissie, Crissie, Khrissy

CHRISTA (German) a short form of Christina. History: Christa McAuliffe, an American school teacher, was the first civilian on a U.S. space flight. See also Krista.
Chrysta, Crista, Crysta

CHRISTABEL (Latin, French) beautiful Christian.
Christabell, Christabella, Christabelle, Christable, Cristabel, Kristabel

CHRISTAIN (Greek) an alternate form of Christina.
Christana, Christann, Christanna

CHRISTAL (Latin) an alternate form of Crystal. (Scottish) a form of Christina.
Christalene, Christalin, Christaline, Christall, Christalle, Christalyn, Christelle, Christle, Chrystal

CHRISTELLE (French) a form of Christal.
Christel, Christele, Christell, Chrystel, Chrystelle

CHRISTEN, Christin (Greek) alternate forms of Christina. See also Kristen.
Christan, Christyn, Chrystan, Chrysten, Chrystyn, Crestienne

CHRISTENA, Christen (Greek) alternate forms of Christina.

CHRISTI, Christie (Greek) short forms of Christina, Christine. See also Kristi.
Christy, Chrysti, Chrystie, Chrysty, Kristi

CHRISTIAN, Christiana, Christianna (Greek) alternate forms of Christina. See also Kristian, Krystian.
Christiane, Christiann, Christi-Ann, Christianne, Christi-Anne, Christianni, Christiaun, Christiean, Christien, Christiena, Christienne, Christinan, Christy-Ann, Christy-Anne, Crystian, Chrystyann, Chrystyanne, Crystiann, Crystianne

CHRISTIN (Greek) a short form of Christina.
Christen, Chrystin

CHRISTINA (Greek) Christian; anointed. See also Khristina, Kristina, Stina, Tina.
Chris, Chrissa, Chrissy, Christa, Christain, Christal, Christeena, Christella, Christen, Christena, Christi, Christian, Christie, Christin, Christinaa, Christine, Christinea, Christinia, Christinna, Christinnah, Christna, Christy, Christyn, Christyna, Christynna, Chrystina, Chrystyna, Cristeena, Cristena, Cristina, Crystina, Chrystena, Cristena

CHRISTINE (French, English) a form of Christina. See also Kirsten, Kristen, Kristine.
Chrisa, Christeen, Christen, Christene, Christi, Christie, Christy, Chrystine, Cristeen, Cristene, Cristine, Crystine

CHRISTOPHE (Greek) Christ-bearer. A feminine form of Christopher.

CHRISTY (English) a short form of Christina, Christine.
Cristy

CHRISTYN (Greek) an alternate form of Christina.
Christyne

CHRYS (English) a form of Chris.
Krys

CHRYSTAL (Latin) an alternate form of Christal.
Chrystale, Chrystalla, Chrystallina, Chrystallynn,

CHU HUA (Chinese) chrysanthemum.

CHUMANI (Lakota) dewdrops.
Chumany

CHUN (Burmese) nature's renewal.

CHYANNE, Chyenne (Cheyenne) alternate forms of Cheyenne.

Chyan, Chyana, Chyane, Chyann, Chyanna, Chyeana, Chyenn, Chyenna, Chyennee

CHYNA, Chynna (Chinese) alternate forms of China.

CIANA (Chinese) an alternate form of China. (Italian) a form of Jane.
Cian, Ciandra, Ciann, Cianna

CIARA, Ciarra (Irish) black. See also Sierra.
Ceara, Chiairah, Ciaara, Ciaera, Ciaira, Ciarah, Ciaria, Ciarrah, Cieara, Ciearra, Ciearria, Ciera, Cierra, Cioria, Cyarra

CICELY (English) a form of Cecilia. See also Sissy.
Cicelia, Cicelie, Ciciley, Cicilia, Cicilie, Cicily, Cile, Cilka, Cilla, Cilli, Cillie, Cilly

CIDNEY (French) an alternate form of Sydney.
Cidnee, Cidni, Cidnie

CIERA, Cierra (Irish) alternate forms of Ciara, Ciarra.
Ceira, Cierah, Ciere, Cieria, Cierrah, Cierre, Cierria, Cierro

CINDERELLA (French, English) little cinder girl. Literature: a fairy tale heroine.
Cindella

CINDY (Greek) moon. (Latin) a familiar form of Cynthia. See also Sindy.
Cindee, Cindi, Cindie, Cyndi

CINTHIA, Cinthya (Greek) alternate forms of Cynthia.
Cinthiya, Cintia

CIRA (Spanish) a form of Cyrilla.

CISSY (American) a familiar form of Cecelia, Cicely.
Cissey, Cissi, Cissie

CLAIRE (French) a form of Clara.
Clair, Klaire, Klarye

CLAIRISSA (Greek) an alternate form of Clarissa.
Clairisa, Clairisse, Claraissa

CLARA (Latin) clear; bright. Music: Clara Shumann was a famous nineteenth-century German composer. See also Chiara, Klara.
Claira, Claire, Clarabelle, Clare, Claresta, Clarice, Clarie, Clarina, Clarinda, Clarine, Clarissa, Clarita

CLARABELLE (Latin) bright and beautiful.
Clarabella, Claribel, Claribell

CLARE (English) a form of Clara.

CLARIE (Latin) a familiar form of Clara.
Clarey, Clari, Clary

CLARICE (Italian) a form of Clara.
Claris, Clarise, Clarisse, Claryce, Cleriese, Klarice, Klarise

CLARISA (Greek) an alternate form of Clarissa.
Claresa, Clarise, Clarisia

CLARISSA (Greek) brilliant. (Italian) a form of Clara. See also Klarissa.
Clairissa, Clarecia, Claressa, Claresta, Clarisa, Clarissia, Claritza, Clarizza, Clarrisa, Clarrissa, Clerissa

CLARITA (Spanish) a form of Clara.
Clairette, Clareta, Claretta, Clarette, Claritza

CLAUDETTE (French) a form of Claudia.
Clauddetta

CLAUDIA (Latin) lame. A feminine form of Claude. See also Gladys, Klaudia.
Claudeen, Claudel, Claudelle, Claudette, Claudex, Claudiana, Claudiane, Claudie, Claudie-Anne, Claudina, Claudine

CLAUDIE (Latin) an alternate form of Claudia.
Claudee

CLEA (Greek) an alternate form of Cleo, Clio.

CLEMENTINE (Latin) merciful. A feminine form of Clement.
Clemence, Clemencia, Clemencie, Clemency, Clementia, Clementina, Clemenza, Clemette

CLEO (Greek) a short form of Cleopatra.
Chleo, Clea

CLEONE (Greek) glorious.
Cleonie, Cleonna, Cliona

CLEOPATRA (Greek) her father's fame. History: a great Egyptian queen.
Cleo

CLETA (Greek) illustrious.

CLIO (Greek) proclaimer; glorifier. Mythology: the muse of history.
Clea

CLOE (Greek) an alternate form of Chloe.
Clo, Cloei, Cloey, Cloie

CLOTILDA (German) heroine.

COCO (Spanish) coconut. See also Koko.

CODI, CODY (English) cushion. See also Kodi.
Coady, Codee, Codey, Codia, Codie

COLBY (English) coal town. Geography: a region in England known for cheese-making. See also Kolby.
Cobi, Cobie, Colbi, Colbie

COLETTE (Greek, French) a familiar form of Nicole.
Coe, Coetta, Coletta, Collet, Collete, Collett, Colletta, Collette, Kolette, Kollette

COLLEEN (Irish) girl. See also Kolina.
Coe, Coel, Cole, Coleen, Colene, Coley, Coline, Colleene, Collen, Collene, Collie, Collina, Colline, Colly

COLLINA (Irish) an alternate form of Colleen.
Colena, Colina, Colinda

CONCETTA (Italian) pure. Religion: refers to the Immaculate Conception.
Concettina, Conchetta

CONCHITA (Spanish) conception.
Chita, Conceptia, Concha, Conciana

CONCORDIA (Latin) harmonious. Mythology: the goddess governing the peace after war.
Con, Cordae, Cordaye

CONNIE (Latin) a familiar form of Constance.
Con, Connee, Conni, Conny, Konnie, Konny

CONNOR (Scottish) wise. (Irish) praised; exhalted.
Connar, Conner, Connery, Conor

CONSTANCE (Latin) constant; firm. History: Constance Motley was the first African-American woman to be appointed as a U.S. federal judge. See also Konstance, Kosta.
Connie, Constancia, Constancy, Constanta, Constantia, Constantina, Constantine, Constanza, Constynse

CONSTANZA (Spanish) a form of Constance.
Constanz, Constanze

CONSUELO (Spanish) consolation. Religion: Santa Maria del Consuelo—Saint Mary of Consolation—is a name for the Virgin Mary.
Consolata, Consuela, Consuella, Consula, Conzuelo, Konsuela, Konsuelo

CORA (Greek) maiden. Mythology: the daughter of Demeter, the goddess of agriculture. See also Kora.
Corah, Coralee, Coretta, Corissa, Corey, Corra

CORABELLE (American) a combination of Cora + Belle.
Corabel, Corabella

CORAL (Latin) coral. See also Koral.
Coraal, Corral

CORALEE (American) a combination of Cora + Lee.
Coralea, Cora-Lee, Coralena, Coralene, Coraley, Coralie, Coraline, Coraly, Coralyn, Corella, Corilee, Koralie

CORALIE (American) an alternate form of Coralee.
Corali, Coralia, Coralina, Coralynn, Coralynne

CORAZON (Spanish) heart.

CORBIN (Latin) raven.
Corbe, Corbi, Corby, Corbyn, Corbynn

CORDASHA (American) a combination of Cora + Dasha.

CORDELIA (Latin) warm hearted. (Welsh) sea jewel. See also Delia, Della.
Cordae, Cordelie, Cordett, Cordette, Cordi, Cordilia, Cordilla, Cordula, Kordelia, Kordula

CORDI (Welsh) a short form of Cordelia.
Cordey, Cordia, Cordie, Cordy

CORETTA (Greek) a familiar form of Cora.
Coreta, Corette, Correta, Corretta, Corrette, Koretta, Korretta

COREY, Cory (Greek) familiar forms of Cora. (Irish) from the hollow. See also Kori.
Coree, Cori, Correy, Correye, Corry

CORI, Corie, Corrie (Irish) alternate forms of Corey.

CORIANN, Corianne (American) combinations of Cori + Ann, Cori + Anne.

Corian, Coriane, Cori-Ann, Corri, Corrie-Ann, Corrianne, Corrie-Anne

CORINA, Corinna (Greek) familiar forms of Corinne. See also Korina.
Coreena, Coriana, Corianna, Corinda, Correna, Corrinna, Coryna

CORINNE (Greek) maiden.
Coreen, Coren, Corin, Corina, Corine, Corinee, Corinn, Corinna, Corrina, Coryn, Corynn, Corynne

CORISSA (Greek) a familiar form of Cora.
Coresa, Coressa, Corisa, Coryssa, Korissa

CORLISS (English) cheerful; good hearted.
Corlisa, Corlise, Corlissa, Corly, Korliss

CORNELIA (Latin) horn colored. A feminine form of Cornelius. See also Kornelia, Nelia, Nellie.
Carna, Carniella, Corneilla, Cornela, Cornelie, Cornella, Cornelle, Cornie, Cornilear, Cornisha, Corny

CORRINA, Corrine (Greek) alternate forms of Corinne.
Correen, Corren, Corrin, Corrinn, Corrinna, Corrinne, Corrinne, Corryn

CORTNEY (English) an alternate form of Courtney.
Cortne, Cortnea, Cortnee, Cortneia, Cortni, Cortnie, Cortny, Cortnye, Corttney

COSETTE (French) a familiar form of Nicole.
Cosetta, Cossetta, Cossette, Cozette

COURTENAY (English) an alternate form of Courtney.
Courtaney, Courtany, Courteney, Courteny

COURTNEE, Courtnie (English) alternate forms of Courtney.
Courtne, Courtnée, Courtnei, Courtneigh, Courtni, Courtnii

COURTNEY (English) from the court. See also Kortney, Kourtney.
Cortney, Courtena, Courtenay, Courtene, Courtnae, Courtnay, Courtnee, Courtny, Courtonie

CRISBELL (American) a combination of Crista + Belle.
Crisbel, Cristabel

CRISTA, Crysta (Italian) forms of Christa.
Cristah

CRISTAL (Latin) an alternate form of Crystal.
Cristalie, Cristalina, Cristalle, Cristel, Cristela, Cristelia, Cristella, Cristelle, Cristhie, Cristle

CRISTEN, Cristin (Irish) forms of Christen, Christin. See also Kristin.
Cristan, Cristyn, Crystan, Crysten, Crystin, Crystyn

CRISTINA, Cristine (Greek) alternate forms of Christina. See also Kristina.
Cristiona, Cristy

CRISTY (English) a familiar form of Cristina. An alternate form of Christy. See also Kristy.
Cristey, Cristi, Cristie, Crysti, Crystie, Crysty

CRYSTAL (Latin) clear, brilliant glass. See also Kristal, Krystal.
Christal, Chrystal, Chrystal-Lynn, Chrystel, Cristal, Crystala, Crystale, Crystalee, Crystalin, Crystall, Crystalle, Crystaly, Crystel, Crystela, Crystelia, Crystelle, Crysthelle, Crystl, Crystle, Crystol, Crystole, Crystyl

CRYSTALIN (American) a form of Crystal.
Crystal-Ann, Cristalanna, Crystal-Anne, Cristalina, Cristallina, Cristalyn, Crystallynn, Crystallynne, Cristilyn, Crystalina, Crystal-Lee, Crystal-Lynn, Crystalyn, Crystalynn

CRYSTINA (Greek) an alternate form of Christina.
Crystin, Crystine, Crystyn, Crystyna, Crystyne

CURRAN (Irish) heroine.
Cura, Curin, Curina, Curinna

CYBELE (Greek) an alternate form of Sybil.
Cybel, Cybil, Cybill, Cybille

CYDNEY (French) an alternate form of Sydney.
Cydne, Cydnee, Cydnei, Cydni, Cydnie

CYERRA (Irish) a form of Ciara.
Cyera, Cyerria

CYNDI (Greek) an alternate form of Cindy.
Cynda, Cyndal, Cyndale, Cyndall, Cyndee, Cyndel, Cyndia, Cyndie, Cyndle, Cyndy

CYNTHIA (Greek) moon. Mythology: another name for Artemis, the moon goddess. See also Hyacinth, Kynthia.
Cindy, Cinthia, Cyneria, Cynethia, Cynithia, Cynthea, Cynthiana, Cynthiann, Cynthie, Cynthria, Cynthy, Cynthya, Cyntia, Cyntreia, Cythia, Synthia

CYRILLA (Greek) ladylike. A feminine form of Cyril.
Cerelia, Cerella, Cira, Cirilla, Cyrella, Cyrille

D

DACEY (Greek) a familiar form of Candace. (Irish) southerner.
Dacee, Dacei, Daci, Dacia, Dacie, Dacy, Daicee, Daici, Daicie, Daicy, Daycee, Daycie, Daycy

DACIA (Irish) an alternate form of Dacey.
Daciah

DAE (English) day. See also Dai.

DAEJA (French) an alternate form of Déja.
Daejah, Daejia

DAELYNN (American) a combination of Dae + Lynn.
Daeleen, Daelena, Daelin, Daelyn, Daelynne

DAESHANDRA (American) a combination of Dae + Shandra.
Daeshandria, Daeshaundra, Daeshaundria, Daeshawndra, Daeshawndria, Daeshondra, Daeshondria

DAESHAWNA (American) a combination of Dae + Shawna.
Daeshan, Daeshaun, Daeshauna, Daeshavon, Daeshawn, Daeshawntia, Daeshon, Daeshona

DAESHONDA (American) a combination of Dae + Shonda.
Daeshanda, Daeshawnda

DAFNY (American) a form of Daphne.
Dafany, Daffany, Daffie, Daffy, Dafna, Dafne, Dafney, Dafnie

DAGMAR (German) glorious.
Dagmara

DAGNY (Scandinavian) day.
Dagna, Dagnanna, Dagne, Dagney, Dagnie

DAHLIA (Scandinavian) valley. Botany: a perennial flower. See also Daliah.
Dahliah, Dahlya, Dahlye

DAI (Japanese) great. See also Dae.
Day, Daye

DAIJA, Daijah (French) alternate forms of Déja.
Daijaah, Daijea, Daijha, Daijhah, Dayja

DAISHA (American) a form of Dasha.
Daesha, Daishae, Daishia, Daishya, Daisia

DAISY (English) day's eye. Botany: a white and yellow flower.

Daisee, Daisey, Daisi, Daisia, Daisie, Dasey, Dasi, Dasie, Dasy, Daysi, Deisy

DAJA, Dajah (French) alternate forms of Déja.
Dajae, Dajai, Daje, Dajha, Dajia

DAKAYLA (American) a combination of the prefix Da + Kayla.
Dakala, Dakila

DAKIRA (American) a combination of the prefix Da + Kira.
Dakara, Dakaria, Dakarra, Dakirah, Dakyra

DAKOTA (Native American) a tribal name.
Dakkota, Dakoda, Dakotah, Dakotha, Dakotta, Dekoda, Dekota, Dekotah, Dekotha

DALE (English) valley.
Dael, Dahl, Daile, Daleleana, Dalena, Dalina, Dayle

DALIA, Daliah (Hebrew) branch. See also Dahlia.
Daelia, Dailia, Daleah, Daleia, Dalialah, Daliyah

DALILA (Swahili) gentle.
Dalela, Dalida, Dalilah, Dalilia

DALISHA (American) a form of Dallas.
Dalisa, Dalishea, Dalishia, Dalishya, Dalisia, Dalissia

DALLAS (Irish) wise.
Dalis, Dalise, Dalisha, Dalisse, Dallace, Dallis, Dallise, Dallus, Dallys, Dalyce, Dalys

DAMARIS (Greek) gentle girl. See also Maris.
Dama, Damar, Damara, Damarius, Damary, Damarylis, Damarys, Dameress, Dameris, Damiris, Dammaris, Dammeris, Damris, Demaras, Demaris

DAMIANA (Greek) tamer, soother. A feminine form of Damian.

Daimenia, Daimiona, Damia, Damiann, Damianna, Damianne, Damien, Damienne, Damiona, Damon, Demion

DAMICA (French) friendly.
Damee, Dameeka, Dameka, Damekah, Damicah, Damicia, Damicka, Damie, Damieka, Damika, Damikah, Damyka, Demeeka, Demeka, Demekah, Demica, Demicah

DAMITA (Spanish) small noblewoman.
Damee, Damesha, Dameshia, Damesia, Dametia, Dametra, Dametrah

DAMONICA (American) a combination of the prefix Da + Monica.
Damonec, Damoneke, Damonik, Damonika, Damonique, Diamoniqua, Diamonique

DANA (English) from Denmark; bright as day.
Daina, Dainna, Danah, Danaia, Danan, Danarra, Dane, Danean, Danna, Dayna

DANAE (Greek) Mythology: the mother of Perseus.
Danaë, Danay, Danayla, Danays, Danai, Danea, Danee, Dannae, Denae, Denee

DANALYN (American) a combination of Dana + Lynn.
Danalee, Donaleen

DANEIL (Hebrew) an alternate form of Danielle.
Daneal, Daneala, Daneale, Daneel, Daneela, Daneila

DANELLA (American) a form of Danielle.
Danayla, Danela, Danelia, Danelle, Danna, Donella, Donnella

DANELLE (Hebrew) an alternate form of Danielle.
Danael, Danalle, Danel, Danele, Danell, Danella, Donelle, Donnelle

DANESHA, Danisha (American) alternate forms of Danessa.
Daneisha, Daneshia, Daniesha, Danishia

DANESSA (American) a combination of Danielle + Vanessa. See also Doneshia.
Danasia, Danesa, Danesha, Danessia, Daniesa, Danisa, Danissa

DANESSIA (American) an alternate form of Danessa.
Danesia, Danieshia, Danisia, Danissia

DANETTE (American) a form of Danielle.
Danetra, Danett, Danetta, Donnita

DANI (Hebrew) a familiar form of Danielle.
Danee, Danie, Danne, Dannee, Danni, Dannie, Danny, Dannye, Dany

DANIA, Danya (Hebrew) short forms of Danielle.
Daniah, Danja, Dannia, Danyae

DANICA, Danika (Hebrew) alternate forms of Danielle. (Slavic) morning star.
Daneca, Daneeka, Daneekah, Danicah, Danicka, Danieka, Danikah, Danikla, Danneeka, Dannica, Dannika, Dannikah, Danyka, Denica, Donica, Donika, Donnaica, Donnica, Donnika

DANICE (American) a combination of Danielle + Janice.
Donice

DANIELA (Italian) a form of Danielle.
Daniellah, Dannilla, Danijela

DANIELAN (Spanish) a form of Danielle.

DANIELLE (Hebrew, French) God is my judge. A feminine form of Daniel.
Daneen, Daneil, Daneille, Danelle, Dani, Danial, Danialle, Danica, Daniel, Daniela, Danielan, Daniele, Danielka, Daniell, Daniella, Danilka, Danille, Danit, Dannielle, Danyel, Donniella

DANILLE (American) a form of Danielle.
Danila, Danile, Danilla, Dannille

DANIT (Hebrew) an alternate form of Danielle.
Danett, Danis, Danisha, Daniss, Danita, Danitra, Danitrea, Danitria, Danitza, Daniz

DANNA (Hebrew) a short form of Danella.
Dannah

DANIELLA (English) an alternate form of Dana.
Danka, Danniella, Danyella

DANNIELLE (Hebrew, French) an alternate form of Danielle.
Danniel, Danniele, Danniell

DANYEL, Danyell, Danyelle (American) forms of Danielle.
Daniyel, Danyae, Danyail, Danyaile, Danyal, Danyale, Danyea, Danyele, Danyiel, Danyielle, Danyle, Donnyale, Donnyell, Donyale, Donyell

DAPHNE (Greek) laurel tree.
Dafny, Daphane, Daphany, Dapheney, Daphna, Daphnee, Daphnique, Daphnit, Daphny

DAPHNEE (Greek) an alternate form of Daphne.
Daphaney, Daphanie, Daphney, Daphni, Daphnie

DARA (Hebrew) compassionate.
Dahra, Daira, Dairah, Darah, Daraka, Daralea, Daralee, Daraleigh, Daralie, Daravie, Darda, Darice, Darisa, Darissa, Darja, Darra, Darrah

DARBY (Irish) free. (Scandinavian) deer estate.
Darb, Darbe, Darbee, Darbi, Darbie, Darbra, Darbye

DARCELLE (French) a form of Darci.
Darcel, Darcell, Darcella, Darselle

DARCI, Darcy (Irish) dark. (French) fortress.
Darcee, Darcelle, Darcey, Darcie, Darsey, Darsi, Darsie

DARIA (Greek) wealthy. A feminine form of Darius.
Dari, Dariya, Darria, Darya, Daryia

DARIAN, Darrian (Greek) alternate forms of Daron.
Dariana, Dariane, Dariann, Darianna, Darianne, Dariyan, Dariyanne, Darriana, Darriane, Darriann, Darrianna, Darrianne, Derrian, Driana

DARIELLE (French) an alternate form of Daryl.
Dariel, Dariela, Dariell, Darriel, Darrielle

DARIEN, Darrien (Greek) alternate forms of Daron.
Dariene, Darienne, Darriene

DARILYNN (American) a form of Darlene.
Daralin, Daralyn, Daralynn, Daralynne, Darilin, Darilyn, Darilynne, Darlin, Darlyn, Darlynn, Darlynne, Darylin, Darylyn, Darylynn, Darylynne

DARION, Darrion (Irish) alternative forms of Daron.
Dariona, Darione, Darionna, Darionne, Darriona, Darrionna

DARLA (English) a short form of Darlene.
Darlecia, Darli, Darlice, Darlie, Darlis, Darly, Darlys

DARLENE (French) little darling. See also Daryl.
Darilynn, Darla, Darlean, Darlee, Darleen, Darleene, Darlena, Darlenia, Darlenne, Darletha, Darlin, Darline, Darling, Darlyn, Darlynn, Darlynne

DARNEE (Irish) a familiar form of Darnelle.

DARNELLE (English) hidden place.
Darnee, Darnel, Darnell, Darnella, Darnesha, Darnetta, Darnette, Darnice, Darniece, Darnita, Darnyell

DARNESHA, Darnisha (American) forms of Darnelle.
Darneisha, Darneishia, Darneshea, Darneshia, Darnesia, Darniesha, Darnishia, Darnisia, Darrenisha

DARON (Irish) great. A feminine form of Darren.
Darian, Darien, Darion, Daronica, Daronice, Darron, Daryn

DARSELLE (French) an alternate form of Darcelle.
Darsel, Darsell, Darsella

DARU (Hindi) pine tree.

DARYL (French) a short form of Darlene. (English) beloved.
Darelle, Darielle, Daril, Darilynn, Darrel, Darrell, Darrelle, Darreshia, Darryl, Darryll, Daryll, Darylle

DARYN (Greek) gifts. (Irish) great. A feminine form of Darren.
Daron, Daryan, Daryne, Darynn, Darynne

DASHA, Dasia (Russian) forms of Dorothy.
Daisha, Dashae, Dashenka, Dashia, Dashiah, Dasiah, Daysha

DASHAWNA (American) a combination of the prefix Da + Shawna.
Dashawn, Dashawnna, Dashay, Dashell, Dayshana, Dayshawnna, Dayshona, Deshawna

DASHIKI (Swahili) loose-fitting shirt worn in Africa.
Dashi, Dashika, Dashka, Desheka, Deshiki

DASHONDA (American) a combination of the prefix Da + Shonda.
Dashawnda, Dishante

DAVALINDA (American) a combination of Davida + Linda.
Davalynda, Davelinda, Davilinda, Davylinda

DAVALYNDA (American) an alternate form of Davalinda.
Davelynda, Davilynda, Davylynda

DAVALYNN (American) a combination of Davida + Lynn.
Davalin, Davalyn, Davalynne, Davelin, Davelyn, Davelynn, Davelynne, Davilin, Davilyn, Davilynn, Davilynne, Dayleen, Devlyn

DAVIDA (Hebrew) beloved. A feminine form of David. See also Vida.
Daveta, Davetta, Davette, Davika, Davita

DAVINA (Scottish) a form of Davida. See also Vina.
Dava, Davannah, Davean, Davee, Daveen, Daveena, Davene, Daveon, Davey, Davi, Daviana, Davie, Davin, Davinder, Davine, Davineen, Davinia, Davinna, Davonna, Davria, Devean, Deveen, Devene, Devina

DAVISHA (American) a combination of the prefix Da + Aisha.
Daveisha, Davesia, Davis, Davisa

DAVONNA (Scottish, English) an alternate form of Davina, Devonna.
Davion, Daviona, Davionna, Davon, Davona, Davonda, Davone, Davonia, Davonne, Davonnia

DAWN (English) sunrise, dawn.
Dawana, Dawandrea, Dawanna, Dawin, Dawna, Dawne, Dawnee, Dawnetta, Dawnisha, Dawnlynn, Dawnn, Dawnrae

DAWNA (English) an alternate form of Dawn.
Dawnna, Dawnya

DAWNYELLE (American) a combination of Dawn + Danielle.
Dawnele, Dawnell, Dawnelle, Dawnyel, Dawnyella

DAWNISHA (American) a form of Dawn.
Dawnesha, Dawni, Dawniell, Dawnielle, Dawnisia, Dawniss, Dawnita, Dawnnisha, Dawnysha, Dawnysia

DAYANA (Latin) an alternate form of Diana.
Dayanara, Dayani, Dayanna, Dayanne, Dayanni, Deyanaira, Dyani, Dyanna, Dyia

DAYLE (English) an alternate form of Dale.
Dayla, Daylan, Daylea, Daylee

DAYNA (Scandinavian) a form of Dana.
Daynah, Dayne, Daynna, Deyna

DAYSHA (American) a form of Dasha.
Daysa, Dayshalie, Daysia, Deisha

DAYSI, Deysi (English) alternate forms of Daisy.
Daysee, Daysia, Daysie, Daysy, Deysia, Deysy

DAYTON, Daytona (English) day town; bright, sunny town.
Daytonia

DEANA (Latin) divine. (English) valley. A feminine form of Dean.
Deanah, Deane, Deanielle, Deanisha, Deanna, Deeana, Deeann, Deeanna, Deena

DEANDRA (American) a combination of Dee + Andrea.
Dandrea, Deandre, Deandré, Deandrea, Deandree, Deandreia, Deandria, Deanndra, Deaundra, Deaundria, Deeandra, Deyaneira, Deondra, Diandra, Diandre, Diandrea, Diondria, Dyandra

DEANGELA (Italian) a combination of the prefix De + Angela.
Deangala, Deangalique, Deangle

DEANNA (Latin) an alternate form of Deana, Diana.
Deaana, Deahana, Deandra, Deandre, Déanna, Deannia, Deeanna, Deena

DEANNE (Latin) an alternate form of
Diane.
*Deahanne, Deane, Deann, Déanne, Deeann,
Dee-Ann, Deeanne*

DEBBIE (Hebrew) a short form of
Deborah.
*Debbee, Debbey, Debbi, Debby, Debee, Debi,
Debie*

DEBORAH (Hebrew) bee. Bible: a great
Hebrew prophetess.
*Deb, Debbie, Debbora, Debborah, Deberah,
Debor, Debora, Deboran, Deborha, Deborrah,
Debra, Debrena, Debrina, Debroah, Devora,
Dobra*

DEBRA (American) a short form of
Deborah.
Debbra, Debbrah, Debrah, Debrea, Debria

DEDRA (American) a form of Deirdre.
Deeddra, Deedra, Deedrea, Deedrie

DEDRIANA (American) a combination
of Dedra + Adriana.
Dedranae

DEE (Welsh) black, dark.
*De, Dea, Deah, Dede, Dedie, Deea, Deedee,
Dee Dee, Didi*

DEENA (American) a form of Deana,
Dena, Dinah.

DEIDRA, Deidre (Irish) alternate forms
of Deirdre.
*Deidrah, Deidrea, Deidrie, Diedra, Diedre,
Dierdra*

DEIRDRE (Irish) sorrowful; wanderer.
*Dedra, Deerdra, Deerdre, Deidra, Deidre,
Deirdree, Didi, Diedra, Dierdre, Diérdre,
Dierdrie*

DEISY (English) an alternate form of
Daisy.
Deisi, Deissy

DEITRA (Greek) a short form of
Demetria.
Deetra, Detria

DÉJA (French) before.
*Daeja, Daija, Deejay, Dejae, Déjah, Dejai,
Dejanae, Dejanelle, Dejon*

DEJANAE (French) an alternate form
of Déja.
*Dajahnae, Dajona, Dejana, Dejanah,
Dejanae, Dejanai, Dejanay, Dejane, Dejanea,
Dejanee, Dejanna, Dejannaye, Dejena,
Dejonae*

DEJON (French) an alternate form of
Déja.
*Daijon, Dajan, Dejone, Dejonee, Dejonelle,
Dejonna*

DEKA (Somali) pleasing.
Dekah

DELACY (American) a combination
of the prefix De + Lacy.
Delaceya

DELAINEY (Irish) an alternate form
of Delaney.
Delaine, Delainee, Delaini, Delainie, Delainy

DELANA (German) noble protector.
*Dalanna, Dalayna, Daleena, Dalena,
Dalenna, Dalina, Dalinda, Dalinna, Delaina,
Delania, Delanya, Delayna, Deleena, Delena,
Delenya, Delina, Dellaina*

DELANEY (Irish) descendant of the
challenger. (English) an alternate form
of Adeline.
*Dalaney, Dalania, Dalene, Daleney, Daline,
Del, Delainey, Delane, Delanee, Delanie,
Delany, Delayne, Delayney, Delaynie,
Deleani, Déline, Della, Dellaney*

DELANIE (Irish) an alternate form of
Delaney.
Delani

DELFINA (Greek) an alternate form
of Delphine. (Spanish) dolphin.
Delfeena, Delfine

DELIA (Greek) visible; from Delos. (German, Welsh) a short form of Adelaide, Cordelia. Mythology: a festival of Apollo held every five years in ancient Greece.
Dehlia, Delea, Deli, Deliah, Deliana, Delianne, Delinda, Dellia, Dellya, Delya

DELICIA (English) delightful.
Delecia, Delesha, Delice, Delisa, Delise, Delisha, Delishia, Delisiah, Delya, Delys, Delyse, Delysia, Doleesha

DELILAH (Hebrew) brooder. Bible: the companion of Samson. See also Lila.
Dalialah, Dalila, Daliliah, Delila, Delilia

DELLA (English) a short form of Adelaide, Cordelia, Delaney.
Del, Dela, Dell, Delle, Delli, Dellie, Dells

DELORES (Spanish) an alternate form of Dolores.
Delora, Delore, Deloria, Delories, Deloris, Delorise, Delorita, Delsie

DELPHINE (Greek) from Delphi. See also Delfina.
Delpha, Delphe, Delphi, Delphia, Delphina, Delphinia, Delvina

DELSIE (English) a familiar form of Delores.
Delsa, Delsey, Delza

DELTA (Greek) door. Linguistics: the fourth letter in the Greek alphabet. Geography: a triangular land mass at the mouth of a river.
Delte, Deltora, Deltoria, Deltra

DEMETRIA (Greek) cover of the earth. Mythology: Demeter was the Greek goddess of the harvest.
Deitra, Demeta, Demeteria, Demetra, Demetriana, Demetrianna, Demetrias, Demetrice, Demetriona, Demetris, Demetrish, Demetrius, Demi, Demita, Demitra, Demitria, Dymitra

DEMI (Greek) a short form of Demetria. (French) half.
Demia, Demiah, Demii, Demmi, Demmie, Demy

DENA (Hebrew) an alternate form of Dinah. (English, Native American) valley. See also Deana.
Deane, Deena, Deeyn, Denae, Denah, Dene, Denea, Deney, Denna, Deonna

DENAE (Hebrew) an alternate form of Dena.
Denaé, Denay, Denee, Deneé

DENI (French) a short form of Denise.
Deney, Denie, Denni, Dennie, Denny, Dinnie, Dinny

DENICA, Denika (Slavic) alternate forms of Danica, Danika.
Denikah, Denikia

DENISE (French) Mythology: follower of Dionysus, the god of wine. A feminine form of Dennis.
Danice, Danise, Denese, Deni, Denice, Denicy, Deniece, Denisha, Denisse, Denize, Dennise, Dennys, Denyce, Denys, Denyse

DENISHA (American) a form of Denise.
Deneesha, Deneichia, Deneisha, Deneishea, Denesha, Deneshia, Deniesha, Denishia

DENISSE (French) an alternate form of Denise.
Denesse, Denissa

DEONNA (English) an alternate form of Dena.
Deon, Deona, Deonah, Deondra, Deonne

DERIKA (German) ruler of the people. A feminine form of Derek.
Dereka, Derekia, Derica, Dericka, Derrica, Derricka, Derrika

DERRY (Irish) redhead.
Deri, Derie

DERYN (Welsh) bird.

Derien, Derienne, Derion, Derin, Deron, Derren, Derrin, Derrine, Derrion, Derriona, Deryne

DESARAE (French) an alternate form of Desiree.
Desara, Desarai, Desaraie, Desaray, Desare, Desaré, Desarea, Desaree, Desarie, Dezarae

DESERAE, Desirae (French) alternate forms of Desiree.
Desera, Deserai, Deseray, Desere, Deseree, Deseret, Deseri, Deserie, Deserrae, Deserray, Deserré, Dessirae, Dezeray, Dezere, Dezerea, Dezrae, Dezyrae

DESHAWNA (American) a combination of the prefix De + Shawna.
Dashawna, Deshan, Deshane, Deshaun, Deshawn, Desheania, Deshona, Deshonna

DESHAWNDA (American) a combination of the prefix De + Shawnda.
Deshanda, Deshandra, Deshaundra, Deshawndra, Deshonda

DESI (French) a short form of Desiree.
Désir, Desira, Dezi, Dezia, Dezzia, Dezzie

DESIREE (French) desired, longed for. See also Dessa.
Chesarey, Desarae, Deserae, Desi, Desirae, Desirah, Desirai, Desiray, Desire, Desirea, Desireah, Desirée, Désirée, Desirey, Desiri, Desray, Desree, Dessie, Dessire, Dezarae, Dezirae, Deziree

DESSA (Greek) wanderer. (French) an alternate form of Desiree.

DESTA (Ethiopian) happy. (French) a short form of Destiny.
Desti, Destie, Desty

DESTANY (French) an alternate form of Destiny.
Destanee, Destaney, Destani, Destanie, Destannee, Destannie

DESTINEE, Destini, Destinie (French) alternate forms of Destiny.
Desteni, Destiana, Destine, Destinée, Destnie

DESTINEY (French) an alternate form of Destiny.

DESTINY (French) fate.
Desnine, Desta, Destany, Destenee, Destenie, Desteny, Destin, Destinee, Destiney, Destini, Destinie, Destonie, Destynee, Dezstany

DESTYNEE, Destyni (French) alternate forms of Destiny.
Desty, Destyn, Destyne, Destyne, Destynie

DEVA (Hindi) divine. Religion: the Hindu moon goddess.
Deeva

DEVAN (Irish) an alternate form of Devin.
Devana, Devane, Devanee, Devaney, Devani, Devanie, Devann, Devanna, Devannae, Devanne, Devany

DEVI (Hindi) goddess. Religion: the Hindu goddess of power and destruction.

DEVIN (Irish) poet.
Devan, Deven, Devena, Devenje, Deveny, Devine, Devinn, Devinne, Devyn

DEVON (English) a short form of Devonna.
Deaven, Devion, Devione, Devionne, Devone, Devoni, Devonne

DEVONNA (English) from Devonshire.
Davonna, Devon, Devona, Devonda, Devondra, Devonia

DEVORA (Hebrew) an alternate form of Deborah.
Deva, Devorah, Devra, Devrah

DEVYN (Irish) an alternate form of Devin.
Deveyn, Devyne, Devynn, Devynne

DEXTRA (Latin) adroit, skillful.
Dekstra, Dextria

DEZARAE, Dezirae, Deziree (French) alternate forms of Desiree.
Dezaraee, Dezarai, Dezaray, Dezare, Dezaree, Dezarey, Dezerie, Deziray, Dezirea, Dezirée, Dezorae, Dezra

DI (Latin) a short form of Diana, Diane.
Dy

DIA (Latin) a short form of Diana, Diane.

DIAMOND (Latin) precious gem.
Diamantina, Diamon, Diamonda, Diamonde, Diamonia, Diamonique, Diamonte, Diamontina, Dyamond

DIANA (Latin) divine. Mythology: the goddess of the hunt, the moon, and fertility. See also Deanna, Deanne, Dyan.
Daiana, Daianna, Dayana, Dayanna, Di, Dia, Dianah, Dianalyn, Dianarose, Dianatris, Dianca, Diandra, Diane, Dianelis, Diania, Dianielle, Dianita, Dianna, Dianys, Didi

DIANE, Dianne (Latin) alternate forms of Diana.
Deane, Deanne, Deeane, Deeanne, Di, Dia, Diahann, Dian, Diani, Dianie, Diann

DIANNA (Latin) an alternate form of Diana.
Diahanna, Diannah

DIANTHA (Greek) divine flower.
Diandre, Dianthe

DIEDRA (Irish) an alternate form of Deirdre.
Didra, Diedre

DILLAN (Irish) loyal, faithful.
Dillon, Dillyn

DILYS (Welsh) perfect; true.

DINA (Hebrew) a short form of Dinah.
Dinna, Dyna

DINAH (Hebrew) vindicated. Bible: a daughter of Jacob and Leah.
Dina, Dinnah, Dynah

DINKA (Swahili) people.

DIONNA (Greek) an alternative form of Dionne.
Deona, Deondra, Deonia, Deonna, Deonyia, Diona, Diondra, Diondrea

DIONNE (Greek) divine queen. Mythology: the mother of Aphrodite, the goddess of love.
Deonne, Dion, Dione, Dionee, Dionis, Dionna, Dionte

DIOR (French) golden.
Diora, Diore, Diorra, Diorre

DITA (Spanish) a form of Edith.
Ditka, Ditta

DIVINIA (Latin) divine.
Devina, Devinae, Devinia, Devinie, Devinna, Diveena, Divina, Divine, Diviniea, Divya

DIXIE (French) tenth. (English) wall; dike. Geography: a nickname for the American South.
Dix, Dixee, Dixi, Dixy

DIZA (Hebrew) joyful.
Ditza, Ditzah, Dizah

DODIE (Greek) a familiar form of Dorothy. (Hebrew) beloved.
Doda, Dode, Dodee, Dodi, Dody

DOLLY (American) a short form of Dolores, Dorothy.
Dol, Doll, Dollee, Dolley, Dolli, Dollie, Dollina

DOLORES (Spanish) sorrowful. Religion: Santa Maria de los Dolores—Saint Mary of the Sorrows—is a name for the Virgin Mary. See also Lola.
Delores, Deloria, Dolly, Dolorcitas, Dolorita, Doloritas

DOMINICA, Dominika (Latin) belonging to the Lord. A feminine form of Dominic. See also Mika.
Domenica, Domenika, Domineca, Domineka, Dominga, Domini, Dominick, Dominicka, Dominique, Dominixe, Domino, Dominyika, Domka, Domnicka, Domonica, Domonice, Domonika

DOMINIQUE, Domonique (French) forms of Dominica, Dominika.
Domanique, Domeneque, Domenique, Domineque, Dominiqua, Domino, Dominoque, Dominque, Dominuque, Domique, Domminique, Domoniqua

DOMINO (English) a short form of Dominica, Dominique.

DONA (Italian) an alternate form of Donna. (English) world leader; proud ruler. A feminine form of Donald.
Donae, Donah, Donalda, Donaldina, Donelda, Donellia, Doni

DOÑA (Italian) an alternate form of Donna.
Donail, Donalea, Donalisa, Donay, Doni, Donia, Donie, Donise, Donitrae

DONATA (Latin) gift.
Donatha, Donato, Donatta, Donetta, Donette, Donita, Donnette, Donnita, Donte

DONDI (American) a familiar form of Donna.
Dondra, Dondrea, Dondria

DONESHIA, Donisha (American) alternate forms of Danessa.
Donasha, Donashay, Doneisha, Doneishia, Donesha, Donisa, Donisha, Donishia, Donneshia, Donnisha

DONNA (Italian) lady.
Doña, Dondi, Donnae, Donnalee, Donnalen, Donnay, Donne, Donnell, Donni, Donnie, Donnise, Donny, Dontia, Donya

DONNIELLA (American) a form of Danielle.

Donella, Doniele, Doniell, Doniella, Donielle, Donnella, Donnielle, Donnyella, Donyelle

DORA (Greek) gift. A short form of Adora, Eudora, Pandora, Theodora.
Dorah, Doralia, Doralie, Doralisa, Doraly, Doralynn, Doran, Dorchen, Dore, Dorece, Doree, Doreece, Doreen, Dorelia, Dorella, Dorelle, Doresha, Doressa, Doretta, Dori, Dorielle, Dorika, Doriley, Dorilis, Dorinda, Dorion, Dorita, Doro, Dory

DORALYNN (English) a combination of Dora + Lynn.
Doralin, Doralyn, Doralynne, Dorlin

DOREEN (Greek) an alternate form of Dora. (Irish) moody, sullen. (French) golden.
Doreena, Dorena, Dorene, Dorina, Dorine

DORETTA (American) a form of Dora, Dorothy.
Doretha, Dorette, Dorettie

DORI, Dory (American) familiar forms of Dora, Doria, Doris, Dorothy.
Dore, Dorey, Dorie, Dorree, Dorri, Dorrie, Dorry

DORIA (Greek) an alternate form of Dorian.
Dori

DORIAN (Greek) from Doris, Greece.
Dorean, Doriana, Doriane, Doriann, Dorianna, Dorianne, Dorin, Dorina, Dorriane

DORINDA (Spanish) a form of Dora.

DORIS (Greek) sea. Mythology: wife of Nereus and mother of the Nereids, or sea nymphs.
Dori, Dorice, Dorisa, Dorise, Dorris, Dorrise, Dorrys, Dory, Dorys

DOROTHEA (Greek) an alternate form of Dorothy. See also Thea.
Dorethea, Dorotea, Doroteya, Dorotha, Dorothia, Dorotthea, Dorthea, Dorthia

DOROTHY (Greek) gift of God. See also
Dasha, Dodie, Lolotea, Theodora.
Dasya, Do, Doa, Doe, Dolly, Doortje, Dorathy,
Dordei, Dordi, Doretta, Dori, Dorika,
Doritha, Dorka, Dorle, Dorlisa, Doro,
Dorolice, Dorosia, Dorota, Dorothea,
Dorothee, Dorothi, Dorothie, Dorottya,
Dorte, Dortha, Dorthy, Dory, Dosi, Dossie,
Dosya, Dottie

DORRIT (Greek) dwelling. (Hebrew)
generation.
Dorit, Dorita, Doritt

DOTTIE, Dotty (Greek) familiar forms
of Dorothy.
Dot, Dottee

DREW (Greek) courageous; strong.
(Latin) a short form of Drusilla.
Dru, Drue

DRINKA (Spanish) a form of
Alexandria.
Dreena, Drena, Drina

DRUSI (Latin) a short form of Drusilla.
Drucey, Druci, Drucie, Drucy, Drusey, Drusie,
Drusy

DRUSILLA (Latin) descendant of
Drusus, the strong one. See also Drew.
Drewsila, Drucella, Drucill, Drucilla, Druscilla,
Druscille, Drusi

DULCE (Latin) sweet.
Delcina, Delcine, Douce, Doucie, Dulcea,
Dulcey, Dulci, Dulcia, Dulciana, Dulcibel,
Dulcibella, Dulcie, Dulcine, Dulcinea, Dulcy,
Dulse, Dulsea

DULCINEA (Spanish) sweet. Literature:
Don Quixote's love interest.

DUSCHA (Russian) soul; sweet-heart;
term of endearment.
Duschah, Dusha, Dushenka

DUSTI, Dusty (English) short forms of
Dustine.
Dustee, Dustie

DUSTINE (German) valiant fighter.
(English) brown rock, quarry. A
feminine form of Dustin.
Dusteena, Dusti, Dustin, Dustina, Dustyn

DYAMOND, Dymond (Latin) alternate
forms of Diamond.
Dyamin, Dyamon, Dyamone, Dymin,
Dymon, Dymonde, Dymone, Dymonn

DYANA (Latin) an alternate form of
Diana. (Native American) deer.
Dyan, Dyane, Dyani, Dyann, Dyanna,
Dyanne

DYLAN (Welsh) sea.
Dylaan, Dylaina, Dylana, Dylane, Dylanee,
Dylanie, Dylann, Dylanna, Dylen, Dylin,
Dyllan, Dylynn

DYLLIS (Welsh) sincere.
Dilys, Dylis, Dylys

DYNASTY (Latin) powerful ruler.
Dynastee, Dynasti, Dynastie

DYSHAWNA (American) a
combination of the prefix Dy +
Shawna.
Dyshanta, Dyshawn, Dyshonda, Dyshonna

E

EARLENE (Irish) pledge. (English)
noblewoman. A feminine form of Earl.
Earla, Earlean, Earlecia, Earleen, Earlena,
Earlina, Earlinda, Earline, Erla, Erlana,
Erlene, Erlenne, Erlina, Erlinda, Erline,
Erlisha

EARTHA (English) earthy.
Ertha

EASTER (English) Easter time. History:
a name for a child born on Easter.
Eastan, Eastlyn, Easton

EBONE, Ebonee (Greek) alternate forms of Ebony.
Abonee, Ebanee, Eboné, Ebonea, Ebonne, Ebonnee

EBONI, Ebonie (Greek) alternate forms of Ebony.
Ebanie, Ebeni, Ebonni, Ebonnie

EBONY (Greek) a hard, dark wood.
Abony, Eban, Ebanie, Ebany, Ebbony, Ebone, Eboney, Eboni, Ebonie, Ebonique, Ebonisha, Ebonye, Ebonyi

ECHO (Greek) repeated sound. Mythology: the nymph who pined for the love of Narcissus until only her voice remained.
Echoe, Ecko, Ekko, Ekkoe

EDA (Irish, English) a short form of Edana, Edith.

EDANA (Irish) ardent; flame.
Eda, Edan, Edanna

EDDA (German) an alternate form of Hedda.
Etta

EDDY (American) a familiar form of Edwina.
Eady, Eddi, Eddie, Edy

EDELINE (English) noble; kind.
Adeline, Edelyne, Ediline, Edilyne

EDEN (Babylonian) a plain. (Hebrew) delightful. Bible: the earthly paradise.
Eaden, Ede, Edena, Edene, Edenia, Edin, Edyn

EDIE (English) a familiar form of Edith.
Eadie, Edi, Edy, Edye, Eyde, Eydie

EDITH (English) rich gift. See also Dita.
Eadith, Eda, Ede, Edetta, Edette, Edie, Edit, Edita, Edite, Editha, Edithe, Editta, Ediva, Edyta, Edyth, Edytha, Edythe

EDNA (Hebrew) rejuvenation. Mythology: the wife of Enoch, according to ancient eastern legends.
Adna, Adnisha, Ednah, Edneisha, Edneshia, Ednisha, Ednita, Edona

EDRIANNA (Greek) an alternate form of Adrienne.
Edria, Edriana, Edrina

EDWINA (English) prosperous friend. A feminine form of Edwin. See also Winnie.
Eddy, Edina, Edweena, Edwena, Edwine, Edwyna, Edwynn

EFFIA (Ghanian) born on Friday.

EFFIE (Greek) spoken well of. (English) a short form of Alfreda, Euphemia.
Effi, Effia, Effy, Ephie

EILEEN (Irish) a form of Helen. See also Aileen, Ilene.
Eilean, Eileena, Eileene, Eilena, Eilene, Eiley, Eilie, Eilieh, Eilina, Eiline, Eilleen, Eillen, Eilyn, Eleen, Elene

EKATERINA (Russian) a form of Katherine.
Ekaterine, Ekaterini

ELA (Polish) a form of Adelaide.

ELAINA (French) a form of Helen.
Elainea, Elainia, Elainna

ELAINE (French) a form of Helen. See also Lainey, Laine.
Eilane, Elain, Elaina, Elaini, Elan, Elana, Elane, Elania, Elanie, Elanit, Elauna, Elayna, Ellaine

ELANA (Greek) a short form of Eleanor. See also Ilana, Lana.
Elan, Elanee, Elaney, Elani, Elania, Elanie, Elanna, Elanni

ELAYNA (French) an alternate form of Elaina.
Elayn, Elaynah, Elayne, Elayni

ELBERTA (English) a form of Alberta.
Elbertha, Elberthina, Elberthine, Elbertina, Elbertine

ELDORA (Spanish) golden, gilded.
Eldoree, Eldorey, Eldori, Eldoria, Eldorie, Eldory

ELEANOR (Greek) light. An alternate form of Helen. History: Anna Eleanor Roosevelt was a U.S. delegate to the United Nations, a writer, and the thirty-second First Lady of the U.S. See also Elana, Ella, Ellen, Leanore, Lena, Lenore, Leonore, Leora, Nellie, Nora, Noreen.
Elana, Elanor, Elanore, Eleanora, Eleanore, Elena, Eleni, Elenor, Elenorah, Elenore, Eleonor, Eleonore, Elianore, Elinor, Elinore, Elladine, Ellenor, Ellie, Elliner, Ellinor, Ellinore, Elna, Elnore, Elynor, Elynore

ELEANORA (Greek) an alternate form of Eleanor. See also Lena.
Elenora, Eleonora, Elianora, Ellenora, Ellenorah, Elnora, Elynora

ELECTRA (Greek) shining; brilliant. Mythology: the daughter of Agamemnon, leader of the Greeks in the Trojan War.
Elektra

ELENA (Greek) an alternate form of Eleanor. (Italian) a form of Helen.
Eleana, Eleen, Eleena, Elen, Elene, Elenitsa, Elenka, Elenna, Elenoa, Elenola, Elina, Ellena, Lena

ELENI (Greek) a familiar form of Eleanor.
Elenie, Eleny

ELEORA (Hebrew) the Lord is my light.
Eliora, Elira, Elora

ELEXIS (Greek) an alternate form of Alexis.
Elexas, Elexes, Elexess, Elexeya, Elexia, Elexiah

ELEXUS (Greek) an alternate form of Alexius, Alexus.
Elexius, Elexsus, Elexxus, Elexys

ELFRIDA (German) peaceful. See also Freda.
Elfrea, Elfreda, Elfredda, Elfreeda, Elfreyda, Elfrieda, Elfryda

ELGA (German) an alternate form of Helga. (Norwegian) pious.
Elgiva

ELIA (Hebrew) a short from of Eliana.
Eliah

ELIANA (Hebrew) my God has answered me. A feminine form of Eli, Elijah. See also Iliana.
Elia, Eliane, Elianna, Ellianna, Liana, Liane

ELIANE (Hebrew) an alternate form of Eliana.
Elianne, Elliane, Ellianne

ELICIA (Hebrew) an alternate form of Elisha. See also Alicia.
Elecia, Elica, Elicea, Elicet, Elichia, Eliscia, Elisia, Elissia, Ellecia, Ellicia

ELIDA, Elide (Latin) alternate forms of Alida.
Elidee, Elidia, Elidy

ELISA (Spanish, Italian, English) a short form of Elizabeth. See also Alisa, Ilisa.
Elecea, Eleesa, Elesa, Elesia, Elisia, Elisya, Ellisa, Ellisia, Ellissa, Ellissia, Ellissya, Ellisya, Elysa, Elysia, Elyssia, Elyssya, Elysya, Lisa

ELISABETH (Hebrew) an alternate form of Elizabeth.
Elisabet, Elisabeta, Elisabethe, Elisabetta, Elisabette, Elisabith, Elisebet, Elisheba, Elisheva

ELISE (French, English) a short form of Elizabeth, Elysia. See also Ilise, Liese, Lisette, Lissie.

Eilis, Eilise, Elese, Élise, Elisee, Elisie, Elisse, Elizé, Ellice, Ellise, Ellyce, Ellyse, Ellyze, Elsey, Elsie, Elsy, Elyce, Elyci, Elyse, Elyze, Lisel, Lisl, Lison

ELISHA (Greek) an alternate form of Alisha. (Hebrew) consecrated to God. See also Ilisha, Lisha.
Eleacia, Eleasha, Eleesha, Eleisha, Elesha, Eleshia, Eleticia, Elicia, Elishah, Elisheva, Elishia, Elishua, Eliska, Ellesha, Ellexia, Ellisha, Elsha, Elysha, Elyshia

ELISSA, Elyssa (Greek, English) forms of Elizabeth. Short forms of Melissa. See also Alissa, Alyssa, Lissa.
Elissah, Ellissa, Ellyssa, Ilissa, Ilyssa

ELITA (Latin, French) chosen. See also Lida, Lita.
Elitia, Elitia, Elitie, Ellita, Ellitia, Ellitie, Ilida, Ilita, Litia

ELIZA (Hebrew) a short form of Elizabeth. See also Aliza.
Eliz, Elizaida, Elizalina, Elize, Elizea

ELIZABET (Hebrew) an alternate form of Elizabeth.
Elizabete, Elizabette

ELIZABETH (Hebrew) consecrated to God. Bible: the mother of John the Baptist. See also Bess, Beth, Betsy, Betty, Elsa, Ilse, Libby, Liese, Liesel, Lisa, Lisbeth, Lisette, Lissa, Lissie, Liz, Liza, Lizabeta, Lizabeth, Lizbeth, Lizina, Lizzy, Veta, Yelisabeta, Zizi.
Alizabeth, Eliabeth, Elisa, Elisabeth, Elise, Elissa, Eliza, Elizabee, Elizabet, Elizaveta, Elizebeth, Elka, Elsabeth, Elsbeth, Elschen, Elspeth, Elysabeth, Elzbieta, Elzsébet, Helsa, Ilizzabet, Lusa

ELIZAVETA (Polish, English) a form of Elizabeth.
Elisavet, Elisaveta, Elisavetta, Elisveta, Elizavet, Elizavetta, Elizveta, Elsveta, Elzveta

ELKA (Polish) a form of Elizabeth.
Ilka

ELKE (German) a form of Adelaide, Alice.
Elki, Ilki

ELLA, Elle (Greek) short forms of Eleanor. (English) elfin; beautiful fairy-woman.
Ellah, Ellamae, Ellia, Ellie

ELLEN (English) a form of Eleanor, Helen.
Elen, Elenee, Eleny, Elin, Elina, Elinda, Ellan, Ellena, Ellene, Ellie, Ellin, Ellon, Ellyn, Ellynn, Ellynne, Elyn

ELLICE (English) an alternate form of Elise.
Ellecia, Ellyce, Elyce

ELLIE, Elly (English) short forms of Eleanor, Ella, Ellen.
Ele, Elie, Ellee, Elleigh, Elli

ELMA (Turkish) sweet fruit.

ELMIRA (Arabic, Spanish) an alternate form of Almira.
Elmeera, Elmera, Elmeria, Elmyra

ELNORA (American) a combination of Ella + Nora.

ELODIE (American) a form of Melody.
Elodee, Elodia, Elody

ELOISE (French) a form of Louise.
Elois, Eloisa, Eloisia

ELORA (American) a short form of Elnora.
Ellora, Elloree, Elorie

ELSA (Hebrew) a short form of Elizabeth. (German) noble. See also Ilse.
Ellsa, Ellse, Else, Elsia, Elsie, Elsje

ELSBETH (German) a form of Elizabeth.
Elsbet, Elzbet, Elzbieta

ELSIE (German) a familiar form of Elsa, Helsa.
Ellsie, Ellsie, Ellsy, Elsi, Elsy

ELSPETH (Scottish) a form of Elizabeth.
Elspet, Elspie

ELVA (English) elfin. See also Alva, Alvina.
Elvia, Elvie

ELVINA (English) an alternate form of Alvina.
Elvenea, Elvinea, Elvinia, Elvinna

ELVIRA (Latin) white; blond. (German) closed up. (Spanish) elfin. Geography: the town in Spain that hosted the first Ecumenical Council in 300 A.D.
Elva, Elvera, Elvire, Elwira, Vira

ELYSE (Latin) an alternate form of Elysia.
Ellysa, Ellyse, Elyce, Elys, Elysee, Elysse

ELYSIA (Latin) sweet; blissful. Mythology: Elysium was the dwelling place of happy souls.
Elise, Elishia, Ellicia, Elycia, Elyssa, Ilysha, Ilysia

ELYSSA (Latin) an alternate form of Elysia.
Ellyssa

EMALEE (Latin) an alternate form of Emily.
Emaili, Emalea, Emaleigh, Emali, Emalia, Emalie

EMANI (Arabic) an alternate form of Iman.
Eman, Emane, Emaneé, Emanie, Emann

EMANUELLE (Hebrew) an alternate form of Emmanuelle.
Emanual, Emanuel, Emanuela, Emanuella

EMBER (French) an alternate form of Amber.
Emberlee, Emberly

EMELIA, Emelie (Latin) alternate forms of Emily.
Emellie

EMELY (Latin) an alternate form of Emily.
Emelly

EMERALD (French) bright green gemstone.
Emelda, Esmeralda

EMERY (German) industrious leader.
Emeri, Emerie

EMILEE, Emilie (English) forms of Emily.
Emile, Emilea, Emileigh, Émilie, Emiliee, Emillee, Emillie, Emméie, Emmilee, Emylee

EMILIA (Italian) a form of Amelia, Emily.
Emalia, Emelia, Emila

EMILY (Latin) flatterer. (German) industrious. A feminine form of Emil. See also Amelia, Emma, Millie.
Eimile, Em, Emaily, Emalee, Emeli, Emelia, Emelie, Emelita, Emely, Emilee, Emiley, Emili, Emilia, Emilie, Émilie, Emilis, Emilka, Emillie, Emilly, Emmaline, Emmaly, Emmélie, Emmey, Emmi, Emmie, Emmilly, Emmily, Emmy, Emmye, Emyle

EMILYANN (American) a combination of Emily + Ann.
Emileane, Emileann, Emileanna, Emileanne, Emiliana, Emiliann, Emilianna, Emilianne, Emillyane, Emillyann, Emillyanna, Emillyanne, Emliana, Emliann, Emlianna, Emlianne

EMMA (German) a short form of Emily. See also Amy.
Em, Ema, Emmah, Emmy

EMMALEE (American) a combination of Emma + Lee. A form of Emily.
Emalea, Emalee, Emilee, Emmalea, Emmalei, Emmaleigh, Emmaley, Emmali, Emmalia, Emmalie, Emmaliese, Emmalyse, Emylee

EMMALINE (French) a form of Emily.

Emalina, Emaline, Emelina, Emeline,
Emilienne, Emilina, Emiline, Emmalina,
Emmalene, Emmeline, Emmiline

EMMALYNN (American) a combination
of Emma + Lynn.
Emelyn, Emelyne, Emelynne, Emilyn,
Emilynn, Emilynne, Emlyn, Emlynn,
Emlynne, Emmalyn, Emmalynne

EMMANUELLE (Hebrew) God is with
us. A feminine form of Emmanuel.
Emanuelle, Emmanuela, Emmanuella

EMMY (German) a familiar form of
Emma.
Emi, Emie, Emiy, Emmi, Emmie, Emmye,
Emy

EMMYLOU (American) a combination
of Emmy + Lou.
Emlou, Emmalou, Emmelou, Emmilou,
Emylou

ENA (Irish) a form of Helen.
Enna

ENID (Welsh) life; spirit.

ENRICA (Spanish) a form of Henrietta.
See also Rica.
Enrieta, Enrietta, Enrika, Enriqua, Enriqueta,
Enriquetta, Enriquette

EPPIE (English) a familiar form of
Euphemia.
Effie, Effy, Eppy

ERICA (Scandinavian) ruler of all.
(English) brave ruler. A feminine form
of Eric. See also Arica, Rica, Ricki.
Ericca, Ericha, Ericka, Errica

ERICKA, Erika (Scandanavian)
alternate forms of Erica.
Erickah, Erikaa, Erikah, Erikka, Erricka,
Errika, Eyka, Erykka, Eyrika

ERIN (Irish) peace. History: another
name for Ireland. See also Arin.

Earin, Earrin, Eran, Eren, Erena, Erene,
Ereni, Eri, Erian, Erina, Erine, Erinetta,
Erinn, Erri, Eryn

ERINN (Irish) an alternate form of Erin.
Erinna, Erinne

ERMA (Latin) a short form of Ermine,
Hermina. See also Irma.
Ermelinda

ERMINE (Latin) an alternate form of
Hermina.
Erma, Ermin, Ermina, Erminda, Erminia,
Erminie

ERNA (English) a short form of
Ernestine.

ERNESTINE (English) earnest, sincere.
A feminine form of Ernest.
Erna, Ernaline, Ernesia, Ernesta, Ernestina,
Ernesztina

ERYN (Irish) an alternate form of Erin.
Eiryn, Eryne, Erynn, Erynne

ESHE (Swahili) life.
Eisha, Esha

ESMÉ (French) a familiar form of
Esmeralda. A form of Amy.
Esma, Esme, Esmëe

ESMERALDA (Greek, Spanish) a form
of Emerald.
Emelda, Esmé, Esmerelda, Esmerilda,
Esmiralda, Ezmerelda, Ezmirilda

ESPERANZA (Spanish) hope. See also
Speranza.
Esparanza, Espe, Esperance, Esperans,
Esperansa, Esperanta, Esperanz, Esperenza

ESSENCE (Latin) life; existence.
Essa, Essenc, Essencee, Essences, Essenes,
Essense, Essynce

ESSIE (English) a short form of Estelle,
Esther.
Essa, Essey, Essie, Essy

ESTEE (English) a short form of Estelle, Esther.
Esta, Estée, Esti

ESTEFANI, Estefania, Estefany (Spanish) forms of Stephanie.
Estafania, Estefana, Estefane, Estefanie

ESTELLE (French) a form of Esther. See also Stella, Trella.
Essie, Estee, Estel, Estela, Estele, Esteley, Estelina, Estelita, Estell, Estella, Estellina, Estellita, Esthella

ESTEPHANIE (Spanish) a form of Stephanie.
Estephania, Estephani, Estephany

ESTHER (Persian) star. Bible: the Jewish captive whom Ahasuerus made his queen. See also Hester.
Essie, Estee, Ester, Esthur, Eszter, Eszti

ESTRELLA (French) star.
Estrela, Estrelinha, Estrell, Estrelle, Estrellita

ETHANA (Hebrew) strong; firm. A feminine form of Ethan.

ETHEL (English) noble.
Ethelda, Ethelin, Etheline, Ethelle, Ethelyn, Ethelynn, Ethelynne, Ethyl

ÉTOILE (French) star.

ETTA (German) little. (English) a short form of Henrietta.
Etka, Etke, Etti, Ettie, Etty, Itke, Itta

EUDORA (Greek) honored gift. See also Dora.

EUGENIA (Greek) born to nobility. A feminine form of Eugene. See also Gina.
Eugenie, Eugenina, Eugina, Evgenia

EUGENIE (Greek) an alternate form of Eugenia.
Eugenee, Eugénie

EULALIA (Greek) well spoken. See also Ula.
Eula, Eulalee, Eulalie, Eulalya, Eulia

EUN (Korean) silver.

EUNICE (Greek) happy; victorious. Bible: the mother of Saint Timothy. See also Unice.
Euna, Eunique, Eunise, Euniss

EUPHEMIA (Greek) spoken well of, in good repute. History: a fourth-century Christian martyr.
Effam, Effie, Eppie, Eufemia, Euphan, Euphemie, Euphie

EURYDICE (Greek) wide, broad. Mythology: the wife of Orpheus.
Euridice, Euridyce, Eurydyce

EUSTACIA (Greek) productive. (Latin) stable; calm. A feminine form of Eustace. See also Stacey.
Eustasia

EVA (Greek) a short form of Evangelina. (Hebrew) an alternate form of Eve. See also Ava, Chava.
Éva, Evah, Evalea, Evalee, Evike

EVALINE (French) a form of Evelyn.
Evalin, Evalina, Evalyn, Evalynn, Eveleen, Evelene, Evelina, Eveline

EVANGELINA (Greek) bearer of good news.
Eva, Evangelene, Evangelia, Evangelica, Evangeline, Evangelique, Evangelyn, Evangelynn

EVANIA (Greek) a feminine form of Evan. (Irish) young warrior.
Evan, Evana, Evanka, Evann, Evanna, Evanne, Evany, Eveania, Evvanne, Evvunea, Evyan

EVE (Hebrew) life. An alternate form of Chava. Bible: the first woman created by God. (French) a short form of Evonne. See also Hava, Naeva, Vica, Yeva.
Eva, Evie, Evita, Evuska, Evyn, Ewa, Yeva

EVELIN (English) an alternate form of Evelyn.
Evelina, Eveline

EVELYN (English) hazelnut.
Avalyn, Aveline, Evaleen, Evalene, Evaline, Evalyn, Evalynn, Evalynne, Eveleen, Evelin, Evelyna, Evelyne, Evelynn, Evelynne, Evline, Ewalina

EVERETT (German) couragrous as a boar.

EVETTE (French) an alternate form of Yvette. A familiar form of Evonne. See also Ivette.
Evett

EVIE (Hungarian) a form of Eve.
Evey, Evi, Evicka, Evike, Evka, Evuska, Evvie, Evvy, Evy, Ewa

EVITA (Spanish) a form of Eve.

EVLINE (English) an alternate form of Evelyn.
Evleen, Evlene, Evlin, Evlina, Evlyn, Evlynn, Evlynne

EVONNE (French) an alternate form of Yvonne. See also Ivonne.
Evanne, Eve, Evenie, Evenne, Evény, Evette, Evin, Evon, Evona, Evone, Evoni, Evonna, Evonnie, Evony, Evyn, Evynn, Eyona, Eyvone

EZRI (Hebrew) helper; strong.
Ezra, Ezria

F

FABIA (Latin) bean grower. A feminine form of Fabian.
Fabiana, Fabienne, Fabiola, Fabra, Fabria

FABIANA (Latin) an alternate form of Fabia.
Fabyana

FABIENNE (Latin) an alternate form of Fabia.
Fabian, Fabiann, Fabianne, Fabiene, Fabreanne

FABIOLA, Faviola (Latin) alternate forms of Fabia.
Fabiole, Fabyola, Faviana, Faviolha

FAITH (English) faithful; fidelity. See also Faye, Fidelity.
Fayth, Faythe

FAIZAH (Arabic) victorious.

FALDA (Icelandic) folded wings.
Faida, Fayda

FALINE (Latin) catlike.
Faleen, Falena, Falene, Falin, Falina, Fallyn, Fallyne, Faylina, Fayline, Faylyn, Faylynn, Faylynne, Felenia, Felina

FALLON (Irish) grandchild of the ruler.
Falan, Falen, Fallan, Fallen, Fallonne, Falon, Falyn, Falynn, Falynne, Phalon

FANCY (French) betrothed. (English) whimsical; decorative.
Fanchette, Fanchon, Fanci, Fancia, Fancie

FANNIE, Fanny (American) familiar forms of Frances.
Fan, Fanette, Fani, Fania, Fannee, Fanney, Fanni, Fannia, Fany, Fanya

FANTASIA (Greek) imagination.
Fantasy, Fantasya, Fantaysia, Fantazia, Fiantasi

FARAH, Farrah (English) beautiful; pleasant.
Fara, Farra, Fayre

FAREN, Farren (English) wanderer.
Faran, Fare, Farin, Faron, Farrahn, Farran, Farrand, Farrin, Farron, Farryn, Farye, Faryn, Feran, Ferin, Feron, Ferran, Ferren, Ferrin, Ferron, Ferryn

FATIMA (Arabic) daughter of the Prophet. History: the daughter of Muhammad.
Fatema, Fathma, Fatimah, Fatime, Fatma, Fatmah, Fatme, Fattim

FAWN (French) young deer.
Faun, Fawna, Fawne

FAWNA (French) an alternate form of Fawn.
Fauna, Fawnia, Fawnna

FAYE (French) fairy; elf. (English) an alternate form of Faith.
Fae, Fay, Fayann, Fayanna, Fayette, Fayina, Fey

FAYOLA (Nigerian) lucky.
Fayla, Feyla

FELECIA (Latin) an alternate form of Felicia.
Flecia

FELICA (Spanish) a short form of Felicia.
Falisa, Felisa, Felisca, Felissa, Feliza

FELICE (Latin) a short form of Felicia.
Felece, Felicie, Felise, Felize, Felyce, Felysse

FELICIA (Latin) fortunate; happy. A feminine form of Felix. See also Lecia, Phylicia.
Falecia, Faleshia, Falicia, Fela, Felecia, Felica, Felice, Felicidad, Feliciona, Felicity, Felicya, Felisea, Felisha, Felisia, Felisiana, Felissya, Felita, Felixia, Felizia, Felka, Fellcia, Felycia, Felysia, Felyssia, Fleasia, Fleichia, Fleishia, Flichia

FELICITY (English) a form of Felicia.
Falicity, Felicita, Felicitas, Félicité, Feliciti, Felisita, Felisity

FELISHA (Latin) an alternate form of Felicia.
Faleisha, Falesha, Falisha, Falleshia, Feleasha, Feleisha, Felesha, Felishia, Fellishia, Felysha, Flisha

FEMI (French) woman. (Nigerian) love me.
Femie, Femmi, Femmie, Femy

FEODORA (Greek) gift of God. A feminine form of Theodore.
Fedora, Fedoria

FERN (German) a short form of Fernanda. (English) fern.
Ferne, Ferni, Fernlee, Fernleigh, Fernley, Fernly

FERNANDA (German) daring, adventurous. A feminine form of Ferdinand. See also Andee, Nan.
Ferdie, Ferdinanda, Ferdinande, Fern, Fernande, Fernandette, Fernandina, Nanda

FIALA (Czech) violet flower.

FIDELIA (Latin) an alternate form of Fidelity.
Fidela, Fidele, Fidelina

FIDELITY (Latin) faithful, true. See also Faith.
Fidelia, Fidelita

FIFI (French) a familiar form of Josephine.
Feef, Feefee, Fifine

FILIPPA (Italian) a form of Philippa.
Felipa, Filipa, Filippina, Filpina

FILOMENA (Italian) a form of Philomena.
Fila, Filah, Filemon

FIONA (Irish) fair, white.
Fionna

FIONNULA (Irish) white shouldered. See also Nola, Nuala.
Fenella, Fenula, Finella, Finola, Finula

FLAIR (English) style; verve.
Flaire, Flare

FLANNERY (Irish) redhead. Literature: Flannery O'Connor was a renowned American writer.
Flan, Flann, Flanna

FLAVIA (Latin) blond, golden haired.
Flavere, Flaviar, Flavie, Flavien, Flavienne, Flaviere, Flavio, Flavyere, Fulvia

FLAVIE (Latin) an alternate form of Flavia.
Flavi

FLEUR (French) flower.
Fleure, Fleuree, Fleurette

FLO (American) a short form of Florence.

FLORA (Latin) flower. A short form of Florence. See also Lore.
Fiora, Fiore, Fiorenza, Flor, Florann, Florella, Florelle, Floren, Floria, Floriana, Florianna, Florica, Florimel

FLORENCE (Latin) blooming; flowery; prosperous. History: Florence Nightingale, a British nurse, is considered the founder of modern nursing. See also Florida.
Fiorenza, Flo, Flora, Florance, Florencia, Florency, Florendra, Florentia, Florentina, Florentyna, Florenza, Floretta, Florette, Florie, Florina, Florine, Floris, Flossie

FLORIA (Basque) a form of Flora.
Flori, Florria

FLORIDA (Spanish) a form of Florence.
Floridia, Florinda, Florita

FLORIE (English) a familiar form of Florence.
Flore, Flori, Florri, Florrie, Florry, Flory

FLORIS (English) a form of Florence.
Florisa, Florise

FLOSSIE (English) a familiar form of Florence.
Floss, Flossi, Flossy

FOLA (Yoruba) honorable.

FONDA (Latin) foundation. (Spanish) inn.
Fondea, Fonta

FONTANNA (French) fountain.
Fontaine, Fontana, Fontane, Fontanne, Fontayne

FORTUNA (Latin) fortune; fortunate.
Fortoona, Fortune

FRAN (Latin) a short form of Frances.
Frain, Frann

FRANCES (Latin) free; from France. See also Paquita.
Fanny, Fran, Franca, France, Francee, Francena, Francesca, Francess, Francesta, Franceta, Francetta, Francette, Francine, Francis, Francisca, Françoise, Frankie, Frannie, Franny

FRANCESCA (Italian) a form of Frances.
Franceska, Francessca, Francesta, Franchesca, Franzetta

FRANCHESCA (Italian) an alternate form of Francesca.
Cheka, Chekka, Chesca, Cheska, Francheca, Francheka, Franchelle, Franchesa, Francheska, Franchessca, Franchesska

FRANCI (Hungarian) a familiar form of Francine.
Francey, Francie, Francy

FRANCINE (French) a form of Frances.
Franceen, Franceine, Franceline, Francene, Francenia, Franci, Francin, Francina, Francyne

FRANCIS (Latin) an alternate form of Frances.
Francise, Franncia, Francys

FRANCISCA (Italian) a form of Frances.
Franciska, Franciszka, Frantiska, Franziska

FRANÇOISE (French) a form of Frances.

FRANKIE (American) a familiar form of Frances.
Francka, Francki, Franka, Frankey, Franki, Frankia, Franky, Frankye

FRANNIE, Franny (English) familiar forms of Frances.
Frani, Frania, Franney, Franni, Frany

FREDA, Freida, Frida (German) short forms of Alfreda, Elfrida, Frederica, Sigfreda.
Frayda, Fredda, Fredella, Fredia, Fredra, Freeda, Freeha, Freia, Frida, Frideborg, Frieda

FREDDI, Freddie (English) familiar forms of Frederica, Winifred.
Fredda, Freddy, Fredi, Fredia, Fredy, Frici

FREDERICA (German) peaceful ruler. A feminine form of Frederick. See also Alfreda, Rica, Ricki.
Farica, Federica, Freda, Fredalena, Fredaline, Freddi, Freddie, Frederickina, Frederika, Frederike, Frederina, Frederine, Frederique, Fredith, Fredora, Fredreca, Fredrica, Fredricah, Fredricia, Freida, Fritzi, Fryderica

FREDERIKA (German) an alternate form of Frederica.
Fredericka, Fredreka, Fredricka, Fredrika, Fryderyka

FREDERIKE (German) an alternate form of Frederica.
Fredericke, Friederike

FREDERIQUE (French) a form of Frederica.
Frédérique, Rike

FREJA (Scandinavian) noblewoman. Mythology: the Norse goddess of love.
Fraya, Freya

FRITZI (German) a familiar form of Frederica.
Friezi, Fritze, Fritzie, Fritzinn, Fritzline, Fritzy

G

GABRIEL, Gabriele (French) alternate forms of Gabrielle.
Gabbriel, Gabbryel, Gabreal, Gabreale, Gabreil, Gabrial, Gabryel

GABRIELA, Gabriella (Italian) alternate forms of Gabrielle.
Gabriala, Gabrialla, Gabrielia, Gabriellia, Gabrila, Gabrilla, Gabryella

GABRIELLE (French) devoted to God. A feminine form of Gabriel.
Gabbrielle, Gabielle, Gabrealle, Gabriana, Gabriel, Gabriela, Gabriele, Gabriell, Gabriella, Gabrille, Gabrina, Gabriylle, Gabryell, Gabryelle, Gaby, Gavriella

GABY (French) a familiar form of Gabrielle.
Gabbey, Gabbi, Gabbie, Gabby, Gabey, Gabi, Gabie, Gavi, Gavy

GADA (Hebrew) lucky.
Gadah

GAEA (Greek) planet Earth. Mythology: the Greek goddess of Earth.
Gaia, Gaiea, Gaya

GAETANA (Italian) from Gaeta. Geography: a region in southern Italy.
Gaetan, Gaétane, Gaetanne

GAGANDEEP (Sikh) sky's light.
Gagandip, Gagnadeep, Gagndeep

GAIL (Hebrew) a short form of Abigail.
(English) merry, lively.
Gael, Gaela, Gaelle, Gaila, Gaile, Gale,
Gayla, Gayle

GALA (Norwegian) singer.
Galla

GALEN (Greek) healer; calm. (Irish)
little and lively.
Gaelen, Gaellen, Galyn, Gaylaine, Gayleen,
Gaylen, Gaylene, Gaylyn

GALENA (Greek) healer; calm.

GALI (Hebrew) hill; fountain; spring.
Galice, Galie

GALINA (Russian) a form of Helen.
Gailya, Galayna, Galenka, Galia, Galiana,
Galiena, Galinka, Galochka, Galya, Galyna

GANESA (Hindi) fortunate. Religion:
the Hindu god of wisdom and luck.

GANYA (Hebrew) garden of the lord.
Gana, Gani, Gania, Ganice, Ganit

GARDENIA (English) Botany: a sweet-
smelling flower.
Deeni, Denia, Gardena, Gardinia

GARLAND (French) wreath of flowers.

GARNET (English) dark red gem.
Garnetta, Garnette

GARYN (English) spear carrier.
A feminine form of Gary.
Garan, Garen, Garra, Garryn

GASHA (Russian) a familiar form of
Agatha.
Gashka

GAVRIELLA (Hebrew) a form of
Gabrielle.
Gavila, Gavilla, Gavrid, Gavrieela, Gavriela,
Gavrielle, Gavrila, Gavrilla

GAY (French) merry.
Gae, Gai, Gaye

GAYLE (English) an alternate form of
Gail.
Gayla

GAYNA (English) a familiar form of
Guinevere.
Gaynah, Gayner, Gaynor

GEELA (Hebrew) joyful.
Gela, Gila

GEENA (American) a form of Gena.
Geania, Geeana, Geeanna

GELYA (Russian) angelic.

GEMA, Gemma (Latin, Italian) jewel,
precious stone. See also Jemma.
Gem, Gemmey, Gemmie, Gemmy

GEMINI (Greek) twin.
Gemelle, Gemima, Gemina, Geminine,
Gemmina

GEN (Japanese) spring. A short form of
names beginning with 'Gen.'

GENA (French) a form of Gina. A short
form of Geneva, Genevieve, Iphigenia.
Geanna, Geena, Geenah, Gen, Genae,
Genah, Genai, Genea, Geneja, Geni, Genia,
Genie

GENEEN (Scottish) an alternate form of
Jeanine.
Geanine, Geannine, Gen, Genene, Genine,
Gineen, Ginene

GENELL (American) an alternate form
of Jenelle.

GENESIS (Latin) origin; birth.
Genes, Genese, Genesha, Genesia, Genesiss,
Genessa, Genesse, Genessie, Genessis,
Genicis, Genises, Genysis, Yenesis

GENEVA (French) juniper tree. A short
form of Genevieve. Geography: a city
in Switzerland.

Geneva (cont.)
Geena, Gen, Gena, Geneieve, Geneiva, Geneive, Geneve, Ginneva, Janeva, Jeaneva, Jeneva

GENEVIEVE (German, French) an alternate form of Guinevere. See also Gwendolyn.
Gen, Gena, Genaveeve, Genaveve, Genavie, Genavieve, Genavive, Geneva, Geneveve, Genevie, Geneviéve, Genevievre, Genevive, Genovieve, Genvieve, Ginette, Gineveve, Ginevieve, Ginevive, Guinevieve, Guinivive, Gwenevieve, Gwenivive, Jennavieve

GENEVRA (French, Welsh) an alternate form of Guinevere.
Gen, Genever, Genevera, Ginevra

GENICE (American) a form of Janice.
Gen, Genece, Geneice, Genesa, Genesee, Genessia, Genis, Genise

GENITA (American) an alternate form of Janita.
Gen, Genet, Geneta

GENNA (English) a form of Jenna.
Gen, Gennae, Gennay, Genni, Gennie, Genny

GENNIFER (American) a form of Jennifer.
Gen, Genifer, Ginnifer

GENOVIEVE (French) an alternate form of Genevieve.
Genoveva, Genoveve, Genovive

GEORGEANNA (English) a combination of Georgia + Anna.
Georgana, Georganna, Georgeana, Georgiana, Georgianna, Georgyanna, Giorgianna

GEORGEANNE (English) a combination of Georgia + Anne.
Georgann, Georganne, Georgean, Georgeann, Georgie, Georgyann, Georgyanne

GEORGENE (English) a familiar form of Georgia.
Georgeena, Georgeina, Georgena, Georgenia, Georgiena, Georgienne, Georgina, Georgine

GEORGETTE (French) a form of Georgia.
Georgeta, Georgett, Georgetta, Georjetta

GEORGIA (Greek) farmer. A feminine form of George. Art: Georgia O'Keeffe was an American painter known especially for her paintings of flowers. Geography: a southern American state; a country in Eastern Europe. See also Jirina, Jorja.
Georgene, Georgette, Georgie, Giorgia

GEORGIANNA (English) an alternate form of Georgeanna.
Georgiana, Georgiann, Georgianne, Georgie, Georgieann, Georgionna

GEORGIE (English) a familiar form of Georgeanne, Georgia, Georgianna.
Georgi, Georgy, Giorgi

GEORGINA (English) a form of Georgia.
Georgena, Georgene, Georgine, Giorgina, Jorgina

GERALDINE (German) mighty with a spear. A feminine form of Gerald. See also Dena, Jeraldine.
Geralda, Geraldina, Geraldyna, Geraldyne, Gerhardine, Geri, Gerianna, Gerianne, Gerrilee, Giralda

GERALYN (American) a combination of Geraldine + Lynn.
Geralisha, Geralynn, Gerilyn, Gerrilyn

GERARDO (English) brave spearwoman.
Gerardine

GERDA (German) a familiar form of Gertrude. (Norwegian) protector.
Gerta

GERI (American) a familiar form of Geraldine. See also Jeri.
Gerri, Gerrie, Gerry

GERMAINE (French) from Germany. See also Jermaine.
Germain, Germana, Germanee, Germani, Germanie, Germaya, Germine

GERTIE (German) a familiar form of Gertrude.
Gert, Gertey, Gerti, Gerty

GERTRUDE (German) beloved warrior. See also Trudy.
Gerda, Gerta, Gertie, Gertina, Gertraud, Gertrud, Gertruda

GERVAISE (French) skilled with a spear. A feminine form of Jarvis.

GESSICA (Italian) a form of Jessica.
Gesica, Gesika, Gess, Gesse, Gessy

GEVA (Hebrew) hill.
Gevah

GHADA (Arabic) young; tender.
Gada

GHITA (Italian) pearly.
Gita

GIANNA (Italian) a short form of Giovanna. See also Jianna, Johana.
Geona, Geonna, Giana, Gianella, Gianetta, Gianina, Gianinna, Gianne, Giannee, Giannella, Giannetta, Gianni, Giannie, Giannina, Gianny, Gianoula

GIGI (French) a familiar form of Gilberte.
Geegee, G.G., Giggi

GILANA (Hebrew) joyful.
Gila, Gilah

GILBERTE (German) brilliant; pledge; trustworthy. A feminine form of Gilbert. See also Berti.
Gigi, Gilberta, Gilbertina, Gilbertine, Gill

GILDA (English) covered with gold.
Gilde, Gildi, Gildie, Gildy

GILL (Latin, German) a short form of Gilberte, Gillian.
Gili, Gilli, Gillie, Gilly

GILLIAN (Latin) an alternate form of Jillian.
Gila, Gilana, Gilenia, Gili, Gilian, Gill, Gilliana, Gilliane, Gilliann, Gillianna, Gillianne, Gillie, Gilly, Gillyan, Gillyane, Gillyann, Gillyanne, Gyllian, Lian

GIN (Japanese) silver. A short form of names beginning with 'Gin.'

GINA (Italian) a short form of Angelina, Eugenia, Regina, Virginia. See also Jina.
Gena, Gin, Ginah, Ginai, Ginna

GINETTE (English) a form of Genevieve.
Gin, Ginata, Ginett, Ginetta, Ginnetta, Ginnette

GINGER (Latin) flower; spice. A familiar form of Virginia.
Gin, Ginja, Ginjer, Ginny

GINIA (Latin) a familiar form of Virginia.
Gin

GINNIFER (Welsh) an alternate form of Jennifer. (English) white; smooth; soft.
Gin, Ginifer

GINNY (English) a familiar form of Ginger, Virginia. See also Jin, Jinny.
Gin, Gini, Ginney, Ginni, Ginnie, Giny, Gionni, Gionny

GIORDANA (Italian) a form of Jordana.

GIORGIANNA (English) an alternate form of Georgeanna.
Giorgina

GIOVANNA (Italian) a form of Jane.
Geovana, Geovanna, Geovonna, Giavanna, Giavonna, Giovana, Giovanne, Giovanni, Giovannica, Giovonna, Givonnie, Jeveny

GISA (Hebrew) carved stone.
Gazit, Gissa

GISELA (German) an alternate form of Giselle.
Gisella, Gissela, Gissella

GISELLE (German) pledge; hostage. See also Jizelle.
Ghisele, Gisel, Gisela, Gisele, Geséle, Giseli, Gisell, Gissell, Gisselle, Gizela, Gysell

GISSEL, Gisselle (German) alternate forms of Giselle.
Gissell

GITA (Polish) a short form of Margaret. (Yiddish) good.
Gitka, Gitta, Gituska

GITANA (Spanish) gypsy; wanderer.

GITTA (Irish) a short form of Bridget.
Getta

GIULIA (Italian) a form of Julia.
Giulana, Giuliana, Giulianna, Giulliana, Guila, Guiliana, Guilietta

GIZELA (Czech) a form of Giselle.
Gizel, Gizele, Gizella, Gizelle, Gizi, Giziki, Gizus

GLADIS (Irish) an alternate form of Gladys.
Gladi, Gladiz

GLADYS (Latin) small sword. (Irish) princess. (Welsh) a form of Claudia. Botany: a gladiolus flower.
Glad, Gladis, Gladness, Gladwys, Glady, Gwladys

GLENDA (Welsh) a form of Glenna.
Glanda, Glennda, Glynda

GLENNA (Irish) valley, glen. A feminine form of Glenn. See also Glynnis.
Glenda, Glenetta, Glenina, Glenine, Glenn, Glenne, Glennesha, Glennia, Glennie, Glenora, Gleny, Glyn

GLENNESHA (American) a form of Glenna.
Glenesha, Glenisha, Glennisha, Glennishia

GLORIA (Latin) glory. History: Gloria Steinem, a leading American feminist, founded *Ms.* magazine.
Gloresha, Gloriah, Gloribel, Gloriela, Gloriella, Glorielle, Gloris, Glorisha, Glorvina, Glory

GLORIANNE (American) a combination of Gloria + Anne.
Gloriana, Gloriane, Gloriann, Glorianna

GLORY (Latin) an alternate form of Gloria.
Glorey, Glori, Glorie

GLYNNIS (Welsh) a form of Glenna.
Glenice, Glenis, Glenise, Glenyse, Glennis, Glennys, Glenwys, Glenys, Glenyss, Glinnis, Glinys, Glynesha, Glynice, Glynis, Glynisha, Glyniss, Glynitra, Glynys, Glynyss

GOLDA (English) gold. History: Golda Meir was a Russian-born politician who served as Prime Minister of Israel.
Goldarina, Golden, Goldie, Goldina

GOLDIE (English) a familiar form of Golda.
Goldi, Goldy

GOMA (Swahili) joyful dance.

GRACE (Latin) graceful.
Engracia, Graca, Gracia, Gracie, Graciela, Graciella, Gracinha, Graice, Grata, Gratia, Gray, Grayce, Grecia

GRACEANNE (English) a combination of Grace + Anne.
Graceann, Graceanna, Gracen, Graciana, Gracianna, Gracin, Gratiana

GRACIA (Spanish) a form of Grace.
Gracea, Grecia

GRACIE (English) a familiar form of Grace.
Gracee, Gracey, Graci, Gracy, Graecie, Graysie

GRANT (English) great; giving.

GRAYSON (English) bailiff's daughter.
Graison, Graisyn, Grasien, Grasyn, Graysen

GRAZIA (Latin) an alternate form of Grace.
Graziella, Grazielle, Graziosa, Grazyna

GRECIA (Latin) an alternate form of Grace.

GREER (Scottish) vigilant. A feminine form of Gregory.
Grear, Grier

GRETA (German) a short form of Gretchen, Margaret.
Greatal, Greatel, Greeta, Gretal, Grete, Gretel, Gretha, Grethal, Grethe, Grethel, Gretta, Grette, Grieta, Gryta, Grytta

GRETCHEN (German) a form of Margaret.
Greta, Gretchin, Gretchyn

GRICELDA (German) an alternate form of Griselda.
Gricelle

GRISEL (German) a short form of Griselda.
Grisell, Griselle, Grissel, Grissele, Grissell, Grizel

GRISELDA (German) gray woman warrior. See also Selda, Zelda.
Gricelda, Grisel, Griseldis, Griseldys, Griselys, Grishilda, Grishilde, Grisselda, Grissely, Grizelda

GUADALUPE (Arabic) river of black stones. See also Lupe.

Guadalup, Guadelupe, Guadlupe, Guadulupe, Gudalupe

GUDRUN (Scandinavian) battler. See also Runa.
Gudren, Gudrin, Gudrinn, Gudruna

GUILLERMA (Spanish) a form of Wilhelmina.
Guilla, Guillermina

GUINEVERE (French, Welsh) white wave; white phantom. Literature: the wife of King Arthur. See also Gayna, Genevieve, Genevra, Jennifer, Winifred, Wynne.
Generva, Genn, Ginette, Guenevere, Guenna, Guinivere, Guinna, Gwen, Gwenevere, Gwenivere, Gwynnevere

GUNDA (Norwegian) female warrior.
Gundala, Gunta

GURIT (Hebrew) innocent baby.

GURLEEN (Sikh) follower of the guru.

GURPREET (Punjabi) religion.
Gurprit

GUSTA (Latin) a short form of Augusta.
Gus, Gussi, Gussie, Gussy, Gusti, Gustie, Gusty

GWEN (Welsh) a short form of Guinevere, Gwendolyn.
Gwenesha, Gweness, Gweneta, Gwenetta, Gwenette, Gweni, Gwenisha, Gwenita, Gwenn, Gwenna, Gwennie, Gwenny

GWENDA (Welsh) a familiar form of Gwendolyn.
Gwinda, Gwynda, Gwynedd

GWENDOLYN (Welsh) white wave; white browed; new moon. Literature: the wife of Merlin, the magician. See also Genevieve, Gwyneth, Wendy.

Gwendolyn (cont.)
Guendolen, Gwen, Gwendalin, Gwenda,
Gwendalee, Gwendaline, Gwendalyn,
Gwendalynn, Gwendela, Gwendelyn,
Gwendelynn, Gwendilyn, Gwendolen,
Gwendolene, Gwendolin, Gwendoline,
Gwendolyne, Gwendolynn, Gwendolynne,
Gwendylan, Gwyndolyn, Gwynndolen

GWYN (Welsh) a short form of
Gwyneth.
Gwinn, Gwinne, Gwynn, Gwynne

GWYNETH (Welsh) an alternate form
of Gwendolyn. See also Winnie,
Wynne.
Gweneth, Gwenith, Gwenneth, Gwennyth,
Gwenyth, Gwyn, Gwynneth

GYPSY (English) wanderer.
Gipsy, Gypsie, Jipsi

H

HABIBA (Arabic) beloved.
Habibah, Habibeh

HACHI (Japanese) eight; good luck.
Hachiko, Hachiyo

HADARA (Hebrew) adorned with
beauty.
Hadarah

HADASSAH (Hebrew) myrtle tree.
Hadas, Hadasah, Hadassa, Haddasa,
Haddasah

HADIYA (Swahili) gift.
Hadaya, Hadia, Hadiyah, Hadiyyah

HADLEY (English) field of heather.
Hadlea, Hadlee, Hadleigh, Hadli, Hadlie,
Hadly

HADRIANE (Greek, Latin) an alternate
form of Adrienne.

Hadriana, Hadrianna, Hadrianne, Hadriene,
Hadrienne

HAELEY (English) an alternate form of
Hailey.
Haelee, Haeleigh, Haeli, Haelie, Haelleigh,
Haelli, Haellie, Haely

HAGAR (Hebrew) forsaken; stranger.
Bible: Sarah's handmaiden, the mother
of Ishmael.
Haggar

HAIDEE (Greek) modest.
Hady, Haide, Haidi, Haidy, Haydee, Haydy

HAIDEN (English) heather-covered hill.
A feminine form of Hadden.
Haden, Hadyn, Haeden, Haidn, Haidyn

HAILEE (English) an alternate form of
Hayley.
Haile, Hailei, Haileigh, Haillee

HAILEY (English) an alternate form of
Hayley.
Haeley, Haiely, Hailea, Hailley, Hailly, Haily

HAILI, Hailie (English) alternate forms
of Hayley.
Haille, Hailli, Haillie

HALDANA (Norwegian) half-Danish.

HALEE (English) an alternate form of
Haley.
Hale, Halea, Haleah, Haleh, Halei

HALEIGH (English) an alternate form
of Haley.

HALEY (Scandinavian) heroine. See
also Hailey, Hayley.
Halee, Haleigh, Hali, Halley, Hallie, Haly,
Halye

HALI, Halie (English) alternate forms of
Haley.
Haliegh

HALIA (Hawaiian) in loving memory.

HALIMAH (Arabic) gentle; patient.
Halima, Halime

HALINA (Russian) a form of Helen.
Haleen, Haleena, Halena, Halinka

HALLA (African) unexpected gift.
Hala, Hallah, Halle

HALLEY (English) an alternate form of Haley.
Hally, Hallye

HALLIE (Scandinavian) an alternate form of Haley.
Hallee, Hallei, Halleigh, Halli

HALONA (Native American) fortunate.
Halonah, Haloona, Haona

HALSEY (English) Hall's island.
Halsea, Halsie

HAMA (Japanese) shore.

HANA, Hanah (Japanese) flower. (Arabic) happiness. (Slavic) forms of Hannah.
Hanae, Hanan, Haneen, Hanicka, Hanin, Hanita, Hanka

HANAKO (Japanese) flower child.

HANIA (Hebrew) resting place.
Haniya, Hanja, Hannia, Hanniah, Hanya

HANNA (Hebrew) an alternate form of Hannah.

HANNAH (Hebrew) gracious. Bible: the mother of Samuel. See also Anci, Anezka, Ania, Anka, Ann, Anna, Annalie, Anneka, Chana, Nina, Nusi.
Hana, Hanna, Hanneke, Hannele, Hanni, Hannon, Honna

HANNI (Hebrew) a familiar form of Hannah.
Hani, Hanne, Hannie, Hanny

HAPPY (English) happy.
Happi

HARA (Hindi) tawny. Religion: another name for the Hindu goddess Shiva, the destroyer.

HARLEE, Harleigh, Harlie (English) alternate forms of Harley.
Harlei, Harli

HARLEY (English) meadow of the hare. See also Arleigh.
Harlee, Harleey, Harly

HARLEYANN (English) a combination of Harley + Ann.
Harlann, Harlanna, Harlanne, Harleen, Harlene, Harleyanna, Harleyanne, Harliann, Harlianna, Harlianne, Harlina, Harline

HARMONY (Latin) harmonious.
Harmene, Harmeni, Harmon, Harmonee, Harmonei, Harmoni, Harmonia, Harmonie

HARPREET (Punjabi) devoted to God.
Harprit

HARRIET (French) ruler of the household. (English) an alternate form of Henrietta. Literature: Harriet Beecher Stowe was an American writer noted for her novel *Uncle Tom's Cabin*.
Harri, Harrie, Harriett, Harrietta, Harriette, Harriot, Harriott, Hattie

HARU (Japanese) spring.

HASANA (Swahili) she arrived first. A name used for the first-born female twin. See also Huseina.
Hasanna, Hasna, Hassana, Hassna, Hassona

HASINA (Swahili) good.
Haseena, Hasena, Hassina

HATEYA (Moquelumnan) footprints.

HATTIE (English) familiar forms of Harriet, Henrietta.
Hatti, Hatty, Hetti, Hettie, Hetty

HAUSU (Moquelumnan) like a bear yawning upon awakening.

HAVA (Hebrew) an alternate form of Chava. See also Eve.
Havah, Havvah

HAVEN (English) an alternate form of Heaven.
Havan, Havana, Havanna, Havannah, Havyn

HAVIVA (Hebrew) beloved.
Havalee, Havelah, Havi, Hayah

HAYDEN (English) an alternate form of Haiden.
Hayde, Haydin, Haydn, Haydon,

HAYFA (Arabic) shapely.

HAYLEE, Hayleigh, Haylie (English) alternate forms of Hayley.
Hayle, Haylea, Haylei, Hayli, Haylle, Hayllie

HAYLEY (English) hay meadow. See also Hailey, Haley.
Hailee, Haili, Hayilee, Hayly

HAZEL (English) hazelnut tree; commanding authority.
Hazal, Hazaline, Haze, Hazeline, Hazell, Hazelle, Hazen, Hazyl

HEATHER (English) flowering heather.
Heath, Heatherlee, Heatherly

HEAVEN (English) place of beauty and happiness. Bible: where God and angels are said to dwell.
Haven, Heavan, Heavenly, Heavin, Heavon, Heavyn, Hevean, Heven, Hevin

HEDDA (German) battler. See also Edda, Hedy.
Heda, Hedaya, Hedia, Hedvick, Hedvig, Hedvika, Hedwig, Hedwiga, Heida, Hetta

HEDY (Greek) delightful; sweet. (German) a familiar form of Hedda.
Heddey, Heddi, Heddie, Heddy, Hede, Hedi

HEIDI, Heidy (German) short forms of Adelaide.
Heida, Heide, Heidee, Heidie, Heydy, Hidee, Hidi, Hidie, Hidy, Hiede, Hiedi, Hydi

HELEN (Greek) light. See also Aileen, Aili, Alena, Eileen, Elaina, Elaine, Eleanor, Ellen, Galina, Ila, Ilene, Ilona, Jelena, Leanore, Leena, Lelya, Lenci, Lene, Liolya, Nellie, Nitsa, Olena, Onella, Yalena, Yelena.
Elana, Ena, Halina, Hela, Hele, Helena, Helene, Helle, Hellen, Helli, Hellin, Hellon, Hellyn, Helon

HELENA (Greek) an alternate form of Helen. See also Ilena.
Halena, Halina, Helaina, Helana, Helania, Helayna, Heleana, Heleena, Helenia, Helenka, Helenna, Helina, Hellanna, Hellena, Hellenna, Helona, Helonna

HELENE (French) a form of Helen.
Helaine, Helanie, Helayne, Heleen, Heleine, Hèléne, Helenor, Heline, Hellenor

HELGA (German) pious. (Scandinavian) an alternate form of Olga. See also Elga.

HELKI (Native American) touched.
Helkey, Helkie, Helky

HELMA (German) a short form of Wilhelmina.
Halma, Helme, Helmi, Helmine, Hilma

HELOISE (French) a form of Louise.
Héloïse, Hlois

HELSA (Danish) a form of Elizabeth.
Helse, Helsey, Helsi, Helsie, Helsy

HELTU (Moquelumnan) like a bear reaching out.

HENNA (English) a familiar form of Henrietta.
Hena, Henaa, Henah, Heni, Henia, Henny, Henya

HENRIETTA (English) ruler of the household. A feminine form of Henry. See also Enrica, Etta, Yetta.

Harriet, Hattie, Hatty, Hendrika, Heneretta, Henka, Henna, Hennrietta, Hennriette, Henretta, Henrica, Henrie, Henrieta, Henriete, Henriette, Henrika, Henrique, Henriquetta, Henryetta, Hetta, Hettie

HERA (Greek) queen; jealous. Mythology: the queen of heaven and the wife of Zeus.

HERMIA (Greek) messenger. A feminine form of Hermes.

HERMINA (Latin) noble. (German) soldier. A feminine form of Herman. See also Erma, Ermine, Irma.
Herma, Hermenia, Hermia, Herminna

HERMIONE (Greek) earthy.
Hermalina, Hermia, Hermina, Hermine, Herminia

HERMOSA (Spanish) beautiful.

HERTHA (English) child of the earth.
Heartha, Hirtha

HESTER (Dutch) a form of Esther.
Hessi, Hessie, Hessye, Hesther, Hettie

HESTIA (Persian) star. Mythology: the Greek goddess of the hearth and home.
Hestea, Hesti, Hestie, Hesty

HETA (Native American) racer.

HETTA (German) an alternate form of Hedda. (English) a familiar form of Henrietta.

HETTIE (German) a familiar form of Hester, Henrietta.
Hetti, Hetty

HILARY, Hillary (Greek) cheerful, merry. See also Alair.
Hilaree, Hilari, Hilaria, Hilarie, Hilery, Hiliary, Hillaree, Hillari, Hillarie, Hilleary, Hilleree, Hilleri, Hillerie, Hillery, Hillianne, Hilliary, Hillory

HILDA (German) a short form of Brunhilda, Hildegarde.
Helle, Hilde, Hildey, Hildie, Hildur, Hildy, Hulda, Hylda

HILDEGARDE (German) fortress.
Hilda, Hildagard, Hildagarde, Hildegard, Hildred

HINDA (Hebrew) hind; doe.
Hindey, Hindie, Hindy, Hynda

HISA (Japanese) long-lasting.
Hisae, Hisako, Hisay

HITI (Eskimo) hyena.
Hitty

HOA (Vietnamese) flower; peace.
Ho, Hoai

HOLA (Hopi) seed-filled club.

HOLLEY (English) an alternate form of Holly.
Holleah, Hollee

HOLLI, Hollie (English) alternate forms of Holly.
Holeigh, Holleigh

HOLLIS (English) near the holly bushes.
Hollise, Hollyce, Holyce

HOLLY (English) holly tree.
Holley, Holli, Hollie, Hollye

HOLLYANN (English) a combination of Holly + Ann.
Holliann, Hollianna, Hollianne, Hollyanne, Hollyn

HOLLYN (English) a short form of Hollyann.
Holin, Holeena, Hollina, Hollynn

HONEY (Latin) a familiar form of Honora. (English) sweet.
Honalee, Hunney, Hunny

HONG (Vietnamese) pink.

HONORA (Latin) honorable. See also Nora, Onora.
Honey, Honner, Honnor, Honnour, Honor, Honorah, Honorata, Honore, Honoree, Honoria, Honorina, Honorine, Honour, Honoure

HOPE (English) hope.
Hopey, Hopi, Hopie

HORTENSE (Latin) gardener. See also Ortensia.
Hortencia, Hortensia

HOSHI (Japanese) star.
Hoshie, Hoshiko, Hoshiyo

HUA (Chinese) flower.

HUATA (Moquelumnan) basket carrier.

HUNTER (English) hunter.
Hunta, Huntar, Huntter

HUONG (Vietnamese) flower.

HUSEINA (Swahili) an alternate form of Hasana.

HYACINTH (Greek) Botany: a plant with colorful, fragrant flowers. See also Cynthia, Jacinda.
Giacinta, Hyacintha, Hyacinthe, Hyacinthia, Hyacinthie, Hycinth, Hycynth

HYDI, Hydeia (German) alternate forms of Heidi.
Hyde, Hydea, Hydee, Hydia, Hydie, Hydiea

HYE (Korean) graceful.

I

IAN (Hebrew) God is gracious.
Iaian, Iain, Iana, Iann, Ianna, Iannel, Iyana

IANTHE (Greek) violet flower.
Iantha, Ianthia, Ianthina

ICESS (Egyptian) an alternate form of Isis.
Ices, Icesis, Icesse, Icey, Icia, Icis, Icy

IDA (German) hardworking. (English) prosperous.
Idah, Idaia, Idalia, Idalis, Idaly, Idamae, Idania, Idarina, Idarine, Idaya, Ide, Idelle, Idette, Idys

IDALINA (English) a combination of Ida + Lina.
Idaleena, Idaleene, Idalena, Idalene, Idaline

IDALIS (English) an alternate form of Ida.
Idalesse, Idalise, Idaliz, Idallas, Idallis, Idelis, Idelys, Idialis

IDEASHIA (American) a combination of Ida + Iesha.
Idasha, Idaysha, Ideesha, Idesha

IDELLE (Welsh) a form of Ida.
Idell, Idella, Idil

IESHA (American) a form of Aisha.
Ieachia, Ieaisha, Ieasha, Ieashe, Ieesha, Ieeshia, Ieisha, Ieishia, Iescha, Ieshah, Ieshea, Iesheia, Ieshia, Iiesha, Iisha

IGNACIA (Latin) fiery, ardent. A feminine form of Ignatius.
Ignacie, Ignasha, Ignashia, Ignatia, Ignatzia

IKIA (Hebrew) God is my salvation. (Hawaiian) a feminine form of Isaiah.
Ikaisha, Ikea, Ikeea, Ikeia, Ikeisha, Ikeishi, Ikeishia, Ikesha, Ikeshia, Ikeya, Ikeyia, Ikiea, Ikiia

ILA (Hungarian) a form of Helen.

ILANA (Hebrew) tree.
Ilaina, Ilane, Ilani, Ilania, Ilainie, Illana, Illane, Illani, Ilania, Illanie, Ilanit

ILEANA (Hebrew) an alternate form of Iliana.
Ilea, Ileah, Ileane, Ileanna, Ileanne, Illeana

ILENA (Greek) an alternate form of Helena.
Ileana, Ileena, Ileina, Ilina, Ilyna

ILENE (Irish) a form of Helen. See also Aileen, Eileen.
Ileen, Ileene, Iline, Ilyne

ILIANA (Greek) from Troy.
Ileana, Ili, Ilia, Iliani, Illiana, Illiani, Illianna, Illyana, Illyanna

ILIMA (Hawaiian) flower of Oahu.

ILISA (Scottish, English) an alternate form of Alisa, Elisa.
Ilicia, Ilissa, Iliza, Illisa, Illissa, Illysa, Illyssa, Ilycia, Ilysa, Ilysia, Ilyssa, Ilyza

ILISE (German) a form of Elise.
Ilese, Illytse, Ilyce, Ilyse

ILISHA (Hebrew) an alternate form of Alisha, Elisha. See also Lisha.
Ileshia, Ilishia, Ilysha, Ilyshia

ILKA (Hungarian) a familiar form of Ilona.
Ilke, Milka, Milke

ILONA (Hungarian) a form of Helen.
Ilka, Illona, Illonia, Illonya, Ilonka, Ilyona

ILSE (German) a form of Elizabeth. See also Elsa.
Ilsa, Ilsey, Ilsie, Ilsy

IMA (German) a familiar form of Amelia. (Japanese) presently.

IMALA (Native American) strong minded.

IMAN (Arabic) believer.
Aman, Imana, Imane, Imani

IMANI (Arabic) an alternate form of Iman.
Amani, Emani, Imahni, Imanie, Imanii, Imonee, Imoni

IMELDA (German) warrior.
Imalda, Irmhilde, Melda

IMENA (African) dream.
Imee, Imene

IMOGENE (Latin) image, likeness.
Emogen, Emogene, Imogen, Imogenia, Imojean, Imojeen, Innogen, Innogene

INA (Irish) a form of Agnes.
Ena, Inanna, Inanne

INDIA (Hindi) from India.
Indea, Indeah, Indee, Indeia, Indeya, Indi, Indiah, Indian, Indiana, Indianna, Indie, Indieya, Indiya, Indy, Indya

INDIGO (Latin) dark blue color.
Indiga, Indygo

INDIRA (Hindi) splendid. Religion: the god of heaven. History: Indira Nehru Gandi was an Indian politician and prime minister.
Indiara, Indra, Indre, Indria

INES, Inez (Spanish) forms of Agnes. See also Ynez.
Inés, Inesa, Inesita, Inésita, Inessa

INGA (Scandinavian) a short form of Ingrid.
Ingaberg, Ingaborg, Inge, Ingeberg, Ingeborg, Ingela

INGRID (Scandinavian) hero's daughter; beautiful daughter.
Inga, Inger

INOA (Hawaiian) name.

IOANA (Romanian) a form of Joan.
Ioani, Ioanna

IOLA (Greek) dawn; violet colored. (Welsh) worthy of the Lord.
Iole, Iolee, Iolia

IOLANA (Hawaiian) soaring like a hawk.

IOLANTHE (English) a form of Yolanda. See also Jolanda.
Iolanda, Iolande

IONA (Greek) violet flower.
Ione, Ioney, Ioni, Ionia, Iyona, Iyonna

IPHIGENIA (Greek) sacrifice.
Mythology: the daughter of the Greek
leader Agamemnon. See also Gena.

IRENE (Greek) peaceful. Mythology: the
goddess of peace. See also Orina, Rena,
Rene, Yarina.
Irén, Irien, Irina, Jereni

IRINA (Russian) a form of Irene.
*Eirena, Erena, Ira, Irana, Iranda, Iranna,
Irena, Irenea, Irenka, Iriana, Irin, Irinia,
Irinka, Irona, Ironka, Irusya, Iryna, Irynka,
Rina*

IRIS (Greek) rainbow. Mythology: the
goddess of the rainbow and messenger
of the gods.
Irisa, Irisha, Irissa, Irita, Irys, Iryssa

IRMA (Latin) an alternate form of Erma.
Irmina, Irminia

ISABEAU (French) a form of Isabel.

ISABEL (Spanish) consecrated to God.
A form of Elizabeth. See also Bel, Belle,
Chavella, Ysabel.
*Isabal, Isabeau, Isabeli, Isabelita, Isabella,
Isabelle, Ishbel, Isobel, Issie, Izabel, Izabele,
Izabella*

ISABELLA (Italian) a form of Isabel.
Isabela, Isabelia, Isabello

ISABELLE (French) a form of Isabel.
Isabele, Isabell

ISADORA (Latin) gift of Isis.
Isidora

ISELA (Scottish) an alternate form of
Isla.
Isel

ISHA (American) a form of Aisha.
*Ishae, Ishana, Ishanaa, Ishanda, Ishanee,
Ishaney, Ishani, Ishanna, Ishaun, Ishawna,
Ishaya, Ishenda, Ishia, Iysha*

ISHI (Japanese) rock.
Ishiko, Ishiyo, Shiko, Shiyo

ISIS (Egyptian) supreme goddess.
Mythology: the goddess of the moon,
maternity, and fertility.
Icess, Issis, Isys

ISLA (Scottish) Geography: the Isla
River in Scotland.
Isela

ISOBEL (Spanish) an alternate form of
Isabel.
Isobell, Isobella, Isobelle

ISOKA (Benin) gift from god.
Soka

ISOLDE (Welsh) fair lady. Literature: a
princess in the Arthurian legends; a
heroine in the medieval romance *Tristan
and Isolde.* See also Yseult.
Isolda, Isolt, Izolde

ISSIE (Spanish) a familiar form of Isabel.
Isa, Issi, Issy, Iza

ITA (Irish) thirsty.

ITALIA (Italian) from Italy.
Itali, Italie, Italy, Italya

ITAMAR (Hebrew) palm island.
Isamar, Isamari, Isamaria, Ithamar, Ittamar

ITZEL (Spanish) protected.
*Itcel, Itchel, Itesel, Itsel, Itssel, Itza, Itzallana,
Itzayana, Itzell, Ixchel*

IVA (Slavic) a short form of Ivana.
Ivah

IVANA (Slavic) God is gracious. A
feminine form of Ivan. See also
Yvanna.
*Iva, Ivanah, Ivania, Ivanka, Ivanna, Ivannia,
Ivany*

IVEREM (Tiv) good fortune; blessing.

IVETTE (French) an alternate form of Yvette. See also Evette.
Ivet, Ivete, Iveth, Ivetha, Ivett, Ivetta

IVONNE (French) an alternate form of Yvonne. See also Evonne.
Ivon, Ivona, Ivone, Ivonna, Iwona, Iwonka, Iwonna, Iwonne

IVORY (Latin) made of ivory.
Ivoory, Ivori, Ivorie, Ivorine, Ivree

IVRIA (Hebrew) from the land of Abraham.
Ivriah, Ivrit

IVY (English) ivy tree.
Ivey, Ivie

IYABO (Yoruba) mother has returned.

IYANA, Iyanna (Hebrew) alternate forms of Ian.
Iyanah, Iyannah, Iyannia

IZABELLA (Spanish) an alternate form of Isabel.
Izabela, Izabell, Izabellah, Izabelle, Izobella

IZUSA (Native American) white stone.

J

JABREA, Jabria (American) a combination of the prefix Ja + Brea.
Jabreal, Jabree, Jabreea, Jabreena, Jabrelle, Jabreona, Jabri, Jabriah, Jabriana, Jabrie, Jabriel, Jabrielle, Jabrienna, Jabrina

JACALYN (American) a form of Jacqueline.
Jacalynn, Jacolyn, Jacolyne, Jacolynn

JACELYN (American) a form of Jocelyn.
Jaceline, Jacelyne, Jacelynn, Jacilyn, Jacilyne, Jacilynn, Jacylyn, Jacylyne, Jacylynn

JACEY, Jacy (Greek) familiar forms of Jacinda. (American) combinations of the initials J. + C.
Jace, Jac-E, Jacee, Jaci, Jacie, Jacylin, Jaice, Jaicee

JACI, Jacie (Greek) alternate forms of Jacey.
Jacci, Jacia, Jacie, Jaciel, Jaici, Jaicie

JACINDA, Jacinta (Greek) beautiful, attractive. (Spanish) a form of Hyacinth.
Jacenda, Jacenta, Jacey, Jacinthe, Jacintia, Jacynthe, Jakinda, Jaxine

JACINTHE (Spanish) an alternate form of Jacinda.
Jacinte, Jacinth, Jacintha

JACKALYN (American) a form of Jacqueline.
Jackalene, Jackalin, Jackaline, Jackalynn, Jackalynne, Jackelin, Jackeline, Jackelyn, Jackelynn, Jackelynne, Jackilin, Jackilyn, Jackilynn, Jackilynne, Jackolin, Jackoline, Jackolyn, Jackolynn, Jackolynne

JACKELINE, Jackelyn (American) forms of Jacqueline.
Jackelin, Jackelline, Jackellyn, Jockeline

JACKI, Jackie (American) familiar forms of Jacqueline.
Jackee, Jackey, Jackia, Jackielee, Jacky, Jackye

JACKLYN (American) a short form of Jacqueline.
Jacklin, Jackline, Jacklyne, Jacklynn, Jacklynne

JACKQUEL (French) an alternate form of Jacqueline.
Jackqueline, Jackquetta, Jackquiline, Jackquilyn, Jackquilynn, Jackquilynne

JACLYN (American) a short form of Jacqueline.
Jacleen, Jaclin, Jacline, Jaclyne, Jaclynn

JACOBI (Hebrew) supplanter, substitute. A feminine form of Jacob.
Coby, Jacoba, Jacobee, Jacobette, Jacobia, Jacobina, Jacoby, Jacolbi, Jacolbia, Jacolby

JACQUALINE (French) an alternate form of Jacqueline.
Jacqualin, Jacqualine, Jacqualyn, Jacqualyne, Jacqualynn

JACQUELIN (French) an alternate form of Jacqueline.
Jacquelina

JACQUELINE (French) supplanter, substitute; little Jacqui. A feminine form of Jacques.
Jacalyn, Jackalyn, Jackeline, Jacki, Jacklyn, Jackquel, Jaclyn, Jacqueena, Jacqueine, Jacquel, Jacqueleen, Jacquelene, Jacquelin, Jacquelyn, Jacquelynn, Jacquena, Jacquene, Jacquenetta, Jacquenette, Jacqui, Jacquiline, Jacquine, Jakelin, Jaquelin, Jaqueline, Jaquelyn, Jocqueline

JACQUELYN, Jacquelynn (French) alternate forms of Jacqueline.
Jackquelyn, Jackquelynn, Jacquelyne, Jacquelynne,

JACQUI (French) a short form of Jacqueline.
Jacquay, Jacqué, Jacquee, Jacqueta, Jacquete, Jacquetta, Jacquette, Jacquie, Jacquise, Jacquita, Jaquay, Jaqui, Jaquie, Jaquiese, Jaquina, Jaquita

JACQULIN, Jacqulyn (American) forms of Jacqueline.
Jackquilin, Jacqul, Jacqulin, Jacqulyne, Jacqulynn, Jacqulynne, Jacquoline

JACQUILINE (French) an alternate form of Jacqueline.
Jacquil, Jacquilin, Jacquilyn, Jacquilyne, Jacquilynn

JACYNTHE (Spanish) an alternate form of Jacinda.
Jacynda, Jacynta, Jacynth, Jacyntha

JADA (Spanish) an alternate form of Jade.
Jadah, Jadda, Jadae, Jadzia, Jadziah, Jaeda, Jaedra, Jayda

JADE (Spanish) jade.
Jada, Jadea, Jadeann, Jadee, Jaden, Jadera, Jadi, Jadie, Jadienne, Jady, Jadyn, Jaedra, Jaida, Jaide, Jaiden, Jayde, Jayden

JADELYN (American) a combination of Jade + Lynn.
Jadalyn, Jadelaine, Jadeline, Jadelyne, Jadelynn, Jadielyn

JADEN (Spanish) an alternate form of Jade.
Jadeen, Jadena, Jadene, Jadeyn, Jadin, Jadine, Jaeden, Jaedine

JADYN (Spanish) an alternate form of Jade.
Jadynn, Jaedyn, Jaedynn

JAE (Latin) jaybird. (French) a familiar form of Jacqueline.
Jaea, Jaey, Jaya

JAEL (Hebrew) mountain goat; climber. See also Yael.
Jaela, Jaelee, Jaeli, Jaelie, Jaelle, Jahla, Jahlea

JAELYN, Jaelynn (American) a combination of Jae + Lynn.
Jaeleen, Jaelin, Jaelinn, Jaelyn, Jailyn, Jalyn, Jalynn, Jayleen, Jaylyn, Jaylynn, Jaylynne

JAFFA (Hebrew) an alternate form of Yaffa.
Jaffice, Jaffit, Jafit, Jafra

JAHA (Swahili) dignified.
Jahaida, Jahaira, Jaharra, Jahayra, Jahida, Jahira, Jahitza

JAI (Tai) heart.

JAIDA, Jaide (Spanish) alternate forms of Jade.
Jaidah, Jaidan

JAIDEN, Jaidyn (Spanish) alternate forms of Jade.
Jaidey, Jaidi, Jaidin, Jaidon

JAILYN (American) an alternate form of Jaelyn.
Jaileen, Jailen, Jailene, Jailin, Jailine

JAIME (French) I love.
Jaima, Jaimee, Jaimey, Jaimie, Jaimini, Jaimme, Jaimy, Jamee

JAIMEE (French) an alternate form of Jaime.

JAIMIE (French) an alternate form of Jaime.
Jaimi, Jaimmie

JAIRA (Spanish) Jehovah teaches.
Jairah, Jairy

JAKEISHA (American) a combination of Jakki + Aisha.
Jakeisia, Jakesha, Jakisha

JAKELIN (American) a form of Jacqueline.
Jakeline, Jakelyn, Jakelynn, Jakelynne

JAKKI (American) an alternate form of Jacki, Jackie.
Jakala, Jakea, Jakeela, Jakeida, Jakeita, Jakela, Jakelia, Jakell, Jakena, Jaketta, Jakevia, Jaki, Jakia, Jakiah, Jakira, Jakita, Jakiya, Jakiyah, Jakke, Jakkia

JALEESA (American) an alternate form of Jalisa.
Jaleasa, Jalece, Jalecea, Jaleesah, Jaleese, Jaleesia, Jaleisa, Jaleisha, Jaleisya

JALENA (American) a combination of Jane + Lena.
Jalaina, Jalana, Jalani, Jalanie, Jalayna, Jalean, Jaleen, Jaleena, Jaleene, Jalen, Jalene, Jalina, Jaline, Jallena, Jalyna, Jelayna, Jelena, Jelina, Jelyna

JALESA, Jalessa (American) alternate forms of Jalisa.
Jalese, Jalesha, Jaleshia, Jalesia

JALIA, Jalea (American) combination of Jae + Leah.
Jaleah, Jalee, Jaleea, Jaleeya, Jaleia, Jalitza

JALILA (Arabic) great.
Jalile

JALISA, Jalissa (American) combinations of Jae + Lisa.
Jaleesa, Jalesa, Jalise, Jalisha, Jalisia, Jalysa

JALYN, Jalynn (American) combinations of Jae + Lynn. See also Jaylyn.
Jaelin, Jaeline, Jaelyn, Jaelyne, Jaelynn, Jaelynne, Jalin, Jaline, Jalyne, Jalynne

JALYSA (American) an alternate form of Jalisa.
Jalyse, Jalyssa, Jalyssia

JAMAICA (Spanish) Geography: an island in the Caribbean.
Jameca, Jamecia, Jameica, Jameika, Jameka, Jamica, Jamika, Jamoka, Jemaica, Jemika, Jemyka

JAMANI (American) a form of Jami.
Jamana

JAMARIA (American) combinations of Jae + Maria.
Jamar, Jamara, Jamarea, Jamaree, Jamari, Jamarie, Jameira, Jamerial, Jamira

JAMECIA (Spanish) an alternate form of Jamaica.

JAMEE (French) an alternate form of Jaime.

JAMEIKA, Jameka (Spanish) alternate forms of Jamaica.
Jamaika, Jamaka, Jamecka, Jamekia, Jamekka

JAMESHA (American) a form of Jami.
Jameisha, Jamese, Jameshia, Jameshyia, Jamesia, Jamesica, Jamesika, Jamesina, Jamessa, Jameta, Jametta, Jamiesha, Jamisha, Jammesha, Jammisha

JAMEY (English) an alternate form of Jami, Jamie.

JAMI, Jamie (Hebrew) supplanter, substitute. (English) feminine forms of James.
Jama, Jamani, Jamay, Jamesha, Jamey, Jamia, Jamii, Jamis, Jamise, Jammie, Jamy, Jamye, Jayme, Jaymee, Jaymie

JAMIA (English) an alternate form of Jami, Jamie.
Jamea, Jamiah, Jamiea, Jamiya, Jamiyah, Jamya, Jamyah

JAMICA (Spanish) an alternate form of Jamaica.
Jamika

JAMILA (Arabic) beautiful. See also Yamila.
Jahmela, Jahmelia, Jahmil, Jahmilla, Jameela, Jameelah, Jameeliah, Jameila, Jamela, Jamelia, Jameliah, Jamell, Jamella, Jamelle, Jamely, Jamelya, Jamiela, Jamielee, Jamilah, Jamilee, Jamilia, Jamiliah, Jamilla, Jamillah, Jamille, Jamillia, Jamilya, Jamyla, Jemeela, Jemelia, Jemila, Jemilla

JAMILYNN (English) a combination of Jami + Lynn.
Jamielin, Jamieline, Jamielyn, Jamielyne, Jamielynn, Jamielynne, Jamilin, Jamiline, Jamilyn, Jamilyne, Jamilynne

JAMMIE (American) a form of Jami.
Jammi, Jammice, Jammise

JAMONICA (American) a combination of Jamie + Monica.
Jamoni

JAMYLIN (American) a form of Jamilynn.
Jamylin, Jamyline, Jamylyn, Jamylyne, Jamylynn, Jamylynne, Jaymylin, Jaymyline, Jaymylyn, Jaymylyne, Jaymylynn, Jaymylynne

JAN (English) a short form of Jane, Janet, Janice.
Jania, Jandy

JANA (Slavic) a form of Jane. See also Yana.
Janalee, Janalisa, Janna, Janne

JANAE, Janay (American) forms of Jane.
Janaé, Janaea, Janaeh, Janah, Janai, Janaya, Janaye, Janea, Janee, Janée, Jannae, Jannay, Jenae, Jenay, Jenaya, Jennae, Jennay, Jennaya, Jennaye

JANAI (American) an alternate form of Janae.
Janaiah, Janaira, Janaiya

JANALYNN (American) a combination of Jana + Lynn.
Janalin, Janaline, Janalyn, Janalyne, Janalynne

JANAN (Arabic) heart; soul.
Jananee, Janani, Jananie, Janann, Jananni

JANE (Hebrew) God is gracious. A feminine form of John. See also Chavon, Jean, Joan, Juanita, Seana, Shana, Shawna, Sheena, Shona, Shunta, Sinead, Zaneta, Zanna, Zhana.
Jaine, Jan, Jana, Janae, Janay, Janelle, Janessa, Janet, Jania, Janice, Janie, Janika, Janine, Janis, Janka, Jannie, Jasia, Jayna, Jayne, Jenica

JANEL, Janell (French) alternate forms of Janelle.
Janiel, Jannel, Jannell, Janyll, Jaynel, Jaynell

JANELLE (French) a form of Jane.
Janel, Janela, Janele, Janelis, Janell, Janella, Janelli, Janellie, Janelly, Janely, Janelys, Janielle, Janille, Jannelle, Jannellies, Jaynelle

JANESHA (American) an alternate form of Janessa.
Janeisha, Janeshia, Janiesha, Janisha, Janishia, Jannesha, Jannisha, Janysha, Jenesha, Jenisha, Jennisha

JANESSA (American) a form of Jane.
Janeesa, Janesa, Janesea, Janesha, Janesia, Janeska, Janessi, Janessia, Janiesa, Janissa,

*Jannesa, Jannessa, Jannisa, Jannissa,
Janyssa, Jenesa, Jenessa, Jenissa, Jennisa,
Jennissa*

JANET (English) a form of Jane. See also
Jessie, Yanet.
*Jan, Janeta, Janete, Janeth, Janett, Janette,
Jannet, Janot, Jante, Janyte*

JANETH (English) an alternate form of
Janet.
Janetha, Janith, Janneth

JANETTE, Jannette (French) forms of
Janet.
Janett, Janetta, Jannett, Jannetta

JANICE (Hebrew) God is gracious.
(English) a familiar form of Jane. See
also Genice.
*Jan, Janece, Janecia, Janeice, Janiece,
Janizzette, Jannice, Janniece, Janyce, Jenice,
Jhanice, Jynice*

JANIE (English) a familiar form of Jane.
Janey, Jani, Janiyh, Jannie, Janny, Jany

JANIKA (Slavic) a form of Jane.
*Janaca, Janeca, Janecka, Janeika, Janeka,
Janica, Janick, Janicka, Janieka, Janikka,
Janikke, Janique, Janka, Jankia, Jannica,
Jannick, Jannika, Janyca, Jenica, Jenicka,
Jenika, Jeniqua, Jenique, Jennica, Jennika,
Jonika*

JANINE (French) a form of Jane.
*Janean, Janeann, Janeanne, Janeen,
Janenan, Janene, Janina, Jannen, Jannina,
Jannine, Jannyne, Janyne, Jeannine, Jeneen,
Jenine*

JANIS (English) a form of Jane.
*Janees, Janese, Janesey, Janess, Janesse,
Janise, Jannis, Jannise, Janys, Jenesse, Jenis,
Jennise, Jennisse*

JANITA (American) a form of Juanita.
See also Genita.
*Janitra, Janitza, Janneta, Jaynita, Jenita,
Jennita*

JANNA (Hebrew) a short form of
Johana. (Arabic) harvest of fruit.
Janaya, Janaye, Jannae, Jannah, Jannai

JANNIE (English) a familiar form of Jan,
Jane.
Janney, Janny

JAQUANA (American) a combination
of Jacqueline + Anna.
*Jaqua, Jaquai, Jaquanda, Jaquania,
Jaquanna*

JAQUELEN (American) a form of
Jacqueline.
Jaquala, Jaquera, Jaqulene, Jaquonna

JAQUELIN, Jaqueline (French)
alternate forms of Jacqueline.
*Jaqualin, Jaqualine, Jaquelina, Jaquline,
Jaquella*

JAQUELYN (French) an alternate form
of Jacqueline.
Jaquelyne, Jaquelynn, Jaquelynne

JARDENA (Hebrew) an alternate form
of Jordan. (French, Spanish) garden.
*Jardan, Jardana, Jardane, Jarden, Jardenia,
Jardin, Jardine, Jardyn, Jardyne*

JARIAN (American) a combination of
Jane + Marian.

JARITA (Arabic) earthen water jug.
*Jara, Jaretta, Jari, Jaria, Jarica, Jarida,
Jarietta, Jarika, Jarina, Jaritta, Jaritza,
Jarixa, Jarnita, Jarrika, Jarrine*

JAS (American) a short form of Jasmine.
Jase, Jass, Jaz, Jazz, Jazze, Jazzi

JASIA (Polish) a form of Jane.
*Jaisha, Jasa, Jasea, Jasha, Jashae, Jashala,
Jashona, Jashonte, Jasie, Jassie, Jaysa*

JASLEEN, Jaslyn (Latin) alternate
forms of Jocelyn.
*Jaslene, Jaslien, Jaslin, Jasline, Jaslynn,
Jaslynne*

JASMAIN (Persian) an alternate form of Jasmine.
Jasmaine, Jasmane, Jassmain, Jassmaine

JASMARIE (American) a combination of Jasmine + Marie.
Jasmari

JASMIN (Persian) an alternate form of Jasmine.
Jasimin, Jasman, Jasmeen, Jasmen, Jasmon, Jassmin, Jassminn

JASMINE (Persian) jasmine flower. See also Jessamine, Yasmin.
Jas, Jasma, Jasmain, Jasme, Jasmeet, Jasmene, Jasmin, Jasmina, Jasminne, Jasmira, Jasmit, Jasmyn, Jassma, Jassmin, Jassmine, Jassmit, Jassmon, Jassmyn, Jazmin, Jazmyn, Jazzmin

JASMYN, Jasmyne (Persian) alternate forms of Jasmine.
Jasmynn, Jasmynne, Jassmyn

JASPREET (Punjabi) virtuous.
Jaspar, Jasparit, Jasparita, Jasper, Jasprit, Jasprita, Jasprite

JATARA (American) a combination of Jane + Tara.
Jataria, Jatarra, Jatori, Jatoria

JAVANA (Malayan) from Java.
Javanna, Javanne, Javona, Javonna, Jawana, Jawanna, Jawn

JAVIERA (Spanish) owner of a new house. A feminine form of Javier. See also Xaviera.
Javeera, Viera

JAVONA, Javonna (Malayan) alternate forms of Javana.
Javon, Javonda, Javone, Javoni, Javonne, Javonni, Javonya

JAYA (Hindi) victory.
Jaea, Jaia

JAYCEE (American) a combination of the initials J. + C.

Jacee, Jacey, Jaci, Jacie, Jacy, Jayce, Jaycey, Jayci, Jaycie, Jaycy

JAYDA (Spanish) an alternate form of Jada.
Jaydah, Jeyda

JAYDE (Spanish) an alternate form of Jade.
Jayd

JAYDEE (American) a combination of the initials J. + D.
Jadee, Jadey, Jadi, Jadie, Jady, Jaydey, Jaydi, Jaydie, Jaydy

JAYDEN (Spanish) an alternate form of Jade.
Jaydeen, Jaydene, Jaydin, Jaydn, Jaydon

JAYE (Latin) jaybird.
Jae, Jay

JAYLA (American) a short form of Jaylene.
Jaylaa, Jaylah, Jayli, Jaylia, Jayliah, Jaylie

JAYLENE (American) an alternate form of Jaylyn.
Jayelene, Jayla, Jaylan, Jayleana, Jaylee, Jayleen, Jayleene, Jaylen, Jaylenne

JAYLIN (American) an alternate form of Jaylyn.
Jayline, Jaylinn

JAYLYN, Jaylynn (American) combinations of Jaye + Lynn. See also Jalyn.
Jaylene, Jaylin, Jaylyne, Jaylynne

JAYME, Jaymie (English) alternate forms of Jami.
Jaymi, Jaymia, Jaymine, Jaymini

JAYMEE, Jaymi (English) alternate forms of Jami.

JAYNA (Hebrew) an alternate form of Jane.
Jaynae, Jaynah, Jaynna

JAYNE (Hindi) victorious. (English) a form of Jane.
Jayn, Jaynie, Jaynne

JAYNIE (English) a familiar form of Jayne.
Jaynee, Jayni

JAZLYN (American) a combination of Jazmin + Lynn.
Jasleen, Jazaline, Jazalyn, Jazleen, Jazlene, Jazlin, Jazline, Jazlon, Jazlynn, Jazlynne, Jazzalyn, Jazzleen, Jazzlene, Jazzlin, Jazzline, Jazzlyn, Jazzlynn, Jazzlynne

JAZMIN, Jazmine (Persian) alternate forms of Jasmine.
Jazmaine, Jazman, Jazmen, Jazminn, Jazmon, Jazzmit

JAZMYN, Jazmyne (Persian) alternate forms of Jasmine.
Jazmynn, Jazmynne, Jazzmyn, Jazzmyne

JAZZMIN, Jazzmine (Persian) alternate forms of Jasmine.
Jazzman, Jazzmeen, Jazzmen, Jazzmene, Jazzmenn, Jazzmon

JEAN, Jeanne (Scottish) God is gracious. Forms of Jane, Joan. See also Kini.
Jeana, Jeanann, Jeancie, Jeane, Jeaneia, Jeanette, Jeaneva, Jeanice, Jeanie, Jeanine, Jeanmaria, Jeanmarie, Jeanna, Jeanné, Jeannie, Jeannita, Jeannot, Jeantelle

JEANA, Jeanna (Scottish) alternate forms of Jean.
Jeanae, Jeannae, Jeannia

JEANETTE, Jeannett (French) forms of Jean.
Jeanet, Jeanete, Jeanett, Jeanetta, Jeanita, Jeannete, Jeannetta, Jeannette, Jeannita, Jenet, Jenett, Jenette, Jennet, Jennett, Jennetta, Jennette, Jennita, Jinetta, Jinette

JEANIE, Jeannie (Scottish) a familiar form of Jean.
Jeannee, Jeanney, Jeani, Jeanny, Jeany

JEANINE, Jenine (Scottish) alternate forms of Jean. See also Geneen.
Jeaneane, Jeaneen, Jeanene, Jeanina, Jeannina, Jeannine, Jennine

JELENA (Russian) a form of Helen. See also Yelena.
Jalaine, Jalane, Jalani, Jalanna, Jalayna, Jalayne, Jaleen, Jaleena, Jaleene, Jalena, Jalene, Jelaina, Jelaine, Jelana, Jelane, Jelani, Jelanni, Jelayna, Jelayne, Jelean, Jeleana, Jeleen, Jeleena, Jelene

JELISA (American) a combination of Jean + Lisa.
Jalissa, Jelesha, Jelessa, Jelise, Jelissa, Jellese, Jellice, Jelysa, Jelyssa, Jillisa, Jillissa, Julissa

JEM (Hebrew) a short form of Jemima.
Gem, Jemi, Jemia, Jemiah, Jemie, Jemm, Jemmi, Jemmy

JEMIMA (Hebrew) dove.
Jamim, Jamima, Jem, Jemimah, Jemma

JEMMA (Hebrew) a short form of Jemima. (English) a form of Gemma.
Jemmia, Jemmiah, Jemmie, Jemmy

JENA, Jenae (Arabic) alternate forms of Jenna.
Jenah, Jenai, Jenal, Jenay, Jenaya, Jenea

JENDAYA (Zimbabwean) thankful.
Daya, Jenda, Jendayah

JENELLE (American) a combination of Jenny + Nell.
Genell, Jeanell, Jeanelle, Jenall, Jenalle, Jenel, Jenela, Jenele, Jenell, Jenella, Jenille, Jennel, Jennell, Jennella, Jennelle, Jennielle, Jennille, Jinelle, Jinnell

JENESSA (American) an alternate form of Jenisa.
Jenesa, Jenese, Jenesia, Jenessia, Jennesa, Jennese, Jennessa, Jinessa

JENICA (Romanian) a form of Jane.
Jeneca, Jenika, Jenikka, Jennica, Jennika

JENIFER, Jeniffer (Welsh) alternate forms of Jennifer.
Jenefer

JENILEE (American) a combination of Jennifer + Lee.
Jenalea, Jenalee, Jenaleigh, Jenaly, Jenelea, Jenelee, Jeneleigh, Jenely, Jenelly, Jenileigh, Jenily, Jennalee, Jennely, Jennielee, Jennilea, Jennilee, Jennilie

JENISA (American) a combination of Jennifer + Nisa.
Jenessa, Jenisha, Jenissa, Jenisse, Jennisa, Jennise, Jennisha, Jennissa, Jennisse, Jennysa, Jennyssa, Jenysa, Jenyse, Jenyssa, Jenysse

JENKA (Czech) a form of Jane.

JENNA (Arabic) small bird. (Welsh) a short form of Jennifer. See also Gen.
Jena, Jennae, Jennah, Jennai, Jennat, Jennay, Jennaya, Jennaye, Jhenna

JENNI, Jennie (Welsh) familiar forms of Jennifer.
Jeni, Jenne, Jenné, Jennee, Jenney, Jennia, Jennier, Jennita, Jennora, Jensine

JENNIFER (Welsh) white wave; white phantom. An alternate form of Guinevere. See also Gennifer, Ginnifer, Yenifer.
Jen, Jenifer, Jeniffer, Jenipher, Jenna, Jennafer, Jenni, Jenniferanne, Jenniferlee, Jenniffe, Jenniffer, Jenniffier, Jennifier, Jennilee, Jenniphe, Jennipher, Jenny, Jennyfer

JENNILEE (American) a combination of Jenny + Lee.
Jennalea, Jennalee, Jennielee, Jennilea, Jennilie, Jinnalee

JENNILYN, Jennilynn (American) a combination of Jenni + Lynn.
Jennalin, Jennaline, Jennalyn, Jenalynann, Jenelyn, Jenilyn, Jennalyne, Jennalynn, Jennalynne, Jennilin, Jenniline, Jennilyne, Jennilynne

JENNY (Welsh) a familiar form of Jennifer.
Jenney, Jenni, Jennie, Jeny, Jinny

JENNYFER (Welsh) an alternate form of Jennifer.
Jenyfer

JERALDINE (English) a form of Geraldine.
Jeraldeen, Jeraldene, Jeraldina, Jeraldyne, Jeralee, Jeri

JERENI (Russian) a form of Irene.
Jerena, Jerenae, Jerina

JERI, Jerri, Jerrie (American) short forms of Jeraldine. See also Geri.
Jera, Jerae, JeRae, Jeree, Jeriel, Jerilee, Jerinda, Jerra, Jerrah, Jerrece, Jerree, Jerriann, Jerrilee, Jerrine, Jerry, Jerrylee, Jerryne, Jerzy

JERICA (American) a combination of Jeri + Erica.
Jereca, Jerecka, Jerice, Jericka, Jerika, Jerrica, Jerrice, Jeryka

JERILYN (American) a combination of Jeri + Lynn.
Jeralin, Jeraline, Jeralyn, Jeralyne, Jeralynn, Jeralynne, Jerelin, Jereline, Jerelyn, Jerelyne, Jerelynn, Jerelynne, Jerilin, Jeriline, Jerilyne, Jerilynn, Jerilynne, Jerrilin, Jerriline, Jerrilyn, Jerrilyne, Jerrilynn, Jerrilynne, Jerrylea

JERMAINE (French) an alternate form of Germaine.
Jermain, Jerman, Jermanay, Jermanaye, Jermane, Jermanee, Jermani, Jermanique, Jermany, Jermayne, Jermecia, Jermia, Jermice, Jermicia, Jermika, Jermila

JERRICA (American) an alternate form of Jerica.
Jerreka, Jerricah, Jerricca, Jerricha, Jerricka, Jerrieka, Jerrika

JERUSHA (Hebrew) inheritance.
Jerushah, Yerusha

JESENIA, Jessenia (Arabic) flower.
Jescenia, Jessennia, Jessenya

JESICA, Jesika (Hebrew) alternate
forms of Jessica.
Jesicca, Jesikah, Jesikkah

JESSA (American) a short form of
Jessalyn, Jessamine, Jessica.
Jesa, Jesha, Jessah

JESSALYN (American) a combination
of Jessica + Lynn.
*Jesalin, Jesaline, Jesalyn, Jesalyne, Jesalynn,
Jesalynne, Jesilin, Jesiline, Jesilyn, Jesilyne,
Jesilynn, Jesilynne, Jessa, Jessalin, Jessaline,
Jessalyne, Jessalynn, Jessalynne, Jesselin,
Jesseline, Jesselyn, Jesselyne, Jesselynn,
Jesselynne, Jesslyn*

JESSAMINE (French) a form of
Jasmine.
*Jessa, Jessamin, Jessamon, Jessamy,
Jessamyn, Jessemin, Jessemine, Jessimin,
Jessimine, Jessmin, Jessmine, Jessmon,
Jessmy, Jessmyn*

JESSE, Jessi (Hebrew) alternate forms
of Jessie.
Jese, Jesi, Jesie

JESSECA (Hebrew) an alternate form of
Jessica.
Jesseeca, Jesseeka

JESSICA (Hebrew) wealthy. A feminine
form of Jesse. Literature: a name
perhaps invented by Shakespeare for
a character in his play *The Merchant
of Venice*. See also Gessica, Yessica.
*Jesica, Jesika, Jessa, Jessaca, Jessca, Jesscia,
Jesseca, Jessia, Jessicah, Jessicca, Jessicia,
Jessicka, Jessie, Jessika, Jessiqua, Jessy,
Jessyca, Jessyka, Jezeca, Jezica, Jezika, Jezyca*

JESSIE, Jessy (Hebrew) short forms of
Jessica. (Scottish) forms of Janet.
*Jescie, Jesey, Jess, Jesse, Jessé, Jessee, Jessey,
Jessi, Jessia, Jessiya, Jessye*

JESSIKA (Hebrew) an alternate form of
Jessica.
Jessieka

JESSLYN (American) an alternate form
of Jessalyn.
Jessilyn, Jessilynn, Jesslin, Jesslynn, Jesslynne

JESSYCA, Jessyka (Hebrew) alternate
forms of Jessica.

JÉSUSA (Hebrew) God is my salvation.
(Spanish) a feminine form of Jésus.

JETTA (English) jet black gem.
(American) a familiar form of Jevette.
Jeta, Jetia, Jetje, Jette, Jettie

JEVETTE (American) a combination of
Jean + Yvette.
Jetta, Jeva, Jeveta, Jevetta

JEWEL (French) precious gem.
*Jewelann, Jewelia, Jeweliana, Jeweliann,
Jewelie, Jewell, Jewelle, Jewellee, Jewellene,
Jewellie, Juel, Jule*

JEZEBEL (Hebrew) unexalted; impure.
Bible: the wife of King Ahab.
*Jesibel, Jessabel, Jessebel, Jez, Jezabel,
Jezabella, Jezabelle, Jezebell, Jezebella,
Jezebelle*

JIANNA (Italian) an alternate form of
Gianna.
Jiana, Jianina, Jianine, Jianni, Jiannini

JIBON (Hindi) life.

JILL (English) a short form of Jillian.
Jil, Jilli, Jillie, Jilly

JILLAINE (Latin) an alternate form of
Jillian.
*Jilaine, Jilane, Jilayne, Jillana, Jillane, Jillann,
Jillanne, Jillayne*

JILLEEN (Irish) a form of Jillian.
*Jileen, Jilene, Jiline, Jillene, Jillenne, Jilline,
Jillyn*

JILLIAN (Latin) youthful. An alternate
form of Julia. See also Gillian.
*Jilian, Jiliana, Jiliann, Jilianna, Jilianne,
Jilienna, Jilienne, Jill, Jillaine, Jilliana,
Jilliane, Jilliann, Jillianne, Jileen, Jillien,
Jillienne, Jillion, Jilliyn*

JIMI (Hebrew) supplanter, substitute.
(American) a feminine form of Jimmy.
*Jimae, Jimaria, Jimee, Jimella, Jimena, Jimia,
Jimiah, Jimie, Jimiyah, Jimmeka, Jimmet,
Jimmi, Jimmia, Jimmie*

JIMISHA (American) a combination of
Jimi + Aisha.
Jimica, Jimicia, Jimmicia, Jimysha

JIN (Japanese) tender. (American) a
short form of Ginny, Jinny.

JINA (Italian) an alternate form of Gina.
(Swahili) baby with a name.
Jena, Jinae, Jinan, Jinda, Jinna, Jinnae

JINNY (Scottish) a familiar form of
Jenny. (American) a familiar form
of Virginia. See also Ginny.
Jin, Jinnee, Jinney, Jinni, Jinnie

JIRINA (Czech) a form of Georgia.
Jirah, Jireh

JIZELLE (American) a form of Giselle.
*Jessel, Jezel, Jezell, Jezella, Jezelle, Jisel, Jisela,
Jisell, Jisella, Jiselle, Jissel, Jissell, Jissella,
Jisselle, Jizel, Jizella, Joselle*

JO (American) a short form of Joanna,
Jolene, Josephine.
Joangie, Joetta, Joette, Joey

JOAN (Hebrew) God is gracious. An
alternate form of Jane. History: Joan of
Arc was a fifteenth-century heroine
and resistance fighter. See also Ioana,
Jean, Juanita, Siobahn.
*Joane, Joaneil, Joanel, Joanelle, Joanie,
Joanmarie, Joann, Joannanette, Joanne,
Joannel, Joanny, Jonni*

JOANA, Joanna (English) a form of
Joan. See also Yoanna.
*Janka, Jhoana, Jo, Jo-Ana, Joandra, Joanka,
Joananna, Jo-Anie, Joanka, Jo-Anna,
Joannah, Jo-Annie, Joeana, Joeanna, Johana,
Johanna, Johannah*

JOANIE, Joannie (Hebrew) familiar
forms of Joan.
*Joanee, Joani, Joanni, Joenie, Johanie,
Johnnie, Joni*

JOANNE (English) a form of Joan.
*Joanann, Joananne, Joann, Jo-Ann, Jo-Anne,
Joayn, Joeann, Joeanne*

JOANNY (Hebrew) a familiar form of
Joan.
Joany

JOAQUINA (Hebrew) God will
establish.
Joaquine

JOBETH (English) a combination of
Jo + Beth.
Joby

JOBY (Hebrew) afflicted. A feminine
form of Job. (English) a familiar form
of Jobeth.
*Jobey, Jobi, Jobie, Jobina, Jobita, Jobrina,
Jobye, Jobyna*

JOCACIA (American) a combination
of Joy + Acacia.

JOCELIN, Joceline (Latin) alternate
forms of Jocelyn.
Jocelina, Jocelinn

JOCELYN (Latin) joyous. See also
Yocelin, Yoselin.
*Jacelyn, Jasleen, Jocelin, Jocelle, Jocelyne,
Jocelynn, Joci, Jocia, Jocilyn, Jocilynn,
Jocinta, Joclyn, Joclynn, Josalyn, Joscelin,
Joselin, Joselyn, Joshlyn, Josilin, Jossalin,
Josselyn, Joycelyn*

JOCELYNE (Latin) an alternate form
of Jocelyn.
Joceline, Jocelynne, Joclynne

JODI, Jodie, Jody (American) familiar forms of Judith.
Jodee, Jodele, Jodell, Jodelle, Jodevea, Jodey, Jodia, Jodiee, Jodilee, Jodi-Lee, Jodilynn, Jodi-Lynn, Joedi, Joedy

JODIANN (American) a combination of Jodi + Ann.
Jodene, Jodi-Ann, Jodianna, Jodi-Anna, Jodianne, Jodi-Anne, Jodine, Jodyann, Jody-Ann, Jodyanna, Jody-Anna, Jodyanne, Jody-Anne, Jodyne

JOELLE (Hebrew) God is willing. A feminine form of Joel.
Joela, Joele, Joelee, Joeli, Joelia, Joelie, Joell, Joella, Joëlle, Joelli, Joelly, Joely, Joyelle

JOELYNN (American) a combination of Joelle + Lynn.
Joeleen, Joelene, Joeline, Joellen, Joellyn, Joelyn, Joelyne

JOHANA, Johanna, Johannah (German) forms of Joanna. See also Gianna.
Janna, Joahna, Johanah, Johanka, Johanne, Johnna, Johonna, Jonna, Joyhanna, Joyhannah

JOHANIE, Johannie (Hebrew) alternate forms of Joanie.
Johani, Johanni, Johanny, Johany

JOHNNA, Jonna (American) forms of Johana, Joanna.
Jahna, Jahnaya, Jhona, Jhonna, Johna, Johnda, Johnnielynn, Johnnie-Lynn, Johnnquia, Joncie, Jonda, Jondrea, Jontel, Jutta

JOHNNIE (Hebrew) an alternate form of Joanie.
Johni, Johnie, Johnni, Johnny

JOHNNESSA (American) a combination of Johnna + Nessa.
Jahnessa, Johneatha, Johnecia, Johnesha, Johnetra, Johnisha, Johnishi, Johnnise, Jonyssa

JOI (Latin) an alternate form of Joy.
Joia, Joie

JOKLA (Swahili) beautiful robe.

JOLANDA (Greek) an alternate form of Yolanda. See also Iolanthe.
Jola, Jolan, Jolán, Jolande, Jolander, Jolanka, Jolánta, Jolantha, Jolanthe

JOLEEN, Joline (English) alternate forms of Jolene.
Joleena, Joleene, Jolleen, Jollene

JOLENE (Hebrew) God will add, God will increase. (English) a form of Josephine.
Jo, Jolaine, Jolana, Jolane, Jolanna, Jolanne, Jolanta, Jolayne, Jole, Jolean, Joleane, Joleen, Jolena, Joléne, Jolenna, Jolin, Jolina, Jolinda, Joline, Jolinn, Jolinna, Jolleane, Jolleen, Jolline

JOLIE (French) pretty.
Jole, Jolea, Jolee, Joleigh, Joley, Joli, Jolibeth, Jollee, Jollie, Jolly, Joly, Jolye

JOLISA (American) a combination of Jo + Lisa.
Joleesa, Joleisha, Joleishia, Jolieasa, Jolise, Jolisha, Jolisia, Jolissa, Jolysa, Jolyssa, Julissa

JOLYNN (American) a combination of Jo + Lynn.
Jolyn, Jolyne, Jolynne

JONATHA (Hebrew) gift of God. A feminine form of Jonathan.
Johnasha, Johnasia, Jonesha, Jonisha

JONELLE (American) a combination of Joan + Elle.
Jahnel, Jahnell, Jahnelle, Johnel, Johnell, Johnella, Johnelle, Jonel, Jonell, Jonella, Jonyelle, Jynell, Jynelle

JONESHA, Jonisha (American) forms of Jonatha.
Joneisha, Jonesa, Joneshia, Jonessa, Jonisa, Jonishia, Jonneisha, Jonnesha, Jonnessia

JONI (American) a familiar form of Joan.
Jona, Jonae, Jonai, Jonann, Jonati, Joncey, Jonci, Joncie, Jonice, Jonie, Jonilee, Joni-lee, Jonis, Jony

JONIKA (American) a form of Janika.
Johnica, Johnique, Johnquia, Johnnica, Johnnika, Joneeka, Joneika, Jonica, Joniqua, Jonique

JONINA (Hebrew) dove. A feminine form of Jonah. See also Yonina.
Jona, Jonita, Jonnina

JONITA (Hebrew) an alternate form of Jonina. See also Yonita.
Johnetta, Johnette, Johnita, Johnittia, Jonati, Jonetia, Jonetta, Jonette, Jonit, Jonnita, Jonta, Jontae, Jontaé, Jontaya

JONNI, Jonnie (American) familiar forms of Joan.
Jonny

JONQUIL (Latin, English) Botany: an ornamental plant with fragrant yellow flowers.
Jonquelle, Jonquie, Jonquill, Jonquille

JONTEL (American) an alternate form of Johnna.
Jontaya, Jontell, Jontelle, Jontia, Jontila, Jontrice

JORA (Hebrew) autumn rain.
Jorah

JORDAN (Hebrew) descending. See also Jardena.
Jordain, Jordaine, Jordana, Jordane, Jordann, Jordanna, Jordanne, Jordany, Jordea, Jordee, Jorden, Jordi, Jordian, Jordie, Jordin, Jordon, Jordyn, Jori, Jorie, Jourdan

JORDANA, Jordanna (Hebrew) alternate forms of Jordan. See also Giordana, Yordana.
Jordannah, Jordina, Jordonna, Jourdana, Jourdanna

JORDEN, Jordin, Jordon (Hebrew) alternate forms of Jordan.
Jordenne, Jordine

JORDYN (Hebrew) an alternate form of Jordan.
Jordyne, Jordynn, Jordynne

JORI, Jorie (Hebrew) familiar forms of Jordan.
Jorai, Jorea, Joree, Jorée, Jorey, Jorian, Jorin, Jorina, Jorine, Jorita, Jorre, Jorrey, Jorri, Jorrian, Jorrie, Jorry, Jory

JORIANN (American) a combination of Jori + Ann.
Jori-Ann, Jorianna, Jori-Anna, Jorianne, Jori-Anne, Jorriann, Jorrianna, Jorrianne, Jorryann, Jorryanna, Jorryanne, Joryann, Joryanna, Joryanne

JORJA (American) a form of Georgia.
Jeorgi, Jeorgia, Jorgana, Jorgi, Jorgia, Jorgina, Jorjana, Jorji

JOSALYN (Latin) an alternate form of Jocelyn.
Josalene, Josalin, Josalind, Josaline, Josalynn, Joshalyne

JOSCELIN, Joscelyn (Latin) alternate forms of Jocelyn.
Josceline, Joscelyne, Joscelynn, Joscelynne, Joselin, Joseline, Joselyn, Joselyne, Joselynn, Joselynne, Joshlyn

JOSEE, Josée (American) familiar forms of Josephine.
Joesee, Josey, Josi, Josina, Josy, Jozee

JOSEFINA (Spanish) a form of Josephine.
Josefa, Josefena, Joseffa, Josefine

JOSELIN, Joseline (Latin) alternate forms of Jocelyn.
Joselina, Joselinne, Josielina

JOSELLE (American) an alternate form of Jizelle.
Joesell, Jozelle

JOSELYN, Joslyn (Latin) alternate forms of Jocelyn.
Joselene, Joselyne, Joselynn, Joshely, Josiline, Josilyn

JOSEPHINE (French) God will add, God will increase. A feminine form of Joseph. See also Fifi, Pepita, Yosepha.
Fina, Jo, Joey, Josee, Josée, Josefina, Josepha, Josephe, Josephene, Josephin, Josephina, Josephyna, Josephyne, Josette, Josey, Josie, Jozephine, Jozie, Sefa

JOSETTE (French) a familiar form of Josephine.
Joesette, Josetta, Joshetta, Jozette

JOSEY, Josie (Hebrew) familiar forms of Josephine.
Josi, Josse, Jossee, Jossie, Josy, Josye

JOSHANN (American) a combination of Joshlyn + Ann.
Joshana, Joshanna, Joshanne

JOSHLYN (Latin) an alternate form of Jocelyn. (Hebrew) God is my salvation. A feminine form of Joshua.
Joshalin, Joshalyn, Joshalynn, Joshalynne, Joshelle, Joshleen, Joshlene, Joshlin, Joshline, Joshlyne, Joshlynn, Joshlynne

JOSIANE, Josianne (American) combinations of Josie + Anne.
Josian, Josie-Ann, Josieann

JOSILIN, Joslin (Latin) alternate forms of Jocelyn.
Josielina, Josiline, Josilyn, Josilyne, Josilynn, Josilynne, Joslin, Josline, Joslyn, Joslyne, Joslynn, Joslynne

JOSSALIN (Latin) an alternate form of Jocelyn.
Jossaline, Jossalyn, Jossalynn, Jossalynne, Josselyn, Josslin, Jossline

JOSSELYN (Latin) an alternate form of Jocelyn.
Josselen, Josselin, Josseline, Jossellen, Jossellin, Jossellyn, Josselyne, Josselynn,

Josselynne, Josslyn, Josslyne, Josslynn, Josslynne

JOURDAN (Hebrew) an alternate form of Jordan.
Jourdain, Jourdann, Jourdanne, Jourden, Jourdian, Jourdon, Jourdyn

JOVANA (Latin) an alternate form of Jovanna.
Jeovana, Jouvan, Jovan, Jovanah, Jovena, Jovian, Jowan, Jowana

JOVANNA (Latin) majestic. A feminine form of Jovan. (Italian) an alternate form of Giovanna. Mythology: Jove, also known as Jupiter, was the supreme Roman god.
Jeovanna, Jovado, Joval, Jovana, Jovann, Jovannie, Jovena, Jovina, Jovon, Jovonda, Jovonia, Jovonna, Jovonnah, Jovonne, Jowanna

JOVANNIE (Italian) a familiar form of Jovanna.
Jovanee, Jovani, Jovanie, Jovanne, Jovanni, Jovanny, Jovonnie

JOVITA (Latin) jovial.
Joveda, Joveta, Jovetta, Jovida, Jovitta

JOY (Latin) joyous.
Joe, Joi, Joya, Joye, Joyeeta, Joyella, Joyia, Joyous, Joyvina

JOYANNE (American) a combination of Joy + Anne.
Joyan, Joyann, Joyanna,

JOYCE (Latin) joyous. A short form of Joycelyn.
Joice, Joycey, Joycie, Joyous, Joysel

JOYCELYN (American) a form of Jocelyn.
Joycelin, Joyceline, Joycelyne, Joycelynn, Joycelynne

JOYLYN (American) a combination of Joy + Lynn.
Joyleen, Joylene, Joylin, Joyline, Joylyne, Joylynn, Joy-Lynn, Joylynne

JOZIE (Hebrew) a familiar form of
Josephine.
Jozee, Jozée, Jozi, Jozy

JUANA (Spanish) a short form of
Juanita.
*Juanell, Juaney, Juanika, Juanit, Juanna,
Juannia*

JUANDALYN (Spanish) an alternate
form of Juanita.
*Jualinn, Juandalin, Juandaline, Juandalyne,
Juandalynn, Juandalynne*

JUANITA (Spanish) a form of Jane,
Joan. See also Kwanita, Nita, Waneta,
Wanika.
*Juana, Juandalyn, Juaneice, Juanequa,
Juanesha, Juanice, Juanicia, Juaniqua,
Juanisha, Juanishia*

JUCI (Hungarian) a form of Judy.
Jucika

JUDITH (Hebrew) praised. Mythology:
the slayer of Holofernes, according to
ancient eastern legend. A feminine
form of Judah. See also Yehudit,
Yudita.
*Giuditta, Ioudith, Jodi, Jodie, Jody, Jude,
Judine, Judit, Judita, Judite, Juditha, Judithe,
Judy, Judyta, Jutka*

JUDY (Hebrew) a familiar form of
Judith.
Juci, Judi, Judie, Judye

JUDYANN (American) a combination of
Judy + Ann.
*Judana, Judiann, Judianna, Judianne,
Judyanna, Judyanne*

JULA (Polish) a form of Julia.
Julca, Julcia, Juliska, Julka

JULENE (Basque) a form of Julia. See
also Yulene.
*Julena, Julina, Juline, Julinka, Juliska,
Julleen, Jullena, Jullene, Julyne*

JULIA (Latin) youthful. A feminine form
of Julius. See also Giulia, Jill, Jillian,
Sulia, Yulia.
*Iulia, Jula, Julea, Juleah, Julene, Juliah,
Juliana, Juliann, Julica, Julie, Juliea, Juliet,
Julija, Julina, Juline, Julisa, Julissa, Julita,
Juliya, Julka, Julyssa*

JULIANA (Czech, Spanish), Julianna
(Hungarian) forms of Julia.
*Julieana, Julieanna, Juliena, Julliana,
Jullianna, Julyana, Julyanna, Yuliana*

JULIANN, Julianne (English) forms of
Julia.
*Julean, Juleann, Julian, Juliane, Julieann,
Julie-Ann, Julieanne, Julie-Anne, Julien,
Juliene, Julienn, Julienne, Jullian*

JULIE (English) a form of Julia.
*Juel, Jule, Julee, Juli, Julie-Lynn, Julie-Mae,
Julle, Jullee, Jullie, Jully, July*

JULIET, Juliette (French) forms of Julia.
*Julet, Julieta, Juliett, Julietta, Jullet, Julliet,
Jullietta*

JULISA, Julissa (Latin) alternate forms
of Julia.
Julis, Julisha, Julysa, Julyssa

JULITA (Spanish) a form of Julia.
Julitta, Julyta

JUMARIS (American) a combination of
Julie + Maris.

JUN (Chinese) truthful.

JUNE (Latin) born in the sixth month.
*Juna, Junea, Junel, Junell, Junella, Junelle,
Junette, Juney, Junia, Junie, Juniet, Junieta,
Junietta, Juniette, Junina, Junita*

JUNO (Latin) queen. Mythology: the
goddess of heaven.

JUSTICE (Latin) an alternate form of
Justine.
*Justis, Justise, Justiss, Justisse, Justus, Justyce,
Justys*

JUSTINA (Italian) a form of Justine.
Jestena, Jestina, Justinna, Justyna

JUSTINE (Latin) just, righteous.
A feminine form of Justin.
*Giustina, Jestine, Juste, Justi, Justice, Justie,
Justina, Justinn, Justy, Justyn, Justyne,
Justynn, Justynne*

K

KACEY, Kacy (Irish) brave. (American)
alternate forms of Casey. A
combination of the initials K. + C.
*K. C., Kace, Kacee, Kaci, Kacie, Kaicee,
Kaicey, Kasey, Kasie, Kaycee, Kayci, Kaycie*

KACHINA (Native American) sacred
dancer.
Kachine

KACI, Kacie (American) alternate
forms of Kacey, Kacy.
Kasci, Kaycie, Kaysie

KACIA (Greek) a short form of Acacia.
Kaycia, Kaysia

KADEDRA (American) a combination
of Kady + Dedra.
*Kadeadra, Kadedrah, Kadedria, Kadeedra,
Kadeidra, Kadeidre, Kadeidria*

KADEJAH (Arabic) an alternate form
of Kadijah.
Kadeija, Kadeijah, Kadejá, Kadejia

KADELYN (American) a combination of
Kady + Lynn.

KADESHA (American) a combination
of Kady + Aisha.
*Kadeesha, Kadeeshia, Kadeesia, Kadeesiah,
Kadeezia, Kadesa, Kadesheia, Kadeshia,
Kadesia, Kadessa, Kadezia*

KADIE (English) an alternate form of
Kady.
Kadi, Kadia, Kadiah

KADIJAH (Arabic) trustworthy.
Kadajah, Kadeeja, Kadeejah, Kadija

KADISHA (American) an alternate
form of Kadesha.
*Kadiesha, Kadieshia, Kadishia, Kadisia,
Kadysha, Kadyshia*

KADY (English) an alternate form of
Katy. A combination of the initials
K. + D. See also Cady.
*K. D., Kade, Kadee, Kadey, Kadie, Kadya,
Kadyn, Kaidi, Kaidy, Kayde, Kaydee, Kaydey,
Kaydi, Kaydie, Kaydy*

KAEDÉ (Japanese) maple leaf.

KAELA (Hebrew, Arabic) beloved,
sweetheart. A short form of Kalila,
Kelila.
Kaelah, Kaelea, Kaeleah, Kaelee, Kaeli, Kayla

KAELEE, Kaeli (American) forms of
Kaela.
*Kaelei, Kaeleigh, Kaeley, Kaelia, Kaelie,
Kaelii, Kaelly, Kaely, Kaelye*

KAELIN (American) an alternate form
of Kaelyn.
Kaeleen, Kaelene, Kaelina, Kaelinn, Kalan

KAELYN (American) a combination of
Kae + Lynn. See also Caelin, Kaylyn.
Kaelan, Kaelen, Kaelin, Kaelynn, Kaelynne

KAETLYN (Irish) an alternate form of
Kaitlin.
Kaetlin, Kaetlynn

KAGAMI (Japanese) mirror.

KAHSHA (Native American) fur robe.
Kasha, Kashae, Kashia

KAI (Hawaiian) sea. (Hopi, Navaho)
willow tree.
Kae, Kaie

KAIA (Greek) earth. Mythology: Gaia was the earth goddess.
Kaiah, Kaija

KAILA (Hebrew) laurel; crown.
Kailah, Kailea, Kaileah, Kailee, Kailey, Kayla

KAILEE, Kailey (American) familiar forms of Kaila. Alternate forms of Kaylee.
Kaile, Kaileh, Kaileigh, Kaili, Kailia, Kailie, Kailli, Kaillie, Kaily, Kailya

KAILYN, Kailynn (American) forms of Kaitlin.
Kailan, Kaileen, Kaileena, Kailen, Kailena, Kailene, Kaileyne, Kailin, Kailina, Kailon, Kailynne

KAIROS (Greek) last, final, complete. Mythology: the last goddess born to Jupiter.
Kaira, Kairra

KAISHAWN (American) a combination of Kai + Shawna.
Kaeshun, Kaisha, Kaishala, Kaishon

KAITLIN (Irish) pure. An alternate form of Caitlin. See also Katelin.
Kaetlyn, Kailyn, Kailynn, Kaitlan, Kaitland, Kaitleen, Kaitlen, Kaitlind, Kaitlinn, Kaitlinne, Kaitlon, Kaytlin

KAITLYN, Kaitlynn (Irish) an alternate form of Caitlyn.
Kaitelynne, Kaitlynne

KAIYA (Japanese) forgiveness.
Kaiyah, Kaiyia

KALA (Arabic) a short form of Kalila. An alternate form of Cala.
Kalah, Kalla, Kallah

KALAMA (Hawaiian) torch.

KALANI (Hawaiian) chieftain; sky.
Kailani, Kalanie, Kaloni

KALARE (Latin, Basque) bright; clear.

KALEA (Hawaiian) bright; clear.
Kahlea, Kahleah, Kailea, Kaileah, Kaleah, Kaleeia, Kaleia, Kalia, Kallea, Kalleah, Kaylea, Kayleah, Khalea, Khaleah

KALEE, Kaleigh, Kaley, Kalie (American) alternate forms of Caley, Kaylee.
Kalei, Kalleigh, Kalley, Kally, Kaly

KALEI (Hawaiian) flower wreath.
Kahlei, Kailei, Kallei, Kaylei, Khalei

KALENA (Hawaiian) pure. See also Kalina.
Kaleen, Kaleena, Kalene, Kalenea, Kalenna

KALERE (Swahili) short woman.
Kaleer

KALI (Sanskrit) energy; black goddess; time the destroyer. (Hawaiian) hesitating. Religion: a name for the Hindu goddess Shakti. See also Cali.
Kalee, Kaleigh, Kaley, Kalie, Kallee, Kalley, Kalli, Kallie, Kally, Kallye, Kaly

KALIA (Hawaiian) an alternate form of Kalea.
Kaliah, Kaliea, Kalieya

KALIFA (Somali) chaste; holy.

KALILA (Arabic) beloved, sweetheart. See also Kaela.
Kahlila, Kala, Kaleela, Kalilla, Kaylil, Kaylila, Kelila, Khalila, Khalilah, Khalillah, Kylila, Kylilah, Kylillah

KALINA (Slavic) flower. (Hawaiian) a form of Karen. See also Kalena.
Kalin, Kalinna, Kalyna, Kalynah, Kalynna

KALINDA (Hindi) sun.
Kaleenda, Kalindi, Kalynda, Kalyndi

KALISA (American) a combination of Kate + Lisa.
Kalise, Kalissa, Kalysa, Kalyssa

KALISHA (American) a combination of Kate + Aisha.
Kaleesha, Kaleisha, Kalishia

KALISKA (Moquelumnan) coyote chasing deer.

KALLAN (Slavic) stream, river.
Kalahn, Kalan, Kalen, Kallen, Kallon, Kalon

KALLE (Finnish) a form of Carol.
Kaille, Kaylle

KALLI, Kallie (Greek) alternate forms of Callie. Familiar forms of Kalliope, Kallista, Kalliyan.
Kalle, Kallee, Kalley, Kallita, Kally

KALLIOPE (Greek) beautiful voice. Mythology: Calliope was the muse of epic poetry.
Kalli, Kallie, Kallyope

KALLISTA (Greek) an alternate form of Callista.
Kalesta, Kalista, Kallesta, Kalli, Kallie, Kallysta, Kaysta

KALLIYAN (Cambodian) best.
Kalli, Kallie

KALTHA (English) marigold, yellow flower.

KALUWA (Swahili) forgotten one.
Kalua

KALYCA (Greek) rosebud.
Kalica, Kalika, Kaly

KALYN, Kalynn (American) alternate forms of Kaylyn, Kaylynn.
Kalin, Kallen, Kallin, Kallon, Kallyn, Kalyne, Kalynne

KAMA (Sanskrit) loved one. Religion: the Hindu god of love.

KAMALA (Hindi) lotus.
Kamalah, Kammala

KAMALI (Mahona) spirit guide; protector.
Kamalie

KAMARIA (Swahili) moonlight.

Kamar, Kamara, Kamarae, Kamaree, Kamari, Kamariah, Kamarie, Kamariya, Kamariyah, Kamarya

KAMATA (Moquelumnan) gambler.

KAMBRIA (Latin) an alternate form of Cambria.
Kambra, Kambrie, Kambriea, Kambry

KAMEA (Hawaiian) one and only; precious.
Kameah, Kameo, Kamiya

KAMEKE (Swahili) blind.

KAMEKO (Japanese) turtle child. Mythology: the turtle symbolizes longevity.

KAMERON (American) a form of Cameron.
Kameran, Kamri

KAMI (Italian, North African) a short form of Kamila, Kamilah. (Japanese) divine aura. See also Cami.
Kamie, Kammi, Kammie, Kammy, Kammye, Kamy

KAMILA (Slavic) a form of Camila. See also Millie.
Kameela, Kamela, Kamelia, Kamella, Kami, Kamilah, Kamilia, Kamilka, Kamilla, Kamille, Kamma, Kammilla, Kamyla

KAMILAH (North African) perfect.
Kameela, Kameelah, Kami, Kamillah, Kammilah

KAMIYA (Hawaiian) an alternate form of Kamea.
Kamia, Kamiah, Kamiyah

KAMRI (American) a short form of Kameron. See also Camri.
Kamree, Kamrey, Kamrie, Kamry, Kamrye

KAMRYN (American) a form of Cameron. See also Camryn.
Kameryn, Kamren, Kamrin, Kamron, Kamrynn

KANANI (Hawaiian) beautiful.
Kana, Kanae, Kanan

KANDA (Native American) magical power.

KANDACE, Kandice (Greek) glittering white; glowing. (American) alternate forms of Candace, Candice.
Kandas, Kandess, Kandi, Kandis, Kandise, Kandiss, Kandus, Kandyce, Kandys, Kandyse

KANDI (American) a familiar form of Kandace, Kandice. See also Candi.
Kandhi, Kandia, Kandie, Kandy, Kendi, Kendie, Kendy, Kenndi, Kenndie, Kenndy

KANDRA (American) a form of Kendra. See also Candra.
Kandrea, Kandree, Kandria

KANE (Japanese) two right hands.

KANEISHA, Kanisha (American) alternate forms of Keneisha.
Kaneasha, Kanecia, Kaneesha, Kanesah, Kanesha, Kaneshea, Kaneshia, Kanessa, Kaneysha, Kaniece, Kanishia

KANENE (Swahili) a little important thing.

KANI (Hawaiian) sound.

KANIKA (Mwera) black cloth.
Kanica, Kanicka

KANNITHA (Cambodian) angel.

KANOA (Hawaiian) free.

KANYA (Hindi) virgin. (Tai) young lady. Religion: a name for the Hindu goddess Shakti.
Kanea, Kania, Kaniya, Kanyia

KAPRI (American) an alternate form of Capri.
Kapre, Kapree, Kapria, Kaprice, Kapricia, Kaprisha, Kaprisia

KAPUA (Hawaiian) blossom.

KAPUKI (Swahili) first-born daughter.

KARA (Greek, Danish) pure. An alternate form of Katherine.
Kaira, Kairah, Karah, Karalea, Karaleah, Karalee, Karalie, Kari, Karra

KARAH (Greek, Danish) an alternate form of Kara. (Irish, Italian) an alternate form of Cara.
Karrah

KARALYNN (English) a combination of Kara + Lynn.
Karalin, Karaline, Karalyn, Karalyne, Karalynne

KARELLE (American) a form of Carol.
Karel, Kareli, Karell, Karely

KAREN (Greek) pure. An alternate form of Katherine. See also Carey, Carina, Caryn.
Kaaren, Kalina, Karaina, Karan, Karena, Karin, Karina, Karine, Karna, Karon, Karren, Karron, Karyn, Kerron, Koren

KARENA (Scandinavian) a form of Karen.
Kareen, Kareena, Kareina, Karenah, Karene, Karreen, Karreena, Karrena, Karrene

KARESSA (French) an alternate form of Caressa.

KARI (Greek) pure. (Danish) a form of Caroline, Katherine. See also Carey, Cari, Carrie.
Karee, Karey, Karia, Kariah, Karie, Karrey, Karri, Karrie, Karry, Kary

KARIANE, Karianne (American) combinations of Kari + Anne.
Karian, Kariana, Kariann, Karianna

KARIDA (Arabic) untouched, pure.
Kareeda, Karita

KARILYNN (American) a combination of Kari + Lynn.

Kareelin, Kareeline, Kareelinn, Kareelyn,
Kareelyne, Kareelynn, Kareelynne, Karilin,
Kariline, Karilinn, Karilyn, Karilyne,
Karilynne, Karylin, Karyline, Karylinn,
Karylyn, Karylyne, Karylynn, Karylynne

KARIMAH (Arabic) generous.
Kareema, Kareemah, Karima, Karime

KARIN (Scandinavian) a form of Karen.
Kaarin, Kareen, Karina, Karine, Karinne,
Karrin, Kerrin

KARINA (Russian) a form of Karen.
Kaarina, Karinna, Karrina, Karryna,
Karyna, Karynna

KARINE (Russian) a form of Karen.
Karrine, Karryne, Karyne

KARIS (Greek) graceful.
Karess, Karice, Karise, Karisse, Karris, Karys,
Karyss

KARISSA (Greek) an alternate form of
Carissa.
Karese, Karesse, Karisa, Karisha, Karishma,
Karisma, Karissimia, Kariza, Karrisa,
Karrissa, Karysa, Karyssa, Kerisa

KARLA (German) an alternate form
of Carla. (Slavic) a short form of
Karoline.
Karila, Karilla, Karle, Karlene, Karlicka,
Karlinka, Karlisha, Karlisia, Karlitha,
Karlla, Karlon, Karlyn

KARLEE, Karleigh (American)
alternate forms of Karley, Karly.
See also Carlee.
Karlea, Karleah, Karlei

KARLENE, Karlyn (American) forms
of Karla. See also Carleen.
Karleen, Karlen, Karlena, Karlign, Karlin,
Karlina, Karlinna, Karlyan, Karlynn,
Karlynne

KARLEY, Karly (Latin) little and
womanly. (American) forms of Carly.
Karlee, Karley, Karlie, Karlyan, Karlye

KARLI, Karlie (American) alternate
forms of Karley, Karly. See also Carli.

KARLOTTE (American) a form of
Charlotte.
Karlita, Karletta, Karlette, Karlotta

KARMA (Hindi) fate, destiny; action.

KARMEL (Hebrew) an alternate form of
Carmela.
Karmeita, Karmela, Karmelina, Karmella,
Karmelle, Karmiella, Karmielle, Karmyla

KARMEN (Latin) song. A form of
Carmen.
Karman, Karmencita, Karmin, Karmina,
Karmine, Karmita, Karmon, Karmyn,
Karmyne

KAROLANE (American) a combination
of Karoll + Anne.
Karolan, Karolann, Karolanne, Karol-Anne

KAROLINA, Karoline (Slavic) forms
of Caroline. See also Carolina.
Karaleen, Karalena, Karalene, Karalin,
Karaline, Karileen, Karilena, Karilene,
Karilin, Karilina, Kariline, Karleen, Karlen,
Karlena, Karlene, Karling, Karoleena,
Karolena, Karolinka, Karroleen, Karrolena,
Karrolene, Karrolin, Karroline

KAROLL (Slavic) a form of Carol.
Karel, Karilla, Karily, Karol, Karola, Karole,
Karoly, Karrol, Karyl, Kerril

KAROLYN (American) a form of
Carolyn.
Karalyn, Karalyna, Karalynn, Karalynne,
Karilyn, Karilyna, Karilynn, Karilynne,
Karlyn, Karlynn, Karlynne, Karolyna,
Karolynn, Karolynne, Karrolyn, Karrolyna,
Karrolynn, Karrolynne

KARRI, Karrie (American) forms of
Carrie.
Kari, Karie, Karry, Kary

KARSEN, Karsyn (English) daughter
of Kar. Feminine forms of Carson.
Karson

KARUNA (Hindi) merciful.

KARYN (American) a form of Karen.
Karyne, Karynn, Karynna, Kerrynn, Kerrynne

KASA (Hopi) fur robe.

KASANDRA (Greek) an alternate form of Kassandra.
Kasander, Kasandria, Kasandra, Kasaundra, Kasondra, Kasoundra

KASEY, Kasie (Irish) brave. (American) forms of Casey, Kacey.
Kaisee, Kaisie, Kasci, Kascy, Kasee, Kasi, Kassee, Kassey, Kasy, Kasya, Kaysci, Kaysea, Kaysee, Kaysey, Kaysi, Kaysie, Kaysy

KASHAWNA (American) a combination of Kate + Shawna.
Kasha, Kashae, Kashana, Kashanna, Kashauna, Kashawn, Kasheana, Kasheanna, Kasheena, Kashena, Kashonda, Kashonna

KASHMIR (Sanskrit) Geography: a state in India.
Cashmere, Kashmear, Kashmere, Kashmia, Kashmira, Kasmir, Kasmira, Kazmir, Kazmira

KASI (Hindi) from the holy city.

KASIA (Polish) a form of Katherine. See also Cassia.
Kashia, Kasiah, Kasian, Kasienka, Kasja, Kaska, Kassa, Kassia, Kassya, Kasya

KASINDA (Umbundu) our last baby.

KASSANDRA (Greek) an alternate form of Cassandra.
Kassandr, Kassandre, Kassandré, Kassaundra, Kassi, Kassondra, Kassondria, Kassundra, Kazandra, Khrisandra, Krisandra, Krissandra

KASSI, Kassie (American) familiar forms of Kassandra, Kassidy. See also Cassie.
Kassey, Kassia, Kassy

KASSIDY (Irish) clever. (American) an alternate form of Cassidy.
Kassadee, Kassadi, Kassadie, Kassadina, Kassady, Kasseday, Kassedee, Kassi, Kassiddy, Kassidee, Kassidi, Kassidie, Kassity, Kassydi

KATALINA (Irish) an alternate form of Caitlin. See also Catalina.
Kataleen, Kataleena, Katalena, Katalin, Katalyn, Katalynn

KATARINA (Czech) a form of Katherine.
Kata, Katareena, Katarena, Katarin, Katarine, Katarinna, Katarinne, Katarrina, Kataryna, Katarzyna, Katinka, Katrika, Katrinka

KATE (Greek) pure. (English) a short form of Katherine.
Kait, Kata, Katee, Kati, Katica, Katie, Katka, Katy, Katya

KATEE, Katey (English) familiar forms of Kate, Katherine.

KATELIN (Irish) an alternate form of Caitlin. See also Kaitlin.
Kaetlin, Katalin, Katelan, Kateland, Kateleen, Katelen, Katelene, Katelind, Kateline, Katelinn, Katelun, Kaytlin

KATELYN, Katelynn (Irish) alternate forms of Caitlin.
Kaetlyn, Kaetlynn, Kaetlynne, Katelyne, Katelynne, Kaytlyn, Kaytlynn, Kaytlynne

KATERINA (Slavic) a form of Katherine.
Katenka, Katerine, Katerini, Katerinka

KATHARINE (Greek) an alternate form of Katherine.
Katharaine, Katharin, Katharina, Katharyn

KATHERINE (Greek) pure. See also Carey, Catherine, Ekaterina, Kara, Karen, Kari, Kasia, Katerina, Yekaterina.

Ekaterina, Ekatrinna, Kasienka, Kasin, Kat, Katarina, Katchen, Kate, Katee, Kathann, Kathanne, Katharine, Kathereen, Katheren, Katherene, Katherenne, Katherin, Katherina, Katheryn, Katheryne, Kathi, Kathleen, Kathrine, Kathryn, Kathy, Kathyrine, Katia, Katina, Katlaina, Katoka, Katreeka, Katrina, Kay, Kitty

KATHI, Kathy (English) familiar forms of Katherine, Kathleen. See also Cathi.
Kaethe, Katha, Kathe, Kathee, Kathey, Kathi, Kathie, Katka, Katla, Kató

KATHLEEN (Irish) a form of Katherine. See also Cathleen.
Katheleen, Kathelene, Kathi, Kathileen, Kathlean, Kathleena, Kathleene, Kathlene, Kathlin, Kathlina, Kathlyn, Kathlyne, Kathlynn, Kathy, Katleen

KATHRINE (Greek) an alternate form of Katherine.
Kathreen, Kathreena, Kathrene, Kathrin, Kathrina

KATHRYN (English) a form of Katherine.
Kathren, Kathryne, Kathrynn, Kathrynne

KATI (Estonian) a form of Kate.
Katja, Katya, Katye

KATIA, Katya (Russian) forms of Katherine.
Cattiah, Katiya, Kattia, Kattiah, Katyah

KATIE (English) a familiar form of Kate.
Katee, Kati, Kātia, Katti, Kattie, Katy, Kayte, Kaytee, Kaytie

KATILYN (Irish) an alternate form of Katlyn.
Katilin, Katilynn

KATLIN (Irish) an alternate form of Katlyn.
Katlina, Katline

KATLYN (Greek) pure. (Irish) an alternate form of Katelin.

Kaatlain, Katilyn, Katland, Katlin, Katlynd, Katlyne, Katlynn, Katlynne

KATRIEL (Hebrew) God is my crown.
Katrelle, Katri, Katrie, Katry, Katryel

KATRINA (German) a form of Katherine. See also Catrina, Trina.
Katreen, Katreena, Katrene, Katri, Katrice, Katricia, Katrien, Katrin, Katrine, Katrinia, Katriona, Katryn, Katryna, Kattrina, Kattryna, Katus, Katuska

KATY (English) a familiar form of Kate. See also Cady.
Kady, Katey, Katty, Kayte

KAULANA (Hawaiian) famous.
Kaula, Kauna, Kahuna

KAVERI (Hindi) Geographical: a sacred river in India.

KAVINDRA (Hindi) poet.

KAWENA (Hawaiian) glow.
Kawana, Kawona

KAY (Greek) rejoicer. (Teutonic) a fortified place. (Latin) merry. A short form of Katherine.
Caye, Kae, Kai, Kaye, Kayla

KAYA (Hopi) wise child. (Japanese) resting place.
Kaja, Kayah, Kayia

KAYCEE (American) a combination of the initials K. + C.
Kayce, Kaysee, Kaysey, Kaysi, Kaysie, Kaysii

KAYDEE (American) a combination of the initials K. + D.
Kayda, Kayde, Kayden, Kaydi, Kaydie

KAYLA (Arabic, Hebrew) laurel; crown. An alternate form of Kaela, Kaila. See also Cayla.
Kaylah, Kaylea, Kaylee, Kayleen, Kaylene, Kaylia, Keila, Keyla

KAYLAH (Arabic, Hebrew) an alternate form of Kayla.
Kayleah, Kaylia, Keylah

KAYLAN, Kaylen (Hebrew) alternate forms of Kayleen.
Kaylana, Kayland, Kaylani, Kaylann, Kaylean, Kayleana, Kayleanna, Kaylenn

KAYLEE (American) a form of Kayla. See also Caeley, Kalee.
Kailee, Kayle, Kayleigh, Kayley, Kayli, Kaylie

KAYLEEN, Kaylene (Hebrew) beloved, sweetheart. Alternate forms of Kayla.
Kaylan, Kayleena, Kayleene, Kaylen, Kaylena

KAYLEIGH (American) an alternate form of Kaylee.
Kaylei

KAYLEY, Kayli, Kaylie (American) alternate forms of Kaylee.

KAYLIN (American) an alternate form of Kaylyn.
Kaylon

KAYLYN, Kaylynn (American) combinations of Kay + Lynn. See also Kaelyn.
Kalyn, Kalynn, Kayleen, Kaylene, Kaylin, Kaylyna, Kaylyne, Kaylynne

KAYTLIN, Kaytlyn (Irish) alternate forms of Kaitlin.
Kaytlan, Kaytlann, Kaytlen, Kaytlyne, Kaytlynn, Kaytlynne

KEAIRA (Irish) an alternate form of Keara.
Keair, Keairah, Keairra, Keairre, Keairrea

KEALA (Hawaiian) path.

KEANA, Keanna (German) bold; sharp. (Irish) beautiful. Feminine forms of Keane.
Keanah, Keanne, Keanu, Keenan, Keeyana, Keeyanah, Keeyanna, Keeyona. Keeyonna, Keiana, Keianna, Keona, Keonna

KEANDRA, Keondra (American) forms of Kenda.
Keandrah, Keandre, Keandrea, Keandria, Kedeana, Kedia, Keonda, Keondre, Keondria

KEARA (Irish) dark; black. Religion: an Irish saint.
Keaira, Kearah, Kearia, Kearra, Keera, Keerra, Keiara, Keiarah, Keiarra, Keira, Kera

KEARSTEN, Keirsten (Greek) alternate forms of Kirstin.
Kearstin, Kearston, Kearstyn, Keirstan, Keirstein, Keirstin, Keirston, Keirstyn, Keirstynne

KEELEY, Keely (Irish) alternate forms of Kelly.
Kealee, Kealey, Keali, Kealie, Keallie, Kealy, Keela, Keelan, Keele, Keelee, Keeleigh, Keeli, Keelia, Keelie, Keellie, Keelye, Keighla, Keilee, Keileigh, Keiley, Keilly, Kiela, Kiele, Kieley, Kielly, Kiely

KEELYN (Irish) an alternate form of Kellyn.
Kealyn, Keelin, Keilan, Kielyn

KEENA (Irish) brave.
Keenya, Kina

KEESHA (American) an alternate form of Keisha.
Keesa, Keeshae, Keeshana, Keeshanne, Keeshawna, Keeshonna, Keeshya, Keiosha

KEI (Japanese) reverent.

KEIANA, Keianna (Irish) alternate forms of Keana, Keanna.
Keiann, Keiannah, Keionna

KEIKI (Hawaiian) child.
Keikana, Keikann, Keikanna, Keikanne

KEIKO (Japanese) happy child.

KEILA (Arabic, Hebrew) an alternate form of Kayla.
Keilah, Kela, Kelah

KEILANI (Hawaiian) glorious chief.
Kaylani, Keilan, Keilana, Keilany, Kelana,
Kelanah, Kelane, Kelani, Kelanie

KEIRA (Irish) an alternate form of
Keara.
Keiara, Keiarra, Keirra, Keirrah, Kera,
Keyeira

KEISHA (American) a short form of
Keneisha.
Keasha, Keashia, Keesha, Keishaun,
Keishauna, Keishawn, Kesha, Keysha,
Kiesha, Kisha, Kishanda

KEITA (Scottish) woods; enclosed place.
Keiti

KEKONA (Hawaiian) second-born child.

KELCEY, Kelci, Kelcie (Scottish)
alternate forms of Kelsey.
Kelse, Kelcee, Kelcy

KELILA (Hebrew) crown, laurel.
See also Kaela, Kayla, Kalila.
Kelilah, Kelula

KELLEY (Irish) an alternate form of
Kelly.

KELLI, Kellie (Irish) familiar forms of
Kelly.
Keleigh, Keli, Kelia, Keliah, Kelie, Kellee,
Kelleigh, Kellia, Kellisa

KELLY (Irish) brave warrior. See also
Caeley.
Keeley, Keely, Kelley, Kelley, Kelli, Kellie,
Kellye

KELLYANNE (Irish) a combination of
Kelly + Anne.
Kelliann, Kellianne, Kellyann

KELLYN (Irish) a combination of
Kelly + Lyn.
Keelyn, Kelleen, Kellen, Kellene, Kellina,
Kelline, Kellynn, Kellynne

KELSEA (Scottish) an alternate form of
Kelsey.
Kelcea, Kelcia, Kelsa, Kelsae, Kelsay, Kelse

KELSEY (Scandinavian, Scottish) ship
island. (English) an alternate form of
Chelsey.
Kelcey, Kelda, Kellsee, Kellsei, Kellsey, Kellsie,
Kellsy, Kelsea, Kelsei, Kelsey, Kelsi, Kelsie,
Kelsy, Kelsye

KELSI, Kelsie, Kelsy (Scottish) forms
of Chelsea.
Kalsie, Kelci, Kelcie, Kellsi

KENDA (English) water baby. (Dakota)
magical power. Astrology: a child born
under Cancer, Scorpio, or Pisces.
Keandra, Kendra, Kennda

KENDAL (English) an alternate form of
Kendall.
Kendahl, Kendale, Kendalie, Kendalin,
Kendalyn, Kendalynn, Kendel, Kendele,
Kendil, Kindal

KENDALL (English) ruler of the valley.
Kendal, Kendalla, Kendalle, Kendell,
Kendelle, Kendera, Kendia, Kendyl, Kinda,
Kindall, Kindi, Kindle, Kynda, Kyndal,
Kyndall, Kyndel

KENDRA (English) an alternate form of
Kenda.
Kandra, Kendrah, Kendre, Kendrea,
Kendreah, Kendria, Kenndra, Kentra,
Kentrae, Kindra, Kyndra

KENDYL (English) an alternate form
of Kendall.
Kendyle, Kendyll

KENEISHA (American) a combination
of the prefix Ken + Aisha.
Kaneisha, Keisha, Keneesha, Kenesha,
Keneshia, Kenisha, Kenneisha, Kennesha,
Kenneshia, Keosha, Kineisha

KENENZA (English) an alternate form
of Kennice.
Kenza

KENIA (Hebrew) an alternate form of
Kenya.
Keniya, Kennia

KENISHA (American) an alternate form of Keneisha.
Kenisa, Kenise, Kenishia, Kenissa, Kennisa, Kennisha, Kennysha

KENNA (Irish) a short form of Kennice.

KENNEDY (Irish) helmeted chief. History: John F. Kennedy was the thirty-fifth U.S. president.
Kenedee, Kenedey, Kenedi, Kenedie, Kenedy, Kenidee, Kenidi, Kenidie, Kenidy, Kennadee, Kennadi, Kennadie, Kennady, Kennedee, Kennedey, Kennedi, Kennedie, Kennidee, Kennidi, Kennidy, Kynnedi

KENNICE (English) beautiful. A feminine form of Kenneth.
Kanice, Keneese, Kenenza, Kenese, Kennise

KENYA (Hebrew) animal horn. Geography: a country in Africa.
Keenya, Kenia, Kenja, Kenyah, Kenyana, Kenyatta, Kenyia

KENYATTA (American) a form of Kenya.
Kenyata, Kenyatah, Kenyatte, Kenyattia, Kenyatta, Kenyette

KENZIE (Scottish) light skinned. (Irish) a short form of Mackenzie.
Kenzea, Kenzee, Kenzey, Kenzi, Kenzia, Kenzy, Kinzie

KEONA, Keonna (Irish) alternate forms of Keana.
Keiona, Keionna, Keoana, Keoni, Keonia, Keonnah, Keonni, Keonnia

KEOSHA (American) a short form of Keneisha.
Keoshae, Keoshi, Keoshia, Keosia

KERANI (Hindi) sacred bells. See also Rani.
Kera, Kerah, Keran, Kerana

KEREN (Hebrew) animal's horn.
Kerrin, Keryn

KERENSA (Cornish) loving, affectionate.
Karensa, Karenza, Kerenza

KERI, Kerri, Kerrie (Irish) alternate forms of Kerry.
Keriann, Kerianne, Kerriann, Kerrianne

KERRY (Irish) dark haired. Geography: a county in Ireland.
Keary, Keiry, Keree, Kerey, Keri, Kerri, Kerrie, Kerryann, Kerryanne, Kery, Kiera, Kierra

KERSTIN (Scandinavian) an alternate form of Kirsten.
Kerstan, Kerste, Kerstein, Kersten, Kerstie, Kerstien, Kerston, Kerstyn, Kerstynn

KESARE (Latin) long haired. (Basque) a feminine form of Caesar.

KESHA (American) an alternate form of Keisha.
Keshah, Keshal, Keshala, Keshan, Keshana, Keshara, Keshawn, Keshawna, Keshawnna

KESHIA (American) an alternate form of Keisha. A short form of Keneisha.
Kecia, Keishia, Keschia, Keshea, Kesia, Kesiah, Kessia, Kessiah

KESI (Swahili) born during difficult times.

KESSIE (Ashanti) chubby baby.
Kess, Kessa, Kesse, Kessey, Kessi

KEVYN (Irish) beautiful. A feminine form of Kevin.
Keva, Kevan, Keven, Kevia, Keviana, Kevinna, Kevina, Kevion, Kevionna, Kevon, Kevona, Kevone, Kevonia, Kevonna, Kevonne, Kevonya, Kevynn

KEYANA, Keyanna (American) alternate forms of Kiana.
Keya, Keyanah, Keyanda, Keyandra, Keyannah

KEYARA (Irish) an alternate form of Kiara.
Keyarah, Keyari, Keyarra, Keyera, Keyerah, Keyerra

KEYONA, Keyonna (American) alternate forms of Kiana.
Keyonda, Keyondra, Keyonnia, Keyonnie

KEYSHA (American) an alternate form of Keisha.
Keyosha, Keyoshia, Keyshana, Keyshanna, Keyshawn, Keyshawna, Keyshia, Keyshla, Keyshona, Keyshonna

KEZIAH (Hebrew) cinnamonlike spice. Bible: one of the daughters of Job.
Kazia, Kaziah, Ketzi, Ketzia, Ketziah, Kezi, Kezia, Kizzy

KHADIJAH (Arabic) trustworthy. History: Muhammed's first wife.
Khadaja, Khadajah, Khadeeja, Khadeejah, Khadeja, Khadejah, Khadejha, Khadija, Khadije, Khadijia, Khadijiah

KHALIDA (Arabic) immortal, everlasting.
Khali, Khalia, Khaliah, Khalidda, Khalita

KHRISSA (American) a form of Chrissa.
Khrishia, Khryssa, Krisha, Krisia, Krissa, Krysha, Kryssa

KHRISTINA (Russian, Scandinavian) a form of Kristina, Christina.
Khristeen, Khristen, Khristin, Khristine, Khyristya, Khristyana, Khristyna, Khrystyne

KI (Korean) arisen.

KIA (African) season's beginning. (American) a short form of Kiana.
Kiah

KIANA (American) a combination of the prefix Ki + Ana.
Keanna, Keiana, Keyana, Keyona, Khiana, Khianah, Khianna, Ki, Kiahna, Kiane, Kiani, Kiania, Kianna, Kiauna, Kiandra, Kiandria, Kiauna, Kiaundra, Kiyana, Kyana

KIANNA (American) an alternate form of Kiana.
Kiannah, Kianne, Kianni

KIARA (Irish) little and dark. A feminine form of Kieran.
Keyara, Kiarra, Kieara, Kiearah, Kiearra, Kyara

KIARIA, Kiarra, Kichi (Japanese) fortunate.

KIELE (Hawaiian) gardenia; fragrant blossom.
Kiela, Kieley, Kieli, Kielli, Kielly

KIERA, Kierra (Irish) alternate forms of Kerry.
Kierana, Kieranna, Kierea

KIERSTEN, Kierstin (Scandanavian) alternate forms of Kirsten.
Keirstan, Kerstin, Kierstan, Kierston, Kierstyn, Kierstynn

KIKI (Spanish) a familiar form of names ending in 'queta.'

KIKU (Japanese) chrysanthemum.
Kiko

KILEY (Irish) attractive; from the straits.
Kilea, Kilee, Kileigh, Kili, Kilie, Kylee, Kyli, Kylie

KIM (Vietnamese) needle. (English) a short form of Kimberly.
Kima, Kimette, Kym

KIMANA (Shoshone) butterfly.
Kiman, Kimani

KIMBER (English) a short form of Kimberly.
Kimbra

KIMBERLEE, Kimberley (English) alternate forms of Kimberly.
Kimbalee, Kimberlea, Kimberlei, Kimberleigh, Kimbley

KIMBERLY (English) chief, ruler.
Cymberly, Cymbre, Kim, Kimba, Kimbely, Kimber, Kimbereley, Kimberely, Kimberlee, Kimberli, Kimberlie, Kimberlyn, Kimbery, Kimbria, Kimbrie, Kimbry, Kimmie, Kymberly

KIMBERLYN (English) an alternate form of Kimberly.
Kimberlin, Kimberlynn

KIMI (Japanese) righteous.
Kimia, Kimika, Kimiko, Kimiyo, Kimmi, Kimmie, Kimmy

KIMMIE (English) a familiar form of Kimberly.
Kimee, Kimme, Kimmee, Kimmi, Kimmy, Kimy

KINA (Hawaiian) from China.

KINEISHA (American) an alternate form of Keneisha.
Kineesha, Kinesha, Kineshia, Kinisha, Kinishia

KINETA (Greek) energetic.
Kinetta

KINI (Hawaiian) a form of Jean.
Kina

KINSEY (English) offspring; relative.
Kinsee, Kinsley, Kinza, Kinze, Kinzee, Kinzey, Kinzi, Kinzie, Kinzy

KINSLEY (American) a form of Kinsey.
Kinslee, Kinslie, Kinslyn

KIOKO (Japanese) happy child.
Kiyo, Kiyoko

KIONA (Native American) brown hills.
Kionah, Kioni, Kionna

KIRA (Persian) sun. (Latin) light. A feminine form of Cyrus.
Kirah, Kiri, Kiria, Kiro, Kirra, Kirrah, Kirri

KIRAN (Hindi) ray.

KIRBY (Scandinavian) church village. (English) cottage by the water.
Kirbee, Kirbi

KIRIMA (Eskimo) hill.

KIRSI (Hindi) amaranth blossoms.
Kirsie

KIRSTA (Scandinavian) an alternate form of Kirsten.

KIRSTEN (Greek) Christian; annointed. (Scandinavian) a form of Christine.
Karsten, Kearsten, Keirstan, Kerstin, Kiersten, Kirsteni, Kirsta, Kirstan, Kirstene, Kirstie, Kirstin, Kirston, Kirsty, Kirstyn, Kjersten, Kursten, Kyersten, Kyrsten, Kyrstin

KIRSTIN (Scandinavian) an alternate form of Kirsten.
Karstin, Kirsteen, Kirstien, Kirstine

KIRSTIE, Kirsty (Scandinavian) familiar forms of Kirsten.
Kerstie, Kirsta, Kirste, Kirstee, Kirstey, Kirsti, Kjersti, Kyrsty

KIRSTYN (Greek) an alternate form of Kirsten.
Kirstynn

KISA (Russian) kitten.
Kisha, Kiska, Kissa, Kiza

KISHI (Japanese) long and happy life.

KISSA (Ugandan) born after twins.

KITA (Japanese) north.

KITRA (Hebrew) crowned.

KITTY (Greek) a familiar form of Katherine.
Ketter, Ketti, Ketty, Kit, Kittee, Kitteen, Kittey, Kitti, Kittie

KIWA (Japanese) borderline.

KIYANA (American) an alternate form of Kiana.
Kiya, Kiyah, Kiyan, Kiyani, Kiyanna, Kiyenna

KIZZY (American) a familiar form of Keziah.
Kezi, Kissie, Kizzi, Kizzie

KLARA (Hungarian) a form of Clara.
Klára, Klari, Klarika

KLARISE (German) an alternate form of Klarissa.
Klarice, Kláris, Klaryce

KLARISSA (German) clear, bright. (Italian) an alternate form of Clarissa.
Klarisa, Klarise, Klarrisa, Klarrissa, Klarrissia, Klarisza, Klarysa, Klaryssa, Kleresa

KLAUDIA (American) a form of Claudia.
Klaudija

KLOE (American) a form of Chloe.
Khloe, Kloee, Kloey, Klohe, Kloie

KODI (American) a form of Codi.
Kodee, Kodey, Kodie, Kody, Kodye, Koedi

KOFFI (Swahili) born on Friday.
Kaffe, Kaffi, Koffe, Koffie

KOKO (Japanese) stork. See also Coco.

KOLBY (American) a form of Colby.
Kobie, Koby, Kolbee, Kolbey, Kolbi, Kolbie

KOLINA (Swedish) a form of Katherine. See also Colleen.
Koleen, Koleena, Kolena, Kolene, Koli, Kolleen, Kollena, Kollene, Kolyn, Kolyna

KONA (Hawaiian) lady. (Hindi) angular. Astrology: born under the sign of Capricorn.
Koni, Konia

KONSTANCE (Latin) an alternate form of Constance.
Konstantina, Konstantine, Konstanza, Konstanze

KORA (Greek) an alternate form of Cora.
Korah, Kore, Koren, Koressa, Koretta, Korra

KORAL (American) a form of Coral.
Korel, Korele, Korella, Korilla, Korral, Korrel, Korrell, Korrelle

KORI (American) a short form of Korina. See also Corey, Cori.
Koree, Korey, Koria, Korie, Korri, Korrie, Korry, Kory

KORINA (Greek) an alternate form of Corina.
Koreena, Korena, Koriana, Korianna, Korine, Korinna, Korreena, Korrina, Korrinna, Koryna, Korynna

KORINE (Greek) an alternate form of Korina.
Koreen, Korene, Koriane, Korianne, Korin, Korinn, Korinne, Korrin, Korrine, Korrinne, Korryn, Korrynne, Koryn, Koryne, Korynn

KORNELIA (Latin) an alternate form of Cornelia.
Karniela, Karniella, Karnis, Kornelija, Kornelis, Kornelya, Korny

KORTNEY (English) an alternate form of Courtney.
Kortnay, Kortnee, Kortni, Kortnie, Kortny

KOSMA (Greek) order; universe.
Cosma

KOSTA (Latin) a short form of Constance.
Kostia, Kostusha, Kostya

KOTO (Japanese) harp.

KOURTNEY (American) a form of Courtney.
Kourtnay, Kourtne, Kourtnee, Kourtnei, Kourtneigh, Kourtni, Kourtny, Kourtynie

KRIS (American) a short form of Kristine. An alternate form of Chris.
Khris, Krissy

KRISSY (American) a familiar form of Kris.
Krissey, Krissi, Krissie

KRISTA (Czech) a form of Christina. See also Christa.
Khrissa, Khrista, Khryssa, Khrysta, Krissa, Kryssa, Krysta

KRISTAL (Latin) an alternate form of Crystal.
Kristale, Kristall, Kristill, Kristl, Kristle, Kristy

KRISTAN (Greek) an alternate form of Kristen.
Kristana, Kristanna, Kristanne, Kriston, Krystan, Krystane

KRISTEN (Greek) Christian; annointed. (Scandinavian) a form of Christine.
Christen, Kristan, Kristene, Kristien, Kristin, Kristyn, Krysten

KRISTI, Kristie (Scandinavian) short forms of Kristine.
Christi

KRISTIAN, Kristiana (Greek) Christian; anointed. Alternate forms of Christian.
Khristian, Kristian, Kristiane, Kristiann, Kristi-Ann, Kristianna, Kristianne, Kristi-Anne, Kristienne, Kristyan, Kristyana, Kristy-Ann, Kristy-Anne

KRISTIN (Scandinavian) an alternate form of Kristen. See also Cristen.
Kristiin, Krystin

KRISTINA (Greek) Christian; annointed. (Scandinavian) a form of Christina. See also Cristina.
Khristina, Kristena, Kristina, Kristeena, Kristena, Kristinka, Krystina

KRISTINE (Scandinavian) a form of Christine.
Kris, Kristeen, Kristene, Kristi, Kristie, Kristy, Krystine, Krystyne

KRISTY (American) a familiar form of Kristine, Krystal. See also Cristy.
Kristi, Kristia, Kristie, Krysia, Krysti

KRISTYN (Greek) an alternate form of Kristen.
Kristyne, Kristynn

KRYSTA (Polish) a form of Krista.
Krystah, Krystka

KRYSTAL (American) clear, brilliant glass. A form of Crystal.
Kristabel, Kristal, Krystalann, Krystalanne, Krystale, Krystall, Krystalle, Krystel, Krystil, Krystle, Krystol

KRYSTALEE (American) a combination of Krystal + Lee.
Kristalea, Kristaleah, Kristalee, Krystalea, Krystaleah, Krystlea, Krystleah, Krystlee, Krystlelea, Krystleleah, Krystlelee

KRYSTALYNN (American) a combination of Krystal + Lynn.
Kristaline, Kristalyn, Kristalynn, Kristilyn, Kristilynn, Kristlyn, Krystaleen, Krystalene, Krystalin, Krystalina, Krystallyn, Krystalyn, Krystalynne

KRYSTEL (Latin) an alternate form of Krystal.
Kristel, Kristell, Kristelle, Krystelle

KRYSTEN (Greek) an alternate form of Kristen.
Krystene, Krystyn, Krystyne

KRYSTIAN, Krystiana (Greek) alternate forms of Christian.
Krystiana, Krystianna, Krystianne, Krysty-Ann, Krystyan, Kristyana, Krystyanna, Krystyanne, Krysty-Anne, Krystyen

KRYSTIN (Czech) a form of Kristin.

KRYSTINA (Greek) an alternate form of Kristina.
Krysteena, Krystena, Krystyna, Krystynka

KRYSTLE (American) an alternate form of Krystal.
Krystl, Krystyl

KUDIO (Swahili) born on Monday.

KUMA (Japanese) bear.

KUMIKO (Japanese) girl with braids.
Kumi

KUMUDA (Sanskrit) lotus flower.

KUNIKO (Japanese) child from the country.

KUNTO (Twi) third-born.

KURI (Japanese) chestnut.

KUSA (Hindi) God's grass.

KWANITA (Zuni) a form of Juanita.

KWASHI (Swahili) born on Sunday.

KWAU (Swahili) born on Thursday.

KYANA (American) an alternate form of Kiana.
Kyanah, Kyani, Kyann, Kyanna, Kyanne, Kyanni, Kyeana, Kyeanna

KYARA (Irish) an alternate form of Kiara.
Kiyara, Kiyera, Kiyerra, Kyarah, Kyaria, Kyarie, Kyarra, Kyera, Kyerra

KYLA (Irish) attractive. (Yiddish) crown; laurel.
Khyla, Kylah, Kylea, Kyleah, Kylia

KYLE (Irish) attractive.
Kial, Kiele, Kylee, Kyleigh, Kylene, Kylie

KYLEE (Irish) a familiar form of Kyle.
Kylea, Kyleah, Kylie, Kyliee

KYLEIGH (Irish) an alternate form of Kyle.
Kyliegh

KYLENE (Irish) an alternate form of Kyle.
Kyleen, Kylen, Kylyn, Kylynn

KYLIE (West Australian Aboriginal) curled stick; boomerang. (Irish) a familiar form of Kyle.
Keiley, Keilley, Keilly, Keily, Kiley, Kye, Kylee, Kyley, Kyli, Kyllie

KYMBERLY (English) an alternate form of Kimberly.
Kymber, Kymberlee, Kymberleigh, Kymberley, Kymberli, Kymberlie, Kymberlyn, Kymberlynn, Kymberlynne

KYNDAL, Kyndall (English) alternate forms of Kendall.
Kyndahl, Kyndalle, Kyndel, Kyndell, Kyndelle, Kyndle, Kyndol

KYNTHIA (Greek) an alternate form of Cynthia.
Kyndi

KYOKO (Japanese) mirror.

KYRA (Greek) ladylike. An alternate form of Cyrilla.
Keera, Keira, Kira, Kyrah, Kyrene, Kyria, Kyriah, Kyriann, Kyrie

L

LACEY, Lacy (Greek) familiar forms of Larissa. (Latin) cheerful.
Lacee, Laci, Lacie, Lacye

LACHANDRA (American) a combination of the prefix La + Chandra.
Lachanda, Lachandice

LACI, Lacie (Latin) alternate forms of Lacey.
Lacia, Laciann, Lacianne

LACRECIA (Latin) an alternate form of Lucretia.
Lacrasha, Lacreash, Lacreasha, Lacreashia, Lacreisha, Lacresha, Lacreshia, Lacresia, Lacretia, Lacricia, Lacriesha, Lacrisah, Lacrisha, Lacrishia, Lacrissa

LADA (Russian) Mythology: the goddess of beauty.

LADASHA (American) a combination of the prefix La + Dasha.
Ladaesha, Ladaisa, Ladaisha, Ladaishea, Ladaishia, Ladashiah, Ladaseha, Ladashia, Ladasia, Ladassa, Ladaysha, Ladesha, Ladisha, Ladosha

LADEIDRA (American) a combinatione of the prefix La + Deidra.
Ladedra, Ladiedra

LADONNA (American) a combination of the prefix La + Donna.
Ladan, Ladana, Ladon, Ladona, Ladonne, Ladonya

LAELA (Arabic, Hebrew) an alternate form of Leila.
Lael, Laelle

LAHELA (Hawaiian) a form of Rachel.

LAILA (Arabic) an alternate form of Leila.
Lailah, Laili, Lailie

LAINE, Layne (French) short forms of Elaine.
Lain, Laina, Lainah, Lainee, Lainna, Layna

LAINEY, Layney (French) familiar forms of Elaine.
Laini, Lainie, Laynee, Layni, Laynie

LAJILA (Hindi) shy, coy.

LAJUANA (American) a combination of the prefix La + Juana.
Lajuanna, Lawana, Lawanna, Lawanza, Lawanze, Laweania

LAKA (Hawaiian) attractive; seductive; tame. Mythology: the goddess of the hula dance.

LAKAYLA (American) a combination of the prefix La + Kayla.
Lakala, Lakaya, Lakeila, Lakela, Lakella

LAKEISHA (American) a combination of the prefix La + Keisha. See also Lekasha.
Lakaiesha, Lakaisha, Lakasha, Lakashia, Lakaysha, Lakaysia, Lakeasha, Lakecia, Lakeesh, Lakeesha, Lakeeshia, Lakesha, Lakeshia, Lakeysha, Lakezia, Lakicia, Lakieshia, Lakisha

LAKEN, Lakin, Lakyn (American) short forms of Lakendra.
Lakena, Lakyna, Lakynn

LAKENDRA (American) a combination of the prefix La + Kendra.
Lakanda, Lakedra, Laken, Lakenda

LAKENYA (American) a combination of the prefix La + Kenya.
Lakeena, Lakeenna, Lakeenya, Lakena, Lakenia, Lakinja, Lakinya, Lakwanya, Lekenia, Lekenya

LAKESHA, Lakeshia, Lakisha (American) alternate forms of Lakeisha.
Lakecia, Lakeesha, Lakesa, Lakese, Lakeseia, Lakeshya, Lakesi, Lakesia, Lakeyshia, Lakiesha

LAKETA (American) a combination of the prefix La + Keita.
Lakeeta, Lakeetah, Lakeita, Lakeitha, Lakeithia, Laketha, Laketia, Laketta, Lakieta, Lakietha, Lakita, Lakitia, Lakitra, Lakitri, Lakitta

LAKIA (Arabic) found treasure.
Lakiea, Lakkia

LAKOTA (Dakota) a tribal name.
Lakoda, Lakohta, Lakotah

LAKRESHA (American) a form of Lucretia.
Lacresha, Lacreshia, Lacresia, Lacretia, Lacrisha, Lakreshia, Lakrisha, Lekresha, Lekresia

LAKYA (Hindi) born on Thursday.
Lakeya, Lakeyah, Lakieya, Lakiya, Lakyia

LALA (Slavic) tulip.
Lalah, Lalla

LALASA (Hindi) love.

LALEH (Persian) tulip.
Lalah

LALI (Spanish) a form of Lulani.
Lalia, Lalli, Lally

LALITA (Greek) talkative. (Sanskrit) charming; candid. Religion: a name for the Hindu goddess Shakti.

LALLIE (English) babbler.
Lalli, Lally

LAMESHA (American) a combination of the prefix La + Mesha.
Lamees, Lameesha, Lameise, Lameisha, Lameshia, Lamisha, Lamishia, Lemisha

LAMIA (German) bright land. A feminine form of Lambert.
Lama, Lamiah

LAMIS (Arabic) soft to the touch.
Lamese, Lamise

LAMONICA (American) a combination of the prefix La + Monica.
Lamoni, Lamonika

LAMYA (Arabic) dark lipped.
Lama

LAN (Vietnamese) flower.

LANA (Latin) woolly. (Irish) attractive, peaceful. A short form of Alana, Elana. (Hawaiian) floating; bouyant.
Lanae, Lanai, Lanata, Lanay, Laneah, Laneetra, Lanette, Lanna, Lannah

LANDA (Basque) another name for the Virgin Mary.

LANDON (English) open, grassy meadow.
Landan, Landen, Landin, Landyn, Landynne

LANDRA (German, Spanish) counselor.
Landrea

LANE (English) narrow road.
Laina, Laney, Layne

LANEISHA (American) a combination of the prefix La + Keneisha.
Laneasha, Lanecia, Laneesha, Laneise, Laneishia, Lanesha, Laneshe, Laneshea, Laneshia, Lanesia, Lanessa, Lanesse, Lanisha, Lanishia

LANEY (English) a familiar form of Lane.
Lanie, Lanni, Lanny, Lany

LANI (Hawaiian) sky; heaven. A short form of Atalanta, 'Aulani, Leilani.
Lanee, Lanei, Lania, Lanie, Lanita, Lanney, Lanni, Lannie

LAPORSHA (American) a combination of the prefix La + Porsha.
Laporcha, Laporche, Laporscha, Laporsche, Laporschia, Laporshe, Laporshia, Laportia

LAQUEENA (American) a combination of the prefix La + Queenie.
Laqueen, Laquena, Laquenetta, Laquinna

LAQUINTA (American) a combination of the prefix La + Quintana.
Laquanta, Laqueinta, Laquenda, Laquenta, Laquinda

LAQUISHA (American) a combination of the prefix La + Queisha.
Laquasha, Laquaysha, Laqueisha, Laquesha, Laquiesha

LAQUITA (American) a combination of the prefix La + Queta.
Laqeita, Laqueta, Laquetta, Laquia, Laquiata, Laquieta, Laquitta, Lequita

LARA (Greek) cheerful. (Latin) shining; famous. Mythology: the daughter of the river god Almo. A short form of Laraine, Larissa, Laura.
Larae, Larah, Laretta, Larette

LARAINE (Latin) an alternate form of Lorraine.
Lara, Laraene, Larain, Larane, Larayn, Larayne, Laraynna, Larein, Lareina, Lareine, Laren, Larenn, Larenya, Lauraine, Laurraine

LARINA (Greek) seagull.
Larena, Larine

LARISA (Greek) an alternate form of
Larissa.
Lareesa, Lareese, Laresa, Laris, Larise,
Larisha, Larrisa, Larysa, Laurisa

LARISSA (Greek) cheerful. See also
Lacey.
Lara, Laressa, Larisa, Larissah, Larrissa,
Larryssa, Laryssa, Laurissa, Laurissah

LARK (English) skylark.

LASHAE, Lashay (American)
combinations of the prefix La + Shay.
Lasha, Lashai, Lashaia, Lashaya, Lashaye,
Lashea

LASHANA (American) a combination
of the prefix La + Shana.
Lashanay, Lashane, Lashanna, Lashannon,
Lashona, Lashonna

LASHANDA (American)
a combination of the prefix
La + Shanda.
Lashandra, Lashanta, Lashante

LASHAWNA (American)
a combination of the prefix
La + Shawna.
Lashaun, Lashauna, Lashaune, Lashaunna,
Lashaunta, Lashawn, Lashawnd,
Lashawnda, Lashawndra, Lashawne,
Lashawnia, Leshawn, Leshawna

LASHONDA (American) a combination
of the prefix La + Shonda.
Lachonda, Lashaunda, Lashaundra, Lashon,
Lashond, Lashonde, Lashondia, Lashondra,
Lashonta, Lashunda, Lashundra, Lashunta,
Lashunte, Leshande, Leshandra, Leshondra,
Leshundra

LATANYA (American) a combination
of the prefix La + Tanya.
Latana, Latandra, Latania, Latanja,
Latanna, Latanua, Latonshia

LATARA (American) a combination of
the prefix La + Tara.

LATASHA (American) a combination
of the prefix La + Tasha.
Latacha, Latacia, Latai, Lataisha, Latashia,
Latasia, Lataysha, Letasha, Letashia,
Letasiah

LATAVIA (American) a combination of
the prefix La + Tavia.

LATEEFAH (Arabic) pleasant.
(Hebrew) pat, caress.
Lateefa, Latifa, Latifah, Latipha

LATESHA (American) a form of Letitia.
Lataeasha, Lateasha, Lateashia, Latecia,
Lateicia, Lateisha, Latesa, Lateshia, Latessa,
Lateysha, Latisa, Latissa, Leteisha, Leteshia

LATIA (American) a combination of
the prefix La + Tia.
Latea, Lateia, Lateka

LATIKA (Hindi) elegant.
Lateeka, Lateka

LATISHA (Latin) joy. An alternate form
of Leticia. (American) a combination
of the prefix La + Tisha.
Laetitia, Laetizia, Latashia, Lateasha,
Lateashia, Latecia, Lateesha, Lateicia,
Lateisha, Latice, Laticia, Latiesha, Latishia,
Latishya, Latissa, Latitia, Latysha

LATONA (Latin) Mythology: the
powerful goddess who bore Apollo
and Diana.
Latonna, Latonnah

LATONYA (Latin) an alternate form of
Latona. (American) a combination
of the prefix La + Tonya.
Latoni, Latonia

LATORIA (American) a combination
of the prefix La + Tori.
Latoira, Latorio, Latorja, Latorray,
Latorreia, Latory, Latorya, Latoyra,
Latoyria

LATOSHA (American) a combination
of the prefix La + Tosha.
Latoshia, Latoshya, Latosia

LATOYA (American) a combination of the prefix La + Toya.
Latoia, Latoiya, LaToya, Latoyia, Latoye, Latoyia, Latoyita, Latoyo

LATRICE (American) a combination of the prefix La + Trice.
Latrece, Latreece, Latreese, Latresa, Latrese, Latressa, Letreece, Letrice

LATRICIA (American) a combination of the prefix La + Tricia.
Latrecia, Latresh, Latresha, Latreshia, Latrica, Latrisha, Latrishia

LAURA (Latin) crowned with laurel. A feminine form of Laurence.
Lara, Laurah, Lauralee, Laurelen, Laurella, Lauren, Lauricia, Laurie, Laurka, Laury, Lauryn, Lavra, Lolly, Lora, Loretta, Lori, Lorinda, Lorna, Loura

LAUREL (Latin) laurel tree.
Laural, Laurell, Laurelle, Lorel, Lorelle

LAUREN (English) a form of Laura.
Lauran, Laureen, Laurena, Laurene, Laurien, Laurin, Laurine, Lawren, Loren, Lorena

LAURENCE (Latin) crowned with laurel.
Laurencia, Laurens, Laurent, Laurentana, Laurentina, Lawrencia

LAURIANNA (English) a combination of Laurie + Anne.
Laurana, Laurann, Laureana, Laureanne, Laureen, Laureena, Laurian, Lauriana, Lauriane, Laurianna, Laurie Ann, Laurie Anne, Laurina

LAURIE (English) a familiar form of Laura.
Lari, Larilia, Laure, Lauré, Lauri, Lawrie

LAURY (English) a familiar form of Laura.

LAURYN (English) a familiar form of Laura.
Laurynn

LAVEDA (Latin) cleansed, purified.
Lavare, Lavetta, Lavette

LAVELLE (Latin) cleansing.
Lavella

LAVENA (Latin) an alternate form of Lavina. (Irish, French) joy.

LAVERNE (Latin) springtime. (French) grove of alder trees. See also Verna.
Laverine, Lavern, Laverna, La Verne

LAVINA (Latin) purified; woman of Rome. See also Vina.
Lavena, Lavenia, Lavinia, Lavinie, Levenia, Levinia, Livinia, Louvinia, Lovina, Lovinia

LAVONNA (American) a combination of the prefix La + Yvonne.
Lavon, Lavonda, Lavonder, Lavondria, Lavone, Lavonia, Lavonica, Lavonn, Lavonne, Lavonnie, Lavonya

LAWAN (Tai) pretty.
Lawanne

LAWANDA (American) a combination of the prefix La + Wanda.
Lawonda, Lawynda

LAYCE (American) a form of Lacey.
Laycee, Layci, Laycia, Laycie, Laysa, Laysea, Laysie

LAYLA (Hebrew, Arabic) an alternate form of Leila.
Laylah, Layli, Laylie

LE (Vietnamese) pearl.

LEA (Hawaiian) Mythology: the goddess of canoe makers.

LEAH (Hebrew) weary. Bible: the wife of Jacob. See also Lia.
Lea, Léa, Lee, Leea, Leeah, Leia

LEALA (French) faithful, loyal.
Lealia, Lealie, Leial

LEAN, Leann, Leanne (English) forms of Leeann, Lian.
Leana, Leane, Leanna

LEANDRA (Latin) like a lioness.
Leanda, Leandre, Leandrea, Leandria, Leeanda, Leeandra

LEANNA, Leeanna (English) alternate forms of Liana.
Leana, Leeana, Leianna

LEANORE (Greek) an alternate form of Eleanor. (English) a form of Helen.
Leanora, Lanore

LECIA (Latin) a short form of Felecia.
Leasia, Leecia, Leesha, Leesia, Lesha, Leshia, Lesia

LEDA (Greek) lady. Mythology: the Queen of Sparta and the mother of Helen of Troy.
Ledah, Lyda, Lydah

LEE (Chinese) plum. (Irish) poetic. (English) meadow. A short form of Ashley, Leah.
Lea, Leigh

LEEANN, Leeanne (English) a combination of Lee + Ann. A form of Lian.
Leane, Leean, Leian, Leiann, Leianne

LEENA (Estonian) a form of Helen.

LEEZA (Hebrew) a short form of Aleeza. (English) an alternate form of Lisa, Liza.
Leesa

LEI (Hawaiian) a familiar form of Leilani.

LEIGH, Leigha (English) alternate forms of Lee.
Leighann, Leighanna, Leighanne

LEIKO (Japanese) arrogant.

LEILA (Hebrew) dark beauty; night. (Arabic) born at night. Literature: the heroine of the epic Persian poem *Leila and Majnum*. See also Laela, Layla, Lila.
Laila, Leela, Leelah, Leilah, Leilia, Lela, Lelah, Leland, Lelia, Leyla

LEILANI (Hawaiian) heavenly flower; heavenly child.
Lailanee, Lailani, Lailanie, Lailany, Lailoni, Lani, Lei, Leilany, Leiloni, Leilony, Lelani, Lelania

LEIRE (Basque) Religion: another name for the Virgin Mary.

LEKASHA (American) an alternate form of Lakeishia.
Lekeesha, Lekeisha, Lekesha, Lekeshia, Lekesia, Lekicia, Lekisha

LELI (Swiss) a form of Magdalen.
Lelie

LELIA (Greek) fair speech.
Leliah, Lelika, Lelita, Lellia

LELYA (Russian) a form of Helen.

LENA (Greek) a short form of Eleanor. (Hebrew) dwelling or lodging. (Latin) temptress. (Norwegian) illustrious. Music: Lena Horne, a well-known African-American singer.
Lenah, Lene, Lenee, Leni, Lenka, Lenna, Lennah, Lina, Linah

LENCI (Hungarian) a form of Helen.
Lency

LENE (German) a form of Helen.
Leni, Line

LENEISHA (American) a combination of the prefix Le + Keneisha.
Lenece, Lenesha, Leniesha, Lenieshia, Leniesia, Leniessia, Lenisa, Lenise, Lenisha, Lennise, Lennisha, Lynesha

LENIA (German) an alternate form of Leona.

Lenayah, Lenda, Lenea, Leneen, Lenna, Lennah, Lennea, Leny

LENITA (Latin) gentle.
Leneta, Lenette, Lennette

LENORE (Greek, Russian) a form of Eleanor.
Lenni, Lenor, Lenora, Lenorah

LEONA (German) brave as a lioness. A feminine form of Leon. See also Lona.
Lenia, Leoine, Leola, Leolah, Leonae, Leonah, Leondra, Leone, Leonelle, Leonia, Leonice, Leonicia, Leonie, Leonissa, Leonna, Leonne, Liona

LEONIE (German) a familiar form of Leona.
Leoni, Léonie, Leony

LEONORE (Greek) an alternate form of Eleanor. See also Nora.
Leonor, Leonora, Leonorah, Léonore

LEONTINE (Latin) like a lioness.
Leona, Leonine, Leontyne, Léontyne

LEORA (Greek) a familiar form of Eleanor. (Hebrew) light. See also Liora.
Leorah, Leorit

LEOTIE (Native American) prairie flower.

LERA (Russian) a short form of Valera.
Lerka

LESLEY (Scottish) gray fortress.
Leslea, Leslee, Leslie, Lesly, Lezlee, Lezley

LESLIE (Scottish) an alternate form of Lesley.
Leslei, Lesleigh, Lesli, Lesslie, Lezli

LESLY (Scottish) an alternate form of Lesley.
Leslye, Lessly, Lezly

LETA (Greek) a short form of Aleta. (Latin) glad. (Swahili) bringer.
Lita, Lyta

LETICIA (Latin) joy. See also Latisha, Tisha.
Laticia, Leisha, Leshia, Let, Leta, Letesa, Letesha, Leteshia, Letha, Lethia, Letice, Letichia, Letisha, Letishia, Letisia, Letissa, Letita, Letitia, Letiticia, Letiza, Letizia, Letty, Letycia, Loutitia

LETTY (English) a familiar form of Leticia.
Letta, Letti, Lettie

LEVANA (Hebrew) moon; white. (Latin) risen. Mythology: the goddess of newborn babies.
Lévana, Levania, Levanna, Levenia, Lewana, Livana

LEVANI (Fijian) anointed with oil.

LEVIA (Hebrew) joined, attached.
Leevya, Levi, Levie

LEVINA (Latin) flash of lightning.
Levene

LEVONA (Hebrew) spice, incense.
Leavonia, Levonat, Levonna, Levonne, Livona

LEWANA (Hebrew) an alternate form of Levana.
Lebhanah, Lewanna

LEXANDRA (Greek) a short form of Alexandra.
Lisandra

LEXI, Lexie (Greek) familiar forms of Alexandra.
Leksi, Lexey, Lexy

LEXIA (Greek) a familiar form of Alexandra.
Leska, Lesya, Lexa, Lexane, Lexina, Lexine

LEXIS (Greek) a short form of Alexius, Alexus.
Laexis, Lexius, Lexsis, Lexxis

LEXUS (Greek) a short form of Alexis.
Lexuss, Lexxus, Lexyss

LEYA (Spanish) loyal. (Tamil) the constellation Leo.
Leyah, Leyla

LIA (Greek) bringer of good news. (Hebrew, Dutch, Italian) dependent. See also Leah.
Liah

LIAN (Chinese) graceful willow. (Latin) a short form of Gillian, Lillian.
Lean, Leeann, Liane, Liann, Lianne

LIANA, Lianna (Hebrew) short forms of Eliana. (Latin) youth. (French) bound, wrapped up; tree covered with vines. (English) meadow.
Leanna

LIANE, Lianne (Hebrew) short forms of Eliane. (English) forms of Lian.
Leeanne

LIBBY (Hebrew) a familiar form of Elizabeth.
Ibby, Lib, Libbee, Libbey, Libbie

LIBERTY (Latin) free.
Liberti, Libertie

LICIA (Greek) a short form of Alicia.
Licha, Lishia, Lisia, Lycia

LIDA (Greek) happy. (Latin) a short form of Alida, Elita. (Slavic) loved by people.
Leeda, Lidah, Lidochka, Lyda

LIDE (Latin, Basque) life.

LIDIA (Greek) an alternate form of Lydia.
Lidea, Lidi, Lidija, Lidiya, Lidka, Lidya

LIEN (Chinese) lotus.
Lienne

LIESABET (German) a short form of Elizabeth.
Liesbeth, Lisbete

LIESE (German) a familiar form of Elise, Elizabeth.
Liesa, Lieschen, Lise

LIESEL (German) a familiar form of Elizabeth.
Leesel, Leesl, Leezel, Leezl, Liesl, Liezel, Liezl, Lisel

LILA (Arabic) night. (Hindi) free will of god. (Persian) lilac. A short form of Dalila, Delilah, Lillian.
Lilah, Lilia, Lyla, Lylah

LILAC (Sanskrit) lilac; blue−purple.

LILIA (Persian) an alternate form of Lila.
Lili

LILIAN (Latin) an alternate form of Lillian.
Liliane, Liliann, Lilianne

LILIANA (Latin) an alternate form of Lillian.
Lileana, Lilliana, Lilianna, Lilliana, Lillianna

LILIBETH (English) a combination of Lilly + Beth.
Lilibet, Lillibeth, Lillybeth, Lilybet, Lilybeth

LILITH (Arabic) of the night; night demon. Mythology: the first wife of Adam, according to ancient eastern legends.
Lillis, Lily

LILLIAN (Latin) lily flower.
Lian, Lil, Lila, Lilas, Lileane, Lilia, Lilian, Liliana, Lilias, Liliha, Lilja, Lilla, Lilli, Lillia, Lilliane, Lilliann, Lillianne, Lillyann, Lis, Liuka

LILLYANN (Latin) an alternate form of Lilian. (English) a combination of Lilly + Ann.
Lillyan, Lillyanne, Lily, Lilyan, Lilyana, Lilyann, Lilyanna, Lilyanne

LILY (Latin, Arabic) a familiar form of Lilith, Lillian, Lillyann.
Lil, Líle, Lili, Lilie, Lilijana, Lilika, Lilike, Liliosa, Lilium, Lilka, Lille, Lilli, Lillie, Lilly

LIMBER (Tiv) joyful.

LIN (Chinese) beautiful jade. (English) a short form of Lynn.
Linh, Linn

LINA (Greek) light. (Latin) an alternate form of Lena. (Arabic) tender.

LINDA (Spanish) pretty.
Lind, Lindy, Linita, Lynda

LINDSAY (English) an alternate form of Lindsey.
Lindsi, Linsay, Lyndsay

LINDSEY (English) linden tree island; camp near the stream.
Lind, Lindsea, Lindsee, Lindsi, Linsey, Lyndsey, Lynsey

LINDSI (American) a familiar form of Lindsay, Lindsey.
Lindsie, Lindsy, Lindze, Lindzee, Lindzey, Lindzy

LINDY (Spanish) a familiar form of Linda.
Linde, Lindee, Lindey, Lindi, Lindie

LINETTE (Welsh) idol. (French) bird.
Lanette, Linet, Linnet, Linnetta, Linnette, Lyannette, Lynette

LING (Chinese) delicate, dainty.

LINNEA (Scandinavian) lime tree. History: the national flower of Sweden.
Lin, Linae, Linea, Linnae, Linnaea, Linneah, Lynea, Lynnea

LINSEY (English) an alternate form of Lindsey.
Linsea, Linsee, Linsi, Linsie, Linsy, Linzee, Linzey, Linzi, Linzie, Linzy, Linzzi, Lynsey

LIOLYA (Russian) a form of Helen.

LIORA (Hebrew) light. See also Leora.

LIRIT (Hebrew) poetic; lyrical, musical.

LIRON (Hebrew) my song.
Leron, Lerone, Lirone

LISA (Hebrew) consecrated to God. (English) a short form of Elizabeth.
Leeza, Liesa, Liisa, Lise, Lisenka, Lisette, Liszka, Litsa, Lysa

LISBETH (English) a short form of Elizabeth.
Lisbet

LISE (German) a form of Lisa.

LISETTE, Lissette (French) forms of Lisa. (English) familiar forms of Elise, Elizabeth.
Liset, Liseta, Lisete, Liseth, Lisett, Lisetta, Lisettina, Lisset, Lissete, Lissett, Lizet, Lizette, Lysette

LISHA (Hebrew) a short form of Alisha, Elisha, Ilisha. (Arabic) darkness before midnight.
Lishe

LISSA (Greek) honey bee. A short form of Elissa, Elizabeth, Melissa, Millicent.
Lyssa

LISSIE (American) a familiar form of Allison, Elise, Elizabeth.
Lissee, Lissey, Lissi, Lissy, Lissye

LITA (Latin) a familiar form of names ending in 'lita.'
Leta, Litah, Litta

LITONYA (Moquelumnan) darting hummingbird.

LIV (Latin) a short form of Livia, Olivia.

LIVANA (Hebrew) an alternate form of Levana. Astrological: born under the sign of Cancer.
Livna, Livnat

LIVIA (Hebrew) crown. A familiar form of Olivia. (Latin) olive.
Levia, Liv, Livie, Livy, Livya, Livye

LIVIYA (Hebrew) brave lioness; royal crown.
Leviya, Levya, Livya

LIVONA (Hebrew) an alternate form of Levona.

LIZ (English) a short form of Elizabeth.

LIZA (American) a short form of Elizabeth.
Leeza, Lizela, Lizka, Lyza

LIZABETA (Russian) a form of Elizabeth.
Lizabetah, Lizaveta, Lizonka

LIZABETH (English) a short form of Elizabeth.
Lisabet, Lisabeth, Lisabette, Lizabette

LIZBETH (English) a short form of Elizabeth.
Lizbet, Lizbett

LIZET, Lizette (French) alternate forms of Lisette.
Lizet, Lizete, Lizeth, Lizett, Lizzet, Lizzeth, Lizzette

LIZINA (Latvian) a familiar form of Elizabeth.

LIZZY (American) a familiar form of Elizabeth.
Lizzie, Lizy

LOGAN (Irish) meadow.
Logann, Loganne, Logen, Loghan, Logun, Logyn, Logynn

LOIS (German) famous warrior. An alternate form of Louise.

LOLA (Spanish) a familiar form of Carlota, Dolores, Louise.
Lolah, Lolita

LOLITA (Spanish) sorrowful. A familiar form of Lola.
Lita, Lulita

LOLLY (English) a familiar form of Laura.

LOLOTEA (Zuni) a form of Dorothy.

LOMASI (Native American) pretty flower.

LONA (Latin) lioness. (German) a short form of Leona. (English) solitary.
Loni, Lonna

LONDON (English) fortress of the moon. Geography: the capital of Great Britain.
Landyn, Londen, Londun, Londyn

LONI (American) a form of Lona.
Lonee, Lonie, Lonni, Lonnie

LORA (Latin) crowned with laurel. (American) a form of Laura.
Lorah, Lorane, Lorann, Lorra, Lorrah, Lorrane

LORE (Latin) a short form of Flora. (Basque) flower.
Lor

LORELEI (German) alluring. Mythology: the siren of the Rhine River who lured sailors to their deaths. See also Lurleen.
Loralee, Loralei, Lorali, Loralie, Loralyn, Loreal, Lorelea, Loreli, Lorilee, Lorilyn

LORELLE (American) a form of Laurel.

LOREN (American) an alternate form of Lauren.
Loreen, Lorena, Lorin, Lorne, Lorren, Lorrin, Lorryn, Loryn, Lorynn, Lorynne

LORENA (English) an alternate form of Lauren, Loren.
Lorene, Lorenea, Lorenia, Lorenna, Lorina, Lorrina, Lorrine, Lurana

LORENZA (Latin) an alternate form of Laura.
Laurencia, Laurentia, Laurentina

LORETTA (English) a familiar form of Laura.
Larretta, Lauretta, Laurette, Loretah, Lorette, Lorita, Lorretta, Lorrette

LORI (Latin) crowned with laurel. (French) a short form of Lorraine. (American) a familiar form of Laura.
Loree, Lorey, Loria, Lorianna, Lorianne, Lorie, Lorree, Lorri, Lorrie, Lory

LORIN (American) an alternate forn of Loren.
Lorine

LORINDA (Spanish) a form of Laura.

LORIS (Greek) a short form of Chloris. (Latin) thong. (Dutch) clown.
Laurice, Laurys, Lorice

LORNA (Latin) crowned with laurel. An alternate form of Laura. Literature: probably coined by Richard Blackmore in his novel *Lorna Doone*.
Lorrna

LORRAINE (Latin) sorrowful. (French) from Lorraine. See also Rayna.
Laraine, Lorain, Loraine, Lorayne, Lorein, Loreine, Lori, Lorine, Lorrain, Lorraina, Lorrayne, Lorreine

LOTTE (German) a short form of Charlotte.
Lotie, Lotta, Lottchen, Lottey, Lottie, Lotty, Loty

LOTUS (Greek) lotus.

LOU (American) a short form of Louise, Luella.
Lu

LOUAM (Ethiopian) sleep well.

LOUISA (English) a familiar form of Louise. Literature: Louisa May Alcott was an American writer and reformer best known for her novel *Little Women*.
Aloisa, Eloisa, Heloisa, Lou, Louisian, Louisane, Louisina, Louiza, Lovisa, Luisa, Luiza, Lujza, Lujzika

LOUISE (German) famous warrior. A feminine form of Louis. See also Alison, Eloise, Heloise, Lois, Lola, Ludovica, Luella, Lulu.
Loise, Lou, Louisa, Louisette, Louisiane, Louisine, Lowise, Loyce, Loyise, Luise

LOURDES (French) from Lourdes, France. Geography: a town in France. Religion: a place where the Virgin Mary was said to have appeared.

LOVE (English) love; kindness; charity.
Lovely, Lovewell, Lovey, Lovie, Lovy, Luv, Luvvy

LOVISA (German) an alternate form of Louisa.

LUANN (Hebrew, German) graceful woman warrior. (Hawaiian) happy; relaxed. (American) a combination of Louise + Anne.
Louann, Louanne, Lu, Lua, Luan, Luane, Luanna, Luanne, Luanni, Luannie

LUANNA (German) an alternate form of Luann.
Lewanna, Louanna, Luana, Luwana

LUBOV (Russian) love.
Luba, Lubna, Lubochka, Lyuba, Lyubov

LUCERNE (Latin) lamp; circle of light. Geography: a lake in Switzerland.
Lucerna, Lucero

LUCERO (Latin) an alternate form of Lucerne.

LUCETTA (English) a familiar form of Lucy.
Lucette

LUCIA (Italian, Spanish) a form of Lucy.
Luciana, Lucianna

LUCIE (French) a familiar form of Lucy.

LUCILLE (English) a familiar form of Lucy.
Lucila, Lucile, Lucilla

LUCINDA (Latin) a familiar form of Lucy. See also Cindy.

LUCINE (Basque) a form of Lucy. (Arabic) moon.
Lucienne, Lucina, Lucyna, Lukene, Lusine, Luzine

LUCITA (Spanish) a form of Lucy.
Lusita

LUCRETIA (Latin) rich; rewarded.
Lacrecia, Lucrece, Lucréce, Lucrecia, Lucreecia, Lucresha, Lucreshia, Lucrezia, Lucrisha, Lucrishia

LUCREZIA (Italian) a form of Lucretia. History: Lucrezia Borgia was the Duchess of Ferrara and a patron of learning and the arts.

LUCY (Latin) light; bringer of light. A feminine form of Lucius.
Luca, Luce, Lucetta, Luci, Lucia, Lucida, Lucie, Lucija, Lucika, Lucille, Lucinda, Lucine, Lucita, Luciya, Lucya, Luzca, Luzi

LUDMILLA (Slavic) loved by the people. See also Mila.
Ludie, Ludka, Ludmila, Lyuba, Lyudmila

LUDOVICA (German) an alternate form of Louise.
Ludovika, Ludwiga

LUELLA (German) a familiar form of Louise. (English) elf.
Loella, Lou, Louella, Ludella, Luelle, Lula, Lulu

LUISA (Spanish) a form of Louisa.

LULANI (Polynesian) highest point of heaven.

LULU (Arabic) pearl. (German) a familiar form of Louise, Luella. (English) soothing, comforting. (Native American) hare.
Loulou, Lula, Lulie

LUNA (Latin) moon.
Lunetta, Lunette, Lunneta, Lunnete

LUPE (Latin) wolf. (Spanish) a short form of Guadalupe.
Lupi, Lupita, Luppi

LUPITA (Latin) an alternate form of Lupe.

LURLEEN, Lurlene (German) alternate forms of Lorelei. (Scandinavian) war horn.
Lura, Lurette, Lurline

LUSA (Finnish) a form of Elizabeth.

LUSELA (Moquelumnan) like a bear swinging its foot when licking it.

LUVENA (Latin, English) little; beloved.
Lovena, Lovina, Luvenia, Luvina

LUYU (Moquelumnan) like a pecking bird.

LUZ (Spanish) light. Religion: Santa Maria de Luz is another name for the Virgin Mary.
Luzi, Luzija

LYCORIS (Greek) twilight.

LYDA (Greek) a short form of Lidia, Lydia.

LYDIA (Greek) from Lydia, an ancient land once ruled by Midas. (Arabic) strife.
Lidia, Lidija, Lidiya, Lyda, Lydie, Lydië

LYLA (French) island. (English) a feminine form of Lyle.
Lila, Lilah

LYNDA (Spanish) pretty. (American) a form of Linda.
Lyndah, Lynde, Lyndi, Lynnda

LYNDELL (English) an alternate form of Lynelle.
Lyndall, Lyndel, Lyndella

LYNDI (Spanish) a familiar form of Lynda.
Lyndee, Lindie, Lyndy, Lynndie, Lynndy

LYNDSAY (American) a form of Lindsay.
Lyndsaye

LYNDSEY (English) linden tree island; camp near the stream. (American) a form of Lindsey.
Lyndsea, Lyndsee, Lyndsi, Lyndsie, Lyndsy, Lyndzee, Lyndzey, Lyndzi, Lyndzie, Lynndsie

LYNELLE (English) pretty.
Linel, Linell, Linnell, Lyndell, Lynel, Lynell, Lynella, Lynnell

LYNETTE (Welsh) idol. (English) a form of Linette.
Lynett, Lynetta, Lynnet, Lynnette

LYNN, Lynne (English) waterfall; pool below a waterfall.
Lin, Lina, Linley, Linn, Lyn, Lynlee, Lynley, Lynna, Lynnae, Lynnea

LYNNELL (English) an alternate form of Lynelle.
Linnell, Lynnelle

LYNSEY (American) an alternate form of Lyndsey.
Lynnsey, Lynnzey, Lynsie, Lynsy, Lynzee, Lynzey, Lynzi, Lynzie, Lynzy

LYRA (Greek) lyre player.
Lyre, Lyric, Lyrica, Lyrie, Lyris

LYSANDRA (Greek) liberator. A feminine form of Lysander.
Lisandra, Lysandre, Lytle

LYSANNE (American) a combination of Lysandra + Anne.
Lisanne, Lizanne

M

MAB (Irish) joyous. (Welsh) baby. Literature: the name of the Fairy Queen in Edmund Spenser's epic romance *The Faerie Queene*.
Mabry

MABEL (Latin) lovable. A short form of Amabel.
Mabelle, Mable, Mabyn, Maible, Maybel, Maybeline, Maybelle, Maybull

MACAWI (Dakota) generous; motherly.

MACAYLA (American) an alternate form of Makayla.
Macaela, Macaila, Macala, Macalah, Macaylah, Macayle, Macayli, Mackayla

MACEY, Macie, Macy (Polish) familiar forms of Macia.
Macee, Maci, Macye

MACHAELA (Hebrew) an alternate form of Mickaela.
Machael, Machaelah, Machaelie, Machaila, Machala, Macheala

MACHIKO (Japanese) fortunate child.
Machi

MACIA (Polish) a form of Miriam.
Macelia, Macey, Machia, Macie, Macy, Masha, Mashia

MACKENNA (American) a form of Mackenzie.
Mackena, Makenna, Mckenna

MACKENZIE (Irish) daughter of the wise leader. See also Kenzie.
Macenzie, Mackenna, Mackensi, Mackensie, Mackenze, Mackenzee, Mackenzey, Mackenzi, Mackenzia, Mackenzy, Mackenzye, Mackinsey, Mackynze, Makenzie, McKenzie, Mckinzie, Mekenzie, Mykenzie

MACKINSEY (Irish) an alternate form of Mackenzie.
Mackinsie, Mackinze, Mackinzee, Mackinzey, Mackinzi, Mackinzie

MADA (English) a short form of Madaline, Magdalen.
Madda, Mahda

MADALINE (English) an alternate form of Madeline.
Mada, Madailéin, Madaleen, Madaleine, Madalene, Madalin, Madaline

MADALYN (Greek) an alternate form of Madeline.
Madalyne, Madalynn, Madalynne

MADDIE (English) a familiar form of Madeline.
Maddi, Maddy, Mady, Maidie, Maydey

MADDISON (English) an alternate form of Madison.
Maddisan, Maddisen, Maddisson, Maddisyn, Maddyson

MADELAINE (French) a form of Madeline.
Madelane, Madelayne

MADELEINE (French) a form of Madeline.
Madalaine, Madalayne, Madelaine, Madelein, Madeliene

MADELENA (English) an alternate form of Madeline.
Madalaina, Madalena, Madalina, Maddalena, Madelaina, Madeleina, Madelina, Madelyna

MADELINE (Greek) high tower. (English) from Magdala, England. An alternate form of Magdalen. See also Lena, Lina, Maud.
Madaline, Madalyn, Maddie, Madel, Madelaine, Madeleine, Madelena, Madelene, Madelia, Madella, Madelle, Madelon, Madelyn, Madge, Madilyn, Madlen, Madlin, Madline, Madlyn, Madolyn, Maida

MADELYN (Greek) an alternate form of Madeline.
Madelyne, Madelynn, Madelynne, Madilyn, Madlyn, Madolyn

MADGE (Greek) a familiar form of Madeline, Margaret.
Madgi, Madgie, Mady

MADILYN (Greek) an alternate form of Madeline.
Madilen, Madiline, Madilyne, Madilynn

MADISEN (English) an alternate form of Madison.
Madisan, Madisin, Madissen, Madisun

MADISON (English) good; daughter of Maud.
Maddison, Madisen, Madisson, Madisyn, Madyson, Mattison

MADISYN (English) an alternate form of Madison.
Madissyn, Madisynn, Madisynne

MADOLYN (Greek) an alternate form of Madeline.
Madoline, Madolyne, Madolynn, Madolynne

MADONNA (Latin) my lady.
Madona

MADRONA (Spanish) mother.
Madre, Madrena

MADYSON (English) an alternate form of Madison.
Madysen, Madysun

MAE (English) an alternate form of May. History: Mae Jemison was the first African-American woman in space.
Maelea, Maeleah, Maelen, Maelle, Maeona

MAEGAN (Irish) an alternate form of Megan.
Maegen, Maeghan, Maegin

MAEKO (Japanese) honest child.
Mae, Maemi

MAEVE (Irish) joyous. History: a first-century queen of Ireland. See also Mavis.
Maevi, Maevy, Maive, Mayve

MAGALI, Magaly (Hebrew) from the high tower.
Magalie, Magally

MAGAN, Magen (Greek) alternate forms of Megan.
Maggen, Maggin

MAGDA (Czech, Polish, Russian) a form of Magdalen.
Mahda, Makda

MAGDALEN (Greek) high tower. Bible: Magdala was the home of Saint Mary Magdalen. See also Madeline, Malena, Marlene.
Mada, Magda, Magdala, Magdaleen, Magdalena, Magdalene, Magdaline, Magdalyn, Magdalynn, Magdelane, Magdelene, Magdeline, Magdelyn, Magdlen, Magdolna, Maggie, Magola, Maighdlin, Mala, Malaine

MAGDALENA (Greek) an alternate form of Magdalen.
Magdalina, Magdelana, Magdelena, Magdelina

MAGENA (Native American) coming moon.

MAGGIE (Greek) pearl. (English) a familiar form of Magdalen, Margaret.
Mag, Magge, Maggee, Maggi, Maggia, Maggie, Maggiemae, Maggy, Magi, Magie, Mags

MAGGY, Meggy (English) alternate forms of Maggie.
Maggey, Magy

MAGNOLIA (Latin) flowering tree. See also Nollie.
Nola

MAHAL (Filipino) love.

MAHALA (Arabic) fat, marrow; tender. (Native American) powerful woman.

Mahalah, Mahalar, Mahalla, Mahela, Mahila, Mahlah, Mahlaha, Mehala, Mehalah

MAHALIA (American) a form of Mahala.
Mahaley, Mahaliah, Mahalie, Mahayla, Mahaylah, Mahaylia, Mahelea, Maheleah, Mahelia, Mahilia, Mehalia

MAHARENE (Ethiopian) forgive us.

MAHESA (Hindi) great lord. Religion: a name for the Hindu goddess Shiva.
Maheesa, Mahisa

MAHILA (Sanskrit) woman.

MAHINA (Hawaiian) moon glow.

MAHIRA (Hebrew) energetic.
Mahri

MAHOGONY (Spanish) rich; strong.
Mahagony, Mahoganey, Mahogani, Mahoganie, Mahogany, Mahogney, Mahogny, Mohogany, Mohogony

MAI (Japanese) brightness. (Vietnamese) flower. (Navajo) coyote.

MAIA (Greek) mother; nurse. (English) kinswoman; maiden. Mythology: the loveliest of the Pleiades, the seven daughters of Atlas, and the mother of Hermes. See also Maya.
Maiah, Maie, Maiya

MAIDA (Greek) a short form of Madeline. (English) maiden.
Maidel, Mayda, Maydena

MAIJA (Finnish) a form of Mary.
Maiji, Maikki

MAIKA (Hebrew) a familiar form of Michaela.
Maikala, Maikka, Maiko

MAIRA, Maire (Irish) forms of Mary.
Maairah, Mair, Mairi, Mairim, Mairin, Mairona, Mairwen

MAISIE (Scottish) a familiar form of Margaret.
Maisa, Maise, Maisey, Maisi, Maisy, Maizie, Maycee, Maysie, Mayzie, Mazey, Mazie, Mazy, Mazzy, Mysie, Myzie

MAITA (Spanish) a form of Martha.
Maite, Maitia

MAITLYN (American) a combination of Maita + Lynn.
Maitlan, Maitland, Maitlynn, Mattilyn

MAIYA (Greek) an alternate form of Maia.
Maiyah

MAJA (Arabic) a short form of Majidah.
Majal, Majalisa, Majalyn, Majalynn

MAJIDAH (Arabic) splendid.
Maja, Majida

MAKAELA, Makaila (American) forms of Michaela.
Makaelah, Makaelee, Makaella, Makaely, Makail, Makailah, Makailee, Makailla, Makaillah, Makealah, Makell

MAKALA (Hawaiian) myrtle.
Makalae, Makalah, Makalai, Makalea, Makalee, Makaleh, Makaleigh, Makaley, Makalia, Makalie, Makalya, Makela, Makelah, Makell, Makella

MAKANA (Hawaiian) gift, present.

MAKANI (Hawaiian) wind.

MAKARA (Hindi) born during the lunar month of Capricorn.

MAKAYLA (American) a form of Michaela.
Macayla, Makaylah, Makaylee, Makayleigh, Makayli, Makaylia, Makaylla, Makell, Makyla, Makylah, Mckayla, Mekayla, Mikayla

MAKELL (American) a short form of Makaela, Makala, Makayla.
Makele, Makelle, Mckell, Mekel

MAKENNA (American) an alternate form of Mackenna.
Makena, Makennah, Mikenna

MAKENZIE (Irish) an alternate form of Mackenzie.
Makense, Makensey, Makensie, Makenze, Makenzee, Makenzey, Makenzi, Makenzy, Makenzye, Makinzey, Makynzey, Mekenzie, Mykenzie

MALA (Greek) a short form of Magdalen.
Malana, Malee, Mali

MALANA (Hawaiian) bouyant, light.

MALAYA (Filipino) free.
Malayaa, Malayah, Malayna, Malea, Maleah

MALENA (Swedish) a familiar form of Magdalen.
Malen, Malenna, Malin, Malina, Maline, Malini, Malinna

MALHA (Hebrew) queen.
Maliah, Malkah, Malkia, Malkiah, Malkie, Malkiya, Malkiyah, Miliah

MALI (Tai) jasmine flower. (Hungarian) a short form of Malika.
Malea, Malee, Maley

MALIA (Hawaiian, Zuni) a form of Mary. (Spanish) a form of Maria.
Malea, Maleah, Maleeya, Maleeyah, Maleia, Maliah, Maliasha, Malie, Maliea, Maliya, Maliyah, Malli, Mally

MALIKA (Hungarian) industrious.
Malak, Maleeka, Maleka, Mali, Maliaka, Malik, Malikah, Malikee, Maliki, Malikia, Malky

MALINA (Hebrew) tower. (English) from Magdala, England. (Native American) soothing.
Malin, Maline, Malina, Malinna, Mallie

MALINDA (Greek) an alternate form of Melinda.
Malinde, Malinna, Malynda

MALINI (Hindi) gardener. Religion: the Hindu god of the earth.
Maliny

MALISSA (Greek) an alternate form of Melissa.
Malisa, Malisah, Malyssa

MALLALAI (Pashto) beautiful.

MALLEY (American) a familiar form of Mallory.
Mallee, Malli, Mallie, Mally, Maly

MALLORIE (French) an alternate form of Mallory.
Malerie, Mallari, Mallerie, Malloreigh, Mallori

MALLORY (German) army counselor. (French) unlucky.
Maliri, Mallary, Mallauri, Mallery, Malley, Malloree, Mallorey, Mallorie, Malorie, Malory, Malorym, Malree, Malrie, Mellory

MALORIE, Malory (German) alternate forms of Mallory.
Malarie, Maloree, Malori, Melorie, Melory

MALVA (English) a form of Melba.
Malvi, Malvy

MALVINA (Scottish) a form of Melvina. Literature: a name created by the eighteenth-century romantic poet James MacPherson.
Malvane, Malvi

MAMIE (American) a familiar form of Margaret.
Mame, Mamee, Mami, Mammie, Mamy, Mamye

MAMO (Hawaiian) saffron flower; yellow bird.

MANA (Hawaiian) psychic; sensitive.
Manal, Manali, Manna, Mannah

MANAR (Arabic) guiding light.
Manayra

MANDA (Latin) a short form of Amanda. (Spanish) woman warrior.
Mandy

MANDARA (Hindi) calm. Religion: a Hindu mythical tree that makes worries disappear.

MANDEEP (Punjabi) enlightened.

MANDISA (Xhosa) sweet.

MANDY (Latin) lovable. A familiar form of Amanda, Manda, Melinda.
Mandee, Mandi, Mandie

MANETTE (French) a form of Mary.

MANGENA (Hebrew) song, melody.
Mangina

MANI (Chinese) a mantra repeated in Tibetan Buddhist prayer to impart understanding.
Manee

MANKA (Polish, Russian) a form of Mary.

MANON (French) a familiar form of Marie.
Mannon

MANPREET (Punjabi) mind full of love.
Manprit

MANSI (Hopi) plucked flower.
Mancey, Manci, Mancie, Mansey, Mansie, Mansy

MANUELA (Spanish) a form of Emmanuelle.
Manuala, Manuelita, Manuella, Manuelle

MANYA (Russian) a form of Mary.

MARA (Greek) a short form of Amara. (Slavic) a form of Mary.
Mahra, Marae, Marah, Maralina, Maraline, Marra

MARABEL (English) a form of Mirabel.
Marabella, Marabelle

MARANDA (Latin) an alternate form of Miranda.

MARAYA (Hebrew) an alternate form of Mariah.
Mareya

MARCELA (Latin) an alternate form of Marcella.
Marcele, Marcelen, Marcelia, Marcelina, Marceline, Maricela

MARCELEN (English) a form of Marcella.
Marcelen, Marcelin, Marcelina, Marceline, Marcellin, Marcellina, Marcelline, Marcelyn, Marcilen

MARCELLA (Latin) martial, warlike. Mythology: Mars was the god of war. A feminine form of Marcellus.
Mairsil, Marca, Marce, Marceil, Marcela, Marcelen, Marcell, Marcelle, Marcello, Marcena, Marchella, Marchelle, Marci, Marcia, Marcie, Marciella, Marcile, Marcilla, Marcille, Marella, Marsella, Marselle, Marsiella

MARCENA (Latin) an alternate form of Marcella, Marcia.
Maracena, Marceen, Marcene, Marcenia, Marceyne, Marcina

MARCI, Marcie (English) familiar forms of Marcella, Marcia.
Marca, Marcee, Marcita, Marcy, Marsi, Marsie

MARCIA (Latin) martial, warlike. An alternate form of Marcella. See also Marquita.
Marcena, Marchia, Marci, Marciale, Marcie, Marcsa, Marsha, Martia

MARCIANN (American) a combination of Marci + Ann.
Marciane, Marcianna, Marcianne, Marcyane, Marcyanna, Marcyanne

MARCILYNN (American) a combination of Marci + Lynn.

Marcilen, Marcilin, Marciline, Marcilyn, Marcilyne, Marcilynne, Marcylen, Marcylin, Marcyline, Marcylyn, Marcylyne, Marcylynn, Marcylynne

MARCY (English) an alternate form of Marci.
Marsey, Marsy

MARDI (French) born on Tuesday. (Aramaic) a familiar form of Martha.

MARE (Irish) a form of Mary.
Mair, Maire

MARELDA (German) renowned warrior.
Marella, Marilda

MAREN (Latin) sea. (Aramaic) a form of Mary. See also Marina.
Marin, Marine, Marinn, Miren

MARESA, Maressa (Latin) alternate forms of Marisa.
Maresha, Meresa

MARETTA (English) a familiar form of Margaret.
Maret, Marette

MARGARET (Greek) pearl. History: Margaret Hilda Thatcher served as British prime minister. See also Gita, Greta, Gretchen, Marjorie, Markita, Meg, Megan, Peggy, Reet, Rita.
Madge, Maergrethe, Maggie, Maisie, Mamie, Maretta, Marga, Margalo, Marganit, Margara, Maretha, Margarett, Margarette, Margarida, Margarit, Margarita, Margaro, Margaux, Marge, Margeret, Margeretta, Margerette, Margery, Margetta, Margiad, Margie, Margisia, Margit, Margo, Margot, Margret, Marguerite, Meta

MARGARIT (Greek) an alternate form of Margaret.
Margalide, Margalit, Margalith, Margarid, Margaritt, Margerit

MARGARITA (Italian, Spanish) a form of Margaret.

Margareta, Margaretta, Margarida,
Margaritis, Margaritta, Margeretta,
Margharita, Margherita, Margrieta,
Margrita, Marguarita, Marguerita,
Margurita

MARGAUX (French) a form of
Margaret.
Margeaux

MARGE (English) a short form
of Margaret, Marjorie.
Margie

MARGERY (English) a form of
Margaret.
Margerie, Margorie

MARGIE (English) a familiar form
of Marge, Margaret.
Margey, Margi, Margy

MARGIT (Hungarian) a form of
Margaret.
Marget, Margette, Margita

MARGO, Margot (French) forms
of Margaret.
Mago, Margaro

MARGRET (German) a form of
Margaret.
Margreta, Margrete, Margreth, Margrett,
Margretta, Margrette, Margrieta, Margrita

MARGUERITE (French) a form of
Margaret.
Margarete, Margaretha, Margarethe,
Margarite, Margerite, Marguaretta,
Marguarette, Marguarite, Marguerette,
Margurite

MARI (Japanese) ball. (Spanish) a form
of Mary.

MARIA (Hebrew) bitter; sea of
bitterness. (Italian, Spanish) a form of
Mary.
Maie, Malia, Marea, Mareah, Mariabella,
Mariae, Mariesa, Mariessa, Mariha, Marija,
Mariya, Mariyah, Marja, Marya

MARIAH (Hebrew) an alternate form
of Mary. See also Moriah.
Maraia, Maraya, Mariyah, Marriah, Meriah

MARIAM (Hebrew) an alternate form
of Miriam.
Mariama, Mariame, Mariem, Meryam

MARIAN (English) an alternate form of
Maryann.
Mariana, Mariane, Mariann, Marianne,
Mariene, Marion, Marrian, Marriann

MARIANA, Marianna (Spanish) forms
of Marian.
Marriana, Marrianna, Maryana, Maryanna

MARIANE, Marianne (English)
alternate forms of Marian.
Marrianne, Maryanne

MARIBEL (French) beautiful. (English)
a combination of Maria + Bell.
Marabel, Marbelle, Mariabella, Maribella,
Maribelle, Maridel, Marybel, Marybella,
Marybelle

MARICE (Italian) a form of Mary.
See also Maris.
Marica, Marise, Marisse

MARICELA (Latin) an alternate form
of Marcella.
Maricel, Mariceli, Maricelia, Maricella,
Maricely

MARIDEL (English) a form of Maribel.

MARIE (French) a form of Mary.
Maree, Marietta, Marrie

MARIEL, Marielle (German, Dutch)
forms of Mary.
Marial, Marieke, Marielana, Mariele,
Marieli, Marielie, Marieline, Mariell,
Mariellen, Marielsie, Mariely, Marielys

MARIELA, Mariella (German, Dutch)
forms of Mary.

MARIETTA (Italian) a familiar form of
Marie.

Marietta (cont.)
Maretta, Marette, Mariet, Mariette, Marrietta

MARIEVE (American) a combination of Mary + Eve.

MARIGOLD (English) Botany: a plant with yellow or orange flowers.
Marygold

MARIKA (Dutch, Slavic) a form of Mary.
Marica, Marieke, Marija, Marijke, Marikah, Marike, Marikia, Marikka, Mariska, Mariske, Marrika, Maryk, Maryka, Merica, Merika

MARIKO (Japanese) circle.

MARILEE (American) a combination of Mary + Lee.
Marili, Marilie, Marily, Marrilee, Marylea, Marylee, Merrilee, Merrili, Merrily

MARILLA (Hebrew, German) a form of Mary.
Marella, Marelle

MARILOU (American) an alternate form of Marylou.
Marilu, Mariluz

MARILYN (Hebrew) Mary's line or descendants. See also Merilyn.
Maralin, Maralyn, Maralyne, Maralynn, Maralynne, Marelyn, Marilin, Marillyn, Marilyne, Marilynn, Marilynne, Marlyn, Marolyn, Marralynn, Marrilin, Marrilyn, Marrilynn, Marrilynne, Marylin, Marylinn, Marylyn, Marylyne, Marylynn, Marylynne

MARINA (Latin) sea. See also Maren.
Mareena, Marena, Marenka, Marinae, Marinah, Marinda, Marindi, Marinka, Marinna, Marrina, Maryna, Merina, Mirena

MARINI (Swahili) healthy; pretty.

MARION (French) a form of Mary.
Marrian, Marrion, Maryon, Maryonn

MARIS (Greek) a short form of Amaris, Damaris. (Latin) sea. See also Marice.
Maries, Marise, Marris, Marys, Maryse, Meris

MARISA (Latin) sea.
Maresa, Mariesa, Mariessa, Marisela, Marissa, Marita, Mariza, Marrisa, Marrissa, Marysa, Maryse, Maryssa, Merisa

MARISELA (Latin) an alternate form of Marisa.
Mariseli, Marisella, Marishelle, Marissela

MARISHA (Russian) a familiar form of Mary.
Mareshah, Marishenka, Marishka, Mariska

MARISOL (Spanish) sunny sea.
Marise, Marizol, Marysol

MARISSA (Latin) an alternate form of Maris, Marisa.
Maressa, Marisa, Marisha, Marissah, Marisse, Marizza, Marrissa, Marrissia, Maryssa, Merissa, Morissa

MARIT (Aramaic) lady.
Marita, Marite

MARITA (Spanish) a form of Marissa.
Marité, Maritha

MARITZA (Arabic) blessed.
Maritsa, Maritssa

MARIYAN (Arabic) purity.
Mariya, Mariyah, Mariyana, Mariyanna

MARJA (Finnish) a form of Mary.
Marjae, Marjatta, Marjie

MARJAN (Persian) coral. (Polish) a form of Mary.
Marjaneh, Marjanna

MARJIE (Scottish) a familiar form of Marjorie.
Marje, Marjey, Marji, Marjy

MARJOLAINE (French) marjoram.

MARJORIE (Greek) a familiar form of
Margaret. (Scottish) a form of Mary.
*Majorie, Marge, Margeree, Margerey,
Margerie, Margery, Margorie, Margory,
Marjarie, Marjary, Marjerie, Marjery, Marjie,
Marjorey, Marjori, Marjory*

MARKAYLA (American) a
combination or Mary + Kayla.
*Marka, Markaiah, Markaya, Markayel,
Markeela, Markel*

MARKEISHA (English) a combination
of Mary + Keisha.
*Markasha, Markeisa, Markeisia, Markesha,
Markeshia, Markesia, Markiesha, Markisha,
Markishia, Marquesha*

MARKITA (Czech) a form of Margaret.
*Marka, Markeah, Markeda, Markee,
Markeeta, Marketa, Marketta, Marki,
Markia, Markie, Markieta, Markita,
Markitha, Markketta, Merkate*

MARLA (English) a short form of
Marlena, Marlene.
Marlah, Marlea, Marleah

MARLANA (English) a form of
Marlena.
*Marlaena, Marlaina, Marlainna, Marlania,
Marlanna, Marlayna, Marleana*

MARLEE (English) a form of Marlene.
Marlea, Marleah, Marleigh

MARLENA (German) a form of
Marlene.
*Marla, Marlaina, Marlana, Marlanna,
Marleena, Marlina, Marlinda, Marlyna,
Marna*

MARLENE (Greek) high tower. (Slavic)
a form of Magdalen.
*Marla, Marlaine, Marlane, Marlayne,
Marlee, Marleen, Marleene, Marlen,
Marlena, Marlenne, Marley, Marlin, Marline,
Marlyne*

MARLEY (English) a familiar form of
Marlene.
Marlee, Marli, Marlie, Marly

MARLIS (English) a combination of
Maria + Lisa.
*Marles, Marlisa, Marlise, Marlys, Marlyse,
Marlyssa*

MARLO (English) a form of Mary.
Marlon, Marlow, Marlowe

MARLYN (Hebrew) a short form of
Marilyn.
Marlynn, Marlynne

MARMARA (Greek) sparkling, shining.
Marmee

MARNI (Hebrew) an alternate form of
Marnie.
Marnia, Marnique

MARNIE (Hebrew) a short form of
Marnina.
*Marna, Marnay, Marne, Marnee, Marney,
Marni, Marnisha, Marnja, Marny, Marnya,
Marnye*

MARNINA (Hebrew) rejoice.

MAROULA (Greek) a form of Mary.

MARQUISE (French) noblewoman.
*Markese, Marquees, Marquese, Marquice,
Marquies, Marquiese, Marquis, Marquisa,
Marquisee, Marquisha, Marquisse, Marquiste*

MARQUISHA (American) a form of
Marquise.
Marquiesha, Marquisia

MARQUITA (Spanish) a form of
Marcia.
*Marquatte, Marqueda, Marquedia, Marquee,
Marqueita, Marquet, Marqueta, Marquetta,
Marquette, Marquia, Marquida, Marquietta,
Marquitra, Marquitia, Marquitta*

MARRIM (Chinese) tribal name in
Manpur state.

MARSALA (Italian) from Marseille,
France.
Marsali, Marseilles

MARSHA (English) a form of Marcia.
Marcha, Marshae, Marshay, Marshel,
Marshele, Marshell, Marshia, Marshiela

MARTA (English) a short form of
Martha, Martina.
Martá, Martä, Marte, Martia, Marttaha,
Merta

MARTHA (Aramaic) lady; sorrowful.
Bible: a sister of the Virgin Mary. See
also Mardi.
Maita, Marta, Martaha, Marth, Marthan,
Marthe, Marthy, Marti, Marticka, Martita,
Mattie, Matty, Martus, Martuska, Masia

MARTI (English) a familiar form of
Martha, Martina.
Martie, Marty

MARTINA (Latin) martial, warlike. A
feminine form of Martin. See also Tina.
Marta, Martel, Martella, Martelle, Martene,
Marthena, Marthina, Marthine, Marti,
Martine, Martinia, Martino, Martisha,
Martosia, Martoya, Martricia, Martrina,
Martyna, Martyne, Martynne

MARTIZA (Arabic) blessed.

MARU (Japanese) round.

MARUCA (Spanish) a form of Mary.
Maruja, Maruska

MARVELLA (French) marvelous.
Marva, Marvel, Marvela, Marvele, Marvelle,
Marvely, Marvetta, Marvette, Marvia,
Marvina

MARY (Hebrew) bitter; sea of bitterness.
An alternate form of Miriam. Bible: the
mother of Jesus. See also Maija, Malia,
Maren, Mariah, Marjorie, Maura,
Maureen, Miriam, Mitzi, Moira, Mollie,
Muriel.
Maira, Maire, Manette, Manka, Manon,
Manya, Mara, Mare, Maree, Maren, Marella,
Marelle, Mari, Maria, Maricara, Marice,
Marie, Mariel, Mariela, Marika, Marilla,
Marilyn, Marion, Mariquilla, Mariquita,
Marisha, Marja, Marjan, Marlo, Maroula,
Maruca, Marye, Maryla, Marynia, Masha,
Mavra, Mendi, Mérane, Meridel, Mhairie,
Mirja, Molara, Morag, Moya

MARYA (Arabic) purity; bright
whiteness.
Maryah

MARYAM (Hebrew) an alternate form
of Miriam.
Maryama

MARYANN, Maryanne (English)
combinations of Mary + Ann.
Marian, Marryann, Maryan, Meryem

MARYBETH (American) a combination
of Mary + Beth.
Maribeth, Maribette

MARYELLEN (American) a
combination of Mary + Ellen.
Mariellen

MARYJANE (American) a combination
of Mary + Jane.

MARYJO (American) a combination of
Mary + Jo.
Marijo, Maryjoe

MARYKATE (American) a combination
of Mary + Kate.
Mary-Kate

MARYLOU (American) a combination
of Mary + Lou.
Marilou, Marylu

MARYSSA (Latin) an alternate form of
Marissa.
Maryse, Marysia

MASAGO (Japanese) sands of time.

MASANI (Luganda) gap toothed.

MASHA (Russian) a form of Mary.
Mashka, Mashenka

MASHIKA (Swahili) born during the rainy season.
Masika

MATANA (Hebrew) gift.
Matat

MATHENA (Hebrew) gift of God. (English) a feminine form of Matthau.

MATHILDE (German) an alternate form of Matilda.
Mathilda

MATILDA (German) powerful battler. See also Maud, Tilda, Tillie.
Máda, Mahaut, Maitilde, Malkin, Mat, Matelda, Mathilde, Matilde, Mattie, Matty, Matusha, Matylda

MATRIKA (Hindi) mother. Religion: a name for the Hindu goddess Shakti.
Matrica

MATSUKO (Japanese) pine tree.

MATTEA (Hebrew) gift of God.
Matea, Mathea, Mathia, Matia, Matte, Matthea, Matthia, Mattia, Matya

MATTIE, Matty (English) familiar forms of Martha, Matilda.
Matte, Mattey, Matti, Mattye

MATUSHA (Spanish) a form of Matilda.
Matuja, Matuxa

MAUD, Maude (English) short forms of Madeline, Matilda. See also Madison.
Maudie, Maudine, Maudlin

MAURA (Irish) dark. An alternate form of Mary, Maureen. See also Moira.
Maurah, Maure, Maurette, Mauricette, Maurita

MAUREEN (French) dark. (Irish) a form of Mary.
Maura, Maurene, Maurine, Mo, Moreen, Morena, Morene, Morine, Morreen, Moureen

MAURELLE (French) dark; elfin.
Mauriel, Mauriell, Maurielle

MAURISE (French) dark skinned; moor; marshland. A feminine form of Maurice.
Maurisa, Maurissa, Maurita, Maurizia

MAUSI (Native American) plucked flower.

MAUVE (French) violet colored.

MAVIS (French) song thrush bird. See also Maeve.
Mavies, Mavin, Mavine, Mavon, Mavra

MAXIE (English) a familiar form of Maxine.
Maxi, Maxy

MAXINE (Latin) greatest. A feminine form of Maximillian.
Max, Maxa, Maxeen, Maxena, Maxene, Maxie, Maxima, Maxime, Maximiliane, Maxina, Maxna, Maxyne

MAY (Latin) great. (Arabic) discerning. (English) flower; month of May. See also Mae, Maia.
Maj, Mayberry, Maybeth, Mayday, Maydee, Maydena, Maye, Mayela, Mayella, Mayetta, Mayrene

MAYA (Hindi) God's creative power. (Greek) mother; grandmother. (Latin) great. An alternate form of Maia.
Mayam, Mya

MAYBELINE (Latin) a familiar form of Mabel.

MAYGAN, Maygen (Irish) an alternate form of Megan.
Mayghan, Maygon

MAYLYN (American) a combination of May + Lynn.
Mayelene, Mayleen, Maylen, Maylene, Maylin, Maylon, Maylynn, Maylynne

MAYOREE (Tai) beautiful.
Mayra, Mayree, Mayariya

MAYRA (Tai) an alternate form of Mayoree.

MAYSA (Arabic) walks with a proud stride.

MAYSUN (Arabic) beautiful.

MAZEL (Hebrew) lucky.
Mazal, Mazala, Mazella

MCKAYLA (American) an alternate form of Makayla.
Mckaela, Mckaila, Mckala, Mckaylah, Mckayle, Mckaylee, Mckayleh, Mckayleigh, Mckayli, Mckaylia, Mckaylie

MCKELL (American) an alternate form of Makell.
Mckelle

MCKENNA (American) an alternate form of Mackenna.
Mckena, Mckennah, Mckinna, Mckinnah

MCKENZIE (Scottish) an alternate form of Mackenzie.
Mckennzie, Mckensee, Mckensey, McKensi, Mckensi, Mckensie, Mckensy, Mckenze, Mckenzee, Mckenzey, Mckenzi, Mckenzy, Mckenzye, Mekensie, Mekenzi, Mekenzie

MCKINLEY (Irish) daughter of the learned ruler.
Mckinlee, Mckinleigh, Mckinlie, Mckinnley

MCKINZIE (Irish) an alternate form of Mackenzie.
Mckinsey, Mckinze, Mckinzea, Mckinzee, Mckinzi, Mckinzy, Mckynze, Mckynzie

MEAD, Meade (Greek) honey wine.

MEAGAN (Irish) an alternate form of Megan.
Maegan, Meagain, Meagann, Meagen, Meagin, Meagnah, Meagon

MEAGHAN (Welsh) a form of Megan.
Maeghan, Meaghann, Meaghen, Meahgan

MEARA (Irish) mirthful.

MEDA (Native American) prophet; priestess.

MEDEA (Greek) ruling. (Latin) middle. Mythology: a sorceress who helped Jason get the Golden Fleece.
Medeia

MEDINA (Arabic) History: the site of Muhammed's tomb.
Medinah

MEDORA (Greek) mother's gift. Literature: a character in Lord Byron's poem 'Corsair.'

MEENA (Hindi) blue semiprecious stone; bird.

MEG (English) a short form of Margaret, Megan.

MEGAN (Greek) pearl; great. (Irish) a form of Margaret.
Maegan, Magan, Magen, Meagan, Meaghan, Magen, Maygan, Maygen, Meg, Megane, Megann, Megean, Megen, Meggan, Meggen, Meggie, Meghan, Megyn, Meygan

MEGANE (Irish) an alternate form of Megan.
Magana, Meganna, Meganne

MEGARA (Greek) first. Mythology: Hercules's first wife.

MEGGIE (English) a familiar form of Margaret, Megan.
Meggi, Meggy

MEGHAN (Welsh) a form of Megan.
Meeghan, Meehan, Megha, Meghana, Meghane, Meghann, Meghanne, Meghean, Meghen, Mehgan, Mehgen

MEHADI (Hindi) flower.

MEHIRA (Hebrew) speedy; energetic.
Mahira

MEHITABEL (Hebrew) benefited by trusting God.
Mehetabel, Mehitabelle, Hetty, Hitty

MEHRI (Persian) kind; lovable; sunny.

MEI (Chinese) a short form of Meiying. (Hawaiian) great.
Meiko

MEIRA (Hebrew) light.
Meera

MEIT (Burmese) affectionate.

MEIYING (Chinese) beautiful flower.
Mei

MEKA (Hebrew) a familiar form of Michaela.

MEKAYLA (American) an alternate form of Makayla.
Mekaela, Mekaila, Mekayela, Mekaylia

MEL (Portuguese, Spanish) sweet as honey.

MELA (Hindi) religious service. (Polish) a form of Melanie.

MELANA (Russian) a form of Melanie.
Melanna, Melashka, Melenka, Milana

MELANIE (Greek) dark skinned.
Malania, Malanie, Meila, Meilani, Meilin, Melaine, Melainie, Melana, Melane, Melanee, Melaney, Melani, Melania, Mélanie, Melanka, Melanney, Melannie, Melany, Melanya, Melasya, Melayne, Melenia, Mella, Mellanie, Melonie, Melya, Milena, Milya

MELANTHA (Greek) dark flower.

MELBA (Greek) soft; slender. (Latin) mallow flower.
Malva, Melva

MELE (Hawaiian) song; poem.

MELESSE (Ethiopian) eternal.
Mellesse

MELIA (German) a short form of Amelia.
Melcia, Melea, Meleah, Meleia, Meleisha, Meli, Meliah, Melida, Melika, Mema

MELINA (Latin) canary yellow. (Greek) a short form of Melinda.
Melaina, Meleana, Meleena, Melena, Meline, Melinia, Melinna, Melynna

MELINDA (Greek) honey. See also Linda, Melina, Mindy.
Maillie, Malinda, Melinde, Melinder, Mellinda, Melynda, Melyne, Milinda, Milynda, Mylenda, Mylinda, Mylynda

MELIORA (Latin) better.
Melior, Meliori, Mellear, Melyor, Melyora

MELISA (Greek) an alternate form of Melissa.
Melesa, Mélisa, Melise, Melisha, Melishia, Melisia, Meliza, Melizah, Mellisa, Melosa, Milisa, Mylisa, Mylisia

MELISANDE (French) a form of Melissa, Millicent.
Lisandra, Malisande, Malissande, Malyssandre, Melesande, Melisandra, Melisandre, Mélisandré, Melisenda, Melissande, Melissandre, Mellisande, Melond, Melysande, Melyssandre

MELISSA (Greek) honey bee. See also Elissa, Lissa, Melisande, Millicent.
Malissa, Mallissa, Melessa, Meleta, Melisa, Mélissa, Melisse, Melissia, Mellie, Mellissa, Melly, Melyssa, Milissa, Millie, Milly, Missy, Molissia, Mollissa, Mylissa, Mylissia

MELITA (Greek) a form of Melissa. (Spanish) a short form of Carmelita.
Malita, Meleeta, Melitta, Melitza, Melletta, Molita

MELLY (American) a familiar form of names beginning with 'Mel.' See also Millie.
Meli, Melie, Melli, Mellie

MELODY (Greek) melody. See also Elodie.
Meladia, Melodee, Melodey, Melodi, Melodia, Melodie, Melodyann, Melodye

MELONIE (American) an alternate form of Melanie.
Melloney, Mellonie, Mellony, Melonee, Meloney, Meloni, Melonie, Melonnie, Melony

MELOSA (Spanish) sweet; tender.

MELVINA (Irish) armored chief. A feminine form of Melvin. See also Malvina.
Melevine, Melva, Melveen, Melvena, Melvene, Melvonna

MELYNE (Greek) a short form of Melinda.
Melyn, Melynn, Melynne

MELYSSA (Greek) an alternate form of Melissa.

MENA (Greek) a short form of Philomena. (German, Dutch) strong. History: Mena was the first king of Egypt.
Menah

MENDI (Basque) a form of Mary.
Menda, Mendy

MERANDA (Latin) an alternate form of Miranda.
Merana, Merandah, Merandia, Merannda

MÉRANE (French) a form of Mary.
Meraine, Merrane

MERCEDES (Latin) reward, payment. (Spanish) merciful.
Mercades, Mercadez, Mercadie, Meceades, Merced, Mercede, Mercedees, Mercedeez, Mercedez, Mercedies, Mercedis, Mersade, Mersades

MERCIA (English) a form of Marcia. History: the name of an ancient British kingdom.

MERCY (English) compassionate, merciful. See also Merry.
Mercey, Merci, Mercie, Mercille, Mersey

MEREDITH (Welsh) protector of the sea.
Meredeth, Meredithe, Meredy, Meredyth, Meredythe, Meridath, Merideth, Meridie, Meridith, Merridie, Merridith, Merry

MERI (Finnish) sea. (Irish) a short form of Meriel.

MERIEL (Irish) shining sea.
Meri, Merial, Meriol, Meryl

MERILYN (English) a combination of Merry + Lynn. See also Marilyn.
Merelyn, Merlyn, Merralyn, Merrelyn, Merrilyn

MERISSA (Latin) an alternate form of Marissa.
Merisa, Merisha

MERLE (Latin, French) blackbird.
Merl, Merla, Merlina, Merline, Merola, Murle, Myrle, Myrleen, Myrlene, Myrline

MERRY (English) cheerful, happy. A familiar form of Mercy, Meredith.
Merie, Merree, Merri, Merrie, Merrielle, Merrilee, Merrili, Merrilyn, Merris, Merrita

MERYL (German) famous. (Irish) shining sea. An alternate form of Meriel, Muriel.
Meral, Merel, Merrall, Merrell, Merril, Merrile, Merrill, Merryl, Meryle, Meryll

MESHA (Hindi) born in the lunar month of Aries.
Meshal

META (German) a short form of Margaret.
Metta, Mette, Metti

MHAIRIE (Scottish) a form of Mary.
Mhaire, Mhairi, Mhari, Mhary

MIA (Italian) mine. A familiar form of Michaela, Michelle.
Mea, Meah, Miah

MICAELA (Hebrew) an alternate form of Michaela.
Macaela, Micaella, Micaila, Micala, Miceala

MICAH (Hebrew) a short form of Michaela. Bible: one of the Old Testament prophets.
Meecah, Mica, Micha, Mika, Myca, Mycah

MICAYLA, Michayla (Hebrew) alternate forms of Michaela.
Micayle, Micaylee, Michaylah

MICHAELA (Hebrew) who is like God? A feminine form of Michael.
Machaela, Maika, Makaela, Makaila, Makala, Makayla, Mia, Micaela, Micayla, Michael, Michaelann, Michala, Michayla, Michealia, Michaelina, Michaeline, Michaell, Michaella, Michaelyn, Michaila, Michal, Michala, Micheal, Micheala, Michelia, Michelina, Michelle, Michely, Michelyn, Micheyla, Micheline, Micki, Miguela, Mikaela, Mikala, Misha, Mycala, Mychael, Mychal

MICHALA (Hebrew) an alternate form of Michaela.
Michalann, Michale, Michalene, Michalin, Mchalina, Michalisha, Michalla, Michalle, Michayla, Michayle, Michela

MICHELE (Italian) a form of Michaela.
Michaelle, Michal, Michela

MICHELLE (French) who is like God? A form of Michaela. See also Shelley.
Machealle, Machele, Machell, Machella, Machelle, Mechelle, Meichelle, Meschell, Meshell, Meshelle, Mia, Michel, Michéle, Michell, Michella, Michellene, Michellyn, Mischel, Mischelle, Mishael, Mishaela, Mishayla, Mishell, Mishelle, Mitchele, Mitchelle

MICHI (Japanese) righteous way.
Miche, Michee, Michiko

MICKI (American) a familiar form of Michaela.
Mickee, Mickeeya, Mickia, Mickie, Micky, Mickya, Miquia

MIDORI (Japanese) green.

MIEKO (Japanese) prosperous.
Mieke

MIELIKKI (Finnish) pleasing.

MIETTE (French) small; sweet.

MIGINA (Omaha) new moon.

MIGNON (French) cute; graceful.
Mignonette, Minnionette, Minnonette, Minyonette, Minyonne

MIGUELA (Spanish) a form of Michaela.
Micquel, Miguelina, Miguelita, Miquel, Miquela, Miquella

MIKA (Hebrew) an alternate form of Micah. (Japanese) new moon. (Russian) God's child. (Native American) wise racoon.
Mikah, Mikka

MIKAELA (Hebrew) an alternate form of Michaela.
Mekaela, Mekala, Mickael, Mickaela, Mickala, Mickalla, Mickeel, Mickell, Mickelle, Mikael, Mikail, Mikaila, Mikal, Mikalene, Mikalovna, Mikalyn, Mikayla, Mikea, Mikeisha, Mikeita, Mikel, Mikela, Mikele, Mikell, Mikella, Mikesha, Mikeya, Mikhaela, Mikie, Mikiela, Mikkel, Mikyla, Mykaela

MIKALA (Hebrew) an alternate form of Michaela.
Mickala, Mikalah, Mikale, Mikalea, Mikalee, Mikaleh

MIKAYLA (American) a form of Mikaela.
Mekayla, Mickayla, Mikala, Mikayle, Mikyla

MIKHAELA (American) a form of Mikaela.
Mikhail, Mikhaila, Mikhala, Mikhalea, Mikhayla, Mikhelle

MIKI (Japanese) flower stem.
Mikia, Mikiala, Mikie, Mikita, Mikiyo, Mikki, Mikkie, Mikkiya, Mikko, Miko

MILA (Italian, Slavic) a short form of Camilla, Ludmilla. (Russian) dear one.
Milah, Milla

MILADA (Czech) my love.
Mila, Milady

MILAGROS (Spanish) miracle.
Mila, Milagritos, Milagro, Milagrosa, Mirari

MILANA (Italian) from Milan, Italy.
Milan, Milane, Milani, Milanka, Milanna, Milanne

MILDRED (English) gentle counselor.
Mil, Mila, Mildrene, Mildrid, Millie, Milly

MILENA (Greek, Hebrew, Russian) a form of Ludmilla, Magdalen, Melanie.
Mila, Milène, Milenia, Milenny, Milini, Millini

MILETA (German) generous, merciful. A feminine form of Milo.

MILIA (German) industrious. A short form of Amelia, Emily.
Mila, Milka, Milla, Milya

MILIANI (Hawaiian) caress.
Milanni, Miliany

MILILANI (Hawaiian) heavenly caress.
Milliani

MILISSA (Greek) an alternate form of Melissa.
Milessa, Milisa, Millisa, Millissa

MILKA (Czech) a form of Amelia.
Milica, Milika

MILLICENT (Greek) an alternate form of Melissa. (English) industrious. See also Lissa, Melisande.
Melicent, Meliscent, Mellicent, Mellisent, Melly, Milicent, Milisent, Millie, Milliestone, Millisent, Milly, Milzie, Missy

MILLIE, Milly (English) familiar forms of Amelia, Camille, Emily, Kamila, Melissa, Mildred, Millicent.
Mili, Milla, Millee, Milley, Millie, Mylie

MIMA (Burmese) woman.
Mimma

MIMI (French) a familiar form of Miriam.

MINA (German) love. (Persian) blue sky. (Hindi) born in the lunar month of Pisces. (Arabic) harbor. (Japanese) south. A short form of names ending in 'mina.'
Meena, Mena, Min

MINAL (Native American) fruit.

MINDA (Hindi) knowledge.

MINDY (Greek) a familiar form of Melinda.
Mindee, Mindi, Mindie, Mindyanne, Mindylee, Myndy

MINE (Japanese) peak; mountain range.
Mineko

MINERVA (Latin) wise. Mythology: the goddess of wisdom.
Merva, Minivera, Minnie, Myna

MINETTE (French) faithful defender
Minnette, Minnita

MINKA (Polish) a short form of Wilhelmina.

MINNA (German) a short form of Wilhelmina.
Mina, Minka, Minnie, Minta

MINNIE (American) a familiar form of Mina, Minerva, Minna, Wilhelmina.
Mini, Minie, Minne, Minni, Minny

MINOWA (Native American) singer.
Minowah

MINTA (English) Literature: originally coined by playwright Sir John Vanbrugh in his comedy *The Confederacy.*
Minty

MINYA (Osage) older sister.

MIO (Japanese) three times as strong.

MIRA (Latin) wonderful. (Spanish) look, gaze. A short form of Almira, Amira, Marabel, Mirabel, Miranda.
Mirae, Mirra, Mirah

MIRABEL (Latin) beautiful.
Mira, Mirabell, Mirabella, Mirabelle, Mirable

MIRACLE (Latin) wonder, marvel.

MIRANDA (Latin) strange; wonderful; admirable. Literature: the heroine of Shakespeare's *The Tempest.* See also Randi.
Maranda, Marenda, Meranda, Mira, Miran, Miranada, Mirandia, Mirinda, Mirindé, Mironda, Mirranda, Muranda, Myranda

MIREILLE (Hebrew) God spoke. (Latin) wonderful.
Mireil, Mirel, Mirella, Mirelle, Mirelys, Mireya, Mireyda, Mirielle, Mirilla, Myrella, Myrilla

MIREYA (Hebrew) an alternate form of Mireille.
Mireea, Miriah, Miryah

MIRI (Gypsy) a short form of Miriam.
Miria, Miriah

MIRIAM (Hebrew) bitter, sea of bitterness. Bible: the original form of Mary. See also Macia, Mimi, Mitzi.
Mairwen, Mariam, Maryam, Miram, Mirham, Miri, Miriain, Miriama, Miriame, Mirian, Mirit, Mirjam, Mirjana, Mirriam, Mirrian, Miryam, Miryan, Myriam

MISHA (Russian) a form of Michaela.
Mischa, Mishae

MISSY (English) a familiar form of Melissa, Millicent.
Missi, Missie

MISTY (English) shrouded by mist.
Missty, Mistee, Mistey, Misti, Mistie, Mistin, Mistina, Mistral, Mistylynn, Mystee, Mysti, Mystie

MITRA (Hindi) god of daylight. (Persian) angel.
Mita

MITUNA (Moquelumnan) like a fish wrapped up in leaves.

MITZI (German) a form of Mary, Miriam.
Mieze, Mitzee, Mitzie, Mitzy

MIWA (Japanese) wise eyes.
Miwako

MIYA (Japanese) temple.
Miyah, Miyana, Miyanna

MIYO (Japanese) beautiful generation.
Miyoko, Miyuko

MIYUKI (Japanese) snow.

MOANA (Hawaiian) ocean; fragrance.

MOCHA (Arabic) chocolate-flavored coffee.
Moka

MODESTY (Latin) modest.
Modesta, Modeste, Modestia, Modestie, Modestina, Modestine, Modestus

MOESHA (American) a short form of Monisha.
Myesha

MOHALA (Hawaiian) flowers in bloom.
Moala

MOIRA (Irish) great. A form of Mary. See also Maura.
Moirae, Moirah, Moire, Moya, Moyra, Moyrah

MOLARA (Basque) a form of Mary.

MOLLIE, Molly (Irish) familiar forms of
Mary.
*Moli, Molie, Moll, Mollee, Molley, Molli,
Mollissa*

MONA (Greek) a short form of Monica,
Ramona, Rimona. (Irish) noble.
*Moina, Monah, Mone, Monea, Monna,
Moyna*

MONET (French) Art: Claude Monet
was a leading French impressionist
remembered for his paintings of water
lilies.
Monae, Monay, Monee

MONICA (Greek) solitary. (Latin)
advisor.
*Mona, Monca, Monee, Monia, Monic,
Monice, Monicia, Monicka, Monika,
Monique, Monise, Monn, Monnica, Monnie,
Monya*

MONIFA (Yoruba) I have my luck.

MONIKA (German) a form of Monica.
Moneka, Monieka, Monike, Monnika

MONIQUE (French) a form of Monica.
*Moneeke, Moneik, Moniqua, Moniquea,
Moniquie, Munique*

MONISHA (American) a combination
of Monica + Aisha.
Moesha, Moneisha, Monishia

MONTANA (Spanish) mountain.
Montanna

MORA (Spanish) blueberry.
Morae, Morea, Moria, Morita

MORELA (Polish) apricot.
Morelia, Morelle

MORENA (Irish) a form of Maureen.

MORGAN (Welsh) seashore. Literature:
Morgan Le Fay was the half-sister of
King Arthur.

*Morgana, Morgance, Morgane, Morganetta,
Morganette, Morganica, Morgann,
Morganna, Morganne, Morgen, Morghan,
Morgyn, Morrigan*

MORGHAN (Welsh) an alternate form
of Morgan.
Morghen, Morghin, Morghyn

MORIAH (Hebrew) God is my teacher.
(French) dark skinned. Bible: the name
of the mountain on which the temple
of Solomon was built. See also Mariah.
Moria, Moriel, Morit, Morria, Morriah

MORIE (Japanese) bay.

MOROWA (Akan) queen.

MORRISA (Latin) dark skinned; moor;
marshland. A feminine form of Morris.
Morisa, Morissa, Morrissa

MOSELLE (Hebrew) drawn from the
water. A feminine form of Moses.
(French) a white wine.
Mozelle

MOSI (Swahili) first-born.

MOSWEN (Tswana) white.

MOUNA (Arabic) wish, desire.
Moona, Moonia, Mounia, Muna, Munia

MRENA (Slavic) white eyes.
Mren

MUMTAZ (Arabic) distinguished.

MURA (Japanese) village.

MURIEL (Arabic) myrrh. (Irish) shining
sea. A form of Mary. See also Meryl.
*Merial, Meriel, Meriol, Merrial, Merriel,
Muire, Murial, Muriell, Murielle*

MUSETTA (French) little bagpipe.
Musette

MUSLIMAH (Arabic) devout believer.

MYA (Burmese) emerald.
My, Myah, Myia, Myiah

MYESHA (American) an alternate form of Moesha.
Myeisha, Myeshia, Myiesha, Myisha

MYKAELA, Mykayla (American) forms of Mikaela.
Mykael, Mykaila, Mykal, Mykala, Mykaleen, Mykel, Mykela, Mykyla

MYLA (English) merciful.

MYLENE (Greek) dark.
Mylaine, Mylana, Mylee, Myleen

MYRA (Latin) fragrant ointment. A feminine form of Myron.
Mayra, Myrena, Myria

MYRANDA (Latin) an alternate form of Miranda.
Myrandah, Myrandia, Myrannda

MYRIAM (American) a form of Miriam.
Myriame, Myryam

MYRNA (Irish) beloved.
Merna, Mirna, Morna, Muirna

MYRTLE (Greek) dark green shrub.
Mertis, Mertle, Mirtle, Myrta, Myrtia, Myrtias, Myrtice, Myrtie, Myrtilla, Myrtis

N

NABILA (Arabic) born to nobility.
Nabeela, Nabiha, Nabilah

NADDA (Arabic) generous; dewy.
Nada

NADETTE (French) a short form of Bernadette.

NADIA (French, Slavic) hopeful.
Nadea, Nadenka, Nadezhda, Nadiah, Nadie, Nadija, Nadijah, Nadine, Nadiya, Nadiyah, Nadja, Nadjae, Nadjah, Nadka, Nadusha, Nady, Nadya

NADINE (French, Slavic) a form of Nadia.
Nadean, Nadeana, Nadeen, Nadena, Nadene, Nadien, Nadin, Nadina, Nadyne, Naidene, Naidine

NADIRA (Arabic) rare, precious.
Naadirah, Nadirah

NAEVA (French) a form of Eve.
Nahvon

NAFUNA (Luganda) born feet first.

NAGIDA (Hebrew) noble; prosperous.
Nagda, Nageeda

NAHID (Persian) Mythology: another name for Venus, the goddess of love and beauty.

NAHIMANA (Dakota) mystic.

NAIDA (Greek) water nymph.
Naiad, Naiya, Nayad, Nyad

NAILA (Arabic) successful.
Nailah

NAIRI (Armenian) land of canyons. History: a name for ancient Armenia.
Naira, Naire, Nayra

NAIYA (Greek) an alternate form of Naida.
Naia, Naiyana, Naja, Najah, Naya

NAJAM (Arabic) star.
Naja, Najma

NAJILA (Arabic) brilliant eyes.
Naja, Najah, Najia, Najja, Najla

NAKEISHA (American) a combination of the prefix Na + Keisha.
Nakeesha, Nakesha, Nakeshea, Nakeshia, Nakeysha, Nakiesha, Nakisha, Nekeisha

NAKEITA (American) a form of Nikita.
Nakeeta, Nakeitha, Nakeithra, Nakeitra, Nakeitress, Nakeitta, Nakeittia, Naketta, Nakieta, Nakitha, Nakitia, Nakitta, Nakyta

NAKIA (Arabic) pure.
Nakea, Nakeia, Nakeya, Nakeyah, Nakeyia, Nakiah, Nakiaya, Nakiea, Nakiya, Nakiyah, Nekia

NAKITA (American) a form of Nikita.
Nakkita, Naquita

NALANI (Hawaiian) calm as the heavens.
Nalanie, Nalany

NAMI (Japanese) wave.
Namika, Namiko

NAN (German) a short form of Fernanda. (English) an alternate form of Ann.
Nana, Nanice, Nanine, Nanna, Nanon

NANA (Hawaiian) spring.

NANCI (English) an alternate form of Nancy.
Nancie, Nancsi, Nansi

NANCY (English) gracious. A familiar form of Nan.
Nainsi, Nance, Nancee, Nancey, Nanci, Nancine, Nancye, Nanette, Nanice, Nanncey, Nanncy, Nanouk, Nansee, Nansey, Nanuk

NANETTE (French) a form of Nancy.
Nan, Nanete, Nannette, Nettie, Nineta, Ninete, Ninetta, Ninette, Nini, Ninita, Ninnetta, Ninnette, Nynette

NANI (Greek) charming. (Hawaiian) beautiful.
Nanni, Nannie, Nanny

NAOMI (Hebrew) pleasant, beautiful. Bible: a friend of Ruth.
Naoma, Naomia, Naomie, Naomy, Navit, Neoma, Neomi, Noami, Noemi, Noma, Nomi, Nyomi

NAOMIE (Hebrew) an alternate form of Naomi.
Naome, Naomee, Noemie

NARA (Greek) happy. (English) north. (Japanese) oak.
Narah

NARCISSA (Greek) daffodil. A feminine form of Narcissus. Mythology: the youth who fell in love with his own reflection.
Narcessa, Narcisa, Narcisse, Narcyssa, Narissa, Narkissa

NARELLE (Australian) woman from the sea.
Narel

NARI (Japanese) thunder.
Narie, Nariko

NARMADA (Hindi) pleasure giver.

NASHAWNA (American) a combination of the prefix Na + Shawna.
Nashan, Nashana, Nashanda, Nashaun, Nashauna, Nashaunda, Nashauwna, Nashawn, Nasheena, Nashounda, Nashuana

NASHOTA (Native American) double; second-born twin.

NASTASIA (Greek) an alternate form of Anastasia.
Nastasha, Nastashia, Nastasja, Nastassa, Nastassia, Nastassiya, Nastassja, Nastassya, Nastasya, Nastazia, Nastisija, Nastka, Nastusya, Nastya

NASYA (Hebrew) miracle.
Nasia, Nasyah

NATA (Sanskrit) dancer. (Latin) swimmer. (Polish, Russian) a form of Natalie. (Native American) speaker; creator. See also Nadia.
Natia, Natka, Natya

NATACHA (Russian) an alternate form of Natasha.
Natachia, Natacia, Naticha

NATALEE, Natali (Latin) alternate forms of Natalie.
Natale, Nataleh, Nataleigh, Nattlee

NATALIA (Russian) a form of Natalie.
See also Talia.
Nacia, Natala, Natalea, Nataliia, Natalija,
Natalina, Nataliya, Nataliyah, Natalja,
Natalka, Natallea, Natallia, Natalya,
Nathalia, Natka

NATALIE (Latin) born on Christmas
day. See also Nata, Natasha, Noel,
Talia.
Nat, Natalee, Natali, Natalia, Nataliee,
Nataline, Natalle, Natallie, Nataly, Natelie,
Nathalie, Nathaly, Natie, Natilie, Natlie,
Nattalie, Nattilie

NATALINE (Latin) an alternate form
of Natalie.
Natalene, Nataléne, Natalyn

NATALLE (French) a form of Natalie.
Natale

NATALY (Latin) an alternate form of
Natalie.
Nathaly, Natally, Natallye

NATANE (Arapaho) daughter.
Natanne

NATANIA (Hebrew) gift of God.
A feminine form of Nathan.
Natanya, Natée, Nathania, Nathenia,
Netania, Nethania

NATARA (Arabic) sacrifice.
Natori, Natoria

NATASHA (Russian) a form of Natalie.
See also Stacey, Tasha.
Nahtasha, Natacha, Natasa, Natascha,
Natashah, Natashea, Natashenka, Natashia,
Natashiea, Natashja, Natashka, Natasia,
Natassia, Natassija, Natassja, Natasza,
Natausha, Natawsha, Natesha, Nateshia,
Nathasha, Nathassha, Natisha, Natishia,
Natosha, Netasha, Notosha

NATESA (Hindi) godlike; goddess.
Religion: another name for the Hindu
goddess Shakti.
Natisa, Natissa

NATHALIE, Nathaly (Latin) alternate
forms of Natalie.
Nathalee, Nathali, Nathalia, Nathalya

NATIE (English) a familiar form of
Natalie.
Nati, Natti, Nattie, Natty

NATOSHA (Russian) an alternate form
of Natasha.
Natoshia, Natoshya, Netosha, Notosha

NAVA (Hebrew) beautiful; pleasant.
Navah, Naveh, Navit

NAYELY (Irish) an alternate form of
Neila.
Naeyli, Nayelia, Nayelli, Nayelly, Nayla

NEALA (Irish) an alternate form
of Neila.
Nayela, Naylea, Naylia, Nealia, Neela,
Neelia, Neila

NECHA (Spanish) a form of Agnes.
Necho

NECI (Hungarian) fiery, intense.
Necia, Necie

NEDA (Slavic) born on Sunday.
Nedah, Nedi, Nedia, Neida

NEDDA (English) prosperous guardian.
A feminine form of Edward.
Neddi, Neddie, Neddy

NEELY (Irish) a familiar form of Neila,
Nelia.
Nealee, Nealie, Nealy, Neelee, Neeley, Neeli,
Neelie, Neili, Neilie

NEEMA (Swahili) born during
prosperous times.

NEENA (Spanish) an alternate form of
Nina.
Neenah, Nena

NEILA (Irish) champion. A feminine
form of Neil. See also Neala, Neely.
Nayely, Neilah, Neile, Neilia, Neilla, Neille

NEKEISHA (American) an alternate form of Nakeisha.
Nechesa, Neikeishia, Nekesha, Nekeshia, Nekiesha, Nekisha, Nekysha

NEKIA (Arabic) an alternate form of Nakia.
Nekeya, Nekiya, Nekiyah, Nekya, Nekiya

NELIA (Spanish) yellow. (Latin) a familiar form of Cornelia.
Neelia, Neely, Neelya, Nela, Neli, Nelka, Nila

NELLE (Greek) stone.

NELLIE, Nelly (English) familiar forms of Cornelia, Eleanor, Helen, Prunella.
Nel, Neli, Nell, Nella, Nelley, Nelli, Nellianne, Nellice, Nellis, Nelma

NENET (Egyptian) born near the sea. Mythology: the goddess of the sea.

NEOLA (Greek) youthful.
Neolla

NEONA (Greek) new moon.

NEREIDA (Greek) an alternate form of Nerine.
Nereyda, Nereyida, Nerida

NERINE (Greek) sea nymph.
Nereida, Nerina, Nerita, Nerline

NERISSA (Greek) sea nymph. See also Rissa.
Narice, Narissa, Nerice, Nerisa, Nerisse, Nerrisa, Nerys, Neryssa

NESSA (Greek) a short form of Agnes. (Scandinavian) promontory. See also Nessie.
Nesa, Nesha, Neshia, Nesiah, Nessia, Nesta, Nevsa, Neysa, Neysha, Neyshia

NESSIE (Greek) a familiar form of Agnes, Nessa, Vanessa.
Nese, Neshie, Nesho, Nesi, Ness, Nessi, Nessy, Nest, Neys

NETA (Hebrew) plant, shrub. See also Nettie.
Netia, Netta, Nettia

NETIS (Native American) trustworthy.

NETTIE (French) a familiar form of Annette, Nanette, Antoinette.
Neti, Netie, Netta, Netti, Netty, Nety

NEVA (Spanish) snow. (English) new. Geography: a river in Russia.
Neiva, Neve, Nevia, Neyva, Nieve, Niva, Nivea, Nivia

NEVADA (Spanish) snow. Geography: a western American state.
Neiva, Neva

NEVINA (Irish) worshipper of the saint. A feminine form of Nevin. History: a well-known Irish saint.
Neveen, Nevein, Nevena, Neveyan, Nevin, Nivena

NEYLAN (Turkish) fulfilled wish.
Neya, Neyla

NEZA (Slavic) a form of Agnes.

NIA (Irish) a familiar form of Neila. Mythology: a legendary Welsh woman.
Neya, Niah, Niajia, Niya, Nya

NIABI (Osage) fawn.

NICHELLE (American) a combination of Nicole + Michelle. Culture: Nichelle Nichols was the first African-American woman featured in a television drama *Star Trek*.
Nichele, Nichell, Nishelle

NICHOLE (French) an alternate form of Nicole.
Nichol, Nichola, Nicholas, Nicholle

NICKI (French) a familiar form of Nicole.
Nicci, Nickey, Nickeya, Nickia, Nickie, Nickiya, Nicky, Niki

NICKOLE (French) an alternate form of Nicole.
Nickol

NICOLA (Italian) a form of Nicole.
Nacola, Necola, Nichola, Nickola, Nicolea, Nicolla, Nikkola, Nikola, Nikolia, Nykola

NICOLE (French) victorious people. A feminine form of Nicholas. See also Colette, Cosette, Nikita.
Nacole, Necole, Nica, Nichole, Nicia, Nicki, Nickole, Nicol, Nicola, Nicolette, Nicoli, Nicolie, Nicoline, Nicolle, Nikayla, Nikelle, Nikki, Niquole, Nocole, Nycole

NICOLETTE (French) an alternate form of Nicole.
Nicholette, Nicoletta, Nicollete, Nicollette, Nikkolette, Nikoleta, Nikoletta, Nikolette

NICOLINE (French) a familiar form of Nicole.
Nicholine, Nicholyn, Nicoleen, Nicolene, Nicolina, Nicolyn, Nicolyne, Nicolynn, Nicolynne, Nikolene, Nikolina, Nikoline

NICOLLE (French) an alternate form of Nicole.
Nicholle

NIDA (Omaha) Mythology: an elflike creature.
Nidda

NIDIA (Latin) nest.
Nidi, Nidya

NIESHA (Scandinavian) an alternate form of Nissa. (American) pure.
Neisha, Neishia, Neissia, Nesha, Neshia, Nesia, Nessia, Niessia, Nisha, Nyesha

NIGE (Latin) dark night. A feminine form of Nigel.
Nigea, Nigela, Nija, Nijae, Nijah

NIKA (Russian) belonging to God.
Nikka

NIKAYLA, Nikelle (American) forms of Nicole.
Nikeille, Nikel, Nikela, Nikelie

NIKE (Greek) victorious. Mythology: the goddess of victory.

NIKI (Russian) a short form of Nikita.
Nikia, Nikiah

NIKITA (Russian) victorious people. A form of Nicole.
Nakeita, Nakita, Niki, Nikitah, Nikitia, Nikitta, Nikki, Nikkita, Niquita, Niquitta

NIKKI (American) a familiar form of Nicole, Nikita.
Nicki, Nikia, Nikkea, Nikkey, Nikkia, Nikkiah, Nikkie, Nikko, Nikky

NIKOLE (French) an alternate form of Nicole.
Nikkole, Nikkolie, Nikola, Nikole, Nikolena, Nicolia, Nikolina, Nikolle

NILA (Latin) Geography: the Nile River in Egypt. (Irish) an alternate form of Neila.
Nilah, Nilesia, Nyla

NILI (Hebrew) Botany: a pea plant that yields indigo.

NIMA (Hebrew) thread. (Arabic) blessing.
Nema, Niama, Nimali

NINA (Hebrew) a familiar form of Hannah. (Spanish) girl. (Native American) mighty.
Neena, Ninah, Ninacska, Ninja, Ninna, Ninon, Ninosca, Ninoshka

NINON (French) a form of Nina.

NIREL (Hebrew) light of God.
Nirali, Nirelle

NIRVELI (Hindi) water child.

NISA (Arabic) woman.

NISHA (American) an alternate form of Niesha, Nissa.
Niasha, Nishay

NISHI (Japanese) west.

NISSA (Hebrew) sign, emblem. (Scandinavian) friendly elf; brownie. See also Nyssa.
Nisha, Nisse, Nissie, Nissy

NITA (Hebrew) planter. (Spanish) a short form of Anita, Juanita. (Choctaw) bear.
Nitai, Nitha, Nithai, Nitika

NITARA (Hindi) deeply rooted.

NITASHA (American) a form of Natasha.
Nitasia, Niteisha, Nitisha, Nitishia

NITSA (Greek) a form of Helen.

NITUNA (Native American) daughter.

NITZA (Hebrew) flower bud.
Nitzah, Nitzana, Nitzanit, Niza, Nizah

NIXIE (German) water sprite.

NIYA (Irish) an alternate form of Nia.
Niyah, Niyana, Niyia, Nyia

NIZANA (Hebrew) an alternate form of Nitza.
Nitzana, Nitzania, Zana

NOEL (Latin) Christmas. See also Natalie.
Noël, Noela, Noelani, Noele, Noeleen, Noelene, Noelia, Noeline, Noelle, Noelyn, Noelynn, Nohely, Noleen, Novelenn, Novelia, Nowel, Noweleen, Nowell

NOELANI (Hawaiian) beautiful one from heaven.
Noela

NOELLE (French) Christmas. A form of Noel.
Noell, Noella, Noelleen, Noelly, Noellyn

NOEMI (Hebrew) an alternate form of Naomi.
Noam, Noemie, Noemy, Nohemi, Nomi

NOEMIE (Hebrew) an alternate form of Noemi.

NOEMY (Hebrew) an alternate form of Noemi.
Noamy

NOGA (Hebrew) morning light.

NOHELY (Latin) an alternate form of Noel.
Noeli, Noelie, Noely, Nohal, Noheli

NOKOMIS (Dakota) moon daughter.

NOLA (Latin) small bell. (Irish) famous; noble. A short form of Fionnula. A feminine form of Nolan.
Nuala

NOLETA (Latin) unwilling.
Nolita

NOLLIE (English) a familiar form of Magnolia.
Nolia, Nolle, Nolley, Nolli, Nolly

NOMA (Hawaiian) a form of Norma.

NONA (Latin) ninth.
Nonah, Noni, Nonia, Nonie, Nonna, Nonnah, Nonya

NOOR (Aramaic) an alternate form of Nura.
Noorie, Nour, Nur

NORA (Greek) light. A familiar form of Eleanor, Honora, Leonore.
Norah, Noreen

NOREEN (Irish) a form of Eleanor, Nora. (Latin) a familiar form of Norma.
Noorin, Noreena, Noreene, Noren, Norena, Norene, Norina, Norine, Nureen

NORELL (Scandinavian) from the north.
Narell, Narelle, Norela, Norelle, Norely

NORI (Japanese) law, tradition.
Noria, Norico, Noriko, Norita

NORMA (Latin) rule, precept.
Noma, Noreen, Normi, Normie

NOVA (Latin) new. A short form of Novella, Novia. (Hopi) butterfly chaser. Astronomy: a star that releases bright bursts of energy.

NOVELLA (Latin) newcomer.
Nova, Novela

NOVIA (Spanish) sweetheart.
Nova, Novka, Nuvia

NU (Burmese) tender. (Vietnamese) girl.
Nue

NUALA (Irish) a short form of Fionnula.
Nola, Nula

NUELA (Spanish) a form of Amelia.

NUNA (Native American) land.

NUNCIATA (Latin) messenger.
Nunzia

NURA (Aramaic) light.
Noor, Noora, Noorah, Noura, Nurah

NURIA (Aramaic) the Lord's light.
Nuri, Nuriel, Nurin

NURITA (Hebrew) Botany: a flower with red and yellow blossoms.
Nurit

NURU (Swahili) daylight.

NUSI (Hungarian) a form of Hannah.

NUWA (Chinese) mother goddess. Mythology: the creator of mankind and order.

NYA (Irish) an alternate form of Nia.
Nyaa, Nyah, Nyia

NYCOLE (French) an alternate form of Nicole.
Nychelle, Nycolette, Nycolle

NYDIA (Latin) nest.
Nyda

NYESHA (American) an alternate form of Niesha.
Nyeisha, Nyeshia

NYLA (Irish) an alternate form of Nila.
Nylah

NYOKO (Japanese) gem, treasure.

NYOMI (Hebrew) an alternate form of Naomi.
Nyome, Nyomee, Nyomie

NYREE (Maori) sea.
Nyra, Nyrie

NYSSA (Greek) beginning. See also Nissa.
Nisha, Nissi, Nissy, Nyasia, Nysa

NYUSHA (Russian) a form of Agnes.
Nyushenka, Nyushka

OBA (Yoruba) Mythology: the goddess who rules the rivers.

OBELIA (Greek) needle.

OCEANA (Greek) ocean. Mythology: Oceanus was the god of water.
Ocean, Oceananna, Oceane, Oceania, Oceanna, Oceanne, Oceaonna, Oceon

OCTAVIA (Latin) eighth. A feminine form of Octavio. See also Tavia.
Octabia, Octaviah, Octaviais, Octavice, Octavie, Octavienne, Octavio, Octavious, Octavise, Octavya, Octivia, Otavia, Ottavia

ODEDA (Hebrew) strong; courageous.

ODELE (Greek) melody, song.
Odelet, Odelette, Odell, Odelle

ODELIA (Greek) ode; melodic. (Hebrew) I will praise God. (French) wealthy. A feminine form of Odell. See also Odetta.
Oda, Odeelia, Odeleya, Odelina, Odelinda, Odelyn, Odila, Odile, Odilia

ODELLA (English) wood hill.
Odela, Odelle, Odelyn

ODERA (Hebrew) plough.

ODESSA (Greek) odyssey, long voyage.
Adesha, Adeshia, Adessa, Adessia, Odessia

ODETTA (German, French) a form of Odelia.
Oddetta, Odette

ODINA (Algonquin) mountain.

OFELIA (Greek) an alternate form of Ophelia.
Ofeelia, Ofilia

OFIRA (Hebrew) gold.
Ofarrah, Ophira

OFRA (Hebrew) an alternate form of Aphra.
Ofrat

OGIN (Native American) wild rose.

OHANNA (Hebrew) God's gracious gift.

OKALANI (Hawaiian) heaven.
Okilani

OKI (Japanese) middle of the ocean.
Okie

OKSANA (Latin) an alternate form of Osanna.
Oksanna

OLA (Greek) a short form of Olesia. (Scandinavian) ancestor. A feminine form of Olaf.

OLATHE (Native American) beautiful.
Olathia

OLEDA (Spanish) an alternate form of Alida. See also Leda.
Oleta, Olida, Olita

OLENA (Russian) a form of Helen.
Oleena, Olenka, Olenna, Olenya, Olya

OLESIA (Greek) an alternate form of Alexandra.
Cesya, Ola, Olecia, Oleesha, Oleishia, Olesha, Olesya, Olexa, Olice, Olicia, Olisha, Olishia, Ollicia

OLETHA (Scandinavian) nimble.
Oleta, Yaletha

OLETHEA (Latin) truthful. See also Alethea.
Oleta

OLGA (Scandinavian) holy. See also Helga, Olivia.
Olenka, Olia, Olja, Ollya, Olva, Olya

OLIANA (Polynesian) oleander.

OLINA (Hawaiian) filled with happiness.

OLINDA (Greek) an alternate form of Yolanda. (Latin) scented. (Spanish) protector of property.

OLISA (Ibo) God.

OLIVE (Latin) olive tree.
Oliff, Oliffe, Olivet, Olivette

OLIVIA (Latin) olive tree. (English) a form of Olga. See also Liv, Livia.
Alivia, Alyvia, Olevia, Oliva, Olivea, Oliveia, Olivetta, Olivi, Olivianne, Olivya, Oliwia, Ollie, Olva, Olyvia

OLLIE (English) a familiar form of Olivia.
Olla, Olly, Ollye

OLWEN (Welsh) white footprint.
Olwenn, Olwin, Olwyn, Olwyne, Olwynne

OLYMPIA (Greek) heavenly.
Olimpia, Olympe, Olympie

OLYVIA (Latin) an alternate form of Olivia.

OMA (Hebrew) reverent. (German) grandmother. (Arabic) highest. A feminine form of Omar.

OMAIRA (Arabic) red.
Omar, Omara, Omarah, Omari, Omaria, Omarra

OMEGA (Greek) last, final, end. Linguistics: the last letter in the Greek alphabet.

ONA (Latin, Irish) an alternate form of Oona, Una. (English) river.

ONATAH (Iroquois) daughter of the earth and the corn spirit.

ONAWA (Native American) wide awake.
Onaja, Onajah

ONDINE (Latin) an alternate form of Undine.
Ondene, Ondina, Ondyne

ONDREA (Czech) a form of Andrea.
Ohndrea, Ohndreea, Ohndreya, Ohndria, Ondraya, Ondreana, Ondreea, Ondreya, Ondria, Ondrianna, Ondriea

ONEIDA (Native American) eagerly awaited.
Onida, Onyda

ONELLA (Hungarian) a form of Helen.

ONESHA (American) a combination of Ondrea + Aisha.
Oneshia, Onesia, Onessa, Onessia, Onethia, Oniesha, Onisha

ONI (Yoruba) born on holy ground.
Onnie

ONORA (Latin) an alternate form of Honora.
Onoria, Onorine, Ornora

OONA (Latin, Irish) an alternate form of Una.
Ona, Onna, Onnie, Oonagh, Oonie

OPA (Choctaw) owl.

OPAL (Hindi) precious stone.
Opale, Opalina, Opaline

OPHELIA (Greek) helper. Literature: Hamlet's love interest in the Shakespearean play *Hamlet*.
Filia, Ofelia, Ophélie, Ophilia, Phelia

OPRAH (Hebrew) an alternate form of Orpah.
Ophra, Ophrah, Opra

ORA (Greek) an alternate form of Aura. (Latin) prayer. (Spanish) gold. (English) seacoast.
Orah, Orlice, Orra

ORABELLA (Latin) an alternate form of Arabella.
Orabel, Orabela, Orabelle

ORALEE (Hebrew) the Lord is my light. See also Yareli.
Areli, Orali, Oralit, Orelie, Orlee, Orli, Orly

ORALIA (French) a form of Aurelia. See also Oriana.
Oralis, Oriel, Orielda, Orielle, Oriena, Orlena, Orlene

OREA (Greek) mountains.
Oreal, Oria, Oriah

ORELA (Latin) announcement from the gods; oracle.
Oreal, Orella, Orelle, Oriel, Orielle

ORENDA (Iroquois) magical power.

ORETHA (Greek) an alternate form of Aretha.
Oreta, Oretta, Orette

ORIANA (Latin) dawn, sunrise. (Irish) golden.

Oriana (cont.)
Orane, Orania, Orelda, Orelle, Ori, Oria, Orian, Oriane, Orianna, Orieana, Oryan

ORINA (Russian) a form of Irene.
Orya, Oryna

ORINDA (Hebrew) pine tree. (Irish) light skinned, white. A feminine form of Oren.
Orenda

ORINO (Japanese) worker's field.
Ori

ORIOLE (Latin) golden; black and orange bird.
Auriel, Oriel, Oriell, Oriella, Oriola

ORLA (Irish) golden woman.
Orlagh, Orlie, Orly

ORLANDA (German) famous throughout the land. A feminine form of Orlando.
Orlandia, Orlantha, Orlenda, Orlinda

ORLENDA (Russian) eagle.

ORLI (Hebrew) light.
Orlice, Orlie, Orly

ORMANDA (Latin) noble. (German) mariner, seaman. A feminine form of Orman.
Orma

ORNICE (Hebrew) cedar tree. (Irish) pale; olive colored.
Orna, Ornah, Ornat, Ornette, Ornit

ORPAH (Hebrew) runaway. See also Oprah.
Orpa, Orpha, Orphie

ORQUIDEA (Spanish) orchid.
Orquidia

ORSA (Greek) an alternate form of Ursula. (Latin) bearlike. A feminine form of Orson. See also Ursa.
Orsaline, Orse, Orsel, Orselina, Orseline, Orsola

ORTENSIA (Italian) a form of Hortense.

ORVA (French) golden; worthy. (English) brave friend.

OSANNA (Latin) praise the Lord.
Oksana, Osana

OSEN (Japanese) one thousand.

OSEYE (Benin) merry.

OSMA (English) devine protector. A feminine form of Osmond.
Ozma

OTILIE (Czech) lucky heroine.
Otila, Otilia, Otka, Ottili, Otylia

OVIA (Latin, Danish) egg.

OWENA (Welsh) born to nobility; young warrior. A feminine form of Owen.

OYA (Moquelumnan) called forth.

OZ (Hebrew) strength.

OZARA (Hebrew) treasure, wealth.

P

PACA (Spanish) a short form of Pancha. See also Paka.

PADGET (French) an alternate form of Page.
Padgett, Paget, Pagett

PADMA (Hindi) lotus.

PAGE (French) young assistant.
Padget, Pagen, Pagi, Payge

PAIGE (English) young child.
Payge

PAISLEY (Scottish) patterned fabric made in Paisley, Scotland.
Paislay, Paislee, Paisleyann, Paisleyanne, Paizlei, Paizleigh, Paizley, Pasley, Pazley

PAITON (English) warrior's town.
Paiten, Paityn, Paityne, Paiyton, Paten, Patton

PAKA (Swahili) kitten. See also Paca.

PAKUNA (Moquelumnan) deer bounding while running downhill.

PALILA (Polynesian) bird.

PALLAS (Greek) wise. Mythology: another name for Athena, the goddess of wisdom.

PALMA (Latin) palm tree.
Pallma, Palmira

PALMIRA (Spanish) a form of Palma.
Pallmirah, Pallmyra, Palmer, Palmyra

PALOMA (Spanish) dove. See also Aloma.
Palloma, Palometa, Palomita, Paluma, Peloma

PAMELA (Greek) honey.
Pam, Pama, Pamala, Pamalla, Pamelia, Pamelina, Pamella, Pamila, Pamilla, Pammela, Pammi, Pammie, Pammy, Pamula

PANCHA (Spanish) free; from France. A feminine form of Pancho.
Paca, Panchita

PANDITA (Hindi) scholar.

PANDORA (Greek) highly gifted. Mythology: a young woman who received many gifts from the gods, such as beauty, wisdom, and creativity. See also Dora.
Pandi, Pandorah, Pandorra, Pandorrah, Pandy, Panndora, Panndorah, Panndorra, Panndorrah

PANSY (Greek) flower; fragrant. (French) thoughtful.
Pansey, Pansie

PANTHEA (Greek) all the gods.
Pantheia, Pantheya

PANYA (Swahili) mouse; tiny baby. (Russian) a familiar form of Stephanie.
Panyia

PANYIN (Fanti) older twin.

PAOLA (Italian) a form of Paula.
Paoli, Paolina

PAPINA (Moquelumnan) vine growing on an oak tree.

PAQUITA (Spanish) a form of Frances.
Paqua

PARI (Persian) fairy eagle.

PARIS (French) Geography: the capital of France. Mythology: the Trojan prince who started the Trojan war by abducting Helen.
Parice, Paries, Parisa, Parise, Parish, Parisha, Pariss, Parissa, Parisse, Parris, Parys, Parysse

PARKER (English) park keeper.
Park, Parke

PARRIS (French) an alternate form of Paris.
Parrise, Parrish, Parrisha, Parrys, Parrysh

PARTHENIA (Greek) virginal.
Partheenia, Parthenie, Parthinia, Pathina

PARVENEH (Persian) butterfly.

PASCALE (French) born on Easter or Passover. A feminine form of Pascal.
Pascalette, Pascaline, Pascalle, Paschale, Paskel

PASHA (Greek) sea.
Palasha, Pascha, Pasche, Pashae, Pashe, Pashel, Pashka, Pasia, Passia

PASSION (Latin) passion.
Pashion, Pashonne, Pasion, Passionaé,
Passionate, Passionette

PASUA (Swahili) born by Caesarean
section.

PAT (Latin) a short form of Patricia,
Patsy.

PATI (Moquelumnan) fish baskets made
of willow branches.

PATIA (Latin, English) a familiar form
of Patience, Patricia. (Gypsy, Spanish)
leaf.

PATIENCE (English) patient.
Paciencia, Patia, Patiance, Patient, Patince,
Patishia

PATRA (Greak, Latin) an alternate form
of Petra.

PATRICE (French) a form of Patricia.
Patrease, Patrece, Patreece, Patreese,
Patreice, Patriece, Patryce, Pattrice

PATRICIA (Latin) noblewoman. A
feminine form of Patrick. See also
Payton, Peyton, Tricia, Trisha, Trissa.
Pat, Patia, Patresa, Patrica, Patrice, Patricea,
Patriceia, Patrichea, Patriciana, Patricianna,
Patricja, Patricka, Patrickia, Patrisha,
Patrishia, Patrisia, Patrissa, Patrizia,
Patrizzia, Patrycia, Patrycja, Patsy, Patty

PATSY (Latin) a familiar form of Patricia.
Pat, Patsey, Patsi

PATTY (English) a familiar form of Patricia.
Patte, Pattee, Patti, Pattie

PAULA (Latin) small. A feminine form
of Paul. See also Pavla, Polly.
Paliki, Paola, Paulane, Paulann, Paule,
Paulette, Paulina, Pauline, Paulla, Pavia

PAULETTE (Latin) a familiar form of
Paula.
Paulet, Paulett, Pauletta, Paulita, Paullett,
Paulletta, Paullette

PAULINA (Slavic) a form of Paula.
Paulena, Paulene, Paulenia, Pauliana,
Paulianne, Paullena, Paulyna, Pawlina,
Polena, Polina, Polinia

PAULINE (Latin) a familiar form of Paula.
Pauleen, Paulene, Paulien, Paulin, Paulyne,
Paulynn, Pouline

PAUSHA (Hindi) lunar month of
Capricorn.

PAVLA (Czech, Russian) a form
of Paula.
Pavlina, Pavlinka

PAXTON (Latin) peaceful town.
Paxtin, Paxtynn

PAYGE (English) an alternate form
of Paige.

PAYTON (Irish) a form of Patricia.
Paydon, Paytan, Payten, Paytin, Paytn,
Paytton

PAZ (Spanish) peace.

PAZI (Ponca) yellow bird.

PAZIA (Hebrew) golden.
Paz, Paza, Pazice, Pazit

PEACE (English) peaceful.

PEARL (Latin) jewel.
Pearle, Pearleen, Pearlena, Pearlene,
Pearlette, Pearlina, Pearline, Pearlisha,
Pearlyn, Perl, Perla, Perle, Perlette, Perlie,
Perline, Perlline

PEGGY (Greek) a familiar form of
Margaret.
Peg, Pegeen, Pegg, Peggey, Peggi, Peggie, Pegi

PEKE (Hawaiian) a form of Bertha.

PELA (Polish) a short form of Penelope.
Pele

PELAGIA (Greek) sea.
Pelage, Pelageia, Pelagie, Pelga, Pelgia,
Pellagia

PELIPA (Zuni) a form of Philippa.

PEMBA (Bambara) the power that controls all life.

PENDA (Swahili) loved.

PENELOPE (Greek) weaver. Mythology: the clever and loyal wife of Odysseus, a Greek hero.
Pela, Pen, Penelopa, Penna, Pennelope, Penny, Pinelopi

PENI (Carrier) mind.

PENINAH (Hebrew) pearl.
Penina, Peninit, Peninnah, Penny

PENNY (Greek) a familiar form of Penelope, Peninah.
Penee, Peni, Penney, Penni, Pennie

PEONY (Greek) flower.
Peonie

PEPITA (Spanish) a familiar form of Josephine.
Pepa, Pepi, Peppy, Peta

PEPPER (Latin) condiment from the pepper plant.

PERAH (Hebrew) flower.

PERDITA (Latin) lost. Literature: a character in Shakespeare's play *The Winter's Tale.*
Perdida, Perdy

PERFECTA (Spanish) flawless.

PERI (Greek) mountain dweller. (Persian) fairy or elf.
Perita

PERLA (Latin) an alternate form of Pearl.
Pearla

PERLIE (Latin) a familiar form of Pearl.
Pearley, Pearlie, Pearly, Perley, Perli, Perly, Purley, Purly

PERNELLA (Greek, French) rock. (Latin) a short form of Petronella.
Parnella, Pernel, Pernell, Pernelle

PERRI (Greek, Latin) small rock; traveler. (French) pear tree. (Welsh) daughter of Harry. A feminine form of Perry.
Perre, Perrey, Perriann, Perrie, Perrin, Perrine, Perry

PERSEPHONE (Greek) springtime. Mythology: the goddess of spring.
Persephanie, Persephany, Persephonie

PERSIS (Latin) from Persia.
Perssis, Persy

PETA (Blackfoot) golden eagle.

PETRA (Greek, Latin) small rock. A short form of Petronella. A feminine form of Peter.
Patra, Pet, Peta, Petena, Peterina, Petraann, Petrice, Petrina, Petrine, Petrova, Petrovna, Pier, Pierce, Pietra

PETRONELLA (Greek) small rock. (Latin) of the Roman clan Petronius.
Pernella, Peternella, Petra, Petrona, Petronela, Petronella, Petronelle, Petronia, Petronija, Petronilla, Petronille

PETULA (Latin) seeker.
Petulah

PETUNIA (Native American) flower.

PEYTON (Irish) an alternate form of Patricia.
Peyden, Peydon, Peyten, Peytyn

PHAEDRA (Greek) bright.
Faydra, Phae, Phaidra, Phe, Phedre

PHALLON (Irish) an alternate form of Fallon.
Phalaine, Phalen, Phallan, Phallie, Phalon, Phalyn

PHEBE (Greek) an alternate form of Phoebe.
Pheba, Pheby

PHEODORA (Greek, Russian) an alternate form of Feodora.
Phedora, Phedorah, Pheodorah, Pheydora, Pheydorah

PHILANA (Greek) lover of mankind. A feminine form of Philander.
Phila, Philanna, Philene, Philiane, Philina, Philine

PHILANTHA (Greek) lover of flowers.

PHILICIA (Latin) an alternate form of Phylicia.
Philecia, Philesha, Philica, Philicha, Philycia

PHILIPPA (Greek) lover of horses. A feminine form of Philip. See also Filippa.
Phil, Philipa, Philippe, Phillipina, Phillippine, Phillie, Philly, Pippa, Pippy

PHILOMENA (Greek) love song; loved one. Bible: a first-century saint. See also Filomena, Mena.
Philoméne, Philomina

PHOEBE (Greek) shining.
Phaebe, Phebe, Pheobe, Phoebey

PHYLICIA (Greek) a form of Felicia. (Latin) fortunate; happy.
Philicia, Phylecia, Phylesha, Phylesia, Phylica, Phylisha, Phylisia, Phylissa, Phyllecia, Phyllicia, Phyllisha, Phyllisia, Phyllissa, Phyllyza

PHYLLIDA (Greek) an alternate form of Phyllis.
Fillida, Philida, Phillida, Phillyda

PHYLLIS (Greek) green bough.
Filise, Fillys, Fyllis, Philis, Phillis, Philliss, Philys, Philyss, Phylis, Phyllida, Phyllis, Phylliss, Phyllys

PIA (Italian) devout.

PIEDAD (Spanish) devoted; pious.

PIER (French) a form of Petra.
Pierette, Pierrette, Pierra, Pierre

PIERCE (English) a form of Petra.

PILAR (Spanish) pillar, column. Religion: honoring the Virgin Mary, the pillar of the Catholic Church.
Peelar, Pilár, Pillar

PING (Chinese) duckweed. (Vietnamese) peaceful.

PINGA (Hindi) bronze; dark. Religion: another name for the Hindu goddess Shakti.

PIPER (English) pipe player.

PIPPA (English) a short form of Phillipa.

PIPPI (French) rosy cheeked.
Pippen, Pippie, Pippin, Pippy

PITA (African) fourth daughter.

PLACIDIA (Latin) serene.
Placida

PLEASANCE (French) pleasant.
Pleasence

POLLA (Arabic) poppy.
Pola

POLLY (Latin) a familiar form of Paula.
Paili, Pali, Pauli, Paulie, Pauly, Poll, Pollee, Polley, Polli, Pollie

POLLYAM (Hindi) goddess of the plague. Religion: the Hindu name invoked to ward off bad spirits.

POLLYANNA (English) a combination of Polly + Anna. Literature: an overly optimistic heroine created by Eleanor Poiter.

POLOMA (Choctaw) bow.

POMONA (Latin) apple. Mythology: the goddess of fruit and fruit trees.

PONI (African) second daughter.

POPPY (Latin) poppy flower.
Popi, Poppey, Poppi, Poppie

PORA, Poria (Hebrew) fruitful.

PORCHA (Latin) an alternate form of Portia.
Porchae, Porchai, Porche, Porchia, Porcia

PORSCHA, Porsche (German) forms of Portia.
Porcsha, Porcshe, Porschah, Porschê, Porschea, Porschia, Pourche

PORSHA (Latin) an alternate form of Portia.
Porshai, Porshay, Porshe, Porshea, Porshia

PORTIA (Latin) offering. Literature: the heroine of Shakespeare's play *The Merchant of Venice.*
Porcha, Porscha, Porsche, Porsha, Portiea

PRECIOUS (French) precious; dear.
Pracious, Preciouse, Precisha, Prescious, Preshious, Presious

PRESLEY (English) priest's meadow.
Preslea, Preslee, Preslei, Presli, Preslie, Presly, Preslye, Pressley, Presslie, Pressly

PRIMA (Latin) first, beginning; first child.
Prema, Primalia, Primetta, Primina, Priminia

PRIMAVERA (Italian, Spanish) spring.

PRIMROSE (English) primrose flower.
Primula

PRINCESS (English) daughter of royalty.
Princcess, Princes, Princesa, Princessa, Princetta, Princie, Princilla

PRISCILLA (Latin) ancient.
Cilla, Piri, Precila, Precilla, Prescilla, Presilla, Pressilia, Pricila, Pricilla, Pris, Prisca, Priscela, Priscella, Priscila, Priscilia, Priscill, Priscille, Priscillia, Prisella, Prisila, Prisilla, Prissila, Prissilla, Prissy, Pryscylla, Prysilla

PRISSY (Latin) a familiar form of Priscilla.
Prisi, Priss, Prissi, Prissie

PRIYA (Hindi) beloved; sweet natured.
Pria

PROCOPIA (Latin) declared leader. A feminine form of Prokopius.

PROMISE (Latin) promise, pledge.
Promis, Promiss, Promys, Promyse

PRU (Latin) a short form of Prudence.
Prue

PRUDENCE (Latin) cautious; discreet.
Pru, Prudencia, Prudens, Prudy

PRUDY (Latin) a familiar form of Prudence.
Prudee, Prudi, Prudie

PRUNELLA (Latin) brown; little plum. See also Nellie.
Prunela

PSYCHE (Greek) soul. Mythology: a beautiful mortal loved by Eros, the Greek god of love.

PUA (Hawaiian) flower.

PUALANI (Hawaiian) heavenly flower.
Puni

PURITY (English) purity.
Pura, Pureza, Purisima

PYRALIS (Greek) fire.
Pyrene

Q

QADIRA (Arabic) powerful.
Kadira

QAMRA (Arabic) moon.
Kamra

QITARAH (Arabic) fragrant.

QUAASHIE (Ewe) born on Sunday.

QUADEISHA (American) a
combination of Qadira + Aisha.
*Qudaisha, Quadaishia, Quadajah, Quadasha,
Quadasia, Quadayshia, Quadaza, Quadejah,
Quadesha, Quadeshia, Quadiasha, Quaesha*

QUANEISHA (American) a
combination of the prefix Qu +
Niesha.
*Quaneasa, Quanece, Quanecia, Quaneice,
Quanesha, Quanisha, Quansha, Quarnisha,
Queisha, Qwanisha, Qynisha*

QUANESHA (American) an alternate
form of Quaneisha.
*Quamesha, Quaneesha, Quaneshia,
Quanesia, Quanessa, Quanessia, Quannesha,
Quanneshia, Quannezia, Quayneshia,
Quinesha*

QUANIKA (American) a combination of
the prefix Qu + Nika.
*Quanikka, Quanikki, Quaniqua, Quanique,
Quantenique, Quawanica, Queenika,
Queenique*

QUANISHA (American) an alternate
form of Quaneisha.
*Quaniesha, Quanishia, Quaynisha,
Queenisha, Quenisha, Quenishia*

QUARTILLA (Latin) fourth.
Quantilla

QUBILAH (Arabic) agreeable.

QUEEN (English) queen. See also Quinn.
Queena, Queenie, Quenna

QUEENIE (English) an alternate form
of Queen.
Queenation, Queeneste, Queeny

QUEISHA (American) a short form of
Quaneisha.
Qeysha, Queshia, Queysha

QUENBY (Scandinavian) feminine.

QUENISHA (American) a combination
of Queen + Aisha.
*Queneesha, Quenesha, Quennisha, Quensha,
Quinesha, Quinisha*

QUENNA (English) an alternate form
of Queen.
Quenell, Quenessa

QUERIDA (Spanish) dear; beloved.

QUESTA (French) searcher.

QUETA (Spanish) a short form of names
ending in 'queta' or 'quetta.'
Quenetta, Quetta

QUIANA (American) a combination of
the prefix Qu + Anna.
*Quian, Quianah, Quianda, Quiane, Quiani,
Quianita, Quianna, Quianne, Quionna*

QUINBY (Scandinavian) queen's estate.

QUINCY (Irish) fifth.
Quincee, Quincey, Quinci, Quincia, Quincie

QUINELLA (Latin) an alternate form of
Quintana.

QUINESHA, Quinisha (American)
alternate forms of Quenisha.
*Quineshia, Quinessa, Quinessia, Quinisa,
Quinishia, Quinnesha, Quinneshia,
Quinnisha, Quneasha, Quonesha, Quonisha,
Quonnisha*

QUINETTA (Latin) an alternate form
of Quintana.
*Queenetta, Queenette, Quinette, Quinita,
Quinnette*

QUINN (German, English) queen.
See also Queen.
Quin, Quinna, Quinne, Quynn

QUINSHAWNA (American) a
combination of Quinn + Shauna.
Quinshea

QUINTANA (Latin) fifth. (English) queen's lawn. A feminine form of Quentin, Quintin. See also Quinella, Quinetta.
Quinntina, Quinta, Quintanna, Quintara, Quintarah, Quintia, Quintila, Quintilla, Quintina, Quintona, Quintonice

QUINTESSA (Latin) essence. See also Tess.
Quintaysha, Quintesa, Quintesha, Quintessia, Quintice, Quinticia, Quintisha, Quintosha

QUINTRELL (American) a combination of Quinn + Trella.
Quintela, Quintella, Quintrelle

QUITERIE (Latin, French) tranquil.
Quita

QWANISHA (American) an alternate form of Quaneisha.
Qwanechia, Qwanesha, Qwanessia, Qwantasha

R

RABECCA (Hebrew) an alternate form of Rebecca.
Rabecka, Rabeca, Rabekah

RABI (Arabic) breeze.
Rabia, Rabiah

RACHAEL (Hebrew) an alternate form of Rachel.
Rachaele, Rachaell, Rachail, Rachalle

RACHEAL (Hebrew) an alternate form of Rachel.

RACHEL (Hebrew) female sheep. Bible: the wife of Jacob. See also Lahela, Rae, Rochelle.
Racha, Rachael, Rachal, Racheal, Rachela, Rachelann, Rachele, Rachelle, Racquel,

Raechel, Rahel, Rahela, Rahil, Raiche, Raquel, Rashel, Rashelle, Ray, Raycene, Raychel, Raychelle, Rey, Ruchel

RACHELLE (French) a form of Rachel. See also Shelley.
Rachalle, Rachell, Rachella, Raechell, Raechelle, Raeshelle, Rashel, Rashele, Rashell, Rashelle, Raychell, Rayshell, Ruchelle

RACQUEL (French) a form of Rachel.
Rackel, Racquell, Racquella, Racquelle

RADELLA (German) counselor.

RADEYAH (Arabic) content, satisfied.
Radeeyah, Radhiya, Radiah, Radiyah

RADINKA (Slavic) full of life; happy, glad.

RADMILLA (Slavic) worker for the people.

RADWA (Arabic) Geography: a mountain in Medina, Saudi Arabia.

RAE (English) doe. (Hebrew) a short form of Rachel.
Raeh, Raeneice, Raeneisha, Raesha, Ray, Raye, Rayetta, Rayette, Rayma, Rey

RAEANN (American) a combination of Rae + Ann. See also Rayanne.
Raea, Raean, Raeanna, Raeannah, Raeona, Reanna, Raeanne

RAECHEL (Hebrew) an alternate form of Rachel.
Raechael, Raechal, Raechele, Raechell, Raechyl

RAEDEN (Japanese) Mythology: the thunder god. A feminine form of Raiden.
Raeda, Raedeen

RAEGAN (Irish) an alternate form of Reganne.
Raegen, Raegene, Raegine, Raegyn

RAELENE (American) a combination of Rae + Lee.
Rael, Raela, Raelani, Raele, Raeleah, Raelee, Raeleen, Raeleia, Raeleigh, Raeleigha, Raelein, Raelene, Raelennia, Raelesha, Raelin, Raelina, Raelle, Raelyn, Raelynn

RAELYN, Raelynn (American) alternate forms of Raelene.
Raelynda, Raelyne, Raelynne

RAENA (German) an alternate form of Raina.
Raenah, Raenia, Raenie, Raenna, Raeonna, Raeyauna, Raeyn, Raeyonna

RAEVEN (English) an alternate form of Raven.
Raevin, Raevion, Raevon, Raevonna, Raevyn, Raevynne, Raewyn, Raewynne, Raivan, Raiven, Raivin, Raivyn

RAFA (Arabic) happy; prosperous.

RAFAELA (Hebrew) an alternate form of Raphaela.
Rafaelia, Rafaella

RAGAN (Irish) an alternate form of Reganne.
Ragean, Rageane, Rageen, Ragen, Ragene, Rageni, Ragenna, Raggan, Raygan, Raygen, Raygene, Rayghan, Raygin

RAGINE (English) an alternate form of Regina.
Raegina, Ragin, Ragina, Raginee

RAGNILD (Scandinavian) Mythology: a warrior goddess.
Ragna, Ragnell, Ragnhild, Rainell, Renilda, Renilde

RAHEEM (Punjabi) compassionate God.
Raheema, Rahima

RÁIDAH (Arabic) leader.

RAINA (German) mighty. (English) a short form of Regina. See also Rayna.
Raeinna, Raena, Raheena, Rain, Rainah, Rainai, Raine, Rainea, Rainna, Reanna

RAINBOW (English) rainbow.
Rainbeau, Rainbeaux, Rainbo, Raynbow

RAINE (Latin) a short form of Regina. An alternate form of Raina, Rane.
Rainee, Rainey, Raini, Rainie, Rainy, Reyne

RAISA (Russian) a form of Rose.
Raisah, Raissa, Raiza, Raysa, Rayza, Razia

RAIZEL (Yiddish) a form of Rose.
Rayzil, Razil, Reizel, Resel

RAJA (Arabic) hopeful.
Raia, Rajaah, Rajae, Rajah, Rajai

RAKU (Japanese) pleasure.

RALEIGH (Irish) an alternate form of Riley.
Ralea, Raleiah, Raley

RAMA (Hebrew) lofty, exalted. (Hindi) godlike. Religion: another name for the Hindu goddess Shiva.
Ramah

RAMAN (Spanish) an alternate form of Ramona.

RAMANDEEP (Sikh) covered by the light of the Lord's love.

RAMLA (Swahili) fortuneteller.
Ramlah

RAMONA (Spanish) mighty; wise protector. See also Mona.
Raman, Ramonda, Raymona, Romona, Romonda

RAMSEY (English) ram's island.
Ramsha, Ramsi, Ramsie, Ramza

RAN (Japanese) water lily. (Scandinavian) destroyer. Mythology: the sea goddess who destroys.

RANA (Sanskrit) royal. (Arabic) gaze, look.
Rahna, Rahni, Rani

RANAIT (Irish) graceful; prosperous.
Rane, Renny

RANDALL (English) protected.
Randa, Randah, Randal, Randalee, Randel, Randell, Randelle, Randi, Randilee, Randilynn, Randlyn, Randy, Randyl

RANDI, Randy (English) familiar forms of Miranda, Randall.
Rande, Randee, Randeen, Randene, Randey, Randie, Randii

RANE (Scandinavian) queen.
Raine

RANI (Sanskrit) queen. (Hebrew) joyful. A short form of Kerani.
Rahni, Ranee, Raney, Rania, Ranie, Ranice, Ranique, Ranni, Rannie

RANITA (Hebrew) song; joyful.
Ranata, Ranice, Ranit, Ranite, Ranitta, Ronita

RANIYAH (Arabic) gazing.
Ranya, Ranyah

RAPA (Hawaiian) moonbeam.

RAPHAELA (Hebrew) healed by God. Bible: one of the four archangels.
Rafaella, Raphaella, Raphaelle

RAPHAELLE (French) a form of Raphaela.
Rafaelle, Raphael, Raphaele

RAQUEL (French) a form of Rachel.
Rakel, Rakhil, Rakhila, Raqueal, Raquela, Raquella, Raquelle, Rickelle, Rickquel, Ricquel, Ricquelle, Rikell, Rikelle, Rockell

RASA (Lithuanian) morning dew.
Rasyte

RASHA (Arabic) young gazelle.
Rahshea, Rahshia, Rashae, Rashai, Rashea, Rashi, Rashia

RASHAWNA (American) a combination of the prefix Ra + Shawna.
Rashana, Rashanae, Rashanah, Rashanda, Rashane, Rashani, Rashanna, Rashanta, Rashaun, Rashauna, Rashaunda, Rashaundra, Rashaune, Rashawn, Rashawnda, Rashawnna, Rashon, Rashona, Rashonda, Rashunda

RASHEL, Rashelle (American) forms of Rachel.
Rashele, Rashell, Rashella

RASHIDA (Swahili, Turkish) righteous.
Rahshea, Rahsheda, Rahsheita, Rashdah, Rasheda, Rashedah, Rasheeda, Rasheedah, Rasheeta, Rasheida, Rashidah, Rashidi

RASHIEKA (Arabic) descended from royalty.
Rasheeka, Rasheika, Rasheka, Rashika, Rasika

RASIA (Greek) rose.

RATANA (Tai) crystal.
Ratania, Ratanya, Ratna, Rattan, Rattana

RATRI (Hindi) night. Religion: another name for the Hindu goddess Shakti.

RAULA (French) wolf counselor. A feminine form of Raoul.
Raoula, Raulla, Raulle

RAVEN (English) blackbird.
Raeven, Raveen, Raveena, Raveenn, Ravena, Ravene, Ravenn, Ravenna, Ravennah, Ravenne, Raveon, Ravin, Ravon, Ravyn, Rayven, Revena

RAVIN (English) an alternate form of Raven.
Ravi, Ravina, Ravine, Ravinne, Ravion,

RAVYN (English) an alternate form of Raven.
Ravynn

RAWNIE (Gypsy) fine lady.
Rawan, Rawna, Rhawnie

RAYA (Hebrew) friend.
Raia, Raiah, Raiya, Ray, Rayah

RAYANNE (American) an alternate form of Raeann.
Rayane, Ray-Ann, Rayan, Rayana, Rayann, Rayanna, Rayeanna, Rayona, Rayonna, Reyan, Reyana, Reyann, Reyanna, Reyanne

RAYCHEL, Raychelle (Hebrew) alternate forms of Rachel.
Raychael, Raychele, Raychell, Raychil

RAYLENE (American) a combination of Rae + Lyn.
Ralina, Rayel, Rayele, Rayelle, Rayleana, Raylee, Rayleen, Rayleigh, Raylena, Raylin, Raylinn, Raylona, Raylyn, Raylynn, Raylynne

RAYMONDE (German) wise protector. A feminine form of Raymond.
Rayma, Raymae, Raymie

RAYNA (Scandinavian) mighty. (Yiddish) pure, clean. (French) a familiar form of Lorraine. (English) king's advisor. A feminine form of Reynold. See also Raina.
Raynah, Rayne, Raynell, Raynelle, Raynette, Rayona, Rayonna, Reyna

RAYVEN (English) an alternate form of Raven.
Rayvan, Rayvana, Rayvein, Rayvenne, Rayveona, Rayvin, Rayvon, Rayvonia

RAYYA (Arabic) thirsty no longer.

RAZI (Aramaic) secretive.
Rayzil, Rayzilee, Raz, Razia, Raziah, Raziela, Razilee, Razili

RAZIYA (Swahili) agreeable.

REA (Greek) poppy flower.
Reah

REAGAN (Irish) an alternate form of Reganne.
Reagen, Reaghan, Reagine

REANNA (German, English) an alternate form of Raina. (American) an alternate form of Raeann.
Reannah

REANNE (American) an alternate form of Raeann, Reanna.
Reana, Reane, Reann, Reannan, Reanne, Reannen, Reannon, Reeana

REBA (Hebrew) fourth-born child. A short form of Rebecca. See also Reva, Riva.
Rabah, Reeba, Rheba

REBECA (Hebrew) an alernate form of Rebecca.
Rebbeca, Rebecah

REBECCA (Hebrew) tied, bound. Bible: the wife of Isaac. See also Becca, Becky.
Rabecca, Reba, Rebbecca, Rebeca, Rebeccah, Rebeccea, Rebeccka, Rebecha, Rebecka, Rebeckah, Rebeckia, Rebecky, Rebekah, Rebeque, Rebi, Reveca, Riva, Rivka

REBEKAH (Hebrew) an alternate form of Rebecca.
Rebeka, Rebekha, Rebekka, Rebekkah, Rebekke, Revecca, Reveka, Revekka, Rifka

REBI (Hebrew) a familiar form of Rebecca.
Rebbie, Rebe, Rebie, Reby, Ree, Reebie

REENA (Greek) peaceful.
Reen, Reenie, Rena, Reyna

REET (Estonian) a form of Margaret.
Reatha, Reta, Retha

REGAN (Irish) an alternate form of Reganne.
Regane, Reghan

REGANNE (Irish) little ruler. A feminine form of Reagan.
Raegan, Ragan, Reagan, Regin

REGGIE (English) a familiar form of Regina.
Reggi, Reggy, Regi, Regia, Regie

REGINA (Latin) queen. (English) king's advisor. A feminine form of Reginald. Geography: the capital of Saskatchewan. See also Gina.
Ragine, Raina, Raine, Rega, Regena, Regennia, Reggie, Regiena, Regine, Reginia, Regis, Reina, Rena

REGINE (Latin) an alternate form of Regina.
Regin

REI (Japanese) polite, well behaved.
Reiko

REILLY (Irish) an alternate form of Riley.
Reilee, Reileigh, Reiley, Reili, Reilley, Reily

REINA (Spanish) a short form of Regina. See also Reyna.
Reinah, Reine, Reinette, Reinie, Reinna, Reiny, Reiona, Renia, Rina

REKHA (Hindi) thin line.
Reka, Rekia, Rekiah, Rekiya

REMEDIOS (Spanish) remedy.

REMI (French) from Rheims.
Raymi, Remee, Remie, Remy

REMINGTON (English) raven estate.
Remmington

REN (Japanese) arranger; water lily; lotus.

RENA (Hebrew) song; joy. A familiar form of Irene, Regina, Renata, Sabrina, Serena.
Reena, Rina, Rinna, Rinnah

RENAE (French) an alternate form of Renée.
Renay

RENATA (French) an alternate form of Renée.
Ranata, Rena, Renada, Renatta, Renita, Rennie, Renyatta, Rinada, Rinata

RENE (Greek) a short form of Irene, Renée.
Reen, Reenie, Reney, Rennie

RENÉE (French) born again.
Renae, Renata, Renay, Rene, Renea, Reneigh, Renell, Renelle, Renne

RENITA (French) an alternate form of Renata.
Reneeta, Renetta, Renitza

RENNIE (English) a familiar form of Renata.
Reni, Renie, Renni

RESEDA (Spanish) fragrant mignonette blossom.

RESHAWNA (American) a combination of the prefix Re + Shawna.
Resaunna, Reshana, Reshaunda, Reshawnda, Reshawnna, Reshonda, Reshonn, Reshonta

RESI (German) a familiar form of Theresa.
Resia, Ressa, Resse, Ressie, Reza, Rezka, Rezi

RETA (African) shaken.
Reeta, Retta, Rheta, Rhetta

REUBENA (Hebrew) behold a daughter. A feminine form of Reuben.
Reubina, Reuvena, Rubena, Rubenia, Rubina, Rubine, Rubyna

REVA (Latin) revived. (Hebrew) rain; one-fourth. An alternate form of Reba, Riva.
Ree, Reeva, Revia, Revida

REVECA, Reveka (Slavic) forms of Rebecca, Rebekah.
Reve, Revecca, Revekka, Rivka

REXANNE (American) queen. A feminine form of Rex.
Rexan, Rexana, Rexann, Rexanna

REYHAN (Turkish) sweet-smelling flower.

REYNA (Greek) peaceful. (English) an alternate form of Reina.
Reyana, Reyanna, Reyni, Reynna

REYNALDA (German) king's advisor. A feminine form of Reynold.

RÉZ (Latin, Hungarian) copper-colored hair.

REZA (Czech) a form of Theresa.
Rezi, Rezka

RHEA (Greek) brook, stream. Mythology: the mother of Zeus.
Rheá, Rhéa, Rhealyn, Rheanna, Rhia, Rhianna

RHEANNA, Rhianna (Greek) alternate forms of Rhea.
Rheana, Rheann, Rheanne, Rhiana, Rhiauna

RHIAN (Welsh) a short form of Rhiannon.
Rhianne, Rhyan, Rhyann, Rhyanne, Rian, Riane, Riann, Rianne, Riayn

RHIANNON (Welsh) witch; nymph; goddess.
Rheannan, Rheannin, Rheannon, Rheanon, Rhian, Rhianen, Rhianna, Rhiannan, Rhiannen, Rhianon, Rhianwen, Rhinnon, Rhyanna, Riana, Riannon, Rianon

RHODA (Greek) from Rhodes.
Rhode, Rhodeia, Rhodie, Rhody, Roda, Rodi, Rodie, Rodina

RHONA (Scottish) powerful, mighty. (English) king's advisor. A feminine form of Ronald.
Rhonae, Rhonnie

RHONDA (Welsh) grand.
Rhondene, Rhondiesha, Ronda, Ronelle, Ronnette

RIA (Spanish) river.
Riah

RIANA, Rianna (Irish) short forms of Briana.
Reana, Reanna, Rhianna, Rhyanna, Riana, Rianah

RICA (Spanish) a short form of Erica, Frederica, Ricarda. See also Enrica, Sandrica, Terrica, Ulrica.
Ricca, Rieca, Riecka, Rieka, Rikka, Riqua, Rycca

RICARDA (Spanish) rich and powerful ruler. A feminine form of Richard.
Rica, Richanda, Richarda, Richi, Ricki

RICHAEL (Irish) saint.

RICHELLE (German, French) a form of Ricarda.
Richel, Richela, Richele, Richell, Richella, Richia

RICKELLE (American) a form of Raquel.
Rickel, Rickela, Rickell

RICKI, Rikki (American) familiar forms of Erica, Frederica, Ricarda.
Rica, Ricci, Riccy, Rici, Rickee, Rickia, Rickie, Rickilee, Rickina, Rickita, Ricky, Ricquie, Riki, Rikia, Rikita, Rikka, Rikke, Rikkia, Rikkie, Rikky, Riko

RICQUEL (American) a form of Raquel.
Rickquell, Ricquelle, Rikell, Rikelle

RIDA (Arabic) favored by God.

RIHANA (Arabic) sweet basil.
Rhiana, Rhianna, Riana, Rianna

RIKA (Swedish) ruler.
Ricka

RILEE (Irish) an alternate form of Riley.
Rielee, Rielle

RILEY (Irish) valiant.
Raleigh, Reilly, Rieley, Rielly, Riely, Rilee, Rileigh, Rilie

RILLA (German) small brook.

RIMA (Arabic) white antelope.
Reem, Reema, Reemah, Rema, Remah, Rhymia, Rim, Ryma

RIMONA (Hebrew) pomegranate.
See also Mona.

RIN (Japanese) park. Geography: a
Japanese village.
Rini, Rynn

RINA (English) a short form of names
ending in 'rina.'
Reena, Rena

RINAH (Hebrew) joyful.
Rina

RIONA (Irish) saint.

RISA (Latin) laughter.
Reesa, Resa

RISHA (Hindi) born during the lunar
month of Taurus.
Rishah, Rishay

RISHONA (Hebrew) first.
Rishina, Rishon

RISSA (Greek) a short form of Nerissa.
Risa, Rissah, Ryssa, Ryssah

RITA (Sanskrit) brave; honest. (Greek) a
short form of Margarita.
*Reatha, Reda, Reeta, Reida, Reitha, Rheta,
Riet, Ritah, Ritamae, Ritamarie*

RITSA (Greek) a familiar form of
Alexandra.
Ritsah, Ritsi, Ritsie, Ritsy

RIVA (Hebrew) a short form of Rebecca.
(French) river bank. See also Reba,
Reva.
Rivalee, Rivi, Rivvy

RIVER (Latin, French) stream, water.
Rivana, Rivanna, Rivers, Riviane

RIVKA (Hebrew) a short form of
Rebecca.
Rivca, Rivcah, Rivkah

RIZA (Greek) a form of Theresa.
Riesa, Rizus, Rizza

ROANNA (American) a combination of
Rose + Anna.
Ranna, Roana, Roanda, Roanne

ROBBI, Robbie (English) familiar forms
of Roberta.
Robby, Robbye, Robey, Robi, Robia, Roby

ROBERTA (English) famous brilliance.
A feminine form of Robert. See also
Bobbette, Bobbi, Robin.
*Roba, Robbi, Robbie, Robena, Robertena,
Robertina*

ROBIN (English) robin. An alternate
form of Roberta.
*Robann, Robbin, Robeen, Roben, Robena,
Robian, Robina, Robine, Robinette, Robinia,
Robinn, Robinta, Robyn*

ROBINETTE (English) a familiar form
of Robin.
Robernetta, Robinet, Robinett, Robinita

ROBYN (English) an alternate form of
Robin.
*Robbyn, Robbynn, Robyne, Robynn,
Robynne*

ROCHELLE (Hebrew) an alternate form
of Rachel. (French) large stone. See also
Shelley.
*Reshelle, Roch, Rocheal, Rochealle, Rochel,
Rochele, Rochell, Rochella, Rochette,
Rockelle, Roshele, Roshell, Roshelle*

ROCIO (Spanish) dewdrops.
Rocío

RODERICA (German) famous ruler.
A feminine form of Roderick.
*Rica, Rika, Rodericka, Roderika, Rodreicka,
Rodricka, Rodrika*

RODNAE (English) island clearing.
Rodna, Rodnetta, Rodnicka

RODNEISHA (American) a
combination of Rodnae + Aisha.
*Rodesha, Rodisha, Rodishah, Rodnecia,
Rodnesha, Rodneshia, Rodneycia,
Rodneysha, Rodnisha*

ROHANA (Hindi) sandalwood. (American) a combination of Rose + Hannah.
Rochana, Rohena

ROHINI (Hindi) woman.

ROLANDA (German) famous throughout the land. A feminine form of Roland.
Ralna, Rolande, Rolando, Rolaunda, Roleesha, Rolene, Rolinda, Rollande, Rolonda

ROLENE (German) an alternate form of Rolanda.
Rolaine, Rolena, Rolleen, Rollene

ROMA (Latin) from Rome.
Romai, Rome, Romeise, Romeka, Romelle, Romesha, Rometta, Romia, Romilda, Romilla, Romina, Romini, Romma, Romonia

ROMAINE (French) from Rome.
Romana, Romanda, Romanelle, Romania, Romanique, Romany, Romayne, Romona, Romy

ROMY (French) a familiar form of Romaine. (English) a familiar form of Rosemary.
Romi, Romie

RONA (Scandinavian) a short form of Rhona.
Rhona, Roana, Ronalda, Ronna, Ronnae, Ronnay, Ronne, Ronni, Ronsy

RONAELE (Greek) Eleanor spelled backwards.
Ronalee, Ronni, Ronnie, Ronny

RONDA (Welsh) an alternate form of Rhonda.
Rondai, Rondesia, Rondi, Rondie, Ronelle, Ronnette, Ronni, Ronnie, Ronny

RONDELLE (French) short poem.
Rhondelle, Rondel, Ronndelle

RONEISHA (American) a combination of Rhonda + Aisha.
Roneasha, Ronecia, Ronee, Roneeka, Roneesha, Roneice, Ronese, Ronesha, Roneshia, Ronesia, Ronessa, Ronessia, Ronichia, Ronicia, Roniesha, Ronisha, Ronneisha, Ronnesa, Ronnesha, Ronneshia, Ronni, Ronnie, Ronniesha, Ronny

RONELLE (Welsh) an alternate form of Rhonda, Ronda.
Ranell, Ranelle, Ronel, Ronella, Ronielle, Ronnella, Ronnelle

RONISHA (American) an alternate form of Roneisha.
Ronise, Ronnise, Ronnisha, Ronnishia

RONLI (Hebrew) joyful.
Ronia, Ronice, Ronit, Ronlee, Ronlie, Ronni, Ronnie, Ronny

RONNETTE (Welsh) a familiar form of Rhonda, Ronda.
Ronetta, Ronette, Ronit, Ronita, Ronnetta, Ronni, Ronnie, Ronny

RONNI, Ronnie, Ronny (American) familiar forms of Veronica and names beginning with 'Ron.'
Rone, Ronee, Roni, Ronnee, Ronney

RORI, Rory (Irish) famous brilliance; famous ruler. Feminine forms of Robert, Roderick.
Rorie

ROS, Roz (English) short forms of Rosalind, Rosalyn.
Rozz, Rozzey, Rozzi, Rozzie, Rozzy

ROSA (Italian, Spanish) a form of Rose. History: Rosa Parks inspired the American civil rights movement by refusing to give up her bus seat to a white man in Montgomery, Alabama. See also Charo, Roza.

ROSABEL (French) beautiful rose.
Rosabelia, Rosabella, Rosabelle, Rosebelle

ROSALBA (Latin) white rose.
Rosalva, Roselba

ROSALIE (English) a form of Rosalind.
*Rosalea, Rosalee, Rosaleen, Rosaleigh,
Rosalene, Rosalia, Rosealee, Rosealie,
Roselee, Roseli, Roselia, Roselie, Roseley,
Rosely, Rosilee, Rosli, Rozali, Rozália,
Rozalie, Rozele*

ROSALIND (Spanish) fair rose.
*Ros, Rosalie, Rosalinda, Rosalinde, Rosalyn,
Rosalynd, Rosalynde, Roselind, Roselyn,
Rosie, Roz, Rozalind, Rozland*

ROSALINDA (Spanish) an alternate
form of Rosalind.
Rosalina

ROSALYN (Spanish) an alternate form
of Rosalind.
*Ros, Rosaleen, Rosalin, Rosaline, Rosalyne,
Rosalynn, Rosalynne, Rosilyn, Roslin,
Roslyn, Roslyne, Roslynn, Roz, Rozalyn,
Rozlyn*

ROSAMOND (German) famous
guardian.
*Rosamund, Rosamunda, Rosemonde,
Rozamond*

ROSANNA, Roseanna (English)
combinations of Rose + Anna.
*Ranna, Roanna, Rosana, Rosannah,
Roseana, Roseannah, Rosehanah,
Rosehannah, Rosie, Rossana, Rossanna,
Rozana, Rozanna*

ROSANNE, Roseanne (English)
combinations of Rose + Ann.
*Roanne, Rosan, Rosann, Roseann, Rose
Ann, Rose Anne, Rossann, Rossanne,
Rozann, Rozanne*

ROSARIO (Filipino, Spanish) rosary.
Rosarah, Rosaria, Rosarie, Rosary, Rosaura

ROSE (Latin) rose. See also Chalina,
Raisa, Raizel, Roza.
*Rada, Rasia, Rasine, Rois, Róise, Rosa,
Rosea, Rosella, Roselle, Roses, Rosetta, Rosie,
Rosina, Rosita, Rosse*

ROSELANI (Hawaiian) heavenly rose.

ROSELYN (Spanish) an alternate form
of Rosalind.
*Roseleen, Roselene, Roselin, Roseline,
Roselyne, Roselynn, Roselynne*

ROSEMARIE (English) a combination
of Rose + Marie.
*Rosamaria, Rosamarie, Rosemari,
Rosemaria, Rose Marie*

ROSEMARY (English) a combination
of Rose + Mary.
Romi, Romy

ROSETTA (Italian) a form of Rose.
Roseta, Rosette

ROSHAN (Sanskrit) shining light.

ROSHAWNA (American) a
combination of Rose + Shawna.
*Roshan, Roshana, Roshanda, Roshani,
Roshann, Roshanna, Roshanta, Roshaun,
Roshauna, Roshaunda, Roshawn,
Roshawnda, Roshawnna, Roshona,
Roshonda, Roshowna, Roshunda*

ROSIE (English) a familiar form of
Rosalind, Rosanna, Rose.
Rosey, Rosi, Rosio, Rosse, Rosy, Rozsi, Rozy

ROSINA (English) a familiar form of
Rose.
*Rosena, Rosenah, Rosene, Rosheen, Rozena,
Rozina*

ROSITA (Spanish) a familiar form of
Rose.
Roseeta, Roseta, Rozeta, Rozita, Rozyte

ROSLYN (Scottish) an alternate form
of Rossalyn.
Roslin, Roslynn, Rosslyn, Rosslynn

ROSSALYN (Scottish) cape;
promontory.
Roslyn, Rosselyn, Rosylin, Roszaliyn

ROWAN (English) tree with red berries.
(Welsh) an alternate form of Rowena.
Rowana

ROWENA (Welsh) fair haired. (English) famous friend. Literature: Ivanhoe's love interest in Sir Walter Scott's novel *Ivanhoe*.
Ranna, Ronni, Row, Rowan, Rowe, Roweena, Rowen, Rowina

ROXANA, Roxanna (Persian) alternate forms of Roxann, Roxanne.
Rocsana, Roxannah

ROXANN, Roxanne (Persian) sunrise. Literature: the heroine of Edmond Rostand's play *Cyrano de Bergerac*.
Rocxann, Roxan, Roxana, Roxane, Roxanna, Roxianne, Roxy

ROXY (Persian) a familiar form of Roxann.
Roxi, Roxie

ROYALE (English) royal.
Royal, Royalene, Royalle, Roylee, Roylene, Ryal, Ryale

ROYANNA (English) queenly, royal. A feminine form of Roy.
Roya

ROZA (Slavic) a form of Rosa.
Roz, Rozalia, Roze, Rozel, Rozele, Rozell, Rozella, Rozelli, Rozia, Rozsa, Rozsi, Rozyte, Rozza, Rozzie

ROZENE (Native American) rose blossom.
Rozena, Rozina, Rozine, Ruzena

RUANA (Hindi) stringed musical instrument.
Ruan, Ruon

RUBENA (Hebrew) an alternate form of Reubena.
Rubenia, Rubina, Rubine, Rubinia, Rubyn, Rubyna

RUBI (French) an alternate form of Ruby.
Ruba, Rubbie, Rubee, Rubia, Rubie

RUBY (French) precious stone.
Rubby, Rubetta, Rubette, Rubey, Rubi, Rubiann, Rubyann, Rubye

RUCHI (Hindi) one who wishes to please.

RUDEE (German) famous wolf. A feminine form of Rudolph.
Rudeline, Rudell, Rudella, Rudi, Rudie, Rudina, Rudy

RUDRA (Hindi) seeds of the rudraksha plant.

RUE (German) famous. (French) street. (English) regretful; strong-scented herbs.
Ru, Ruey

RUFFINA (Italian) redhead.
Rufeena, Rufeine, Rufina, Ruphyna

RUI (Japanese) affectionate.

RUKAN (Arabic) steady; confident.

RULA (Latin, English) ruler.

RUNA (Norwegian) secret; flowing.
Runna

RUPERTA (Spanish) a form of Roberta.

RUPINDER (Sanskrit) beautiful.

RURI (Japanese) emerald.
Ruriko

RUSALKA (Czech) wood nymph. (Russian) mermaid.

RUSSHELL (French) redhead; fox colored. A feminine form of Russell.
Rushell, Rushelle, Russellynn, Russhelle

RUSTI (English) redhead.
Russet, Rustie, Rusty

RUTH (Hebrew) friendship. Bible: friend of Naomi.
Rutha, Ruthalma, Ruthe, Ruthella, Ruthetta, Ruthie, Ruthven

RUTHANN (American) a combination of Ruth + Ann.
Ruthan, Ruthanna, Ruthannah, Ruthanne, Ruthina, Ruthine

RUTHIE (Hebrew) a familiar form of Ruth.
Ruthey, Ruthi, Ruthy

RUZA (Czech) rose.
Ruzena, Ruzenka, Ruzha, Ruzsa

RYAN, Ryann (Irish) little ruler.
Raiann, Raianne, Rhyann, Riana, Riane, Ryana, Ryane, Ryanna, Ryanne, Rye, Ryen, Ryenne

RYBA (Czech) fish.

RYLEE (Irish) valiant.
Rye, Ryelee, Rylea, Ryleigh, Ryley, Rylie, Rylina, Rylyn

RYLEIGH, Rylie (Irish) alternate forms of Rylee.
Ryelie, Ryli, Rylleigh, Ryllie

RYLEY (Irish) an alternate form of Rylee.
Ryeley, Rylly, Ryly

RYO (Japanese) dragon.
Ryoko

S

SAARAH (Arabic) princess.

SABA (Greek) a form of Sheba. (Arabic) morning.
Sabaah, Sabah, Sabba, Sabbah

SABI (Arabic) young girl.

SABINA (Latin) History: the Sabine were a tribe in ancient Italy. See also Bina.
Sabeen, Sabena, Sabienne, Sabin, Sabine, Sabinka, Sabinna, Sabiny, Saby, Sabyne, Savina, Sebina, Sebinah

SABIYA (Arabic) morning; eastern wind.
Saba, Sabaya, Sabiyah

SABLE (English) sable; sleek.
Sabel, Sabela, Sabella

SABRA (Hebrew) thorny cactus fruit. History: a name for native-born Israelis, who were said to be hard on the outside and soft and sweet on the inside. (Arabic) resting.
Sabera, Sabira, Sabrah, Sabre, Sabrea, Sabreah, Sabree, Sabreea, Sabri, Sabria, Sabriah, Sabriya, Sebra

SABREENA (English) an alternate form of Sabrina.
Sabreen, Sabrena, Sabrene

SABRINA (Latin) boundary line. (Hebrew) a familiar form of Sabra. (English) princess. See also Bree, Brina, Rena, Zabrina.
Sabre, Sabreena, Sabrinas, Sabrinah, Sabrine, Sabrinia, Sabrinna, Sabryna, Sebree, Sebrina, Subrina

SABRYNA (English) an alternate form of Sabrina.
Sabrynna

SACHA (Russian) an alternate form of Sasha.
Sache, Sachia

SACHI (Japanese) blessed; lucky.
Saatchi, Sachie, Sachiko

SADA (Japanese) chaste. (English) a form of Sadie.
Sadá, Sadah, Sadako

SADE (Hebrew) an alternate form of Chadee, Sarah, Shardae, Sharday.
Sáde, Sadé, Sadea, Sadee, Shaday

SADELLA (American) a combination of Sade + Ella.
Sadelle, Sydel, Sydell, Sydella, Sydelle

SADHANA (Hindi) devoted.

SADIE (Hebrew) a familiar form of
Sarah. See also Sada.
*Saddie, Sadee, Sadey, Sadi, Sadiey, Sady,
Sadye, Saide, Saidee, Saidey, Saidi, Saidia,
Saidie, Saidy, Sayde, Saydee, Seidy*

SADIRA (Persian) lotus tree. (Arabic)
star.
Sadra

SADIYA (Arabic) lucky, fortunate.
*Sadi, Sadia, Sadiah, Sadiyah, Sadiyyah,
Sadya*

SADZI (Carrier) sunny disposition.

SAFFRON (English) Botany: a plant
with purple or white flowers whose
orange stigmas are used as a spice.
Safron

SAFIYA (Arabic) pure; serene; best friend.
Safa, Safeya, Saffa, Safia, Safiyah

SAGARA (Hindi) ocean.

SAGE (English) wise. Botany: an herb
with healing powers.
Sagia, Saige, Salvia

SAHARA (Arabic) desert; wilderness.
*Sahar, Saharah, Sahari, Saheer, Saher,
Sahira, Sahra, Sahrah*

SAI (Japanese) talented.
Saiko

SAIDA (Hebrew) an alternate form of
Sarah. (Arabic) happy; fortunate.
Saidah

SAIGE (English) an alternate form of
Sage.

SAIRA (Hebrew) an alternate form
of Sara.
Sairah, Sairi

SAKAË (Japanese) prosperous.

SAKARI (Hindi) sweet.
Sakkara

SAKI (Japanese) cloak; rice wine.

SAKTI (Hindi) energetic. An alternate
form of Shakti.

SAKUNA (Native American) bird.

SAKURA (Japanese) cherry blossom;
wealthy; prosperous.

SALA (Hindi) sala tree. Religion: the
sacred tree under which Buddha died.

SALALI (Cherokee) squirrel.

SALAMA (Arabic) peaceful. See also
Zulima.

SALENA (French) an alternate form
of Salina.
*Saleana, Saleen, Saleena, Salene, Salenna,
Sallene*

SALIMA (Arabic) safe and sound;
healthy.
Saleema, Salema, Salim, Salimah, Salma

SALINA (French) solemn, dignified.
Salena, Salin, Salinah, Salinda, Saline

SALLIANN (English) a combination
of Sally + Ann.
*Sallian, Sallianne, Sallyann, Sally-Ann,
Sallyanne, Sally-Anne*

SALLY (English) princess. A familiar
form of Sarah. History: Sally Ride, an
American astronaut, became the first
U.S. woman in space.
*Sal, Salaid, Sallee, Salletta, Sallette, Salley,
Salli, Sallie*

SALOME (Hebrew) peaceful. History:
Salome Alexandra was a ruler of
ancient Judea. Bible: the sister of King
Herod.
Saloma, Salomé, Salomey, Salomi

SALVADORA (Spanish) savior.

SALVIA (Latin) a form of Sage.
(Spanish) healthy; saved.
Sallvia, Salviana, Salviane, Salvina, Salvine

SAMALA (Hebrew) asked of God.
Samale, Sammala

SAMANTA (Hebrew) an alternate form
of Samantha.
Samantah, Smanta

SAMANTHA (Aramaic) listener.
(Hebrew) told by God.
Sam, Samana, Samanath, Samanatha,
Samanitha, Samanithia, Samanta, Samanth,
Samanthe, Samanthi, Samanthia, Samatha,
Sami, Sammanth, Sammantha, Semantha,
Simantha, Smantha, Symantha

SAMARA (Latin) elm-tree seed.
Saimara, Samaira, Samar, Samarah,
Samari, Samaria, Samariah, Samarie,
Samarra, Samarrea, Samary, Samera,
Sameria, Samira, Sammar, Sammara,
Samora

SAMATHA (Hebrew) an alternate form
of Samantha.
Sammatha

SAMEH (Hebrew) listener. (Arabic)
forgiving.
Samaiya, Samaya

SAMI (Hebrew) a short form of
Samantha, Samuela. (Arabic) praised.
Samia, Samiah, Samiha, Samina, Sammey,
Sammi, Sammie, Sammijo, Sammy,
Sammyjo, Samya, Samye

SAMIRA (Arabic) entertaining.
Samirah, Samire, Samiria, Samirra, Samyra

SAMONE (Hebrew) an alternate form
of Simone.
Samoan, Samoane, Samon, Samona,
Samoné, Samonia

SAMUELA (Hebrew) heard God, asked
of God. A feminine form of Samuel.
Samala, Samelia, Samella, Sami, Samielle,
Samille, Sammile, Samuelle

SAMUELLE (Hebrew) an alternate
form of Samuela.
Samuella

SANA (Arabic) mountaintop; splendid;
brilliant.
Sanaa, Sanáa, Sanaah, Sane, Sanah

SANCIA (Spanish) holy, sacred.
Sanceska, Sancha, Sancharia, Sanchia,
Sancie, Santsia, Sanzia

SANDEEP (Punjabi) enlightened.
Sandip

SANDI (Greek) a familiar form of
Sandra.
Sandee, Sandia, Sandie, Sandiey, Sandine,
Sanndie

SANDRA (Greek) defender of mankind.
A short form of Alexandra, Cassandra.
History: Sandra Day O'Connor was the
first woman appointed to the U.S.
Supreme Court. See also Zandra.
Sahndra, Sandi, Sandira, Sandrea, Sandria,
Sandrica, Sandy, Sanndra, Saundra

SANDREA (Greek) an alternate form
of Sandra.
Sandreea, Sandreia, Sandrell, Sandria,
Sanndria

SANDRICA (Greek) an alternate form
of Sandra. See also Rica.
Sandricka, Sandrika

SANDRINE (Greek) an alternate form
of Alexandra.
Sandreana, Sandrene, Sandrenna,
Sandrianna, Sandrina

SANDY (Greek) a familiar form of
Cassandra, Sandra.
Sandya, Sandye

SANNE (Hebrew, Dutch) lily.
Sanea, Saneh, Sanna, Sanneen

SANTANA (Spanish) saint.
Santa, Santaniata, Santanna, Santanne,
Santena, Santenna, Shantana

SANTINA (Spanish) little saint.
Santinia

SANURA (Swahili) kitten.
Sanora

SANUYE (Moquelumnan) red clouds at sunset.

SANYA (Sanskrit) born on Saturday.
Saneiya, Sania, Sanyia

SANYU (Luganda) happiness.

SAPATA (Native American) dancing bear.

SAPPHIRA (Hebrew) a form of Sapphire.
Safira, Sapheria, Saphira, Saphyra, Sephira

SAPPHIRE (Greek) blue gemstone.
Saffire, Saphire, Saphyre, Sapphira

SARA (Hebrew) an alternate form of Sarah.
Saira, Sarae, Saralee, Sarra, Sera

SARAH (Hebrew) princess. Bible: the wife of Abraham and mother of Isaac. See also Sadie, Saida, Sally, Saree, Sharai, Shari, Zara, Zarita.
Sahra, Sara, Saraha, Sarahann, Sarahi, Sarai, Sarann, Saray, Sarha, Sariah, Sarina, Sarita, Sarolta, Sarotte, Sarrah, Sasa, Sayra, Sorcha

SARAI, Saray (Hebrew) alternate forms of Sarah.
Saraya

SARALYN (American) a combination of Sarah + Lynn.
Saralena, Saraly, Saralynn

SAREE (Hebrew) a familiar form of Sarah. (Arabic) noble.
Sareeka, Sareka, Sari, Sarika, Sarka, Sarri, Sarrie, Sary

SARIAH (Hebrew) an alternate form of Sarah.
Saria, Sarie

SARILA (Turkish) waterfall.

SARINA (Hebrew) a familiar form of Sarah.
Sareen, Sareena, Saren, Sarena, Sarene, Sarenna, Sarin, Sarine, Sarinna, Sarinne

SARITA (Hebrew) a familiar form of Sarah.
Saretta, Sarette, Sarit, Saritia, Saritta

SAROLTA (Hungarian) a form of Sarah.

SAROTTE (French) a form of Sarah.

SARRAH (Hebrew) an alternate form of Sarah.
Sarra

SASA (Hungarian) a form of Sarah, Sasha. (Japanese) assistant.

SASHA (Russian) defender of mankind. A short form of Alexandra. See also Zasha.
Sacha, Sahsha, Sasa, Sascha, Saschae, Sashae, Sashah, Sashai, Sashana, Sashay, Sashea, Sashel, Sashenka, Sashey, Sashi, Sashia, Sashira, Sashsha, Sashya, Sasjara, Sauscha, Sausha, Shasha, Shashi, Shashia

SASS (Irish) Saxon.
Sassie, Sassoon, Sassy

SATARA (American) a combination of Sarah + Tara.
Sataria, Satarra, Sateriaa, Saterra, Saterria

SATIN (French) smooth, shiny.
Satinder

SATINKA (Native American) sacred dancer.

SATO (Japanese) sugar.
Satu

SAUNDRA (English) a form of Sandra, Sondra.
Saundee, Saundi, Saundie, Saundy

SAURA (Hindi) sun worshiper. Astrology: born under the sign of Leo.

SAVANA, Savanna (Spanish) alternate forms of Savannah.
Saveena, Savhana, Savhanna, Savina, Savine, Savona, Savonna

SAVANAH (Spanish) an alternate form of Savannah.
Savhannah

SAVANNAH (Spanish) treeless plain.
Sahvannah, Savana, Savanah, Savanha, Savanna, Savannha, Savauna, Savonnah, Savonne, Sevan, Sevanah, Sevanh, Sevann, Sevanna, Svannah

SAWA (Japanese) swamp. (Moquelumnan) stone.

SAWYER (English) wood worker.
Sawyar, Sawyor

SAYDE, Saydee (Hebrew) alternate forms of Sadie.
Saydi, Saydia, Saydie, Saydy

SAYO (Japanese) born at night.

SAYRA (Hebrew) an alternate form of Sarah.
Sayrah, Sayre, Sayri

SCARLETT (English) bright red. Literature: Scarlett O'Hara is the heroine of Margaret Mitchell's novel *Gone with the Wind*.
Scarlet, Scarlette, Scarlotte, Skarlette

SCHYLER (Dutch) sheltering.
Schuyla, Schuyler, Schuylia, Schylar

SCOTTI (Scottish) from Scotland. A feminine form of Scott.
Scota, Scotia, Scottie, Scotty

SEANA, Seanna (Irish) forms of Jane. See also Shauna, Shawna.
Seaana, Sean, Seane, Seann, Seannae, Seannah, Seannalisa, Seanté, Sianna, Sina

SEBASTIANE (Greek) venerable. (Latin) revered. (French) a feminine form of Sebastian.
Sebastene, Sebastia, Sebastian, Sebastiana, Sebastien, Sebastienne

SEBLE (Ethiopian) autumn.

SEBRINA (English) an alternate form of Sabrina.
Sebrena, Sebrenna, Sebria, Sebriana

SECILIA (Latin) an alternate form of Cecilia.
Saselia, Sasilia, Sesilia, Sileas

SECUNDA (Latin) second.

SEDA (Armenian) forest voices.

SEDNA (Eskimo) well-fed. Mythology: the goddess of sea animals.

SEELIA (English) a form of Sheila.

SEEMA (Greek) sprout. (Afghani) sky; profile.
Seemah, Sima, Simah

SEFA (Swiss) a familiar form of Josefina.

SEIRRA (Irish) an alternate form of Sierra.
Seiara, Seiarra, Seira, Seirria

SEKI (Japanese) wonderful.
Seka

SELA (English) a short form of Selena.
Seeley, Selah

SELAM (Ethiopian) peaceful.

SELDA (German) a short form of Griselda. (Yiddish) an alternate form of Zelda.
Seldah, Selde, Sellda, Selldah

SELENA (Greek) moon. Mythology: Selene was the goddess of the moon. See also Celena.
Saleena, Sela, Selana, Seleana, Seleena, Selen, Selenah, Selene, Séléné, Selenia, Selenna, Selina, Sena, Syleena, Sylena

SELENE (Greek) an alternate form of Selena.
Seleni, Selenie, Seleny

SELIA (Latin) a short form of Cecilia.
Seel, Seil, Sela, Silia

SELIMA (Hebrew) peaceful. A feminine form of Solomon.
Selema, Selemah, Selimah

SELINA (Greek) an alternate form of Celina, Selena.
Selie, Selin, Selinda, Seline, Selinia, Selinka, Sellina, Selyna, Selyne, Selynne, Sylina

SELMA (German) devine protector. (Irish) fair, just. (Scandinavian) divinely protected. (Arabic) secure. A feminine form of Anselm. See also Zelma.
Sellma, Sellmah, Selmah

SEMA (Turkish) heaven; divine omen.
Semaj

SEN (Japanese) Mythology: a magical forest elf that lives for thousands of years.

SENALDA (Spanish) sign.
Sena, Senda, Senna

SENECA (Iroquoian) a tribal name.
Senaka, Seneka, Senequa, Senequae, Senequai, Seneque

SEPTIMA (Latin) seventh.

SEQUOIA (Cherokee) giant redwood tree.
Seqoiyia, Seqouyia, Seqoya, Sequoi, Sequoiah, Sequora, Sequoya, Sequoyah, Sikoya

SERAFINA (Hebrew) burning; ardent. Bible: Seraphim are the highest order of angels.
Sarafina, Serafine, Seraphe, Seraphin, Seraphina, Seraphine, Seraphita, Serapia, Serofina

SERENA (Latin) peaceful. See also Rena.
Sarina, Saryna, Seraina, Serana, Sereen, Sereina, Seren, Serenah, Serene, Serenea, Serenia, Serenna, Serina, Serreana, Serrena, Serrenna

SERENITY (Latin) peaceful.
Serenidy, Serenitee, Serenitey, Sereniti, Serenitiy, Serinity, Serrennity

SERILDA (Greek) armed warrior woman.

SERINA (Latin) an alternate form of Serena.
Sereena, Serin, Serine, Serreena, Serrin, Serrina, Seryna

SEVILLA (Spanish) from Seville.
Seville

SHABA (Spanish) rose.
Shabana, Shabina

SHADA (Native American) pelican.
Shadae, Shadea, Shadeana, Shadee, Shadi, Shadia, Shadiah, Shadie, Shadiya, Shaida

SHADAY (American) a form of Sade.
Shadai, Shadaia, Shadaya, Shadayna, Shadei, Shadeziah, Shaiday

SHADRIKA (American) a combination of the prefix Sha + Rika.
Shadreeka, Shadreka, Shadrica, Shadricka, Shadrieka

SHAE (Irish) an alternate form of Shea.
Shaenel, Shaeya, Shai, Shaia

SHAELEE (Irish) an alternate form of Shea.
Shaeleigh, Shaeley, Shaelie, Shaely

SHAELYN (Irish) an alternate form of Shea.
Shael, Shaelaine, Shaelan, Shaelanie, Shaelanna, Shaeleen, Shaelene, Shaelin, Shaeline, Shaelyne, Shaelynn, Shae-Lynn, Shaelynne

SHAFIRA (Swahili) distinguished.
Shaffira

SHAHAR (Arabic) moonlit.
Shahara

SHAHINA (Arabic) falcon.
Shaheen, Shaheena, Shahi, Shahin

SHAHLA (Afghani) beautiful eyes.
Shaila, Shailah, Shalah

SHAIANNE (Cheyenne) an alternate form of Cheyenne.
Shaeen, Shaeine, Shaian, Shaiana, Shaiandra, Shaiane, Shaiann, Shaianna

SHAILA (Latin) an alternate form of Sheila.
Shaela, Shaelea, Shaeyla, Shailah, Shailee, Shailey, Shaili, Shailie, Shailla, Shaily, Shailyn, Shailynn

SHAINA (Yiddish) beautiful.
Shaena, Shainah, Shaine, Shainna, Shajna, Shanie, Shayna, Shayndel, Sheina, Sheindel

SHAJUANA (American) a combination of the prefix Sha + Juanita. See also Shawanna.
Shajuan, Shajuanda, Shajuanita, Shajuanna, Shajuanza

SHAKA (Hindi) an alternate form of Shakti. A short form of names beginning with 'Shak.' See also Chaka.
Shakah, Shakha

SHAKARAH (American) a combination of the prefix Sha + Kara.
Shacara, Shacari, Shaccara, Shaka, Shakari, Shakkara, Shikara

SHAKAYLA (Arabic) an alternate form of Shakila.
Shakaela, Shakail, Shakaila, Shakala

SHAKEENA (American) a combination of the prefix Sha + Keena.
Shaka, Shakeina, Shakeyna, Shakina, Shakyna

SHAKEITA (American) a combination of the prefix Sha + Keita. See also Shaqueita.
Shaka, Shakeeta, Shakeitha, Shakeithia, Shaketa, Shaketha, Shakethia, Shaketia, Shakita, Shakitra, Sheketa, Shekita, Shikita, Shikitha

SHAKERA (Arabic) an alternate form of Shakira.
Chakeria, Shakeira, Shakeirra, Shakerah, Shakeria, Shakeriah, Shakeriay, Shakerra, Shakerri, Shakerria, Shakerya, Shakeryia, Shakeyra

SHAKIA (American) a combination of the prefix Sha + Kia.
Shakeeia, Shakeeyah, Shakeia, Shakeya, Shakiya, Shekeia, Shekia, Shekiah, Shikia

SHAKILA (Arabic) pretty.
Chakila, Shaka, Shakayla, Shakeela, Shakeena, Shakela, Shakelah, Shakilah, Shakyla, Shekila, Shekilla, Shikeela

SHAKIRA (Arabic) thankful. A feminine form of Shakir.
Shaakira, Shacora, Shaka, Shakeera, Shakeerah, Shakeeria, Shakera, Shakiera, Shakierra, Shakir, Shakirah, Shakirat, Shakirea, Shakirra, Shakora, Shakuria, Shakyra, Shaquira, Shekiera, Shekira, Shikira

SHAKTI (Hindi) divine woman. Religion: the Hindu goddess who controls time and destruction.
Sakti, Shaka, Sita

SHAKYRA (Arabic) an alternate form of Shakira.
Shakyria

SHALANA (American) a combination of the prefix Sha + Lana.
Shalaana, Shalain, Shalaina, Shalaine, Shaland, Shalanda, Shalane, Shalann, Shalaun, Shalauna, Shalayna, Shalayne, Shalaynna, Shallan, Shelan, Shelanda

SHALEAH (American) a combination of the prefix Sha + Leah.
Shalea, Shalee, Shaleea, Shalia, Shaliah

SHALEISHA (American) a combination of the prefix Sha + Aisha.
Shalesha, Shalesia, Shalicia, Shalisha

SHALENA (American) a combination of the prefix Sha + Lena.
Shaleana, Shaleen, Shaleena, Shalen, Shálena, Shalene, Shalené, Shalenna, Shalina, Shalinda, Shaline, Shalini, Shalinna, Shelayna, Shelayne, Shelena

SHALISA (American) a combination of the prefix Sha + Lisa.
Shalesa, Shalese, Shalessa, Shalice, Shalicia, Shaliece, Shalise, Shalisha, Shalishea, Shalisia, Shalissa, Shalisse, Shalyce, Shalys, Shalyse

SHALITA (American) a combination of the prefix Sha + Lita.
Shaleta, Shaletta, Shalida, Shalitta

SHALONA (American) a combination of the prefix Sha + Lona.
Shalon, Shalone, Shálonna, Shalonne

SHALONDA (American) a combination of the prefix Sha + Ondine.
Shalonde, Shalondine, Shalondra, Shalondria

SHALYN (American) a combination of the prefix Sha + Lynn.
Shalin, Shalina, Shalinda, Shaline, Shalyna, Shalynda, Shalyne, Shalynn, Shalynne

SHAMARA (Arabic) ready for battle.
Shamar, Shamarah, Shamare, Shamarea, Shamaree, Shamari, Shamaria, Shamariah, Shamarra, Shamarri, Shammara, Shamora, Shamori, Shamorra, Shamorria, Shamorriah

SHAMEKA (American) a combination of the prefix Sha + Meka.
Shameaka, Shameakah, Shameca, Shamecca, Shamecha, Shamecia, Shameika, Shameke, Shamekia

SHAMIKA (American) a combination of the prefix Sha + Mika.
Shameeca, Shameeka, Shamica, Shamicia, Shamicka, Shamieka, Shamikia

SHAMIRA (Hebrew) precious stone. A eminine form of Shamir.
Shamir, Shamiran, Shamiria, Shamyra

SHAMIYA (American) a combination of the prefix Sha + Mia.
Shamea, Shamia, Shamiah, Shamiyah, Shamyia, Shamyiah, Shamyne

SHANA (Hebrew) God is gracious (Irish) a form of Jane.
Shaana, Shan, Shanae, Shanda, Shandi, Shane, Shania, Shanna, Shannah, Shauna, Shawna

SHANAE (Irish) an alternate form of Shana.
Shanay, Shanea

SHANDA (American) a form of Chanda, Shana.
Shandae, Shandah, Shandra, Shannda

SHANDI (English) a familiar form of Shana.
Shandee, Shandeigh, Shandey, Shandice, Shandie

SHANDRA (American) an alternate form of Shanda. See also Chandra.
Shandrea, Shandreka, Shandri, Shandria, Shandriah, Shandrice, Shandrie, Shandry

SHANE (Irish) an alternate form of Shana.
Shanea, Shaneah, Shanee, Shanée, Shanie

SHANEISHA (American) a combination of the prefix Sha + Aisha.
Shanesha, Shaneshia, Shanessa, Shanisha, Shanissha

SHANEKA (American) an alternate form of Shanika.
Shanecka, Shaneeka, Shaneekah, Shaneequa, Shaneeque, Shaneika, Shaneikah, Shanekia, Shanequa, Shaneyka, Shonneka

SHANEL, Shanell, Shanelle
(American) forms of Chanel.
Schanel, Schanell, Shanella, Shanelly,
Shannel, Shannell, Shannelle, Shenel,
Shenela, Shenell, Shenelle, Shenelly, Shinelle,
Shonelle, Shynelle

SHANETA (American) a combination
of the prefix Sha + Neta.
Seanette, Shaneeta, Shanetha, Shanethis,
Shanetta, Shanette, Shineta, Shonetta

SHANI (Swahili) marvelous.

SHANIA (American) a form of Shana.
Shanasia, Shanaya, Shaniah, Shaniya,
Shanya, Shenia

SHANICE (American) a form of Janice.
See also Chanise.
Chenise, Shanece, Shaneese, Shaneice,
Shanese, Shanicea, Shaniece, Shanise,
Shanneice, Shannice, Shanyce, Sheneice

SHANIDA (American) a combination of
the prefix Sha + Ida.
Shaneeda, Shannida

SHANIKA (American) a combination
of the prefix Sha + Nika.
Shaneka, Shanica, Shanicca, Shanicka,
Shanieka, Shanike, Shanikia, Shanikka,
Shanikqua, Shanikwa, Shaniqua, Shenika,
Shineeca, Shonnika

SHANIQUA (American) an alternate
form of Shanika.
Shaniqa, Shaniquah, Shanique, Shaniquia,
Shaniquwa, Shaniqwa, Shenequa, Sheniqua,
Shinequa, Shiniqua

SHANISE (American) an alternate form
of Shanice.
Shanisa, Shanisha, Shanisia, Shanissa,
Shanisse, Shineese

SHANITA (American) a combination
of the prefix Sha + Nita.
Shanitha, Shanitra, Shanitta, Shinita

SHANLEY (Irish) hero's child.
Shanlee, Shanleigh, Shanlie, Shanly

SHANNA (Irish) an alternate form of
Shana, Shannon.
Shanea, Shannah, Shannea

SHANNEN (Irish) an alternate form
of Shannon.
Shanen, Shanena, Shanene

SHANNON (Irish) small and wise.
Shanan, Shanadoah, Shann, Shanna,
Shannan, Shanneen, Shannen, Shannie,
Shannin, Shannyn, Shanon

SHANTA, Shantae, Shante (French)
alternate forms of Chantal.
Shantai, Shantay, Shantaya, Shantaye,
Shanté, Shantea, Shantee, Shantée,
Shanteia

SHANTAL (American) an alternate
form of Shantel.
Shantall, Shontal

SHANTANA (American) a form of
Santana.
Shantan, Shantanae, Shantanell,
Shantanickia, Shantanika, Shantanna

SHANTARA (American) a combination
of the prefix Sha + Tara.
Shantaria, Shantarra, Shantera, Shanteria,
Shanterra, Shantira, Shontara, Shuntara

SHANTECA (American) a combination
of the prefix Sha + Teca.
Shantecca, Shanteka, Shantika, Shantikia

SHANTEL, Shantell (American) song.
Forms of Chantel.
Seantelle, Shanntell, Shanta, Shantal,
Shantae, Shantale, Shante, Shanteal,
Shanteil, Shantele, Shantella, Shantelle,
Shantrell, Shantyl, Shantyle, Shauntel,
Shauntell, Shauntelle, Shauntrel, Shauntrell,
Shauntrella, Shentel, Shentelle, Shontal,
Shontalla, Shontalle, Shontel, Shontelle

SHANTERIA (American) an alternate
form of Shantara.
Shanterica, Shanterria, Shanterrie,
Shantieria, Shantirea, Shonteria

SHANTESA (American) a combination of the prefix Sha + Tess.
Shantese, Shantice, Shantise, Shantisha, Shontecia, Shontessia

SHANTIA (American) a combination of the prefix Sha + Tia.
Shanteya, Shanti, Shantida, Shantie, Shaunteya, Shauntia, Shontia

SHANTILLE (American) a form of Chantilly.
Shanteil, Shantil, Shantilli, Shantillie, Shantilly, Shantyl, Shantyle

SHANTINA (American) a combination of the prefix Sha + Tina.
Shanteena, Shontina

SHANTORA (American) a combination of the prefix Sha + Tory.
Shantoia, Shantori, Shantoria, Shantory, Shantorya, Shantoya, Shanttoria

SHANTRICE (American) a combination of the prefix Sha + Trice. See also Chantrice.
Shantrece, Shantrecia, Shantreece, Shantreese, Shantrese, Shantress, Shantrezia, Shantricia, Shantriece, Shantris, Shantrisse, Shontrice

SHANY (Swahili) marvellous, wonderful.
Shaney, Shannai, Shannea, Shanni, Shannia, Shannie, Shanny, Shanya

SHAPPA (Native American) red thunder.

SHAQUANDA (American) a combination of the prefix Sha + Wanda.
Shaquan, Shaquana, Shaquand, Shaquandey, Shaquandra, Shaquandria, Shaquanera, Shaquani, Shaquania, Shaquanna, Shaquanta, Shaquantae, Shaquantay, Shaquante, Shaquantia, Shaquona, Shaquonda, Shaquondra, Shaquondria

SHAQUEITA, Shaquita (American) alternate forms of Shakeita.
Shaqueta, Shaquetta, Shaquette, Shaquitta, Shequida, Shequita, Shequittia

SHAQUILA, Shaquilla (American) forms of Shakila.
Shaquail, Shaquia, Shaquil, Shaquilah, Shaquile, Shaquill, Shaquillah, Shaquille, Shaquillia, Shequela, Shequele, Shequila, Shquiyla

SHAQUIRA (American) a form of Shakira.
Shaquirah, Shaquire, Shaquirra, Shaqura, Shaqurah, Shaquri

SHARA (Hebrew) a short form of Sharon.
Shaara, Sharah, Sharal, Sharala, Sharalee, Sharlyn, Sharlynn, Sharra, Sharrah

SHARAI (Hebrew) princess. An alternate form of Sarah. See also Sharon.
Sharae, Sharaé, Sharah, Sharaiah, Sharay, Sharaya, Sharayah

SHARAN (Hindi) protector.
Sharaine, Sharanda, Sharanjeet

SHARDAE, Sharday (Punjabi) charity. (Yoruba) honored by royalty. (Arabic) runaway. An alternate form of Chardae.
Sade, Shadae, Sharda, Shar-Dae, Shardai, Shar-Day, Sharde, Shardea, Shardee, Shardée, Shardei, Shardeia, Shardey

SHAREE (English) a form of Shari.
Shareen, Shareena, Sharine

SHARI (French) beloved, dearest. An alternate form of Cheri. (Hungarian) a form of Sarah. See also Sharita, Sheree, Sherry.
Shara, Share, Sharee, Sharia, Shariah, Sharian, Shariann, Sharianne, Sharie, Sharra, Sharree, Sharri, Sharrie, Sharry, Shary

SHARICE (French) an alternate form of Cherise.
Shareese, Sharesse, Sharese, Sharica, Sharicka, Shariece, Sharis, Sharise, Sharish, Shariss, Sharissa, Sharisse, Sharyse

SHARIK (African) child of God.

SHARISSA (American) a form of Sharice.
Sharesa, Sharessia, Sharisa, Sharisha, Shereeza, Shericia, Sherisa, Sherissa

SHARITA (French) a familiar form of Shari. (American) a form of Charity. See also Sherita.
Shareeta, Sharrita

SHARLA (French) a short form of Sharlene, Sharlotte.

SHARLENE (French) little and womanly. A form of Charlene.
Scharlane, Scharlene, Shar, Sharla, Sharlaina, Sharlaine, Sharlane, Sharlanna, Sharlee, Sharleen, Sharleine, Sharlena, Sharleyne, Sharline, Sharlyn, Sharlyne, Sharlynn, Sharlynne, Sherlean, Sherleen, Sherlene, Sherline

SHARLOTTE (American) a form of Charlotte.
Sharlet, Sharlett, Sharlott, Sharlotta

SHARMA (American) a short form of Sharmaine.
Sharmae, Sharme

SHARMAINE (American) a form of Charmaine.
Sharma, Sharmain, Sharman, Sharmane, Sharmanta, Sharmayne, Sharmeen, Sharmene, Sharmese, Sharmin, Sharmine, Sharmon, Sharmyn

SHARNA (Hebrew) an alternate form of Sharon.
Sharnae, Sharnay, Sharne, Sharnea, Sharnease, Sharnee, Sharneese, Sharnell, Sharnelle, Sharnese, Sharnett, Sharnetta, Sharnise

SHARON (Hebrew) desert plain. An alternate form of Sharai.
Shaaron, Shara, Sharai, Sharan, Shareen, Sharen, Shari, Sharin, Sharna, Sharonda, Sharone, Sharran, Sharren, Sharrin, Sharron, Sharrona, Sharyn, Sharyon, Sheren, Sheron, Sherryn

SHARONDA (Hebrew) an alternate form of Sharon.
Sharronda, Sheronda, Sherrhonda

SHARRONA (Hebrew) an alternate form of Sharon.
Sharona, Sharone, Sharonia, Sharonna, Sharony, Sharronne, Sheron, Sherona, Sheronna, Sherron, Sherronna, Sherronne, Shirona

SHATARA (Hindi) umbrella. (Arabic) good; industrious. (American) a combination of Sharon + Tara.
Shatarea, Shatari, Shataria, Shatarra, Shataura, Shateira, Shatera, Shaterah, Shateria, Shaterra, Shaterri, Shaterria, Shatherian, Shatierra, Shatiria

SHATORIA (American) a combination of the prefix Sha + Tory.
Shatora, Shatorea, Shatori, Shatorri, Shatorria, Shatory, Shatorya, Shatoya

SHAUNA (Hebrew) God is gracious. (Irish) an alternate form of Shana. See also Seana, Shona.
Shaun, Shaunah, Shaunda, Shaune, Shaunee, Shauneen, Shaunelle, Shaunette, Shauni, Shaunice, Shaunicy, Shaunie, Shaunika, Shaunisha, Shaunna, Shaunnea, Shaunta, Shaunua, Shaunya

SHAUNDA (Irish) an alternate form of Shauna. See also Shanda, Shawnda, Shonda.
Shaundal, Shaundala, Shaundel, Shaundela, Shaundell, Shaundelle, Shaundra, Shaundrea, Shaundree, Shaundria, Shaundrice

SHAUNTA (Irish) an alternate form of Shauna. See also Shawnta, Shonta.

Shaunta (cont.)
Schunta, Shauntae, Shauntay, Shaunte,
Shauntea, Shauntee, Shauntée, Shaunteena,
Shauntei, Shauntia, Shauntier, Shauntrel,
Shauntrell, Shauntrella

SHAVON (American) an alternate form
of Shavonne.
Schavon, Schevon, Shavan, Shavana,
Shavaun, Shavona, Shavonda, Shavone,
Shavonia, Shivon

SHAVONNE (American) a combination
of the prefix Sha + Yvonne. See also
Siobhan.
Shavanna, Shavon, Shavondra, Shavonn,
Shavonna, Shavonni, Shavonnia,
Shavonnie, Shavontae, Shavonte, Shavonté,
Shavoun, Shivaun, Shivawn, Shivonne,
Shyvon, Shyvonne

SHAWANNA (American) a
combination of the prefix Sha +
Wanda. See also Shajuana, Shawna.
Shawan, Shawana, Shawanda, Shawante,
Shiwani

SHAWNA (Hebrew) God is gracious.
(Irish) a form of Jane. An alternate
form of Shana, Shauna. See also Seana,
Shona.
Sawna, Shaw, Shawn, Shawnae, Shawnai,
Shawnea, Shawnee, Shawneen, Shawneena,
Shawnell, Shawnette, Shawnna, Shawnra,
Shawnta, Sheona, Siân, Siana, Sianna

SHAWNDA (Irish) an alternate form of
Shawna. See also Shanda, Shaunda,
Shonda.
Shawndal, Shawndala, Shawndan,
Shawndel, Shawndra, Shawndrea,
Shawndree, Shawndreel, Shawndrell,
Shawndria

SHAWNEE (Irish) an alternate form of
Shawna.
Shawne, Shawneea, Shawney, Shawni,
Shawnie

SHAWNIKA (American) a combination
of Shawna + Nika.
Shawnaka, Shawnequa, Shawneika,
Shawnicka

SHAWNTA (Irish) an alternate form of
Shawna. See also Shaunta, Shonta.
Shawntae, Shawntay, Shawnte, Shawnté,
Shawntee, Shawntell, Shawntelle,
Shawnteria, Shawntia, Shawntil, Shawntile,
Shawntill, Shawntille, Shawntina,
Shawntish, Shawntrese, Shawntriece

SHAY, Shaye (Irish) alternate forms of
Shea.
Shaya, Shayah, Shayda, Shayha, Shayia,
Shayla, Shey, Sheye

SHAYLA (Irish) an alternate form of
Shay.
Shaylagh, Shaylah, Shaylain, Shaylan,
Shaylea, Shayleah, Shaylla, Shaylyn, Sheyla

SHAYLEE (Irish) an alternate form of
Shea.
Shaylei, Shayleigh, Shayley, Shayli, Shaylie,
Shayly, Shealy

SHAYLYN (Irish) an alternate form of
Shea.
Shaylin, Shaylina, Shaylinn, Shaylynn,
Shaylynne, Shealyn, Sheylyn

SHAYNA (Hebrew) beautiful. A form of
Shaina.
Shaynae, Shaynah, Shayne, Shaynee,
Shayney, Shayni, Shaynie, Shaynna,
Shaynne, Shayny, Sheana, Sheanna

SHEA (Irish) fairy palace.
Shae, Shay, Shaylee, Shaylyn, Shealy,
Shaelee, Shaelyn, Shealyn, Sheann,
Sheannon, Sheanta, Sheaon, Shearra,
Sheatara, Sheaunna, Sheavon

SHEBA (Hebrew) a short form of
Bathsheba. Geography: an ancient
country of South Arabia.
Saba, Sabah, Shebah, Sheeba

SHEENA (Hebrew) God is gracious.
(Irish) a form of Jane.
Sheenagh, Sheenah, Sheenan, Sheeneal,
Sheenika, Sheenna, Sheina, Shena, Shiona

SHEILA (Latin) blind. (Irish) a form of
Cecelia. See also Cheyla, Zelizi.
*Seelia, Seila, Selia, Shaila, Sheela, Sheelagh,
Sheelah, Sheilagh, Sheilah, Sheileen,
Sheiletta, Sheilia, Sheillynn, Sheilya, Shela,
Shelagh, Shelah, Shelia, Shiela, Shila, Shilah,
Shilea, Shyla*

SHELBI, Shelbie (English) alternate
forms of Shelby.
Shelbbie, Shellbi, Shellbie

SHELBY (English) ledge estate.
*Chelby, Schelby, Shel, Shelbe, Shelbee,
Shelbey, Shelbi, Shelbie, Shelbye, Shellby*

SHELDON (English) farm on the ledge.
*Sheldina, Sheldine, Sheldrina, Sheldyn,
Shelton*

SHELEE (English) an alternate form of
Shelley.
*Shelee, Sheleen, Shelena, Sheley, Sheli,
Shelia, Shelina, Shelinda, Shelita*

SHELISA (American) a combination
of Shelley + Lisa.
*Sheleza, Shelica, Shelicia, Shelise, Shelisse,
Sheliza*

SHELLEY, Shelly (English) meadow on
the ledge. (French) familiar forms of
Michelle. See also Rochelle.
*Shelee, Shell, Shella, Shellaine, Shellana,
Shellany, Shellee, Shellene, Shelli, Shellian,
Shelliann, Shellie, Shellina*

SHELSEA (American) a form of
Chelsea.
Shellsea, Shellsey, Shelsey, Shelsie, Shelsy

SHENA (Irish) an alternate form of
Sheena.
*Shenada, Shenae, Shenah, Shenay, Shenda,
Shene, Shenea, Sheneda, Shenee, Sheneena,
Shenica, Shenika, Shenina, Sheniqua,
Shenita, Shenna, Shennae, Shennah,
Shenoa*

SHERA (Aramaic) light.
*Sheera, Sheerah, Sherae, Sherah, Sheralee,
Sheralle, Sheralyn, Sheralynn, Sheralynne,
Sheray, Sheraya*

SHEREE (French) beloved, dearest.
An alternate form of Shari.
*Scherie, Sheeree, Shere, Shereé, Sherrelle,
Shereen, Shereena*

SHERELLE (French) an alternate form of
Cherelle, Sheryl.
*Sherel, Sherell, Sheriel, Sherrel, Sherrell,
Sherrelle, Shirelle*

SHERI, Sherri (French) alternate forms
of Sherry.
Sheria, Sheriah, Sherie, Sherrie

SHERIAN (American) a combination
of Sheri + Ann.
Sherianne, Sherrina

SHERICE (French) an alternate form of
Cherise.
*Scherise, Sherece, Shereece, Sherees,
Shereese, Sherese, Shericia, Sherise, Sherisse,
Sherrish, Sherryse, Sheryce*

SHERIDAN (Irish) wild.
*Sherida, Sheridane, Sherideen, Sheriden,
Sheridian, Sheridon, Sherridan, Sherridon*

SHERIKA (Punjabi) relative. (Arabic)
easterner.
*Shereka, Sherica, Shericka, Sherrica,
Sherricka, Sherrika*

SHERISSA (French) a form of Sherry,
Sheryl.
Shereeza, Sheresa, Shericia, Sherrish

SHERITA (French) a form of Sherry,
Sheryl. See also Sharita.
Shereta, Sheretta, Sherette, Sherrita

SHERLEEN (French, English) an
alternate form of Sheryl, Shirley.
*Sherileen, Sherlene, Sherlin, Sherlina,
Sherline, Sherlyn, Sherlyne, Sherlynne,
Shirlena, Shirlene, Shirlina, Shirlyn*

SHERRY (French) beloved, dearest. An alternate form of Shari. A familiar form of Sheryl. See also Sheree.
Sherey, Sheri, Sherissa, Sherrey, Sherri, Sherria, Sherriah, Sherrie, Sherye, Sheryy

SHERYL (French) beloved. An alternate form of Cheryl. A familiar form of Shirley. See also Sherry.
Sharel, Sharil, Sharilyn, Sharyl, Sharyll, Sheral, Sherell, Sheriel, Sheril, Sherill, Sherily, Sherilyn, Sherissa, Sherita, Sherleen, Sherral, Sherrelle, Sherril, Sherrill, Sherryl, Sherylly

SHERYLYN (American) a combination of Sheryl + Lynn. See also Cherilyn.
Sharolin, Sharolyn, Sharyl-Lynn, Sheralyn, Sherilyn, Sherilynn, Sherilynne, Sherralyn, Sherralynn, Sherrilyn, Sherrilynn, Sherrilynne, Sherrylyn, Sherryn, Sherylanne

SHEVONNE (American) a combination of the prefix She + Yvonne.
Shevaun, Shevon, Shevonda, Shevone

SHEYENNE (Cheyenne) an alternate form of Cheyenne. See also Shyann, Shyanne.
Shayhan, Sheyan, Sheyane, Sheyann, Sheyanna, Sheyannah, Sheyanne, Sheyen, Sheyene, Shiante, Shyanne

SHIANNE (Cheyenne) an alternate form of Cheyenne.
She, Shian, Shiana, Shianah, Shianda, Shiane, Shiann, Shianna, Shiannah, Shiany, Shieana, Shieann, Shieanne, Shiena, Shiene, Shienna

SHIFRA (Hebrew) beautiful.
Schifra, Shifrah

SHIKA (Japanese) gentle deer.
Shi, Shikah, Shikha

SHILO (Hebrew) God's gift. Geography: a site near Jerusalem. Bible: a sanctuary for the Israelites where the Ark of the Covenant was kept.
Shiloh

SHINA (Japanese) virtuous; wealthy. (Chinese) an alternate form of China.
Shinae, Shinay, Shine, Shinna

SHINO (Japanese) bamboo stalk.

SHIQUITA (American) a form of Chiquita.
Shiquata, Shiquitta

SHIRA (Hebrew) song.
Shirah, Shiray, Shire, Shiree, Shiri, Shirit, Shyra

SHIRLENE (English) an alternate form of Shirley.
Shirleen, Shirline, Shirlynn

SHIRLEY (English) bright meadow. See also Sheryl.
Sherlee, Sherleen, Sherley, Sherli, Sherlie, Shir, Shirl, Shirlee, Shirlie, Shirly, Shirlly, Shurlee, Shurley

SHIVANI (Hindi) life and death.
Shiva, Shivana, Shivanie, Shivanna

SHIZU (Japanese) silent.
Shizue, Shizuka, Shizuko, Shizuyo

SHONA (Irish) a form of Jane. An alternate form of Shana, Shauna, Shawna.
Shiona, Shonagh, Shonah, Shonalee, Shonda, Shone, Shonee, Shonette, Shoni, Shonie, Shonna, Shonnah, Shonta

SHONDA (Irish) an alternate form of Shona. See also Shanda, Shaunda, Shawnda.
Shondalette, Shondalyn, Shondel, Shondelle, Shondi, Shondia, Shondie, Shondra, Shondreka, Shounda

SHONTA (Irish) an alternate form of Shona. See also Shaunta, Shawnta.
Shontá, Shontae, Shontai, Shontalea, Shontasia, Shontavia, Shontaviea, Shontay, Shontaya, Shonte, Shonté, Shontedra, Shontee, Shonteral, Shonti, Shontol, Shontoy, Shontrail, Shountáe

SHOSHANA (Hebrew) lily.
An alternate form of Susan.
Shosha, Shoshan, Shoshanah, Shoshane,
Shoshanha, Shoshann, Shoshanna,
Shoshannah, Shoshauna, Shoshaunah,
Shoshawna, Shoshona, Shoshone,
Shoshonee, Shoshoney, Shoshoni, Shoushan,
Shushana, Sosha, Soshana

SHU (Chinese) kind, gentle.

SHUG (American) a short form of
Sugar.

SHULA (Arabic) flaming, bright.
Shulah

SHULAMITH (Hebrew) peaceful.
See also Sula.
Shulamit, Sulamith

SHUNTA (Irish) an alternate form of
Shonta.
Shuntae, Shunté, Shuntel, Shuntell,
Shuntelle, Shuntia

SHURA (Russian) a form of Alexandra.
Schura, Shurah, Shuree, Shureen, Shurelle,
Shuritta, Shurka, Shurlana

SHYANN, Shyanne (Cheyenne)
alternate forms of Cheyenne. See also
Sheyenne.
Shyan, Shyana, Shyandra, Shyane, Shynee,
Shyanna, Shyannah, Shye, Shyene,
Shyenna, Shyenne

SHYLA (English) an alternate form of
Sheila.
Shya, Shyah, Shylah, Shylan, Shylayah,
Shylana, Shylane, Shyle, Shyleah, Shylee,
Shyley, Shyli, Shylia, Shylie, Shylo, Shyloe,
Shyloh, Shylon, Shylyn

SHYRA (Hebrew) an alternate form of
Shira.
Shyrae, Shyrah, Shyrai, Shyrie, Shyro

SIARA (Irish) an alternate form of
Sierra.
Siarah, Siarra, Siarrah, Sieara

SIANNA (Irish) an alternate form of
Seana.
Sian, Siana, Sianae, Sianai, Sianey, Siannah,
Sianne, Sianni, Sianny, Siany

SIBETA (Moquelumnan) finding a fish
under a rock.

SIBLEY (Greek) an alternate form of
Sybil. (English) sibling; friendly.
Sybley

SIDNEY (French) an alternate form
of Sydney.
Sidne, Sidnee, Sidnei, Sidneya, Sidni, Sidnie,
Sidny, Sidnye

SIDONIA (Hebrew) enticing.
Sydania, Syndonia

SIDONIE (French) from Saint Denis,
France. Geography: an ancient
Phoenician city. See also Sydney.
Sedona, Sidaine, Sidanni, Sidelle, Sidoine,
Sidona, Sidonae, Sidonia, Sidony

SIDRA (Latin) star child.
Sidrah, Sidras

SIENNA (American) a form of Ciana.
Seini, Siena

SIERA (Irish) an alternte form of Sierra.
Sierah, Sieria

SIERRA (Irish) black. (Spanish) saw
toothed. Geography: a rugged range of
mountains that, when viewed from a
distance, has a jagged profile. See also
Ciara.
Seara, Searria, Seera, Seirra, Siara, Siearra,
Siera, Sierrah, Sierre, Sierrea, Sierriah,
Syerra

SIGFREDA (German) victorious peace.
See also Freda.
Sigfreida, Sigfrida, Sigfrieda, Sigfryda

SIGMUNDA (German) victorious
protector.
Sigmonda

SIGNE (Latin) sign, signal. (Scandinavian) a short form of Sigourney.
Sig, Signa, Signy, Singna, Singne

SIGOURNEY (English) victorious conquerer.
Signe, Sigournee, Sigourny

SIGRID (Scandinavian) victorious counselor.
Siegrid, Siegrida, Sigritt

SIHU (Native American) flower; bush.

SIKO (African) crying baby.

SILVIA (Latin) an alternate form of Sylvia.
Silivia, Silva, Silvya

SIMCHA (Hebrew) joyful.

SIMONE (Hebrew) she heard. (French) a feminine form of Simon.
Samone, Siminie, Simmi, Simmie, Simmona, Simmone, Simoane, Simona, Simonetta, Simonette, Simonia, Simonina, Simonne, Somone, Symone

SIMRAN (Sikh) absorbed in God.
Simren, Simrin, Simrun

SINA (Irish) an alternate form of Seana.
Seena, Sinai, Sinaia, Sinan, Sinay

SINCLAIRE (French) prayer. Religion: name honoring Saint Clair.
Sinclair

SINDY (American) a form of Cindy.
Sinda, Sindal, Sindee, Sindi, Sindia, Sindie, Sinnedy, Synda, Syndal, Syndee, Syndey, Syndi, Syndia, Syndie, Syndy

SINEAD (Irish) a form of Jane.
Seonaid, Sine, Sinéad

SIOBHAN (Irish) a form of Joan. See also Shavonne.
Shibahn, Shibani, Shibhan, Shioban, Shobana, Shobha, Shobhana, Siobahn, Siobhana, Siobhann, Siobhon, Siovaun, Siovhan

SIRENA (Greek) enchanter. Mythology: sirens were half-woman, half-bird creatures whose singing so enchanted sailors, they crashed their ships into nearby rocks.
Sireena, Sirene, Sirine, Syrena, Syrenia, Syrenna, Syrina

SISIKA (Native American) songbird.

SISSY (American) a familiar form of Cecelia.
Sisi, Sisie, Sissey, Sissie

SITA (Hindi) an alternate form of Shakti.
Sitah, Sitarah, Sitha, Sithara

SITI (Swahili) respected woman.

SKYE (Arabic) water giver. (Dutch) a short form of Skyler. Geography: an island in the Hebrides, Scotland.
Ski, Skie, Skii, Skky, Sky, Skya, Skyy

SKYLAR (Dutch) an alternate form of Skyler.
Skyela, Skyelar, Skyla, Skylair, Skyylar

SKYLER (Dutch) sheltering.
Skila, Skilah, Skye, Skyeler, Skyelur, Skyla, Skylar, Skylee, Skylena, Skyli, Skylia, Skylie, Skylin, Skyllar, Skylor, Skylyn, Skylynn, Skylyr, Skyra

SLOANE (Irish) warrior.
Sloan, Sloanne

SOCORRO (Spanish) helper.

SOFIA (Greek) an alternate form of Sophia. See also Zofia, Zsofia.
Sofeea, Sofeeia, Soffi, Sofi, Soficita, Sofie, Sofija, Sofiya, Sofka, Sofya

SOLADA (Tai) listener.

SOLANA (Spanish) sunshine.
Solande, Solanna, Soleil, Solena, Soley, Solina, Solinda

SOLANGE (French) dignified.

SOLEDAD (Spanish) solitary.
Sole, Soleda

SOLENNE (French) solemn, dignified.
Solaine, Solene, Soléne, Solenna, Solina, Soline, Solonez, Souline, Soulle

SOMA (Hindi) lunar. Astrological: born under the sign of Cancer.

SOMMER (English) summer; summoner. (Arabic) black. See also Summer.
Somara, Somer, Sommar, Sommara, Sommers

SONDRA (Greek) defender of mankind. A short form of Alexandra.
Saundra, Sondre, Sonndra, Sonndre

SONIA (Russian, Slavic) an alternate form of Sonya.
Sonica, Sonida, Sonita, Sonna, Sonni, Sonnia, Sonnie, Sonny

SONJA (Scandinavian) a form of Sonya.
Sonjae, Sonjia

SONYA (Greek) wise. (Russian, Slavic) a form of Sophia.
Sonia, Sonja, Sonnya, Sonyae, Sunya

SOOK (Korean) pure.

SOPHEARY (Cambodian) beautiful girl.

SOPHIA (Greek) wise. See also Sonya, Zofia.
Sofia, Sophie

SOPHIE (Greek) a familiar form of Sophia. See also Zocha.
Sophey, Sophi, Sophy

SOPHRONIA (Greek) wise; sensible.
Soffrona, Sofronia

SORA (Native American) chirping songbird.

SORAYA (Persian) princess.
Suraya

SORREL (French) reddish brown. Botany: a wild herb.

SOSO (Native American) tree squirrel dining on pine nuts; chubby-cheeked baby.

SOUZAN (Persian) burning fire.
Sousan, Souzanne

SPENCER (English) dispenser of provisions.
Spenser

SPERANZA (Italian) a form of Esperanza.
Speranca

SPRING (English) springtime.
Spryng

STACEY, Stacy (Greek) resurrection. (Irish) a short form of Anastasia, Eustacia, Natasha.
Stace, Stacee, Staceyan, Staceyann, Staicy, Stasey, Stasya, Stayce, Staycee, Staci, Steacy

STACI, Stacie (Greek) alternate forms of Stacey.
Stacci, Stacia, Stayci

STACIA (English) a short form of Anastasia.
Stasia, Staysha

STARLA (English) an alternate form of Starr.
Starrla

STARLEEN (English) an alternate form of Starr.
Starleena, Starlena, Starlene, Starlin, Starlyn, Starlynn, Starrlen

STARLEY (English) a familiar form of Starr.
Starle, Starlee, Staly

STARLING (English) bird.

STARR (English) star.
Star, Staria, Starisha, Starla, Starleen, Starlet, Starlette, Starley, Starlight, Starre, Starri, Starria, Starrika, Starrsha, Starsha, Starshanna, Startish

STASYA (Greek) a familiar form of
Anastasia. (Russian) a form of Stacey.
Stasa, Stasha, Stashia, Stasia, Stasja, Staska

STEFANI, Steffani (Greek) alternate
forms of Stephanie.
*Stafani, Stefanni, Steffane, Steffanee, Stefini,
Stefoni*

STEFANIE (Greek) an alternate form
of Stephanie.
*Stafanie, Staffany, Stefane, Stefanee,
Stefaney, Stefania, Stefanié, Stefanija,
Stefannie, Stefcia, Stefenie, Steffanie, Steffi,
Stefinie, Stefka*

STEFANY, Steffany (Greek) alternate
forms of Stephanie.
Stefanny, Stefanya, Steffaney

STEFFI (Greek) a familiar form of
Stefanie, Stephanie.
*Stefa, Stefcia, Steffee, Steffie, Steffy, Stefi,
Stefka, Stefy, Stepha, Stephi, Stephie, Stephy*

STELLA (Latin) star. (French) a familiar
form of Estelle.
Steile, Stellina

STEPANIA (Russian) a form of
Stephanie.
*Stepa, Stepahny, Stepanida, Stepanie,
Stepanyda, Stepfanie, Stephana*

STEPHANI (Greek) an alternate form
of Stephanie.
Stephania, Stephanni

STEPHANIE (Greek) crowned. A
feminine form of Stephan. See also
Estefani, Estephanie, Panya, Stevie,
Zephania.
*Stamatios, Stefani, Stefanie, Stefany, Steffie,
Stepania, Stephaija, Stephaine, Stephanas,
Stephane, Stephanee, Stephani, Stephanida,
Stéphanie, Stephanine, Stephann,
Stephannie, Stephany, Stephene, Stephenie,
Stephianie, Stephney, Stesha, Steshka,
Stevanee*

STEPHANY (Greek) an alternate form
of Stephanie.
Stephaney, Stephanye

STEPHENE (Greek) an alternate form
of Stephanie.
Stephina, Stephine, Stephyne

STEPHENIE (Greek) an alternate
form of Stephanie.
*Stephena, Stephenee, Stepheney, Stepheni,
Stephenny, Stepheny, Stephine, Stephinie*

STEPHNEY (Greek) an alternate form
of Stephanie.
Stephne, Stephni, Stephnie, Stephny

STERLING (English) valuable; silver
penny.

STEVIE (Greek) a familiar form of
Stephanie.
*Steva, Stevana, Stevanee, Stevee, Stevena,
Stevey, Stevi, Stevy, Stevye*

STINA (German) a form of Christina.
Steena, Stena, Stine, Stinna

STOCKARD (English) stockyard.

STORMIE (English) an alternate form of
Stormy.
Stormee, Stormi, Stormii

STORMY (English) impetuous by
nature.
Storm, Storme, Stormey, Stormie, Stormm

SUCHIN (Tai) beautiful thought.

SUE (Hebrew) a short form of Susan,
Susanna.

SUEANN, Sueanna (American)
combinations of Sue + Ann,
Sue + Anna.
Suann, Suanna, Suannah, Suanne, Sueanne

SUELA (Spanish) consolation.
Suelita

SUGAR (American) sweet as sugar.
Shug

SUGI (Japanese) cedar tree.

SUKE (Hawaiian) a form of Susan.

SUKEY (Hawaiian) a familiar form of
Susan.
Suka, Sukee, Suki, Sukie, Suky

SUKHDEEP (Sikh) light of peace and
bliss.
Sukhdip

SUKI (Japanese) loved one.
(Moquelumnan) eagle eyed.
Sukie

SULA (Greek, Hebrew) a short form of
Shulamith, Ursula. (Icelandic) large
seabird.

SULETU (Moquelumnan) soaring bird.

SULIA (Latin) an alternate form of Julia.
Suliana

SULWEN (Welsh) bright as the sun.

SUMALEE (Tai) beautiful flower.

SUMATI (Hindi) unity.

SUMAYA (American) a combination
of Sue + Maya.
Sumayah, Sumayya, Sumayyah

SUMI (Japanese) elegant, refined.
Sumiko

SUMMER (English) summertime.
See also Sommer.
*Sumer, Summar, Summerann,
Summerbreeze, Summerhaze, Summerine,
Summerlee, Summerlin, Summerlyn,
Summerlynn, Summers, Sumrah, Summyr,
Sumyr*

SUN (Korean) obedient.
*Suncance, Sundee, Sundeep, Sundi, Sundip,
Sundrenea, Sunta, Sunya*

SUNEE (Tai) good.
Suni

SUN-HI (Korean) good; joyful.

SUNI (Zuni) native; member of our tribe.
*Sunita, Sunitha, Suniti, Sunne, Sunni,
Sunnie, Sunnilei*

SUNKI (Hopi) swift.
Sunkia

SUNNY (English) bright, cheerful.
Sunni, Sunnie

SUNSHINE (English) sunshine.
Sunshyn, Sunshyne

SURATA (Pakistani) blessed joy.

SURI (Todas) pointy nose.
Suree, Surena, Surenia

SURYA (Pakistani) Mythology: a sun
god.
Suria, Suriya, Surra

SUSAMMI (French) a combination
of Susan + Aimee.
Suzami, Suzamie, Suzamy

SUSAN (Hebrew) lily. See also
Shoshana, Sukey, Zsa Zsa, Zusa.
*Sawsan, Siusan, Sosan, Sosana, Sue, Suesan,
Sueva, Suisan, Suke, Susana, Susann,
Susanna, Suse, Susen, Susette, Susie, Suson,
Suzan, Suzanna, Suzannah, Suzanne,
Suzette*

SUSANA (Hebrew) an alternate form
of Susan.
Susanah, Susane

SUSANNA, Susannah (Hebrew)
alternate forms of Susan. See also
Xuxa, Zanna, Zsuzsanna.
*Sonel, Sosana, Sue, Suesanna, Susana,
Susanah, Susanka, Susette, Susie, Suzanna*

SUSE (Hawaiian) a form of Susan.

SUSETTE (French) a familiar form of
Susan, Susanna.
Susetta

SUSIE, Suzie (American) familiar forms of Susan, Susanna.
Suse, Susey, Susi, Sussi, Sussy, Susy, Suze, Suzi, Suzy, Suzzie

SUZANNA, Suzannah (Hebrew) alternate forms of Susan.
Suzana, Suzenna, Suzzanna

SUZANNE (English) a form of Susan.
Susanne, Suszanne, Suzane, Suzann, Suzzane, Suzzann, Suzzanne

SUZETTE (French) a form of Susan.
Suzetta, Suzzette

SUZU (Japanese) little bell.
Suzue, Suzuko

SUZUKI (Japanese) bell tree.

SVETLANA (Russian) bright light.
Sveta, Svetochka

SYÀ (Chinese) summer.

SYBELLA (English) a form of Sybil.
Sebila, Sibbella, Sibeal, Sibel, Sibell, Sibella, Sibelle, Sibilla, Sibylla, Sybel, Sybelle, Sybila, Sybilla

SYBIL (Greek) prophet. Mythology: sibyls were oracles who relayed the messages of the gods. See also Cybele, Sibley.
Sib, Sibbel, Sibbie, Sibbill, Sibby, Sibeal, Sibel, Sibyl, Sibylle, Sibylline, Sybella, Sybille, Syble

SYDNEE (French) an alternate form of Sydney.
Sydne, Sydnea, Sydnei

SYDNEY (French) from Saint Denis, France. A feminine form of Sidney. See also Sidonie.
Cidney, Cydney, Sidney, Sy, Syd, Sydel, Sydelle, Sydna, Sydnee, Sydni, Sydnie, Sydny, Sydnye, Syndona, Syndonah

SYDNI, Sydnie (French) alternate forms of Sydney.

SYING (Chinese) star.

SYLVANA (Latin) forest.
Silvaine, Silvana, Silvanna, Silviane, Sylva, Sylvaine, Sylvanah, Sylvania, Sylvanna, Sylvie, Sylvina, Sylvinnia, Sylvonah, Sylvonia, Sylvonna

SYLVIA (Latin) forest. Literature: Sylvia Plath was a well-known American writer and poet. See also Silvia, Xylia.
Sylvette, Sylvie, Sylwia

SYLVIANNE (American) a combination of Sylvia + Anne.
Sylvian

SYLVIE (Latin) a familiar form of Sylvia.
Silvi, Silvie, Silvy, Sylvi

SYMONE (Hebrew) an alternate form of Simone.
Symmeon, Symmone, Symona, Symoné, Symonne

SYMPHONY (Greek) symphony, harmonious sound.
Symfoni, Symphanie, Symphany, Symphanée, Symphoni, Symphoni

SYREETA (Hindi) good traditions. (Arabic) companion.
Syretta, Syrrita

T

TABATHA (Greek, Aramaic) an alternate form of Tabitha.
Tabathe, Tabathia, Tabbatha

TABBY (English) a familiar form of Tabitha.
Tabbi

TABIA (Swahili) talented.
Tabea

TABETHA (Greek, Aramaic) an alternate form of Tabitha.

TABINA (Arabic) follower of
Muhammed.

TABITHA (Greek, Aramaic) gazelle.
Tabatha, Tabbee, Tabbetha, Tabbey, Tabbi,
Tabbie, Tabbitha, Tabby, Tabetha, Tabiatha,
Tabita, Tabithia, Tabotha, Tabtha, Tabytha

TABYTHA (Greek, Aramaic) an
alternate form of Tabitha.
Tabbytha

TACEY (English) a familiar form of
Tacita.
Tace, Tacee, Taci, Tacy, Tacye

TACI (Zuni) washtub. (English) an
alternate form of Tacey.
Tacia, Taciana, Tacie

TACITA (Latin) silent.
Tacey

TADITA (Omaha) runner.
Tadeta, Tadra

TAELOR (English) an alternate form
of Taylor.
Taelar, Taeler, Taellor, Taelore, Taelyr

TAESHA (Latin) an alternate form
of Tisha. (American) a combination
of the prefix Ta + Aisha.
Tadasha, Taeshayla, Taeshia, Taheisha,
Tahisha, Taiesha, Taisha, Taishae, Teasha,
Teashia, Teisha, Tesha

TAFFY (Welsh) beloved.
Taffia, Taffine, Taffye, Tafia, Tafisa, Tafoya

TAHIRA (Arabic) virginal, pure.
Taheera, Taheerah, Tahera, Tahere, Taheria,
Taherri, Tahiara, Tahirah, Tahireh

TAHLIA (Greek, Hebrew) an alternate
form of Talia.
Tahleah, Tahleia

TAILOR (English) an alternate form of
Taylor.
Tailar, Tailer, Taillor, Tailyr

TAIMA (Native American) loud
thunder.
Taimi, Taimia, Taimy

TAIPA (Moquelumnan) flying quail.

TAITE (English) cheerful.
Tate, Tayte, Tayten

TAJA (Hindi) crown.
Taiajára, Taija, Tajae, Tajah, Tahai, Tehya,
Teja, Tejah, Tejal

TAKA (Japanese) honored.

TAKALA (Hopi) corn tassel.

TAKARA (Japanese) treasure.
Takarah, Takaria, Takarra, Takra

TAKAYLA (American) a combination of
the prefix Ta + Kayla.
Takayler, Takeyli

TAKEISHA (American) a combination
of the prefix Ta + Keisha.
Takecia, Takesha, Takeshia, Takesia, Takisha,
Takishea, Takishia, Tekeesha, Tekeisha,
Tekeshi, Tekeysia, Tekisha, Tikesha, Tikisha,
Tokesia, Tykeisha

TAKENYA (Hebrew) animal horn.
(Moquelumnan) falcon. (American)
a combination of the prefix Ta +
Kenya.
Takenia, Takenja

TAKERIA (American) an alternate
form of Takira.
Takera, Takeri, Takerian, Takerra, Takerria,
Takierria, Takoria

TAKI (Japanese) waterfall.
Tiki

TAKIA (Arabic) worshiper.
Takeia, Takeiyah, Takeya, Takeyah, Takhiya,
Takiah, Takija, Takiya, Takiyah, Takkia,
Takya, Takyah, Takyia, Taqiyya, Taquaia,
Taquaya, Taquiia, Tekeiya, Tekeiyah, Tekeyia,
Tekiya, Tekiyah, Tikia, Tykeia, Tykia

TAKILA (American) a form Tequila.
Takayla, Takeila, Takela, Takelia, Takella,
Takeyla, Takiela, Takilah, Takilla, Takilya,
Takyla, Takylia, Tatakyla, Tehilla, Tekeila,
Tekela, Tekelia, Tekilaa, Tekilia, Tekilla,
Tekilyah, Tekla

TAKIRA (American) a combination of
the prefix Ta + Kira.
Takara, Takarra, Takeara, Takeera, Takeira,
Takeirah, Takera, Takiara, Takiera, Takierah,
Takierra, Takirah, Takiria, Takirra, Takora,
Takyra, Takyrra, Taquera, Taquira, Tekeria,
Tikara, Tikira, Tykera

TALA (Native American) stalking wolf.

TALASI (Hopi) corn tassel.
Talasea, Talasia

TALEAH (American) a form of Talia.
Talaya, Talayah, Talayia, Talea, Taleana,
Taleea, Taleéi, Talei, Taleia, Taleiya, Tylea,
Tyleah, Tylee

TALEISHA (American) a combination
of Talia + Aisha.
Taileisha, Taleise, Talesha, Talicia, Taliesha,
Talisa, Talisha, Talysha, Telisha, Tilisha,
Tyleasha, Tyleisha, Tylicia, Tylisha, Tylishia

TALENA (American) a combination of
the prefix Ta + Lena.
Talayna, Talihna, Taline, Tallenia, Talná,
Tilena, Tilene, Tylena

TALESHA (American) an alternate
form of Taleisha.
Taleesha, Talesa, Talese, Taleshia, Talesia,
Tallese, Tallesia, Tylesha, Tyleshia, Tylesia

TALIA (Greek) blooming. (Hebrew) dew
from heaven. (Latin, French) birthday.
A short form of Natalie. See also Thalia.
Tahlia, Taleah, Taliah, Taliatha, Taliea,
Taliyah, Talley, Tallia, Tallya, Talya, Tylia

TALINA (American) a combination of
Talia + Lina.
Talin, Talinda, Taline, Tallyn, Talyn, Talynn,
Tylina, Tyline

TALISA (English) an alternate form of
Tallis.
Talisha, Talishia, Talisia, Talissa, Talysa,
Talysha, Talysia, Talyssa

TALITHA (Arabic) young girl.
Taleetha, Taletha, Talethia, Taliatha, Talita,
Talithia, Taliya, Telita, Tiletha

TALIYAH (Greek) an alternate form
of Talia.
Taleya, Taleyah, Talieya, Talliyah, Talya,
Talyah, Talyia

TALLEY (French) a familiar form of
Talia.
Tali, Talle, Tallie, Tally, Taly, Talye

TALLIS (French, English) forest.
Talice, Talisa, Talise, Tallys

TALLULAH (Choctaw) leaping water.
Tallou, Talula

TAM (Vietnamese) heart.

TAMA (Japanese) jewel.
Tamaa, Tamah, Tamaiah, Tamala, Tema

TAMAKA (Japanese) bracelet.
Tamaki, Tamako, Timaka

TAMAR (Hebrew) a short form of
Tamara. (Russian) History: a twelfth-
century Georgian queen.
Tamer, Tamor, Tamour

TAMARA (Hebrew) palm tree. See also
Tammy.
Tamar, Tamará, Tamarae, Tamarah,
Tamaria, Tamarin, Tamarla, Tamarra,
Tamarria, Tamarrian, Tamarsha, Tamary,
Tamera, Tamira, Tamma, Tammara, Tamora,
Tamoya, Tamra, Tamura, Tamyra, Temara,
Temarian, Thama, Thamar, Thamara,
Thamarra, Timara, Tomara, Tymara

TAMASSA (Hebrew) an alternate form
of Thomasina.
Tamasin, Tamasine, Tamsen, Tamsin,
Tamzen, Tamzin

TAMEKA (Aramaic) twin.
Tameca, Tamecia, Tamecka, Tameeka, Tamekia, Tamiecka, Tamieka, Temeka, Timeeka, Timeka, Tomeka, Tomekia, Trameika, Tymeka, Tymmeeka, Tymmeka

TAMERA (Hebrew) an alternate form of Tamara.
Tamer, Tamerai, Tameran, Tameria, Tamerra, Tammera, Thamer, Timera

TAMESHA (American) a combination of the prefix Ta + Mesha.
Tameesha, Tameisha, Tameshia, Tameshkia, Tameshya, Tamisha, Tamishia, Tamnesha, Temisha, Timesha, Timisha, Tomesha, Tomiese, Tomise, Tomisha, Tramesha, Tramisha, Tymesha

TAMIKA (Japanese) an alternate form of Tamiko.
Tamica, Tamieka, Tamikah, Tamikia, Tamikka, Tammika, Tamyka, Timika, Timikia, Tomika, Tymika, Tymmicka

TAMIKO (Japanese) child of the people.
Tami, Tamika, Tamike, Tamiqua, Tamiyo, Tammiko

TAMILA (American) a combination of the prefix Ta + Mila.
Tamala, Tamela, Tamelia, Tamilla, Tamille, Tamillia, Tamilya

TAMIRA (Hebrew) an alternate form of Tamara.
Tamir, Tamirae, Tamirah, Tamiria, Tamirra, Tamyra, Tamyria, Tamyrra

TAMMI, Tammie (English) alternate forms of Tammy.
Tameia, Tami, Tamia, Tamiah, Tamie, Tamijo, Tamiya

TAMMY (Hebrew) a familiar form of Tamara. (English) twin.
Tamilyn, Tamlyn, Tammee, Tammey, Tammi, Tammie, Tamy, Tamya

TAMRA (Hebrew) a short form of Tamara.
Tammra, Tamrah

TAMSIN (English) a short form of Thomasina.

TANA (Slavic) a short form of Tanya.
Taina, Tanae, Tanaeah, Tanah, Tanairi, Tanairy, Tanalia, Tanara, Tanavia, Tanaya, Tanaz, Tanna, Tannah

TANDY (English) team.
Tanda, Tandalaya, Tandi, Tandie, Tandis, Tandra, Tandrea, Tandria

TANEISHA, Tanesha (American) combinations of the prefix Ta + Nesha.
Tahniesha, Taineshia, Tanasha, Tanashia, Tanaysia, Taneasha, Taneesha, Taneshea, Taneshia, Taneshya, Tanesia, Tanesian, Tanessa, Tanessia, Taniesha, Tannesha, Tanneshia, Tanniecia, Tanniesha, Tantashea

TANEYA (Russian, Slavic) an alternate form of Tanya.
Tanea, Taneah, Tanee, Taneé, Taneia

TANGIA (American) a combination of the prefix Ta + Angela.
Tangela, Tangi, Tangie, Tanja, Tanji, Tanjia, Tanjie

TANI (Japanese) valley. (Slavic) stand of glory. A familiar form of Tania.
Tahnee, Tahni, Tahnie, Tanee, Taney, Tanie, Tany

TANIA (Russian, Slavic) fairy queen. A form of Tanya, Titania.
Taneea, Tani, Taniah, Tanija, Tanika, Tanis, Taniya, Tannia, Tannis, Tanniya, Tannya, Tarnia

TANIEL (American) a combination of Tania + Danielle.
Taniele, Tanielle, Teniel, Teniele, Tenielle

TANIKA (American) a form of Tania.
Tanikka, Tanikqua, Taniqua, Tanique, Tannica, Tianeka, Tianika

TANIS, Tannis (Slavic) forms of Tania, Tanya.

Tanis (cont.)
Tanas, Tanese, Taniese, Tanise, Tanisia, Tanka, Tannese, Tanniece, Tanniese, Tannis, Tannise, Tannus, Tannyce, Tenice, Tenise, Tenyse, Tiannis, Tonise, Tranice, Tranise, Tynice, Tyniece, Tyniese, Tynise

TANISHA (American) a combination of the prefix Ta + Nisha.
Tahniscia, Tahnisha, Tanasha, Tanashea, Tanicha, Taniesha, Tanish, Tanishah, Tanishia, Tanitia, Tannicia, Tannisha, Tenisha, Tenishka, Tinisha, Tonisha, Tonnisha, Tynisha

TANISSA (American) a combination of the prefix Tania + Nissa.
Tanesa, Tanisa, Tannesa, Tannisa, Tennessa, Tranissa

TANITA (American) a combination of the prefix Ta + Nita.
Taneta, Tanetta, Tanitra, Tanitta, Teneta, Tenetta, Tenita, Tenitta, Tyneta, Tynetta, Tynette, Tynita, Tynitra, Tynitta

TANITH (Phoenician) Mythology: the goddess of love.
Tanitha

TANNER (English) leather worker, tanner.
Tannor

TANSY (Greek) immortal. (Latin) tenacious, persistent.
Tancy, Tansee, Tansey, Tanshay, Tanzey

TANYA (Russian, Slavic) fairy queen. A short form of Tatiana.
Tahnee, Tahnya, Tana, Tanaya, Taneya, Tania, Tanis, Taniya, Tanka, Tannis, Tannya, Tanoya, Tany, Tanyia, Taunya, Tawnya, Thanya

TAO (Chinese, Vietnamese) peach.

TARA (Aramaic) throw; carry. (Irish) rocky hill. (Arabic) a measurement.
Taira, Tairra, Taraea, Tarah, Taráh, Tarai, Taralee, Tarali, Tarasa, Tarasha, Taraya, Tarha, Tari, Tarra, Taryn, Tayra, Tehra

TARANEH (Persian) melody.

TAREE (Japanese) arching branch.
Tarea, Tareya, Tari, Taria

TARI (Irish) a familiar form of Tara.
Taria, Tarika, Tarila, Tarilyn, Tarin, Tarina, Tarita

TARISSA (American) a combination of Tara + Rissa.
Taris, Tarisa, Tarise, Tarisha

TARRA (Irish) an alternate form of Tara.
Tarrah

TARYN (Irish) an alternate form of Tara.
Taran, Tareen, Tareena, Taren, Tarene, Tarin, Tarina, Tarren, Tarrena, Tarrin, Tarrina, Tarron, Tarryn, Taryna

TASARLA (Gypsy) dawn.

TASHA (Greek) born on Christmas day. (Russian) a short form of Natasha. See also Tashi, Tosha.
Tacha, Tachiana, Tahsha, Tasenka, Tashae, Tashana, Tashay, Tashe, Tashee, Tasheka, Tashka, Tasia, Taska, Taysha, Thasha, Tiaisha, Tysha

TASHANA (American) a combination of the prefix Ta + Shana.
Tashan, Tashanda, Tashani, Tashanika, Tashanna, Tashiana, Tashianna, Tashina, Tishana, Tishani, Tishanna, Tishanne, Toshanna, Toshanti, Tyshana

TASHARA (American) a combination of the prefix Ta + Shara.
Tashar, Tasharah, Tasharia, Tasharna, Tasharra, Tashera, Tasherey, Tasheri, Tasherra, Tashira, Tashirah

TASHAWNA (American) a combination of the prefix Ta + Shawna.
Tashauna, Tashauni, Tashaunie, Tashaunna, Tashawanna, Tashawn, Tashawnda, Tashawnna, Tashawnnia, Tashonda, Tashondra, Tiashauna, Tishawn, Tishunda,

Tishunta, Toshauna, Toshawna, Tyshauna,
Tyshawna

TASHEENA (American) a combination
of the prefix Ta + Sheena.
Tasheana, Tasheeana, Tasheeni, Tashena,
Tashenna, Tashennia, Tasheona, Tashina,
Tisheena, Tosheena, Tysheana, Tysheena,
Tyshyna

TASHELLE (American) a combination
of the prefix Ta + Shelley.
Tachell, Tashell, Techell, Techelle, Teshell,
Teshelle, Tochell, Tochelle, Toshelle, Tychell,
Tychelle, Tyshell, Tyshelle

TASHI (Slavic) a form of Tasha. (Hausa)
a bird in flight.
Tashia, Tashie, Tashika, Tashima, Tashiya

TASIA (Slavic) a familiar form of Tasha.
Tachia, Tashea, Tasiya, Tassi, Tassia,
Tassiana, Tassie, Tasya

TASSOS (Greek) an alternate form
of Theresa.

TATA (Russian) a familiar form of
Tatiana.
Tate, Tatia

TATE (English) a short form of Tatum.
An alternate form of Taite, Tata.

TATIANA (Slavic) fairy queen.
A feminine form of Tatius. See also
Tanya, Tiana.
Tata, Tatania, Tatanya, Tateana, Tati, Tatia,
Tatianna, Tatie, Tatihana, Tatiyana, Tatjana,
Tatyana, Tiatiana

TATIANNA (Slavic) an alternate form
of Tatiana.
Taitiann, Taitianna, Tateanna, Tateonna,
Tationna

TATIYANA (Slavic) an alternate form
of Tatiana.
Tateyana, Tatiayana, Tatiyanna, Tatiyona,
Tatiyonna

TATUM (English) cheerful.
Tate, Tatumn

TATYANA (Slavic) an alternate form
of Tatiana.
Tatyanah, Tatyani, Tatyanna, Tatyannah,
Tatyona, Tatyonna

TAURA (Latin) bull. Astrology: Taurus is
a sign of the zodiac.
Taurae, Tauria, Taurina

TAURI (English) an alternate form of
Tory.
Taure, Taurie, Taury

TAVIA (Latin) a short form of Octavia.
See also Tawia.
Taiva, Tauvia, Tava, Tavah, Tavita

TAVIE (Scottish) twin. A feminine form
of Tavish.
Tavey, Tavi

TAWANNA (American) a combination
of the prefix Ta + Wanda.
Taiwana, Taiwanna, Taquana, Taquanna,
Tawan, Tawana, Tawanda, Tawanne,
Tequana, Tequanna, Tequawna, Tewanna,
Tewauna, Tiquana, Tiwanna, Tiwena,
Towanda, Towanna, Tywania, Tywanna

TAWIA (African) born after twins.
(Polish) a form of Tavia.

TAWNI (English) an alternate form of
Tawny.
Tauni, Taunia, Tawnia, Tawnie, Tawnnie,
Tiawni

TAWNY (Gypsy) little one. (English)
brownish yellow, tan.
Tahnee, Tany, Tauna, Tauné, Taunisha,
Tawnee, Tawnesha, Tawney, Tawni, Tawnyell,
Tiawna

TAWNYA (American) a combination
of Tawny + Tonya.
Tawna

TAYA, Taye (English) short forms of
Taylor.
Tay, Tayah, Tayana, Tayiah, Tayna, Tayra,
Taysha, Taysia, Tayva, Tayvonne, Teya,
Teyanna, Teyona, Teyuna, Tiaya, Tiya, Tiyah,
Tiyana, Tye

TAYLA (English) a short form of Taylor.
Taylah, Tayleah, Taylee, Tayleigh, Taylie, Teila

TAYLAR (English) an alternate form of Taylor.
Talar, Tayla, Taylah, Taylare, Tayllar

TAYLER (English) an alternate form of Taylor.
Tayller

TAYLOR (English) tailor.
Taelor, Tailor, Taiylor, Talor, Talora, Taya, Taye, Tayla, Taylar, Tayler, Tayllor, Tayllore, Tayloir, Taylorann, Taylore, Taylorr, Taylour, Taylur, Teylor

TAZU (Japanese) stork; longevity.
Taz, Tazi, Tazia

TEAGAN (Welsh) beautiful, attractive.
Taegen, Teage, Teagen, Teaghan, Teaghanne, Teaghen, Teagin, Teague, Teegan, Teeghan, Tegan, Tegwen, Teigan, Tejan, Tiegan, Tigan, Tijan, Tijana

TEAIRA (Latin) an alternate form of Tiara.
Teairra, Teairre, Teairria, Teara, Tearah, Teareya, Teari, Tearia, Teariea, Tearra, Tearria

TEAL (English) river duck; blue green.
Teala, Teale, Tealia, Tealisha

TEANNA (American) a combination of the prefix Te + Anna. An alternate form of Tina.
Tean, Teana, Teanah, Teann, Teannah, Teanne, Teaunna, Teena, Teuana

TECA (Hungarian) a form of Theresa.
Techa, Teka, Tica, Tika

TECLA (Greek) God's fame.
Tekla, Theckla

TEDDI (Greek) a familiar form of Theodora.
Tedde, Teddey, Teddie, Teddy, Tedi, Tediah, Tedy

TEDRA (Greek) a short form of Theodora.
Teddra, Teddreya, Tedera, Teedra, Teidra

TEGAN (Welsh) an alternate form of Teagan.
Tega, Tegen, Teggan, Teghan, Tegin, Tegyn, Teigen

TELISHA (American) an alternate form of Taleisha.
Teleesha, Teleisia, Telesa, Telesha, Teleshia, Telesia, Telicia, Telisa, Telishia, Telisia, Telissa, Telisse, Tellisa, Tellisha, Telsa, Telysa

TEMIRA (Hebrew) tall.
Temora, Timora

TEMPEST (French) stormy.
Tempesta, Tempeste, Tempestt, Tempist, Tempistt, Tempress, Tempteste

TENESHA, Tenisha (American) combinations of the prefix Te + Niesha.
Tenecia, Teneesha, Teneisha, Teneshia, Tenesia, Tenessa, Teneusa, Teniesha, Tenishia

TENNILLE (American) a combination of the prefix Te + Nellie.
Taniel, Tanille, Teneal, Teneil, Teneille, Teniel, Tenille, Tenneal, Tenneill, Tenneille, Tennia, Tennie, Tennielle, Tennile, Tineal, Tiniel, Tonielle, Tonille

TEODORA (Czech) a form of Theodora.
Teadora

TEONA, Teonna (Greek) alternate forms of Tiana, Tianna.
Teon, Teoni, Teonia, Teonie, Teonney, Teonnia, Teonnie

TEQUILA (Spanish) an alcoholic cocktail. See also Takila.
Taquela, Taquella, Taquila, Taquilla, Tequilia, Tequilla, Tiquila, Tiquilia

TERA, Terra (Latin) earth. (Japanese) swift arrow.
Terah, Terai, Teria, Terrae, Terrah, Terria, Tierra

TERALYN (American) a combination of Terri + Lynn.
Taralyn, Teralyn, Teralynn, Terralin, Terralyn

TERESA (Greek) reaper. An alternate form of Theresa. See also Tressa.
Taresa, Taressa, Tarissa, Terasa, Tercza, Tereasa, Tereatha, Terese, Teresea, Teresha, Teresia, Teresina, Teresita, Tereska, Tereson, Teressa, Teretha, Tereza, Terezia, Terezie, Terezilya, Terezinha, Terezka, Terezsa, Terisa, Terisha, Teriza, Terrasa, Terresa, Terresha, Terresia, Terressa, Terrosina, Tersa, Tersea, Teruska, Terza, Teté, Tyresa, Tyresia

TERESE (Greek) an alternate form of Teresa.
Tarese, Taress, Taris, Tarise, Tereece, Tereese, Teress, Terez, Teris, Terrise

TERI (Greek) reaper. A familiar form of Theresa.
Terie

TERRELLE (Greek) an alternate form of Theresa.
Tarrell, Teral, Terall, Terel, Terell, Teriel, Terral, Terrall, Terrell, Terrella, Terriel, Terriell, Terrielle, Terrill, Terryelle, Terryl, Terryll, Terrylle, Teryl, Tyrell, Tyrelle

TERRENE (Latin) smooth. A feminine form of Terrence.
Tareena, Tarena, Teran, Teranee, Tereena, Terena, Terencia, Terene, Terenia, Terentia, Terina, Terran, Terren, Terrena, Terrin, Terrina, Terron, Terrosina, Terryn, Terun, Teryn, Teryna, Terynn, Tyreen, Tyrene

TERRI (Greek) reaper. A familiar form of Theresa.
Terree, Terria, Terrie

TERRIANN (American) a combination of Terri + Ann.
Teran, Terian, Teriann, Terianne, Teriyan, Terria, Terrian, Terrianne, Terryann

TERRIANNA (American) a combination of Terri + Anna.
Teriana, Terianna, Terriana, Terriauna, Terrina, Terriona, Terrionna, Terriyana, Terriyanna, Terryana, Terryauna, Tyrina

TERRICA (American) a combination of Terri + Erica. See also Rica.
Tereka, Terica, Tericka, Terika, Terreka, Terricka, Terrika, Tyrica, Tyricka, Tyrika, Tyrikka, Tyronica

TERRY (Greek) a short form of Theresa.
Tere, Teree, Terelle, Terene, Teri, Terie, Terrey, Terri, Terrie, Terrye, Tery

TERRY-LYNN (American) a combination of Terry + Lynn.
Terelyn, Terelynn, Terri-Lynn, Terrilynn, Terrylynn

TERTIA (Latin) third.
Tercia, Tercina, Tercine, Terecena, Tersia, Terza

TESS (Greek) a short form of Quintessa, Theresa.
Tes, Tese

TESSA (Greek) reaper. A short form of Theresa.
Tesa, Tesah, Tesha, Tesia, Tessah, Tessia, Tezia

TESSIE (Greek) a familiar form of Theresa.
Tesi, Tessey, Tessi, Tessy, Tezi

TETSU (Japanese) strong as iron.

TETTY (English) a familiar form of Elizabeth.

TEVY (Cambodian) angel.
Teva

TEYLOR (English) an alternate form of Taylor.
Teighlor, Teylar

THADDEA (Greek) courageous. (Latin) praiser. A feminine form of Thaddeus.
Thada, Thadda

THALASSA (Greek) sea, ocean.

THALIA (Greek) an alternate form of Talia. Mythology: the Muse of comedy.
Thaleia, Thalie, Thalya

THANA (Arabic) happy occasion.
Thaina, Thania, Thanie

THANH (Vietnamese) bright blue. (Punjabi) good place.
Thantra, Thanya

THAO (Vietnamese) respectful of parents.

THEA (Greek) goddess. A short form of Althea.
Theo

THELMA (Greek) willful.
Thelmalina

THEMA (African) queen.

THEODORA (Greek) gift of God. See also Dora, Dorothy, Feodora.
Taedra, Teddi, Tedra, Teodora, Teodory, Teodosia, Theda, Thedorsha, Thedrica, Theo, Theodore, Theodoria, Theodorian, Theodosia, Theodra

THEONE (Greek) gift of God.
Theondra, Theoni, Theonie

THEOPHANIA (Greek) God's appearance. See also Tiffany.
Theo, Theophanie

THEOPHILA (Greek) loved by God.
Theo

THERESA (Greek) reaper. See also Resi, Reza, Riza, Tassos, Teca, Terrelle, Tracey, Tracy, Zilya.
Teresa, Teri, Terri, Terry, Tersea, Tess, Tessa, Tessie, Theresia, Theresina, Theresita, Theressa, Thereza, Therisa, Therissie, Thersa, Thersea, Tresha, Tressa, Trice

THERESE (Greek) an alternate form of Theresa.
Terese, Thérése, Theresia, Theressa, Therra, Therressa, Thersa

THETA (Greek) Linguistics: a letter in the Greek alphabet.

THETIS (Greek) disposed. Mythology: the mother of Achilles.

THI (Vietnamese) poem.
Thia, Thy, Thya

THIRZA (Hebrew) pleasant.
Therza, Thirsa, Thirzah, Thursa, Thurza, Thyrza, Tirshka, Tirza

THOMASINA (Hebrew) twin. A feminine form of Thomas. See also Tamassa.
Tamsin, Thomasa, Thomasia, Thomasin, Thomasine, Thomazine, Thomencia, Thomethia, Thomisha, Thomsina, Toma, Tomasa, Tomasina, Tomasine, Tomina, Tommie, Tommina

THORA (Scandinavian) thunder. A feminine form of Thor.
Thordia, Thordis, Thorri, Thyra, Tyra

THUY (Vietnamese) gentle.

TIA (Greek) princess. (Spanish) aunt.
Téa, Teah, Teeya, Teia, Ti, Tiakeisha, Tialeigh, Tiamarie, Tianda, Tiandria, Tiante, Tiia, Tiye, Tyja

TIANA, Tianna (Greek) princess. (Latin) short forms of Tatiana.
Teana, Teanna, Tiahna, Tianah, Tiane, Tianea, Tianee, Tiani, Tiann, Tiannah, Tianne, Tianni, Tiaon, Tiauna, Tiena, Tiona, Tionna, Tiyana

TIARA (Latin) crowned.
Teair, Teaira, Teara, Téare, Tearia, Tearria, Teearia, Teira, Teirra, Tiaira, Tiare, Tiarea, Tiareah, Tiari, Tiaria, Tiarra, Tiera, Tierra, Tyara

TIARRA (Latin) an alternate form of Tiara.
Tiairra, Tiarrah, Tyarra

TIAUNA (Greek) an alternate form of Tiana.
Tiaunah, Tiaunia, Tiaunna

TIBERIA (Latin) Geography: the Tiber River in Italy.
Tib, Tibbie, Tibby

TICHINA (American) a combination of the prefix Ti + China.
Tichian, Tichin, Tichinia

TIDA (Tai) daughter.

TIERA, Tierra (Latin) alternate forms of Tiara.
Tieara, Tiéra, Tierah, Tierre, Tierrea, Tierria

TIERNEY (Irish) noble.
Tieranae, Tierani, Tieranie, Tieranni, Tierany, Tiernan, Tiernee, Tierny

TIFF (Latin) a short form of Tiffani, Tiffanie, Tiffany.

TIFFANI, Tiffanie (Latin) alternate forms of Tiffany.
Tephanie, Tifanee, Tifani, Tifanie, Tiff, Tiffanee, Tiffayne, Tiffeni, Tiffenie, Tiffennie, Tiffiani, Tiffianie, Tiffine, Tiffini, Tiffinie, Tiffni, Tiffy, Tiffynie, Tifni

TIFFANY (Greek) a short form of Theophania. (Latin) trinity. See also Tyfany.
Taffanay, Taffany, Tifaney, Tifany, Tiff, Tiffaney, Tiffani, Tiffanie, Tiffanny, Tiffeney, Tiffiany, Tiffiney, Tiffiny, Tiffnay, Tiffney, Tiffny, Tiffy, Tiphanie, Triffany

TIFFY (Latin) a familiar form of Tiffani, Tiffany.
Tiffey, Tiffi, Tiffie

TIJUANA (Spanish) Geography: a border town in Mexico.
Tajuana, Tajuanna, Thejuana, Tiajuana, Tiajuanna, Tiawanna

TILDA (German) a short form of Matilda.
Tilde, Tildie, Tildy, Tylda, Tyldy

TILLIE (German) a familiar form of Matilda.
Tilia, Tilley, Tilli, Tillia, Tilly, Tillye

TIMI (English) a familiar form of Timothea.
Timia, Timie, Timmi, Timmie

TIMOTHEA (English) honoring God. A feminine form of Timothy.
Thea, Timi

TINA (Spanish, American) a short form of Augustine, Martina, Christina, Valentina.
Teanna, Teena, Teina, Tena, Tenae, Tinai, Tine, Tinea, Tinia, Tiniah, Tinna, Tinnia, Tyna, Tynka

TINBLE (English) sound bells make.
Tynble

TINESHA (American) a combination of the prefix Ti + Niesha.
Timnesha, Tinecia, Tineisha, Tinesa, Tineshia, Tinessa, Tinisha, Tinsia

TINISHA (American) an alternate form of Tenesha.
Tiniesha, Tinieshia, Tinishia, Tinishya

TIONA, Tionna (American) forms of Tiana.
Teona, Teonna, Tionda, Tiondra, Tiondre, Tioné, Tionette, Tioni, Tionia, Tionie, Tionja, Tionnah, Tionne, Tionya, Tyonna

TIPHANIE (Latin) an alternate form of Tiffany.
Tiphanee, Tiphani, Tiphany

TIPONYA (Native American) great horned owl.
Tipper

TIPPER (Irish) water pourer. (Native American) a short form of Tiponya.

TIRA (Hindi) arrow.
Tirah, Tirea, Tirena

TIRTHA (Hindi) ford.

TIRZA (Hebrew) pleasant.
Thersa, Thirza, Tierza, Tirsa, Tirzah, Tirzha, Tyrzah

TISA (Swahili) ninth-born.
Tisah, Tysa, Tyssa

TISH (Latin) a short form of Tisha.

TISHA (Latin) joy. A short form of
Leticia.
*Taesha, Tesha, Teisha, Tiesha, Tieshia, Tish,
Tishal, Tishia, Tysha, Tyshia*

TITA (Greek) giant. (Spanish) a short
form of names ending in 'tita.'
A feminine form of Titus.

TITANIA (Greek) giant. Mythology: the
Titans were a race of giants.
*Tania, Teata, Titanna, Titanya, Titiana,
Tiziana, Tytan, Tytania, Tytiana*

TITIANA (Greek) an alternate form
of Titania.
*Titianay, Titiania, Titianna, Titiayana,
Titionia, Titiyana, Titiyanna, Tityana*

TIVONA (Hebrew) nature lover.

TIWA (Zuni) onion.

TIYANA (Greek) an alternate form of
Tiana.
Tiyan, Tiyani, Tiyania, Tiyanna, Tiyonna

TOBI (Hebrew) God is good. A feminine
form of Tobias.
*Tobe, Tobee, Tobey, Tobie, Tobit, Toby, Tobye,
Tova, Tovah, Tove, Tovi, Tybi, Tybie*

TOCARRA (American) a combination
of the prefix To + Cara.
Tocara, Toccara

TOINETTE (French) a short form of
Antoinette.
*Toinetta, Tola, Tonetta, Tonette, Toni,
Toniette, Twanette*

TOKI (Japanese) hopeful.
Toko, Tokoya, Tokyo

TOLA (Polish) a form of Toinette.
Tolsia

TOMI (Japanese) rich.
Tomie, Tomiju

TOMMIE (Hebrew) a short form of
Thomasina.
Tomme, Tommi, Tommia, Tommy

TOMO (Japanese) intelligent.
Tomoko

TONESHA (American) a combination
of the prefix To + Niesha.
*Toneisha, Toneisheia, Tonesha, Tonesia,
Toniece, Tonisha, Tonneshia*

TONI (Greek) flourishing. (Latin)
praiseworthy. A short form of
Antoinette, Antonia, Toinette.
*Tonee, Toney, Tonia, Tonie, Toniee, Tonni,
Tonnie, Tony, Tonye*

TONIA (Latin, Slavic) an alternate form
of Toni, Tonya.
*Tonea, Toniah, Toniea, Tonja, Tonje, Tonna,
Tonni, Tonnia, Tonnie, Tonnja*

TONISHA (American) an alternate
form of Tonesha.
Toniesha, Tonisa, Tonise, Tonisia, Tonnisha

TONYA (Slavic) fairy queen.
Tonia, Tonnya, Tonyea, Tonyetta, Tonyia

TOPAZ (Latin) golden yellow gem.

TOPSY (English) on top. Literature: a
slave in Harriet Beecher Stowe's novel
Uncle Tom's Cabin.
Toppsy, Topsey, Topsie

TORA (Japanese) tiger.

TORI (Japanese) bird. (English) an
alternate form of Tory.
Toria, Toriana, Torie, Torri, Torrie, Torrita

TORIA (English) an alternate form of
Tori.
Toriah, Torria

TORIANA (English) an alternate form
of Tori.

Torian, Toriane, Toriann, Torianna, Torianne, Toriauna, Torin, Torina, Torine, Torinne, Torion, Torionna, Torionne, Toriyanna, Torrina

TORIE, Torrie (English) alternate forms of Tori.
Tore, Toree, Torei, Torre, Torree

TORILYN (English) a combination of Tori + Lynn.
Torilynn, Torrilyn, Torrilynn

TORRI (English) an alternate form of Tori.

TORY (Latin) a short form of Victoria. (English) victorious.
Tauri, Torey, Tori, Torrey, Torreya, Torry, Torrye, Torya, Torye, Toya

TOSHA (Punjabi) armaments. (Polish) a familiar form of Antonia. (Russian) an alternate form of Tasha.
Toshea, Toshia, Toshiea, Toshke, Tosia, Toska

TOSHI (Japanese) mirror image.
Toshie, Toshiko, Toshikyo

TOSKI (Hopi) squash bug.

TOTSI (Hopi) moccasins.

TOTTIE (English) a familiar form of Charlotte.
Tota, Totti, Totty

TOVAH (Hebrew) good.
Tova, Tovia

TOYA (Spanish) a form of Tory.
Toia, Toyanika, Toyanna, Toyea, Toylea, Toyleah, Toylenn, Toylin, Toylyn

TRACEY (Greek) a familiar form of Theresa. (Latin) warrior.
Trace, Tracee, Tracell, Traci, Tracie, Tracy, Traice, Trasey, Treesy

TRACI, Tracie (Latin) alternate forms of Tracey.
Tracia, Tracilee, Tracilyn, Tracilynn, Tracina, Traeci

TRACY (Greek) a familiar form of Theresa. (Latin) warrior.
Treacy

TRALENA (Latin) a combination of Tracy + Lena.
Traleen, Tralene, Tralin, Tralinda, Tralyn, Tralynn, Tralynne

TRANESHA (American) a combination of the prefix Tra + Niesha.
Traneice, Traneis, Traneise, Traneisha, Tranese, Traneshia, Tranice, Traniece, Traniesha, Tranisha, Tranishia

TRASHAWN (American) a combination of the prefix Tra + Shawn.
Trashan, Trashana, Trashauna, Trashon, Trayshauna

TRAVA (Czech) spring grasses.

TREASURE (Latin) treasure, wealth; valuable.
Treasa, Treasur, Treasuré, Treasury

TRELLA (Spanish) a familiar form of Estelle.

TRESHA (Greek) an alternate form of Theresa.
Trescha, Trescia, Treshana, Treshia

TRESSA (Greek) a short form of Theresa. See also Teresa.
Treaser, Tresa, Tresca, Trese, Treska, Tressia, Tressie, Trez, Treza, Trisa

TREVINA (Irish) prudent. (Welsh) homestead. A feminine form of Trevor.
Treva, Trevanna, Trevena, Trevenia, Treveon, Trevia, Treviana, Trevien, Trevin, Trevona

TREVONA (Irish) an alternate form of Trevina.
Trevion, Trevon, Trevonia, Trevonna, Trevonne, Trevonye

TRIANA (Greek) an alternate form of Trina. (Latin) third.
Tria, Triann, Trianna, Trianne

TRICE (Greek) a short form of Theresa.
Treece

TRICIA (Latin) an alternate form of Trisha.
Trica, Tricha, Trichelle, Tricina, Trickia

TRILBY (English) soft hat.
Tribi, Trilbie, Trillby

TRINA (Greek) pure. A short form of Katrina. (Hindi) points of sacred kusa grass.
Treena, Treina, Trenna, Triana, Trinia, Trinchen, Trind, Trinda, Trine, Trinette, Trini, Trinica, Trinice, Triniece, Trinika, Trinique, Trinisa, Tryna

TRINI (Greek) an alternate form of Trina.
Trinia, Trinie

TRINITY (Latin) triad. Religion: the Father, the Son, and the Holy Spirit.
Trinita, Trinite, Trinitee, Triniti, Trinnette, Trinty

TRISH (Latin) a short form of Beatrice, Trisha.
Trishell, Trishelle

TRISHA (Latin) noblewoman. A familiar form of Patricia. (Hindi) thirsty. See also Tricia.
Treasha, Trish, Trishann, Trishanna, Trishanne, Trishara, Trishia, Trishna, Trissha, Trycia

TRISSA (Latin) a familiar form of Patricia.
Trisa, Trisanne, Trisia, Trisina, Trissi, Trissie, Trissy, Tryssa

TRISTA (Latin) a short form of Tristen.
Trisatal, Tristess, Tristia, Trysta, Trystia

TRISTAN (Latin) bold.
Trista, Tristane, Tristanni, Tristany, Tristen, Tristian, Tristiana, Tristin, Triston, Trystan, Trystyn

TRISTEN (Latin) an alternate form of Tristan.
Tristene, Trysten

TRISTIN (Latin) an alternate form of Tristan.
Tristina, Tristine, Tristinye, Tristn, Trystin

TRISTON, Trystyn (Latin) alternate forms of Tristan.
Tristony, Trystyn

TRIXIE (American) a familiar form of Beatrice.
Tris, Trissie, Trissina, Trix, Trixi, Trixy

TROYA (Irish) foot soldier.
Troi, Troia, Troiana, Troiya, Troy

TRUDEL (Dutch) a form of Trudy.

TRUDY (German) a familiar form of Gertrude.
Truda, Trude, Trudel, Trudessa, Trudey, Trudi, Trudie

TRYCIA (latin) an alternate form of Trisha.

TRYNA (Greek) an alternate form of\ Trina.
Tryane, Tryanna, Trynee

TRYNE (Dutch) pure.
Trine

TSIGANA (Hungarian) an alternate form of Zigana.
Tsigane, Tzigana, Tzigane

TU (Chinese) jade.

TUESDAY (English) second day of the week.
Tuesdae, Tuesdea, Tuesdee, Tuesdey, Tusdai

TULA (Hindi) born in the lunar month of Capricorn.
Tulah, Tulla, Tullah, Tuula

TULLIA (Irish) peaceful, quiet.
Tulia, Tulliah

TULSI (Hindi) basil, a sacred Hindi herb.
Tulsia

TURQUOISE (French) blue green, semi-precious stone originally brought to Europe through Turkey.
Turkois, Turkoise, Turkoys, Turkoyse

TUSA (Zuni) prairie dog.

TUYEN (Vietnamese) angel.

TUYET (Vietnamese) snow.

TWYLA (English) woven of double thread.
Twila, Twilla

TYANNA (American) a combination of the prefix Ty + Anna.
Tya, Tyana, Tyann, Tyannah, Tyanne, Tyannia

TYEISHA (American) an alternate form of Tyesha.
Tyeesha, Tyeishia, Tyieshia, Tyisha, Tyishea, Tyishia

TYESHA (American) a combination of the prefix Ty + Aisha.
Tyasha, Tyashia, Tyasia, Tyasiah, Tyeisha, Tyeshia, Tyeyshia, Tyisha

TYFANY (American) a short form of Tiffany.
Tyfani, Tyfanny, Tyffani, Tyffanni, Tyffany, Tyffini, Typhanie, Typhany

TYKEISHA (American) an alternate form of Takeisha.
Tkeesha, Tykeisa, Tykeishia, Tykesha, Tykeshia, Tykeysha, Tykeza, Tykisha

TYKERA (American) an alternate form of Takira.
Tykeira, Tykeirah, Tykereiah, Tykeria, Tykeriah, Tykerria, Tykiera, Tykierra, Tykira, Tykiria, Tykirra

TYLER (English) tailor.
Tyller, Tylor

TYNA (Czech) a short form of Kristina.
Tynae, Tynea, Tynia

TYNE (English) river.
Tine, Tyna, Tynelle, Tynessa, Tynetta

TYNESHA (American) a combination of the prefix Ty + Niesha.
Tynaise, Tynece, Tyneicia, Tynesa, Tynesha, Tyneshia, Tynessia, Tyniesha, Tynisha, Tyseisha

TYNISHA (American) an alternate form of Tynesha.
Tyneisha, Tyneisia, Tynisa, Tynise, Tynishi

TYRA (Scandinavian) battler. Mythology: Tyr was the god of battle.
Tyraa, Tyrah, Tyran, Tyree, Tyria

TYSHANNA (American) a combination of the prefis Ty + Shawna.
Tyshana, Tyshanae, Tyshane, Tyshaun, Tyshaunda, Tyshawn, Tyshawna, Tyshawnah, Tyshawnda, Tyshawnna, Tysheann, Tysheanna, Tyshonia, Tyshonna, Tyshonya

TYTIANA (Greek) an alternate form of Titania.
Tytana, Tytanna, Tyteana, Tyteanna, Tytianna, Tytianni, Tytionna, Tytiyana, Tytiyanna, Tytyana, Tytyauna

U

U (Korean) gentle.

UDELE (English) prosperous.
Uda, Udella, Udelle, Yudelle

ULA (Basque) the Virgin Mary. (Irish) sea jewel. (Spanish) a short form of Eulalia. (Scandinavian) wealthy.
Uli, Ulla

ULANI (Polynesian) cheerful.
Ulana, Ulane

ULIMA (Arabic) astute; wise.
Ullima

ULLA (Latin) a short form of Ursula. (German, Swedish) willful.
Ulli

ULRICA (German) wolf ruler; ruler of all. A feminine form of Ulric. See also Rica.
Ulka, Ullrica, Ullricka, Ullrika, Ulrika, Ulrike

ULTIMA (Latin) last, endmost, farthest.

ULULANI (Hawaiian) heavenly inspiration.

ULVA (German) wolf.

UMA (Hindi) mother. Religion: another name for the Hindu goddess Shakti.

UMAY (Turkish) hopeful.
Umai

UMEKO (Japanese) plum blossom child; patient.
Ume, Umeyo

UNA (Latin) one; united. (Irish) a form of Agnes. (Hopi) good memory. See also Oona.
Unna, Uny

UNDINE (Latin) little wave. Mythology: the Undines were water sprites. See also Ondine.
Undeen, Undene

UNICE (English) a form of Eunice.

UNIKA (American) a form of Unique.
Unica, Unicka, Unik, Unikqua, Unikue

UNIQUE (Latin) only one.
Unika, Uniqia, Uniqua, Uniquia

UNITY (English) unity.
Uinita, Unita, Unitee

UNN (Norwegian) she who is loved.

UNNA (German) woman.

URANIA (Greek) heavenly. Mythology: the Muse of astronomy.
Urainia, Uranie, Uraniya, Uranya

URBANA (Latin) city dweller.
Urbanah, Urbanna

URIKA (Omaha) useful to everyone.
Ureka

URIT (Hebrew) bright.
Urice

URSA (Greek) a short form of Ursula. (Latin) an alternate form of Orsa.
Ursey, Ursi, Ursie, Ursy

URSULA (Greek) little bear. See also Sula, Ulla, Vorsila.
Irsaline, Ursa, Ursala, Ursel, Ursela, Ursella, Ursely, Ursilla, Ursillane, Ursola, Ursule, Ursulina, Ursuline, Urszula, Urszuli, Urzula

USHA (Hindi) sunrise.

USHI (Chinese) ox. Astrology: a sign of the zodiac.

UTA (German) rich. (Japanese) poem.
Utako

UTINA (Native American) woman of my country.
Utahna, Utona, Utonna

VAIL (English) valley.
Vale, Vayle

VAL (Latin) a short form of Valentina, Valerie.

VALA (German) singled out.
Valla

VALARIE (Latin) an alternate form of Valerie.
Valarae, Valaree, Valarey, Valari, Valaria, Vallarie

VALDA (German) famous ruler. A feminine form of Valdemar.
Valida, Velda

VALENCIA (Spanish) strong. Geography: a region in eastern Spain.
Valecia, Valence, Valenica, Valentia, Valenzia

VALENE (Latin) a short form of Valentina.
Valaine, Valean, Valeda, Valeen, Valen, Valena, Valeney, Valien, Valina, Valine, Vallan, Vallen

VALENTINA (Latin) strong. History: Valentina Tereshkova, a Soviet cosmonaut, was the first woman in space. See also Tina, Valene, Valli.
Val, Valantina, Vale, Valenteen, Valentena, Valentijn, Valentin, Valentine, Valiaka, Valtina, Valyn, Valynn

VALERA (Russian) a form of Valerie. See also Lera.

VALERIA (Latin) an alternate form of Valerie.
Valaria, Valeriana, Valeriane, Veleria

VALERIE (Latin) strong.
Vairy, Val, Valarie, Vale, Valera, Valeree, Valeri, Valeria, Valérie, Valery, Valka, Valleree, Valleri, Vallerie, Valli, Vallirie, Valora, Valorie, Valry, Valya, Velerie, Waleria

VALERY (Latin) an alternate form of Valerie.
Valerye, Vallary, Vallery

VALESKA (Slavic) glorious ruler. A feminine form of Vladislav.
Valesca, Valese, Valeshia, Valeshka, Valezka, Valisha

VALLI (Latin) a familiar form of Valentina, Valerie. Botany: a plant native to India.
Vallie, Vally

VALMA (Finnish) loyal defender.

VALONIA (Latin) shadow valley.
Vallon, Valona

VALORA (Latin) an alternate form of Valerie.
Valoria, Valorya, Velora

VALORIE (Latin) an alternate form of Valerie.
Vallori, Vallory, Valori, Valory

VANDA (German) an alternate form of Wanda.
Vandana, Vandella, Vandetta, Vandi, Vannda

VANESA (Greek) an alternate form of Vanessa.
Vanesha, Vaneshah, Vanesia, Vanisa

VANESSA (Greek) butterfly. Literature: a name invented by Jonathan Swift as a nickname for Esther Vanhomrigh. See also Nessie.
Van, Vanassa, Vanesa, Vaneshia, Vanesse, Vanessia, Vanessica, Vanetta, Vaneza, Vaniece, Vaniessa, Vanija, Vanika, Vanissa, Vanita, Vanna, Vannesa, Vannessa, Vanni, Vannie, Vanny, Varnessa, Venessa

VANETTA (English) a form of Vanessa.
Vaneta, Vanita, Vanneta, Vannetta, Vannita, Venetta

VANIA, Vanya (Russian) familiar forms of Anna.
Vanija, Vanina, Vaniya, Vanja, Vanka, Vannia

VANITY (English) vain.
Vaniti, Vanitty

VANNA (Greek) a short form of Vanessa. (Cambodian) golden.
Vana, Vanae, Vanelly, Vannah, Vannalee, Vannaleigh, Vannie, Vanny

VANNESA, Vannessa (Greek) alternate forms of Vanessa.
Vannesha, Vanneza

VANORA (Welsh) white wave.
Vannora

VANTRICE (American) a combination of the prefix Van + Trice.
Vantrece, Vantricia, Vantrisa, Vantrissa

VARDA (Hebrew) rose.
Vadit, Vardia, Vardice, Vardina, Vardis, Vardit

VARVARA (Latin) a form of Barbara.
Vara, Varenka, Varina, Varinka, Varya, Varyusha, Vava, Vavka

VASHTI (Persian) lovely. Bible: the wife of Ahasuerus, king of Persia.
Vashtee, Vashtie, Vashty

VEANNA (American) a combination of the prefix Ve + Anna.
Veeana, Veena, Veenaya, Veeona

VEDA (Sanskrit) wise. Religion: the Vedas are the sacred writings of Hinduism.
Vedad, Vedis, Veeda, Veida, Veleda, Vida

VEDETTE (Italian) sentry; scout. (French) movie star.
Vedetta

VEGA (Arabic) falling star.

VELDA (German) an alternate form of Valda.

VELIKA (Slavic) great, wondrous.

VELMA (German) a familiar form of Vilhelmina.
Valma, Vellma, Vilma, Vilna

VELVET (English) velvety.

VENECIA (Italian) from Venice.
Vanecia, Vanetia, Veneise, Venesa, Venesha, Venesher, Venesse, Venessia, Venetia, Venette, Venezia, Venice, Venicia, Veniece, Veniesa, Venise, Venisha, Venishia, Venita, Venitia, Venize, Vennesa, Vennice, Vennisa, Vennise, Vonitia, Vonizia

VENESSA (Latin) a form of Vanessa.
Veneese, Venesa, Venese, Veneshia, Venesia, Venisa, Venissa, Vennessa

VENUS (Latin) love. Mythology: the goddess of love and beauty.
Venis, Venusa, Venusina, Vinny

VERA (Latin) true. (Slavic) faith. A short form of Elvera, Veronica. See also Verena, Wera.
Vara, Veera, Veira, Veradis, Verasha, Vere, Verka, Verla, Viera, Vira

VERBENA (Latin) sacred plants including olive, laurel, and myrtle.
Verbeena, Verbina

VERDA (Latin) young, fresh.
Verdi, Verdie, Viridiana, Viridis

VERDAD (Spanish) truthful.

VERENA (Latin) truthful. A familiar form of Vera, Verna.
Verene, Verenis, Vereniz, Verina, Verine, Verinka, Veroshka, Verunka, Verusya, Virna

VERENICE (Latin) an alternate form of Varonica.
Verenis, Verenise, Vereniz

VERITY (Latin) truthful.
Verita, Veritie

VERLENE (Latin) a combination of Veronica + Lena.
Verleen, Verlena, Verlin, Verlina, Verlinda, Verline, Verlyn

VERNA (Latin) springtime. (French) a familiar form of Laverne. See also Verena, Wera.
Verasha, Verla, Verne, Vernetia, Vernetta, Vernette, Vernia, Vernice, Vernita, Verusya, Viera, Virida, Virna, Virnell

VERNICE (Latin) a form of Bernice, Verna.

Vernese, Vernesha, Verneshia, Vernessa, Vernica, Vernicca, Verniece, Vernika, Vernique, Vernis, Vernise, Vernisha, Vernisheia, Vernissia

VERONICA (Latin) true image. See also Ronni, Weronika.
Varonica, Vera, Veranique, Verenice, Verhonica, Verinica, Verohnica, Veron, Verona, Verone, Veronic, Véronic, Veronice, Veronika, Veronique, Véronique, Veronne, Veronnica, Veruszhka, Vironica, Vron, Vronica

VERONIKA (Latin) an alternate form of Veronica.
Varonika, Veronick, Véronick, Veronik, Veronike, Veronka, Veronkia, Veruka

VERONIQUE, Véronique (French) forms of Veronica.

VESPERA (Latin) evening star.

VESTA (Latin) keeper of the house. Mythology: the goddess of the home.
Vessy, Vest, Vesteria

VETA (Slavic) a familiar form of Elizabeth.
Veeta, Vita

VI (Latin, French) a short form of Viola, Violet.
Vye

VIANCA (Spanish) a form of Bianca.
Vianeca, Vianica

VIANEY (American) a familiar form of Vianna.
Vianney, Viany

VIANNA (American) a combination of Vi + Anna.
Viana, Vianey, Viann, Vianne

VICA (Hungarian) a form of Eve.

VICKI, Vickie (Latin) familiar forms of Victoria.

Vic, Vicci, Vicke, Vickee, Vickiana, Vickilyn, Vickki, Vicky, Vika, Viki, Vikie, Vikki, Vikky

VICKY (Latin) a familiar form of Victoria.
Viccy, Vickey, Viky, Vikkey, Vikky

VICTORIA (Latin) victorious. See also Tory, Wicktoria, Wisia.
Vicki, Vicky, Victoire, Victoriana, Victorianna, Victorie, Victorina, Victorine, Victoriya, Victorria, Victorriah, Victory, Victorya, Viktoria, Vitoria, Vyctoria

VIDA (Sanskrit) an alternate form of Veda. (Hebrew) a short form of Davida.
Vidamarie

VIDONIA (Portuguese) branch of a vine.
Vedonia, Vidonya

VIENNA (Latin) Geography: the capital of Austria.
Veena, Vena, Venna, Vienette, Vienne, Vina

VIKTORIA (Latin) an alternate form of Victoria.
Viktorie, Viktorija, Viktorina, Viktorine, Viktorka

VILHELMINA (German) an alternate form of Wilhelmina.
Velma, Vilhelmine, Vilma

VILLETTE (French) small town.
Vietta

VILMA (German) a short form of Vilhemina.

VINA (Hebrew) a short form of Davina. (Hindi) Mythology: a musical instrument played by the Hindu goddess of wisdom. (Spanish) vineyard. See also Lavina. (English) a short form of Alvina.
Veena, Vena, Viña, Vinesha, Vinessa, Vinia, Viniece, Vinique, Vinisha, Viñita, Vinna, Vinni, Vinnie, Vinny, Vinora, Vyna

VINCENTIA (Latin) victor, conqueror. A feminine form of Vincent.
Vicenta, Vincenta, Vincentena, Vincentina, Vincentine, Vincenza, Vincy, Vinnie

VIÑITA (Spanish) an alternate form of Vina.
Viñeet, Viñeeta, Viñetta, Viñette, Viñitha, Viñta, Viñti, Viñtia, Vyñetta, Vyñette

VIOLA (Latin) violet; stringed instrument in the violin family. Literature: the heroine of Shakespeare's play *Twelfth Night*.
Vi, Violaine, Violanta, Violante, Viole, Violeine

VIOLET (French) Botany: a plant with purplish blue flowers.
Vi, Violeta, Violette, Vyolet, Vyoletta, Vyolette

VIOLETA (French) an alternate form of Violet.
Violetta

VIRGILIA (Latin) rod bearer, staff bearer. A feminine form of Virgil.
Virgillia

VIRGINIA (Latin) pure, virginal. Literature: Virginia Woolf was a well-known British writer. See also Gina, Ginger, Ginny, Jinny.
Verginia, Verginya, Virge, Virgen, Virgenia, Virgenya, Virgie, Virgine, Virginie, Virginië, Virginio, Virginnia, Virgy, Virjeana

VIRGINIE (French) a form of Virginia.

VIRIDIANA (Latin) an alternate form of Viridis.

VIRIDIS (Latin) green.
Virdis, Virida, Viridia, Viridiana

VIRTUE (Latin) virtuous.

VITA (Latin) life.
Veeta, Veta, Vitaliana, Vitalina, Vitel, Vitella, Vitia, Vitka, Vitke

VITORIA (Spanish) a form of Victoria.
Vittoria

VIV (Latin) a short form of Vivian.

VIVA (Latin) a short form of Aviva, Vivian.
Vica, Vivan, Vivva

VIVECA (Latin) an alternate form of Vivian.
Viv, Vivecca, Vivecka, Viveka, Vivica, Vivieca, Vyveca

VIVIAN (Latin) full of life.
Vevay, Vevey, Viv, Viva, Viveca, Vivee, Vivi, Vivia, Viviana, Viviane, Viviann, Vivianne, Vivie, Vivien, Vivienne, Vivina, Vivion, Vivyan, Vivyann, Vivyanne, Vyvyan, Vyvyann, Vyvyanne

VIVIANA (Latin) an alternate form of Vivian.
Viv, Vivianna, Vivyana, Vyvyana

VONDRA (Czech) loving woman.
Vonda, Vondrea

VONEISHA (American) a combination of Yvonne + Aisha.
Voneishia, Vonesha, Voneshia

VONNA (French) an alternate form of Yvonne.
Vona

VONNY (French) a familiar form of Yvonne.
Vonney, Vonni, Vonnie

VONTRICIA (American) a combination of Yvonne + Tricia.
Vontrece, Vontrese, Vontrice, Vontriece

VORSILA (Greek) an alternate form of Ursula.
Vorsilla, Vorsula, Vorsulla, Vorsyla

W

WADD (Arabic) beloved.

WAHEEDA (Arabic) one and only.

WAINANI (Hawaiian) beautiful water.

WAKANA (Japanese) plant.

WAKANDA (Dakota) magical power.
Wakenda

WAKEISHA (American) a combination of the prefix Wa + Keisha.
Wakeishia, Wakesha, Wakeshia, Wakesia

WALAD (Arabic) newborn.
Waladah, Walidah

WALDA (German) powerful; famous. A feminine form of Waldo.
Waldina, Waldine, Walida, Wallda, Welda

WALERIA (Polish) a form of Valerie.
Wala

WALKER (English) cloth; walker.
Wallker

WALLIS (English) from Wales. A feminine form of Wallace.
Wallie, Walliss, Wally, Wallys

WANDA (German) wanderer. See also Wendy.
Vanda, Wahnda, Wandah, Wandely, Wandie, Wandis, Wandja, Wandzia, Wannda, Wonda, Wonnda

WANDIE (German) a familiar form of Wanda.
Wandi, Wandy

WANETA (Native American) charger. See also Juanita.
Waneeta, Wanita, Wanite, Wanneta, Waunita, Wonita, Wonnita, Wynita

WANETTA (English) pale face.
Wanette, Wannetta, Wannette

WANIKA (Hawaiian) a form of Juanita.
Wanicka

WARDA (German) guardian. A feminine form of Ward.
Wardah, Wardeh, Wardena, Wardenia, Wardia, Wardine

WASHI (Japanese) eagle.

WATTAN (Japanese) homeland.

WAUNA (Moquelumnan) snow geese honking.
Waunakee

WAVA (Slavic) a form of Barbara.

WAVERLY (English) quaking aspen-tree meadow.
Waverley, Waverli, Wavierlee

WAYNESHA (American) a combination of Waynette + Niesha.
Wayneesha, Wayneisha, Waynie, Waynisha

WAYNETTE (English) wagon maker. A feminine form of Wayne.
Waynel, Waynelle, Waynetta, Waynlyn

WEEKO (Dakota) pretty girl.

WEHILANI (Hawaiian) heavenly adornment.

WENDA (Welsh) an alternate form of Wendy.
Wendaine, Wendayne

WENDELLE (English) wanderer.
Wendaline, Wendall, Wendalyn, Wendeline, Wendella, Wendelline, Wendelly

WENDI (Welsh) an alternate form of Wendy.
Wendie

WENDY (Welsh) white; light skinned. A familiar form of Gwendolyn, Wanda.
Wenda, Wende, Wendee, Wendey, Wendi, Wendye, Wuendy

WERA (Polish) a form of Vera. See also Verna.
Wiera, Wiercia, Wierka

WERONIKA (Polish) a form of Veronica.
Weronikra

WESISA (Musoga) foolish.

WESLEE (English) western meadow. A feminine form of Wesley.
Weslea, Wesleigh, Weslene, Wesley, Wesli, Weslia, Weslie, Weslyn

WHITLEY (English) white field.
Whitely, Whitlee, Whitleigh, Whitlie, Whittley

WHITNEY (English) white island.
Whiteney, Whitne, Whitné, Whitnee, Whitneigh, Whitnie, Whitny, Whitnye, Whytne, Whytney, Witney

WHITNIE (English) an alternate form of Whitney.
Whitani, Whitnei, Whitni, Whytni, Whytnie

WHITTNEY (English) an alternate form of Whitney.
Whittaney, Whittanie, Whittany, Whitteny, Whittnay, Whittnee, Whittney, Whittni, Whittnie

WHOOPI (English) happy; excited.
Whoopie, Whoopy

WICKTORIA (Polish) a form of Victoria.
Wicktorja, Wiktoria, Wiktorja

WILDA (German) untamed. (English) willow.
Willda, Wylda

WILEEN (English) a short form of Wilhelmina.
Wilene, Willeen, Willene

WILHELMINA (German) determined guardian. A feminine form of Wilhelm, William. See also Billie, Guillerma, Helma, Minka, Minna, Minnie.
Vilhelmina, Wileen, Wilhelmine, Willa, Willamina, Willamine, Willemina, Willette, Williamina, Willie, Willmina, Willmine, Wilma, Wimina

WILIKINIA (Hawaiian) a form of Virginia.

WILLA (German) a short form of Wilhelmina.
Willabella, Willette, Williabelle

WILLETTE (English) a familiar form of Wilhelmina, Willa.
Wiletta, Wilette, Willetta, Williette

WILLIE (English) a familiar form of Wilhelmina.
Willi, Willina, Willisha, Willishia, Willy

WILLOW (English) willow tree.
Willough

WILMA (German) a short form of Wilhelmina.
Williemae, Wilmanie, Wilmayra, Wilmetta, Wilmette, Wilmina, Wilmyne, Wylma

WILONA (English) desired.
Willona, Willone, Wilone

WIN (German) a short form of Winifred. See also Edwina.
Wyn

WINDA (Swahili) hunter.

WINDY (English) windy.
Windee, Windey, Windi, Windie, Wyndee, Wyndy

WINEMA (Moquelumnan) woman chief.

WINIFRED (German) peaceful friend. (Welsh) an alternate form of Guinevere. See also Freddi, Una, Winnie.
Win, Winafred, Winefred, Winefride, Winfreda, Winfrieda, Winiefrida, Winifrid, Winifryd, Winnafred, Winnefred, Winniefred, Winnifred, Winnifrid, Wynafred, Wynifred, Wynnifred

WINNA (African) friend.
Winnah

WINNIE (English) a familiar form of Edwina, Gwyneth, Winnifred, Winona, Wynne. History: Winnie Mandela kept the anti-aparteid movement alive in South Africa while her husband, Nelson Mandela, was imprisoned. Literature: the lovable bear in A. A. Milne's children's story *Winnie the Pooh*.
Wina, Winne, Winney, Winni, Winny, Wynnie

WINOLA (German) charming friend.
Wynola

WINONA (Lakota) oldest daughter.
Wanona, Wenona, Wenonah, Winnie, Winonah, Wynonna

WINTER (English) winter.
Wintr, Wynter

WIRA (Polish) a form of Elvira.
Wiria, Wirke

WISIA (Polish) a form of Victoria.
Wicia, Wikta

WREN (English) wren, songbird.

WYANET (Native American) legendary beauty.
Wyaneta, Wyanita, Wynette

WYNNE (Welsh) white, light skinned. A short form of Blodwyn, Guinivere, Gwyneth.
Winnie, Wyn, Wynn

WYNONNA (Lakota) an alternate form of Winona.
Wynnona, Wynona

WYNTER (English) an alternate form of Winter.
Wynteria

WYOMING (Native American) Geography: a western American state.
Wy, Wye, Wyoh, Wyomia

X

XANDRA (Greek) an alternate form of Zandra. (Spanish) a short form of Alexandra.
Xander, Xandrea, Xandria

XANTHE (Greek) yellow, blond. See also Zanthe.
Xanne, Xantha, Xanthia, Xanthippe

XANTHIPPE (Greek) an alternate form of Xanthe. History: Socrates's wife.
Xantippie

XAVIERA (Basque) owner of the new house. (Arabic) bright. A feminine form of Xavier. See also Javiera, Zaviera.
Xavia, Xaviére, Xavyera, Xiveria

XELA (Quiché) my mountain home.

XENA (Greek) an alternate form of Xenia.

XENIA (Greek) hospitable. See also Zena, Zina.
Xeenia, Xena, Xenea, Xenya, Xinia

XIANG (Chinese) fragrant.

XIOMARA (Teutonic) glorious forest.
Xiomaris, Xiomayra

XIU MEI (Chinese) beautiful plum.

XOCHITL (Aztec) place of many flowers.
Xochil, Xochilt, Xochilth, Xochiti

XUAN (Vietnamese) spring.

XUXA (Portuguese) a familiar form of Susanna.

XYLIA (Greek) a form of Sylvia.
Xylina, Xylona

Y

YACHNE (Hebrew) hospitable.

YADIRA (Hebrew) friend.
Yadirah, Yadirha, Yadyra

YAEL (Hebrew) strength of God. See also Jael.
Yaeli, Yaella, Yeala

YAFFA (Hebrew) beautiful. See also Jaffa.
Yafeal, Yaffit, Yafit

YAHAIRA (Hebrew) an alternate form of Yakira.
Yahara, Yahayra, Yahira

YAJAIRA (Hebrew) an alternate form of Yakira.
Yahaira, Yajara, Yajayra, Yajhaira

YAKIRA (Hebrew) precious; dear.
Yahaira, Yajaira

YALANDA (Greek) an alternate form of Yolanda.
Yalando, Yalonda, Ylana, Ylanda

YALENA (Greek, Russian) an alternate form of Helen. See also Lena, Yelena.

YALETHA (American) a form of Oletha.
Yelitsa

YAMARY (American) a combination of the prefix Ya + Mary.
Yamairy, Yamarie, Yamaris, Yamayra

YAMELIA (American) an alternate form of Amelia.
Yameily, Yamelya, Yamelys

YAMILA (Arabic) an alternate form of Jamila.
Yamela, Yamely, Yamil, Yamile, Yamilet, Yamiley, Yamilla, Yamille

YAMINAH (Arabic) right, proper.
Yamina, Yamini, Yemina, Yeminah, Yemini

YAMKA (Hopi) blossom.

YAMUNA (Hindi) sacred river.

YANA (Slavic) an alternate form of Jana.
Yanae, Yanah, Yanay, Yanaye, Yanesi, Yanet, Yaneth, Yaney, Yani, Yanik, Yanina, Yanis, Yanisha, Yanitza, Yanixia, Yanna, Yannah, Yanni, Yannica, Yannick, Yannina

YANABA (Navajo) brave.

YANELI (American) a combination of the prefix Ya + Nellie.
Yanela, Yanelis, Yaneliz, Yanelle, Yanelli, Yanely, Yanelys

YANET (American) a form of Janet.
Yanete, Yaneth, Yanethe, Yanette, Yannet, Yanneth, Yannette

YÁNG (Chinese) sun.

YARELI (American) a form of Oralee.
Yarely, Yaresly

YARINA (Slavic) a form of Irene.
Yaryna

YARITZA (American) a combination of Yana + Ritsa.
Yaritsa, Yaritza

YARKONA (Hebrew) green.

YARMILLA (Slavic) market trader.

YASHIRA (Afghani) hamble; takes it easy. (Arabic) wealthy. A feminine form of Yasir.

YASMEEN (Persian) an alternate form of Yasmin.
Yasemeen, Yasemin, Yasmeena, Yasmen, Yasmene, Yasmeni, Yasmenne, Yassmeen, Yassmen

YASMIN, Yasmine (Persian) jasmine flower. Alternate forms of Jasmine.
Yashmine, Yasiman, Yasimine, Yasma, Yasmain, Yasmaine, Yasmina, Yasminda, Yasmon, Yasmyn, Yazmin, Yesmean, Yesmeen, Yesmin, Yesmina, Yesmine, Yesmyn

YASU (Japanese) resting, calm.
Yasuko, Yasuyo

YAZMIN (Persian) an alternate form of Yasmin.
Yazmeen, Yazmen, Yazmene, Yazmina, Yazmine, Yazmyn, Yazmyne, Yazzmien, Yazzmine, Yazzmine, Yazzmyn

YECENIA (Arabic) an alternate form of Yesenia.

YEHUDIT (Hebrew) an alternate form of Judith.
Yudit, Yudita, Yuta

YEI (Japanese) flourishing.

YEIRA (Hebrew) light.

YEKATERINA (Russian) a form of Katherine.

YELENA (Russian) a form of Helen, Jelena. See also Lena, Yalena.
Yeleana, Yelen, Yelenna, Yelenne, Yelina, Ylena, Ylenia, Ylenna

YELISABETA (Russian) a form of Elizabeth.
Yelizaveta

YEMENA (Arabic) from Yemen.
Yemina

YEN (Chinese) yearning; desirous.
Yeni, Yenih, Yenny

YENENE (Native American) shaman.

YENIFER (Welsh) an alternate form of Jennifer.
Yenefer, Yennifer

YEO (Korean) mild.
Yee

YEPA (Native American) snow girl.

YERA (Basque) Religion: a name for the Virgin Mary.

YESENIA (Arabic) flower.
Yasenya, Yecenia, Yesinia, Yesnia, Yessenia

YESICA (Hebrew) an alternate form of Jessica.
Yesika, Yesiko

YESSENIA (Arabic) an alternate form of Yesenia.
Yessena, Yessenya, Yissenia

YESSICA (Hebrew) an alternate form of Jessica.
Yessika, Yesyka

YETTA (English) a short form of Henrietta.
Yette, Yitta, Yitty

YEVA (Ukrainian) a form of Eve.

YIESHA (Arabic, Swahili) an alternate form of Aisha.
Yiasha

YÍN (Chinese) silver.

YNEZ (Spanish) a form of Agnes. See also Inez.
Ynes, Ynesita

YOANNA (Hebrew) an alternate form of Joanna.
Yoana, Yohana, Yohanka, Yohanna, Yohannah

YOCELIN, Yocelyn (Latin) alternate forms of Jocelyn.
Yoceline, Yocelyne, Yuceli

YOI (Japanese) born in the evening.

YOKI (Hopi) bluebird.
Yokie

YOKO (Japanese) good girl.
Yo

YOLIE (Greek) a familiar form of Yolanda.
Yola, Yoley, Yoli, Yoly

YOLANDA (Greek) violet flower. See also Iolanthe, Jolanda, Olinda.
Yalanda, Yolie, Yolaine, Yolana, Yoland, Yolande, Yolane, Yolanna, Yolantha, Yolanthe, Yolette, Yolonda, Yorlanda, Youlanda, Yulanda, Yulonda

YOLUTA (Native American) summer flower.

YOMARA (American) a combination of Yolanda + Tamara.
Yomaira, Yomarie, Yomira

YON (Burmese) rabbit. (Korean) lotus blossom.
Yona, Yonna

YONÉ (Japanese) wealth; rice.

YONINA (Hebrew) an alternate form of Jonina.
Yona, Yonah

YONITA (Hebrew) an alternate form of Jonita.
Yonat, Yonati, Yonit

YOOMEE (Coos) star.
Yoome

YORDANA (Basque) descendant. See also Jordana.

YORI (Japanese) reliable.
Yoriko, Yoriyo

YOSELIN (Latin) an alternate form of Jocelyn.
Yoseline, Yoselyn, Yosselin, Yosseline, Yosselyn

YOSEPHA (Hebrew) a form of Josephine.
Yosefa, Yosifa, Yuseffa

YOSHI (Japanese) good; respectful.
Yoshie, Yoshiko, Yoshiyo

YOVELA (Hebrew) joyful heart; rejoicer.

YSABEL (Spanish) an alternate form of Isabel.
Ysabell, Ysabella, Ysabelle, Ysbel, Ysbella, Ysobel

YSANNE (American) a combination of Ysabel + Ann.
Ysande, Ysann, Ysanna

YSEULT (German) ice rule. (Irish) fair; light skinned. (Welsh) an alternate form of Isolde.
Yseulte, Ysolt

YUANA (Spanish) an alternate form of Juana.
Yuan, Yuanna

YUDELLE (English) an alternate form of Udele
Yudela, Yudell, Yudella

YUDITA (Russian) a form of Judith.
Yudit, Yudith, Yuditt

YUKI (Japanese) snow.
Yukie, Yukiko, Yukiyo

YULENE (Basque) a form of Julia.
Yuleen

YULIA (Russian) a form of Julia.
Yula, Yulenka, Yulinka, Yulka, Yulya

YULIANA (Spanish) an alternate form of Juliana.
Yulenia, Yuliani

YURI (Japanese) lily.
Yuree, Yuriko, Yuriyo

YVANNA (Slavic) an alternate form of Ivana.
Yvan, Yvana, Yvannia

YVETTE (French) a familiar form of Yvonne. See also Evette, Ivette.
Yavette, Yevett, Yevette, Yevetta, Yvet, Yveta, Yvett, Yvetta

YVONNE (French) young archer. (Scandanavian) yew wood; bow wood. A feminine form of Ivar. See also Evonne, Ivonne, Vonna, Vonny, Yvette.
Yavanda, Yavanna, Yavanne, Yavonda, Yavonna, Yavonne, Yveline, Yvon, Yvone, Yvonna, Yvonnah, Yvonnia, Yvonnie, Yvonny

Z

ZABRINA (American) an alternate form of Sabrina.
Zabreena, Zabrinia, Zabrinna, Zabryna

ZACHARIE (Hebrew) God remembered. A feminine form of Zachariah.
Zacari, Zacceaus, Zacchaea, Zachary, Zachoia, Zackaria, Zackeisha, Zackeria, Zakaria, Zakaya, Zakeshia, Zakiah, Zakiria, Zakiya, Zakiyah, Zechari

ZACHARY (Hebrew) an alternate form of Zacharie.
Zackery, Zakary

ZADA (Arabic) fortunate, prosperous.
Zaida, Zayda, Zayeda

ZAFINA (Arabic) victorious.

ZAFIRAH (Arabic) successful; victorious.

ZAHAR (Hebrew) daybreak; dawn.
Zahara, Zaharra, Zahera, Zahira, Zahirah, Zeeherah

ZAHAVAH (Hebrew) golden.
Zachava, Zachavah, Zechava, Zechavah, Zehava, Zehavi, Zehavit, Zeheva, Zehuva

ZAHRA (Swahili) flower. (Arabic) white.
Zahara, Zahraa, Zahrah, Zahreh, Zahria

ZAIRA (Hebrew) an alternate form of Zara.
Zaire, Zairea, Zirrea

ZAKIA (Swahili) smart. (Arabic) chaste.
Zakea, Zakeia, Zakiah, Zakiya

ZAKIRA (Hebrew) an alternate form of Zacharie.
Zaakira, Zakiera, Zakierra, Zakir, Zakirah, Zakiria, Zakiriya, Zykarah, Zykera, Zykeria, Zykerria, Zykira, Zykuria

ZAKIYA (Arabic) an alternate form of Zakia.
Zakeya, Zakeyia, Zakiyaa, Zakiyah, Zakiyya, Zakiyyah, Zakkiyya, Zakkiyyah, Zakkyyah

ZALIKA (Swahili) born to royalty.
Zuleika

ZALTANA (Native American) high mountain.

ZANDRA (Greek) an alternate form of Sandra.
Zahndra, Zandrea, Zandria, Zandy, Zanndra, Zondra

ZANETA (Spanish) a form of Jane. A feminine form of Zane.
Zanita, Zanitra

ZANNA (Spanish) a form of Jane. (English) a short form of Susanna.
Zaina, Zainah, Zainna, Zana, Zanae, Zanah, Zanella, Zanette, Zannah, Zannette, Zannia, Zannie

ZANTHE (Greek) an alternate form of Xanthe.
Zanth, Zantha

ZARA (Hebrew) an alternate form of Sarah, Zora.
Zaira, Zarah, Zarea, Zaree, Zareea, Zareen, Zareena, Zareh, Zareya, Zari, Zaria, Zariya, Zarria

ZARIFA (Arabic) successful.

ZARITA (Spanish) a form of Sarah.

ZASHA (Russian) an alternate form of Sasha.
Zascha, Zashenka, Zashka, Zasho

ZAVIERA (Spanish) a form of Xaviera.
Zavera, Zavirah

ZAWATI (Swahili) gift.

ZAYIT (Hebrew) olive.

ZAYNAH (Arabic) beautiful.
Zayn, Zayna

ZEA (Latin) grain.

ZELDA (German) a short form of Griselda. (Yiddish) gray haired. See also Selda.
Zelde, Zella, Zellda

ZELENE (English) sunshine.
Zeleen, Zelena, Zeline

ZELIA (Spanish) sunshine.
Zele, Zelene, Zelie, Zélie, Zelina

ZELIZI (Basque) a form of Sheila.

ZELMA (German) an alternate form of Selma.

ZEMIRAH (Hebrew) song of joy.

ZENA (Greek) an alternate form of Xenia. (Ethiopian) news. (Persian) woman. See also Zina.
Zanae, Zanah, Zeena, Zeenat, Zeenet, Zeenia, Zeenya, Zein, Zeina, Zenah, Zenana, Zenea, Zenia, Zenna, Zennah, Zennia, Zenya

ZENAIDE (Greek) Mythology: a daughter of Zeus.
Zenaida, Zenaïde, Zenayda, Zenochka

ZENDA (Persian) sacred; feminine.

ZENOBIA (Greek) sign, symbol. History: a queen who ruled the city of Palmyra in the Arabian desert.
Zeba, Zeeba, Zenobie, Zenovia

ZEPHANIA, Zephanie (Greek) alternate forms of Stephanie.
Zepania, Zephanas, Zephany

ZEPHYR (Greek) west wind.
Zefiryn, Zephra, Zephria, Zephyer, Zephyrine

ZERA (Hebrew) seeds.
Zerah, Zeriah

ZERDALI (Turkish) wild apricot.

ZERLINA (Latin, Spanish) beautiful dawn. Music: a character in Mozart's opera *Don Giovanni*.
Zerla, Zerlinda

ZERRIN (Turkish) golden.
Zerren

ZETA (English) rose. Linguistics: the last letter in the Greek alphabet.
Zayit, Zetana, Zetta

ZETTA (Portuguese) rose.

ZHANA, Zhane (Slavic) forms of Jane.
Zhanae, Zhanay, Zhanaya, Zhané, Zhanea, Zhanee, Zhaney, Zhani, Zhaniah, Zhanna

ZHEN (Chinese) chaste.

ZIA (Latin) grain. (Arabic) light.
Zea

ZIGANA (Hungarian) gypsy girl.
See also Tsigana.
Zigane

ZIHNA (Hopi) one who spins tops.

ZILLA (Hebrew) shadow.
Zila, Zillah, Zylla

ZILPAH (Hebrew) dignified. Bible:
Jacob's wife.
Zilpha, Zylpha

ZILYA (Russian) a form of Theresa.

ZIMRA (Hebrew) song of praise.
Zamora, Zemira, Zemora, Zimria

ZINA (Greek) an alternate form of
Xenia, Zena. (African) secret spirit.
(English) hospitable.
Zinah, Zine

ZINNIA (Latin) Botany: a plant with
beautiful, rayed, colorful flowers.
Zinia, Zinny, Zinnya, Zinya

ZIPPORAH (Hebrew) bird. Bible:
Moses' wife.
Zipora, Ziporah, Zipporia, Ziproh

ZITA (Spanish) rose. (Arabic) mistress.
A short form of names ending in 'sita'
or 'zita.'
Zeeta, Zyta, Zytka

ZIVA (Hebrew) bright; radiant.
Zeeva, Ziv, Zivanka, Zivi, Zivit

ZIZI (Hungarian) a familiar form of
Elizabeth.
Zsi Zsi

ZOCHA (Polish) an alternate form
of Sophie.

ZOE (Greek) life.
Zoé, Zoë, Zoee, Zoelie, Zoeline, Zoelle, Zoey,
Zoi, Zoie, Zowe, Zowey, Zowie, Zoya

ZOEY (Greek) an alternate form of Zoe.
Zooey

ZOFIA (Slavic) an alternate form of
Sophia. See also Sofia.
Zofka, Zsofia

ZOHAR (Hebrew) shining, brilliant.
Zoheret

ZOHRA (Hebrew) blossom.

ZOHREH (Persian) happy.
Zahreh, Zohrah

ZOLA (Italian) piece of earth.
Zoela, Zoila

ZONA (Latin) belt, sash.
Zonia

ZONDRA (Greek) an alternate form
of Zandra.
Zohndra

ZORA (Slavic) aurora; dawn. See also
Zara.
Zorah, Zorana, Zoreen, Zoreena, Zorna,
Zorra, Zorrah, Zorya

ZORINA (Slavic) golden.
Zorana, Zori, Zorie, Zorine, Zorna, Zory

ZOYA (Slavic) a form of Zoe.
Zoia, Zoyara, Zoyechka, Zoyenka, Zoyya

ZSA ZSA (Hungarian) a familiar form
of Susan.
Zhazha

ZSOFIA (Hungarian) a form of Sofia.
Zofia, Zsofi, Zsofika

ZSUZSANNA (Hungarian) a form of
Susanna.
Zsuska, Zsuzsa, Zsuzsi, Zsuzsika, Zsuzska

ZUDORA (Sanskrit) laborer.

ZULEIKA (Arabic) brilliant.
Zeleeka, Zul, Zulay, Zulekha, Zuleyka

ZULIMA (Arabic) an alternate form
of Salama.
Zuleima, Zulema, Zulemah, Zulimah

ZURAFA (Arabic) lovely.
  Ziraf, Zuruf

ZURI (Basque) white; light skinned.
  (Swahili) beautiful.
  Zuria, Zurie, Zurisha, Zury

ZUSA (Czech, Polish) a form of Susan.
  Zuzana, Zuzanka, Zuzia, Zuzka, Zuzu

ZUWENA (Swahili) good.
  Zwena

ZYTKA (Polish) rose.

Boys' names

AAKASH (Hindi) an alternate form of Akash.

AARON (Hebrew) enlightened. (Arabic) messenger. Bible: the brother of Moses and the first high priest of the Jews. See also Ron.
Aahron, Aaran, Aaren, Aareon, Aarin, Aaronn, Aarron, Aaryn, Aeron, Aharon, Ahran, Ahren, Aranne, Arek, Aren, Ari, Arin, Aron, Aronek, Aronne, Aronos, Arran, Arron

ABAN (Persian) Mythology: a figure associated with water and the arts.

ABASI (Swahili) stern.

ABBEY (Hebrew) a familiar form of Abe.
Abey, Abbie, Abby

ABBOTT (Hebrew) father; abbot.
Ab, Abba, Abbah, Abbán, Abbé, Abbot, Abott

ABBUD (Arabic) devoted.

ABDIRAHMAN (Arabic) an alternate form of Abdulrahman.
Abdirehman

ABDUL (Arabic) servant.
Abdal, Abdeel, Abdel, Abdoul, Abdual, Abdull, Abul

ABDULAZIZ (Arabic) servant of the Mighty.
Abdelazim, Abdelaziz, Abdulazaz, Abdulazeez

ABDULLAH (Arabic) servant of Allah.
Abdalah, Abdalla, Abdallah, Abduala, Abdualla, Abduallah, Abdulah, Abdulahi, Abdulha, Abdulla, Abdullahi

ABDULRAHMAN (Arabic) servant of the Merciful.
Abdelrahim, Abdelrahman, Abdirahman, Abdolrahem, Abdularahman, Abdurrahman, Abdurram

ABE (Hebrew) a short form of Abel, Abraham.

ABEL (Hebrew) breath. (Assyrian) meadow. (German) a short form of Abelard. Bible: Adam and Eve's second son.
Abe, Abele, Abell, Able, Adal, Avel

ABELARD (German) noble; resolute.
Ab, Abalard, Abel, Abelardo, Abelhard, Abilard, Adalard, Adelard

ABI (Turkish) older brother.

ABIAH (Hebrew) God is my father.
Abia, Abiel, Abija, Abijah, Abisha, Abishai, Aviya, Aviyah

ABIE (Hebrew) a familiar form of Abraham.

ABIEL (Hebrew) an alternate form of Abiah.

ABIR (Hebrew) strong.

ABISHA (Hebrew) gift of God.
Abijah, Abishai

ABNER (Hebrew) father of light. Bible:
the commander of King Saul's army.
Ab, Avner, Ebner

ABRAHAM (Hebrew) father of many
nations. Bible: the first Hebrew
patriarch. See also Avram, Bram,
Ibrahim.
*Abarran, Abe, Aberham, Abey, Abhiram,
Abie, Abrahaim, Abrahame, Abrahamo,
Abrahan, Abrahán, Abraheem, Abrahem,
Abrahim, Abrahm, Abram, Abramo,
Abrán, Abrao, Arram, Avram*

ABRAHAN (Hebrew) an alternate form
of Abraham.
Abrahon

ABRAM (Hebrew) a short form of
Abraham. See also Bram.
Abramo, Abrams, Avram

ABSALOM (Hebrew) father of peace.
Bible: the son of King David. See also
Avshalom, Axel.
Absalaam, Absalon, Abselon, Absolum

ACAR (Turkish) bright.

ACE (Latin) unity.
Acer, Acey, Acie

ACHILLES (Greek) Mythology: a hero
of the Trojan war. Literature: the hero
of Homer's epic *The Iliad*.
*Achill, Achille, Achillea, Achillios, Akil,
Akili, Akilles*

ACKERLEY (English) meadow of oak
trees.
*Accerley, Ackerlea, Ackerleigh, Ackersley,
Acklea, Ackleigh, Ackley, Acklie*

ACTON (English) oak-tree settlement.

ADAHY (Cherokee) in the woods.

ADAIR (Scottish) oak-tree ford.
Adaire, Adare

ADAM (Phoenician) man; mankind.
(Hebrew) earth; man of the red earth.
Bible: the first man created by God.
See also Adamson, Addison, Damek,
Keddy, Macadam.
*Ad, Adama, Adamec, Adamo, Adão, Adas,
Addam, Addams, Addis, Addy, Adem,
Adham, Adhamh, Adné, Adok, Adomas*

ADAMEC (Czech) a form of Adam.
*Adamek, Adamik, Adamka, Adamko,
Adamok*

ADAMSON (Hebrew) son of Adam.
Adams, Adamsson, Addamson

ADAN (Irish) an alternate form of
Aidan.
Aden, Adian, Adin

ADAR (Syrian) ruler, prince. (Hebrew)
noble; exalted.
Addar

ADARIUS (American) a combination of
Adam + Darius.
*Adareus, Adarias, Adarrius, Adarro,
Adarruis, Adaruis, Adauris*

ADDISON (English) son of Adam.
*Addis, Addisen, Addisun, Addyson, Adison,
Adisson, Adyson*

ADDY (Hebrew) a familiar form of
Adam, Adlai. (German) a familiar form
of Adelard.
Addey, Addi, Addie, Ade, Adi

ADE (Yoruba) royal.

ADELARD (German) noble;
courageous.
*Adal, Adalar, Adalard, Addy, Adel, Adél,
Adelar*

ADEN (Arabic) Geography: a region in
southern Yemen. (Irish) an alternate
form of Aidan, Aiden.

ADHAM (Arabic) black.

ADIL (Arabic) just; wise.
Adeel, Adeele

ADIN (Hebrew) pleasant.

ADIR (Hebrew) majestic; noble.
Adeer

ADIV (Hebrew) pleasant; gentle.
Adeev

ADLAI (Hebrew) my ornament.
Ad, Addy, Adley

ADLER (German) eagle.
Ad, Addler, Adlar

ADLI (Turkish) just; wise.

ADMON (Hebrew) peony.

ADNAN (Arabic) pleasant.
Adnaan

ADNEY (English) noble's island.
Adny

ADOLF (German) noble wolf. History:
Adolf Hitler led Germany to defeat in
World War II. See also Dolf.
Ad, Adolfo, Adolfus, Adolph

ADOLFO (Spanish) a form of Adolf.
Adolpho

ADOLPH (German) an alternate form
of Adolf.
Adolphe, Adolpho, Adolphus, Adulphus

ADOM (Akan) help from God.

ADON (Greek) a short form of Adonis.
(Hebrew) Lord.

ADONIS (Greek) highly attractive.
Mythology: the attractive youth loved
by Aphrodite.
Adon, Adonnis, Adonys

ADRI (Indo-Pakistani) rock. (Hindi)
Religion: a minor Hindu god.
Adrey

ADRIAN (Greek) rich. (Latin) dark.
(Swedish) a short form of Hadrian.

*Adarian, Ade, Adorjan, Adrain, Adreian,
Adreyan, Adri, Adriaan, Adriane, Adriann,
Adrianne, Adriano, Adriean, Adrien, Adrik,
Adrion, Adrionn, Adrionne, Adron,
Adryan, Adryn, Adryon*

ADRIANO (Italian) a form of Adrian.
Adrianno

ADRIEL (Hebrew) member of God's
flock.
Adrial

ADRIEN (French) a form of Adrian.
Adriene, Adrienne

ADRIK (Russian) a form of Adrian.
Adric

AENEAS (Greek) praised. Literature:
the Trojan hero of Virgil's epic *Aeneid*.
See also Eneas.

AFRAM (African) Geography: a river
in Ghana, Africa.

AFTON (English) from Afton, England.
Affton

AGAMEMNON (Greek) resolute.
Mythology: the King of Mycenae who
led the Greeks in the Trojan War.

AGNI (Hindi) Religion: the Hindu fire
god.

AGU (Ibo) leopard.

AGUSTIN (Latin) an alternate form of
Augustine.
*Agostino, Agoston, Aguistin, Agustine,
Agustis, Agusto, Agustus*

AHAB (Hebrew) father's brother.
Literature: the captain of the Pequod
in Herman Melville's novel *Moby Dick*.

AHANU (Native American) laughter.

AHDIK (Native American) caribou;
reindeer.

AHEARN (Scottish) lord of the horses. (English) heron.
Ahearne, Aherin, Ahern, Aherne, Hearn

AHIR (Turkish) last.

AHMAD (Arabic) most highly praised. See also Muhammad.
Achmad, Achmed, Ahamad, Ahamada, Ahamed, Ahmaad, Ahmaud, Amad, Amahd, Amed

AHMED (Swahili) praiseworthy.

AHSAN (Arabic) charitable.

AIDAN (Irish) fiery.
Adan, Aden, Aiden, Aydan, Ayden, Aydin

AIDEN, Ayden (Irish) an alternate form of Aidan.
Aden, Aidon, Aidyn, Aydean

AIKEN (English) made of oak.
Aicken, Aikin, Ayken, Aykin

AIMERY (German) an alternate form of Emery.
Aime, Aimerey, Aimeric, Amerey, Aymeric, Aymery

AIMON (French) house. (Irish) an alternate form of Eamon.

AINDREA (Irish) a form of Andrew.
Aindreas

AINSLEY (Scottish) my own meadow.
Ainsleigh, Ainslie, Ansley, Aynslee, Aynsley, Aynslie

AIZIK (Russian) a form of Isaac.

AJALA (Yoruba) potter.

AJAY (Punjabi) victorious; undefeatable. (American) a combination of the initials A. + J.
Aj, Aja, Ajae, Ajai, Ajaye, Ajaz, Ajé, Ajee, Ajit

AJIT (Sanskrit) unconquerable.
Ajeet, Ajith

AKAR (Turkish) flowing stream.
Akara

AKASH (Hindi) sky.
Aakash, Akasha, Akshay

AKBAR (Arabic) great.

AKECHETA (Sioux) warrior.

AKEEM, Akim (Hebrew) short forms of Joachim.
Achim, Ackeem, Ackim, Ahkieme, Akeam, Akee, Akiem, Akima, Arkeem

AKEMI (Japanese) dawn.

AKIL (Arabic) intelligent. Geography: a river in the Basque region.
Ahkeel, Akeel, Akeil, Akeyla, Akhil, Akiel, Akila, Akilah, Akile, Akili

AKINS (Yoruba) brave.

AKIRA (Japanese) intelligent.
Akihito, Akio, Akiyo

AKIVA (Hebrew) an alternate form of Jacob.
Akiba, Kiva

AKMAL (Arabic) perfect.

AKSEL (Norwegian) father of peace.
Aksell

AKSHAY (American) a form of Akash.
Akshaj, Akshaya

AKSHAT (Sanskrit) uninjurable.

AKULE (Native American) he looks up.

AL (Irish) a short form of Alan, Albert, Alexander.

ALADDIN (Arabic) height of faith. Literature: the hero of a story in the *Arabian Nights*.
Ala, Alaa, Alaaddin, Aladean, Aladin, Aladino

ALAIN (French) a form of Alan.
Alaen, Alainn, Alayn, Allain

ALAIRE (French) joyful.

ALAM (Arabic) universe.

ALAN (Irish) handsome; peaceful.
Ailan, Ailin, Al, Alaan, Alain, Alair, Aland,
Alande, Alando, Alani, Alann, Alano,
Alanson, Alante, Alao, Allan, Allen, Alon,
Alun

ALARIC (German) ruler of all. See also
Ulrich.
Alarick, Alarico, Alarik, Aleric, Allaric,
Allarick, Alric, Alrick, Alrik

ALASTAIR (Scottish) a form of
Alexander.
Alaisdair, Alaistair, Alaister, Alasdair,
Alasteir, Alaster, Alastor, Aleister, Alester,
Alistair, Allaistair, Allastair, Allaster,
Allastir, Allysdair, Alystair

ALBAN (Latin) from Alba, Italy, a city
on a white hill.
Albain, Albany, Albean, Albein, Alby,
Auban, Auben

ALBERN (German) noble; courageous.

ALBERT (German, French) noble and
bright. See also Elbert, Ulbrecht.
Adelbert, Ailbert, Al, Albertik, Alberto,
Alberts, Albie, Albrecht, Alby, Alvertos,
Aubert

ALBERTO (Italian) a form of Albert.
Berto

ALBIE, Alby (German, French) familiar
forms of Albert.
Albee, Albi

ALBIN (Latin) an alternate form of
Alvin.
Alben, Albeno, Albinek, Albino, Albins,
Albinson, Alby, Auben

ALBION (Latin) white cliffs. Geography:
a reference to the white cliffs in
Dover, England.

ALCOTT (English) old cottage.
Alcot, Alkot, Alkott, Allcot, Allcott, Allkot,
Allkott

ALCANDOR (Greek) manly; strong.

ALDAIR (German, English) an alternate
form of Alder.
Aldahir, Aldayr

ALDEN (English) old; wise protector.
Aldan, Aldean, Aldin, Aldous, Elden

ALDER (German, English) alder tree.
Aldair

ALDO (Italian) old; elder.

ALDOUS (German) a form of Alden.
Aldis, Aldo, Aldon, Aldus, Elden

ALDRED (English) old; wise counselor.
Alldred, Eldred

ALDRICH (English) wise counselor.
Aldric, Aldrick, Aldridge, Aldrige, Aldritch,
Alldric, Alldrich, Alldrick, Alldridge,
Eldridge

ALDWIN (English) old friend.
Aldwyn, Eldwin

ALEC, Alek (Greek) short forms
of Alexander.
Aleck, Alekko, Elek

ALEJÁNDRO (Spanish) a form of
Alexander.
Alejándra, Aléjo, Alexjándro

ALEKSANDAR, Aleksander (Greek)
alternate forms of Alexander.
Aleksandor, Aleksandr, Aleksandras,
Aleksandur

ALEKSEI (Russian) a form of
Alexander.
Aleks, Aleksey, Aleksi, Aleksis, Aleksy,
Alexei, Alexey

ALEKZANDER, Alexzander (Greek)
alternate forms of Alexander.

Alekzander (cont.)
*Alekxander, Alekxzander, Alexkzandr,
Alexzandr, Alexzandyr*

ALEM (Arabic) wise.

ALERIC (German) an alternate form
of Alaric.
Alerick, Alleric, Allerick

ALERON (Latin) winged.

ALESSANDRO (Italian) a form of
Alexander.
Alessand, Allessandro

ALEX (Greek) a short form of
Alexander.
Alax, Alix, Allax, Allex, Elek

ALEXANDER (Greek) defender of
mankind. History: Alexander the
Great was the conquerer of the Greek
Empire. See also Alastair, Alistair,
Iskander, Jando, Leks, Lex, Lexus,
Macallister, Oleksandr, Olés, Sander,
Sándor, Sandro, Sandy, Sasha, Xan,
Xander, Zander, Zindel.
*Al, Alec, Alecsandar, Alejándro, Alek,
Alekos, Aleksandar, Aleksander, Aleksei,
Alekzander, Alessandro, Alex, Alexandar,
Alexandor, Alexandr, Alexandre,
Alexandro, Alexandros, Alexi, Alexis,
Alexxander, Alexzander, Alic, Alick,
Alisander, Alixander,*

ALEXANDRE (French) a form of
Alexander.

ALEXANDRO (Greek) an alternate
form of Alexander.
Alexandras, Alexandros, Alexandru

ALEXI (Greek) a short form of
Alexander.
Alexe, Alexee, Alexey, Alexie, Alexio, Alexy

ALEXIS (Greek) a short form of
Alexander.
*Alexei, Alexes, Alexey, Alexios, Alexius,
Alexiz, Alexsis, Alexsus, Alexus*

ALFIE (English) a familiar form of Alfred.
Alfy

ALFONSO (Italian, Spanish) a form of
Alphonse.
*Affonso, Alfons, Alfonse, Alfonsus, Alfonza,
Alfonzo, Alfonzus*

ALFORD (English) old river ford.

ALFRED (English) elf counselor; wise
counselor. See also Fred.
*Ailfrid, Ailfryd, Alf, Alfeo, Alfie, Alfredo,
Alured*

ALFREDO (Italian, Spanish) a form of
Alfred.
Alfrido

ALGER (German) noble spearman.
(English) a short form of Algernon.
See also Elger.
Algar, Allgar

ALGERNON (English) bearded, wearing
a moustache.
Algenon, Alger, Algie, Algin, Algon

ALGIE (English) a familiar form of
Algernon.
Algee, Algia, Algy

ALGIS (German) spear.

ALI (Arabic) greatest. (Swahili) exalted.
Aly

ALIC (Greek) a short form of
Alexander.
Alick, Aliek, Alik, Aliko

ALIM (Arabic) scholar.

ALISANDER (Greek) an alternate form
of Alexander.
*Alissander, Alissandre, Alsandair,
Alsandare, Alsander*

ALISTAIR (English) a form of
Alexander.
*Alisdair, Alistaire, Alistar, Alister, Allistair,
Allistar, Allister, Allistir, Alstair*

ALIXANDER (Greek) an alternate form of Alexander.
Alixandre, Alixandru, Alixzander

ALLAN (Irish) an alternate form of Alan.
Allayne

ALLARD (English) noble, brave.
Alard, Ellard

ALLEN (Irish) an alternate form of Alan.
Alen, Alley, Alleyn, Alleyne, Allie, Allin, Allon, Allyn

ALMON (Hebrew) widower.

ALOIS (German) a short form of Aloysius.
Aloys

ALOISIO (Spanish) a form of Louis.

ALOK (Sanskrit) victorious cry.

ALON (Hebrew) oak.

ALONSO, Alonzo (Spanish) forms of Alphonse.
Alano, Alanzo, Alon, Alonza, Elonzo, Lon, Lonnie, Lonso, Lonzo

ALOYSIUS (German) famous warrior. An alternate form of Louis.
Alaois, Alois, Aloisius, Aloisio

ALPHONSE (German) noble and eager.
Alf, Alfie, Alfonso, Alonzo, Alphons, Alphonsa, Alphonso, Alphonsus, Alphonza, Alphonzus, Fonzie

ALPHONSO (Italian) a form of Alphonse.
Alphanso, Alphonzo, Fonso

ALPIN (Irish) attractive.
Alpine

ALROY (Spanish) king.

ALSTON (English) noble's settlement.
Allston, Alstun

ALTAIR (Greek) star. (Arabic) flying eagle.

ALTMAN (German) old man.
Altmann, Atman

ALTON (English) old town.
Alten

ALVA (Hebrew) sublime.
Alvah

ALVAN (German) an alternate form of Alvin.
Alvand

ALVAR (Swedish) Botany: a small shrub native to Sweden. (English) army of elves.
Alvara

ALVARO (Spanish) just; wise.

ALVERN (Latin) spring.
Elvern

ALVIN (Latin) white; light skinned. (German) friend to all; noble friend; friend of elves. See also Albin, Elvin.
Aloin, Aluin, Aluino, Alvan, Alven, Alvie, Alvino, Alvy, Alvyn, Alwin, Elwin

ALVIS (Scandinavian) all-knowing.

ALWIN (German) an alternate form of Alvin.
Ailwyn, Alwyn, Alwynn, Aylwin

AMADEO (Italian) a form of Amadeus.

AMADEUS (Latin) loves God. Music: Wolfgang Amadeus Mozart was a famous eighteenth-century Austrian composer.
Amad, Amadeaus, Amadée, Amadeo, Amadei, Amadio, Amadis, Amado, Amador, Amadou, Amando, Amedeo, Amodaos

AMAL (Hebrew) worker. (Arabic) hopeful.

AMANDEEP (Punjabi) light of peace.
Amandip, Amanjit, Amanjot, Amanpreet

AMANDO (French) a form of
Amadeus.
Amand, Amandio, Amaniel, Amato

AMANI (Arabic) believer.
Amanee

AMAR (Punjabi) immortal. (Arabic)
builder.
*Amare, Amaree, Amari, Amario, Amaris,
Amarjit, Amaro, Amarpreet, Amarri,
Ammar, Ammer*

AMATO (French) loved.
Amatto

AMBAR (Sanskrit) sky.
Amber

AMBROSE (Greek) immortal.
*Ambie, Ambroise, Ambros, Ambrosi,
Ambrosio, Ambrosius, Ambrus, Amby*

AMEER (Hebrew) an alternate form
of Amir.
Ameir, Amer, Amere

AMERIGO (Teutonic) industrious.
History: Amerigo Vespucci was the
explorer for whom America is named.
Americo, Americus

AMES (French) friend.

AMICUS (English, Latin) beloved friend.
Amico

AMIEL (Hebrew) God of my people.
Ammiel

AMIN (Hebrew, Arabic) trust-worthy;
honest. (Hindi) faithful.
Amine

AMIR (Hebrew) proclaimed. (Punjabi)
wealthy; king's minister. (Arabic)
prince.
Aamer, Aamir, Ameer, Amire, Amiri

AMISH (Sanskrit) honest.

AMIT (Punjabi) unfriendly. (Arabic)
highly praised.
Amitan, Amreet

AMMON (Egyptian) hidden. Mythology:
the ancient god associated with
reproduction and life.
Amman

AMOL (Hindi) priceless, valuable.
Amul

AMON (Hebrew) trustworthy; faithful.

AMORY (German) an alternate form
of Emory.
Amery, Amor

AMOS (Hebrew) burdened, troubled.
Bible: an Old Testament prophet.
Amose

AMRAM (Hebrew) mighty nation.
Amarien, Amran, Amren

AMRIT (Sanskrit) nectar.

AN (Chinese, Vietnamese) peaceful.
Ana

ANAND (Hindi) blissful.
Ananda, Anant, Ananth

ANASTASIUS (Greek) resurrection.
*Anas, Anastacio, Anastacios, Anastagio,
Anastas, Anastase, Anastasi, Anastasio,
Anastasios, Anastice, Anastisis, Anaztáz,
Athanasius*

ANATOLE (Greek) east.
*Anatol, Anatoley, Anatoli, Anatolijus,
Anatolio, Anatoliy, Anatoly, Anitoly*

ANCHALI (Taos) painter.

ANDERS (Swedish) a form of Andrew.
Ander

ANDERSON (Swedish) son of Andrew.
Andersen

ANDONIOS (Greek) an alternate form of Anthony.
Andoni, Andonis, Andonny

ANDOR (Hungarian) a form of Andrew.

ANDRÁS (Hungarian) a form of Andrew.
Andraes, Andri, Andris, Andrius, Andriy, Aundras, Aundreas

ANDRE, André (French) forms of Andrew.
Andra, Andrae, Andrecito, Andree, Andrei, Aundre, Aundré

ANDREA (Greek) an alternate form of Andrew.
Andrean, Andreani, Andrian

ANDREAS (Greek) an alternate form of Andrew.
Andres, Andries

ANDREI (Bulgarian, Romanian, Russian) a form of Andrew.
Andreian, Andrej, Andrey, Andreyan, Andrie, Aundrei

ANDRES (Spanish) a form of Andrew.
Andras, Andrés, Andrez

ANDREW (Greek) strong; manly; courageous. Bible: one of the Twelve Apostles. See also Bandi, Drew, Endre, Evangelos, Kendrew, Ondro.
Aindrea, Anders, Andery, Andonis, Andor, András, Andre, André, Andrea, Andreas, Andrei, Andres, Andrews, Andru, Andrue, Andrus, Andy, Anker, Anndra, Antal, Audrew

ANDROS (Polish) sea. Mythology: the god of the sea.
Andris, Andrius, Andrus

ANDY (Greek) a short form of Andrew.
Andino, Andis, Andje

ANEURIN (Welsh) honorable; gold. See also Nye.
Aneirin

ANFERNEE (Greek) an alternate form of Anthony.
Anferney, Anfernie, Anferny, Anfranee, Anfrene, Anfrenee, Anpherne

ANGEL (Greek) angel. (Latin) messenger. See also Gotzon.
Ange, Angell, Angelo, Angie, Angy

ANGELO (Italian) a form of Angel.
Angeleo, Angelito, Angello, Angelos, Anglo

ANGUS (Scottish) exceptional; outstanding. Mythology: Angus Og was the Celtic god of laughter, love, and wisdom. See also Ennis, Gus.
Aeneas, Aonghas

ANH (Vietnamese) peace; safety.

ANIBAL (Phoenician) an alternate form of Hannibal.

ANIL (Hindi) wind god.
Aneel, Anel, Aniel, Aniello

ANKA (Turkish) phoenix.

ANKER (Danish) a form of Andrew.
Ankur

ANNAN (Scottish) brook. (Swahili) fourth-born son.

ANNAS (Greek) gift from God.
Anis, Anish, Anna, Annais

ANNO (German) a familiar form of Johann.

ANOKI (Native American) actor.

ANSEL (French) follower of a nobleman.
Ancell, Ansa, Ansell

ANSELM (German) divine protector. See also Elmo.
Anse, Anselme, Anselmi, Anselmo

ANSIS (Latvian) an alternate form of Janis.

ANSLEY (Scottish) an alternate form of Ainsley.
Anslea, Anslee, Ansleigh, Anslie, Ansly, Ansy

ANSON (German) divine. (English) Anne's son.
Ansun

ANTAL (Hungarian) a form of Anthony.
Antek, Anti, Antos

ANTARES (Greek) giant, red star. Astronomy: the brightest star in the constellation Scorpio.
Antar, Antario, Antarious, Antarius, Antarr, Antarus

ANTAVAS (Lithuanian) a form of Anthony.
Antae, Antaeus, Antavious, Antavius, Ante, Anteo

ANTHANY (Latin, Greek) an alternate form of Anthony.
Antanee, Antanie, Antenee, Anthan, Antheny, Anthine, Anthney

ANTHONIE (Latin, Greek) an alternate form of Anthony.
Anthone, Anthonee, Anthoni, Anthonia

ANTHONY (Latin) praiseworthy. (Greek) flourishing. See also Tony.
Anathony, Andonios, Andor, András, Anothony, Antal, Antavas, Anfernee, Anthany, Anthawn, Anthey, Anthian, Anthino, Anthone, Anthoney, Anthonie, Anthonio, Anthonu, Anthonysha, Anthoy, Anthyoine, Anthyonny, Antione, Antjuan, Antoine, Anton, Antonio, Antony, Antwan, Antwon

ANTIONE (French) a form of Anthony.
Antion, Antionio, Antionne, Antiono

ANTJUAN (Spanish) a form of Anthony.
Antajuan, Anthjuan, Antuan, Antuane

ANTOAN (Vietnamese) safe, secure.

ANTOINE (French) a form of Anthony.
Anntoin, Anthoine, Antoiné, Antoinne, Atoine

ANTON (Slavic) a form of Anthony.
Anthon, Antone, Antonn, Antonne, Antons, Antos

ANTONIO (Italian) a form of Anthony. See also Tino, Tonio.
Anthonio, Antinio, Antoinio, Antoino, Antonello, Antoneo, Antonin, Antonín, Antonino, Antonnio, Antonios, Antonius, Antonyia, Antonyio, Antonyo

ANTONY (Latin) an alternate form of Anthony.
Antin, Antini, Antius, Antoney, Antoni, Antonie, Antonin, Antonios, Antonius, Antonyia, Antonyio, Antonyo, Anty

ANTTI (Finnish) manly.
Anthey, Anthi, Anti

ANTWAN (Arabic) a form of Anthony.
Antaw, Antawan, Antawn, Anthawn, Antowan, Antowaun, Antowine, Antowne, Antowyn, Antuwan, Antwain, Antwaina, Antwaine, Antwainn, Antwaion; Antwane, Antwann, Antwanne, Antwarn, Antwaun, Antwen, Antwian, Antwine, Antwuan, Antwun, Antwyné

ANTWON (Arabic) a form of Anthony.
Antown, Antuwon, Antwion, Antwione, Antwoan, Antwoin, Antwoine, Antwone, Antwonn, Antwonne, Antwoun, Antwyon, Antwyone, Antyon, Antyonne, Antywon

ANWAR (Arabic) luminous.
Anour, Anouar, Anwi

APIATAN (Kiowa) wooden lance.

APOLLO (Greek) manly. Mythology: the god of prophecy, healing, music, poetry, truth, and the sun. See also Polo.
Apolinar, Apolinario, Apollos, Apolo, Apolonio, Appollo

AQUILA (Latin, Spanish) eagle.
Acquilla, Aquil, Aquilas, Aquileo, Aquiles, Aquilino, Aquilla, Aquille, Aquillino

ARALDO (Spanish) a form of Harold.
Aralodo, Aralt, Aroldo, Arry

ARAM (Syrian) high, exalted.
Ara, Aramia, Arra, Arram

ARAMIS (French) Literature: one of the title characters in Alexandre Dumas's novel *The Three Musketeers*.
Airamis, Aramith, Aramys

ARAN (Tai) forest.

ARCHER (English) bowman.
Archie

ARCHIBALD (German) bold. See also Arkady.
Arch, Archaimbaud, Archambault, Archibaldo, Archibold, Archie

ARCHIE (German, English) a familiar form of Archer, Archibald.
Archy

ARDAL (Irish) a form of Arnold.
Ardale

ARDELL (Latin) eager; industrious.
Ardel

ARDEN (Latin) ardent; fiery.
Ard, Ardan, Ardene, Ardian, Ardie, Ardin, Ardn, Arduino

ARDON (Hebrew) bronzed.

AREN (Danish) eagle; ruler.

ARETINO (Greek, Italian) victorious.

ARGUS (Danish) watchful, vigilant.
Agos

ARI (Greek) a short form of Aristotle. (Hebrew) a short form of Ariel.
Aria, Arias, Arie, Arieh, Arih, Arij, Ario, Arri, Ary, Arye

ARIAN (Greek) an alternate form of Arion.
Ariana, Ariane, Ariann, Arianne, Arrian, Aryan

ARIC (German) an alternate form of Richard. (Scandinavian) an alternate form of Eric.
Aaric, Arec, Areck, Arich, Arick, Ariek, Arik, Arrek, Arric, Arrick, Arrik, Aryk

ARIEL (Hebrew) lion of God. Bible: another name for Jerusalem. Literature: the name of a spirit in the Shakespearean play *The Tempest*.
Airel, Arel, Areli, Ari, Ariell, Ariya, Ariyel, Arrial, Arriel

ARIES (Greek) Mythology: Ares was the Greek god of war. (Latin) ram.
Ares, Arie, Ariez

ARIF (Arabic) knowledgeable.
Areef

ARION (Greek) enchanted. Mythology: a magic horse. (Hebrew) melodious.
Arian, Arien, Ario, Arione, Aryon

ARISTIDES (Greek) son of the best.
Aris, Aristedes, Aristeed, Aristide, Aristides, Aristidis

ARISTOTLE (Greek) best; wise. History: a third-century B.C. philosopher who tutored Alexander the Great.
Ari, Aris, Aristito, Aristo, Aristokles, Aristotelis

ARJUN (Hindi) white, milk-colored.
Arjen, Arjin, Arju, Arjuna, Arjune

ARKADY (Russian) a form of Archibald.
Arcadio, Arkadi, Arkadij, Arkadiy

ARKIN (Norwegian) son of the eternal king.
Aricin, Arkeen, Arkyn

ARLEDGE (English) lake with the hares.
Arlidge, Arlledge

ARLEN (Irish) pledge.
Arlan, Arland, Arlend, Arlin, Arlinn, Arlyn, Arlynn

ARLEY (English) a short form of Harley.
Arleigh, Arlie, Arly

ARLO (German) an alternate form of Charles. (Spanish) barberry. (English) fortified hill. An alternate form of Harlow.

ARMAN (Persian) desire, goal.
Armaan, Armahn, Armaine

ARMAND (Latin) noble. (German) soldier. An alternate form of Herman. See also Mandek.
Armad, Arman, Armanda, Armando, Armands, Armanno, Armaude, Armenta, Armond

ARMANDO (Spanish) a form of Armand.
Armondo

ARMANI (Hebrew) an alternate form of Armon.
Arman, Armann, Armoni, Armonie, Armonio, Armonni, Armony

ARMON (Hebrew) high fortress, stronghold.
Armani, Armen, Armin, Armino, Armonn, Armons

ARMSTRONG (English) strong arm.

ARNAUD (French) a form of Arnold.
Arnauld, Arnault, Arnoll

ARNE (German) an alternate form of Arnold.
Arna, Arnay, Arnel, Arnele, Arnell, Arnelle

ARNETTE (English) little eagle.
Arnat, Arnet, Arnett, Arnetta, Arnot, Arnott

ARNIE (German) a familiar form of Arnold.
Arney, Arni, Arnny, Arny

ARNO (German) eagle wolf. (Czech) a short form of Ernest.
Arnou, Arnoux

ARNOLD (German) eagle ruler.
Ardal, Arnald, Arnaldo, Arnaud, Arne, Arnie, Arno, Arnol, Arnoldas, Arnoldo, Arnoll, Arndt, Arnulfo

ARNON (Hebrew) rushing river.
Arnan

ARNULFO (German) an alternate form of Arnold.

ARON, Arron (Hebrew) alternate forms of Aaron.
Arrion

AROON (Tai) dawn.

ARRAN (Hebrew) an alternate form of Aaron. (Scottish) island dweller. Geography: an island off the coast of Scotland.
Arren, Arrin, Arryn, Aryn

ARRIGO (Italian) a form of Harry.
Alrigo, Arrighetto

ARRIO (Spanish) warlike.
Ario, Arrow, Arryo, Aryo

ARSENIO (Greek) masculine; virile. History: Saint Arsenius was a teacher in the Roman Empire.
Arsen, Arsène, Arsenius, Arseny, Arsinio

ARSHA (Persian) venerable.

ART (English) a short form of Arthur.

ARTEMUS (Greek) gift of Artemis. Mythology: Artemis was the goddess of the hunt and the moon.
Artemas, Artemio, Artemis, Artimas, Artimis, Artimus

ARTHUR (Irish) noble; lofty hill. (Scottish) bear. (English) rock. (Icelandic) follower of Thor. See also Turi.
Art, Artair, Artek, Arth, Arther, Arthor, Artie, Artor, Arturo, Artus, Aurthar, Aurther, Aurthur

ARTIE (English) a familiar form of Arthur.
Arte, Artian, Artis, Arty, Atty

ARTURO (Italian) a form of Arthur.
Arthuro, Artur

ARUN (Cambodian, Hindi) sun.
Aruns

ARUNDEL (English) eagle valley.

ARVE (Norwegian) heir, inheritor.

ARVEL (Welsh) wept over.
Arval, Arvell, Arvelle

ARVID (Hebrew) wanderer. (Norwegian) eagle tree. See also Ravid.
Arv, Arvad, Arve, Arvie, Arvind, Arvinder, Arvydas

ARVIN (German) friend of the people; friend of the army.
Arv, Arvie, Arvind, Arvinder, Arvon, Arvy

ARYEH (Hebrew) lion.

ASA (Hebrew) physician, healer. (Yoruba) falcon.
Asaa, Ase

ASÁD (Arabic) lion.
Asaad, Asad, Asid, Assad, Azad

ASADEL (Arabic) prosperous.
Asadour, Asadul, Asael

ASCOT (English) eastern cottage; style of necktie. Geography: a famous racetrack near Windsor castle.

ASGARD (Scandinavian) court of the gods.

ASH (Hebrew) ash tree.
Ashby

ASHANTI (Swahili) from a tribe in West Africa.
Ashan, Ashani, Ashante, Ashantee, Ashaunte

ASHBY (Scandinavian) ash-tree farm. (Hebrew) an alternate form of Ash.
Ashbey

ASHER (Hebrew) happy; blessed.
Ashar, Ashor, Ashur

ASHFORD (English) ash-tree ford.
Ash, Ashtin

ASHLEY (English) ash-tree meadow.
Ash, Asheley, Ashelie, Ashely, Ashlan, Ashlee, Ashleigh, Ashlen, Ashlie, Ashlin, Ashling, Ashlinn, Ashlone, Ashly, Ashlyn, Ashlynn, Aslan

ASHON (Swahili) seventh-born son.

ASHTON (English) ash-tree settlement.
Ashtan, Ashten, Ashtian, Ashtin, Ashtion, Ashtonn, Ashtun, Ashtyn

ASHUR (Swahili) Mythology: the principle Assyrian deity.

ASHWANI (Hindi) first. Religion: the first of the twenty-seven galaxies revolving around the moon.
Ashwan

ASHWIN (Hindi) star.

ASIEL (Hebrew) created by God.

ASKER (Turkish) soldier.

ASPEN (English) aspen tree.

ASTON (English) eastern town.
Asten, Astin

ASWAD (Arabic) dark skinned, black.

ATA (Fante) twin.

ATEK (Polish) a form of Tanek.

ATHAN (Greek) immortal.

ATHERTON (English) town by a spring.

ATID (Tai) sun.

ATIF (Arabic) caring.
Ateef, Atef

ATLAS (Greek) lifted; carried.
Mythology: Atlas was forced to carry
the world on his shoulders as a
punishment for feuding with Zeus.

ATLEY (English) meadow.
Atlea, Atlee, Atleigh, Atli, Attley

ATTILA (Gothic) little father. History:
the Hun leader who conquered the
Goths.
*Atalik, Atila, Atilio, Atilla, Atiya, Attal,
Attilio*

ATWATER (English) at the water's
edge.

ATWELL (English) at the well.

ATWOOD (English) at the forest.

ATWORTH (English) at the farmstead.

AUBERON (German) an alternate form
of Oberon.
Auberron, Aubrey

AUBREY (German) noble; bearlike.
(French) a familiar form of Auberon.
See also Avery.
*Aubary, Aube, Aubery, Aubie, Aubré,
Aubree, Aubreii, Aubrie, Aubry, Aubury*

AUBURN (Latin) reddish brown.

AUDEN (English) old friend.

AUDIE (German) noble; strong.
(English) a familiar form of Edward.
Audi, Audiel, Audley, Audy

AUDON (French) old; rich.
Audelon

AUDREY (English) noble strength.
Audra, Audre, Audrea, Audrius, Audry

AUDRIC (English) wise ruler.
Audrick, Audrik

AUDUN (Scandinavian) deserted,
desolate.

AUGIE (Latin) a familiar form
of August.
Auggie, Augy

AUGUST (Latin) a short form of
Augustine, Augustus.
Agosto, Augie, Auguste, Augusto

AUGUSTINE (Latin) majestic. Religion:
Saint Augustine was the first
Archbishop of Canterbury. See also
Austin, Gus, Tino.
*August, Agustin, Augustin, Augustinas,
Augustino, Austen, Austin, Auston, Austyn*

AUGUSTUS (Latin) majestic; venerable.
History: a name used by Roman
emperors such as Augustus Caesar.
August

AUKAI (Hawaiian) seafarer.

AUNDRE (Greek) an alternate form
of Andre.
*Aundrae, Aundray, Aundrea, Aundrey,
Aundry*

AUREK (Polish) golden haired.

AURELIO (Latin) a short form of
Aurelius.
Aurel, Aurele, Aureli, Aurellio

AURELIUS (Latin) golden. History:
Marcus Aurelius Antoninus was a
second-century A.D. philosopher and
emperor of Rome.
*Arelian, Areliano, Aurèle, Aureliano,
Aurelien, Aurélien, Aurelio, Aurey, Auriel,
Aury*

AURICK (German) protecting ruler.
Auric

AUSTEN, Auston, Austyn (Latin) short forms of Augustine.
Austan, Austun, Austyne

AUSTIN (Latin) a short form of Augustine.
Astin, Austine, Oistin, Ostin

AVEL (Greek) breath.

AVENT (French) born during Advent.
Aventin, Aventino

AVERILL (French) born in April. (English) boar-warrior.
Ave, Averel, Averell, Averiel, Averil, Averyl, Averyll, Avrel, Avrell, Avrill, Avryll

AVERY (English) a form of Aubrey.
Avary, Aveary, Avere, Averee, Averey, Averi, Averie, Avrey, Avry

AVI (Hebrew) God is my father.
Avian, Avidan, Avidor, Aviel, Avion

AVIV (Hebrew) youth; springtime.

AVNER (Hebrew) an alternate form of Abner.
Avneet, Avniel

AVRAM (Hebrew) an alternate form of Abraham, Abram.
Arram, Avraam, Avraham, Avrahom, Avrohom, Avrom, Avrum

AVSHALOM (Hebrew) father of peace. See also Absalom.
Avsalom

AWAN (Native American) somebody.

AXEL (Latin) axe. (German) small oak tree; source of life. (Scandinavian) a form of Absalom.
Aksel, Ax, Axe, Axell, Axil, Axill, Axl, Axle, Axyle

AYDIN (Turkish) intelligent.

AYERS (English) heir to a fortune.

AYINDE (Yoruba) we gave praise and he came.

AYLMER (English) an alternate form of Elmer.
Aillmer, Ailmer, Allmer, Ayllmer

AYMIL (Greek) an alternate form of Emil.

AYMON (French) a form of Raymond.

AYO (Yoruba) happiness.

AZAD (Turkish) free.

AZEEM (Arabic) an alternate form of Azim.
Aseem, Asim

AZI (Nigerian) youth.

AZIM (Arabic) defender.
Azeem

'AZIZ (Arabic) strong.

AZIZI (Swahili) precious.

AZRIEL (Hebrew) God is my aid.

AZURIAH (Hebrew) aided by God.
Azaria, Azariah, Azuria

B

BADEN (German) bather.
Baeden, Bayden, Baydon

BAHIR (Arabic) brilliant, dazzling.

BAHRAM (Persian) ancient king.

BAILEY (French) bailiff, steward.
Bail, Bailee, Bailie, Bailio, Baillie, Baily, Bailye, Baley, Bayley

BAIN (Irish) a short form of Bainbridge.
Baine, Bayne, Baynn

BAINBRIDGE (Irish) fair bridge.
Bain, Baynbridge, Bayne, Baynebridge

BAIRD (Irish) bard, traveling minstrel; poet.
Bairde, Bard

BAKARI (Swahili) noble promise.
Bacari, Baccari, Bakarie

BAKER (English) baker. See also Baxter.
Bakir, Bakory, Bakr

BAL (Sanskrit) child born with lots of hair.

BALASI (Basque) flat footed.

BALBO (Latin) stammerer.
Bailby, Balbi, Ballbo

BALDEMAR (German) bold; famous.
Baldemer, Baldomero, Baumar, Baumer

BALDER (Scandinavian) bald. Mythology: the Norse god of light, summer, and innocence.
Baldier, Baldur, Baudier

BALDRIC (German) brave ruler.
Baldrick, Baudric

BALDWIN (German) bold friend.
Bald, Baldovino, Balduin, Baldwinn, Baldwyn, Baldwynn, Balldwin, Baudoin

BALFOUR (Scottish) pasture land.
Balfor, Balfore

BALIN (Hindi) mighty soldier.
Bali, Baylen, Baylin, Baylon, Valin

BALLARD (German) brave; strong.
Balard

BALRAJ (Hindi) strongest.

BALTAZAR (Greek) an alternate form of Balthasar.
Baltasar

BALTHASAR (Greek) God save the king. Bible: one of the Three Wise Men.

Badassare, Baldassare, Baltazar, Balthasaar, Balthazar, Balthazzar, Baltsaros, Belshazar, Belshazzar, Boldizsár

BANCROFT (English) bean field.
Ban, Bancrofft, Bank, Bankroft, Banky, Binky

BANDI (Hungarian) a form of Andrew.
Bandit

BANE (Hawaiian) a form of Bartholomew.

BANNER (Scottish, English) flag bearer.
Bannor, Banny

BANNING (Irish) small and fair.
Bannie, Banny

BARAK (Hebrew) lightning bolt. Bible: the valiant warrior who helped Deborah.
Barrak

BARAN (Russian) ram.
Baren

BARASA (Kikuyu) meeting place.

BARCLAY (Scottish, English) birch tree meadow.
Bar, Barcley, Barklay, Barkley, Barklie, Barrclay, Berkeley

BARD (Irish) an alternate form of Baird.
Bar, Barde, Bardia, Bardiya, Barr

BARDOLF (German) bright wolf. Literature: the name of a drunken fool who appeared in four Shakespearean plays.
Bardo, Bardolph, Bardou, Bardoul, Bardulf, Bardulph

BARDRICK (Teutonic) axe ruler.
Bardric, Bardrik

BARIS (Turkish) peaceful.

BARKER (English) lumberjack; advertiser at a carnival.

BARLOW (English) bare hillside.
Barlowe, Barrlow, Barrlowe

BARNABAS (Greek, Hebrew, Aramaic, Latin) son of the missionary. Bible: disciple of Paul.
Bane, Barna, Barnaba, Barnabus, Barnaby, Barnebas, Barnebus, Barney

BARNABY (English) a form of Barnabas.
Barnabe, Barnabé, Barnabee, Barnabey, Barnabi, Barnabie, Bernabé, Burnaby

BARNARD (English) a form of Bernard.
Barn, Barnard, Barnhard, Barnhardo

BARNES (English) bear; son of Barnett.

BARNETT (English) nobleman; leader.
Barn, Barnet, Barney, Baronet, Baronett, Barrie, Barron, Barry

BARNEY (English) a familiar form of Barnabas, Barnett.
Barnie, Barny

BARNUM (German) barn; storage place. (English) baron's home.
Barnham

BARON (German, English) nobleman, baron.
Baaron, Barion, Baronie, Barrin, Barrion, Barron, Baryn, Bayron, Berron

BARRETT (German) strong as a bear.
Bar, Baret, Barrat, Barret, Barretta, Barrette, Barry, Berrett, Berrit

BARRIC (English) grain farm.
Barrick, Beric, Berric, Berrick, Berrik

BARRINGTON (English) Geography: a town in England.

BARRY (Welsh) son of Harry. (Irish) spear, marksman. (French) gate, fence.
Baris, Barri, Barrie, Barris, Bary

BART (Hebrew) a short form of Bartholomew, Barton.
Barrt, Bartel, Bartie, Barty

BARTHOLOMEW (Hebrew) son of Talmaí. Bible: one of the Twelve Apostles. See also Jerney, Parlan, Parthalán.
Balta, Bane, Bart, Bartek, Barth, Barthel, Barthelemy, Barthélemy, Barthélmy, Bartho, Bartholo, Bartholomaus, Bartholome, Bartholomeo, Bartholomeus, Bartholomieu, Bartimous, Bartlet, Barto, Bartolome, Bartolomé, Bartolomeo, Bartolomeô, Bartolommeo, Bartome, Bartz, Bat

BARTLET (English) a form of Bartholomew.
Bartlett, Bartley

BARTO (Spanish) a form of Bartholomew.
Bardo, Bardol, Bartol, Bartoli, Bartolo, Bartos

BARTON (English) barley farm; Bart's town.
Barrton, Bart

BARTRAM (English) an alternate form of Bertram.
Barthram

BARUCH (Hebrew) blessed.
Boruch

BASAM (Arabic) smiling.
Basem, Basim, Bassam

BASIL (Greek, Latin) royal, kingly. Religion: a saint and leading scholar of the early Christian Church. Botany: an herb used in cooking. See also Vasilis, Wasili.
Bas, Basal, Base, Baseal, Basel, Basle, Basile, Basilio, Basilios, Basilius, Bassel, Bazek, Bazel, Bazil, Bazyli

BASIR (Turkish) intelligent, discerning.
Bashar, Basheer, Bashir, Bashiyr, Bechir, Bhasheer

BASSETT (English) little person.
Basett, Basit, Basset, Bassit

BASTIEN (German) a short form of
Sebastian.
Baste, Bastiaan, Bastian, Bastion

BAT (English) a short form of
Bartholomew.

BAUL (Gypsy) snail.

BAVOL (Gypsy) wind; air.

BAXTER (English) an alternate form of
Baker.
Bax, Baxie, Baxty, Baxy

BAY (Vietnamese) seventh son. (French)
chestnut brown color; evergreen tree.
(English) howler.

BAYARD (English) reddish brown hair.
Baiardo, Bay, Bayardo, Bayerd, Bayrd

BAYLEY (French) an alternate form
of Bailey.
Baylee, Bayleigh, Baylie, Bayly

BEACAN (Irish) small.
Beacán, Becan

BEACHER (English) beech trees.
Beach, Beachy, Beech, Beecher, Beechy

BEAGAN (Irish) small.
Beagen, Beagin

BEALE (French) an alternate form of
Beau.
Beal, Beall, Bealle, Beals

BEAMAN (English) beekeeper.
Beamann, Beamen, Beeman, Beman

BEAMER (English) trumpet player.

BEASLEY (English) field of peas.

BEATTIE (Latin) blessed; happy;
bringer of joy. A masculine form
of Beatrice.
Beatie, Beatty, Beaty

BEAU (French) handsome.
Beale, Beaux, Bo

BEAUFORT (French) beautiful fort.

BEAUMONT (French) beautiful
mountain.

BEAUREGARD (French) handsome;
beautiful; well regarded.

BEAVER (English) beaver.
Beav, Beavo, Beve, Bevo

BEBE (Spanish) baby.

BECK (English, Scandinavian) brook.
Beckett

BEDE (English) prayer. Religion: the
patron saint of scholars.

BELA (Czech) white. (Hungarian) bright.
Béla, Belaal, Belal, Belall, Belay, Bellal

BELDEN (French, English) pretty valley.
Beldin, Beldon, Bellden, Belldon

BELEN (Greek) arrow.

BELL (French) handsome. (English) bell
ringer.

BELLAMY (French) beautiful friend.
Belamy, Bell, Bellamey, Bellamie

BELLO (African) helper or promoter
of Islam

BELMIRO (Portuguese) good looking;
attractive.

BEM (Tiv) peace.
Behm

BEN (Hebrew) a short form of Benjamin.
Behn, Benio, Benn, Benne, Benno

BEN-AMI (Hebrew) son of my people.
Baram, Barami

BENEDICT (Latin) blessed. See also
Venedictos, Venya.
*Benci, Bendick, Bendict, Bendino, Bendix,
Bendrick, Benedetto, Benedick, Benedicto,
Benedictus, Benedikt, Bengt, Benito, Benoit*

BENEDIKT (German, Slavic) a form
of Benedict.
Bendek, Bendik, Benedek, Benedik

BENGT (Scandinavian) a form of
Benedict.
Beng, Benke, Bent

BENIAM (Ethiopian) a form of
Benjamin.
Beneyam, Beniamin, Beniamino

BENITO (Italian) a form of Benedict.
History: Benito Mussolini led Italy
during World War II.
Benedo, Benino, Benno, Beno, Betto, Beto

BENJAMEN (Hebrew) an alternate
form of Benjamin.
Benejamen, Benjermen, Benjjmen

BENJAMIN (Hebrew) son of my right
hand. See also Peniamina, Veniamin.
*Behnjamin, Bejamin, Bemjiman, Ben,
Benejaminas, Bengamin, Beniam, Benja,
Benjahmin, Benjaim, Benjam, Benjamaim,
Benjaman, Benjamen, Benjamine,
Benjaminn, Benjamino, Benjamon,
Benjamyn, Benjamynn, Benjemin,
Benjermain, Benjermin, Benji, Benjie,
Benjiman, Benjy, Benkamin, Bennjamin,
Benny, Benyamin, Benyamino, Binyamin,
Mincho*

BENJIMAN (Hebrew) an alternate form
of Benjamin.
Benjimen, Benjimin, Benjimon, Benjmain

BENJIRO (Japanese) enjoys peace.

BENNETT (Latin) little blessed one.
*Benet, Benett, Bennet, Benette, Bennete,
Bennette*

BENNY (Hebrew) a familiar form of
Benjamin.
Bennie

BENO (Hebrew) son. (Mwera) band
member.

BENOIT (French) a form of Benedict.
(English) Botany: a yellow, flowering
rose plant.
Benott

BENONI (Hebrew) son of my sorrow.
Bible: Ben-Oni was the son of Jacob
and Rachel.
Ben-Oni

BENSON (Hebrew) son of Ben. A short
form of Ben Zion.
Bensan, Bensen, Benssen, Bensson

BENTLEY (English) moor; coarse grass
meadow.
Bent, Bentlea, Bentlee, Bentlie, Lee

BENTON (English) Ben's town; town on
the moors.
Bent

BENZI (Hebrew) a familiar form of Ben
Zion.

BEN ZION (Hebrew) son of Zion.
Benson, Benzi

BEPPE (Italian) a form of Joseph.
Beppy

BER (English) boundary. (Yiddish) bear.

BEREDEI (Russian) a form of Hubert.
Berdry, Berdy, Beredej, Beredy

BERG (German) mountain.
Berdj, Berge, Bergh, Berje

BERGEN (German, Scandinavian) hill
dweller.
Bergin, Birgin

BERGER (French) shepherd.

BERGREN (Scandinavian) mountain
stream.
Berg

BERK (Turkish) solid, rugged.

BERKELEY (English) an alternate form of Barclay.
Berk, Berkely, Berkie, Berkley, Berklie, Berkly, Berky

BERL (German) an alternate form of Burl.
Berle, Berlie, Berlin, Berlyn

BERLYN (German) boundary line. See also Burl.
Berlin, Burlin

BERN (German) a short form of Bernard.
Berne

BERNAL (German) strong as a bear.
Bernald, Bernaldo, Bernel, Bernhald, Bernhold, Bernold

BERNARD (German) brave as a bear. See also Bjorn.
Barnard, Bear, Bearnard, Benek, Ber, Berend, Bern, Bernabé, Bernadas, Bernardel, Bernardin, Bernardo, Bernardus, Bernardyn, Bernarr, Bernat, Bernek, Bernal, Bernel, Bernerd, Berngards, Bernhard, Bernhards, Bernhardt, Bernie, Bjorn, Burnard

BERNARDO (Spanish) a form of Bernard.
Barnardino, Barnardo, Barnhardo, Benardo, Bernardino, Bernhardo, Berno, Burnardo, Nardo

BERNIE (German) a familiar form of Bernard.
Berney, Berni, Berny, Birney, Birnie, Birny, Burney

BERRY (English) berry; grape.
Berrie

BERSH (Gypsy) one year.

BERT (German, English) bright, shining. A short form of Berthold, Berton, Bertram, Bertrand, Egbert, Filbert.
Bertie, Bertus, Birt, Burt

BERTHOLD (German) bright; illustrious; brilliant ruler.
Bert, Berthoud, Bertold, Bertolde

BERTIE (English) a familiar form of Bert, Egbert.
Bertie, Berty, Birt, Birtie, Birty

BERTÍN (Spanish) distinguished friend.
Berti

BERTO (Spanish) a short form of Alberto.

BERTON (English) bright settlement; fortified town.
Bert

BERTRAM (German) bright; illustrious. (English) bright raven. See also Bartram.
Beltran, Beltrán, Beltrano, Bert, Berton, Bertrae, Bertraim, Bertraum, Bertron

BERTRAND (German) bright shield.
Bert, Bertran, Bertrando, Bertranno

BERWYN (English) harvest son; powerful friend. Astrology: a name for babies born under the signs of Virgo, Capricorn, and Taurus.
Berwin, Berwynn, Berwynne

BEVAN (Welsh) son of Evan.
Beavan, Beaven, Beavin, Bev, Beve, Beven, Bevin, Bevo, Bevon

BEVERLY (English) beaver meadow.
Beverlea, Beverleigh, Beverley, Beverlie

BEVIS (French) from Beauvais, France; bull.
Beauvais, Bevys

BHAGWANDAS (Hindi) servant of God.

BICKFORD (English) axe-man's ford.

BIENVENIDO (Filipino) welcome.

BIJAN (Persian) ancient hero.
Bihjan, Bijann, Bijhan, Bijhon, Bijon

BILAL (Arabic) chosen.
Bila, Bilaal, Bilale, Bile, Bilel, Billaal, Billal

BILL (German) a short form of William.
Bil, Billee, Billijo, Billye, Byll, Will

BILLY (German) a familiar form of Bill, William.
Bille, Billey, Billie, Billy, Bily, Willie

BINAH (Hebrew) understanding; wise.
Bina

BING (German) kettle-shaped hollow.

BINH (Vietnamese) peaceful.

BINKENTIOS (Greek) a form of Vincent.

BINKY (English) a familiar form of Bancroft, Vincent.
Bink, Binkentios, Binkie

BIRCH (English) white; shining; birch tree.
Birk, Burch

BIRGER (Norwegian) rescued.

BIRKEY (English) island with birch trees.
Birk, Birkie, Birky

BIRKITT (English) birch-tree coast.
Birk, Birket, Birkit, Burket, Burkett, Burkitt

BIRLEY (English) meadow with the cow barn.
Birlee, Birlie, Birly

BIRNEY (English) island with a brook.
Birne, Birnie, Birny, Burney, Burnie, Burny

BIRTLE (English) hill with birds.

BISHOP (Greek) overseer. (English) bishop.
Bish, Bishup

BJORN (Scandinavian) a form of Bernard.
Bjarne

BLACKBURN (Scottish) black brook.

BLADE (English) knife, sword.
Bladen, Bladon, Bladyn, Blae, Blaed, Blayde

BLADIMIR (Russian) an alternate form of Vladimir.
Bladimer

BLAINE (Irish) thin, lean. (English) river source.
Blain, Blane, Blayne

BLAIR (Irish) plain, field. (Welsh) place.
Blaire, Blare, Blayr, Blayre

BLAISE, Blaize (French) forms of Blaze.
Ballas, Balyse, Blais, Blaisot, Blas, Blase, Blasi, Blasien, Blasius, Blass, Blaz, Blaze, Blayz, Blayze, Blayzz

BLAKE (English) attractive; dark.
Blaik, Blaike, Blakely, Blakeman, Blakey, Blayke

BLAKELY (English) dark meadow.
Blakelee, Blakeleigh, Blakeley, Blakelie, Blakelin, Blakelyn, Blakeny, Blakley, Blakney

BLANCO (Spanish) light skinned, white, blond.

BLANE (Irish) an alternate form of Blaine.
Blaney, Blanne

BLAYNE (Irish) an alternate form of Blaine.
Blayn, Blayney

BLAZE (Latin) stammerer. (English) flame; trail mark made on a tree.
Balázs, Biaggio, Biagio, Blaise, Blaize, Blazen, Blazer

BLISS (English) blissful; joyful.

BLY (Native American) high.

BLYTHE (English) carefree; merry, joyful.
Blithe, Blyth

BO (English) a form of Beau, Beauregard. (German) a form of Bogart.
Boe

BOAZ (Hebrew) swift; strong.
Bo, Boas, Booz, Bos, Boz

BOB (English) a short form of Robert.
Bobb, Bobby, Bobek, Rob

BOBBY (English) a familiar form of Bob, Robert.
Bobbey, Bobbi, Bobbie, Bobbye, Boby

BOBEK (Czech) a form of Bob, Robert.

BODEN (Scandinavian) sheltered. (French) messenger, herald.
Bodie, Bodin, Bodine, Bodyne, Boe

BODIE (Scandinavian) a familiar form of Boden.
Boddie, Bode, Bodee, Bodey, Bodhi, Bodi, Boedee, Boedi, Boedy

BODIL (Norwegian) mighty ruler.

BODUA (Akan) animal's tail.

BOGART (German) strong as a bow. (Irish, Welsh) bog, marshland.
Bo, Bogey, Bogie, Bogy

BOHDAN (Ukranian) a form of Donald.
Bogdan, Bogdashka, Bogdon, Bohden, Bohdon

BONARO (Italian, Spanish) friend.
Bona, Bonar

BONAVENTURE (Italian) good luck.

BOND (English) tiller of the soil.
Bondie, Bondon, Bonds, Bondy

BONIFACE (Latin) do-gooder.
Bonifacio, Bonifacius, Bonifacy

BOOKER (English) book-maker; book lover; Bible lover.
Bookie, Books, Booky

BOONE (Latin, French) good. History: Daniel Boone was an American frontiersman.
Bon, Bone, Bonne, Boonie, Boony

BOOTH (English) hut. (Scandinavian) temporary dwelling.
Boot, Boote, Boothe

BORAK (Arabic) lightning. Mythology: the horse that carried Muhammed to seventh heaven.

BORDEN (French) cottage. (English) valley of the boar; boar's den.
Bord, Bordie, Bordy

BORG (Scandinavian) castle.

BORIS (Slavic) battler, warrior. Religion: the patron saint of Moscow.
Boriss, Borja, Borris, Borya, Boryenka, Borys

BORKA (Russian) fighter.
Borkinka

BOSEDA (Tiv) born on Saturday.

BOSLEY (English) grove of trees.

BOTAN (Japanese) blossom, bud.

BOUREY (Cambodian) country.

BOURNE (Latin, French) boundary. (English) brook, stream.

BOUTROS (Arabic) a form of Peter.

BOWEN (Welsh) son of Owen.
Bow, Bowe, Bowie

BOWIE (Irish) yellow haired. History: Colonel James Bowie was an American scout.
Bow, Bowen

BOYCE (French) woods, forest.
Boice, Boise, Boy, Boycey, Boycie

BOYD (Scottish) yellow haired.
Boid, Boyde

BRAD (English) a short form of
Bradford, Bradley.
Bradd, Brade

BRADBURN (English) broad stream.

BRADEN (English) broad valley.
Bradan, Bradden, Bradeon, Bradin, Bradine,
Bradyn, Braeden, Braiden, Brayden, Bredan,
Bredon

BRADFORD (English) broad river
crossing.
Brad, Braddford, Ford

BRADLEE (English) an alternate form
of Bradley.
Bradlea, Bradleigh, Bradlie

BRADLEY (English) broad meadow.
Brad, Braddly, Bradlay, Bradlee, Bradly,
Bradlyn, Bradney

BRADLY (English) an alternate form
of Bradley.

BRADON (English) broad hill.
Braedon, Braidon, Braydon

BRADSHAW (English) broad forest.

BRADY (Irish) spirited. (English) broad
island.
Bradey, Bradi, Bradie, Bradye, Braidy

BRADYN (English) an alternate form
of Braden.
Bradynne, Breidyn

BRAEDEN, Braiden (English) alternate
forms of Braden.
Braedan, Braedin, Braedyn, Braidyn

BRAEDON (English) an alternate form
of Bradon.
Breadon

BRAGI (Scandinavian) poet. Mythology:
the god of poetry and music.
Brage

BRAHAM (Hindi) creator.
Braheem, Braheim, Brahiem, Brahima, Brahm

BRAINARD (English) bold raven;
prince.
Brainerd

BRAM (Hebrew) a short form of
Abraham, Abram. (Scottish) bramble,
brushwood.
Brame, Bramm, Bramdon

BRAMWELL (English) bramble-bush
spring.
Brammel, Brammell, Bramwel, Bramwyll

BRANCH (Latin) paw; claw; tree
branch.

BRAND (English) firebrand; sword.
A short form of Brandon.
Brandall, Brande, Brandel, Brandell,
Brander, Brandley, Brandol, Brandt, Brandy,
Brann

BRANDEIS (Czech) dweller on a
burned clearing.
Brandis

BRANDEN (English) beacon valley.
Brandden, Brandene, Brandin, Brandine,
Brandyn, Breandan

BRANDON (English) beacon hill.
Bran, Brand, Brandan, Branddon, Brandone,
Brandonn, Brandyn, Branndan, Branndon,
Brannon, Breandon, Brendon

BRANDT (English) an alternate form of
Brant.

BRANDY (Dutch) brandy.
Branddy, Brandey, Brandi, Brandie

BRANDYN (English) an alternate form
of Branden.
Brandynn

BRANNON (Irish) a form of Brandon.
Branen, Brannan, Brannen, Branon

BRANSON (English) son of Brandon,
Brant.
Bransen, Bransin, Brantson

BRANT (English) proud.
Brandt, Brannt, Brante, Brantley, Branton

BRANTLEY (English) an alternate form of Brant.
Brantlie, Brantly, Brentlee, Brentley, Brently

BRAULIO (Italian) a form of Brawley.
Brauli, Brauliuo

BRAWLEY (English) meadow on the hillside.
Braulio , Brawlee, Brawly

BRAXTON (English) Brock's town.
Brax, Braxdon, Braxston, Braxten, Braxtin, Braxxton

BRAYAN (Irish, Scottish) an alternate form of Brian.
Brayn, Brayon

BRAYDEN (English) an alternate form of Braden.
Braydan, Braydn, Bradyn, Breydan, Breyden, Brydan, Bryden

BRAYDON (English) an alternate form of Bradon.
Braydoon, Brydon, Breydon

BRECK (Irish) freckled.
Brec, Breckan, Brecken, Breckie, Breckin, Breckke, Breckyn, Brek, Brexton

BREDE (Scandinavian) iceberg, glacier.

BRENCIS (Latvian) a form of Lawrence.
Brence

BRENDAN (Irish) little raven. (English) sword.
Breandan, Bren, Brenden, Brendis, Brendon, Brendyn, Brenn, Brennan, Brennen, Brenndan, Brenyan, Bryn

BRENDEN (Irish) an alternate form of Brendan.
Bren, Brendene, Brendin, Brendine, Brennden

BRENDON (English) an alternate form of Brandon.
Brenndon

BRENNAN, Brennen (English, Irish) alternate forms of Brendan.
Bren, Brenan, Brenen, Brenin, Brenn, Brenna, Brennann, Brenner, Brennin, Brennon, Brennor, Brennyn, Brenon

BRENT (English) a short form of Brenton.
Brendt, Brente, Brentson, Brentt

BRENTON (English) steep hill.
Brent, Brentan, Brenten, Brentin, Brentten, Brentton, Brentyn

BRET, Brett (Scottish) from Great Britain. See also Britton.
Bhrett, Braten, Braton, Brayton, Bretin, Bretley, Bretlin, Breton, Brettan, Brette, Bretten, Bretton, Brit, Britt

BREWSTER (English) brewer.
Brew, Brewer, Bruwster

BREYON (Irish, Scottish) an alternate form of Brian.
Breon, Breyan

BRIAN (Irish, Scottish) strong; virtuous; honorable. History: Brian Boru was the most famous Irish king. See also Palaina.
Brayan, Breyon, Briana, Briann, Brianna, Brianne, Briano, Briant, Briante, Briaun, Briayan, Brien, Brience, Brient, Brin, Briny, Brion, Bryan, Bryen

BRIAR (French) heather.
Brier, Brierly, Bryar, Bryer, Bryor

BRICE (Welsh) alert; ambitious. (English) son of Rice.
Bricen, Briceton, Bryce

BRICK (English) bridge.
Bricker, Bricklen, Brickman, Brik

BRIDGER (English) bridge builder.
Bridd, Bridge, Bridgeley, Bridgely

BRIGHAM (English) covered bridge. (French) troops, brigade.
Brig, Brigg, Briggs, Brighton

BRIGHTON (English) bright town.
Breighton, Bright, Brightin, Bryton

BRION (Irish, Scottish) an alternate form of Brian.
Brieon, Brione, Brionn, Brionne

BRIT, Britt (Scottish) alternate forms of Bret, Brett. See also Britton.
Brit, Brityce

BRITTON (Scottish) from Great Britain. See also Bret, Brett, Brit, Britt.
Britain, Briten, Britian, Britin, Briton, Brittain, Brittan, Britten, Brittian, Brittin, Britton

BROCK (English) badger.
Broc, Brocke, Brockett, Brockie, Brockley, Brockton, Brocky, Brok, Broque

BROD (English) a short form of Broderick.
Brode, Broden

BRODERICK (Welsh) son of the famous ruler. (English) broad ridge. See also Roderick.
Brod, Broddie, Brodderick, Brodderrick, Broddy, Broderic, Broderrick, Brodrick,

BRODIE (Irish) an alternate form of Brody.
Brodi, Broedi

BRODRICK (Welsh, English) an alternate form of Broderick.
Broddrick, Brodric, Brodryck

BRODY (Irish) ditch; canal builder.
Brodee, Broden, Brodey, Brodie, Broedy

BROGAN (Irish) a heavy work shoe.
Brogen, Broghan, Broghen

BROMLEY (English) brushwood meadow.

BRON (Afrikaans) source.

BRONISLAW (Polish) weapon of glory.

BRONSON (English) son of Brown.
Bransen, Bransin, Branson, Bron, Bronnie, Bronnson, Bronny, Bronsan, Bronsen, Bronsin, Bronsonn, Bronsson, Bronsun, Bronsyn, Brunson

BROOK (English) brook, stream.
Brooke, Brooker, Brookin, Brooklyn

BROOKS (English) son of Brook.
Brookes, Broox

BROWN (English) brown; bear.

BRUCE (French) brushwood thicket; woods.
Brucey, Brucy, Brue, Bruis

BRUNO (German, Italian) brown haired; brown skinned.
Brunon, Bruns

BRYAN (Irish) strong; virtuous; honorable. An alternate form of Brian.
Brayan, Bryann, Bryant, Bryen

BRYANT (Irish) an alternate form of Bryan.
Bryent

BRYCE (Welsh) an alternate form of Brice.
Brycen, Bryceton, Bryson, Bryston

BRYON (German) cottage. (English) bear.
Bryeon, Bryn, Bryne, Brynn, Brynne, Bryone

BRYSON (Welsh) son of Brice.
Brysan, Brysen, Brysun, Brysyn

BRYTON (English) an alternate form of Brighton.
Brayten, Brayton, Breyton, Bryeton, Brytan, Bryten, Brytin, Brytten, Brytton

BUBBA (German) a boy.
Babba, Babe, Bebba

BUCK (German, English) male deer.
Buckie, Buckley, Buckner, Bucko, Bucky

BUCKLEY (English) deer meadow.
Bucklea, Bucklee

BUCKMINSTER (English) preacher.

BUD (English) herald, messenger.
Budd, Buddy

BUDDY (American) a familiar form of Bud.
Budde, Buddey, Buddie

BUELL (German) hill dweller. (English) bull.

BUFORD (English) ford near the castle.
Burford

BURGESS (English) town dweller; shopkeeper.
Burg, Burges, Burgh, Burgiss, Burr

BURIAN (Ukrainian) lives near weeds.

BURKE (German, French) fortress, castle.
Berk, Berke, Birk, Bourke, Burk, Burkley

BURL (German) a short form of Berlyn. (English) cup bearer; wine servant; knot in a tree.
Berl, Burley, Burlie, Byrle

BURLEIGH (English) meadow with knotted tree trunks.
Burlee, Burley, Burlie, Byrleigh, Byrlee

BURNE (English) brook.
Beirne, Burn, Burnell, Burnett, Burney, Byrn, Byrne

BURNEY (English) island with a brook. A familiar form of Rayburn.

BURR (Swedish) youth. (English) prickly plant.

BURRIS (English) town dweller.

BURT (English) an alternate form of Bert. A short form of Burton.
Burrt, Burtt, Burty

BURTON (English) fortified town.
Berton, Burt

BUSBY (Scottish) village in the thicket; tall military hat made of fur.
Busbee, Buzby, Buzz

BUSTER (American) hitter, puncher.

BUTCH (American) a short form of Butcher.

BUTCHER (English) butcher.
Butch

BUZZ (Scottish) a short form of Busby.
Buzzy

BYFORD (English) by the ford.

BYRAM (English) cattleyard.

BYRD (English) birdlike.
Bird, Birdie, Byrdie

BYRNE (English) an alternate form of Burne.
Byrn, Byrnes

BYRON (French) cottage. (English) barn.
Beyren, Beyron, Biren, Biron, Buiron, Byram, Byran, Byrann, Byren, Byrom, Byrone

C

CABLE (French, English) rope maker.
Cabell

CADAO (Vietnamese) folk song.

CADBY (English) warrior's settlement.

CADDOCK (Welsh) eager for war.

CADE (Welsh) a short form of Cadell.
Cady

CADELL (Welsh) battler.
Cade, Cadel, Cedell

CADEN (American) a form of Kadin.
Cadan, Caddon, Cadian, Cadien, Cadin, Cadon, Cadyn, Caeden, Caedon, Caid, Caiden, Cayden

CADMUS (Greek) from the east. Mythology: the founder of the city of Thebes.

CAELAN (Scottish) a form of Nicholas.
Cael, Caelon, Caelyn, Cailan, Cailean, Caillan, Cailun, Cailyn, Calan, Calen, Caleon, Caley, Calin, Callan, Callon, Callyn, Calon, Calyn, Caylan, Cayley

CAESAR (Latin) long haired. History: a title for Roman emperors. See also Kaiser, Kesar, Sarito.
Caesarae, Caesear, Caeser, Caezar, Caseare, Ceasar, Cesar, Ceseare, Cezar, Cézar, Czar, Seasar

CAHIL (Turkish) young, naive.

CAI (Welsh) a form of Gaius.
Caio, Caius, Caw

CAIN (Hebrew) spear; gatherer. Bible: Adam and Eve's oldest son. See also Kabil, Kane, Kayne.
Cainaen, Cainan, Caine, Cainen, Caineth, Cayn, Cayne

CAIRN (Welsh) landmark made of piled-up stones.
Cairne, Carn, Carne

CAIRO (Arabic) Geography: the capital of Egypt.
Kairo

CAL (Latin) a short form of Calvert, Calvin.

CALDER (Welsh, English) brook, stream.

CALDWELL (English) cold well.

CALE (Hebrew) a short form of Caleb.

CALEB (Hebrew) dog; faithful. (Arabic) bold, brave. Bible: a companion of Moses and Joshua. See also Kaleb, Kayleb.
Caeleb, Calab, Calabe, Cale, Caley, Calib, Calieb, Callob, Calob, Calyb, Cayleb, Caylebb, Caylib, Caylob

CALEN, Calin (Scottish) alternate forms of Caelan.
Caelen, Caelin, Caellin, Cailen, Cailin, Caillin, Calean, Callen, Caylin

CALEY (Irish) a familiar form of Caleb.
Calee, Caleigh

CALHOUN (Irish) narrow woods. (Scottish) warrior.
Colhoun, Colhoune, Colquhoun

CALLAHAN (Irish) Religion: a Catholic saint.
Calahan, Callaghan

CALLUM (Irish) dove.
Callam, Calum, Calym

CALVERT (English) calf herder.
Cal, Calbert, Calvirt

CALVIN (Latin) bald. See also Kalvin, Vinny.
Cal, Calv, Calvien, Calvon, Calvyn

CAM (Gypsy) beloved. (Scottish) a short form of Cameron.
Camm, Cammie, Cammy, Camy

CAMARON (Scottish) an alternate form of Cameron.
Camar, Camari, Camaran, Camaren

CAMDEN (Scottish) winding valley.
Kamden

CAMERON (Scottish) crooked nose. See also Kameron.

Cameron (cont.)
*Cam, Camaron, Cameran, Cameren,
Camerin, Cameroun, Camerron, Camerson,
Camerun, Cameryn, Camiren, Camiron,
Cammeron, Camron*

CAMILLE (French) young ceremonial
attendant.
Camile

CAMILO (Latin) child born to freedom;
noble.
Camiel, Camillo, Camillus

CAMPBELL (Latin, French) beautiful
field. (Scottish) crooked mouth.
Cam, Camp, Campy

CAMRON (Scottish) a short form of
Cameron.
*Camren, Cammrin, Cammron, Camran,
Camreon, Camrin, Camryn, Camrynn*

CANAAN (French) an alternate form of
Cannon. History: an ancient region
between the Jordan River and the
Mediterranean Sea.
Canan, Canen, Caynan

CANDIDE (Latin) pure; sincere.
Candid, Candido, Candonino

CANNON (French) church official; large
gun. See also Kannon.
*Canaan, Cannan, Cannen, Cannin,
Canning, Canon*

CANUTE (Latin) white haired.
(Scandinavian) knot. History: an
ancient Danish king who won a battle
at Knutsford. See also Knute.
Cnut, Cnute

CAPPI (Gypsy) good fortune.

CAR (Irish) a short form of Carney.

CAREY (Greek) pure. (Welsh) castle;
rocky island. See also Karey.
*Care, Caree, Cari, Carre, Carree, Carrie,
Cary*

CARL (German) farmer. (English) strong
and manly. An alternate form of
Charles. A short form of Carlton.
See also Carroll, Kale, Kalle, Karl,
Karlen, Karol.
*Carle, Carles, Carless, Carlis, Carll, Carlo,
Carlos, Carlson, Carlston, Carlus, Carolos*

CARLIN (Irish) little champion.
*Carlan, Carlen, Carley, Carlie, Carling,
Carlino, Carly*

CARLISLE (English) Carl's island.
Carlyle, Carlysle

CARLITO (Spanish) a familiar form
of Carlos.
Carlitos

CARLO (Italian) a form of Carl, Charles.
Carolo

CARLOS (Spanish) a form of Carl,
Charles.
Carlito

CARLTON (English) Carl's town.
*Carl, Carleton, Carllton, Carlston, Carltonn,
Carltton, Charlton*

CARMEL (Hebrew) vineyard, garden.
See also Carmine.
Carmello, Carmelo, Karmel

CARMICHAEL (Scottish) follower of
Michael.

CARMINE (Latin) song; crimson.
(Italian) a form of Carmel.
*Carmain, Carmaine, Carman, Carmen,
Carmon*

CARNELIUS (Greek, Latin) an
alternate form of Cornelius.
*Carnealius, Carneilius, Carnellius,
Carnilious*

CARNELL (English) defender of the
castle.

CARNEY (Irish) victorious. (Scottish)
fighter. See also Kearney.
Car, Carny, Karney

CARR (Scandinavian) marsh. See also Kerr.
Karr

CARRICK (Irish) rock.
Carooq, Carricko

CARRINGTON (Welsh) rocky town.

CARROLL (German) an alternate form of Carl. (Irish) champion.
Carel, Carell, Cariel, Cariell, Carol, Carole, Carolo, Carols, Carollan, Carolus, Carrol, Cary, Caryl

CARSON (English) son of Carr.
Carsen, Carsino, Carrson, Karson

CARSTEN (Greek) an alternate form of Karsten.
Carston

CARTER (English) cart driver.
Cart

CARTWRIGHT (English) cart builder.

CARVELL (French, English) village on the marsh.
Carvel, Carvelle, Carvellius

CARVER (English) wood-carver; sculptor.

CARY (Welsh) an alternate form of Carey.
Carray, Carry

CASE (Irish) a short form of Casey. (English) a short form of Casimir.

CASEY (Irish) brave.
Case, Casie, Casy, Cayse, Caysey, Kacey, Kasey

CASH (Latin) vain. (Slavic) a short form of Casimir.
Cashe

CASIMIR (Slavic) peacemaker.
Cachi, Cas, Case, Cash, Cashemere, Cashi, Cashmeire, Cashmere, Casimere, Casimire, Casimiro, Castimer, Kasimir, Kazio

CASPER (Persian) treasurer. (German) imperial. See also Gaspar, Jasper, Kasper.
Caspar, Cass

CASS (Irish, Persian) a short form of Casper, Cassidy.

CASSIDY (Irish) clever; curly haired. See also Kazio.
Casidy, Cass, Cassady, Cassie, Kassidy

CASSIE (Irish) a familiar form of Cassidy.
Casi, Casie, Casio, Cassey, Cassy, Casy

CASSIUS (Latin, French) box; protective cover.
Cassia, Cassio, Cazzie

CASTLE (Latin) castle.
Cassle, Castel

CASTOR (Greek) beaver. Astrology: one of the twins in the constellation Gemini. Mythology: one of the patron saints of sailors.
Caster, Caston

CATER (English) caterer.

CATO (Latin) knowledgeable, wise.
Caton, Catón

CAVAN (Irish) handsome. See also Kevin.
Caven, Cavin, Cavan, Cawoun

CAYDEN (American) an alternate form of Caden.
Cayde, Caydin

CAYLAN (Scottish) an alternate form of Caelan.
Caylans, Caylen, Caylon

CAZZIE (American) a familiar form of Cassius.
Caz, Cazz, Cazzy

CEASAR (Latin) an alternate form of Caesar.
Ceaser

CECIL (Latin) blind.
Cece, Cecile, Cecilio, Cecilius, Cecill, Celio, Siseal

CEDRIC (English) battle chieftain. See also Kedrick, Rick.
Cad, Caddaric, Ced, Cederic, Cedrec, Cédric, Cedrick, Cedryche, Sedric

CEDRICK (English) an alternate form of Cedric.
Ceddrick, Cederick, Cederrick, Cedirick, Cedrik

CEEJAY (American) a combination of the initials C. + J.
Cejay, C.J.

CEMAL (Arabic) attractive.

CEPHAS (Latin) small rock. Bible: the term used by Jesus to describe Peter.
Cepheus, Cephus

CERDIC (Welsh) beloved.
Caradoc, Caradog, Ceredig, Ceretic

CEREK (Greek) an alternate form of Cyril. (Polish) lordly.

CESAR (Spanish) a form of Caesar.
Casar, César, Cesare, Cesareo, Cesario, Cesaro, Cessar

CESTMIR (Czech) fortress.

CEZAR (Slavic) a form of Caesar.
Cézar, Cezary, Cezek, Chezrae, Sezar

CHACE (French) an alternate form of Chase.
Chayce

CHAD (English) warrior. A short form of Chadwick. Geography: a country in north-central Africa.
Ceadd, Chaad, Chadd, Chaddie, Chaddy, Chade, Chadleigh, Chadler, Chadley, Chadlin, Chadlyn, Chadmen, Chado, Chadron, Chady

CHADRICK (German) mighty warrior.
Chaddrick, Chaderic, Chaderick, Chadrack, Chadric

CHADWICK (English) warrior's town.
Chad, Chaddwick, Chadvic, Chadwyck

CHAGO (Spanish) a form of Jacob.
Chango, Chanti

CHAIM (Hebrew) life. See also Hyman.
Chai, Chaimek, Haim, Khaim

CHAISE (French) an alternate form of Chase.
Chais, Chaisen, Chaison

CHAL (Gypsy) boy; son.
Chalie, Chalin

CHALMERS (Scottish) son of the lord.
Chalmer, Chalmr, Chamar, Chamarr

CHAM (Vietnamese) hard worker.
Chams

CHAN (Sanskrit) shining. (Spanish) an alternate form of Juan.
Chann, Chano, Chayo

CHANAN (Hebrew) cloud.

CHANCE (English) a short form of Chancellor, Chauncey.
Chanc, Chancee, Chancey, Chancie, Chancy, Chanse, Chansy, Chants, Chantz, Chanze, Chanz, Chaynce

CHANCELLOR (English) recordkeeper.
Chance, Chancelar, Chancelen, Chanceleor, Chanceler, Chanceller, Chancelor, Chanselor, Chanslor

CHANDER (Hindi) moon.
Chand, Chandan, Chandany, Chandara, Chandon

CHANDLER (English) candle maker.
Chandelar, Chandlan, Chandlar, Chandlier, Chandlor, Chandlyr

CHANE (Swahili) dependable.

CHANEY (French) oak.
Chayne, Cheaney, Cheney, Cheyn, Cheyne, Cheyney

CHANKRISNA (Cambodian) sweet-smelling tree.

CHANNING (English) wise. (French) canon; church official.
Chane, Chann

CHANSE (English) an alternate form of Chance.
Chans, Chansey

CHANTE (French) singer.
Chant, Chantha, Chanthar, Chantra, Chantry, Shantae

CHAPMAN (English) merchant.
Chap, Chappie, Chappy

CHARLES (German) farmer. (English) strong and manly. See also Carl, Searlas, Tearlach, Xarles.
Arlo, Chareles, Charels, Charlese, Carlo, Carlos, Charl, Charle, Charlen, Charlie, Charlot, Charlz, Charlzell, Chaz, Chick, Chip, Chuck

CHARLIE (German, English) a familiar form of Charles.
Charle, Charlee, Charley, Charli, Charly

CHARLTON (English) a form of Carlton.
Charlesten, Charleston, Charleton, Charlotin

CHARRO (Spanish) cowboy.

CHASE (French) hunter.
Chace, Chaise, Chasen, Chason, Chass, Chasse, Chastan, Chasten, Chastin, Chastinn, Chaston, Chasyn, Chayse

CHASKA (Sioux) first-born son.

CHAUNCEY (English) chancellor; church official.
Chan, Chance, Chancey, Chaunce, Chauncei, Chauncy, Chaunecy, Chaunesy, Chaunszi

CHAVEZ (Hispanic) a surname used as a first name.

Chavaz, Chaves, Chaveze, Chavies, Chavis, Chavius, Chevez, Cheveze, Cheviez, Chevious, Chevis, Chivass, Chivez

CHAYSE (French) an alternate form of Chase.
Chaysea, Chaysen, Chayson, Chaysten

CHAYTON (Lakota) falcon.

CHAZ (English) a familiar form of Charles.
Chas, Chasz, Chaze, Chazwick, Chazy, Chazz, Chez

CHÉ (Spanish) a familiar form of José. History: Ché Guevarra was a revolutionary who fought at Fidel Castro's side in Cuba.
Chay

CHECHA (Spanish) a familiar form of Jacob.

CHECHE (Spanish) a familiar form of Joseph.

CHEN (Chinese) great, tremendous.

CHENCHO (Spanish) a familiar form of Lawrence.

CHEPE (Spanish) a familiar form of Joseph.
Cepito

CHEROKEE (Cherokee) people of a different speech.
Cherrakee

CHESMU (Native American) gritty.

CHESTER (English) a short form of Rochester.
Ches, Cheslav, Cheston, Chet

CHET (English) a short form of Chester.
Chett, Chette

CHEUNG (Chinese) good luck.

CHEVALIER (French) horseman, knight.
Chev, Chevy

CHEVY (French) a familiar form of Chevalier. Geography: Chevy Chase is a town in Maryland. Culture: a short form of Chevrolet, an American automobile.
Chev, Chevey, Chevi, Chevie, Chevvy, Chewy

CHEYENNE (Cheyenne) a tribal name.
Chayann, Chayanne, Cheyeenne, Cheyene, Chyenne, Shayan

CHI (Chinese) younger generation. (Nigerian) personal guardian angel.

CHICK (English) a familiar form of Charles.
Chic, Chickie, Chicky

CHICO (Spanish) boy.

CHIK (Gypsy) earth.

CHIKE (Ibo) God's power.

CHIKO (Japanese) arrow; pledge.

CHILO (Spanish) a familiar form of Francisco.

CHILTON (English) farm by the spring.
Chil, Chill, Chillton, Chilt

CHIM (Vietnamese) bird.

CHINUA (Ibo) God's blessing.
Chino, Chinou

CHIOKE (Ibo) gift of God.

CHIP (English) a familiar form of Charles.
Chipman, Chipper

CHIRAM (Hebrew) exalted; noble.

CHRIS (Greek) a short form of Christian, Christopher. See also Kris.
Chriss, Christ, Chrys, Cris, Crist

CHRISTAIN (Greek) an alternate form of Christian.
Christai, Christan, Christane, Christaun, Christein

CHRISTIAN (Greek) follower of Christ; anointed. See also Jaan, Kerstan, Khristian, Kit, Krister, Kristian, Krystian.
Chretien, Chris, Christa, Christain, Christé, Christen, Christensen, Christiaan, Christiana, Christiane, Christiann, Christianna, Christianno, Christiano, Christianos, Christien, Christin, Christino, Christion, Christon, Christos, Christyan, Christyon, Chritian, Chrystian, Cristian, Crystek

CHRISTIEN (Greek) an alternate form of Christian.
Christienne, Christinne, Chrystien

CHRISTOFER (Greek) an alternate form of Christopher.
Christafer, Christafur, Christefor, Christerfer, Christifer, Christoffer, Christofher, Christofper, Chrystofer

CHRISTOFF (Russian) a form of Christopher.
Chrisof, Christif, Christof, Cristofe

CHRISTOPHE (French) a form of Christopher.
Christoph

CHRISTOPHER (Greek) Christ-bearer. Religion: the patron saint of travelers and drivers. See also Kester, Kit, Kristopher, Risto, Stoffel, Tobal, Topher.
Chris, Chrisopherson, Christapher, Christepher, Christerpher, Christhoper, Christipher, Christobal, Christofer, Christoff, Christoforo, Christoher, Christopehr, Christoper, Christophe, Christopherr, Christophor, Christophoros, Christophr, Christophre, Christophyer, Christophyr, Christorpher, Christos, Christovao, Christpher, Christphere, Christphor, Christpor, Christrpher, Chrystopher, Cristobal

CHRISTOPHOROS (Greek) an alternate form of Christopher.
Christoforo, Christoforos, Christophor, Christophorus, Christphor, Cristoforo, Cristopher

CHRISTOS (Greek) an alternate form of Christopher. See also Khristos.

CHUCHO (Hebrew) a familiar form of Jesus.

CHUCK (American) a familiar form of Charles.
Chuckey, Chuckie, Chucky

CHUI (Swahili) leopard.

CHUL (Korean) firm.

CHUMA (Ibo) having many beads, wealthy. (Swahili) iron.

CHUMINGA (Spanish) a familiar form of Dominic.
Chumin

CHUMO (Spanish) a familiar form of Thomas.

CHUN (Chinese) spring.

CHUNG (Chinese) intelligent.
Chungo, Chuong

CHURCHILL (English) church on the hill. History: Sir Winston Churchill served as British prime minister and won a Nobel Prize for literature.

CIAN (Irish) ancient.
Céin, Cianán, Kian

CICERO (Latin) chickpea. History: a famous Roman orator and statesman.
Cicerón

CID (Spanish) lord. History: an eleventh-century Spanish soldier and national hero.
Cyd

CIQALA (Dakota) little.

CIRRILLO (Italian) a form of Cyril.
Cirilio, Cirillo, Cirilo, Ciro

CISCO (Spanish) a short form of Francisco.

CLANCY (Irish) red-headed fighter.
Clancey, Claney

CLARE (Latin) a short form of Clarence.
Clair, Clarey, Clary

CLARENCE (Latin) clear; victorious.
Clarance, Clare, Clarrance, Clarrence, Clearence

CLARK (French) cleric; scholar.
Clarke, Clerc, Clerk

CLAUDE (Latin, French) lame.
Claud, Claudan, Claudel, Claudell, Claudey, Claudi, Claudian, Claudianus, Claudie, Claudien, Claudin, Claudio, Claudis, Claudius, Claudy

CLAUDIO (Italian) a form of Claude.

CLAUS (German) a short form of Nicholas. See also Klaus.
Claas, Claes, Clause

CLAY (English) clay pit. A short form of Clayborne, Clayton.
Klay

CLAYBORNE (English) brook near the clay pit.
Claibern, Claiborn, Claiborne, Claibrone, Clay, Claybon, Clayborn, Claybourn, Claybourne, Clayburn, Clebourn

CLAYTON (English) town built on clay.
Clay, Clayten, Cleighton, Cleyton, Clyton, Klayton

CLEARY (Irish) learned.

CLEAVON (English) cliff.
Clavin, Clavion, Clavon, Clavone, Clayvon, Claywon, Clévon, Clevonn, Clyvon

CLEM (Latin) a short form of Clement.
Cleme, Clemmy, Clim

CLEMENT (Latin) merciful. Bible: a disciple of Paul. See also Klement, Menz.
Clem, Clemens, Clément, Clemente, Clementius, Clemmons

CLEMENTE (Italian, Spanish) a form of Clement.
Clemento, Clemenza

CLEON (Greek) famous.
Kleon

CLETUS (Greek) illustrious. History: a Roman pope and martyr.
Cleatus, Cledis, Cleotis, Clete, Cletis

CLEVELAND (English) land of cliffs.
Cleaveland, Cleavland, Cleavon, Cleve, Clevelend, Clevelynn, Clevey, Clevie, Clevon

CLIFF (English) a short form of Clifford, Clifton.
Clif, Clift, Clive, Clyff, Clyph, Kliff

CLIFFORD (English) cliff at the river crossing.
Cliff, Cliford, Clyfford, Klifford

CLIFTON (English) cliff town.
Cliff, Cliffton, Clift, Cliften, Clyfton

CLINT (English) a short form of Clinton.
Klint

CLINTON (English) hill town.
Clenten, Clint, Clinten, Clintion, Clintton, Clynton, Klinton

CLIVE (English) an alternate form of Cliff.
Cleve, Clivans, Clivens, Clyve, Klyve

CLOVIS (German) famous soldier. See also Louis.

CLUNY (Irish) meadow.

CLYDE (Welsh) warm. (Scottish) Geography: a river in Scotland.
Cly, Clywd, Klyde

COBY (Hebrew) a familiar form of Jacob.
Cob, Cobby, Cobe, Cobey, Cobi, Cobia, Cobie

COCHISE (Apache) hardwood. History: a famous Apache warrior and chief.

COCO (French) a familiar form of Jacques.
Coko, Koko

CODEY (English) an alternate form of Cody.
Coday

CODI, Codie (English) alternate forms of Cody.
Coadi, Codea

CODY (English) cushion. History: William Cody (Buffalo Bill) was a sharpshooter and showman in the American 'Wild' West. See also Kody.
Coady, Coddy, Code, Codee, Codell, Codey, Codi, Codiak, Codie, Coedy

COFFIE (Ewe) born on Friday.

COLA (Italian) a familiar form of Nicholas, Nicola.
Colas

COLAR (French) a form of Nicholas.

COLBERT (English) famous seafarer.
Cole, Colt, Colvert, Culbert

COLBY (English) dark; dark haired.
Colbey, Colbi, Colbie, Colbin, Colebee, Coleby, Collby, Kolby

COLE (Greek) a short form of Nicholas. (Latin) cabbage farmer. (English) a short form of Coleman.
Colet, Coley, Colie, Kole

COLEMAN (Latin) cabbage farmer. (English) coal miner.
Cole, Colemann, Colm, Colman, Koleman

COLIN (Greek) a short form of Nicholas.
(Irish) young cub.
*Cailean, Colan, Cole, Colen, Coleon, Colinn,
Collin, Colyn, Kolin*

COLLEY (English) black haired;
swarthy.
Colee, Collie, Collis

COLLIER (English) miner.
Colier, Collayer, Collie, Collyer, Colyer

COLLIN (Scottish) a form of Colin,
Collins.
Collan, Collen, Collian, Collon, Collyn

COLLINS (Greek) son of Colin. (Irish)
holly.
Collin, Collis

COLSON (Greek, English) son of
Nicholas.
Colsen, Coulson

COLT (English) young horse; frisky.
A short form of Colter, Colton.
Colte

COLTEN (English) an alternate form
of Colton.

COLTER (English) herd of colts.
Colt

COLTON (English) coal town.
*Colt, Coltan, Colten, Coltin, Coltinn, Coltn,
Coltrane, Colttan, Coltton, Coltun, Coltyn,
Coltyne, Kolton*

COLUMBA (Latin) dove.
Coim, Colum, Columbia, Columbus

COLWYN (Welsh) Geography: a river
in Wales.
Colwin, Colwinn

COMAN (Arabic) noble. (Irish) bent.
Comán

CONALL (Irish) high, mighty.
*Conal, Connal, Connel, Connell, Connelly,
Connolly*

CONAN (Irish) praised; exalted.
(Scottish) wise.
*Conant, Conary, Connen, Connie, Connon,
Connor, Conon*

CONARY (Irish) an alternate form of
Conan.
Conaire

CONLAN (Irish) hero.
Conlen, Conley, Conlin, Conlyn

CONNER (Irish) an alternate form
of Connor.
Connar, Connary, Conneer, Connery, Konner

CONNIE (English, Irish) a familiar form
of Conan, Conrad, Constantine,
Conway.
Con, Conn, Conney, Conny

CONNOR (Scottish) wise. (Irish) an
alternate form of Conan.
*Conner, Connoer, Connory, Connyr, Conor,
Konner, Konnor*

CONOR (Irish) an alternate form of
Connor.
Conar, Coner, Conour, Konner

CONRAD (German) brave counselor.
Connie, Conrade, Conrado, Corrado, Konrad

CONROY (Irish) wise.
Conry, Roy

CONSTANT (Latin) a short form of
Constantine.

CONSTANTINE (Latin) firm, constant.
History: Constantine the Great was
one of the most famous Roman
emperors. See also Dinos, Konstantin,
Stancio.
*Connie, Constadine, Constandine,
Constandios, Constanstine, Constant,
Constantin, Constantino, Constantinos,
Constantios, Costa*

CONWAY (Irish) hound of the plain.
Connie, Conwy

COOK (English) cook.
Cooke

COOPER (English) barrel maker.
See also Keiffer.
Coop, Couper

CORBETT (Latin) raven.
Corbbitt, Corbet, Corbette, Corbit, Corbitt

CORBIN (Latin) raven.
Corban, Corben, Corbey, Corbie, Corbon,
Corby, Corbyn, Korbin

CORCORAN (Irish) ruddy.

CORDARO (Spanish) an alternate form
of Cordero.
Coradaro, Cordairo, Cordara, Cordarel,
Cordarell, Cordarelle, Cordareo, Cordarin,
Cordario, Cordarion, Cordarious, Cordarius,
Cordarrel, Cordarrell, Cordarris, Cordarrius,
Cordarro, Cordarrol, Cordarus, Cordarryl,
Cordaryal, Corddarro, Corrdarl

CORDELL (French) rope maker.
Cord, Cordae, Cordale, Corday, Cordeal,
Cordeil, Cordel, Cordele, Cordelle, Cordie,
Cordy, Kordell

CORDERO (Spanish) little lamb.
Cordaro, Cordeal, Cordeara, Cordearo,
Cordeiro, Cordelro, Corder, Cordera,
Corderall, Corderias, Corderious, Corderral,
Corderro, Corderryn, Corderun, Corderus,
Cordiaro, Cordierre, Cordy, Corrderio

COREY (Irish) hollow. See also Korey,
Kory.
Core, Coreaa, Coree, Cori, Corian, Corie, Corio,
Correy, Corria, Corrie, Corry, Corrye, Cory

CORMAC (Irish) raven's son. History: a
third-century king of Ireland who
founded schools.
Cormack, Cormick

CORNELIUS (Greek) cornel tree. (Latin)
horn colored. See also Kornel,
Kornelius, Nelek.
Carnelius, Conny, Cornealous, Corneili,
Corneilius, Corneilus, Corneliaus,

Cornelious, Cornelias, Cornelis, Corneliu,
Cornell, Cornellious, Cornellis, Cornellius,
Cornelous, Corneluis, Cornelus, Corney,
Cornie, Cornielius, Corniellus, Corny,
Cournelius, Cournelyous, Nelius, Nellie

CORNELL (French) a form of Cornelius.
Carnell, Cornall, Corneil, Cornel, Cornelio,
Corney, Cornie, Corny, Nellie

CORNWALLIS (English) from
Cornwall.

CORRADO (Italian) a form of Conrad.
Carrado

CORRIGAN (Irish) spearman.
Carrigan, Carrigen, Corrigon, Corrigun,
Korrigan

CORRIN (Irish) spear carrier.
Corin, Corion

CORRY (Latin) a form of Corey.

CORT (German) bold. (Scandinavian)
short. (English) a short form of
Courtney.
Corte, Cortie, Corty, Kort

CORTEZ (Spanish) conqueror. History:
Hernando Cortez was an explorer
who conquered the Aztecs in Mexico.
Cartez, Cortes, Cortis, Cortize, Courtes,
Courtez, Curtez, Kortez

CORWIN (English) heart's companion;
heart's delight.
Corwinn, Corwyn, Corwynn, Corwynne

CORY (Latin) a form of Corey. (French)
a familiar form of Cornell.
Corye

CORYDON (Greek) helmet, crest.
Coridon, Corradino, Cory, Coryden, Coryell

COSGROVE (Irish) victor, champion.

COSMO (Greek) orderly; harmonious;
universe.
Cos, Cosimo, Cosme, Cosmé, Cozmo, Kosmo

COSTA (Greek) a short form of Constantine.
Costandinos, Costantinos, Costas, Costes

COTY (French) slope, hillside.
Cote, Cotee, Cotey, Coti, Cotie, Cotty, Cotye

COURTLAND (English) court's land.
Court, Courtlan, Courtlana, Courtlandt, Courtlin, Courtlind, Courtlon, Courtlyn, Kourtland

COURTNEY (English) court.
Cort, Cortnay, Cortne, Cortney, Court, Courten, Courtenay, Courteney, Courtnay, Courtnee, Curt, Kortney

COWAN (Irish) hillside hollow.
Coe, Coven, Covin, Cowen, Cowey, Cowie

COY (English) woods.
Coye, Coyie, Coyt

COYLE (Irish) leader in battle.

COYNE (French) modest.
Coyan

CRADDOCK (Welsh) love.
Caradoc, Caradog

CRAIG (Irish, Scottish) crag; steep rock.
Crag, Craige, Craigen, Craigery, Craigh, Craigon, Creag, Creg, Cregan, Cregg, Creig, Creigh, Criag, Kraig

CRANDALL (English) crane's valley.
Cran, Crandal, Crandel, Crandell, Crendal

CRAWFORD (English) ford where crows fly.
Craw, Crow, Ford

CREED (Latin) belief.
Creedon

CREIGHTON (English) town near the rocks.
Cray, Crayton, Creighm, Creight, Creighto, Crichton

CREPIN (French) a form of Crispin.

CRISPIN (Latin) curly haired.
Crepin, Cris, Crispian, Crispien, Crispino, Crispo, Krispin

CRISTIAN (Greek) an alternate form of Christian.
Crétien, Cristean, Cristhian, Cristiano, Cristien, Cristino, Cristle, Criston, Cristos, Cristy, Cristyan, Crystek, Crystian

CRISTOBAL (Greek) an alternate form of Christopher.
Cristóbal, Cristoval, Cristovao

CRISTOFORO (Italian) a form of Christopher.
Cristofor

CRISTOPHER (Greek) an alternate form of Christopher.
Cristaph, Cristhofer, Cristifer, Cristofer, Cristoph, Cristophe, Crystapher, Crystifer

CROFTON (Irish) town with cottages.

CROMWELL (English) crooked spring, winding spring.

CROSBY (Scandinavian) shrine of the cross.
Crosbey, Crosbie, Cross

CROSLEY (English) meadow of the cross.
Cross

CROWTHER (English) fiddler.

CRUZ (Portuguese, Spanish) cross.
Cruze, Kruz

CRYSTEK (Polish) a form of Christian.

CSABA (Hungarian) Geography: a city in southwestern Hungary.

CULLEN (Irish) handsome.
Cull, Cullan, Cullie, Cullin

CULLEY (Irish) woods.
Cullie, Cully

CULVER (English) dove.
Colver, Cull, Cullie, Cully

CUNNINGHAM (Irish) village of the milk pail.

CURRAN (Irish) hero.
Curan, Curon, Curr, Curren, Currey, Curri, Currie, Currin, Curry

CURRITO (Spanish) a form of Curtis.
Curcio

CURT (Latin) a short form of Courtney, Curtis. See also Kurt.

CURTIS (Latin) enclosure. (French) courteous. See also Kurtis.
Curio, Currito, Curt, Curtice, Curtiss, Curtus

CUTHBERT (English) brilliant.

CUTLER (English) knife maker.
Cut, Cuttie, Cutty

CY (Persian) a short form of Cyrus.

CYLE (Irish) an alternate form of Kyle.

CYPRIAN (Latin) from the island of Cyprus.
Ciprian, Cipriano, Ciprien, Cyprien

CYRANO (Greek) from Cyrene, an ancient Greek city. Literature: *Cyrano de Bergerac* is a play by Edmond Rostand about a great swordsman whose large nose prevented him from pursuing the woman he loved.

CYRIL (Greek) lordly. See also Kiril.
Cerek, Cerel, Cyrell, Ceril, Ciril, Cirillo, Cirrillo, Cyra, Cyrel, Cyrell, Cyrelle, Cyrill, Cyrille, Cyrillus, Syrell, Syril

CYRUS (Persian) sun. Historial: Cyrus the Great was a king in ancient Persia. See also Kir.
Ciro, Cy, Cyress, Cyris, Cyriss, Cyruss, Syris, Syrus

D

DABI (Basque) a form of David.

DABIR (Arabic) tutor.

DACEY (Latin) from Dacia, an area now in Romania. (Irish) southerner.
Dace, Dache, Dacian, Dacias, Dacio, Dacy, Daicey, Daicy

DADA (Yoruba) curly haired.
Dadi

DAEGEL (English) from Daegel, England.

DAELEN (English) an alternate form of Dale.
Daelan, Daelin, Daelon, Daelyn, Daelyne

DAEMON (Greek) an alternate form of Damian.
Daemean, Daemeon, Daemien, Daemin, Daemion, Daemyen

DAEQUAN (American) an alternate form of Daquan.
Daequane, Daequon, Daequone, Daeqwan

DAESHAWN (American) a combination of the prefix Da + Shawn.
Daesean, Daeshaun, Daeshon, Daeshun, Daisean, Daishaun, Daishawn, Daishon, Daishoun

DAEVON (American) an alternate form of Davon.
Daevion, Daevohn, Daevonne, Daevonte, Daevontey

DAFYDD (Welsh) a form of David.
Dafyd

DAG (Scandinavian) day; bright.
Daeg, Daegan, Dagen, Dagny, Deegan

DAGAN (Hebrew) corn; grain.
Daegan, Daegon, Dagen, Dageon, Dagon

DAGWOOD (English) shining forest.

DAI (Japanese) big.

DAIMIAN (Greek) an alternate form of Damian.
Daiman, Daimean, Daimen, Daimeon, Daimeyon, Daimien, Daimin, Daimion, Daimyan

DAIMON (Greek, Latin) an alternate form of Damon.
Daimone

DAIQUAN (American) an alternate form of Dajuan.
Daekwaun, Daekwon, Daiqone, Daiqua, Daiquane, Daiquawn, Daiquon, Daiqwan, Daiqwon

DAIVON (American) an alternate form of Davon.
Daivain, Daivion, Daivonn, Daivonte, Daiwan

DAJON (American) an alternate form of Dajuan.
Dajean, Dajiawn, Dajin, Dajion, Dajn, Dajohn, Dajonae

DAJUAN (American) a combination of the prefix Da + Juan. See also Dejuan.
Daejon, Daejuan, Daiquan, Dajon, Da Jon, Da-Juan, Dajwan, Dajwoun, Dakuan, Dakwan, Dawan, Dawaun, Dawawn, Dawon, Dawoyan, Dijuan, Diuan, Dujuan, D'Juan, D'juan, Dwaun

DAKARAI (Shona) happy.
Dakairi, Dakar, Dakaraia, Dakari, Dakarri

DAKODA (Dakota) an alternate form of Dakota.
Dacoda, Dacodah, Dakodah, Dakodas

DAKOTA (Dakota) friend; partner; tribal name.
Dac, Dack, Dackota, Dacota, DaCota, Dak, Dakcota, Dakkota, Dakoata, Dakoda, Dakotah, Dakotha, Dakotta, Dekota

DAKOTAH (Dakota) an alternate form of Dakota.
Dakottah

DAKSH (Hindi) efficient.

DALAL (Sanskrit) broker.

DALBERT (English) bright, shining. See also Delbert.

DALE (English) dale, valley.
Dael, Daelen, Dal, Dalen, Daley, Dalibor, Dallan, Dallin, Dallyn, Daly, Dayl, Dayle

DALEN (English) an alternate form of Dale.
Dailin, Dalaan, Dalan, Dalane, Daleon, Dalian, Dalibor, Dalione, Dallan, Dalon, Daylan, Daylen, Daylin, Daylon

DALEY (Irish) assembly. (English) a familiar form of Dale.
Daily, Daly, Dawley

DALLAN (English) an alternate form of Dale.
Dallen, Dallon

DALLAS (Scottish) Geography: a town in Scotland; a city in Texas.
Dal, Dalieass, Dall, Dalles, Dallis, Dalys, Dellis

DALLIN, Dallyn (English) alternate forms of Dale.
Dalin, Dalyn

DALSTON (English) Daegel's place.
Dalis, Dallon

DALTON (English) town in the valley.
Dal, Dalaton, Dallton, Dalt, Daltan, Dalten, Daltin, Daltyn, Daulton, Delton

DALVIN (English) an alternate form of Delvin.
Dalven, Dalvon, Dalvyn

DALZIEL (Scottish) small field.

DAMAR (American) a short form of Damarcus, Damario.
Damare, Damari, Damarre, Damauri

DAMARCUS (American) a combination of the prefix Da + Marcus.
Damacus, Damar, Damarco, Damarcue, Damarick, Damark, Damarkco, Damarkis, Damarko, Damarkus, Damarques, Damarquez, Damarquis, Damarrco

DAMARIO (American) a combination of the prefix Da + Mario.
Damar, Damarea, Damareus, Damaria, Damarie, Damarino, Damarion, Damarious, Damaris, Damarius, Damarrea, Damarrion, Damarrious, Damarrius, Damaryo, Dameris, Damerius

DAMEK (Slavic) a form of Adam.
Damick, Damicke

DAMEON (Greek) an alternate form of Damian.
Damein, Dameion, Dameone

DAMETRIUS (Greek) an alternate form of Demetrius.
Dametri, Dametries, Dametrious, Damitri, Damitric, Damitrie, Damitrious, Damitrius

DAMIAN (Greek) tamer; soother.
Daemon, Daimian, Damaiaon, Damaian, Damaien, Damain, Damaine, Damaion, Damani, Damanni, Damaun, Damayon, Dame, Damean, Dameon, Damián, Damiane, Damiann, Damiano, Damianos, Damien, Damion, Damiyan, Damján, Damyan, Daymian, Dema, Demyan

DAMIEN (Greek) an alternate form of Damian. Religion: Father Damien spent his life serving the leper colony on Molokai island, Hawaii.
Daemien, Daimien, Damie, Damienne, Damyen

DAMION (Greek) an alternate form of Damian.

Damieon, Damiion, Damin, Damine, Damionne, Damiyon, Dammion, Damyon

DAMON (Greek) constant, loyal. (Latin) spirit, demon.
Daemen, Daemon, Daemond, Daimon, Daman, Damen, Damond, Damone, Damoni, Damonn, Damonni, Damonta, Damontae, Damonte, Damontez, Damontis, Damyn, Daymon, Daymond

DAN (Hebrew) a short form of Daniel. (Vietnamese) yes.
Dahn, Danh, Danne

DANA (Scandinavian) from Denmark.
Dain, Daina, Dayna

DANDIN (Hindi) holy man.

DANDRÉ (French) a combination of the prefix De + André.
D'André, Dandrae, D'andrea, Dandras, Dandray, Dandre, Dondrea

DANE (English) from Denmark. See also Halden.
Dain, Daine, Danie, Dayne, Dhane

DANEK (Polish) a form of Daniel.

DANFORTH (English) a form of Daniel.

DANIAL (Hebrew) an alternate form of Daniel.
Danal, Daneal, Danieal, Daniyal, Dannial

DANICK, Dannick (Slavic) familiar forms of Daniel.
Danek, Danieko, Danik, Danika, Danyck

DANIEL (Hebrew) God is my judge. Bible: a great Hebrew prophet. See also Danno, Kanaiela.
Dacso, Dainel, Dan, Daneel, Daneil, Danek, Danel, Danforth, Danial, Danick, Dániel, Daniël, Daniele, Danielius, Daniell, Daniels, Danielson, Danilo, Daniyel, Dan'l, Dannel, Dannick, Danniel, Dannil, Danno, Danny, Dano, Danukas, Dany, Danyel, Danyell, Daoud, Dasco, Dayne, Deniel, Doneal, Doniel, Donois, Dusan, Nelo

DANIELE (Hebrew) an alternate form of Daniel.
Danile, Danniele

DANILO (Slavic) a form of Daniel.
Danielo, Danil, Danila, Danilka, Danylo

DANIOR (Gypsy) born with teeth.

DANLADI (Hausa) born on Sunday.

DANNO (Hebrew) a familiar form of Daniel. (Japanese) gathering in the meadow.
Dannon, Dano

DANNON (American) a form of Danno.
Daenan, Daenen, Dainon, Danaan, Danen, Danon

DANNY, Dany (Hebrew) familiar forms of Daniel.
Daney, Dani, Dannee, Danney, Danni, Dannie, Dannye

DANO (Czech) a form of Daniel.
Danko, Danno

DANTE, Danté (Latin) lasting, enduring.
Danatay, Danaté, Dant, Dantae, Dantay, Dantee, Dauntay, Dauntaye, Daunté, Dauntrae, Deante, Dontae, Donté

DANTRELL (American) a combination of Dante + Darell.
Dantrel, Dantrey, Dantril, Dantyrell, Dontrell

DANYEL (Hebrew) an alternate form of Daniel.
Danya, Danyal, Danyale, Danyele, Danyell, Danyiel, Danyl, Danyle, Danylets, Danylo, Donyell

DAOUD (Arabic) a form of David.
Daudi, Daudy, Dauod, Dawud

DAQUAN (American) a combination of the prefix Da + Quan.

Daequan, Daqon, Daquain, Daquaine, Da'quan, Daquandre, Daquandrey, Daquane, Daquann, Daquantae, Daquante, Daquarius, Daquaun, Daquawn, Daquin, Daquon, Daquone, Daquwon, Daqwain, Daqwan, Daqwane, Daqwann, Daqwon, Daqwone, Dayquan, Dequain, Dequan, Dequann, Dequaun

DAR (Hebrew) pearl.

DARA (Cambodian) stars.

DARAN (Irish) an alternate form of Darren.
Darann, Darawn, Darian, Darran, Dayran, Deran

DARBY (Irish) free. (English) deer park.
Dar, Darb, Darbee, Darbey, Darbie, Derby

DARCY (Irish) dark. (French) from Arcy.
Dar, Daray, D'Aray, Darce, Darcee, Darcel, Darcey, Darcio, D'Arcy, Darsey, Darsy

DAREH (Persian) wealthy.

DARELL (English) a form of Darrell.
Darall, Daralle, Dareal, Darel, Darelle, Darral, Darrall

DAREN (Irish) an alternate form of Darren. (Hausa) born at night.
Dare, Dayren, Dheren

DARIAN, Darrian (Irish) alternative forms of Darren.
Daryan

DARICK (German) an alternate form of Derek.
Darek, Daric, Darico, Darieck, Dariek, Darik, Daryk

DARIEN, Darrien (Irish) alternative forms of Darren.

DARIN (Irish) an alternate form of Darren.
Daryn, Darynn, Dayrin, Dearin, Dharin

DARIO (Spanish) affluent.

DARION, Darrion (Irish) alternative forms of Darren.
Daryeon, Daryon

DARIUS (Greek) wealthy.
Dairus, Dare, Darieus, Darioush, Dariuse, Dariush, Dariuss, Dariusz, Darrius

DARNELL (English) hidden place.
Dar, Darn, Darnall, Darneal, Darneil, Darnel, Darnelle, Darnyell, Darnyll

DARON (Irish) an alternate form of Darren.
Daeron, Dairon, Darone, Daronn, Darroun, Dayron, Dearon, Dharon, Diron

DARRELL (French) darling, beloved; grove of oak trees.
Dare, Darel, Darell, Darral, Darrel, Darrill, Darrol, Darryl, Derrell

DARREN (Irish) great. (English) small; rocky hill.
Daran, Dare, Daren, Darian, Darien, Darin, Darion, Daron, Darran, Darrian, Darrien, Darrience, Darrin, Darrion, Darron, Darryn, Darun, Daryn, Dearron, Deren, Dereon, Derren, Derron

DARRICK (German) an alternate form of Derek.
Darrec, Darrek, Darric, Darrik, Darryk

DARRIN (Irish) an alternate form of Darren.

DARRION (Irish) an alternate form of Darren.
Dairean, Dairion, Darian, Darien, Darion, Darrian, Darrien, Darrione, Darriyun, Derrian, Derrion

DARRIUS (Greek) an alternate form of Darius.
Darreus, Darrias, Darrious, Darris, Darriuss, Darrus, Darryus, Derrious, Derris, Derrius

DARRON (Irish) an alternate form of Darren.
Darriun, Darroun

DARRYL (French) darling, beloved; grove of oak trees. An alternate form of Darrell.
Dahrll, Darryle, Darryll, Daryl, Daryle, Daryll, Derryl

DARSHAN (Hindi) god; godlike. Religion: another name for the Hindu god Shiva.
Darshaun, Darshon

DARTON (English) deer town.
Dartel, Dartrel

DARWIN (English) dear friend. History: Charles Darwin was the naturalist who established the theory of evolution.
Darvin, Darvon, Darwyn, Derwin, Derwynn, Durwin

DARYL (French) an alternate form of Darryl.
Darel, Daril, Darl, Darly, Daryell, Daryle, Daryll, Darylle, Daroyl

DASAN (Pomo) leader of the bird clan.
Dassan

DASHAWN (American) a combination of the prefix Da + Shawn.
Dasean, Dashan, Dashane, Dashante, Dashaun, Dashaunte, Dashean, Dashon, Dashonnie, Dashonte, Dashuan, Dashun, Dashwan, Dayshawn

DAUID (Swahili) a form of David.

DAULTON (English) an alternate form of Dalton.

DAVANTE (American) an alternate form of Davonte.
Davanta, Davantay, Davinte

DAVARIS (American) a combination of Dave + Darius.
Davario, Davarious, Davarius, Davarrius, Davarus

DAVE (Hebrew) a short form of David, Davis.

DAVEY (Hebrew) a familiar form of David.
Davee, Davi, Davie, Davy

DAVID (Hebrew) beloved. Bible: the
first king of Israel. See also Dov,
Havika, Kawika, Taaveti, Taffy, Tevel.
*Dabi, Daevid, Dafydd, Dai, Daivid, Daoud,
Dauid, Dav, Dave, Daved, Daveed, Daven,
Davey, Davidde, Davide, Davidek, Davido,
Davon, Davoud, Davyd, Dawid, Dawit,
Dawud, Dayvid, Dodya, Dov*

DAVIN (Scandinavian) brilliant Finn.
*Daevin, Davion, Davon, Davyn, Dawan,
Dawin, Dawine, Dayvon, Deavan, Deaven*

DAVION (American) a form of Davin.
*Davione, Davionne, Daviyon, Davyon,
Deaveon*

DAVIS (Welsh) son of David.
Dave, Davidson, Davies, Davison

DAVON (American) a form of Davin.
*Daevon, Daivon, Davon, Davone, Davonn,
Davonne, Deavon, Deavone, Devon*

DAVONTE (American) a combination
of Davon + the suffix -te.
*Davante, Davonnte, Davonta, Davontae,
Davontah, Davontai, Davontay, Davontaye,
Davontea, Davontee, Davonti*

DAWAN (American) a form of Davin.
*Dawann, Dawante, Dawaun, Dawayne,
Dawon, Dawone, Dawoon, Dawyne, Dawyun*

DAWIT (Ethiopian) a form of David.

DAWSON (English) son of David.
Dawsyn

DAX (French, English) water.

DAYLON (American) a form of Dillon.
Daylan, Daylen, Daylin, Daylun, Daylyn

DAYMIAN (Greek) an alternate form
of Damian.
*Daymayne, Daymen, Daymeon, Daymiane,
Daymien, Daymin, Dayminn, Daymion,
Daymn*

DAYNE (Scandinavian) a form of Dane.
Dayn

DAYQUAN (American) an alternate
form of of Daquan.
Dayquain, Dayquawane, Dayquin, Dayqwan

DAYSHAWN (American) an alternate
form of of Dashawn.
*Daysean, Daysen, Dayshaun, Dayshon,
Dayson*

DAYTON (English) day town; bright,
sunny town.
*Daeton, Daiton, Daythan, Daython,
Daytona, Daytonn, Deyton*

DAYVON (American) a form of Davin.
*Dayven, Dayveon, Dayvin, Dayvion,
Dayvonn*

DE (Chinese) virtuous.

DEACON (Greek) one who serves.
Deke

DEAN (French) leader. (English) valley.
See also Dino.
Deane, Deen, Dene, Deyn, Deyne

DEANDRE (French) a combination of
the prefix De + André.
*D'andre, D'andré, D'André, D'andrea,
Deandra, Deandrae, Déandre, Deandré,
De André, Deandrea, De Andrea, Deandres,
Deandrey, Deaundera, Deaundra, Deaundray,
Deaundre, De Aundre, Deaundrey, Deaundry,
Deondre, Diandre, Dondre*

DEANGELO (Italian) a combination
of the prefix De + Angelo.
*Dang, Dangelo, D'Angelo, Danglo, Deaengelo,
Deangelio, Deangello, Déangelo, De Angelo,
Deangilio, Deangleo, Deanglo, Deangulo,
Diangelo, Di'angelo*

DEANTE (Latin) an alternate form of
Dante.
*Deanta, Deantai, Deantay, Deanté, De Anté,
Deanteé, Deaunta, Diantae, Diante, Diantey*

DEANTHONY (Italian) a combination of the prefix De + Anthony.
D'anthony, Danton, Dianthony

DEARBORN (English) deer brook.
Dearbourn, Dearburne, Deaurburn, Deerborn

DECARLOS (Spanish) a combination of the prefix De + Carlos.
Dacarlos, Decarlo, Di'carlos

DECHA (Tai) strong.

DECIMUS (Latin) tenth.

DECLAN (Irish) man of prayer. Religion: Saint Declan was a fifth-century Irish bishop.
Deklan

DEDRICK (German) ruler of the people. See also Derek, Theodoric.
Deadrick, Deddrick, Dederick, Dedrek, Dedreko, Dedric, Dedrix, Dedrrick, Deedrick, Diedrich, Diedrick, Dietrich, Detrick

DEEMS (English) judge's child.

DEION (Greek) an alternate form of Dion.
Deione, Deionta, Deionte

DEJUAN (American) a combination of the prefix De + Juan. See also Dajuan.
Dejan, Dejon, Dejuane, Dejun, Dewan, Dewaun, Dewon, Dijaun, Djuan, D'Juan, Dujuan, Dujuane, D'Won

DEKEL (Hebrew, Arabic) palm tree, date tree.

DEKOTA (Dakota) an alternate form of Dakota.
Decoda, Dekoda, Dekodda, Dekotes

DEL (English) a short form of Delbert, Delvin, Delwin.

DELANEY (Irish) descendant of the challenger.
Delaine, Delainey, Delainy, Delan, Delane, Delanny, Delany

DELANO (French) nut tree. (Irish) dark.
Delanio, Delayno, Dellano

DELBERT (English) bright as day. See also Dalbert.
Bert, Del, Dilbert

DELFINO (Latin) dolphin.
Delfine

DÉLÌ (Chinese) virtuous.

DELL (English) small valley. A short form of Udell.

DELLING (Scandinavian) scintillating.

DELMAR (Latin) sea.
Dalmar, Dalmer, Delmare, Delmario, Delmarr, Delmer, Delmor, Delmore

DELON (American) a form of Dillon.
Deloin, Delone, Deloni, Delonne

DELROY (French) belonging to the king. See also Elroy, Leroy.
Delray, Delree, Delroi

DELSHAWN (American) a combination of Del + Shawn.
Delsean, Delshon, Delsin, Delson

DELSIN (Native American) he is so.
Delsy

DELTON (English) an alternate form of Dalton.
Delten, Deltyn

DELVIN (English) proud friend; friend from the valley.
Dalvin, Del, Delavan, Delvian, Delvon, Delvyn, Delwin

DELWIN (English) an alternate form of Delvin.
Dalwin, Dalwyn, Del, Dellwin, Dellwyn, Delwyn, Delwynn

DEMAN (Dutch) man.

DEMARCO (Italian) a combination of the prefix De + Marco.
Damarco, Demarcco, Demarceo, Demarcio, Demarkco, Demarkeo, Demarko, Demarquo, D'Marco

DEMARCUS (American) a combination of the prefix De + Marcus.
Damarcius, Damarcus, Demarces, Demarcis, Demarcius, Demarcos, Demarcuse, Demarkes, Demarkis, Demarkos, Demarkus, Demarqus, D'Marcus

DEMARIO (Italian) a combination of the prefix De + Mario.
Demarea, Demaree, Demareo, Demari, Demaria, Demariea, Demarion, Demarreio, Demariez, Demarious, Demaris, Demariuz, Demarrio, Demerio, Demerrio

DEMARIUS (American) a combination of the prefix De + Marius.

DEMARQUIS (American) a combination of the prefix De + Marquis.
Demarques, Demarquez, Demarqui

DEMBE (Luganda) peaceful.
Damba

DEMETRI, Demitri (Greek) short forms of Demetrius.
Dametri, Damitré, Demeter, Demetre, Demetrea, Demetriel, Demitre, Demitrie, Domotor

DEMETRIS (Greek) a short form of Demetrius.
Demeatric, Demeatrice, Demeatris, Demetres, Demetress, Demetric, Demetrice, Demetrick, Demetrics, Demetricus, Demetrik, Demitrez, Demitries, Demitris

DEMETRIUS (Greek) lover of the earth. Mythology: a follower of Demeter, the goddess of the harvest and fertility. See also Dimitri, Mimis, Mitsos.
Dametrius, Demeitrius, Demeterious, Demetreus, Demetri, Demetrias, Demetrio, Demetrios, Demetrious, Demetris, Demetriu, Demetrium, Demetrois, Demetruis, Demetrus, Demitirus, Demitri, Demitrias, Demitriu, Demitrius, Demitrus, Demtrius, Demtrus, Dimitri, Dimitrios, Dimitrius, Dmetrius, Dymek

DEMICHAEL (American) a combination of the prefix De + Michael.
Dumichael

DEMOND (Irish) a short form of Desmond.
Demonde, Demonds, Demone, Dumonde

DEMONT (French) mountain.
Démont, Demonta, Demontae, Demontay, Demontaz, Demonte, Demontez, Demontre

DEMORRIS (American) a combination of the prefix De + Morris.
Demoris, DeMorris, Demorus

DEMOS (Greek) people.
Demas, Demosthenes

DEMOTHI (Native American) talks while walking.

DEMPSEY (Irish) proud.
Demp, Demps, Dempsie, Dempsy

DEMPSTER (English) one who judges.
Demster

DENBY (Scandinavian) Geography: a Danish village.
Danby, Den, Denbey, Denney, Dennie, Denny

DENHAM (English) village in the valley.

DENHOLM (Scottish) Geography: a town in Scotland.

DENIS (Greek) an alternate form of Dennis.
Denise, Deniz

DENLEY (English) meadow; valley.
Denlie, Denly

DENMAN (English) man from the valley.

DENNIS (Greek) Mythology: a follower of Dionysius, the god of wine. See also Dion, Nicho.
Den, Dénes, Denies, Denis, Deniz, Dennes, Dennet, Dennez, Denny, Dennys, Denya, Denys, Deon, Dinis

DENNISON (English) son of Dennis. See also Dyson, Tennyson.
Den, Denison, Denisson, Dennyson

DENNY (Greek) a familiar form of Dennis.
Den, Denney, Dennie, Deny

DENTON (English) happy home.
Dent, Denten, Dentin

DENVER (English) green valley. Geography: the capital of Colorado.

DENZEL (Cornish) an alternate form of Denzil.
Danzel, Danzell, Dennzel, Denzal, Denzale, Denzall, Denzell, Denzelle, Denzle, Denzsel

DENZIL (Cornish) Geography: a location in Cornwall, England.
Dennzil, Dennzyl, Denzel, Denzial, Denziel, Denzill, Denzyel, Denzyl, Donzell

DEON (Greek) an alternate form of Dennis. See also Dion.
Deion, Deone, Deonn, Deonno

DEONDRE (French) an alternate form of Deandre.
Deiondray, Deiondre, Deondra, Deondrae, Deondray, Deondré, Deondrea, Deondree, Deondrei, Deondrey, Diondra, Diondrae, Diondre, Diondrey

DEONTAE (American) a combination of the prefix De + Dontae.
Deonta, Deontai, Deontay, Deontaye, Deonte, Deonté, Deontea, Deonteya, Deonteye, Deontia, Deontre, Dionte

DEONTE, Deonté (American) alternate forms of Deontae.
D'Ante, Deante, Deontée, Deontie

DEONTRE (American) alternate forms of Deontae.
Deontrae, Deontrais, Deontray, Deontrea, Deontrey, Deontrez, Deontreze, Deontrus

DEQUAN (American) a combination of the prefix De + Quan.
Dequain, Dequane, Dequann, Dequante, Dequantez, Dequantis, Dequaun, Dequavius, Dequawn, Dequian, Dequin, Dequine, Dequinn, Dequion, Dequoin, Dequon, Deqwan, Deqwon, Deqwone

DERECK, Derick (German) alternate forms of Derek.
Derekk, Dericka, Derico, Deriek, Derique, Deryck, Deryk, Deryke, Detrek

DEREK (German) ruler of the people. A short form of Theodoric. See also Dedrick, Dirk.
Darek, Darick, Darrick, Derak, Dereck, Derecke, Derele, Deric, Derick, Derik, Derk, Derke, Derrek, Derrick, Deryek

DERIC, Derik (German) alternate forms of Derek.
Deriek, Derikk

DERMOT (Hebrew) a short form of Jeremiah. (Irish) free from envy. (English) free. See also Kermit.
Der, Dermod, Dermott, Diarmid, Diarmuid

DERON (Hebrew) bird; freedom. (American) a combination of the prefix De + Ron.
Daaron, Daron, Da-Ron, Darone, Darron, Dayron, Dereon, Deronn, Deronne, Derrin, Derrion, Derron, Derronn, Derronne, Derryn, Diron, Duron, Durron, Dyron

DEROR (Hebrew) lover of freedom.
Derori, Derorie

DERREK (German) an alternate form of Derek.
Derrec, Derreck

DERRELL (French) an alternate form of Darrell.
Derel, Derele, Derell, Derelle, Derrel, Dérrell, Derriel, Derril, Derrill, Deryl, Deryll

DERREN (Irish) great. An alternate form of Darren.
Deren, Derran, Derraun, Derreon, Derrian, Derrien, Derrin, Derrion, Derron, Derryn, Deryan, Deryn, Deryon

DERRICK (German) ruler of the people. An alternate form of Derek.
Derric, Derrik, Derryck, Derryk

DERRY (Irish) redhead. Geography: a city in Northern Ireland.
Darrie, Darry, Derri, Derrie, Derrye, Dery

DERRYL (French) an alternate form of Darryl.
Deryl, Deryll

DERWARD (English) deer keeper.

DERWIN (English) an alternate form of Darwin.
Derwyn

DESEAN (American) a combination of the prefix De + Sean.
Dasean, D'Sean, Dusean

DESHANE (American) a combination of the prefix De + Shane.
Deshan, Deshayne

DESHAUN (American) a combination of the prefix De + Shaun.
Deshan, Deshane, Deshann, Deshaon, Deshaune, D'shaun, D'Shaun, Dushaun

DESHAWN (American) a combination of the prefix De + Shawn.
Dashaun, Dashawn, Deshauwn, Deshawan, Deshawon, Deshon, D'shawn, D'Shawn, Dushan, Dushawn

DESHEA (American) a combination of the prefix De + Shea.
Deshay

DÉSHÌ (Chinese) virtuous.

DESHON (American) an alternate form of Deshawn.
Deshondre, Deshone, Deshonn, Deshonte, Deshun, Deshunn

DESIDERIO (Spanish) desired.

DESMOND (Irish) from south Munster.
Demond, Des, Desi, Desimon, Desman, Desmand, Desmane, Desmen, Desmine, Desmon, Desmound, Desmund, Desmyn, Dezmon, Dezmond

DESTIN (French) destiny, fate.
Destan, Desten, Destine, Deston, Destry, Destyn

DESTRY (American) a form of Destin.
Destrey, Destrie

DETRICK (German) an alternate form of Dedrick.
Detrek, Detric, Detrich, Detrik, Detrix

DEVAN (Irish) an alternate form of Devin.
Devaan, Devain, Devane, Devann, Devean, Devun, Diwan

DEVANTE (American) a combination of Devan + the suffix -te.
Devanta, Devantae, Devantay, Devanté, Devantée, Devantez, Devanty, Devaughntae, Devaughnte, Devaunte, Deventae, Deventay, Devente, Divante

DEVAUGHN (American) a form of Devin.
Devaugh, Devaun

DEVAYNE (American) an alternate form of Dewayne.
Devain, Devaine, Devan, Devane, Devayn, Devein, Deveion

DEVEN (Hindi) for God. (Irish) an alternate form of Devin.
Deaven, Deiven, Devein, Devenn, Devven, Diven

DEVERELL (English) riverbank.

DEVIN (Irish) poet.
Deavin, Deivin, Dev, Devan, Devaughn, Deven, Devlyn, Devon, Devvin, Devy, Devyn, Dyvon

DEVINE (Latin) divine. (Irish) ox.
Davon, Devinn, Devon, Devyn, Devyne, Dewine

DEVLIN (Irish) brave, fierce.
Dev, Devlan, Devland, Devlen, Devlon, Devlyn

DEVON (Irish) an alternate form of Devin.
Deavon, Deivon, Deivone, Deivonne, Deveon, Deveone, Devion, Devoen, Devohn, Devonae, Devone, Devoni, Devonio, Devonn, Devonne, Devontaine, Devvon, Devvonne, Dewon, Dewone, Divon, Diwon

DEVONTA (American) a combination of Devon + the suffix -ta.
Deveonta, Devonnta, Devonntae, Devontae, Devontai, Devontay, Devontaye

DEVONTE (American) a combination of Devon + the suffix -te.
Deveonte, Devionte, Devonté, Devontea, Devontee, Devonti, Devontia, Devontre

DEVYN (Irish) an alternate form of Devin.
Devyin, Devynn, Devynne

DEWAYNE (Irish) an alternate form of Dwayne. (American) a combination of the prefix De + Wayne.
Deuwayne, Devayne, Dewain, Dewaine, Dewan, Dewane, Dewaun, Dewaune, Dewayen, Dewean, Dewon, Dewune

DEWEI (Chinese) highly virtuous.

DEWEY (Welsh) prized.
Dew, Dewi, Dewie

DEWITT (Flemish) blond.
Dewitt, Dwight, Wit

DEXTER (Latin) dexterous, adroit. (English) fabric dyer.
Daxter, Decca, Deck, Decka, Dekka, Dex, Dextar, Dextor, Dextrel, Dextron

DEZMON, Dezmond (Irish) alternate forms of Desmond.
Dezman, Dezmand, Dezmen, Dezmin

DIAMOND (English) brilliant gem; bright guardian.
Diaman, Diamanta, Diamante, Diamend, Diamenn, Diamont, Diamonta, Diamonte, Diamund, Dimond, Dimonta, Dimontae, Dimonte

DICK (German) a short form of Frederick, Richard.
Dic, Dicken, Dickens, Dickie, Dickon, Dicky, Dik

DICKRAN (Armenian) History: an ancient Armenian king.
Dicran, Dikran

DICKSON (English) son of Dick.
Dickenson, Dickerson, Dikerson, Diksan

DIDI (Hebrew) a familiar form of Jedidiah, Yedidyah.

DIDIER (French) desired, longed for. A masculine form of Desiree.

DIEDRICH (German) an alternate form of Dedrick, Dietrich.
Didrich, Didrick, Didrik, Diederick

DIEGO (Spanish) a form of Jacob, James.
Iago, Diaz, Jago

DIETBALD (German) an alternate form of Theobald.
Dietbalt, Dietbolt

DIETER (German) army of the people.
Deiter

DIETRICH (German) an alternate form of Dedrick.
Deitrich, Deitrick, Deke, Diedrich, Dietrick, Dierck, Dieter, Dieterich, Dieterick, Dietz

DIGBY (Irish) ditch town; dike town.

DILLAN (Irish) an alternate form of Dillon.
Dilan, Dillian, Dilun, Dilyan

DILLON (Irish) loyal, faithful. See also Dylan.
Daylon, Delon, Dil, Dill, Dillan, Dillen, Dillie, Dillin, Dillion, Dilly, Dillyn, Dilon, Dilyn, Dilynn

DILWYN (Welsh) shady place.
Dillwyn

DIMA (Russian) a familiar form of Vladimir.
Dimka

DIMITRI (Russian) a form of Demetrius.
Dimetra, Dimetri, Dimetric, Dimetrie, Dimitr, Dimitric, Dimitrie, Dimitrik, Dimitris, Dimitry, Dimmy, Dmitri, Dymitr, Dymitry

DIMITRIOS (Greek) an alternate form of Demetrius.
Dhimitrios, Dimitrius, Dimos, Dmitrios

DIMITRIUS (Greek) an alternate form of Demetrius.
Dimetrius, Dimitricus, Dimitrius, Dimetrus, Dmitrius

DINGBANG (Chinese) protector of the country.

DINH (Vietnamese) calm, peaceful.
Din

DINO (German) little sword. (Italian) a form of Dean.
Deano

DINOS (Greek) a familiar form of Constantine, Konstantin.

DINSMORE (Irish) fortified hill.
Dinnie, Dinny, Dinse

DIOGENES (Greek) honest. History: an ancient philosopher who searched the streets for an honest man.
Diogenese

DION (Greek) a short form of Dennis, Dionysus.
Deion, Deon, Dio, Dione, Dionigi, Dionis, Dionn, Dionne, Diontae, Dionte, Diontray

DIONTE (American) an alternate form of Deontae.
Diante, Dionta, Diontae, Diontay, Diontaye, Dionté, Diontea

DIONYSUS (Greek) celebration. Mythology: the god of wine.
Dion, Dionesios, Dionicio, Dionisio, Dionisios, Dionusios, Dionysios, Dionysius, Dunixi

DIQUAN (American) a combination of the prefix Di + Quan.
Diqawan, Diqawn, Diquane

DIRK (German) a short form of Derek, Theodoric.
Derk, Dirck, Dirke, Durc, Durk, Dyrk

DIXON (English) son of Dick.
Dickson, Dix

DMITRI (Russian) an alternate form of Dimitri.
Dmetriy, Dmitiri, Dmitri, Dmitrik, Dmitriy

DOANE (English) low, rolling hills.
Doan

DOB (English) a familiar form of Robert.
Dobie

DOBRY (Polish) good.

DOHERTY (Irish) harmful.
Docherty, Dougherty, Douherty

DOLAN (Irish) dark haired.
Dolin, Dolyn

DOLF, Dolph (German) short forms of Adolf, Adolph, Rudolf, Rudolph.
Dolfe, Dolfi, Dolphe, Dolphus

DOM (Latin) a short form of Dominic.
Dome, Domó

DOMENIC (Latin) an alternte form of Dominic.
Domanick, Domenick

DOMENICO (Italian) a form of Dominic.
Domenic, Domicio, Dominico, Menico

DOMINGO (Spanish) born on Sunday. See also Mingo.
Demingo, Domingos

DOMINIC (Latin) belonging to the Lord. See also Chuminga.
Deco, Demenico, Dom, Domanic, Domeka, Domenic, Domenico, Domini, Dominie, Dominik, Dominique, Dominitric, Dominy, Domminic, Domnenique, Domokos, Domonic, Nick

DOMINICK (Latin) an alternate form of Dominic.
Domiku, Domineck, Dominick, Dominicke, Dominiek, Dominik, Dominnick, Dominyck, Domminick, Dommonick, Domnick, Domokos, Domonick, Donek, Dumin

DOMINIK (Latin) an alternte form of Dominic.
Domenik, Dominiko, Dominyk, Domonik

DOMINIQUE (French) a form of Dominic.
Domeniq, Domeniqu, Domenique, Domenque, Dominiqu, Dominque, Dominiqueia, Domnenique, Domnique, Domoniqu, Domonique, Domunique

DOMOKOS (Hungarian) a form of Dominic.
Dedo, Dome, Domek, Domok, Domonkos

DON (Scottish) a short form of Donald. See also Kona.
Donn

DONAHUE (Irish) dark warrior.
Donohoe, Donohue

DONAL (Irish) a form of Donald.

DONALD (Scottish) world leader; proud ruler. See also Bohdan, Tauno.
Don, Donal, Dónal, Donaldo, Donall, Donalt, Donát, Donaugh, Donnie

DONATIEN (French) gift.
Donathan, Donathon

DONATO (Italian) gift.
Dodek, Donatello, Donati, Donatien, Donatus

DONAVAN (Irish) an alternate form of Donovan.
Donaven, Donavin, Donavon, Donavyn

DONDRE (French) an alternate form of Deandre.
Dondra, Dondrae, Dondray, Dondré, Dondrea

DONG (Vietnamese) easterner.
Duong

DONKOR (Akan) humble.

DONNELL (Irish) brave; dark.
Doneal, Donel, Donele, Donell, Donelle, Donnel, Donnele, Donnelly, Doniel, Donielle, Donnel, Donnelle, Donniel, Donyel, Donyell

DONNELLY (Irish) an alternate form of Donnell.
Donelly, Donlee, Donley

DONNIE, Donny (Irish) familiar forms of Donald.

DONOVAN (Irish) dark warrior.
Dohnovan, Donavan, Donevan, Donevon, Donivan, Donnivan, Donnovan, Donnoven, Donoven, Donovin, Donovon, Donvan

DONTAE, Donté (American) forms of Dante.
Donta, Dontai, Dontao, Dontate, Dontavious, Dontavius, Dontay, Dontaye, Dontea, Dontee, Dontez

DONTRELL (American) an alternate form of Dantrell.

Dontral, Dontrall, Dontray, Dontre,
Dontreal, Dontrel, Dontrelle, Dontriel,
Dontriell

DONZELL (Cornish) an alternate form
of Denzil.
Donzeil, Donzel, Donzelle, Donzello

DOOLEY (Irish) dark hero.
Dooly

DOR (Hebrew) generation.

DORAN (Greek, Hebrew) gift. (Irish)
stranger; exile.
Dore, Dorin, Dorran, Doron, Dorren, Dory

DORIAN (Greek) from Doris, Greece.
See also Isidore.
Dore, Dorey, Dorie, Dorien, Dorin, Dorion,
Dorján, Doron, Dorrian, Dorrien, Dorrin,
Dorrion, Dorron, Dorryen, Dory

DORRELL (Scottish) king's doorkeeper.
See also Durell.
Dorrel, Dorrelle

DOTAN (Hebrew) law.
Dothan

DOUG (Scottish) a short form of Dougal,
Douglas.
Dougie, Dougy, Dugey, Dugie, Dugy

DOUGAL (Scottish) dark stranger.
See also Doyle.
Doug, Dougall, Dugal, Dugald, Dugall,
Dughall

DOUGLAS (Scottish) dark river, dark
stream. See also Koukalaka.
Doug, Douglass, Dougles, Dugaid, Dughlas

DOV (Hebrew) a familiar form of David.
(Yiddish) bear.
Dovid, Dovidas, Dowid

DOVEV (Hebrew) whisper.

DOW (Irish) dark haired.

DOYLE (Irish) a form of Dougal.
Doy, Doyal, Doyel

DRAGO (Italian) a form of Drake.

DRAKE (English) dragon; owner of the
inn with the dragon trademark.
Drago

DRAPER (English) fabric maker.
Dray, Draypr

DRAVEN (American) a combination
of the letter D + Raven.
Dravian, Dravin, Dravion, Dravon,
Dravone, Dravyn, Drayven, Drevon

DRENG (Norwegian) hired hand; brave.

DRESHAWN (American) a
combination of Drew + Shawn.
Dreshaun, Dreshon, Dreshown

DREVON (American) an alternate form
of Draven.
Drevan, Drevaun, Dreven, Drevin, Drevion,
Drevone

DREW (Welsh) wise. (English) a short
form of Andrew.
Drewe, Dru

DRU (English) an alternate form of
Drew.
Druan, Drud, Drue, Drugi, Drui

DRUMMOND (Scottish) druid's
mountain.
Drummund, Drumond, Drumund

DRURY (French) loving. Geography:
Drury Lane is a street in London's
theater district. Literature: according
to a nursery rhyme, Drury Lane is
where the Muffin Man lives.

DRYDEN (English) dry valley.
Dry

DUANE (Irish) an alternate form of
Dwayne.
Deune, Duain, Duaine, Duana

DUARTE (Portuguese) rich guard.
See also Edward.

DUC (Vietnamese) moral.
Duoc, Duy

DUDD (English) a short form of Dudley.
Dud, Dudde, Duddy

DUDLEY (English) common field.
Dudd, Dudly

DUER (Scottish) heroic.

DUFF (Scottish) dark.
Duffey, Duffie, Duffy

DUGAN (Irish) dark.
Doogan, Dougan, Douggan, Duggan

DUKE (French) leader; duke.
Dukey, Dukie, Duky

DUKKER (Gypsy) fortuneteller.

DULANI (Ngoni) cutting.

DUMAKA (Ibo) helping hand.

DUMAN (Turkish) misty, smoky.

DUNCAN (Scottish) brown warrior. Literature: King Duncan was MacBeth's victim in Shakespeare's play *MacBeth*.
Dunc, Dunn

DUNHAM (Scottish) brown.

DUNIXI (Basque) a form of Dionysus.

DUNLEY (English) hilly meadow.

DUNLOP (Scottish) muddy hill.

DUNMORE (Scottish) fortress on the hill.

DUNN (Scottish) a short form of Duncan.
Dun, Dune, Dunne

DUNSTAN (English) brown-stone fortress.
Dun, Dunston

DUNTON (English) hill town.

DUR (Hebrew) stacked up.

DURAND (Latin) an alternate form of Durant.

DURANT (Latin) enduring.
Duran, Durance, Durand, Durante, Durontae, Durrant

DURELL (Scottish, English) king's doorkeeper. See also Dorrell.
Durel, Durial, Durreil, Durrell, Durrelle

DURKO (Czech) a form of George.

DURRIKEN (Gypsy) fortuneteller.

DURRIL (Gypsy) gooseberry.
Durrel, Durrell

DURWARD (English) gatekeeper.
Dur, Ward

DURWIN (English) an alternate form of Darwin.

DUSHAWN (American) a combination of the prefix Du + Shawn.
Dusan, Dusean, Dushan, Dushane, Dushaun, Dushon, Dushun

DUSTIN (German) valiant fighter. (English) brown rock quarry.
Dust, Dustain, Dustan, Dusten, Dustie, Dustine, Dustion, Duston, Dusty, Dustyn, Dustynn

DUSTY (English) a familiar form of Dustin.

DUSTYN (English) an alternate form of Dustin.

DUTCH (Dutch) from the Netherlands; from Germany.

DUVAL (French) a combination of the prefix Du + Val.
Duvall, Duveuil

DWAUN (American) an alternate form of Dajuan.
Dwan, Dwaunn, Dwawn, Dwon, Dwuann

DWAYNE (Irish) dark. See also Dewayne.
Dawayne, Dawyne, Duane, Duwain, Duwan, Duwane, Duwayn, Duwayne, Dwain, Dwaine, Dwan, Dwane, Dwyane, Dywan, Dywane, Dywayne, Dywone

DWIGHT (English) a form of DeWitt.

DYAMI (Native American) soaring eagle.

DYER (English) fabric dyer.

DYKE (English) dike; ditch.
Dike

DYLAN (Welsh) sea. See also Dillon.
Dylane, Dylann, Dylen, Dylian, Dylin, Dyllan, Dyllen, Dyllian, Dyllin, Dyllyn, Dylon, Dylyn

DYLON (Welsh) an alternate form of Dylan.
Dyllion, Dyllon

DYRE (Norwegian) dear heart.

DYSON (English) a short form of Dennison.
Dysen, Dysonn

E

EA (Irish) a form of Hugh.

EACHAN (Irish) horseman.

EAGAN (Irish) very mighty.
Egan, Egon

EAMON (Irish) a form of Edmond, Edmund.
Aimon, Eammon, Eamonn

EAN (English) a form of Ian.
Eaen, Eann, Eayon, Eion, Eon, Eyan, Eyon

EARL (Irish) pledge. (English) nobleman.
Airle, Earld, Earle, Earlie, Earlson, Early, Eorl, Erl, Erle, Errol

EARNEST (English) an alternate form of Ernest.
Earn, Earnesto, Earnie, Eranest

EASTON (English) eastern town.
Eason, Easten, Eastin, Eastton

EATON (English) estate on the river.
Eatton, Eton, Eyton

EB (Hebrew) a short form of Ebenezer.
Ebb, Ebbie, Ebby

EBEN (Hebrew) rock.
Eban, Ebin, Ebon

EBENEZER (Hebrew) foundation stone. Literature: Ebenezer Scrooge is a character in Charles Dickens's *A Christmas Carol.*
Eb, Ebbaneza, Eben, Ebeneezer, Ebeneser, Ebenezar, Eveneser

EBERHARD (German) courageous as a boar. See also Everett.
Eber, Ebere, Eberardo, Eberhardt, Evard, Everard, Everardo, Everhardt, Everhart

EBNER (English) a form of Abner.

EBO (Fante) born on Tuesday.

ED (English) a short form of Edgar, Edsel, Edward.
Edd

EDAN (Scottish) fire.
Edain

EDBERT (English) wealthy; bright.
Ediberto

EDDIE (English) a familiar form of Edgar, Edsel, Edward.
Eddee, Eddy, Edi, Edie

EDDY (English) an alternate form of
Eddie.
Eddye, Edy

EDEL (German) noble.
Adel, Edell, Edelmar, Edelweiss

EDEN (Hebrew) delightful. Bible: the
earthly paradise.
*Eaden, Eadin, Edan, Edenson, Edin, Edyn,
Eiden*

EDER (Hebrew) flock.
Ederick, Edir

EDGAR (English) successful spearman.
See also Garek, Gerik, Medgar.
Ed, Eddie, Edek, Edgard, Edgardo, Edgars

EDGARDO (Spanish) a form of Edgar.

EDISON (English) son of Edward.
Eddison, Edisen, Edson

EDMOND (English) an alternate form
of Edmund.
*Eamon, Edmon, Edmonde, Edmondo,
Edmondson, Esmond*

EDMUND (English) prosperous
protector.
*Eadmund, Eamon, Edmand, Edmaund,
Edmond, Edmun, Edmundo, Edmunds*

EDMUNDO (Spanish) a form of
Edmund.
Edmando, Mundo

EDO (Czech) a form of Edward.

EDOARDO (Italian) a form of Edward.

EDORTA (Basque) a form of Edward.

EDOUARD (French) a form of Edward.
Édoard, Édouard

EDRIC (English) prosperous ruler.
*Eddric, Eddrick, Ederick, Edrek, Edrice,
Edrick, Edrico*

EDSEL (English) rich man's house.
Ed, Eddie, Edsell

EDSON (English) a short form of
Edison.
Eddson, Edsen

EDUARDO (Spanish) a form of
Edward.
Estuardo, Estvardo

EDUR (Basque) snow.

EDWARD (English) prosperous
guardian. See also Audie, Duarte,
Ekewaka, Ned, Ted, Teddy.
*Ed, Eddie, Edik, Edko, Edo, Edoardo, Edorta,
Édouard, Eduard, Eduardo, Edus, Edvard,
Edvardo, Edwardo, Edwards, Edwy, Edzio,
Ekewaka, Etzio, Ewart*

EDWIN (English) prosperous friend.
See also Ned, Ted.
*Eadwinn, Edik, Edlin, Eduino, Edwan,
Edwen, Edwon, Edwyn*

EFRAIN (Hebrew) fruitful.
*Efran, Efrane, Efrayin, Efren, Efrian,
Eifraine*

EFRAT (Hebrew) honored.

EFREM (Hebrew) a short form of
Ephraim.
Efe, Efraim, Efrim, Efrum

EFREN (Hebrew) an alternate form
of Efrain.

EGAN (Irish) ardent, fiery.
Egann, Egen, Egon

EGBERT (English) bright sword.
See also Bert, Bertie.

EGERTON (English) Edgar's town.
Edgarton, Edgartown, Edgerton, Egeton

EGIL (Norwegian) awe inspiring.
Eigil

EGINHARD (German) power of the
sword.
Eginhardt, Einhard, Einhardt, Enno

EGON (German) formidable.

EGOR (Russian) a form of George. See also Igor, Yegor.

EHREN (German) honorable.

EIKKI (Finnish) ever-powerful.

EINAR (Scandinavian) individualist.
Ejnar, Inar

EION (Irish) a form of Ean, Ian.
Eann, Eian, Ein, Eine, Einn

EITAN (Hebrew) an alternate form of Ethan.
Eita, Eithan, Eiton

EJAU (Ateso) we have received.

EKEWAKA (Hawaiian) a form of Edward.

EKON (Nigerian) strong.

ELAM (Hebrew) highlands.

ELAN (Hebrew) tree. (Native American) friendly.
Elann

ELBERT (English) a form of Albert.
Elberto

ELCHANAN (Hebrew) an alternate form of John.
Elchan, Elchonon, Elhanan, Elhannan

ELDEN (English) an alternate form of Alden, Aldous.
Eldan, Eldin

ELDER (English) dweller near the elder trees.

ELDON (English) holy hill.

ELDRED (English) an alternate form of Aldred.
Eldrid

ELDRIDGE (English) an alternate form of Aldrich.
El, Eldred, Eldredge, Eldrege, Eldrid, Eldrige, Elric

ELDWIN (English) an alternate form of Aldwin.
Eldwinn, Eldwyn, Eldwynn

ELEAZAR (Hebrew) God has helped. See also Lazarus.
Elazar, Elazaro, Eleasar, Eléazar, Eliazar, Eliezer

ELEK (Hungarian) a form of Alec, Alex.
Elec, Elic, Elik

ELGER (German) an alternate form of Alger.
Elger, Ellgar, Ellger

ELGIN (English) noble; white.
Elgan, Elgen

ELI (Hebrew) uplifted. A short form of Elijah, Elisha. Bible: the high priest who trained the prophet Samuel. See also Elliot.
Elie, Elier, Ellie, Eloi, Eloy, Ely

ELIA (Zuni) a short form of Elijah.
Eliah, Elio, Eliya, Elya

ELIAN (English) a form of Elijah. See also Trevelyan.
Elion

ELIAS (Greek) a form of Elijah.
Elia, Eliasz, Elice, Eliyas, Ellias, Ellice, Ellis, Elyas, Elyes

ELIAZAR (Hebrew) an alternate form of Eleazar.
Eliasar, Eliazer, Elizar, Elizardo

ELIE (Hebrew) an alternate form of Eli.

ELIEZER (Hebrew) an alternate form of Eleazar.
Elieser

ELIHU (Hebrew) a short form of Eliyahu.
Elih, Eliu, Ellihu

ELIJAH (Hebrew) the Lord is my God. An alternate form of Eliyahu. Bible: a great Hebrew prophet. See also Eli, Elliot, Elisha, Ilias, Ilya.
El, Elia, Elian, Elias, Elija, Elijha, Elijiah, Elijio, Elijuah, Elijuo, Elisjsha, Eliya, Eliyah, Ellis

ELIKA (Hawaiian) a form of Eric.

ELISEO (Hebrew) an alternate form of Elisha.
Elisee, Elisée, Elisei, Elisiah, Elisio

ELISHA (Hebrew) God is my salvation. Bible: a great Hebrew prophet, successor to Elijah. See also Eli, Elijah.
Elijsha, Eliseo, Elish, Elishah, Elisher, Elishia, Elishua, Elysha, Lisha

ELIYAHU (Hebrew) the Lord is my God. The original form of Elijah.
Eliyahou, Elihu

ELKAN (Hebrew) God is jealous.
Elkana, Elkanah, Elkin, Elkins

ELKI (Moquelumnan) hanging over the top.

ELLARD (German) sacred; brave.
Allard, Ellerd

ELLERY (English) elder tree island.
Ellary, Ellerey

ELLIOT, Elliott (English) forms of Eli, Elijah.
Elio, Eliot, Eliott, Eliud, Eliut, Elliotte, Elyot, Elyott

ELLIS (English) a form of Elias.
Elis

ELLISON (English) son of Ellis.
Elison, Ellson, Ellyson, Elson

ELLSWORTH (English) nobleman's estate.
Ellswerth, Elsworth

ELMAN (German) like an elm tree.
Elmen

ELMER (English) noble; famous.
Aylmer, Elemér, Ellmer, Elmir, Elmo

ELMO (Latin) a familiar form of Anselm. (Greek) lovable, friendly. (Italian) guardian. (English) an alternate form of Elmer.

ELMORE (English) moor where the elm trees grow.

ELONZO (Spanish) an alternate form of Alonzo.
Elon, Élon, Elonso

ELOY (Latin) chosen.
Eloi

ELRAD (Hebrew) God rules.
Rad, Radd

ELROY (French) an alternate form of Delroy, Leroy.
Elroi

ELSDON (English) nobleman's hill.

ELSTON (English) noble's town.
Ellston

ELSU (Native American) swooping, soaring falcon.

ELSWORTH (English) noble's estate.

ELTON (English) old town.
Alton, Eldon, Ellton, Elthon, Eltonia

ELVERN (Latin) an alternate form of Alvern.
Elver, Elverne

ELVIN (English) a form of Alvin.
El, Elvyn, Elwin, Elwyn, Elwynn

ELVIO (Spanish) light skinned; blond.

ELVIS (Scandinavian) wise.
El, Elviz, Elvys

ELVY (English) elfin warrior.

ELWELL (English) old well.

ELWOOD (English) old forest. See also
Wood, Woody.

ELY (Hebrew) an alternate form of Eli.
Geography: a river in Wales.
Elya, Elyie

EMAN (Czech) a form of Emmanuel.
Emaney, Emani

EMANUEL (Hebrew) an alternate form
of Emmanuel.
*Emaniel, Emannual, Emannuel, Emanual,
Emanueal, Emanuele, Emanuell, Emanuell,
Emanuelle*

EMERSON (German, English) son of
Emery.
Emmerson, Emreson

EMERY (German) industrious leader.
*Aimery, Emari, Emarri, Emeri, Emerich,
Emerio, Emmerich, Emmerie, Emmery,
Emmo, Emory, Emrick, Emry, Inre, Imrich*

EMIL (Latin) flatterer. (German)
industrious. See also Milko, Milo.
*Aymil, Emiel, Émile, Emilek, Emiliano,
Emilio, Emill, Emils, Emilyan, Emlyn*

ÉMILE (French) a form of Emil.
Emiel, Emile, Emille

EMILIANO (Italian) a form of Emil.
Emilian, Emilion

EMILIEN (Latin) friendly; industrious.

EMILIO (Italian, Spanish) a form of
Emil.
*Emielio, Emileo, Emilio, Emilios, Emillio,
Emilo*

EMLYN (Welsh) a form of Emil.
Emelen, Emlen, Emlin

EMMANUEL (Hebrew) God is with us.
See also Immanuel, Maco, Mango,
Manuel.
*Eman, Emanuel, Emanuell, Emek,
Emmahnuel, Emmanel, Emmaneuol,
Emmanle, Emmanual, Emmanueal,
Emmanuele, Emmanuell, Emmanuelle,
Emmanuil, Enmanuel*

EMMETT (German) industrious; strong.
(English) ant. History: Robert Emmett
was an Irish patriot.
*Em, Emet, Emett, Emitt, Emmet, Emmette,
Emmitt, Emmot, Emmott, Emmy*

EMMITT (German, English) an alternate
form of Emmett.
Emmit

EMORY (German) an alternate form of
Emery.
Amory, Emmory, Emorye

EMRE (Turkish) brother.
Emra, Emrah, Emreson

EMRICK (German) an alternate form
of Emery.
Emeric, Emerick, Emric, Emrique, Emryk

ENAPAY (Sioux) brave appearance;
he appears.

ENDRE (Hungarian) a form of Andrew.
Ender

ENEAS (Greek) an alternate form of
Aeneas.
Eneias, Enné

ENGELBERT (German) bright as an
angel. See also Ingelbert.
Bert, Englebert

ENLI (Dene) that dog over there.

ENNIS (Greek) mine. (Scottish) an
alternate form of Angus.
Eni, Enni

ENOCH (Hebrew) dedicated, consecrated. Bible: the father of Methuselah.
Enoc, Enock, Enok

ENOS (Hebrew) man.
Enosh

ENRIC (Romanian) a form of Henry.
Enrica

ENRICK (Spanish) a form of Henry.
Enricky

ENRICO (Italian) a form of Henry.
Enzio, Enzo, Rico

ENRIKOS (Greek) a form of Henry.

ENRIQUE (Spanish) a form of Henry. See also Quiqui.
Enrigué, Enriqué, Enriquez, Enrrique

ENVER (Turkish) bright; handsome.

ENYETO (Native American) walks like a bear.

ENZI (Swahili) powerful.

EOIN (Welsh) a form of Evan.

EPHRAIM (Hebrew) fruitful. Bible: the second son of Joseph.
Efraim, Efrayim, Efrem, Efren, Ephraen, Ephrain, Ephram, Ephrem, Ephriam

ERASMUS (Greek) lovable.
Érasme, Erasmo, Rasmus

ERASTUS (Greek) beloved.
Éraste, Erastious, Ras, Rastus

ERBERT (German) a short form of Herbert.
Ebert, Erberto

ERCOLE (Italian) splendid gift.

EREK (Scandinavian) an alternate form of Eric.
Erec

ERHARD (German) strong; resolute.
Erhardt, Erhart

ERIBERTO (Italian) a form of Herbert.
Erberto, Heriberto

ERIC (German) a short form of Frederick. (Scandinavian) ruler of all. (English) brave ruler. History: Eric the Red was a Norse hero and explorer.
Aric, Ehrich, Elika, Erek, Éric, Erica, Ericc, Erich, Erick, Erico, Erik, Erikur, Erric, Eryc, Rick

ERICH (Czech, German) a form of Eric.

ERICK (English) an alternate form of Eric.
Errick, Eryck

ERICKSON (English) son of Eric.
Erickzon, Erics, Ericson, Ericsson, Erikson, Erikzzon, Eriqson

ERIK (Scandinavian) an alternate form of Eric.
Erek, Erike, Eriks, Erikur, Errick, Errik, Eryk

ERIKUR (Icelandic) a form of Eric, Erik.

ERIN (Irish) peaceful. History: another name for Ireland.
Erine, Erinn, Erino, Eron, Errin, Eryn, Erynn

ERLAND (English) nobleman's land.
Erlend

ERLING (English) nobleman's son.

ERMANNO (Italian) a form of Herman.
Erman

ERMANO (Spanish) a form of Herman.
Ermin, Ermine, Erminio, Ermon

ERNEST (English) earnest, sincere. See also Arno.
Earnest, Ernestino, Ernesto, Ernestus, Ernie, Erno, Ernst

ERNESTO (Spanish) a form of Ernest.
Ernester, Neto

ERNIE (English) a familiar form of Ernest.
Earnie, Erney, Erny

ERNO (Hungarian) a form of Ernest.
Ernö

ERNST (German) a form of Ernest.
Erns

EROL (Turkish) strong, courageous.
Eroll

ERON (Irish) an alternate form of Erin.
Erran, Erren, Errion, Erron

ERRANDO (Basque) bold.

ERROL (Latin) wanderer. (English) an alternate form of Earl.
Erol, Erold, Erroll, Erryl

ERROMAN (Basque) from Rome.

ERSKINE (Scottish) high cliff. (English) from Ireland.
Ersin, Erskin, Kinny

ERVIN, Erwin (English) sea friend. Alternate forms of Irving, Irwin.
Earvin, Erv, Erven, Ervyn, Erwan, Erwinek, Erwinn, Erwyn, Erwynn

ERVINE (English) a form of Irving.
Erv, Ervin, Ervince, Erving, Ervins

ESAU (Hebrew) rough; hairy. Bible: Jacob's twin brother.
Esaw

ESEQUIEL (Hebrew) an alternate form of Ezekiel.

ESHKOL (Hebrew) grape clusters.

ESKIL (Norwegian) god vessel.

ESMOND (English) rich protector.

ESPEN (Danish) god-bear.

ESSIEN (Ochi) sixth-born son.

ESTE (Italian) east.
Estes

ESTÉBAN (Spanish) a form of Stephen.
Estabon, Esteben, Estefan, Estefano, Estefen, Estephan, Estephen

ESTEBE (Basque) a form of Stephen.

ESTEVAN (Spanish) a form of Stephen.
Esteven, Estevon, Estiven

ESTEVAO (Spanish) a form of Stephen.
Estevez

ETHAN (Hebrew) strong; firm.
Eathan, Eathen, Eathon, Eeathen, Eitan, Etan, Ethaen, Ethe, Ethen, Ethian

ÉTIENNE (French) a form of Stephen.
Etian, Etien, Étienn, Ettien

ETTORE (Italian) steadfast.
Etor, Etore

ETU (Native American) sunny.

EUCLID (Greek) intelligent. History: the founder of Euclidean geometry.

EUGEN (German) a form of Eugene.

EUGENE (Greek) born to nobility. See also Ewan, Gene, Gino, Iukini, Jenö, Yevgenyi, Zenda.
Eoghan, Eugen, Eugéne, Eugeni, Eugenio, Eugenius, Evgeny, Ezven

EUGENIO (Spanish) a form of Eugene.

EULISES (Latin) an alternate form of Ulysses.

EUSTACE (Greek) productive. (Latin) stable, calm. See also Stacey.
Eustache, Eustachius, Eustachy, Eustashe, Eustasius, Eustatius, Eustazio, Eustis, Eustiss

EVAN (Irish) young warrior. (English) a form of John. See also Bevan, Owen.
Eavan, Eoin, Ev, Evaine, Evann, Evans, Even, Evens, Evin, Evon, Evyn, Ewan, Ewen

EVANGELOS (Greek) an alternate
form of Andrew.
Evagelos, Evaggelos, Evangelo

EVELYN (English) hazelnut.
Evelin

EVERARDO (German) strong as a boar.
Everado

EVERETT (English) a form of Eberhard.
*Ev, Evered, Everet, Everette, Everhett, Everit,
Everitt, Everrett, Evert, Evrett*

EVERLEY (English) boar meadow.
Everlea, Everlee

EVERTON (English) boar town.

EVGENY (Russian) a form of Eugene.
See also Zhek.
Evgeni, Evgenij, Evgenyi

EVIN (Irish) an alternate form of Evan.
Evian, Evinn, Evins

EWALD (German) always powerful.
(English) powerful lawman.

EWAN (Scottish) a form of Eugene,
Evan. See also Keon.
Euan, Euann, Euen, Ewen, Ewhen

EWERT (English) ewe herder, shepherd.
Ewart

EWING (English) friend of the law.
Ewin, Ewynn

EXAVIER (Basque) an alternate form
of Xavier.
Exaviar, Exavior, Ezavier

EYOTA (Native American) great.

EZEKIEL (Hebrew) strength of God.
Bible: a Hebrew prophet. See also
Haskel, Zeke.
*Esequiel, Ezakeil, Ezéchiel, Ezeck, Ezeckiel,
Ezeeckel, Ezekeial, Ezekeil, Ezekeyial,
Ezekial, Ezekielle, Ezell, Ezequiel, Eziakah,
Eziechiele*

EZEQUIEL (Hebrew) an alternate form
of Ezekiel.
Esequiel, Eziequel

EZER (Hebrew) an alternate form of
Ezra.

EZRA (Hebrew) helper; strong. Bible: a
prophet and leader of the Israelites.
Esdras, Esra, Ezer, Ezera, Ezrah, Ezri, Ezry

EZVEN (Czech) a form of Eugene.
Esven, Esvin, Ezavin, Ezavine

FABER (German) a form of Fabian.

FABIAN (Latin) bean grower.
*Fabain, Fabayan, Fabe, Fabein, Fabek,
Fabeon, Faber, Fabert, Fabi, Fabiano, Fabien,
Fabin, Fabio, Fabion, Fabius, Fabiyan,
Fabiyus, Fabyan, Fabyen, Faybian, Faybien*

FABIANO (Italian) a form of Fabian.
Fabianno, Fabio

FABIO (Latin) an alternate form of
Fabian. (Italian) a short form of
Fabiano.
Fabbio

FABRIZIO (Italian) craftsman.
Fabrice, Fabricio, Fabrizius

FABRON (French) little blacksmith;
apprentice.
Fabre, Fabroni

FADEY (Ukrainian) a form of Thaddeus.
*Faday, Faddei, Faddey, Faddy, Fade,
Fadeyka, Fadie, Fady*

FADI (Arabic) redeemer.
Fadhi

FADIL (Arabic) generous.
Fadeel, Fadel

FAGAN (Irish) little fiery one.
Fagin

FAHD (Arabic) lynx.
Fahaad, Fahad

FAI (Chinese) beginning.

FAIRFAX (English) blond.
Fair, Fax

FAISAL (Arabic) decisive.
*Faisel, Faisil, Faisl, Faiyaz, Faiz, Faizal,
Faize, Faizel, Faizi, Fasel, Fasil, Faysal,
Fayzal, Fayzel*

FAKHIR (Arabic) excellent.
Fahkry, Fakher

FAKIH (Arabic) thinker; reader of the
Koran.

FALCO (Latin) falconer.
Falcon, Falk, Falke, Falken

FALITO (Italian) a familiar form of
Rafael, Raphael.

FALKNER (English) trainer of falcons.
See also Falco.
*Falconer, Falconner, Faulconer, Faulconner,
Faulkner*

FANE (English) joyful, glad.
Fanes, Faniel

FARAJI (Swahili) consolation.

FARID (Arabic) unique.

FARIS (Arabic) horseman.
Faraz, Fares, Farhaz, Farice, Fariez, Farris

FARLEY (English) bull meadow; sheep
meadow. See also Lee.
*Fairlay, Fairlee, Fairleigh, Fairley, Fairlie,
Far, Farlay, Farlee, Farleigh, Farlie, Farly,
Farrleigh, Farrley*

FARNELL (English) fern-covered hill.
Farnall, Fernald, Fernall, Furnald

FARNHAM (English) field of ferns.
Farnam, Farnum, Fernham

FARNLEY (English) fern meadow.
*Farnlea, Farnlee, Farnleigh, Farnly, Fernlea,
Fernlee, Fernleigh, Fernley*

FAROH (Latin) an alternate form of
Pharaoh.

FAROLD (English) mighty traveler.

FARQUHAR (Scottish) dear.
*Fark, Farq, Farquar, Farquarson, Farque,
Farquharson, Farquy, Farqy*

FARR (English) traveler.
*Faer, Farran, Farren, Farrin, Farrington,
Farron*

FARRELL (Irish) heroic.
Farrel, Farrill, Farryll, Ferrell

FARROW (English) piglet.

FARRUCO (Spanish) a form of Francis,
Francisco.
Frascuelo

FARUQ (Arabic) honest.
Farook, Farooq, Faroque, Farouk, Faruqh

FASTE (Norwegian) firm.

FATH (Arabic) victor.

FATIN (Arabic) clever.

FAUST (Latin) lucky, fortunate. History:
the sixteenth-century German doctor
who inspired many legends.
Faustino, Faustis, Fausto, Faustus

FAUSTINO (Italian) a form of Faust.

FAUSTO (Italian) a form of Faust.

FAVIAN (Latin) understanding.
Favain, Favio, Favyen

FAXON (German) long haired.

FEDERICO (Italian, Spanish) a form
of Frederick.
Federic, Federigo, Federoquito

FEIVEL (Yiddish) God aids.

FELIKS (Russian) a form of Felix.

FELIPE (Spanish) a form of Philip.
Feeleep, Felipino, Felo, Filip, Filippo, Filips, Fillip, Flip

FELIPPO (Italian) a form of Philip.
Felip, Filippo, Lipp, Lippo, Pip, Pippo

FELIX (Latin) fortunate; happy. See also Pitin.
Fee, Felic, Félice, Feliciano, Felicio, Felike, Feliks, Felo, Félix, Felizio, Phelix

FELTON (English) field town.
Felten, Feltin

FENTON (English) marshland farm.
Fen, Fennie, Fenny, Fintan, Finton

FEODOR (Slavic) a form of Theodore.
Dorek, Fedar, Fedinka, Fedor, Fedya, Fyodor

FEORAS (Greek) smooth rock.

FERDINAND (German) daring, adventurous. See also Hernando.
Feranado, Ferd, Ferda, Ferdie, Ferdinánd, Ferdy, Ferdynand, Fernando, Nando

FERENC (Hungarian) a form of Francis.
Feri, Ferke, Ferko

FERGUS (Irish) strong; manly.
Fearghas, Fearghus, Feargus, Ferghus, Fergie, Ferguson, Fergusson

FERMIN (French, Spanish) firm, strong.
Ferman, Firmin, Furman

FERNANDO (Spanish) a form of Ferdinand.
Ferando, Ferdinando, Ferdnando, Ferdo, Fernand, Fernandez, Fernendo

FEROZ (Persian) fortunate.

FERRAN (Arabic) baker.
Feran, Feron, Ferrin, Ferron

FERRAND (French) iron gray hair.
Farand, Farrand, Farrant, Ferrant

FERRELL (Irish) an alternate form of Farrell.
Ferrel, Ferrill, Ferryl

FERRIS (Irish) a form of Peter.
Fares, Faris, Fariz, Farris, Farrish, Feris, Ferriss

FICO (Spanish) a familiar form of Frederick.

FIDEL (Latin) faithful.
Fidele, Fidèle, Fidelio, Fidelis, Fidell, Fido

FIELD (English) a short form of Fielding.
Fields

FIELDING (English) field; field worker.
Field

FIFE (Scottish) from Fife, Scotland.
Fyfe

FIFI (Fante) born on Friday.

FIL (Polish) a form of Phil.
Filipek

FILBERT (English) brilliant. See also Bert.
Filberte, Filberto, Filiberto, Philbert

FILIBERTO (Spanish) a form of Filbert.

FILIP (Greek) an alternate form of Philip.
Filip, Filippo

FILLIPP (Russian) a form of Philip.
Filip, Filipe, Filipek, Filips, Fill, Fillip, Filya

FILMORE (English) famous.
Fillmore, Filmer, Fyllmer, Fylmer, Philmore

FILYA (Russian) a form of Philip.

FINEAS (Irish) a form of Phineas.
Finneas

FINIAN (Irish) light skinned; white.
Finnen, Finnian, Fionan, Fionn, Phinean

FINLAY (Irish) blond-haired soldier.
Findlay, Findley, Finlea, Finlee, Finley, Finn, Finnlea, Finnley

FINN (German) from Finland. (Irish) blond haired; light skinned. A short form of Finlay. (Norwegian) from the Lapland.
Fin, Finnie, Finnis, Finny

FINNEGAN (Irish) light skinned; white.
Finegan

FIORELLO (Italian) little flower.
Fiore

FIRAS (Arabic) persistent.

FIRMAN (French) firm; strong.
Ferman, Firmin

FIRTH (English) woodland.

FISCHEL (Yiddish) a form of Phillip.

FISKE (English) fisherman.
Fisk

FITCH (English) weasel, ermine.
Fitche

FITZ (English) son.
Filz

FITZGERALD (English) son of Gerald.

FITZHUGH (English) son of Hugh.
Hugh

FITZPATRICK (English) son of Patrick.

FITZROY (Irish) son of Roy.

FLAMINIO (Spanish) Religion: a Roman priest.

FLANN (Irish) redhead.
Flainn, Flannan, Flannery

FLAVIAN (Latin) blond, yellow haired.
Flavel, Flavelle, Flavien, Flavio, Flawiusz

FLAVIO (Italian) a form of Flavian.
Flabio, Flavious, Flavius

FLEMING (English) from Denmark; from Flanders.
Flemming, Flemmyng, Flemyng

FLETCHER (English) arrow featherer, arrow maker.
Flecher, Fletch

FLINT (English) stream; flintstone.
Flynt

FLIP (Spanish) a short form of Felipe. (American) a short form of Philip.

FLORENCIO (Italian) a form of Florent.

FLORENT (French) flowering.
Florenci, Florencio, Florentin, Florentino, Florentyn, Florentz, Florinio, Florino

FLORIAN (Latin) flowering, blooming.
Florien, Florrian, Flory, Floryan

FLOYD (English) a form of Lloyd.

FLURRY (English) flourishing, blooming.

FLYNN (Irish) son of the red-haired man.
Flin, Flinn, Flyn

FOLKE (German) an alternate form of Volker.
Folker

FOLUKE (Yoruba) given to God.

FOMA (Bulgarian, Russian) a form of Thomas.
Fomka

FONSO (German, Italian) a short form of Alphonso.
Fonzo

FONTAINE (French) fountain.

FONZIE (German) a familiar form of Alphonse.
Fons, Fonsie, Fonsy, Fonz

FORBES (Irish) prosperous.
Forbe

FORD (English) a short form of names ending in 'ford.'

FORDEL (Gypsy) forgiving.

FOREST (French) an alternate form of Forrest.
Forestt, Foryst

FORESTER (English) forest guardian.
Forrester, Forrie, Forry, Forster, Foss, Foster

FORREST (French) forest; woodsman.
Forest, Forester, Forrestar, Forrester, Forrestt, Forrie

FORTINO (Italian) fortunate, lucky.

FORTUNE (French) fortunate, lucky.
Fortun, Fortunato, Fortuné, Fortunio

FOSTER (Latin) a short form of Forester.

FOWLER (English) trapper of wild fowl.

FRAN (Latin) a short form of Francis.
Franh

FRANCESCO (Italian) a form of Francis.

FRANCHOT (French) a form of Francis.

FRANCIS (Latin) free; from France. Religion: Saint Francis of Assisi was the founder of the Franciscan order. See also Farruco, Ferenc.
Fran, France, Frances, Francesco, Franchot, Francisco, Franciskus, Franco, François, Frang, Frank, Frannie, Franny, Frans, Franscis, Fransis, Franta, Frantisek, Frants, Franus, Frantisek, Franz, Frencis

FRANCISCO (Portuguese, Spanish) a form of Francis. See also Chilo, Cisco, Farruco, Paco, Pancho.
Franco, Fransisco, Fransysco, Frasco, Frisco

FRANCO (Latin) a short form of Francis.
Franko

FRANÇOIS (French) a form of Francis.
Francoise

FRANK (English) a short form of Francis, Franklin. See also Palani, Pancho.
Franc, Franck, Franek, Frang, Franio, Franke, Frankie, Franko

FRANKIE (English) a familiar form of Frank.
Francky, Franke, Frankey, Franki, Franky, Franqui

FRANKLIN (English) free landowner.
Fran, Francklen, Francklin, Francklyn, Francylen, Frank, Frankin, Franklen, Franklinn, Franklyn, Franquelin

FRANKLYN (English) an alternate form of Franklin.
Franklynn

FRANS (Swedish) a form of Francis.
Frants

FRANTISEK (Czech) a form of Francis.
Franta

FRANZ (German) a form of Francis.
Fransz, Frantz, Franzen, Franzie, Franzin, Franzl, Franzy

FRASER (French) strawberry. (English) curly haired.
Fraizer, Frasier, Fraze, Frazer, Frazier

FRAYNE (French) dweller at the ash tree. (English) stranger.
Fraine, Frayn, Frean, Freen, Freyne

FRED (German) a short form of Alfred, Frederick, Manfred.
Fredd, Fredde, Fredo, Fredson

FREDDIE (German) a familiar form of Frederick.
Freddi, Freddy, Fredi, Fredy

FREDDY, Fredy (German) familiar forms of Frederick.

FREDERIC (German) an alternate form of Frederick.
Frédéric, Frederich, Frederric, Fredric, Fredrich

FREDERICK (German) peaceful ruler. See also Dick, Eric, Fico, Peleke, Rick.
Federico, Fico, Fred, Fredderick, Freddie, Freddrick, Freddy, Fredek, Frederic, Frédérick, Frédérick, Frederik, Frederique, Frederrick, Fredo, Fredrick, Fredwick, Fredwyck, Fredy, Friedrich, Fritz

FREDERICO (Spanish) a form of Frederick.
Fredrico, Frederigo

FREDERIK (German) an alternate form of Frederick.
Frédérik, Frederrik, Fredrik

FREDERIQUE (French) a form of Frederick.

FREDO (Spanish) a form of Fred.

FREDRICK (German) an alternate form of Frederick.
Fredric, Fredricka, Fredricks

FREEBORN (English) child of freedom.
Free

FREEMAN (English) free.
Free, Freedman, Freemin, Freemon, Friedman, Friedmann

FREMONT (German) free; noble protector.

FREWIN (English) free; noble friend.
Frewen

FREY (English) lord. (Scandinavian) Mythology: god of prosperity.

FRICK (English) bold.

FRIDOLF (English) peaceful wolf.
Freydolf, Freydulf, Fridulf

FRIEDRICH (German) a form of Frederick.
Friedel, Friedrick, Fridrich, Fridrick, Friedrike, Friedryk, Fryderyk

FRISCO (Spanish) a short form of Francisco.

FRITZ (German) a familiar form of Frederick.
Fritson, Fritts, Fritzchen, Fritzl

FRODE (Norwegian) wise.

FULBRIGHT (German) very bright.
Fulbert

FULLER (English) cloth thickener.

FULTON (English) field near town.

FUNSONI (Ngoni) requested.

FYFE (Scottish) an alternate form of Fife.
Fyffe

FYNN (Ghanian) Geography: another name for the Offin river.

FYODOR (Russian) an alternate form of Theodore.

G

GABBY (American) a familiar form of Gabriel.
Gabbi, Gabbie, Gabi, Gabie, Gaby

GABE (Hebrew) a short form of Gabriel.

GABINO (American) a form of Gabriel.
Gabin, Gabrino

GÁBOR (Hungarian) God is my strength.
Gabbo, Gabko, Gabo

GABRIAL (Hebrew) an alternate form of Gabriel.
Gaberial, Gabrael, Gabraiel, Gabrail, Gabreal, Gabriael, Gabrieal, Gabryalle

GABRIEL (Hebrew) devoted to God. Bible: the Archangel of Annunciation.
Gab, Gabe, Gabby, Gabino, Gabis, Gábor, Gabreil, Gabrel, Gabrell, Gabrial, Gabriël, Gabriele, Gabriell, Gabrielle, Gabrielli, Gabrile, Gabris, Gabryel, Gabys, Gavril, Gebereal, Ghabriel, Riel

GABRIELLI (Italian) a form of Gabriel.
Gabriello

GADI (Arabic) God is my fortune.
Gad, Gaddy, Gadiel

GAETAN (Italian) from Gaeta, a region in southern Italy.
Gaetano, Gaetono

GAGE (French) pledge.
Gager, Gaige, Gaje

GAIGE (French) an alternate form of Gage.

GAIR (Irish) small.
Gaer, Gearr, Geir

GAIUS (Latin) rejoicer. See also Cai.

GALBRAITH (Irish) Scotsman in Ireland.
Galbrait, Galbreath

GALE (Greek) a short form of Galen.
Gael, Gail, Gaile, Gayle

GALEN (Greek) healer; calm. (Irish) little and lively.
Gaelan, Gaelen, Gaelin, Gaelyn, Gailen, Galan, Gale, Galeno, Galin, Galyn, Gaylen

GALENO (Spanish) illuminated child.

GALLAGHER (Irish) eager helper.

GALLOWAY (Irish) Scotsman in Ireland.
Gallway, Galway

GALT (Norwegian) high ground.

GALTON (English) owner of a rented estate.
Gallton

GALVIN (Irish) sparrow.
Gal, Gall, Gallven, Gallvin, Galvan, Galven

GAMAL (Arabic) camel. See also Jamal.
Gamall, Gamel, Gamil

GAMBLE (Scandinavian) old.

GAN (Chinese) daring, adventurous. (Vietnamese) near.

GANNON (Irish) light skinned, white.
Gannan, Gannen, Gannie, Ganny

GANYA (Zulu) clever.

GAR (English) a short form of Gareth, Garnett, Garrett, Garvin.
Garr

GARCIA (Spanish) mighty with a spear.

GARDNER (English) gardener.
Gard, Gardener, Gardie, Gardiner, Gardy

GAREK (Polish) a form of Edgar.

GAREN (English) an alternate form of Garry.
Garan, Garen, Garin, Garion, Garon, Garyn, Garyon

GARETH (Welsh) gentle.
Gar, Garith, Garreth, Garrith, Garth, Garyth

GARETT (Irish) an alternate form of Garrett.
Gared, Garet, Garette, Garhett, Garit, Garitt, Garritt

GARFIELD (English) field of spears; battlefield.

GARLAND (French) wreath of flowers; prize. (English) land of spears; battleground.
Garlan, Garlen, Garllan, Garlund, Garlyn

GARMAN (English) spearman.
Garmann, Garrman

GARNER (French) army guard, sentry.
Garnier

GARNETT (Latin) pomegranate seed; garnet stone. (English) armed with a spear.
Gar, Garnet, Garnie, Garrnett

GARNOCK (Welsh) dweller by the alder river.

GARRAD (English) a form of Garrett.
Gared, Garrard, Garred, Garrod, Gerred, Gerrid, Gerrod, Garrode, Jared

GARRET (Irish) an alternate form of Garrett.
Garrit, Garyt, Gerret, Garrid, Gerrit, Gerrot

GARRETT (Irish) brave spearman. See also Jarrett.
Gar, Gareth, Garett, Garrad, Garret, Garrette, Gerrett, Gerritt, Gerrott

GARRICK (English) oak spear.
Gaerick, Garek, Garick, Garik, Garreck, Garrek, Garric, Garrik, Garryck, Garryk, Gerreck, Gerrick

GARREN, Garrin (English) alternate forms of Garry.
Garran, Garrion, Garron, Garyn, Gerren, Gerron, Gerryn

GARRISON (French) troops stationed at a fort; garrison.
Garison, Garisson, Garris

GARROWAY (English) spear fighter.
Garraway

GARRY (English) an alternate form of Gary.
Garen, Garrey, Garri, Garrie, Garren, Garrin

GARSON (English) son of Gar.

GARTH (Scandinavian) garden, gardener. (Welsh) a short form of Gareth.

GARVEY (Irish) rough peace.
Garbhán, Garrvey, Garrvie, Garv, Garvan, Garvie, Garvy

GARVIN (English) comrade in battle.
Gar, Garvan, Garven, Garvyn, Garwen, Garwin, Garwyn, Garwynn

GARWOOD (English) evergreen forest. See also Wood, Woody.
Garrwood

GARY (German) mighty spearman. (English) a familiar form of Gerald. See also Kali.
Gare, Garey, Gari, Garry

GASPAR (French) a form of Casper.
Gáspár, Gaspard, Gaspare, Gaspari, Gasparo, Gasper, Gazsi

GASTON (French) from Gascony, France.
Gascon, Gastaun

GAUTE (Norwegian) great.

GAUTIER (French) a form of Walter.
Galtero, Gaulterio, Gaultier, Gaultiero, Gauthier

GAVIN (Welsh) white hawk.
Gav, Gavan, Gaven, Gavinn, Gavino, Gavn, Gavohn, Gavon, Gavyn, Gavynn, Gawain

GAVRIEL (Hebrew) man of God.
Gav, Gavi, Gavrel, Gavril, Gavy

GAVRIL (Russian) a form of Gavriel.
Ganya, Gavrilo, Gavrilushka

GAWAIN (Welsh) an alternate form of Gavin.
Gawaine, Gawayn, Gawayne, Gawen, Gwayne

GAYLEN (Greek) an alternate form of Galen.
Gaylin, Gaylinn, Gaylon, Gaylyn

GAYLORD (French) merry lord; jailer.
Gaillard, Gallard, Gay, Gayelord, Gayler,
Gaylor

GAYNOR (Irish) son of the fair-skinned
man.
Gainer, Gainor, Gay, Gayner, Gaynnor

GEARY (English) variable, changeable.
Gearey, Gery

GEDEON (Bulgarian, French) a form of
Gideon.

GEFFREY (English) an alternate form
of Geoffrey. See also Jeffrey.
Gefery, Geff, Geffery, Geffrard

GELLERT (Hungarian) a form of Gerald.

GENA (Russian) a short form of
Yevgenyi.
Genka, Genya, Gine

GENARO (Latin) consecrated to God.
Genereo, Genero, Gennaro

GENE (Greek) born to nobility. A short
form of Eugene.
Genek

GENEK (Polish) a form of Gene.

GENO (Italian) a form of John. A short
form of Genovese.
Genio, Jeno

GENOVESE (Italian) from Genoa, Italy.
Geno, Genovis

GENT (English) gentleman.
Gentle, Gentry

GENTY (Irish, English) snow.

GEOFF (English) a short form of
Geoffrey.

GEOFFERY (English) an alternate form
of Geoffrey.
Geofery

GEOFFREY (English) divinely peaceful.
A form of Jeffrey. See also Giotto,
Godfrey, Gottfried, Jeff.
Geffrey, Geoff, Geoffery, Geoffre, Geoffrie,
Geoffroi, Geoffroy, Geoffry, Geofrey, Geofri,
Gofery

GEORDAN (Scottish) a form of Gordon.
Geordann, Geordian, Geordin, Geordon

GEORDIE (Scottish) a form of George.
Geordi, Geordy

GEORG (Scandinavian) a form of
George.

GEORGE (Greek) farmer. See also
Durko, Egor, Iorgos, Jerzy, Jiri, Joji,
Jörg, Jorge, Jorgen, Joris, Jorrín, Jur,
Jurgis, Keoki, Mahiái, Semer, Yegor,
Yorgos, Yoyi, Yrjo, Yuri, Zhora.
Geordie, Georg, Georgas, Georges, Georget,
Georgi, Georgii, Georgio, Georgios, Georgiy,
Georgy, Gevork, Gheorghe, Giorgio, Giorgos,
Goerge, Goran, Gordios, Gorge, Gorje,
Gorya, Grzegorz, Gyorgy

GEORGES (French) a form of George.
Geórges

GEORGIO (Italian) a form of George.

GEORGIOS (Greek) an alternate form
of George.
Georgious, Georgius

GEORGY (Greek) a familiar form of
George.
Georgie

GEOVANNI, Geovanny (Italian)
alternate forms of Giovanni.
Geovan, Geovani, Geovanne, Geovannee,
Geovannhi, Geovany

GERAINT (English) old.

GERALD (German) mighty spearman.
See also Fitzgerald, Jarell, Jarrell,
Jerald, Jerry, Kharald.
Garald, Garold, Garolds, Gary, Gearalt,
Gellert, Gérald, Geralde, Geraldo, Gerale,

Geraud, Gerek, Gerick, Gerik, Gerold,
Gerrald, Gerrell, Gérrick, Gerrild, Gerrin,
Gerrit, Gerrold, Gerry, Geryld, Giraldo,
Giraud, Girauld

GERALDO (Italian, Spanish) a form of
Gerald.

GERARD (English) brave spearman.
See also Jerard, Jerry.
Garrard, Garrat, Garratt, Gearard, Gerad,
Gerar, Gérard, Gerardo, Geraro, Géraud,
Gerd, Gerek, Gerhard, Gerrard, Gerrit,
Gerry, Girard

GERARDO (Spanish) a form of Gerard.
Gherardo

GÉRAUD (French) a form of Gerard.
Gerrad, Gerraud

GEREK (Polish) a form of Gerard.

GEREMIA (Hebrew) exalted by God.
(Italian) a form of Jeremiah.

GEREMIAH (Italian) a form of
Jeremiah.
Geremia, Gerimiah, Geromiah

GERHARD (German) a form of Gerard.
Garhard, Gerhardi, Gerhardt, Gerhart,
Gerhort

GERIK (Polish) a form of Edgar.
Geric, Gerick

GERMAIN (French) from Germany.
(English) sprout, bud. See also
Jermaine.
Germaine, German, Germane, Germano,
Germayn, Germayne

GEROME (English) a form of Jerome.

GERONIMO (Greek, Italian) a form of
Jerome. History: a famous Apache
chief.
Geronemo

GERRIT (Dutch) a form of Gerald.

GERRY (English) a familiar form of
Gerald, Gerard. See also Jerry.
Geri, Gerre, Gerri, Gerrie, Gerryson

GERSHOM (Hebrew) exiled. (Yiddish)
stranger in exile.
Gersham, Gersho, Gershon, Gerson,
Geurson, Gursham, Gurshan

GERSON (English) son of Gar.
Gersan, Gershawn

GERT (German, Danish) fighter.

GERVAISE (French) honorable.
See also Jervis.
Garvais, Garvaise, Garvey, Gervais, Gervase,
Gervasio, Gervaso, Gervayse, Gervis,
Gerwazy

GERWIN (Welsh) fair love.

GETHIN (Welsh) dusky.
Geth

GHAZI (Arabic) conqueror.

GHILCHRIST (Irish) servant of Christ.
See also Gil.
Gilchrist, Gilcrist, Gilie, Gill, Gilley, Gilly

GHISLAIN (French) pledge.

GI (Korean) brave.

GIA (Vietnamese) family.

GIACINTO (Portuguese, Spanish) an
alternate form of Jacinto.
Giacintho

GIACOMO (Italian) a form of Jacob.
Gaimo, Giacamo, Giaco, Giacobbe, Giacobo,
Giacopo

GIAN (Italian) a form of Giovanni, John.
Gianetto, Giann, Gianne, Giannes, Gianni,
Giannis, Giannos, Ghian

GIANCARLO (Italian) a combination of
John + Charles.
Giancarlos, Gianncarlo

GIANLUCA (Italian) a combination of
John + Lucas.

GIANNI (Italian) a form of Johnny.
Giani, Gionni

GIANPAOLO (Italian) a combination
of John + Paul.
Gianpaulo

GIB (English) a short form of Gilbert.
Gibb, Gibbie, Gibby

GIBOR (Hebrew) powerful.

GIBSON (English) son of Gilbert.
Gibbon, Gibbons, Gibbs, Gillson, Gilson

GIDEON (Hebrew) tree cutter. Bible: the
judge who delivered the Israelites
from captivity.
Gedeon, Gideone, Gidon, Hedeon

GIDON (Hebrew) an alternate form of
Gideon.

GIFFORD (English) bold giver.
Giff, Giffard, Gifferd, Giffie, Giffy

GIG (English) horse-drawn carriage.

GIL (Greek) shield bearer. (Hebrew)
happy. (English) a short form of
Ghilchrist, Gilbert.
Gili, Gill, Gilli, Gillie, Gillis, Gilly

GILAD (Arabic) camel hump; from
Giladi, Saudi Arabia.
Giladi, Gilead

GILAMU (Basque) a form of William.
Gillen

GILBERT (English) brilliant pledge;
trustworthy. See also Gil, Gillett.
*Gib, Gilberto, Gilburt, Giselbert, Giselberto,
Giselbertus, Guilbert*

GILBERTO (Spanish) a form of Gilbert.

GILBY (Scandinavian) hostage's estate.
(Irish) blond boy.
Gilbey, Gillbey, Gillbie, Gillby

GILCHRIST (Irish) an alternate form of
Ghilchrist.

GILEN (Basque, German) illustrious
pledge.

GILES (French) goatskin shield.
Gide, Gilles, Gyles

GILLEAN (Irish) Bible: Saint John's
servant.
Gillan, Gillen, Gillian

GILLESPIE (Irish) son of the bishop's
servant.
Gillis

GILLETT (French) young Gilbert.
Gelett, Gelette, Gillette

GILMER (English) famous hostage.
Gilmar

GILMORE (Irish) devoted to the Virgin
Mary.
Gillmore, Gillmour, Gilmour

GILON (Hebrew) circle.

GILROY (Irish) devoted to the king.
Gilderoy, Gildray, Gildroy, Gillroy, Roy

GINO (Greek) a familiar form of Eugene.
(Italian) a short form of names ending
in 'gene,' 'gino.'
Ghino

GIONA (Italian) a form of Jonah.

GIORDANO (Italian) a form of Jordan.
Giordan, Giordana, Giordin, Guordan

GIORGIO (Italian) a form of George.

GIORGOS (Greek) an alternate form
of George.
Georgos, Giorgios

GIOSIA (Italian) a form of Joshua.

GIOTTO (Italian) a form of Geoffrey.

GIOVANI (Italian) an alternate form of Giovanni.
Giavani, Giovan, Giovane, Giovanie, Giovon

GIOVANNI (Italian) a form of John. See also Jeovanni, Jiovanni.
Geovanni, Geovanny, Gian, Gianni, Giannino, Giovani, Giovann, Giovannie, Giovanno, Giovanny, Giovonathon, Giovonni, Giovonnia, Giovonnie, Givonni

GIOVANNY (Italian) an alternate form of Giovanni.
Giovany

GIPSY (English) wanderer.
Gipson, Gypsy

GIRVIN (Irish) small; tough.
Girvan, Girven, Girvon

GITANO (Spanish) gypsy.

GIULIANO (Italian) a form of Julius.
Giulano, Giulino, Giulliano

GIULIO (Italian) a form of Julius.
Guilano

GIUSEPPE (Italian) a form of Joseph.
Giuseppi, Giuseppino, Giusseppe, Guiseppe, Guiseppi, Guiseppie, Guisseppe

GIUSTINO (Italian) a form of Justin.
Giusto

GIVON (Hebrew) hill; heights.
Givan, Givawn, Givyn

GLADWIN (English) cheerful. See also Win.
Glad, Gladdie, Gladdy, Gladwinn, Gladwyn, Gladwynne

GLANVILLE (English) village with oak trees.

GLEN (Irish) an alternate form of Glenn.
Glyn

GLENDON (Scottish) fortress in the glen.
Glenden, Glendin, Glenn, Glennden, Glennton, Glenton

GLENDOWER (Welsh) from Glyndwer, England.

GLENN (Irish) a short form of Glendon.
Gleann, Glen, Glennie, Glennis, Glennon, Glenny, Glynn

GLENTWORTH (English) from Glenton, England.

GLENVILLE (Irish) village in the glen.

GLYN (Welsh) a form of Glen.
Glin, Glynn

GODDARD (German) divinely firm.
Godard, Godart, Goddart, Godhardt, Godhart, Gothart, Gotthard, Gotthardt, Gotthart

GODFREY (German) a form of Jeffrey. (Irish) God's peace. See also Geoffrey, Gottfried.
Giotto, Godefroi, Godfree, Godfry, Godofredo, Godoired, Godrey, Goffredo, Gofraidh, Gofredo, Gorry

GODWIN (English) friend of God. See also Win.
Godewyn, Godwinn, Godwyn, Goodwin, Goodwyn, Goodwynn, Goodwynne

GOEL (Hebrew) redeemer.

GOLDWIN (English) golden friend. See also Win.
Golden, Goldewin, Goldewinn, Goldewyn, Goldwyn, Goldwynn

GOLIATH (Hebrew) exiled. Bible: the giant Phillistine whom David slew with a slingshot.
Golliath

GOMDA (Kiowa) wind.

GOMER (Hebrew) completed, finished. (English) famous battle.

GONZA (Rutooro) love.

GONZALO (Spanish) wolf.
Goncalve, Gonsalo, Gonsalve, Gonzales, Gonzelee, Gonzolo

GORDON (English) triangular hill.
Geordan, Gord, Gordain, Gordan, Gorden, Gordonn, Gordy

GORDY (English) a familiar form of Gordon.
Gordie

GORE (English) triangular-shaped land; wedge-shaped land.

GORMAN (Irish) small; blue eyed.

GORO (Japanese) fifth.

GOSHEVEN (Native American) great leaper.

GOTTFRIED (German) a form of Geoffrey, Godfrey.
Gotfrid, Gotfrids, Gottfrid

GOTZON (German) a form of Angel.

GOVERT (Dutch) heavenly peace.

GOWER (Welsh) pure.

GOWON (Tiv) rainmaker.
Gowan

GOZOL (Hebrew) soaring bird.
Gozal

GRADY (Irish) noble; illustrious.
Gradea, Gradee, Gradey, Gradleigh, Graidey, Graidy

GRAEME (Scottish) a form of Graham.
Graem

GRAHAM (English) grand home.
Graeham, Graehame, Graehme, Graeme, Grahamme, Grahm, Grahame, Grahme, Gram, Grame, Gramm, Grayeme, Grayham

GRANGER (French) farmer.
Grainger, Grange

GRANT (English) a short form of Grantland.
Grand, Grantham, Granthem, Grantley

GRANTLAND (English) great plains.
Grant

GRANVILLE (French) large village.
Gran, Granvel, Granvil, Granvile, Granvill, Grenville, Greville

GRAY (English) gray haired.
Graye, Grey, Greye

GRAYDEN (English) gray haired.
Graden, Graydan, Graydyn, Greyden

GRAYDON (English) gray hill.
Gradon, Grayton, Greydon

GRAYSON (English) bailiff's son.
See also Sonny.
Graysen, Greyson

GREELEY (English) gray meadow.
Greelea, Greeleigh, Greely

GREENWOOD (English) green forest.
Green, Greener

GREG, Gregg (Latin) short forms of Gregory.
Graig, Greig, Gregson

GREGGORY (Latin) an alternate form of Gregory.
Greggery

GREGOR (Scottish) a form of Gregory.
Gregoor, Grégor, Gregore

GREGORIO (Italian, Portuguese) a form of Gregory.
Gregorios

GREGORY (Latin) vigilant watch-man.
See also Jörn, Krikor.
Gergely, Gergo, Greagoir, Greagory, Greer, Greg, Gregary, Greger, Gregery, Greggory, Grégoire, Gregor, Gregorey, Gregori, Grégorie, Gregorio, Gregorius, Gregors, Gregos, Gregrey, Gregroy, Gregry, Greogry, Gries, Grisha, Grzegorz

GRESHAM (English) village in the pasture.

GREYSON (English) an alternate form of Grayson.
Greysen, Greysten, Greyston

GRIFFIN (Latin) hooked nose.
Griff, Griffen, Griffie, Griffon, Griffy, Gryphon

GRIFFITH (Welsh) fierce chief; ruddy.
Grifen, Griff, Griffeth, Griffie, Griffy, Griffyn, Griffynn, Gryphon

GRIGORI (Bulgarian) a form of Gregory.
Grigoi, Grigor, Grigore, Grigorios, Grigorov, Grigory

GRIMSHAW (English) dark woods.

GRISHA (Russian) a form of Gregory.

GRISWOLD (German, French) gray forest.
Gris, Griz, Grizwald

GROSVENER (French) big hunter.

GROVER (English) grove.
Grove

GUADALUPE (Arabic) river of black stones.
Guadalope

GUALBERTO (Spanish) a form of Walter.
Gualterio

GUALTIERO (Italian) a form of Walter.
Gualterio

GUGLIELMO (Italian) a form of William.

GUIDO (Italian) a form of Guy.

GUILFORD (English) ford with yellow flowers.
Guildford

GUILHERME (Portuguese) a form of William.

GUILLAUME (French) a form of William.
Guillaums, Guilleaume, Guilem, Guyllaume

GUILLERMO (Spanish) a form of William.
Guillerrmo

GUNNAR (Scandinavian) an alternate form of Gunther.
Guner, Gunner

GUNTHER (Scandinavian) battle army; warrior.
Guenter, Guenther, Gun, Gunnar, Guntar, Gunter, Guntero, Gunthar, Günther

GUOTIN (Chinese) polite; strong leader.

GURION (Hebrew) young lion.
Gur, Guri, Guriel

GURPREET (Punjabi) devoted to the guru; devoted to the Prophet.
Gurjeet, Gurmeet, Guruprit

GURVIR (Sikh) guru's warrior.
Gurveer

GUS (Scandinavian) a short form of Angus, Augustine, Gustave.
Guss, Gussie, Gussy, Gusti, Gustry, Gusty

GUSTAF (Swedish) a form of Gustave.
Gustaaf, Gustaff

GUSTAVE (Scandinavian) staff of the Goths. History: Gustavus Adolphus was a king of Sweden. See also Kosti, Tabo, Tavo.
Gus, Gustaf, Gustaff, Gustaof, Gustav, Gustáv, Gustava, Gustaves, Gustavo, Gustavs, Gustavus, Gustik, Gustus, Gusztav

GUSTAVO (Italian, Spanish) a form of Gustave.
Gustabo

GUTHRIE (German) war hero. (Irish) windy place.
Guthrey, Guthry

GUTIERRE (Spanish) a form of Walter.

GUY (Hebrew) valley. (German) warrior. (French) guide. See also Guido.
Guyon

GUYAPI (Native American) candid.

GWAYNE (Welsh) an alternate form of Gawain.
Gwaine, Gwayn

GWIDON (Polish) life.

GWILYM (Welsh) a form of William.
Gwillym

GWYN (Welsh) fair; blessed.
Gwynn, Gwynne

GYASI (Akan) marvelous baby.

GYORGY (Russian) a form of George.
Gyoergy, György, Gyuri, Gyurka

GYULA (Hungarian) youth.
Gyala, Gyuszi

H

HABIB (Arabic) beloved.

HACKETT (German, French) little woodcutter.
Hacket, Hackit, Hackitt

HACKMAN (German, French) woodcutter.

HADAR (Hebrew) glory.

HADDAD (Arabic) blacksmith.

HADDEN (English) heather-covered hill.
Haddan, Haddon, Haden

HADEN (English) an alternate form of Hadden.
Hadin, Hadon, Hadyn, Haeden

HADI (Arabic) guiding to the right.
Hadee, Hady

HADLEY (English) heather-covered meadow.
Had, Hadlea, Hadlee, Hadleigh, Hadly, Lee, Leigh

HADRIAN (Latin, Swedish) dark.
Adrian, Hadrien

HADWIN (English) friend in a time of war.
Hadwinn, Hadwyn, Hadwynn, Hadwynne

HAGAN (German) strong defense.
Haggan

HAGEN (Irish) young, youthful.

HAGLEY (English) enclosed meadow.

HAGOS (Ethiopian) happy.

HAHNEE (Native American) beggar.

HAI (Vietnamese) sea.

HAIDAR (Arabic) lion.
Haider

HAIDEN (English) an alternate form of Hayden.
Haidyn

HAIG (English) enclosed with hedges.

HAILEY (Irish) an alternate form of Haley.
Haile, Haille, Haily, Halee

HAJI (Swahili) born during the pilgrimage to Mecca.

HAKAN (Native American) fiery.

HAKEEM (Arabic) an alternate form of Hakim.
Hakam, Hakem

HAKIM (Arabic) wise. (Ethiopian) doctor.
Hakeem, Hakiem

HAKON (Scandinavian) of Nordic ancestry.
Haaken, Haakin, Haakon, Haeo, Hak, Hakan, Hako

HAL (English) a short form of Halden, Hall, Harold.

HALBERT (English) shining hero.
Bert, Halburt

HALDEN (Scandinavian) half-Danish. See also Dane.
Hal, Haldan, Haldane, Halfdan, Halvdan

HALE (English) a short form of Haley. (Hawaiian) a form of Harry.
Hayle, Heall

HALEN (Swedish) hall.
Hale, Hallen, Haylan, Haylen

HALEY (Irish) ingenious.
Hailey, Hale, Haleigh, Halley, Hayleigh, Hayley, Hayli

HALFORD (English) valley ford.

HALI (Greek) sea.

HALIAN (Zuni) young.

HALIL (Turkish) dear friend.
Halill

HALIM (Arabic) mild, gentle.
Haleem

HALL (English) manor, hall.
Hal, Halstead, Halsted

HALLAM (English) valley.

HALLAN (Engish) dweller at the hall; dweller at the manor.
Halin, Hallene, Hallin

HALLEY (English) meadow near the hall; holy.
Hallie

HALLIWELL (English) holy well.
Hallewell, Hellewell, Helliwell

HALLWARD (English) hall guard.

HALSEY (English) Hal's island.

HALSTEAD (English) manor grounds.
Halsted

HALTON (English) estate on the hill.

HALVOR (Norwegian) rock; protector.
Halvard

HAM (Hebrew) hot. Bible: one of Noah's sons.

HAMAL (Arabic) lamb. Astronomy: a bright star in the constellation of Aries.

HAMAR (Scandinavian) hammer.

HAMID (Arabic) praised. See also Muhammad.
Haamid, Hamaad, Hamadi, Hamd, Hamdrem, Hamed, Hamedo, Hameed, Hamidi, Hammad, Hammed, Humayd

HAMILL (English) scarred.
Hamel, Hamell, Hammill

HAMILTON (English) proud estate.
Hamel, Hamelton, Hamil, Hamill, Tony

HAMISH (Scottish) a form of Jacob, James.

HAMISI (Swahili) born on Thursday.

HAMLET (German, French) little village; home. Literature: one of Shakespeare's tragic heroes.

HAMLIN (German, French) loves his home.
Hamblin, Hamelen, Hamelin, Hamlen, Hamlyn, Lin

HAMMET (English, Scandinavian)
village.
Hammett, Hamnet, Hamnett

HAMMOND (English) village.
Hamond

HAMPTON (English) Geography: a
town in England.
Hamp

HAMZA (Arabic) powerful.
Hamzah, Hamze, Hamzeh, Hamzia

HANALE (Hawaiian) a form of Henry.
Haneke

HANAN (Hebrew) grace.
Hananel, Hananiah, Johanan

HANBAL (Arabic) pure. History:
founder of an Islamic school of
thought.

HANDEL (German, English) a form
of John.

HANFORD (English) high ford.

HANIF (Arabic) true believer.
Haneef, Hanef

HANK (American) a familiar form of
Henry.

HANLEY (English) high meadow.
*Handlea, Handleigh, Handley, Hanlea,
Hanlee, Hanleigh, Hanly, Henlea, Henlee,
Henleigh, Henley*

HANNES (Finnish) a form of John.

HANNIBAL (Phoenician) grace of God.
History: a famous Carthaginian
general who fought the Romans.
Anibal

HANNO (German) a short form of
Johan.
Hanna, Hannah, Hannon, Hannu, Hanon

HANS (Scanadinavian) a form of John.
Hanschen, Hansel, Hants, Hanz

HANSEL (Scandinavian) an alternate
form of Hans.
Haensel, Hansell, Hansl, Hanzel

HANSEN (Scandinavian) son of Hans.
Hanson

HANSH (Hindi) god; godlike. Religion:
another name for the Hindu god Shiva.

HANSON (Scandinavian) an alternate
form of Hansen.
Hansen, Hanssen, Hansson

HANUS (Czech) a form of John.

HAOA (Hawaiian) a form of Howard.

HARA (Hindi) seizer. Religion: another
name for the Hindu god Shiva.

HARALD (Scandinavian) an alternate
form of Harold.
Haraldo, Haralds, Haralpos

HARB (Arabic) warrior.

HARBIN (German, French) little bright
warrior.
Harben, Harbyn

HARCOURT (French) fortified
dwelling.
Court, Harcort

HARDEEP (Punjabi) an alternate form
of Harpreet.

HARDEN (English) valley of the hares.
Hardian, Hardin

HARDING (English) brave man's son.
Hardin

HARDWIN (English) brave friend.

HARDY (German) bold, daring.
Hardie

HAREL (Hebrew) mountain of God.
Harell, Hariel, Harrell

HARFORD (English) ford of the hares.

HARGROVE (English) grove of the hares.
Hargreave, Hargreaves

HARI (Hindi) tawny. Religion: another name for the Hindu god Vishnu.
Hariel, Harin

HARITH (Arabic) cultivator.

HARJOT (Sikh) light of God.
Harjeet, Harjit, Harjodh

HARKIN (Irish) dark red.
Harkan, Harken

HARLAN (English) hare's land; army land.
Harland, Harlen, Harlenn, Harlin, Harlon, Harlyn, Harlynn

HARLAND (English) an alternate form of Harlan.
Harlend

HARLEY (English) hare's meadow; army meadow.
Arley, Harlea, Harlee, Harleigh, Harly

HARLOW (English) hare's hill; army hill. See also Arlo.

HARMAN, Harmon (English) forms of Herman.
Harm, Harmen, Harmond, Harms

HAROLD (Scandinavian) army ruler. See also Jindra.
Araldo, Garald, Garold, Hal, Harald, Haraldas, Haraldo, Haralds, Harry, Heraldo, Herold, Heronim, Herrick, Herryck

HAROUN (Arabic) lofty; exalted.
Haarun, Harin, Haron, Haroon, Harron, Harun

HARPER (English) harp player.
Harp, Harpo

HARPREET (Punjabi) loves God, devoted to God.
Hardeep

HARRIS (English) a short form of Harrison.
Haris, Hariss

HARRISON (English) son of Harry.
Harison, Harreson, Harris, Harrisen, Harrisson

HARROD (Hebrew) hero; conqueror.

HARRY (English) a familiar form of Harold. See also Arrigo, Hale, Parry.
Harm, Harray, Harrey, Harri, Harrie

HART (English) a short form of Hartley.

HARTLEY (English) deer meadow.
Hart, Hartlea, Hartlee, Hartleigh, Hartly

HARTMAN (German) hard; strong.

HARTWELL (English) deer well.
Harwell, Harwill

HARTWIG (German) strong advisor.

HARTWOOD (English) deer forest.
Harwood

HARVEY (German) army warrior.
Harv, Hervé, Hervey, Hervie, Hervy

HARVIR (Sikh) God's warrior.
Harvier

HASAD (Turkish) reaper, harvester.

HASAN (Arabic) an alternate form of Hassan.
Hasaan, Hasain, Hasaun, Hashaan, Hason

HASANI (Swahili) handsome.
Hasan, Hasanni, Hassani, Heseny, Hassen, Hassian, Husani

HASHIM (Arabic) destroyer of evil.
Haashim, Hasham, Hasheem, Hashem

HASIN (Hindi) laughing.
Haseen, Hasen, Hassin, Hazen, Hesen

HASKEL (Hebrew) an alternate form of Ezekiel.
Haskell

HASLETT (English) hazel-tree land.
Haze, Hazel, Hazlett, Hazlitt

HASSAN (Arabic) handsome.
Hasan, Hassen, Hasson

HASSEL (German, English) witches' corner.
Hassal, Hassall, Hassell, Hazael, Hazell

HASTIN (Hindi) elephant.

HASTINGS (Latin) spear. (English) house council.
Hastie, Hasty

HATIM (Arabic) judge.
Hateem, Hatem

HAUK (Norwegian) hawk.
Haukeye

HAVELOCK (Norwegian) sea battler.

HAVEN (Dutch, English) harbor, port; safe place.
Haeven, Havin, Hevin, Hevon, Hovan

HAVIKA (Hawaiian) a form of David.

HAWK (English) hawk.
Hawke, Hawkin, Hawkins

HAWLEY (English) hedged meadow.
Hawleigh, Hawly

HAWTHORNE (English) hawthorn tree.

HAYDEN (English) hedged valley.
Haiden, Haydan, Haydenn, Haydn, Haydon

HAYES (English) hedged valley.
Hayse

HAYWARD (English) guardian of the hedged area.
Haward, Heyvard, Heyward

HAYWOOD (English) hedged forest.
Heywood, Woody

HEARN (Scottish, English) a short form of Ahearn.
Hearne, Herin, Hern

HEATH (English) heath.
Heathe, Heith

HEATHCLIFF (English) cliff near the heath. Literature: the hero of Emily Brontë's novel *Wuthering Heights*.

HEATON (English) high place.

HEBER (Hebrew) ally, partner.

HECTOR (Greek) steadfast. Mythology: the greatest hero of the Trojan war.

HEDLEY (English) heather-filled meadow.
Headley, Headly, Hedly

HEINRICH (German) an alternate form of Henry.
Heindrick, Heiner, Heinreich, Heinrick, Heinrik, Hinrich

HEINZ (German) a familiar form of Henry.

HELAKU (Native American) sunny day.

HELGE (Russian) holy.

HELKI (Moquelumnan) touching.

HELMER (German) warrior's wrath.

HELMUT (German) courageous.
Helmuth

HEMAN (Hebrew) faithful.

HENDERSON (Scottish, English) son of Henry.
Hendrie, Hendries, Hendron, Henryson

HENDRICK (Dutch) a form of Henry.
Hendricks, Hendrickson, Hendrik, Hendriks, Hendrikus, Hendrix, Henning

HENIEK (Polish) a form of Henry.
Henier

HENLEY (English) high meadow.

HENNING (German) an alternate form of Hendrick, Henry.

HENOCH (Yiddish) initiator.
Enoch, Henock, Henok

HENRI (French) a form of Henry.
Henrico, Henrri

HENRICK (Dutch) a form of Henry.
Heinrick, Henerik, Henrich, Henrik, Henryk

HENRIQUE (Portuguese) a form of Henry.

HENRY (German) ruler of the household. See also Arrigo, Enric, Enrick, Enrico, Enrikos, Enrique, Hanale, Honok, Kiki.
Hagan, Hank, Harro, Harry, Heike, Heinrich, Heinz, Hendrick, Henery, Heniek, Henning, Henraoi, Henri, Henrick, Henrim, Henrique, Henrry, Heromin, Hersz

HERALDO (Spanish) a form of Harold.
Herald, Hiraldo

HERB (German) a short form of Herbert.
Herbie, Herby

HERBERT (German) glorious soldier.
Bert, Erbert, Eriberto, Harbert, Hebert, Hébert, Heberto, Herb, Heriberto, Hurbert

HERCULES (Greek) glorious gift. Mythology: a famous Greek hero renowned for his twelve labors.
Herakles, Herc, Hercule, Herculie

HERIBERTO (Spanish) a form of Herbert.
Heribert

HERMAN (Latin) noble. (German) soldier. See also Armand, Ermanno, Ermano, Mandek.
Harmon, Hermaan, Hermann, Hermie, Herminio, Hermino, Hermon, Hermy, Heromin

HERMES (Greek) messenger. Mythology: the messenger for the Greek gods.

HERNAN (German) peacemaker.

HERNANDO (Spanish) a form of Ferdinand.
Hernandes, Hernandez

HERRICK (German) war ruler.
Herrik, Herryck

HERSCHEL (Hebrew) an alternate form of Hershel.
Herchel, Hersch, Herschel, Herschell

HERSH (Hebrew) a short form of Hershel.
Hersch, Hirsch

HERSHEL (Hebrew) deer.
Herschel, Hersh, Hershal, Hershall, Hershell, Herzl, Hirschel, Hirshel

HERTZ (Yiddish) my strife.
Herzel

HERVÉ (French) a form of Harvey.

HESPEROS (Greek) evening star.
Hespero

HESUTU (Moquelumnan) picking up a yellow jacket's nest.

HEW (Welsh) a form of Hugh.
Hewe, Huw

HEWITT (German, French) little smart one.
Hewe, Hewet, Hewett, Hewie, Hewit, Hewlett, Hewlitt, Hugh

HEWSON (English) son of Hugh.

HEZEKIAH (Hebrew) God gives strength.
Hezekyah, Hazikiah, Hezikyah

HIAMOVI (Cheyenne) high chief.

HIBAH (Arabic) gift.

HIDEAKI (Japanese) smart, clever.
Hideo

HIEREMIAS (Greek) God will uplift.

HIERONYMOS (Greek) a form of
Jerome.
*Hierome, Hieronim, Hieronimo, Hieronimos,
Hieronymo, Hieronymus*

HIEU (Vietnamese) respectful.

HILARIO (Spanish) a form of Hilary.

HILARY (Latin) cheerful. See also Ilari.
*Hi, Hilair, Hilaire, Hilarie, Hilario, Hilarion,
Hilarius, Hil, Hill, Hillary, Hillery, Hilliary,
Hillie, Hilly*

HILDEBRAND (German) battle sword.
Hildebrando, Hildo

HILEL (Arabic) new moon.

HILLEL (Hebrew) greatly praised.
Religion: Rabbi Hillel originated the
Talmud.

HILLIARD (German) brave warrior.
*Hillard, Hiller, Hillier, Hillierd, Hillyard,
Hillyer, Hillyerd*

HILMAR (Swedish) famous noble.

HILTON (English) town on a hill.
Hylton

HINTO (Dakota) blue.

HINUN (Native American) spirit of the
storm.

HIPPOLYTE (Greek) horseman.
*Hipolito, Hippolit, Hippolitos, Hippolytus,
Ippolito*

HIRAM (Hebrew) noblest; exalted.
Hi, Hirom, Huram, Hyrum

HIROMASA (Japanese) fair, just.

HIROSHI (Japanese) generous.

HISOKA (Japanese) secretive, reserved.

HIU (Hawaiian) a form of Hugh.

HO (Chinese) good.

HOANG (Vietnamese) finished.

HOBART (German) Bart's hill.
Hobard, Hobbie, Hobby, Hobie, Hoebart

HOBERT (German) Bert's hill.
Hobey

HOBSON (English) son of Robert.
Hobbs, Hobs

HOC (Vietnamese) studious.

HOD (Hebrew) a short form of Hodgson.

HODGSON (English) son of Roger.
Hod

HOGAN (Irish) youth.
Hogin

HOLBROOK (English) brook in the
hollow.
Brook, Holbrooke

HOLDEN (English) hollow in the valley.
Holdan, Holdin, Holdon, Holdun, Holdyn

HOLIC (Czech) barber.

HOLLAND (French) Geography:
A country in the Netherlands.

HOLLEB (Polish) dove.
Hollub, Holub

HOLLIS (English) grove of holly trees.
Hollie, Holly

HOLMES (English) river islands.

HOLT (English) forest.
Holten, Holton

HOMER (Greek) hostage; pledge;
security. Literature: a renowned Greek
poet.

Homar, Homere, Homère, Homero, Homeros, Homerus

HONDO (Shona) warrior.

HONESTO (Filipino) honest.

HONI (Hebrew) gracious.
Choni

HONOK (Polish) a form of Henry.

HONON (Moquelumnan) bear.

HONORATO (Spanish) honorable.

HONORÉ (Latin) honored.
Honor, Honoratus, Honoray, Honorio, Honorius

HONOVI (Native American) strong.

HONZA (Czech) a form of John.

HOP (Chinese) agreeable.

HORACE (Latin) keeper of the hours. Literature: a famous Latin poet.
Horacio, Horaz

HORACIO (Latin) an alternate form of Horace.

HORATIO (Latin) clan name. See also Orris.
Horatius, Oratio

HORST (German) dense grove; thicket.
Hurst

HORTON (English) garden estate.
Hort, Horten, Orton

HOSA (Arapaho) young crow.

HOSEA (Hebrew) salvation. Bible: a Hebrew prophet.
Hose, Hoseia, Hoshea, Hosheah

HOTAH (Lakota) white.

HOTOTO (Native American) whistler.

HOUGHTON (English) settlement on the headland.

HOUSTON (English) hill town. Geography: a city in Texas.
Housten, Houstin, Hustin, Huston

HOWARD (English) watchman. See also Haoa.
Howie, Ward

HOWE (German) high.
Howey, Howie

HOWELL (Welsh) remarkable.
Howel

HOWI (Moquelumnan) turtle dove.

HOWIE (English) a familiar form of Howard, Howland.
Howey

HOWIN (Chinese) loyal swallow.

HOWLAND (English) hilly land.
Howie, Howlan, Howlen

HOYT (Irish) mind; spirit.

HU (Chinese) tiger.

HUBBARD (German) an alternate form of Hubert.

HUBERT (German) bright mind; bright spirit. See also Beredei, Uberto.
Bert, Hobart, Hubbard, Hubbert, Huber, Hubertek, Huberto, Hubertson, Hubie, Huey, Hugh, Hugibert, Huibert, Humberto

HUBERTO (Spanish) a form of Hubert.
Humberto

HUBIE (English) a familiar form of Hubert.
Hube, Hubi

HUD (Arabic) Religion: a Muslim prophet.

HUDSON (English) son of Hud.

HUEY (English) a familiar form of Hugh.
Hughey, Hughie, Hughy, Hui

HUGH (English) a short form of Hubert.
See also Ea, Hewitt, Huxley, Maccoy,
Ugo.
*Fitzhugh, Hew, Hiu, Hue, Huey, Hughes,
Hugo, Hugues*

HUGO (Latin) a form of Hugh.
Ugo

HULBERT (German) brilliant grace.
Bert, Hulbard, Hulburd, Hulburt, Hull

HUMBERT (German) brilliant strength.
See also Umberto.
Hum, Humberto

HUMBERTO (Portuguese) a form of
Humbert.

HUMPHREY (German) peaceful
strength. See also Onofrio, Onufry.
*Hum, Humfredo, Humfrey, Humfrid,
Humfried, Humfry, Hump, Humph,
Humphery, Humphry, Humphrys, Hunfredo*

HUNG (Vietnamese) brave.

HUNT (English) a short form of names
beginning with 'Hunt.'

HUNTER (English) hunter.
Hunt, Huntur

HUNTINGTON (English) hunting
estate.
Hunt, Huntingdon

HUNTLEY (English) hunter's meadow.
Hunt, Huntlea, Huntlee, Huntleigh, Huntly

HURLEY (Irish) sea tide.
Hurlee, Hurleigh

HURST (English) a form of Horst.
Hearst, Hirst

HUSAM (Arabic) sword.

HUSAMETTIN (Turkish) sharp sword.

HUSLU (Native American) hairy bear.

HUSSAIN (Arabic) an alternate form of
Hussein.
*Hossain, Husain, Husani, Husayn, Hussan,
Hussayn*

HUSSEIN (Arabic) little; handsome.
*Hossein, Houssein, Houssin, Huissien,
Huossein, Husein, Husien, Hussain, Hussien*

HUSSIEN (Arabic) an alternate form
of Hussein.
Husian, Hussin

HUTCHINSON (English) son of the
hutch dweller.
Hutcheson

HUTE (Native American) star.
Astronomy: a star in the Big Dipper.

HUTTON (English) house on the jutting
ledge.
Hut, Hutt, Huttan

HUXLEY (English) Hugh's meadow.
Hux, Huxlea, Huxlee, Huxleigh, Lee

HUY (Vietnamese) glorious.

HY (Vietnamese) hopeful. (English) a
short form of Hyman.

HYACINTHE (French) hyacinth.

HYATT (English) high gate.
Hyat

HYDE (English) measure of land equal
to 120 acres.

HYDER (English) tanner, preparer of
animal hides for tanning.

HYMAN (English) a form of Chaim.
*Haim, Hayim, Hayvim, Hayyim, Hy, Hyam,
Hymie*

HYUN-KI (Korean) wise.

HYUN-SHIK (Korean) clever.

I

IAGO (Spanish, Welsh) a form of Jacob, James. Literature: the villain in Shakespeare's *Othello*.
Jago

IAIN (Scottish) an alternate form of Ian.

IAKOBOS (Greek) a form of Jacob.
Iakov, Iakovos, Iakovs

IAN (Scottish) a form of John. See also Ean, Eion.
Iain, Iane, Iann

IANOS (Czech) a form of John.
Iannis

IB (Phoenician, Danish) oath of Baal.

IBAN (Basque) a form of John.

IBON (Basque) a form of Ivor.

IBRAHIM (Arabic) a form of Abraham. (Hausa) my father is exalted.
Ibrahaim, Ibraham, Ibraheem, Ibrahem, Ibrahiem, Ibrahiim, Ibrahmim

ICHABOD (Hebrew) glory is gone. Literature: Ichabod Crane was the main character of Washington Irving's story 'The Legend of Sleepy Hollow.'

IDI (Swahili) born during the Idd festival.

IDRIS (Welsh) eager lord. Religion: a Muslim prophet.
Idrease, Idrees, Idres, Idress, Idreus, Idriece, Idriss, Idrissa, Idriys

IESTYN (Welsh) a form of Justin.

IGASHU (Native American) wanderer; seeker.
Igasho

IGGY (Latin) a familiar form of Ignatius.

IGNACIO (Italian) a form of Ignatius.
Ignazio

IGNATIUS (Latin) fiery, ardent. Religion: Saint Ignatious of Loyola was the founder of the Jesuit order. See also Inigo, Neci.
Iggie, Iggy, Ignac, Ignác, Ignace, Ignacio, Ignacius, Ignatios, Ignatious, Ignatz, Ignaz, Ignazio

IGOR (Russian) a form of Inger, Ingvar. See also Egor, Yegor.
Igoryok

IHSAN (Turkish) compassionate.

IKE (Hebrew) a familiar form of Isaac. History: the nickname of the thirty-fourth U.S. president Dwight D. Eisenhower.
Ikee, Ikey

IKER (Basque) visitation.

ILAN (Hebrew) tree. (Basque) youth.

ILARI (Basque) a form of Hilary.
Ilario

ILIAS (Greek) a form of Elijah.
Illias, Illyas, Ilyas, Ilyes

ILLAN (Basque, Latin) youth.

ILOM (Ibo) my enemies are many.

ILYA (Russian) a form of Elijah.
Ilia, Ilie, Ilija, Iliya, Ilja, Illia, Illya

IMAD (Arabic) supportive; mainstay.

IMAN (Hebrew) a short form of Immanuel.
Imani, Imanni

IMMANUEL (Hebrew) an alternate form of Emmanuel.
Iman, Imanol, Imanuel, Immanual, Immanuele, Immuneal

IMRAN (Arabic) host. Bible: a character in the Old Testament.
Imraan

IMRE (Hungarian) a form of Emery.
Imri

IMRICH (Czech) a form of Emery.
Imrus

INAY (Hindi) god; godlike. Religion: another name for the Hindu god Shiva.

INCE (Hungarian) innocent.

INDER (Hindi) god; godlike. Religion: another name for the Hindu god Shiva.
Inderbir, Inderdeep, Inderjeet, Inderjit, Inderpal, Inderpreet, Inderveer, Indervir, Indra, Indrajit

INDIANA (Hindi) from India.
Indi, Indy

INEK (Welsh) an alternate form of Irvin.

ING (Scandinavian) a short form of Ingmar.
Inge

INGELBERT (German) an alternate form of Engelbert.
Inglebert

INGER (Scandinavian) son's army.
Igor, Ingemar, Ingmar

INGMAR (Scandinavian) famous son.
Ing, Ingamar, Ingamur, Ingemar

INGRAM (English) angel.
Inglis, Ingra, Ingraham, Ingrim

INGVAR (Scandinavian) Ing's soldier.
Igor, Ingevar

INIGO (Basque) a form of Ignatius.
Iñaki, Iniego, Iñigo

INIKO (Ibo) born during bad times.

INNIS (Irish) island.
Innes, Inness, Inniss

INNOCENZIO (Italian) innocent.
Innocenty, Inocenci, Inocencio, Inocente, Inosente

INTEUS (Native American) proud; unashamed.

IOAKIM (Russian) a form of Joachim.
Ioachime, Ioakimo, Iov

IOAN (Greek, Bulgarian, Romanian) a form of John.
Ioane, Ioann, Ioannes, Ioannikios, Ioannis, Ionel

IOKEPA (Hawaiian) a form of Joseph.
Keo

IOLO (Welsh) the Lord is worthy.
Iorwerth

IONAKANA (Hawaiian) a form of Jonathan.

IORGOS (Greek) an alternate form of George.

IOSIF (Greek, Russian) a form of Joseph.

IOSUA (Romanian) a form of Joshua.

IPYANA (Nyakusa) graceful.

IRA (Hebrew) watchful.

IRAM (English) bright.

IRUMBA (Rutooro) born after twins.

IRV (Irish, Welsh, English) a short form of Irvin, Irving.

IRVIN (Irish, Welsh, English) a short form of Irving. See also Ervine.
Inek, Irv, Irven, Irvine, Irvinn, Irvon

IRVING (Irish) handsome. (Welsh) white river. (English) sea friend. See also Ervin, Ervine.
Irv, Irvin, Irvington, Irwin, Irwing

IRWIN (English) an alternate form of Irving. See also Ervin.
Irwinn, Irwyn

ISA (Arabic) a form of Jesus.
Isaah

ISAAC (Hebrew) he will laugh. Bible: the son of Abraham and Sarah. See also Itzak, Izak, Yitzchak.
Aizik, Icek, Ike, Ikey, Ikie, Isaak, Isaakios, Isac, Isacc, Isacco, Isack, Isaic, Ishaq, Isiac, Isiacc, Issac, Issca, Itzak, Izak, Izzy

ISAAK (Hebrew) an alternate form of Isaac.
Isack, Isak, Isik, Issak

ISAIAH (Hebrew) God is my salvation. Bible: an influential Hebrew prophet.
Isa, Isai, Isaia, Isaias, Isaid, Isaih, Isaish, Ishaq, Isia, Isiah, Isiash, Issia, Issiah, Izaiah, Izaiha, Izaya, Izayah, Izayaih, Izayiah, Izeyah, Izeyha

ISAIAS (Hebrew) an alternate form of Isaiah.
Isaiahs, Isais, Izayus

ISAM (Arabic) safeguard.

ISAS (Japanese) meritorious.

ISEKEMU (Native American) slow-moving creek.

ISHAM (English) home of the iron one.

ISHAN (Hindi) direction.
Ishaan, Ishaun

ISHAQ (Arabic) a form of Isaac.
Ishaac, Ishak

ISHMAEL (Hebrew) God will hear. Literature: the narrator of Melville's novel *Moby Dick*.
Isamael, Isamail, Ishma, Ishmail, Ishmale, Ishmeal, Ishmeil, Ishmel, Ishmil, Ismael, Ismail

ISIDORE (Greek) gift of Isis. See also Dorian, Ysidro.
Isador, Isadore, Isadorios, Isidor, Isidro, Issy, Ixidor, Izadore, Izidor, Izidore, Izydor, Izzy

ISIDRO (Greek) an alternate form of Isidore.
Isidoro, Isidoros

ISKANDER (Afghani) a form of Alexander.

ISMAEL (Arabic) a form of Ishmael.

ISMAIL (Arabic) a form of Ishmael.
Ismeil, Ismiel

ISRAEL (Hebrew) prince of God; wrestled with God. History: the nation of Israel took its name from the name given Jacob after he wrestled with the Angel of the Lord.
Iser, Isreal, Israhel, Isrell, Isrrael, Isser, Izrael, Izzy, Yisrael

ISREAL (Hebrew) an alternate form of Israel.
Isrieal

ISSA (Swahili) God is our salvation.

ISSAC (Hebrew) an alternate form of Isaac.
Issacc, Issaic, Issiac

ISSIAH (Hebrew) an alternate form of Isaiah.
Issaiah, Issia

ISTU (Native American) sugar pine.

ISTVÁN (Hungarian) a form of Stephen.
Isti, Istvan, Pista

ITHEL (Welsh) generous lord.

ITTAMAR (Hebrew) island of palms.
Itamar

ITZAK (Hebrew) an alternate form of Isaac, Yitzchak.
Itzik

IUKINI (Hawaiian) a form of Eugene.
Kini

IUSTIN (Bulgarian, Russian) a form of Justin.

IVAN (Russian) a form of John.
Iván, Ivanchik, Ivanichek, Ivann, Ivano, Ivas, Iven, Ivin, Ivon, Ivyn, Vanya

IVAR (Scandinavian) an alternate form of Ivor. See also Yves, Yvon.
Iv, Iva

IVES (English) young archer.
Ive, Iven, Ivey, Yves

IVO (German) yew wood; bow wood.
Ibon, Ivar, Ives, Ivon, Ivonnie, Ivor, Yvo

IVOR (Scandinavian) a form of Ivo.
Ibon, Ifor, Ivar, Iver, Ivory, Ivry

IWAN (Polish) a form of John.

IYAPO (Yoruba) many trials; many obstacles.

IYE (Native American) smoke.

IZAK (Czech) a form of Isaac.
Itzhak, Ixaka, Izaac, Izaak, Izac, Izaic, Izak, Izec, Izeke, Izick, Izik, Izsak, Izsák, Izzak

IZZY (Hebrew) a familiar form of Isaac, Isidore, Israel.
Issy

J

J (American) an initial used as a first name.
J.

JA (Korean) attractive, magnetic.

JAALI (Swahili) powerful.

JAAN (Estonian) a form of Christian.

JAAP (Dutch) a form of Jim.

JABARI (Swahili) fearless.
Jabaar, Jabahri, Jabar, Jabarae, Jabare, Jabaree, Jabarei, Jabarie, Jabarri, Jabarrie, Jabary, Jabbar, Jabbaree, Jabbari, Jaber, Jabiari, Jabier, Jabori, Jaborie

JABEZ (Hebrew) born in pain.
Jabe, Jabes, Jabesh

JABIN (Hebrew) God has created.
Jabain, Jabien, Jabon

JABIR (Arabic) consoler, comforter.
Jabiri, Jabori

JABRIL (Arabic) an alternate form of Jibril.
Jabrail, Jabree, Jabreel, Jabrel, Jabrell, Jabrelle, Jabri, Jabrial, Jabrie, Jabriel, Jabrielle, Jabrille

JABULANI (Shona) happy.

JACAN (Hebrew) trouble.
Jachin

JACARI (American) an alternate form of Jacorey.
Jacarey, Jacaris, Jacarius, Jacarre, Jacarri, Jacarrus, Jacarus, Jacary, Jacaure, Jacauri, Jaccar, Jaccari

JACE (American) a combination of the initials J. + C.
JC, J.C., Jacee, Jacek, Jacey, Jacie, Jaice, Jaicee

JACEN (Greek) an alternate form of Jason.
Jaceon

JACINTO (Portuguese, Spanish) hyacinth. See also Giacinto.
Jacindo, Jacint, Jacinta

JACK (American) a familiar form of Jacob, John. See also Keaka.
Jackie, Jacko, Jackub, Jak, Jax, Jock, Jocko

JACKIE, Jacky (American) familiar forms of Jack.
Jackey

JACKSON (English) son of Jack.
Jacksen, Jacksin, Jacson, Jakson, Jaxon

JACO (Portuguese) a form of Jacob.

JACOB (Hebrew) supplanter, substitute.
Bible: son of Isaac, brother of Esau. See
also Akiva, Chago, Checha, Coby,
Diego, Giacomo, Hamish, Iago, Iakobos,
James, Kiva, Koby, Kuba, Tiago, Yakov,
Yasha, Yoakim.
*Jaap, Jachob, Jack, Jackob, Jackub, Jaco,
Jacobb, Jacobe, Jacobi, Jacobo, Jacoby,
Jacolbi, Jacolby, Jacque, Jacques, Jacub,
Jaecob, Jago, Jaicob, Jaime, Jake, Jakob, Jalu,
Jasha, Jaycob, Jecis, Jeks, Jeska, Jim, Jocek,
Jock, Jocob, Jocobb, Jocoby, Jocolby, Jokubas*

JACOBI, Jacoby (Hebrew) alternate
forms of Jacob.
*Jachobi, Jacobbe, Jacobee, Jacobey, Jacobie,
Jacobii, Jacobis*

JACOBO (Hebrew) an alternate form of
Jacob.

JACOBSON (English) son of Jacob.
Jacobs, Jacobsen, Jacobsin, Jacobus

JACOREY (American) a combination
of Jacob + Corey.
*Jacari, Jacori, Jacoria, Jacorie, Jacoris,
Jacorius, Jacorrey, Jacorrien, Jacorry, Jacory,
Jacouri, Jacourie, Jakari*

JACQUE (French) a familiar form of
Jacob.
Jacquay, Jacqui, Jocque, Jocqui

JACQUES (French) a form of Jacob,
James. See also Coco.
*Jackque, Jackques, Jackquise, Jacot, Jacquan,
Jacquees, Jacquese, Jacquess, Jacquet,
Jacquett, Jacquez, Jacquis, Jacquise, Jaquez,
Jarques, Jarquis*

JACQUEZ, Jaquez (French) alternate
forms of Jacques.
*Jaques, Jaquese, Jaqueus, Jaqueze, Jaquis,
Jaquise, Jaquze, Jocquez*

JACY (Tupi-Guarani) moon.
Jaicy, Jaycee

JADE (Spanish) jade, precious stone.
Jaeid, Jaid, Jaide

JADEN (Hebrew) an alternate form of
Jadon.
Jadee, Jadeen, Jadenn, Jadeon, Jadin, Jaeden

JADON (Hebrew) God has heard.
Jaden, Jadyn, Jaedon, Jaiden, Jaydon

JADRIEN (American) a combination
of Jay + Adrien.
Jad, Jada, Jadd, Jader, Jadrian

JADYN (Hebrew) an alternate form of
Jadon.
Jadyne, Jaedyn

JAEGAR (German) hunter.
Jaager, Jaeger, Jagur

JAE-HWA (Korean) rich, prosperous.

JAEL (Hebrew) mountain goat.
Yael

JAELEN (American) an alternate form
of Jalen.
Jaelan, Jaelaun, Jaelin, Jaelon, Jaelyn

JA'FAR (Sanskrit) little stream.
Jafar, Jafari, Jaffar, Jaffer, Jafur

JAGGER (English) carter.
Jagar, Jager, Jaggar

JAGO (English) an alternate form of James.

JAGUAR (Spanish) jaguar.
Jagguar

JAHI (Swahili) dignified.

JAHLIL (Hindi) an alternate form of
Jalil.
Jahlal, Jahlee, Jahleel, Jahliel

JAHMAR (American) an alternate form
of Jamar.
Jahmare, Jahmari, Jahmarr, Jahmer

JAHVON (Hebrew) an alternate form of Javan.
Jahvan, Jahvine, Jahwaan, Jahwon

JAI (Tai) heart.
Jaie, Jaii

JAIDEN (Hebrew) an alternate form of Jadon.
Jaidan, Jaidon, Jaidyn

JAILEN (American) an alternate form of Jalen.
Jailan, Jailani, Jaileen Jailen, Jailon, Jailyn, Jailynn

JAIME (Spanish) a form of Jacob, James.
Jaimee, Jaimey, Jaimie, Jaimito, Jaimy, Jayme, Jaymie

JAIRO (Spanish) God enlightens.
Jair, Jairay, Jaire, Jairus, Jarius

JAISON (Greek) an alternate form of Jason.
Jaisan, Jaisen, Jaishon, Jaishun

JAIVON (Hebrew) an alternate form of Javan.
Jaiven, Jaivion, Jaiwon

JAJA (Ibo) honored.

JAJUAN (American) a combination of the prefix Ja + Juan.
Ja Juan, Jauan, Jawaun, Jejuan, Jujuan, Juwan

JAKARI (American) an alternate form of Jacorey.
Jakaire, Jakar, Jakaray, Jakarie, Jakarious, Jakarius, Jakarre, Jakarri, Jakarus

JAKE (Hebrew) a short form of Jacob.
Jakie, Jayk, Jayke

JAKEEM (Arabic) uplifted.

JAKOB (Hebrew) an alternate form of Jacob.
Jaekob, Jaikab, Jaikob, Jakab, Jakeb, Jakeob, Jakeub, Jakib, Jakiv, Jakobe, Jakobi, Jakobus, Jakoby, Jakov, Jakovian, Jakub, Jakubek, Jekebs

JAKOME (Basque) a form of James. Bible: another name for Saint James.
Xanti

JAL (Gypsy) wanderer.

JALAN (American) an alternate form of Jalen.
Jalaan, Jalaen, Jalain, Jaland, Jalane, Jalani, Jalanie, Jalann, Jalaun, Jalean, Jallan

JALEEL (Hindi) an alternate form of Jalil.
Jaleell, Jaleil, Jalel

JALEN (American) a combination of the prefix Ja + Len.
Jaelen, Jailen, Jalan, Jaleen, Jalend, Jalene, Jalin, Jallen, Jalon, Jalyn

JALIL (Hindi) god; godlike. Religion: another name for the Hindu god Shiva.
Jahlil, Jalaal, Jalal

JALIN, Jalyn (American) alternate forms of Jalen.
Jalian, Jaline, Jalynn, Jalynne

JALON (American) an alternate form of Jalen.
Jalone, Jaloni, Jalun

JAM (American) a short form of Jamal, Jamar.
Jama

JAMAAL (Arabic) an alternate form of Jamal.

JAMAINE (Arabic) a form of Germain.

JAMAL (Arabic) handsome. See also Gamal.
Jahmal, Jahmall, Jahmalle, Jahmeal, Jahmeel, Jahmeil, Jahmel, Jahmelle, Jahmil, Jahmile, Jaimal, Jam, Jamaal, Jamael, Jamahl, Jamail, Jamaile, Jamala, Jamale, Jamall, Jamalle, Jamar, Jamaul, Jamel, Jamil, Jammal, Jamor, Jamual, Jarmal, Jaumal, Jemal, Jermal, Jomal, Jomall

JAMAR (American) a form of Jamal.
Jam, Jamaar, Jamaari, Jamahrae, Jamair,
Jamara, Jamaras, Jamaraus, Jamarl, Jamarr,
Jamarre, Jamarrea, Jamarree, Jamarri,
Jamarvis, Jamaur, Jamir, Jamire, Jamiree,
Jammar, Jarmar, Jarmarr, Jaumar, Jemaar,
Jemar, Jimar, Jomar

JAMARCUS (American) a combination
of the prefix Ja + Marcus.
Jamarco, Jamarkus, Jemarcus, Jimarcus

JAMARI (American) an alternate form
of Jamario.
Jamare, Jamarea, Jamaree, Jamareh,
Jamaria, Jamarie, Jamaul

JAMARIO (American) a combination of
the prefix Ja + Mario.
Jamareo, Jamari, Jamariel, Jamarious,
Jamaris, Jamarius, Jamariya, Jemario,
Jemarus

JAMARQUIS (American) a
combination of the prefix
Ja + Marquis.
Jamarkees, Jamarkeus, Jamarkis, Jamarqese,
Jamarqueis, Jamarques, Jamarquez,
Jamarquios, Jamarqus

JAMEL (Arabic) an alternate form of
Jamal.
Jameel, Jamele, Jamell, Jamelle, Jammel,
Jamuel, Jamul, Jarmel, Jaumal, Jaumell, Je-
Mell, Jimell

JAMES (Hebrew) supplanter, substitute.
(English) a form of Jacob. Bible: James
the Great and James the Lesser were
two of the Twelve Apostles. See also
Diego, Hamish, Iago, Kimo, Santiago,
Seamus, Seumas, Yago, Yasha.
Jacques, Jago, Jaime, Jaimes, Jakome,
Jamesie, Jamesy, Jamez, Jameze, Jamie,
Jamies, Jamse, Jamyes, Jamze, Jas, Jasha,
Jay, Jaymes, Jem, Jemes, Jim

JAMESON (English) son of James.
Jamerson, Jamesian, Jamison, Jaymeson

JAMIE (English) a familiar form of
James.
Jaime, Jaimey, Jaimie, Jame, Jamee, Jamey,
Jameyel, Jami, Jamia, Jamiah, Jamian,
Jamme, Jammie, Jamiee, Jammy, Jamy,
Jamye, Jayme, Jaymee, Jaymie

JAMIL (Arabic) an alternate form of
Jamal.
Jamiel, Jamiell, Jamielle, Jamile, Jamill,
Jamille, Jamyl, Jarmil

JAMIN (Hebrew) favored.
Jamen, Jamian, Jamien, Jamion, Jamionn,
Jamon, Jamun, Jamyn, Jarmin, Jarmon,
Jaymin

JAMISON (English) son of James.
Jamiesen, Jamieson, Jamis, Jamisen,
Jamyson, Jaymison

JAMON (Hebrew) an alternate form of
Jamin.
Jamohn, Jamone, Jamoni

JAMOND (American) a combination
of James + Raymond.
Jamod, Jamont, Jamonta, Jamontae,
Jamontay, Jamonte, Jarmond

JAMOR (American) a form of Jamal.
Jamoree, Jamori, Jamorie, Jamorius,
Jamorrio, Jamorris, Jamory, Jamour

JAMSHEED (Persian) from Persia.
Jamshaid, Jamshed

JAN (Dutch, Slavic) a form of John.
Jaan, Jana, Janae, Jann, Janne, Jano, Janson,
Jenda, Yan

JANCO (Czech) a form of John.
Jancsi, Janke, Janko

JANDO (Spanish) a form of Alexander.
Jandino

JANEIL (American) a combination of
the prefix Ja + Neil.
Janal, Janel, Janell, Janelle, Janiel, Janielle,
Janile, Janille, Jarnail, Jarneil, Jarnell

JANEK (Polish) a form of John.
Janak, Janik, Janika, Janka, Jankiel, Janko

JANIS (Latvian) a form of John.
Ansis, Jancis, Zanis

JANNE (Finnish) a form of John.
Jann, Jannes

JÁNOS (Hungarian) a form of John.
Jancsi, Jani, Jankia, Jano

JANSON (Scandinavian) son of Jan.
Janse, Jansen, Jansin, Janssen, Jansun, Jantzen, Janzen, Jensen, Jenson

JANTZEN (Scandinavian) an alternate form of Janson.
Janten, Jantsen, Jantson

JANUS (Latin) gate, passageway; born in January. Mythology: the Roman god of beginnings.
Jannese, Jannus, Januario, Janusz

JAPHETH (Hebrew) handsome. (Arabic) abundant. Bible: a son of Noah. See also Yaphet.
Japeth, Japhet

JAQUAN (American) a combination of the prefix Ja + Quan.
Jaequan, Jaiqaun, Jaiquan, Jaqaun, Jaqawan, Jaquaan, Jaquain, Ja'quan, Jaquane, Jaquann, Jaquanne, Jaquavius, Jaquawn, Jaquin, Jaquon, Jaqwan

JAQUARIUS (American) a combination of Jaquan + Darius.
Jaquari, Jaquarious, Jaquaris

JAQUAVIUS (American) an alternate form of Jaquan.
Jaquavas, Jaquaveis, Jaquaveius, Jaquaveon, Jaquaveous, Jaquavias, Jaquavious, Jaquavis, Jaquavus

JAQUON (American) an alternate form of Jaquan.
Jaequon, Jaqoun, Jaquinn, Jaqune, Jaquoin, Jaquone, Jaqwon

JARAD (Hebrew) an alternate form of Jared.
Jaraad, Jaraed

JARAH (Hebrew) sweet as honey.
Jerah

JARDAN (Hebrew) an alternate form of Jordan.
Jarden, Jardin, Jardon

JAREB (Hebrew) contending.
Jarib

JARED (Hebrew) descendant.
Jahred, Jaired, Jarad, Jaredd, Jareid, Jarid, Jarod, Jarred, Jarrett, Jarrod, Jarryd, Jerad, Jered, Jerod, Jerrad, Jerred, Jerrod, Jerryd, Jordan

JAREK (Slavic) born in January.
Janiuszck, Januarius, Januisz, Jarec, Jarrek, Jarric, Jarrick

JARELL (Scandinavian) a form of Gerald.
Jairell, Jarael, Jareil, Jarel, Jarelle, Jariel, Jarrell, Jarryl, Jayryl, Jerel, Jerell, Jerrell, Jharell

JAREN (Hebrew) an alternate form of Jaron.
Jarian, Jarien, Jarin, Jarion

JARETH (American) a combination of Jared + Gareth.
Jarreth, Jereth, Jarreth

JARETT (English) an alternate form of Jarrett.
Jaret, Jarette

JARL (Scandinavian) earl, nobleman.

JARLATH (Latin) in control.
Jarl, Jarlen

JARMAN (German) from Germany.
Jerman

JAROD (Hebrew) an alternate form of Jared.
Jarodd, Jaroid

JARON (Hebrew) he will sing; he will cry out.
Jaaron, Jairon, Jaren, Jarone, Jarren, Jarron, Jaryn, Jayron, Jayronn, Je Ronn, J'ron

JAROSLAV (Czech) glory of spring.
Jarda

JARRED (Hebrew) an alternate form of Jared.
Ja'red, Jarrad, Jarrayd, Jarrid, Jarrod, Jarryd, Jerrid

JARRELL (English) a form of Gerald.
Jarel, Jarell, Jarrel, Jerall, Jerel, Jerell

JARREN (Hebrew) an alternate form of Jaron.
Jarrain, Jarran, Jarrian, Jarrin

JARRETT (English) a form of Garrett, Jared.
Jairett, Jareth, Jarett, Jaretté, Jarhett, Jarratt, Jarret, Jarrette, Jarrot, Jarrott, Jerrett

JARROD (Hebrew) an alternate form of Jared.
Jarod, Jerod, Jerrod

JARRYD (Hebrew) an alternate form of Jared.
Jarrayd, Jaryd

JARVIS (German) skilled with a spear.
Jaravis, Jarv, Jarvaris, Jarvas, Jarvaska, Jarvey, Jarvez, Jarvie, Jarvios, Jarvious, Jarvius, Jarvorice, Jarvoris, Jarvous, Jarvus, Javaris, Jervey, Jervis

JARYN (Hebrew) an alternate form of Jaron.
Jarryn, Jarynn, Jaryon

JAS (Polish) a form of John. (English) a familiar form of James.
Jasio

JASHA (Russian) a familiar form of Jacob, James.
Jascha

JASHAWN (American) a combination of the prefix Ja + Shawn.
Jasean, Jashan, Jashaun, Jashion, Jashon

JASKARAN (Sikh) sings praises to the Lord.
Jaskaren, Jaskarn, Jaskiran

JASMIN (Persian) jasmine flower.
Jasman, Jasmanie, Jasmine, Jasmon, Jasmond

JASON (Greek) healer. Mythology: the hero who led the Argonauts in search of the Golden Fleece.
Jacen, Jaeson, Jahson, Jaison, Jasan, Jasaun, Jase, Jasen, Jasin, Jasson, Jasten, Jasun, Jasyn, Jathan, Jathon, Jay, Jayson

JASPAL (Punjabi) living a virtuous lifestyle.

JASPER (French) green ornamental stone. (English) a form of Casper. See also Kasper.
Jaspar, Jazper, Jespar, Jesper

JASSON (Greek) an alternate form of Jason.
Jassen, Jassin

JATINRA (Hindi) great Brahmin sage.

JAVAN (Hebrew) Bible: son of Japheth.
Jaewan, Jahvaughan, Jahvon, Jaivon, Javante, Javaon, JaVaughn, Javen, Javian, Javien, Javin, Javine, Javoanta, Javon, Javona, Javone, Javonte, Jayvin, Jayvion, Jayvon, Jevan, Jevon

JAVANTE (American) a form of Javan.
Javantae, Javantai, Javantée, Javanti

JAVARIS (English) a form of Jarvis.
Javaor, Javar, Javaras, Javare, Javares, Javari, Javarias, Javaries, Javario, Javarius, Javaro, Javaron, Javarous, Javarre, Javarreis, Javarri, Javarrious, Javarris, Javarro, Javarous, Javarte, Javarus, Javorious, Javoris, Javorius, Javouris

JAVAS (Sanskrit) quick, swift.
Jayvas, Jayvis

JAVIER (Spanish) owner of a new house. See also Xavier.
Jabier, Javer, Javere, Javiar

JAVON (Hebrew) an alternate form of Javan.
Jaavon, Jaevin, Jaevon, Jaewon, Javeon, Javion, Javionne, Javohn, Javona, Javone, Javoney, Javoni, Javonn, Javonne, Javonni, Javonnie, Javonnte, Javoun, Jayvon

JAVONTE (American) a form of Javan.
Javona, Javontae, Javontai, Javontay, Javontaye, Javonté, Javontee, Javonteh, Javontey

JAWAUN (American) an alternate form of Jajuan.
Jawaan, Jawan, Jawann, Jawn, Jawon, Jawuan

JAWHAR (Arabic) jewel; essence.

JAXON (English) an alternate form of Jackson.
Jaxen, Jaxsen, Jaxson, Jaxsun, Jaxun

JAY (French) blue jay. (English) a short form of James, Jason.
Jae, Jai, Jave, Jaye, Jeays, Jeyes

JAYCE (American) a combination of the initials J. + C.
JC, J.C., Jayc, Jaycee, Jay Cee, Jaycey, Jecie

JAYCOB (Hebrew) an alternate form of Jacob.
Jaycub, Jaykob

JAYDE (American) a combination of the initials J. + D.
JD, J.D., Jayd, Jaydee, Jayden

JAYDEN (American) an alternate form of Jayde.
Jaydan, Jaydin, Jaydn, Jaydon

JAYLEE (American) a combination of Jay + Lee.
Jayla, Jayle, Jaylen

JAYLEN (American) a combination of Jay + Len.
Jaylaan, Jaylan, Jayland, Jayleen, Jaylend, Jaylin, Jayln, Jaylon, Jaylun, Jaylund, Jaylyn

JAYLIN (American) an alternate form of Jaylen.
Jaylian, Jayline

JAYLON (American) an alternate form of Jaylen.
Jayleon

JAYLYN (American) an alternate form of Jaylen.
Jaylynd, Jaylynn, Jaylynne

JAYME (English) an alternate form of Jamie.
Jaymie

JAYMES (English) an alternate form of James.
Jaymis, Jayms, Jaymz

JAYQUAN (American) a combination of Jay + Quan.
Jaykwan, Jaykwon, Jayqon, Jayquawn, Jayqunn

JAYSON (Greek) an alternate form of Jason.
Jaycent, Jaysean, Jaysen, Jayshaun, Jayshawn, Jayshon, Jayshun, Jaysin, Jaysn, Jayssen, Jaysson, Jaysun

JAYVON (American) a form of Javon.
Jayvion, Jayvohn, Jayvone, Jayvonn, Jayvontay, Jayvonte, Jaywan, Jaywaun, Jaywin

JAZZ (American) jazz.
Jaz, Jazze, Jazzlee, Jazzman, Jazzmen, Jazzmin, Jazzmon, Jazztin, Jazzton, Jazzy

JEAN (French) a form of John.
Jéan, Jeane, Jeannah, Jeannie, Jeannot, Jeano, Jeanot, Jeanty, Jene

JEB (Hebrew) a short form of Jebediah.
Jebb, Jebi, Jeby

JEBEDIAH (Hebrew) an alternate form of Jedidiah.
Jeb, Jebadia, Jebadiah, Jebadieh, Jebidiah

JED (Hebrew) a short form of Jedidiah. (Arabic) hand.
Jedd, Jeddy, Jedi

JEDIAH (Hebrew) hand of God.
Jedaia, Jedaiah, Jedeiah, Jedi, Yedaya

JEDIDIAH (Hebrew) friend of God, beloved of God. See also Didi.
Jebediah, Jed, Jedadiah, Jeddediah, Jedediah, Jedediha, Jedidia, Jedidiah, Jedidiyah, Yedidya

JEDREK (Polish) strong; manly.
Jedric, Jedrik, Jedrus

JEFF (English) a short form of Jefferson, Jeffrey. A familiar form of Geoffrey.
Jef, Jefe, Jeffe, Jeffey, Jeffie, Jeffy, Jhef

JEFFERSON (English) son of Jeff. History: Thomas Jefferson was the third U.S. president.
Jeferson, Jeff, Jeffers

JEFFERY (English) an alternate form of Jeffrey.
Jefery, Jeffari, Jeffary, Jeffeory, Jefferay, Jeffereoy, Jefferey, Jefferie, Jeffory

JEFFORD (English) Jeff's ford.

JEFFREY (English) divinely peaceful. See also Geffrey, Geoffrey, Godfrey.
Jeff, Jefferies, Jeffery, Jeffre, Jeffree, Jeffrie, Jeffrery, Jeffrie, Jeffries, Jeffry, Jefre, Jefri, Jefry, Jeoffroi, Joffre, Joffrey

JEFFRY (English) an alternate form of Jeffrey.

JEHAN (French) a form of John.
Jehann

JEHU (Hebrew) God lives. Bible: a military commander and king of Israel.
Yehu

JELANI (Swahili) mighty.
Jel, Jelan, Jelanie, Jelaun

JEM (English) a short form of James, Jeremiah.
Jemmie, Jemmy

JEMAL (Arabic) an alternate form of Jamal.
Jemaal, Jemael, Jemale, Jemel

JEMEL (Arabic) an alternate form of Jemal.
Jemeal, Jemehl, Jemehyl, Jemell, Jemelle, Jemello, Jemeyle, Jemile, Jemmy

JEMOND (French) worldly.
Jemon, Jémond, Jemonde, Jemone

JENKIN (Flemish) little John.
Jenkins, Jenkyn, Jenkyns, Jennings

JENÖ (Hungarian) a form of Eugene.
Jenci, Jency, Jenoe, Jensi, Jensy

JENS (Danish) a form of John.
Jense, Jensen, Jenson, Jenssen, Jensy, Jentz

JEOVANNI (Italian) an alternate form of Giovanni.
Jeovahny, Jeovan, Jeovani, Jeovany

JEQUAN (American) a combination of the prefix Je + Quan.
Jeqaun, Jequann, Jequon

JERAD, Jerrad (Hebrew) alternate forms of Jared.
Jeread, Jeredd

JERAHMY (Hebrew) a form of Jeremy.
Jerahmeel, Jerahmeil, Jerahmey

JERALD (English) a form of Gerald.
Jeraldo, Jerold, Jerral, Jerrald, Jerrold, Jerry

JERALL (English) an alternate form of Jarrell.
Jerael, Jerai, Jerail, Jeraile, Jeral, Jerale, Jerall, Jerrail, Jerral, Jerrel, Jerrell, Jerrelle

JERAMIE, Jeramy (Hebrew) alternate forms of Jeremy.
Jerame, Jeramee, Jeramey, Jerami, Jerammie

JERARD (French) a form of Gerard.
Jarard, Jarrard, Jerardo, Jeraude, Jerrard

JERE (Hebrew) a short form of Jeremiah, Jeremy.
Jeré, Jeree

JERED, Jerred (Hebrew) alternate forms of Jared.
Jereed, Jerid, Jerryd, Jeryd

JEREL, Jerell, Jerrell (English) forms of Jarell.
Jerelle, Jeriel, Jeril, Jerrail, Jerral, Jerrall, Jerrel, Jerrill, Jerrol, Jerroll, Jerryl, Jerryll, Jeryl, Jeryle

JEREME, Jeremey (Hebrew) alternate forms of Jeremy.
Jarame

JEREMIAH (Hebrew) God will uplift. Bible: a great Hebrew prophet. See also Dermot, Yeremey, Yirmaya.
Geremiah, Jaramia, Jem, Jemeriah, Jemiah, Jeramiah, Jeramiha, Jere, Jereias, Jeremaya, Jeremi, Jeremia, Jeremial, Jeremias, Jeremija, Jeremy, Jerimiah, Jerimiha, Jerimya, Jermiah, Jermija, Jerry

JEREMIE, Jérémie (Hebrew) alternate forms of Jeremy.
Jeremi, Jérémie, Jeremii

JEREMY (English) a form of Jeremiah.
Jaremay, Jaremi, Jaremy, Jem, Jemmy, Jerahmy, Jeramie, Jeramy, Jere, Jereamy, Jereme, Jeremee, Jeremey, Jeremie, Jérémie, Jeremry, Jérémy, Jeremye, Jereomy, Jeriemy, Jerime, Jerimy, Jermey, Jeromy, Jerremy

JERIAH (Hebrew) Jehovah has seen.

JERICHO (Arabic) city of the moon. Bible: a city conquered by Joshua.
Jeric, Jerick, Jerico, Jerik, Jerric, Jerrick, Jerrico, Jerricoh, Jerryco

JERMAINE (French) an alternate form of Germain. (English) sprout, bud.
Jarman, Jeremaine, Jeremane, Jerimane, Jermain, Jerman, Jermane, Jermanie, Jermanne, Jermany, Jermayn, Jermayne, Jermiane, Jermine, Jer-Mon, Jermone, Jermoney, Jhirmaine

JERMAL (Arabic) an alternate form of Jamal.
Jermael, Jermail, Jermall, Jermaul, Jermel, Jermell, Jermil, Jermol, Jermyll

JERMEY (English) an alternate form of Jeremy.
Jerme, Jermee, Jermere, Jermery, Jermie, Jermy, Jhermie

JERMIAH (Hebrew) an alternate form of Jeremiah.
Jermiha, Jermiya

JERNEY (Slavic) a form of Bartholomew.

JEROD, Jerrod (Hebrew) alternate forms of Jarrod.
Jerode, Jeroid

JEROLIN (Basque, Latin) holy.

JEROME (Latin) holy. See also Geronimo, Hieronymos.
Gerome, Jere, Jeroen, Jerom, Jérome, Jérôme, Jeromo, Jeromy, Jeron, Jerónimo, Jerrome, Jerromy

JEROMY (Latin) an alternate form of Jerome.
Jeromee, Jeromey, Jeromie

JERON (English) a form of Jerome.
Jéron, Jerone, Jeronimo, Jerrin, Jerrion, Jerron, Jerrone, J'ron

JERRETT (Hebrew) a form of Jarrett.
Jeret, Jerett, Jeritt, Jerret, Jerrette, Jerriot, Jerritt, Jerrot, Jerrott

JERRICK (American) a combination of Jerry + Derrick.
Jaric, Jarrick, Jerick, Jerrik

JERRY (German) mighty spearman. (English) a familiar form of Gerald, Gerard. See also Gerry, Kele.
Jehri, Jere, Jeree, Jeris, Jerison, Jerri, Jerrie, Jery

JERVIS (English) a form of Gervaise, Jarvis.

JERZY (Polish) a form of George.
Jersey, Jerzey, Jurek

JESHUA (Hebrew) an alternate form of Joshua.
Jeshuah

JESS (Hebrew) a short form of Jesse.

JESSE (Hebrew) wealthy. Bible: the father of David. See also Yishai.
Jese, Jesee, Jesi, Jess, Jessé, Jessee, Jessie, Jessy

JESSIE (Hebrew) an alternate form of Jesse.
Jesie, Jessi, Jessi

JESSY (Hebrew) an alternate form of Jesse.
Jescey, Jessey, Jessye, Jessyie, Jesy

JESTIN (Welsh) a form of Justin.
Jessten, Jesten, Jeston, Jesstin, Jesston

JESUS (Hebrew) God is my salvation. An alternate form of Joshua. Bible: son of Mary and Joseph, believed by Christians to be the Son of God. See also Chucho, Isa, Yosu.
Jecho, Jessus, Jesu, Jesús, Josu

JESÚS (Hispanic) a form of Jesus.

JETHRO (Hebrew) abundant. Bible: the father-in-law of Moses. See also Yitro.
Jeth, Jethroe, Jetro, Jett

JETT (Hebrew) a short form of Jethro. (English) hard, black mineral.
Jet, Jetson, Jetter, Jetty

JEVAN (Hebrew) an alternate form of Javan.
Jevaun, Jeven, Jevin

JEVON (Hebrew) an alternate form of Javan.
Jevion, Jevohn, Jevone, Jevonn, Jevonne, Jevonnie

JEVONTE (American) a form of Jevon.
Jevonta, Jevontae, Jevontaye, Jevonté

JIBADE (Yoruba) born close to royalty.

JIBBEN (Gypsy) life.
Jibin

JIBRIL (Arabic) archangel of Allah.
Jabril, Jibreel, Jibriel

JILT (Dutch) money.

JIM (Hebrew) supplanter, substitute. (English) a short form of James. See also Jaap.
Jimbo, Jimm, Jimmy

JIMBO (American) a familiar form of Jim.
Jimboo

JIMELL (Arabic) an alternate form of Jamel.
Jimel, Jimelle, Jimill, Jimmell, Jimmelle, Jimmiel, Jimmil

JIMIYU (Abaluhya) born in the dry season.

JIMMIE (English) an alternate form of Jimmy.
Jimi, Jimie, Jimmee, Jimmi

JIMMY (English) a familiar form of Jim.
Jimmey, Jimmie, Jimmye, Jimmyjo, Jimy

JIMOH (Swahili) born on Friday.

JIN (Chinese) gold.
Jinn

JINDRA (Czech) a form of Harold.

JING-QUO (Chinese) ruler of the country.

JIOVANNI (Italian) an alternate form of Giovanni.
Jio, Jiovani, Jiovanie, Jiovann, Jiovannie, Jiovanny, Jiovany, Jiovoni, Jivan

JIRAIR (Armenian) strong; hard working.

JIRI (Czech) a form of George.
Jirka

JIRO (Japanese) second son.

JIVIN (Hindi) life giver.
Jivanta

JO (Hebrew, Japanese) a form of Joe.

JOAB (Hebrew) God is father. See also Yoav.
Joabe, Joaby

JOACHIM (Hebrew) God will establish. See also Akeem, Ioakim, Yehoyakem.
Joacheim, Joakim, Joaquim, Joaquín, Jokin, Jov

JOÃO (Portuguese) a form of John.

JOAQUIM (Portuguese) a form of Joachim.

JOAQUÍN (Spanish) a form of Joachim, Yehoyakem.
Jehoichin, Joaquin, Jocquin, Jocquinn, Joquin, Juaquin

JOB (Hebrew) afflicted. Bible: a righteous man who endured many afflictions.
Jobe, Jobert, Jobey, Jobie, Joby

JOBEN (Japanese) enjoys cleanliness.
Joban, Jobin

JOBO (Spanish) a familiar form of Joseph.

JOBY (Hebrew) a familiar form of Job.
Jobie

JOCK (American) a familiar form of Jacob.
Jocko, Joco, Jocoby, Jocolby

JOCQUEZ (French) an alternate form of Jacquez.
Jocques, Jocquis, Jocquise

JODAN (Hebrew) a combination of Jo + Dan.
Jodahn, Joden, Jodhan, Jodian, Jodin, Jodon, Jodonnis

JODY (Hebrew) a familiar form of Joseph.
Jodey, Jodi, Jodie, Jodiha, Joedy

JOE (Hebrew) a short form of Joseph.
Jo, Joely, Joey

JOEL (Hebrew) God is willing. Bible: an Old Testament Hebrew prophet.
Jôel, Joël, Joell, Joelle, Joely, Jole, Yoel

JOESEPH (Hebrew) an alternate form of Joseph.
Joesph

JOEY (Hebrew) a familiar form of Joe, Joseph.

JOHAN, Johann (German) forms of John. See also Anno, Hanno, Yoan, Yohan.
Joahan, Joan, Joannes, Johahn, Johan, Johanan, Johane, Johannan, Johannes, Johanthan, Johatan, Johathan, Johathon, Johaun, Johon

JOHANNES (German) an alternate form of Johan, Johann.
Johanes, Johannas, Johannus, Johansen, Johanson, Johonson

JOHN (Hebrew) God is gracious. Bible: name honoring John the Baptist and John the Evangelist. See also Elchanan, Evan, Geno, Gian, Giovanni, Handel, Hannes, Hans, Hanus, Honza, Ian, Ianos, Iban, Ioan, Ivan, Iwan, Keoni, Kwam, Ohannes, Sean, Ugutz, Yan, Yanka, Yanni, Yochanan, Yohance, Zane.
Jack, Jacsi, Jaenda, Jahn, Jan, Janak, Janco, Janek, Janis, Janne, János, Jansen, Jantje, Jantzen, Jas, Jean, Jehan, Jen, Jenkin, Jenkyn, Jens, Jhan, Jhanick, Jhon, Jian, Joáo, João, Jock, Joen, Johan, Johann, Johne, Johnl, Johnlee, Johnnie, Johnny, Johnson, Jon, Jonam, Jonas, Jone, Jones, Jonny, Jonté, Jovan, Juan, Juhana

JOHNATHAN (Hebrew) an alternate form of Jonathan.
Jhonathan, Johathe, Johnatan, Johnathann, Johnathaon, Johnathen, Johnathyne, Johnatten, Johniathin, Johnothan, Johnthan

JOHNATHON (Hebrew) an alternate form of Jonathon. See also Yanton.
Johnaton

JOHNNIE (Hebrew) a familiar form of John.
Johnie, Johnier, Johnni, Johnsie, Jonni, Jonnie

JOHNNY (Hebrew) a familiar form of John. See also Gianni.
Jantje, Jhonny, Johney, Johnney, Johny, Jonny

JOHNSON (English) son of John.
Johnston, Jonson

JOJI (Japanese) a form of George.

JOJO (Fante) born on Monday.

JOKIN (Basque) a form of Joachim.

JOLON (Native American) valley of the dead oaks.
Jolyon

JOMAR (American) an alternate form of Jamar.
Jomari, Jomarie, Jomarri

JOMEI (Japanese) spreads light.

JON (Hebrew) an alternate form of John. A short form of Jonathan.
J'on, Joni, Jonn, Jonnie, Jonny, Jony

JONAH (Hebrew) dove. Bible: an Old Testament prophet who was swallowed by a large fish.
Giona, Jona, Yonah, Yunus

JONAS (Lithuanian) a form of John. (Hebrew) he accomplishes.
Jonahs, Jonass, Jonaus, Jonelis, Jonukas, Jonus, Jonutis, Joonas

JONATAN (Hebrew) an alternate form of Jonathan.
Jonatane, Jonate, Jonattan, Jonnattan

JONATHAN (Hebrew) gift of God. Bible: the son of King Saul who became a loyal friend of David. See also Ionakana, Yanton, Yonatan.
Janathan, Johnathan, Johnathon, Jon, Jonatan, Jonatha, Jonathen, Jonathin, Jonathon, Jonathun, Jonathyn, Jonethen, Jonnatha, Jonnathan, Jonnathun, Jonothan, Jonthan

JONATHON (Hebrew) an alternate form of Jonathan.
Joanathon, Johnathon, Jonnathon, Jonothon, Jonthon, Jounathon, Yanaton

JONES (Welsh) son of John.
Joenns, Joness, Jonesy

JONNY (Hebrew) a familiar form of John.
Jonhy, Joni, Jonnee, Jony

JONTAE (French) a combination of Jon + the suffix -tae.
Johntae, Jontay, Jontea, Jonteau, Jontez

JONTAY (American) a form of Jontae.
Johntay, Johnte, Johntez, Jontai, Jonte, Jonté, Jontez

JOOP (Dutch) a familiar form of Joseph.
Jopie

JOOST (Dutch) just.

JOQUIN (Spanish) an alternate form of Joaquin.
Joquan, Joquawn, Joqunn, Joquon

JORA (Hebrew) teacher.
Yora, Jorah

JORAM (Hebrew) Jehovah is exalted.
Joran, Jorim

JORDAN (Hebrew) descending. See also Giordano, Yarden.
Jardan, Jared, Jordaan, Jordae, Jordain, Jordaine, Jordane, Jordani, Jordanio, Jordann, Jordanny, Jordano, Jordany, Jordão, Jordayne, Jorden, Jordian, Jordin, Jordon, Jordun, Jordy, Jordyn, Jorrdan, Jory, Jourdan

JORDEN (Hebrew) an alternate form of Jordan.
Jordenn

JORDON (Hebrew) an alternate form of Jordan.
Jeordon, Johordan

JORDY (Hebrew) a familiar form of Jordan.
Jordi, Jordie

JORDYN (Hebrew) an alternate form of Jordan.

JORELL (American) he saves. Literature: a name inspired by the fictional character Jorel, Superman's father.
Jorel, Jor-El, Jorelle, Jorl, Jorrel, Jorrell

JÖRG (German) a form of George.
Jeorg, Juergen, Jungen, Jürgen

JORGE (Spanish) a form of George.
Jorrín

JORGEN (Danish) a form of George.
Joergen, Jorgan, Jörgen

JORIS (Dutch) a form of George.

JÖRN (German) a familiar form of Gregory.

JORRÍN (Spanish) a form of George.
Jorian, Jorje

JORY (Hebrew) a familiar form of Jordan.
Joar, Joary, Jorey, Jori, Jorie, Jorrie

JOSÉ (Spanish) a form of Joseph. See also Ché, Pepe.
Josean, Josecito, Josee, Joseito, Joselito, Josey

JOSEF (German, Portuguese, Czech, Scandinavian) a form of Joseph.
Joosef, Joseff, Josif, Jozef, József, Juzef

JOSELUIS (Spanish) a combination of Jose + Luis.

JOSEPH (Hebrew) God will add, God will increase. Bible: in the Old Testament, the son of Jesse who came to rule Egypt; in the New Testament, the husband of Mary. See also Beppe, Cheche, Chepe, Giuseppe, Iokepa, Iosif, Osip, Pepa, Peppe, Pino, Sepp, Yeska, Yosef, Yousef, Youssel, Yusif, Yusuf, Zeusef.
Jazeps, Jo, Jobo, Jody, Joe, Joeseph, Joey, Jojo, Joop, Joos, Jooseppi, Jopie, José, Joseba, Josef, Josep, Josephat, Josephe, Josephie, Josephus, Josheph, Josip, Jóska, Joza, Joze, Jozef, Jozeph, Jozhe, Jozio, Jozka, Jozsi, Jozzepi, Jupp, Juziu

JOSH (Hebrew) a short form of Joshua.
Joshe

JOSHA (Hindi) satisfied.

JOSHI (Swahili) galloping.

JOSHUA (Hebrew) God is my salvation. Bible: led the Israelites into the Promised Land. See also Giosia, Iosua, Jesus, Yehoshua.
Jeshua, Johsua, Johusa, Josh, Joshau, Joshaua, Joshauh, Joshawa, Joshawah, Joshia, Joshu, Joshuaa, Joshuah, Joshuea,

Joshuia, Joshula, Joshus, Joshusa, Joshuwa,
Joshwa, Josue, Jousha, Jozshua, Jozsua,
Jozua, Jushua

JOSIAH (Hebrew) fire of the Lord. See
also Yoshiyahu.
Joshiah, Josia, Josiahs, Josian, Josias, Josie

JOSS (Chinese) luck; fate.
Josse, Jossy

JOSUE (Hebrew) an alternate form of
Joshua.
Joshue, Jossue, Josu, Josua, Josuha, Jozus

JOTHAM (Hebrew) may God complete.
Bible: a king of Judah.

JOURDAN (Hebrew) an alternate form
of Jordan.
Jourdain, Jourden, Jourdin, Jourdon,
Jourdyn

JOVAN (Latin) Jove-like, majestic.
(Slavic) a form of John. Mythology:
Jove, also known as Jupiter, was the
supreme Roman god.
Johvan, Johvon, Jovaan, Jovane, Jovani,
Jovanic, Jovann, Jovanni, Jovannis, Jovanny,
Jovany, Jovaughn, Jovaun, Joven, Jovenal,
Jovenel, Jovi, Jovian, Jovin, Jovito, Jovoan,
Jovon, Jovone, Jovonn, Jovonne, Jowan,
Jowaun, Yovan, Yovani

JOVANI, Jovanni (Latin) alternate
forms of Jovan.
Jovanie, Jovannie, Jovoni, Jovonie, Jovonni

JOVANNY, Jovany (Latin) alternate
forms of Jovan.
Jovony

JR (Latin) a short form of Junior.
Jr.

JUAN (Spanish) a form of John. See also
Chan.
Juanch, Juanchito, Juane, Juanito, Juann,
Juaun

JUANCARLOS (Spanish) a
combination of Juan + Carlos.

JUAQUIN (Spanish) an alternate form
of Joaquín.
Juaqin, Juaqine, Juquan, Juaquine

JUBAL (Hebrew) ram's horn. Bible: a
musician and a descendant of Cain.

JUDAH (Hebrew) praised. Bible: the
fourth of Jacob's sons. See also Yehudi.
Juda, Judas, Judd, Jude

JUDAS (Latin) a form of Judah. Bible:
Judas Iscariot was the disciple who
betrayed Jesus.
Jude

JUDD (Hebrew) a short form of Judah.
Jud, Judson

JUDE (Latin) a short form of Judah,
Judas. Bible: one of the Christian
apostles, author of the New Testament
book, 'The Epistle of Saint Jude.'

JUDSON (English) son of Judd.

JUHANA (Finnish) a form of John.
Juha, Juho

JUKU (Estonian) a form of Richard.
Jukka

JULES (French) a form of Julius.
Joles, Jule

JULIAN (Greek, Latin) an alternate
form of Julius.
Jolyon, Julean, Juliaan, Julianne, Juliano,
Julien, Jullian, Julyan

JULIEN (Latin) an alternate form of
Julian.
Juliene, Julienn, Julienne, Jullien, Jullin

JULIO (Hispanic) a form of Julius.

JULIUS (Greek, Latin) youthful, downy
bearded. History: Julius Caesar was a
great Roman emperor. See also
Giuliano.
Jolyon, Julas, Jule, Jules, Julen, Jules, Julian,
Julias, Julie, Julio, Juliusz, Jullius, Juluis

JUMAANE (Swahili) born on Tuesday.

JUMAH (Arabic, Swahili) born on Friday, a holy day in the Islamic religion.
Jimoh, Juma

JUMOKE (Yoruba) loved by everyone.

JUN (Chinese) truthful. (Japanese) obedient; pure.
Junnie

JUNIOR (Latin) young.
Jr, Junious, Junius, Junor

JUPP (German) a form of Joseph.

JUR (Czech) a form of George.
Juraz, Jurek, Jurik, Jurko, Juro

JURGIS (Lithuanian) a form of George.
Jurgi, Juri

JURO (Japanese) best wishes; long life.

JURRIEN (Dutch) God will uplift.
Jore, Jurian, Jurre

JUSTEN (Latin) an alternate form of Justin.
Jasten

JUSTICE (Latin) an alternate form of Justis.
Justic, Justiz, Justyc, Justyce

JUSTIN (Latin) just, righteous. See also Giustino, Iestyn, Iustin, Tutu, Ustin, Yustyn.
Jastin, Jaston, Jestin, Jobst, Joost, Jost, Jusa, Just, Justain, Justan, Justas, Justek, Justen, Justian, Justinas, Justine, Justinian, Justinius, Justinn, Justino, Justins, Justinus, Justo, Juston, Justton, Justukas, Justun, Justyn

JUSTIS (French) just.
Justice, Justs, Justus, Justyse

JUSTYN (Latin) an alternate form of Justin.
Justn, Justyne, Justynn

JUVENAL (Latin) young. Literature: a Roman satiric poet.
Juvon, Juvone

JUWAN (American) an alternate form of Jajuan.
Juvon, Juvone, Juvaun, Juwaan, Juwain, Juwane, Juwann, Juwaun, Juwon, Juwonn, Juwuan, Juwuane, Juwvan, Jwan, Jwon

K

KABIITO (Rutooro) born while foreigners are visiting.

KABIL (Turkish) a form of Cain.
Kabel

KABIR (Hindi) History: a Hindu mystic.
Kabar, Kabeer, Kabier

KABONERO (Runyankore) sign.

KABONESA (Rutooro) difficult birth.

KACEY (Irish) an alternate form of Casey. (American) a combination of the initials K. + C. See also KC.
Kace, Kacee, Kaci, Kacy, Kaesy, Kase, Kasey, Kasie, Kasy, Kaycee

KADAR (Arabic) powerful.
Kader

KADARIUS (American) a combination of Kade + Darius.
Kadairious, Kadarious, Kadaris, Kadarrius, Kadarus, Kaddarrius, Kaderious, Kaderius

KADE (Scottish) wetlands. (American) a combination of the initials K. + D.
Kadee, Kady, Kaid, Kaide, Kaydee

KADEEM (Arabic) servant.
Kadim, Khadeem

KADEN (Arabic) an alternate form of Kadin.
Kadeen, Kadein, Kaidan, Kaiden

KADIN (Arabic) friend, companion.
Caden, Kaden, Kadyn, Kaeden, Kayden

KADIR (Arabic) spring greening.
Kadeer

KADO (Japanese) gateway.

KAEDEN (Arabic) an alternate form of Kadin.
Kaedin, Kaedon, Kaedyn

KAELAN, Kaelin (Irish) alternate forms of Kellen.
Kael, Kaelen, Kaelon, Kaelyn

KAELEB (Hebrew) an alternate form of Kaleb.
Kaelib, Kaelob, Kaelyb, Kailab, Kaileb

KAEMON (Japanese) joyful; right handed.
Kaeman, Kaemen, Kaemin

KAENAN (Irish) an alternate form of Keenan.
Kaenen, Kaenin, Kaenyn

KA'EO (Hawaiian) victorious.

KAFELE (Ngoni) worth dying for.

KAGA (Native American) writer.

KAGAN (Irish) an alternate form of Keegan.
Kage, Kagen, Kaghen, Kaigan

KAHALE (Hawaiian) home.

KAHIL (Turkish) young; inexperienced; naive.
Cahil, Kaheel, Kale, Kayle

KAHLIL (Arabic) an alternate form of Khalíl.
Kahleal, Kahlee, Kahleel, Kahleil, Kahli, Kahliel, Kahlill, Kalel, Kalil

KAHOLO (Hawaiian) runner.

KAHRAMAN (Turkish) hero.

KAI (Welsh) keeper of the keys. (German) an alternate form of Kay. (Hawaiian) sea.
Kae, Kaie, Kaii

KAIKARA (Runyoro) Religion: a Banyoro deity.

KAILEN (Irish) an alternate form of Kellen.
Kail, Kailan, Kailey, Kailin, Kailon, Kailyn

KAILI (Hawaiian) Religion: a Hawaiian deity.
Kailli

KAIN (Welsh, Irish) an alternate form of Kane.
Kainan, Kaine, Kainen, Kainin, Kainon

KAINOA (Hawaiian) name.

KAIPO (Hawaiian) sweetheart.

KAIRO (Arabic) an alternate form of Cairo.
Kaire, Kairee, Kairi

KAISER (German) a form of Caesar.
Kaesar, Kaisar, Kaizer

KAIVEN (American) a form of Kevin.
Kaivan, Kaiven, Kaivon, Kaiwan

KAJ (Danish) earth.
Kai, Kaje

KAKAR (Hindi) grass.

KALA (Hindi) black; time. (Hawaiian) sun. Religion: another name for the Hindu god Shiva.

KALAMA (Hawaiian) torch.
Kalam

KALAN (Irish) an alternate form of Kalen.
Kalane, Kallan

KALANI (Hawaiian) heaven; chief.
Kalan

KALE (Arabic) a short form of Kahlil. (Hawaiian) a familiar form of Carl.
Kalee, Kalen, Kaleu, Kaley, Kali, Kalin, Kalle, Kayle

KALEB (Hebrew) an alternate form of Caleb.
Kaeleb, Kal, Kalab, Kalabe, Kalb, Kale, Kaleob, Kalev, Kalib, Kalieb, Kallb, Kalleb, Kalob, Kaloeb, Kalub, Kalyb, Kilab

KALEN, Kalin (Arabic) alternate forms of Kale. (Irish) alternate forms of Kellen.
Kalan

KALEVI (Finnish) hero.

KALI (Arabic) a short form of Kalil. (Hawaiian) a form of Gary.

KALIL (Arabic) an alternate form of Khalíl.
Kaleel, Kalell, Kali, Kaliel, Kaliil

KALIQ (Arabic) an alternate form of Khaliq.
Kalic, Kalique

KALKIN (Hindi) tenth. Religion: the tenth incarnation of the Hindu god Vishnu.
Kalki

KALLE (Scandinavian) a form of Carl.

KALLEN (Irish) an alternate form of Kellen.
Kallan, Kallin, Kallion, Kallon, Kallun, Kalun

KALON, Kalyn (Irish) alternate forms of Kellen
Kalone, Kalonn, Kalyen, Kalyne, Kalynn

KALOOSH (Armenian) blessed event.

KALVIN (Latin) an alternate form of Calvin.
Kal, Kalv, Kalvan, Kalven, Kalvon, Kalvyn, Vinny

KAMAKA (Hawaiian) face.

KAMAKANI (Hawaiian) wind.

KAMAL (Hindi) lotus. Religion: a Hindu god. (Arabic) perfect, perfection.
Kamaal, Kamel, Kamil

KAMAU (Kikuyu) quiet warrior.

KAMDEN (Scottish) an alternate form of Camden.
Kamdon

KAMERON (Scottish) an alternate form of Cameron.
Kam, Kamaren, Kamaron, Kameran, Kameren, Kamerin, Kamerion, Kamerron, Kamerun, Kameryn, Kamey, Kammeren, Kammeron, Kammy, Kamoryn, Kamran, Kamron

KAMI (Hindi) loving.

KAMIL (Arabic) an alternate form of Kamal.
Kameel

KAMOGA (Luganda) name of a royal Baganda family.

KAMRAN, Kamron (Scottish) alternate forms of Kameron.
Kammron, Kamrein, Kamren, Kamrin, Kamrun, Kamryn

KAMUELA (Hawaiian) a form of Samuel.

KAMUHANDA (Runyankore) born on the way to the hospital.

KAMUKAMA (Runyankore) protected by God.

KAMUZU (Ngoni) medicine.

KAMYA (Luganda) born after twin brothers.

KANA (Japanese) powerful; capable. (Hawaiian) Mythology: a god who took the form of a rope extending from Molokai to Hawaii.

KANAIELA (Hawaiian) a form of
Daniel.
Kana, Kaneii

KANE (Welsh) beautiful. (Irish) tribute.
(Japanese) golden. (Hawaiian) eastern
sky. (English) an alternate form of
Keene. See also Cain.
Kahan, Kain, Kaney, Kayne

KANGE (Lakota) raven.
Kang, Kanga

KANIEL (Hebrew) stalk, reed.
Kan, Kani, Kannie, Kanny

KANNAN (Hindi) Religion: another
name for the Hindu god Krishna.
*Kanaan, Kanan, Kanen, Kanin, Kanine,
Kannen*

KANNON (Polynesian) free. An
alternate form of Cannon.
Kanon

KANOA (Hawaiian) free. (Chinese)
Religion: the Chinese god of mercy.

KANTU (Hindi) happy.

KANU (Swahili) wildcat.

KAORI (Japanese) strong.

KAPILA (Hindi) ancient prophet.
Kapil

KAPONO (Hawaiian) righteous.
Kapena

KARDAL (Arabic) mustard seed.
Karandal, Kardell

KARE (Norwegian) enormous.
Karee

KAREEM (Arabic) noble; distinguished.
Karee, Karem, Kareme, Karim, Karriem

KAREL (Czech) a form of Carl.
Karell, Karil, Karrell

KAREY (Greek) an alternate form of
Carey.
Karee, Kari, Karry, Kary

KARIF (Arabic) born in autumn.
Kareef

KARIISA (Runyankore) herdsman.

KARIM (Arabic) an alternate form of
Kareem.

KARL (German) an alternate form of
Carl.
*Kaarle, Kaarlo, Kale, Kalle, Kalman,
Kálmán, Karcsi, Karel, Kari, Karlen, Karlitis,
Karlo, Karlos, Karlton, Karlus, Karol, Kjell*

KARLEN (Latvian, Russian) a form of
Carl.
*Karlan, Karlens, Karlik, Karlin, Karlis,
Karlon*

KARMEL (Hebrew) an alternate form
of Carmel.

KARNEY (Irish) an alternate form of
Carney.

KAROL (Czech, Polish) a form of Carl.
*Karal, Karolek, Karolis, Karalos, Károly,
Karrel, Karrol*

KARR (Scandinavian) an alternate form
of Carr.

KARSON (English) an alternate form of
Carson.
Karrson, Karsen

KARSTEN (Greek) anointed.
Carsten, Karstan, Karston

KARU (Hindi) cousin. Bible: the cousin
of Moses.
Karun

KARUTUNDA (Runyankore) little.

KARWANA (Rutooro) born during
wartime.

KASEEM (Arabic) divided.
Kasceem, Kaseam, Kaseym, Kasim, Kasseem,
Kassem, Kazeem

KASEKO (Rhodesian) mocked, ridiculed.

KASEM (Tai) happiness.

KASEN (Basque) protected with a
helmet.
Kasean, Kasene, Kaseon, Kasin, Kason,
Kassen

KASEY (Irish) an alternate form of
Casey.
Kaese, Kaesy, Kasay, Kassey

KASHAWN (American) a combination
of the prefix Ka + Shawn.
Kashain, Kashan, Kashaun, Kashen, Kashon

KASIB (Arabic) fertile.

KASIM (Arabic) an alternate form of
Kaseem.
Kassim

KASIMIR (Arabic) peace. (Slavic) an
alternate form of Casimir.
Kasim, Kazimierz, Kazimir, Kazio, Kazmer,
Kazmér, Kázmér

KASIYA (Ngoni) separate.

KASPER (Persian) treasurer. (German)
an alternate form of Casper.
Jasper, Kaspar, Kaspero

KASS (German) blackbird.
Kaese, Kasch, Kase

KASSIDY (Irish) an alternate form
of Cassidy.
Kassady, Kassie, Kassy

KATEB (Arabic) writer.

KATO (Runyankore) second of twins.

KATUNGI (Runyankore) rich.

KAVAN (Irish) handsome.
Cavan, Kavanagh, Kavaugn, Kaven,
Kavenaugh, Kavin, Kavon, Kayvan

KAVEH (Persian) ancient hero.

KAVI (Hindi) poet.

KAVIN, Kavon (Irish) alternate forms
of Kavan.
Kaveon, Kavion, Kavone, Kayvon, Kaywon

KAWIKA (Hawaiian) a form of David.

KAY (Greek) rejoicing. (German)
fortified place. Literature: one of the
knights of King Arthur's Round Table.
Kai, Kaycee, Kaye, Kayson

KAYDEN (Arabic) an alternate form of
Kadin.
Kayde, Kaydee, Kaydin, Kaydn, Kaydon

KAYIN (Nigerian) celebrated. (Yoruba)
long-hoped-for child.

KAYLE (Hebrew) faithful dog. (Arabic) a
short form of Kahlil.
Kayl, Kayla, Kaylee

KAYLEB (Hebrew) an alternate form
of Caleb.
Kaylib, Kaylob, Kaylub

KAYLEN (Irish) an alternate form of
Kellen.
Kaylan, Kaylin, Kaylon, Kaylyn, Kaylynn

KAYNE (Hebrew) an alternate form
of Cain.
Kaynan, Kaynen, Kaynon

KAYODE (Yoruba) he brought joy.

KAYONGA (Runyankore) ash. History:
a great Ankole warrior.

KAZIO (Polish) a form of Casimir,
Kasimir. See also Cassidy.

KAZUO (Japanese) man of peace.

KC (American) a combination of the
initials K. + C. See also Kacey.
Kc, K.C., Kcee, Kcey

KEAGAN (Irish) an alternate form of Keegan.
Keagean, Keagen, Keaghan, Keagyn

KEAHI (Hawaiian) flames.

KEAKA (Hawaiian) a form of Jack.

KEALOHA (Hawaiian) fragrant.
Ke'ala

KEANAN (Irish) an alternate form of Keenan.
Keanen, Keanna, Keannan, Keanon

KEANDRE (American) a combination of the prefix Ke + Andre.
Keandra, Keandray, Keandré, Keandree, Keandrell, Keondre

KEANE (German) bold; sharp. (Irish) handsome. (English) an alternate form of Keene.
Kean

KEANU (Irish) an alternate form of Keenan.
Keaneu, Keani, Keanno, Keano, Keanue, Keeno, Keenu, Kianu

KEARN (Irish) a short form of Kearney.
Kearne

KEARNEY (Irish) an alternate form of Carney.
Kar, Karney, Karny, Kearn, Kearny

KEARY (Irish) an alternate form of Kerry.
Kearie

KEATON (English) where hawks fly.
Keatan, Keaten, Keatin, Keatton, Keatyn, Keeton, Keetun

KEAVEN (Irish) an alternate form of Kevin.
Keavan, Keavon

KEAWE (Hawaiian) strand.

KEB (Egyptian) earth. Mythology: an ancient earth god, also known as Geb.

KEDAR (Hindi) mountain lord. (Arabic) powerful. Religion: another name for the Hindu god Shiva.
Kadar, Kedaar, Keder

KEDDY (Scottish) a form of Adam.
Keddie

KEDEM (Hebrew) ancient.

KEDRICK (English) an alternate form of Cedric.
Keddrick, Kederick, Kedrek, Kedric, Kiedric, Kiedrick

KEEFE (Irish) handsome; loved.

KEEGAN (Irish) little; fiery.
Kaegan, Kagan, Keagan, Keagen, Keeghan, Keegon, Keegun, Kegan, Keigan

KEELAN (Irish) little; slender.
Keelen, Keelin, Keelyn, Keilan, Kelan

KEELEY (Irish) handsome.
Kealey, Kealy, Keeli, Keelian, Keelie, Keely

KEENAN (Irish) little Keene.
Kaenan, Keanan, Keanu, Keenen, Keennan, Keenon, Kenan, Keynan, Kienan, Kienon

KEENE (German) bold; sharp. (English) smart. See also Kane.
Kaene, Keane, Keen, Keenan

KEENEN (Irish) an alternate form of Keenan.
Keenin, Kienen

KEES (Dutch) a form of Kornelius.
Keese, Keesee, Keyes

KEEVON (Irish) an alternate form of Kevin.
Keevan, Keeven, Keevin, Keewan, Keewin

KEGAN (Irish) an alternate form of Keegan.
Kegen, Keghan, Kegon, Kegun

KEHIND (Yoruba) second-born twin.
Kehinde

KEIFFER (German) a form of Cooper.
Keefer, Keifer, Kiefer

KEIGAN (Irish) an alternate form of
Keegan.
Keighan, Keighen

KEIJI (Japanese) cautious ruler.

KEILAN (Irish) an alternate form
of Keelan.
*Keilen, Keilin, Keillene, Keillyn, Keilon,
Keilynn*

KEIR (Irish) a short form of Kieran.

KEITARO (Japanese) blessed.
Keita

KEITH (Welsh) forest. (Scottish) battle
place. See also Kika.
Keath, Keeth, Keithen

KEITHEN (Welsh, Scottish) an alternate
form of Keith.
Keithan, Keitheon, Keithon

KEIVAN (Irish) an alternate form of
Kevin.
Keiven, Keivn, Keivon, Keivone

KEKAPA (Hawaiian) tapa cloth.

KEKIPI (Hawaiian) rebel.

KEKOA (Hawaiian) bold, courageous.

KELBY (German) farm by the spring.
Keelby, Kelbee, Kelbey, Kelbi, Kellby

KELE (Hawaiian) a form of Jerry. (Hopi)
sparrow hawk.
Kelle

KELEMEN (Hungarian) gentle; kind.
Kellman

KELEVI (Finnish) hero.

KELI (Hawaiian) a form of Terry.

KELI'I (Hawaiian) chief.

KELILE (Ethiopian) protected.

KELL (Scandinavian) spring.

KELLAN (Irish) an alternate form of
Kellen.
Keillan

KELLEN (Irish) mighty warrior.
*Kaelan, Kailen, Kalan, Kalen, Kalin, Kallen,
Kalon, Kalyn, Kaylen, Keelan, Kelden, Kelin,
Kellan, Kelle, Kellin, Kellyn, Kelyn, Kelynn*

KELLER (Irish) little companion.

KELLY (Irish) warrior.
Kelle, Kellen, Kelley, Kelli, Kellie, Kely

KELMEN (Basque) merciful.
Kelmin

KELSEY (Scandinavian) island of ships.
*Kelcy, Kelse, Kelsea, Kelsi, Kelsie, Kelso, Kelsy,
Kesley, Kesly*

KELTON (English) keel town; port.
*Kelden, Keldon, Kelson, Kelston, Kelten,
Keltin, Keltonn, Keltyn*

KELVIN (Irish, English) narrow river.
Geography: a river in Scotland.
*Kelvan, Kelven, Kelvon, Kelvyn, Kelwin,
Kelwyn*

KEMAL (Turkish) highest honor.

KEMEN (Basque) strong.

KEMP (English) fighter; champion.

KEMPTON (English) military town.

KEN (Japanese) one's own kind. (Scottish)
a short form of Kendall, Kendrick,
Kenneth.
Kena, Kenn, Keno

KENAN (Irish) an alternate form of
Keenan.

KENAZ (Hebrew) bright.

KENDAL (English) an alternate form of Kendall.
Kendale, Kendali, Kendel, Kendul, Kendyl

KENDALL (English) valley of the river Kent.
Ken, Kendal, Kendell, Kendrall, Kendryll, Kendyll, Kyndall

KENDARIUS (American) a combination of Ken + Darius.
Kendarious, Kendarrious, Kendarrius, Kenderious, Kenderius, Kenderyious

KENDELL (English) an alternate form of Kendall.
Kendelle, Kendrel, Kendrell

KENDREW (Scottish) a form of Andrew.

KENDRICK (Irish) son of Henry. (Scottish) royal chieftain.
Ken, Kenderrick, Kendric, Kendrich, Kenedrick, Kendricks, Kendrik, Kendrix, Kendryck, Kenndrick, Keondric, Keondrick

KENLEY (English) royal meadow.
Kenlea, Kenlee, Kenleigh, Kenlie, Kenly

KENN (Scottish) an alternate form of Ken.

KENNAN (Scottish) little Ken.
Kenna, Kenan, Kenen, Kennen, Kennon

KENNARD (Irish) brave chieftain.
Kenner

KENNEDY (Irish) helmeted chief. History: John F. Kennedy was the thirty-fifth U.S. president.
Kenedy, Kenidy, Kennady, Kennedey

KENNETH (Irish) handsome. (English) royal oath.
Ken, Keneth, Kenneith, Kennet, Kennethen, Kennett, Kennieth, Kennith, Kennth, Kenny, Kennyth, Kenya

KENNY (Scottish) a familiar form of Kenneth.
Keni, Kenney, Kenni, Kennie, Kinnie

KENRICK (English) bold ruler; royal ruler.
Kenric, Kenricks, Kenrik

KENT (Welsh) white; bright. (English) a short form of Kenton. Geography: a county in England.

KENTARO (Japanese) big boy.

KENTON (English) from Kent, England.
Kent, Kenten, Kentin, Kentonn

KENTRELL (English) king's estate.
Kenreal, Kentrel, Kentrelle

KENWARD (English) brave; royal guardian.

KENYA (Hebrew) animal horn. (Russian) a form of Kenneth. Geography: a country in Africa.
Kenyatta

KENYATTA (American) a form of Kenya.
Kenyata, Kenyatae, Kenyatee, Kenyatter, Kenyatti, Kenyotta

KENYON (Irish) white haired, blond.
Kenyan, Kenynn, Keonyon

KENZIE (Scottish) wise leader. See also Mackenzie.
Kensie

KEOKI (Hawaiian) a form of George.

KEOLA (Hawaiian) life.

KEON (Irish) a form of Ewan.
Keeon, Keion, Keionne, Keondre, Keone, Keonne, Keonte, Keony, Keyon, Kian, Kion

KEONI (Hawaiian) a form of John.

KEONTE (American) a form of Keon.
Keonntay, Keonta, Keontae, Keontay, Keontaye, Keontez, Keontia, Keontis, Keontrae, Keontre, Keontrey, Keontrye

KERBASI (Basque) warrior.

KEREL (Afrikaans) young.
Kerell

KEREM (Turkish) noble; kind.
Kereem

KEREY (Gypsy) homeward- bound.
Ker

KERMAN (Basque) from Germany.

KERMIT (Irish) an alternate form of
Dermot.
Kermey, Kermie, Kermitt, Kermy

KERN (Irish) a short form of Kieran.
Kearn, Kerne

KERR (Scandinavian) an alternate form
of Carr.
Karr

KERRICK (English) king's rule.

KERRY (Irish) dark, dark haired.
Keary, Keri, Kerrey, Kerri, Kerrie

KERS (Todas) Botany: an Indian plant.

KERSEN (Indonesian) cherry.

KERSTAN (Dutch) a form of Christian.

KERWIN (Irish) little; dark. (English)
friend of the marshlands.
*Kervin, Kervyn, Kerwinn, Kerwyn, Kerwynn,
Kirwin, Kirwyn*

KESAR (Russian) a form of Caesar.
Kesare

KESHAWN (American) a combination
of the prefix Ke + Shawn.
*Keeshaun, Keeshawn, Keeshon, Kesean,
Keshan, Keshane, Keshaun, Keshayne,
Keshion, Keshon, Keshone, Keshun, Kishan*

KESIN (Hindi) long-haired beggar.

KESSE (Ashanti, Fante) chubby baby.
Kessie

KESTER (English) a form of
Christopher.

KESTREL (English) falcon.
Kes

KEUNG (Chinese) universe.

KEVAN (Irish) an alternate form of
Kevin.
*Kavan, Kewan, Kewane, Kewaun, Keyvan,
Kiwan, Kiwane*

KEVEN (Irish) an alternate form
of Kevin.
Keve, Keveen, Kiven

KEVIN (Irish) handsome. See also
Cavan.
*Kaiven, Keaven, Keevon, Keivan, Kev,
Kevan, Keven, Keverne, Kevian, Kevien,
Kévin, Kevinn, Kevins, Kevis, Kevn, Kevon,
Kevvy, Kevyn, Kyven*

KEVON (Irish) an alternate form of
Kevin.
*Keveon, Kevion, Kevone, Kevonne, Kevontae,
Kevonte, Kevoyn, Kevron, Kewon, Kewone,
Keyvon, Kivon*

KEVYN (Irish) an alternate form of
Kevin.
Kevyon

KEY (English) key; protected.

KEYON (Irish) an alternate form
of Keon.
Keyan, Keyen, Keyin, Keyion

KEYSHAWN (American) a combination
of Key + Shawn.
Keyshan, Keyshaun, Keyshon, Keyshun

KHACHIG (Armenian) small cross.
Khachik

KHAIM (Russian) a form of Chaim.

KHALDUN (Arabic) forever.
Khaldoon, Khaldoun

KHALFANI (Swahili) born to lead.
Khalfan

KHÄLID (Arabic) eternal.
Khaled, Khallid, Khalyd

KHALÍL (Arabic) friend.
Kahlil, Kaleel, Kalil, Khahlil, Khailil, Khailyl, Khalee, Khaleel, Khaleil, Khali, Khalial, Khaliel, Khalihl, Khalill, Khaliyl

KHALIQ (Arabic) creative.
Kaliq, Khalique

KHAMISI (Swahili) born on Thursday.
Kham

KHAN (Turkish) prince.
Khanh

KHARALD (Russian) a form of Gerald.

KHAYRU (Arabic) benevolent.
Khiri, Khiry, Kiry

KHOURY (Arabic) priest.
Khory

KHRISTIAN (Greek) an alternate form of Christian, Kristian.
Khris, Khristan, Khristin, Khriston, Khrystian

KHRISTOPHER (Greek) an alternate form of Kristopher.
Khristofer, Khristophar, Khrystopher

KHRISTOS (Greek) an alternate form of Christos.
Khris, Khristophe, Kristo, Kristos

KIBO (Uset) worldly; wise.

KIBUUKA (Luganda) brave warrior. History: a brave Buganda warrior.

KIDD (English) child; young goat.

KIEFER (German) an alternate form of Keifer.
Kief, Kieffer, Kiefor, Kiffer, Kiiefer

KIEL (Irish) an alternate form of Kyle.
Kiell

KIELE (Hawaiian) gardenia.

KIERAN (Irish) little and dark; little Keir.
Keiran, Keiren, Keiron, Kiaron, Kiarron, Kier, Kieren, Kierian, Kierien, Kierin, Kiernan, Kieron, Kierr, Kierre, Kierron, Kyran

KIERNAN (Irish) an alternate form of Kieran.
Kern, Kernan, Kiernen

KIET (Tai) honor.

KIFEDA (Luo) only boy among girls.

KIHO (Dutooro) born on a foggy day.

KIJIKA (Native American) quiet walker.

KIKA (Hawaiian) a form of Keith.

KIKI (Spanish) a form of Henry.

KILE (Irish) an alternate form of Kyle.
Kilee, Kilen, Kiley, Kiyl, Kiyle

KILLIAN (Irish) little Kelly.
Kilean, Kilian, Kilien, Killie, Killien, Killiean, Killion, Killy

KIM (English) a short form of Kimball.
Kimie, Kimmy

KIMBALL (Greek) hollow vessel. (English) warrior chief.
Kim, Kimbal, Kimbel, Kimbell, Kimble

KIMO (Hawaiian) a form of James.

KIMOKEO (Hawaiian) a form of Timothy.

KIN (Japanese) golden.

KINCAID (Scottish) battle chief.
Kincade, Kinkaid

KINDIN (Basque) fifth.

KING (English) king. A short form of names beginning with 'King.'

KINGSLEY (English) king's meadow.
King, Kings, Kingslea, Kingslie, Kingsly,
Kingzlee, Kinslea, Kinslee, Kinsley, Kinslie,
Kinsly

KINGSTON (English) king's estate.
King, Kinston

KINGSWELL (English) king's well.
King

KINI (Hawaiian) a short form of Iukini.

KINNARD (Irish) tall slope.

KINSEY (English) victorious royalty.
Kinze, Kinzie

KINTON (Hindi) crowned.

KION (Irish) an alternate form of Keon.
Kione, Kionie, Kionne

KIOSHI (Japanese) quiet.

KIPP (English) pointed hill.
Kip, Kippar, Kipper, Kippie, Kippy

KIR (Bulgarian) a familiar form of Cyrus.

KIRAL (Turkish) king; supreme leader.

KIRAN (Sanskrit) beam of light.
Kyran

KIRBY (Scandinavian) church village.
(English) cottage by the water.
Kerbey, Kerbie, Kerby, Kirbey, Kirbie, Kirkby

KIRI (Cambodian) mountain.

KIRIL (Slavic) a form of Cyril.
Kirill, Kiryl, Kyrillos

KIRITAN (Hindi) wearing a crown.

KIRK (Scandinavian) church.
Kerk

KIRKLAND (English) church land.
Kirklin, Kirklind, Kirklynd

KIRKLEY (English) church meadow.

KIRKLIN (English) an alternate form of
Kirkland.
Kirklan, Kirklen, Kirkline, Kirkloun,
Kirklun, Kirklyn, Kirklynn

KIRKWELL (English) church well;
church spring.

KIRKWOOD (English) church forest.

KIRTON (English) church town.

KISHAN (American) an alternate form
of Keshawn.
Kishaun, Kishawn, Kishen, Kishon, Kyshon,
Kyshun

KISTNA (Hindi) sacred, holy.
Geography: a sacred river in India.

KISTUR (Gypsy) skillful rider.

KIT (Greek) a familiar form of Christian,
Christopher, Kristopher.
Kitt, Kitts

KITO (Swahili) jewel; precious child.

KITWANA (Swahili) pledged to live.

KIVA (Hebrew) a short form of Akiva,
Jacob.
Kiba, Kivi, Kiwa

KIYOSHI (Japanese) quiet; peaceful.

KIZZA (Luganda) born after twins.
Kizzy

KJELL (Swedish) a form of Karl.
Kjel

KLAUS (German) a short form of
Nicholas. An alternate form of Claus.
Klaas, Klaes, Klas, Klause

KLAY (English) an alternate form of
Clay.

KLAYTON (English) an alternate form
of Clayton.

KLEEF (Dutch) cliff.

KLEMENT (Czech) a form of Clement.
Klema, Klemenis, Klemens, Klemet, Klemo,
Klim, Klimek, Kliment, Klimka

KLENG (Norwegian) claw.

KNIGHT (English) armored knight.
Knightly

KNOTON (Native American) an
alternate form of Nodin.

KNOWLES (English) grassy slope.
Knolls, Nowles

KNOX (English) hill.

KNUTE (Scandinavian) an alternate
form of Canute.
Knud, Knut

KOBY (Polish) a familiar form of Jacob.
Kobby, Kobe, Kobey, Kobi, Kobia, Kobie

KODI (English) an alternate form of
Kody.
Kode, Kodee, Kodie

KODY (English) an alternate form
of Cody.
Kodey, Kodi, Kodye, Koty

KOFI (Twi) born on Friday.

KOHANA (Lakota) swift.

KOI (Hawaiian) a form of Troy.
(Choctaw) panther.

KOJO (Akan) born on Monday.

KOKA (Hawaiian) Scotsman.

KOKAYI (Shona) gathered together.

KOLBY (English) an alternate form of
Colby.
Kelby, Koalby, Koelby, Kohlbe, Kohlby, Kolbe,
Kolbey, Kolbi, Kolbie, Kolebe, Koleby, Kollby

KOLE (English) an alternate form of
Cole.
Kohl, Kohle

KOLEMAN (English) an alternate form
of Coleman.
Kolemann, Kolemen

KOLIN (English) an alternate form of
Colin.
Kolen, Kollen, Kollin, Kollyn, Kolyn

KOLTON (English) an alternate form of
Colton.
Kolt, Koltan, Kolte, Kolten, Koltin, Koltn,
Koltyn

KOLYA (Russian) a familiar form of
Nikolai, Nikolos.
Kola, Kolenka, Kolia, Kolja

KONA (Hawaiian) a form of Don.
Konala

KONANE (Hawaiian) bright moonlight.

KONDO (Swahili) war.

KONG (Chinese) glorious; sky.

KONNER (Irish) an alternate form
of Conner, Connor.
Konar, Koner

KONNOR (Irish) an alternate form of
Connor.
Kohner, Kohnor, Konor

KONO (Moquelumnan) squirrel eating a
pine nut.

KONRAD (German) a form of Conrad.
Khonrad, Koen, Koenraad, Kon, Konn,
Konney, Konni, Konnie, Konny, Konrád,
Konrade, Konrado, Kord, Kort, Kunz

KONSTANTIN (German, Russian) a
form of Constantine. See also Dinos.
Konstancji, Konstadine, Konstadino,
Konstandinos, Konstantinas, Konstantine,
Konstantinos, Konstantio, Konstanty,
Konstantyn, Konstanz, Konstatino,
Kostadino, Kostadinos, Kostandino,
Kostandinos, Kostantin, Kostantino, Kostas,
Kostenka, Kostya, Kotsos

KONTAR (Akan) only child.

KORB (German) basket.

KORBIN (English) a form of Corbin.
Korban, Korben, Korbyn

KORDELL (English) a form of Cordell.
Kordel

KOREY (Irish) an alternate form of
Corey, Kory.
*Kore, Koree, Korei, Korio, Korre, Korria,
Korrye*

KORNEL (Latin) a form of Cornelius,
Kornelius.
*Kees, Korneil, Kornél, Korneli, Kornelisz,
Kornell, Krelis, Soma*

KORNELIUS (Latin) an alternate form
of Cornelius. See also Kees, Kornel.
*Karnelius, Korneilius, Korneliaus,
Kornelious, Kornellius*

KORRIGAN (Irish) an alternate form of
Corrigan.
Korigan, Korigan, Korrigon, Korrigun

KORT (German, Dutch) an alternate
form of Cort, Kurt.
Kourt

KORTNEY (English) an alternate form
of Courtney.
Kortni, Kourtney

KORUDON (Greek) helmeted one.

KORY (Irish) an alternate form of Corey.
*Korey, Kori, Korie, Korrey, Korri, Korrie,
Korry*

KOSEY (African) lion.
Kosse

KOSMO (Greek) an alternate form of
Cosmo.
Kosmy, Kozmo

KOSTAS (Greek) a short form of
Konstantin.

KOSTI (Finnish) a form of Gustave.

KOSUMI (Moquelumnan) spear fisher.

KOUKALAKA (Hawaiian) a form of
Douglas.

KOURTLAND (English) an alternate
form of Courtland.
*Kortlan, Kortland, Kortlend, Kortlon,
Kourtlin*

KOVIT (Tai) expert.

KRAIG (Irish, Scottish) an alternate
form of Craig.
Kraggie, Kraggy, Krayg, Kreg, Kreig, Kreigh

KRIKOR (Armenian) a form of Gregory.

KRIS (Greek) an alternate form of Chris.
A short form of Kristian, Kristofer,
Kristopher.
Kriss, Krys

KRISCHAN (German) a form of
Christian.
*Krishan, Krishaun, Krishawn, Krishon,
Krishun*

KRISHNA (Hindi) delightful,
pleasurable. Religion: one of the
human incarnations of the Hindu god.
Kistna, Kistnah, Krisha, Krishnah

KRISPIN (Latin) an alternate form of
Crispin.
Krispian, Krispino, Krispo

KRISTER (Swedish) a form of Christian.
Krist, Kristar

KRISTIAN (Greek) an alternate form
of Christian, Khristian.
*Kerstan, Khristos, Kit, Kris, Krischan, Krist,
Kristan, Kristar, Kristek, Kristen, Krister,
Kristien, Kristin, Kristine, Kristinn, Kristion,
Kristjan, Kristo, Kristos, Krists, Krystek,
Krystian, Khrystiyan*

KRISTO (Greek) a short form of
Khristos.

KRISTOFER (Swedish) a form of
Kristopher.
Kris, Kristafer, Kristef, Kristifer, Kristoff,
Kristoffer, Kristofo, Kristofor, Kristofyr,
Kristufer, Kristus, Krystofer

KRISTOFF (Greek) a short form
of Kristofer, Kristopher.
Kristof, Kristóf

KRISTOPHE (French) a form of
Kristopher.

KRISTOPHER (Greek) Christ-bearer.
An alternate form of Christopher.
See also Topher.
Khristopher, Kit, Kris, Krisstopher,
Kristapher, Kristepher, Kristfer, Kristfor,
Kristo, Kristofer, Kristoff, Kristoforo,
Kristoph, Kristophe, Kristophor, Kristos,
Krists, Krisus, Krystopher, Krystupas,
Krzysztof

KRUZ (Spanish) an alternate form
of Cruz.
Kruise, Kruize, Kruse, Kruze

KRYSTIAN (Polish) a form of Christian.
Krys, Krystek, Krystien, Krystin

KUBA (Czech) a form of Jacob.
Kubo, Kubus

KUENG (Chinese) universe.

KUGONZA (Dutooro) love.

KUIRIL (Basque) lord.

KUMAR (Sanskrit) prince.

KUNLE (Yoruba) home filled with
honors.

KUPER (Yiddish) copper.

KURT (Latin, German, French)
courteous; enclosure. A short form
of Kurtis. An alternate form of Curt.
Kirt, Kort, Kuno, Kurtt

KURTIS (Latin, French) an alternate
form of Curtis.
Kirtis, Kirtus, Kurt, Kurtes, Kurtez, Kurtice,
Kurties, Kurtiss, Kurtus, Kurtys

KURUK (Pawnee) bear.

KUZIH (Carrier) good speaker.

KWABENA (Akan) born on Tuesday.

KWACHA (Ngoni) morning.

KWAKO (Akan) born on Wednesday.
Kwaka, Kwaku

KWAM (Zuni) a form of John.

KWAME (Akan) born on Saturday.
Kwamen, Kwami, Kwamin

KWAN (Korean) strong.
Kwane

KWASI (Akan) born on Sunday.
(Swahili) wealthy.
Kwasie, Kwazzi, Kwesi

KWAYERA (Ngoni) dawn.

KWENDE (Ngoni) let's go.

KYELE (Irish) an alternate form of Kyle.

KYLAN (Irish) an alternate form of Kyle.
Kyelen, Kyleen, Kylen, Kylin, Kyline, Kylon,
Kylun

KYLE (Irish) narrow piece of land; place
where cattle graze. (Yiddish) crowned
with laurels.
Cyle, Kiel, Kilan, Kile, Kilen, Kiley, Ky, Kye,
Kyel, Kyele, Kylan, Kylee, Kyler, Kyley, Kylie,
Kyll, Kylle, Kyrell

KYLER (English) a form of Kyle.
Kylar, Kylor

KYNAN (Welsh) chief.

KYNDALL (English) an alternate form
of Kendall.
Kyndal, Kyndel, Kyndell, Kyndle

KYNE (English) royal.

KYRAN (Sanskrit) an alternate form
of Kiran.
Kyren, Kyron, Kyrone

KYROS (Greek) master.

KYVEN (American) a form of Kevin.
Kyvan, Kyvaun, Kyvon, Kywon, Kywynn

L

LABAN (Hawaiian) white.
Labon, Lebaan, Leban, Liban

LABARON (American) a combination
of the prefix La + Baron.
*Labaren, Labarren, Labarron, Labearon,
Labron*

LABIB (Arabic) sensible; intelligent.

LABRENTSIS (Russian) a form of
Lawrence.
Labhras, Labhruinn, Labrencis

LACHLAN (Scottish) land of lakes.
*Lache, Lachlann, Lachunn, Lakelan,
Lakeland*

LADARIAN (American) a combination
of the prefix La + Darian.
*Ladarien, Ladarin, Ladarion, Ladarren,
Ladarrian, Ladarrien, Ladarrin, Ladarrion,
Laderion, Laderrian, Laderrion*

LADARIUS (American) a combination
of the prefix La + Darius.
*Ladarious, Ladaris, Ladarrius, Ladauris,
Laderius, Ladirus*

LADARRIUS (American) an alternate
form of Ladarius.
*Ladarrias, Ladarries, Ladarrious,
Laderrious, Laderris*

LADD (English) attendant.
Lad, Laddey, Laddie, Laddy

LADERRICK (American) a
combination of the prefix
La + Derrick.
Ladarrick, Ladereck, Laderic, Laderricks

LADISLAV (Czech) a form of Walter.
Laco, Lada, Ladislaus

LADO (Fante) second-born son.

LAFAYETTE (French) History:
Marquis de Lafayette was a French
soldier and politician who aided the
American Revolution.
Lafaiete, Lafayett, Lafette, Laffyette

LAINE (English) an alternate form of
Lane.
Lain

LAIRD (Scottish) wealthy landowner.

LAIS (Arabic) lion.

LAJOS (Hungarian) famous; holy.
Lajcsi, Laji, Lali

LAKE (English) lake.
Lakan, Lakane, Lakee, Laken, Lakin

LAKOTA (Dakota) a tribal name.
Lakoda

LAL (Hindi) beloved.

LAMAR (German) famous throughout
the land. (French) sea, ocean.
*Lamair, Lamario, Lamaris, Lamarr,
Lamarre, Larmar, Lemar*

LAMBERT (German) bright land.
*Bert, Lambard, Lamberto, Lambirt,
Lampard, Landbert*

LAMOND (French) world.
*Lammond, Lamon, Lamonde, Lamondo,
Lamondre, Lamund, Lemond*

LAMONT (Scandinavian) lawyer.
*Lamaunt, Lamonta, Lamonte, Lamontie,
Lamonto, Lamount, Lemont*

LANCE (German) a short form of Lancelot.
Lancy, Lantz, Lanz, Launce

LANCELOT (French) attendant. Literature: the knight who loved King Arthur's wife, Queen Guinevere.
Lance, Lancelott, Launcelet, Launcelot

LANDEN (English) an alternate form of Landon.
Landenn

LANDER (Basque) lion man. (English) landowner.
Landers, Landor

LANDO (Portuguese, Spanish) a short form of Orlando, Rolando.

LANDON (English) open, grassy meadow.
Landan, Landen, Landin, Landyn

LANDRY (French, English) ruler.
Landre, Landré, Landrue

LANE (English) narrow road.
Laine, Laney, Lanie, Layne

LANG (Scandinavian) tall man.
Lange

LANGDON (English) long hill.
Landon, Langsdon, Langston

LANGFORD (English) long ford.
Lanford, Lankford

LANGLEY (English) long meadow.
Langlea, Langlee, Langleigh, Langly

LANGSTON (English) long, narrow town.
Langsden, Langsdon

LANGUNDO (Native American) peaceful.

LANI (Hawaiian) heaven.

LANNY (American) a familiar form of Lawrence, Laurence.
Lanney, Lannie, Lennie

LANU (Moquelumnan) running around the pole.

LANZ (Italian) a form of Lance.
Lanzo, Lonzo

LAO (Spanish) a short form of Stanislaus.

LAP (Vietnamese) independent.

LAPIDOS (Hebrew) torches.
Lapidoth

LAQUAN (American) a combination of the prefix La + Quan.
Laquain, Laquann, Laquanta, Laquantae, Laquante, Laquawn, Laquawne, Laquin, Laquinn, Laqun, Laquon, Laquone, Laqwan, Laqwon

LAQUINTIN (American) a combination of the prefix La + Quintin.
Laquentin, Laquenton, Laquintas, Laquinten, Laquintiss, Laquinton

LARAMIE (French) tears of love. Geography: a town in Wyoming on the Overland Trail.
Larami, Laramy, Laremy

LARENZO (Italian, Spanish) an alternate form of Lorenzo.
Larenz, Larenza, Larinzo, Laurenzo

LARKIN (Irish) rough; fierce.
Larklin

LARNELL (American) a combination of Larry + Darnell.

LARON (French) thief.
Laran, La'ron, La Ron, Larone, Laronn, Larron, La Ruan

LARRIMORE (French) armorer.
Larimore, Larmer, Larmor

LARRY (Latin) a familiar form
of Lawrence.
Larrie, Lary

LARS (Scandinavian) a form of
Lawrence.
*Laris, Larris, Larse, Larsen, Larson, Larsson,
Larz, Lasse, Laurans, Laurits, Lavrans, Lorens*

LASALLE (French) hall.
Lasal, Lasalle, Lascell, Lascelles

LASH (Gypsy) a form of Louis.
Lashi, Lasho

LASHAWN (American) a combination
of the prefix La + Shawn.
*Lasaun, Lasean, Lashajaun, Lashan,
Lashane, Lashaun, Lashon, Lashun*

LASHON (American) an alternate form
of Lashawn.
Lashone, Lashonne

LASSE (Finnish) a form of Nicholas.

LÁSZLÓ (Hungarian) famous ruler.
Laci, Lacko, Laslo, Lazlo

LATEEF (Arabic) gentle; pleasant.
Latif, Letif

LATHAM (Scandinavian) barn.
(English) district.
Laith, Lathe, Lay

LATHAN (American) a combination of
the prefix La + Nathan.
Lathaniel, Lathen, Lathyn, Leathan

LATHROP (English) barn, farmstead.
Lathe, Lathrope, Lay

LATIMER (English) interpreter.
Lat, Latimor, Lattie, Latty, Latymer

LATRAVIS (American) a combination
of the prefix La + Travis.
*Latavious, Latavius, Latraveus, Latraviaus,
Latravious, Latravius, Latrayvious,
Latrayvous, Latrivis*

LATRELL (American) a combination
of the prefix La + Kentrell.
*Latreal, Latreil, Latrel, Latrelle, Letreal,
Letrel, Letrell, Letrelle*

LAUDALINO (Portuguese) praised.
Lino

LAUGHLIN (Irish) servant of Saint
Secundinus.
Lanty, Lauchlin, Leachlainn

LAURENCE (Latin) crowned with
laurel. An alternate form of Lawrence.
See also Rance, Raulas, Raulo, Renzo.
*Lanny, Lauran, Laurance, Laureano,
Lauren, Laurencho, Laurencio, Laurens,
Laurent, Laurentij, Laurentios, Laurentiu,
Laurentius, Laurentz, Laurentzi, Laurie,
Laurin, Lauris, Laurits, Lauritz, Laurnet,
Lauro, Laurus, Lavrenti, Lurance*

LAURENCIO (Spanish) a form of
Laurence.

LAURENS (Dutch) a form of Laurence.
Laurenz

LAURENT (French) a form of Laurence.
Laurente

LAURIE (English) a familiar form of
Laurence.
Lauri, Laury, Lorry

LAURIS (Swedish) a form of Laurence.

LAURO (Filipino) a form of Laurence.

LAVALLE (French) valley.
Lavail, Laval, Lavalei, Lavalle, Lavell

LAVAN (Hebrew) white.
Lavane, Lavaughan, Laven, Lavon, Levan

LAVAUGHAN (American) a form
of Lavan.
Lavaughn, Levaughan, Levaughn

LAVE (Italian) lava. (English) lord.

LAVELL (French) an alternate form of LaValle.
Lavel, Lavele, Lavelle, Levele, Levell, Levelle

LAVI (Hebrew) lion.

LAVON (American) a form of Lavan.
Lavion, Lavone, Lavonn, Lavonne, Lavont, Lavonte

LAVRENTI (Russian) a form of Lawrence.
Larenti, Lavrentij, Lavrusha, Lavrik, Lavro

LAWERENCE (Latin) an alternate form of Lawrence.
Lawerance

LAWFORD (English) ford on the hill.
Ford, Law

LAWLER (Irish) mutterer.
Lawlor, Lollar, Loller

LAWRENCE (Latin) crowned with laurel. See also Brencis, Chencho.
Labrentsis, Laiurenty, Lanny, Lanty, Larance, Laren, Larian, Larien, Laris, Larka, Larrance, Larrence, Larry, Lars, Larya, Laurence, Lavrenti, Law, Lawerence, Lawrance, Lawren, Lawrey, Lawrie, Lawron, Lawry, Lencho, Lon, Lóránt, Loreca, Loren, Loretto, Lorenzo, Lorne, Lourenco, Lowrance

LAWSON (English) son of Lawrence.
Lawsen, Layson

LAWTON (English) town on the hill.
Laughton, Law

LAYNE (English) an alternate form of Lane.
Layn, Laynee

LAYTON (English) an alternate form of Leighton.
Laydon, Layten, Layth, Laythan, Laython

LAZARO (Italian) a form of Lazarus.
Lazarillo, Lazarito, Lazzaro

LAZARUS (Greek) a form of Eleazar. Bible: Lazarus was raised from the dead.
Lazar, Lázár, Lazare, Lazarius, Lazaro, Lazaros, Lazorus

LEANDER (Greek) lion-man; brave as a lion.
Ander, Leandro

LEANDRO (Spanish) a form of Leander.
Leandra, Léandre, Leandrew, Leandros

LEBEN (Yiddish) life.
Laben, Lebon

LEBNA (Ethiopian) spirit; heart.

LEDARIUS (American) a combination of the prefix Le + Darius.
Ledarrious, Ledarrius, Lederious, Lederris

LEE (English) a short form of Farley, Leonard, and names containing 'lee.'
Leigh

LEGGETT (French) one who is sent; delegate.
Legate, Legette, Leggitt, Liggett

LEI (Chinese) thunder. (Hawaiian) a form of Ray.

LEIB (Yiddish) roaring lion.
Leibel

LEIF (Scandinavian) beloved.
Laif, Leife, Lief

LEIGH (English) an alternate form of Lee.

LEIGHTON (English) meadow farm.
Lay, Layton, Leigh, Leyton

LEITH (Scottish) broad river.

LEK (Tai) small.

LEKEKE (Hawaiian) powerful ruler.

LEKS (Estonian) a familiar form of Alexander.
Leksik, Lekso

LEL (Gypsy) taker.

LELAND (English) meadowland;
protected land.
Lealand, Lee, Leeland, Leigh, Leighland,
Lelan, Lelann, Lelend, Lelund, Leyland

LEMAR (French) an alternate form of
Lamar.
Lemario, Lemarr

LEMUEL (Hebrew) devoted to God.
Lem, Lemmie, Lemmy

LEN (German) a short form of Leonard.
(Hopi) flute.

LENARD (German) an alternate form
of Leonard.
Lennard

LENCHO (Spanish) a form of Lawrence.
Lenci, Lenzy

LENNART (Swedish) a form of
Leonard.
Lennerd

LENNO (Native American) man.

LENNON (Irish) small cloak; cape.
Lenon

LENNOR (Gypsy) spring; summer.

LENNOX (Scottish) with many elms.
Lennix, Lenox

LENNY (German) a familiar form of
Leonard.
Leni, Lennie, Leny

LEO (Latin) lion. (German) a short form
of Leopold, Leon.
Lavi, Leão, Lee, Leib, Leibel, Leos, Leosko,
Léo, Léocadie, Leos, Leosoko, Lev, Lio, Lion,
Liutas, Lyon, Nardek

LEOBARDO (Italian) a form of
Leonard.

LEON (Greek, German) a short form of
Leonard, Napoleon.
Leo, Léon, Leonas, Léonce, Leoncio, Leondris,
Leone, Leonek, Leonetti, Leoni, Leonid,
Leonidas, Leonirez, Leonizio, Leonon, Leons,
Leontes, Leontios, Leontrae, Liutas

LEONARD (German) brave as a lion.
Leanard, Lee, Len, Lena, Lenard, Lennart,
Lenny, Leno, Leobardo, Leon, Léonard,
Leonardis, Leonardo, Leonart, Leonerd,
Leonhard, Leonidas, Leonnard, Leontes,
Lernard, Lienard, Linek, Lnard, Lon,
Londard, Lonnard, Lonya, Lynnard

LEONARDO (Italian) a form of
Leonard.
Leonaldo, Lionardo

LEONEL (English) little lion. See also
Lionel.
Leonell

LEONHARD (German) an alternate
form of Leonard.
Leonhards

LEONID (Russian) a form of Leonard.
Leonide, Lyonechka, Lyonya

LEONIDAS (Greek) a form of Leonard.
Leonida, Leonides

LEOPOLD (German) brave people.
Leo, Leopoldo, Leorad, Lipót, Lopolda,
Luepold, Luitpold, Poldi

LEOPOLDO (Italian) a form of Leopold.

LEOR (Hebrew) my light.
Leory, Lior

LEQUINTON (American) a combination
of the prefix Le + Quinton.
Lequentin, Lequenton, Lequinn

LERON (French) round, circle.
(American) a combination of the
prefix Le + Ron.
Leeron, Le Ron, Lerone, Liron, Lyron

LEROY (French) king. See also Delroy, Elroy.
Lee, Leeroy, LeeRoy, Leigh, Lerai, Leroi, LeRoi, LeRoy, Roy

LES (Scottish, English) a short form of Leslie, Lester.
Lessie

LESHARO (Pawnee) chief.

LESHAWN (American) a combination of the prefix Le + Shawn.
Lashan, Lesean, Leshaun, Leshon, Leshun

LESLIE (Scottish) gray fortress.
Lee, Leigh, Les, Leslea, Leslee, Lesley, Lesli, Lesly, Lezlie, Lezly

LESTER (Latin) chosen camp. (English) from Leicester, England.
Leicester, Les

LEV (Hebrew) heart. (Russian) a form of Leo. A short form of Leverett, Levi.
Leb, Leva, Levka, Levko, Levushka

LEVERETT (French) young hare.
Lev, Leveret, Leverit, Leveritt

LEVI (Hebrew) joined in harmony. Bible: the son of Jacob; the priestly tribe of Israel.
Leavi, Leevi, Leevie, Lev, Levey, Levie, Levin, Levitis, Levy, Lewi, Leyvi

LEVIN (Hebrew) an alternate form of Levi.
Levine, Levion

LEVON (American) an alternate form of Lavon.
Leevon, Levone, Levonn, Levonne, Levonte, Lyvonne

LEW (English) a short form of Lewis.

LEWIN (English) beloved friend.

LEWIS (English) a form of Louis. (Welsh) an alternate form of Llewellyn.
Lew, Lewes, Lewie, Lewy

LEX (English) a short form of Alexander.
Lexi, Lexie, Lexin

LEXUS (Greek) a short form of Alexander.
Lexis, Lexius, Lexxus

LEYATI (Moquelumnan) shape of an abalone shell.

LÍ (Chinese) strong.

LIAM (Irish) a form of William.
Liem, Lliam, Lyam

LIANG (Chinese) good, excellent.

LIBAN (Hawaiian) an alternate form of Laban.
Libaan, Lieban

LIBERIO (Portuguese) liberation.
Liberaratore, Liborio

LIDIO (Greek, Portuguese) ancient. Geography: an ancient province in Asia Minor.

LIGONGO (Yao) means 'who is this?'

LIKEKE (Hawaiian) a form of Richard.

LIKO (Chinese) protected by Buddha. (Hawaiian) bud.
Like

LIN (Burmese) bright. (English) a short form of Lyndon.
Linh, Linn, Linny, Lyn, Lynn

LINC (English) a short form of Lincoln.
Link

LINCOLN (English) settlement by the pool. History: Abraham Lincoln was the sixteenth U.S. president.
Linc, Lincon, Lyncoln

LINDBERG (German) mountain where linden trees grow.
Lindbergh, Lindburg, Lindy

LINDELL (English) valley of the linden trees.
Lendall, Lendel, Lendell, Lindall, Lindel, Lyndale, Lyndall, Lyndel, Lyndell

LINDEN (English) an alternate form of Lyndon.

LINDLEY (English) linden field.
Lindlea, Lindlee, Lindleigh, Lindly

LINDON (English) an alternate form of Lyndon.
Lin, Lindan

LINDSAY (English) an alternate form of Lindsey.
Linsay

LINDSEY (English) linden-tree island.
Lind, Lindsay, Lindsee, Lindsie, Lindsy, Lindzy, Linsey, Linzie, Linzy, Lyndsay, Lyndsey, Lyndsie, Lynzie

LINFORD (English) linden-tree ford.
Lynford

LINFRED (German) peaceful, calm.

LINLEY (English) flax meadow.
Linlea, Linlee, Linleigh, Linly

LINTON (English) flax town.
Lintonn, Lynton, Lyntonn

LINU (Hindi) lily.

LINUS (Greek) flaxen haired.
Linas, Linux

LINWOOD (English) flax wood.

LIO (Hawaiian) a form of Leo.

LIONEL (French) lion cub. See also Leonel.
Lional, Lionell, Lionello, Lynel, Lynell, Lyonel

LIRON (Hebrew) my song.
Lyron

LISE (Moquelumnan) salmon's head coming out of the water.

LISIMBA (Yao) lion.
Simba

LISTER (English) dyer.

LITTON (English) town on the hill.
Liton

LIU (African) voice.

LIUZ (Polish) light.
Lius

LIVINGSTON (English) Leif's town.
Livingstone

LIWANU (Moquelumnan) growling bear.

LLEWELLYN (Welsh) lionlike.
Lewis, Llewelin, Llewellen, Llewelleyn, Llewellin, Llewlyn, Llywellyn, Llywellynn, Llywelyn

LLOYD (Welsh) gray haired; holy. See also Floyd.
Loy, Loyd, Loyde, Loydie

LOBO (Spanish) wolf.

LOCHLAIN (Irish, Scottish) land of lakes.
Laughlin, Lochlan, Lochlann, Lochlin, Locklynn

LOCKE (English) forest.
Lock, Lockwood

LOE (Hawaiian) a form of Roy.

LOGAN (Irish) meadow.
Llogan, Loagan, Loagen, Loagon, Logann, Logen, Loggan, Loghan, Logon, Logn, Logun, Logunn, Logyn

LOK (Chinese) happy.

LOKELA (Hawaiian) a form of Roger.

LOKNI (Moquelumnan) raining through the roof.

LOMÁN (Irish) bare. (Slavic) sensitive.

LOMBARD (Latin) long bearded.
Bard, Barr

LON (Spanish) a short form of Alonso, Alonzo, Leonard, Lonnie. (Irish) fierce.
Lonn

LONAN (Zuni) cloud.

LONATO (Native American) flint stone.

LONDON (English) fortress of the moon. Geography: the capital of Great Britain.
Londen, Londyn, Lunden, Lundon

LONG (Chinese) dragon. (Vietnamese) hair.

LONNIE (German, Spanish) a familiar form of Alonso, Alonzo.
Lon, Loni, Lonie, Lonnell, Lonney, Lonni, Lonniel, Lonny

LONO (Hawaiian) Mythology: a god of peace and farming.

LONZO (German, Spanish) a short form of Alonso, Alonzo.
Lonso

LOOTAH (Lakota) red.

LOPAKA (Hawaiian) a form of Robert.

LORÁND (Hungarian) a form of Roland.

LÓRÁNT (Hungarian) a form of Lawrence.
Lorant

LORCAN (Irish) little; fierce.

LORD (English) noble title.

LOREN (Latin) a short form of Lawrence.
Lorin, Lorren, Lorrin, Loryn

LORENZO (Italian, Spanish) a form of Lawrence.
Larenzo, Lerenzo, Lewrenzo, Lorenc, Lorence, Lorenco, Lorencz, Lorens, Lorenso, Lorentz, Lorenz, Lorenza, Loretto, Lorinc, Lörinc, Lorinzo, Loritz, Lorrenzo, Lorrie, Lorry, Lourenza, Lourenzo, Lowrenzo, Renzo, Zo

LORETTO (Italian) a form of Lawrence.
Loreto

LORIMER (Latin) harness maker.
Lorrie, Lorrimer, Lorry

LORING (German) son of the famous warrior.
Lorrie, Lorring, Lorry

LORIS (Dutch) clown.

LORITZ (Latin, Danish) laurel.
Lauritz

LORNE (Latin) a short form of Lawrence.
Lorn, Lornie

LORRY (English) an alternate form of Laurie.
Lori, Lorri, Lory

LOT (Hebrew) hidden, covered. Bible: Lot fled from Sodom, but his wife glanced back upon its destruction and was transformed into a pillar of salt.
Lott

LOTHAR (German) an alternate form of Luther.
Lotaire, Lotarrio, Lothair, Lothaire, Lothario, Lotharrio

LOU (German) a short form of Louis.

LOUDON (German) low valley.
Loudan, Louden, Loudin, Lowden

LOUIE (German) a familiar form of Louis.

LOUIS (German) famous warrior. See also Aloisio, Aloysius, Clovis, Luigi.

Louis (cont.)
Lash, Lashi, Lasho, Lewis, Lou, Loudovicus, Louie, Louies, Louise, Lucho, Lude, Ludek, Ludirk, Ludis, Ludko, Ludwig, Lughaidh, Lui, Luigi, Luis, Luiz, Luki, Lutek

LOURDES (French) from Lourdes, France. Geography: a town in France. Religion: a place where the Virgin Mary was said to have appeared.

LOUVAIN (English) Lou's vanity. Geography: a city in Belgium.
Louvin

LOVELL (English) an alternate form of Lowell.
Louvell, Lovel, Lovelle, Lovey

LOWELL (French) young wolf. (English) beloved.
Lovell, Lowe, Lowel

LOYAL (English) faithful, loyal.
Loy, Loyall, Loye, Lyall, Lyell

LUBOMIR (Polish) lover of peace.

LUBOSLAW (Polish) lover of glory.
Lubs, Lubz

LUC (French) a form of Luke.
Luce

LUCA (Italian) a form of Lucius.
Lucca, Luka

LUCAS (German, Irish, Danish, Dutch) a form of Lucius.
Lucais, Lucassie, Lucaus, Luccas, Luccus, Luckas, Lucus

LUCIAN (Latin) an alternate form of Lucius.
Liuz, Lucan, Lucanus, Luciano, Lucianus, Lucias, Lucjan, Lukianos, Lukyan

LUCIANO (Italian) a form of Lucian.
Luca, Lucca, Lucino, Lucio

LUCIEN (French) a form of Lucius.

LUCIO (Italian) a form of Lucius.

LUCIUS (Latin) light; bringer of light.
Loukas, Luc, Luca, Lucais, Lucanus, Lucas, Luce, Lucian, Lucien, Lucio, Lucious, Lucis, Luke, Lusio

LUCKY (American) fortunate.
Luckee, Luckie, Luckson, Lucson

LUDLOW (English) prince's hill.

LUDOVIC (German) an alternate form of Ludwig.
Ludovick, Ludovico

LUDWIG (German) an alternate form of Louis. Music: Ludwig Van Beethoven was a famous nineteenth-century German composer.
Ludovic, Ludvig, Ludvik, Ludwik, Lutz

LUI (Hawaiian) a form of Louis.

LUIGI (Italian) a form of Louis.
Lui, Luiggi, Luigino, Luigy

LUIS, Luiz (Spanish) forms of Louis.
Luise

LUKAS, Lukus (Greek, Czech, Swedish) forms of Luke.
Loukas, Lukais, Lukash, Lukasha, Lukass, Lukasz, Lukaus, Lukkas

LUKE (Latin) a form of Lucius. Bible: author of the 'Gospel of Saint Luke' and 'Acts of the Apostles'—two New Testament books.
Luc, Luchok, Luck, Lucky, Luk, Luka, Lúkács, Lukas, Luken, Lukes, Lukus, Lukyan, Lusio

LUKELA (Hawaiian) a form of Russel.

LUKEN (Basque) bringer of light.
Lucan, Lucane, Lucano, Luk

LUKI (Basque) famous warrior.

LUKMAN (Arabic) prophet.
Luqman

LULANI (Hawaiian) highest point in heaven.

LUMO (Ewe) born face-downward.

LUNDY (Scottish) grove by the island.

LUNN (Irish) warlike.
Lon, Lonn

LUNT (Swedish) grove.

LUSILA (Hindi) leader.

LUSIO (Zuni) a form of Lucius.

LUTALO (Luganda) warrior.

LUTFI (Arabic) kind, friendly.

LUTHER (German) famous warrior. History: the Protestant reformer Martin Luther was one of the central figures of the Reformation.
Lothar, Lutero, Luthor

LUTHERUM (Gypsy) slumber.

LUYU (Moquelumnan) head shaker.

LYALL, Lyell (Scottish) loyal.

LYLE (French) island.
Lisle, Ly, Lysle

LYMAN (English) meadow.
Leaman, Leeman, Lymon

LYNCH (Irish) mariner.
Linch

LYNDAL (English) valley of lime trees.
Lyndale, Lyndall, Lyndel, Lyndell

LYNDON (English) linden-tree hill. History: Lyndon B. Johnson was the thirty-sixth U.S. president.
Lin, Linden, Lindon, Lyden, Lydon, Lyn, Lyndan, Lynden, Lynn

LYNN (English) waterfall; brook.
Lyn, Lynell, Lynette, Lynnard, Lynoll

LYRON (Hebrew) an alternate form of Leron, Liron.

LYSANDER (Greek) liberator.
Lyzander, Sander

M

MAALIK (Punjabi) an alternate form of Malik.
Maalek, Maaliek

MAC (Scottish) son.
Macs

MACADAM (Scottish) son of Adam.
MacAdam, McAdam

MACALLISTER (Irish) son of Alistair.
Macalaster, Macalister, MacAlister, McAlister, McAllister

MACARIO (Spanish) happy; blessed.

MACARTHUR (Irish) son of Arthur.
MacArthur, McArthur

MACAULAY (Scottish) son of righteousness.
Macaulee, Macauley, Macaully, Macauly, Maccauley, Mackauly, Macualay, McCauley

MACBRIDE (Scottish) son of a follower of Saint Brigid.
Macbryde, Mcbride, McBride

MACCOY (Irish) son of Hugh, Coy.
MacCoy, Mccoy, McCoy

MACCREA (Irish) son of grace.
MacCrae, MacCray, MacCrea, Macrae, Macray, Makray, Mccrea, McCrea

MACDONALD (Scottish) son of Donald.
MacDonald, Mcdonald, McDonald, Mcdonna, Mcdonnell, McDonnell

MACDOUGAL (Scottish) son of
Dougal.
MacDougal, Mcdougal, McDougal,
McDougall, Dougal

MACE (French) club. (English) a short
form of Macy, Mason.
Macean, Maceo, Macer, Macey, Macie, Macy

MACGREGOR (Scottish) son of
Gregor.
Macgreggor

Machas (Polish) a form of Michael.

MACK (Scottish) a short form of names
beginning with 'Mac' and 'Mc.'
Macke, Mackey, Mackie, Macklin, Macks,
Macky

MACKENZIE (Irish) son of Kenzie.
Mackensy, Mackenxo, Mackenze, Mackenzey,
Mackenzi, MacKenzie, Mackenzly, Mackenzy,
Mackienzie, Mackinsey, Mackinzie, Makenzie,
McKenzie, Mickenzie

MACKINNLEY (Irish) son of the
learned ruler.
Mackinley, MacKinnley, Mackinnly,
Mckinley

MACKLAIN (Irish) an alternate form
of Maclean.
Macklaine, Macklane

MACLEAN (Irish) son of Leander.
Machlin, Macklain, MacLain, MacLean,
Maclin, Maclyn, Makleen, McLaine, McLean

MACMAHON (Irish) son of Mahon.
MacMahon, McMahon

MACMURRAY (Irish) son of Murray.
McMurray

MACNAIR (Scottish) son of the heir.
Macnair

MACO (Hungarian) a form of
Emmanuel.

MACON (German, English) maker.

MACY (French) Matthew's estate.
Mace, Macey

MADDOCK (Welsh) generous.
Madoc, Madock, Madog

MADDOX (Welsh, English) benefactor's
son.
Maddux, Madox

MADHAR (Hindi) god; godlike.
Religion: another name for the Hindu
god Shiva.

MADISON (English) son of Maude;
good son.
Maddie, Maddison, Maddy, Madisen,
Madisson, Madisyn, Madsen, Son, Sonny

MADONGO (Luganda) uncircumcised.

MADU (Ibo) people.

MAGAR (Armenian) groom's attendant.
Magarious

MAGEE (Irish) son of Hugh.
MacGee, MacGhee, McGee

MAGEN (Hebrew) protector.

MAGNAR (Norwegian) strong; warrior.
Magne

MAGNUS (Latin) great.
Maghnus, Magnes, Manius, Mayer

MAGOMU (Luganda) younger of twins.

MAGUIRE (Irish) son of the beige one.
MacGuire, McGuire, McGwire

MAHAMMED (Arabic) an alternate
form of Muhammad.
Mahamad, Mahamed

MAHDI (Arabic) guided to the right
path.
Mahde, Mahdee, Mahdy

MAHESA (Hindi) great lord. Religion:
another name for the Hindu god Shiva.

MAHI'AI (Hawaiian) a form of George.

MAHIR (Arabic, Hebrew) excellent; industrious.
Maher

MAHKAH (Lakota) earth.

MAHMOUD (Arabic) an alternate form of Muhammad.
Mahamoud, Mahmmoud, Mahmuod

MAHMÚD (Arabic) an alternate form of Muhammad.
Mahmed, Mahmood, Mahmut

MAHOMET (Arabic) an alternate form of Muhammad.
Mehemet, Mehmet

MAHON (Irish) bear.

MAHPEE (Lakota) sky.

MAIMUN (Arabic) lucky.
Maimon

MAIRTIN (Irish) a form of Martin.
Martain, Martainn

MAITIAS (Irish) a form of Mathias.
Maithias

MAITIÚ (Irish) a form of Matthew.

MAITLAND (English) meadowland.

MAJID (Arabic) great, glorious.
Majd, Majde, Majdi, Majdy, Majed, Majeed

MAJOR (Latin) greater; military rank.
Majar, Maje, Majer, Mayer, Mayor

MAKAIO (Hawaiian) a form of Matthew.

MAKALANI (Mwera) writer.

MAKANI (Hawaiian) wind.

MAKARIOS (Greek) happy; blessed.
Macario, Macarios, Maccario, Maccarios

MAKENZIE (Irish) an alternate form of Mackenzie.
Makensie, Makenzy

MAKIN (Arabic) strong.
Makeen

MAKIS (Greek) a form of Michael.

MAKOTO (Japanese) sincere.

MAKS (Hungarian) a form of Max.
Makszi

MAKSIM (Russian) a form of Maximilian.
Maksimka, Maksym, Maxim

MAKSYM (Polish) a form of Maximilian.
Makimus, Maksim, Maksymilian

MAKYAH (Hopi) eagle hunter.

MAL (Irish) a short form of names beginning with 'Mal'.

MALACHI (Hebrew) angel of God. Bible: the last canonical Hebrew prophet.
Maeleachlainn, Mal, Malachai, Malachia, Malachie, Malachy, Malakai, Malake, Malaki, Malchija, Malechy, Málik

MALACHY (Irish) a form of Malachi.

MALAJITM (Sanskrit) garland of victory.

MALCOLM (Scottish) follower of Saint Columba, an early Scottish saint. (Arabic) dove.
Mal, Malcalm, Malcohm, Malcolum, Malcom, Malkolm

MALCOM (Scottish) an alternate form of Malcolm.
Malcome, Malcum, Malkom, Malkum

MALDEN (English) meeting place in a pasture.
Mal, Maldon

MALEK (Arabic) an alternate form of Malik.
Maleak, Maleek, Maleik, Maleka, Maleke, Mallek

MALEKO (Hawaiian) a form of Mark.

MÁLIK (Arabic) a form of Malachi. (Punjabi) lord, master.
Maalik, Mailik, Malak, Malic, Malick, Malicke, Maliek, Maliik, Malik, Malike, Malikh, Maliq, Malique, Mallik, Malyk, Malyq

MALIN (English) strong, little warrior.
Mal, Mallin, Mallon

MALLORY (German) army counselor. (French) wild duck.
Lory, Mal, Mallery, Mallori, Mallorie, Malory

MALONEY (Irish) church going.
Malone, Malony

MALVERN (Welsh) bare hill.
Malverne

MALVIN (Irish, English) an alternate form of Melvin.
Mal, Malvinn, Malvyn, Malvynn

MAMO (Hawaiian) yellow flower; yellow bird.

MANCHU (Chinese) pure.

MANCO (Peruvian) supreme leader. History: a thirteenth-century Incan king.

MANDALA (Yao) flowers.
Manda, Mandela

MANDEEP (Punjabi) mind full of light.
Mandieep

MANDEL (German) almond.
Mandell

MANDEK (Polish) a form of Armand, Herman.
Mandie

MANDER (Gypsy) from me.

MANFORD (English) small ford.

MANFRED (English) man of peace. See also Fred.
Manfret, Manfrid, Manfried, Maniferd, Mannfred, Mannfryd

MANGER (French) stable.

MANGO (Spanish) a familiar form of Emmanuel, Manuel.

MANHEIM (German) servant's home.

MANIPI (Native American) living marvel.

MANIUS (Scottish) a form of Magnus.
Manus, Manyus

MANLEY (English) hero's meadow.
Manlea, Manleigh, Manly

MANN (German) man.
Manin

MANNING (English) son of the hero.

MANNIX (Irish) monk.
Mainchin

MANNY (German, Spanish) a familiar form of Manuel.
Mani, Manni, Mannie, Many

MANO (Hawaiian) shark. (Spanish) a short form of Manuel.
Manno, Manolo

MANOJ (Sanskrit) cupid.

MANSA (Swahili) king. History: a fourteenth-century emperor of Mali.

MANSEL (English) manse; house occupied by a clergyman.
Mansell

MANSFIELD (English) field by the river; hero's field.

MAN-SHIK (Korean) deeply rooted.

MANSÜR (Arabic) divinely aided.
Mansoor, Mansour

MANTON (English) man's town; hero's town.
Mannton, Manten

MANU (Hindi) lawmaker. History: the writer of the Hindi code of conduct. (Hawaiian) bird. (Ghanian) second-born son.

MANUEL (Hebrew) a short form of Emmanuel.
Maco, Mango, Mannuel, Manny, Mano, Manolón, Manual, Manuale, Manue, Manuelli, Manuelo, Manuil, Manyuil, Minel

MANVILLE (French) worker's village. (English) hero's village.
Mandeville, Manvel, Manvil

MAN-YOUNG (Korean) ten thousand years of prosperity.

MANZO (Japanese) third son.

MAONA (Winnebago) creator, earth maker.

MAPIRA (Yao) millet.

MARAR (Watamare) mud; dust.

MARC (French) a form of Mark.

MARCEL (French) a form of Marcellus.
Marcell, Marsale, Marsel

MARCELINO (Italian) a form of Marcellus.
Marceleno, Marcelin, Marcellin, Marcellino

MARCELO, Marcello (Italian) forms of Marcellus.
Marchello, Marsello, Marselo

MARCELLUS (Latin) a familiar form of Marcus.

Marceau, Marcel, Marceles, Marcelias, Marcelino, Marcelis, Marcelius, Marcellas, Marcelleous, Marcellis, Marcellous, Marcelluas, Marcelo, Marcelus, Marcely, Marciano, Marcilka, Marcsseau, Marquel, Marsalis

MARCH (English) dweller by a boundary.

MARCIANO (Italian) a form of Martin.
Marci, Marcio

MARCILKA (Hungarian) a form of Marcellus.
Marci, Marcilki

MARCIN (Polish) a form of Martin.

MARCO (Italian) a form of Marcus. History: Marco Polo was the thirteenth-century Venetian traveler who explored Asia.
Marcko, Marko

MARCOS (Spanish) a form of Marcus.
Marckos, Marcous, Markos, Markose

MARCUS (Latin) martial, warlike.
Marc, Marcas, Marcellus, Marcio, Marckus, Marco, Marcos, Marcous, Marcuss, Marcuus, Marcux, Marek, Mark, Markov, Markus

MAREK (Slavic) a form of Marcus.

MAREN (Basque) sea.

MAREO (Japanese) uncommon.

MARIAN (Polish) a form of Mark.

MARIANO (Italian) a form of Mark.

MARID (Arabic) rebellious.

MARIN (French) sailor.
Marine, Mariner, Marino, Marius, Marriner

MARINO (Italian) a form of Marin.
Marinos, Marinus, Mario, Mariono

MARIO (Italian) an alternate form of Marino.
Marios, Marrio

MARION (French) bitter; sea of bitterness. A masculine form of Mary.
Mareon, Mariano

MARIUS (Latin) a form of Marin. History: a Roman clan name.
Marious

MARK (Latin) an alternate form of Marcus. Bible: author of the New Testament book, 'The Gospel According to Saint Mark.' See also Maleko.
Marc, Marek, Marian, Mariano, Marke, Markee, Markel, Markell, Markey, Marko, Markos, Márkus, Markusha, Marque, Martial, Marx

MARKANTHONY (Italian) a combination of Mark + Anthony.

MARKE (Polish) a form of Mark.

MARKEL, Markell (Latin) alternate forms of Mark.
Markelle, Markelo

MARKES (Portuguese) an alternate form of Marques.
Markess, Markest

MARKESE (French) an alternate form of Marquis.
Markease, Markeece, Markees, Markeese, Markei, Markeice, Markeis, Markeise, Markes, Markez, Markeze, Markice

MARKHAM (English) homestead on the boundary.

MARKIS (French) an alternate form of Marquis.
Markies, Markiese, Markise, Markiss, Markist

MARKO (Latin) an alternate form of Marco, Mark.
Markco

MARKUS (Latin) an alternate form of Marcus.
Markas, Markcus, Markcuss, Markys, Marqus

MARLAND (English) lake land.

MARLEY (English) lake meadow.
Marlea, Marleigh, Marly, Marrley

MARLIN (English) deep-sea fish.
Marlen, Marlion, Marlyn

MARLON (French) a form of Merlin.

MARLOW (English) hill by the lake.
Mar, Marlo, Marlowe

MARMION (French) small.
Marmyon

MARNIN (Hebrew) singer; bringer of joy.

MARO (Japanese) myself.

MARQUAN (American) a combination of Mark + Quan.
Marquane, Marquante

MARQUEL (American) a form of Marcellus.
Marqueal, Marquelis, Marquell, Marquelle, Marquellis, Marquiel, Marquil, Marquiles, Marquill, Marquille, Marquillus, Marqwel, Marqwell

MARQUES (Portuguese) nobleman.
Markes, Markqes, Markques, Markquese, Marqese, Marqesse, Marqez, Marqeze, Marquees, Marquese, Marquess, Marquesse, Marquest, Markqueus, Marquez, Marqus

MARQUEZ (Portuguese) an alternate form of Marques.
Marqueze, Marquiez

MARQUICE (American) a form of Marquis.
Marquaice, Marquece

MARQUIS, Marquise (French) nobleman.
Marcquis, Marcuis, Markis, Markquis, Markquise, Markuis, Marqise, Marquee, Marqui, Marquice, Marquie, Marquies, Marquiss, Marquist, Marquiz, Marquize

MARQUON (American) a combination of Mark + Quon.
Marquin, Marquinn, Marqwan, Marqwon, Marqwyn

MARR (Spanish) divine. (Arabic) forbidden.

MARS (Latin) bold warrior. Mythology: the Roman god of war.

MARSALIS (Italian) a form of Marcellus.
Marsalius, Marsallis, Marsellis, Marsellius, Marsellus

MARSDEN (English) marsh valley.
Marsdon

MARSH (French) a short form of Marshall. (English) swamp land.

MARSHAL (French) an alternate form of Marshall.
Marschal, Marshel

MARSHALL (French) caretaker of the horses; military title.
Marsh, Marshal, Marshell

MARSHAWN (American) a combination of Mark + Shawn.
Marshaine, Marshaun, Marshauwn, Marshean, Marshon, Marshun

MARSTON (English) town by the marsh.

MARTELL (English) hammerer.
Martel, Martele, Martellis

MARTEN (Dutch) a form of Martin.
Maarten, Martein

MARTEZ (Spanish) a form of Martin.
Martaz, Martaze, Martes, Martese, Marteze, Martice, Martiece, Marties, Martiese, Martiez, Martis, Martise, Martize

MARTI (Spanish) a form of Martin.
Martee, Martie

MARTIAL (French) a form of Mark.

MARTIN (Latin) martial, warlike. (French) a form of Martinus. History: Martin Luther King, Jr. led the civic rights movement and won the Nobel Peace Prize. See also Tynek.
Maartin, Mairtin, Marciano, Marcin, Marinos, Marius, Mart, Martan, Marten, Martez, Marti, Martijn, Martinas, Martine, Martinez, Martinho, Martiniano, Martinien, Martinka, Martino, Martins, Marto, Marton, Márton, Marts, Marty, Martyn, Mattin, Mertin, Morten, Moss

MARTINEZ (Spanish) a form of Martin.
Martines

MARTINHO (Portuguese) a form of Martin.

MARTINO (Italian) a form of Martin.
Martinos

MARTINS (Latvian) a form of Martin.

MARTINUS (Latin) martial, warlike.
Martin

MARTY (Latin) a familiar form of Martin.
Martey, Marti, Martie

MARUT (Hindi) Religion: the Hindu god of the wind.

MARV (English) a short form of Marvin.
Marve, Marvi, Marvis

MARVIN (English) lover of the sea.
Marv, Marvein, Marven, Marvion, Marvn, Marvon, Marvyn, Marwin, Marwynn, Mervin

MARWAN (Arabic) history personage.

MARWOOD (English) forest pond.

MASACCIO (Italian) twin.
Masaki

MASAHIRO (Japanese) broad minded.

MASAMBA (Yao) leaves.

MASAO (Japanese) righteous.

MASATO (Japanese) just.

MASHAMA (Shona) surprising.

MASKA (Native American) powerful.

MASLIN (French) little Thomas.
Maslen, Masling

MASON (French) stone worker.
Mace, Maison, Masson, Masun, Masyn,
Sonny

MASOU (Native American) fire god.

MASSEY (English) twin.
Massi

MASSIMO (Italian) greatest.
Massimiliano

MASUD (Arabic, Swahili) fortunate.
Masood, Masoud, Mhasood

MATAI (Basque, Bulgarian) a form of
Matthew.
Máté, Matei

MATALINO (Filipino) bright.

MATEO (Spanish) a form of Matthew.
Matías, Matteo

MATEUSZ (Polish) a form of Matthew.
Matejs, Mateus

MATHE (German) a short form of
Matthew.

MATHER (English) powerful army.

MATHEU (German) a form of Matthew.
Matheau, Matheus, Mathu

MATHEW (Hebrew) an alternate form
of Matthew.

MATHIAS, Matthias (German,
Swedish) forms of Matthew.
Maitias, Mathi, Mathia, Mathis, Matías,
Matthia, Matthieus, Mattia, Mattias, Matus

MATHIEU, Matthieu (French) forms
of Matthew.
Mathie, Mathieux, Mathiew, Matthiew,
Mattieu, Mattieux

MATÍAS (Spanish) a form of Mathias.
Mattias

MATO (Native American) brave.

MATOPE (Rhodesian) our last child.

MATOSKAH (Lakota) white bear.

MATS (Swedish) a familiar form of
Matthew.
Matts, Matz

MATSON (Hebrew) son of Matt.
Matison, Matsen, Mattison, Mattson

MATT (Hebrew) a short form of
Matthew.
Mat

MATTEEN (Afghani) disciplined; polite.

MATTEUS (Scandinavian) a form of
Matthew.

MATTHEW (Hebrew) gift of God. Bible:
author of the New Testament book,
'The Gospel According to Saint
Matthew.'
Mads, Makaio, Maitiú, Mata, Matai, Matek,
Mateo, Mateusz, Matfei, Mathe, Matheson,
Matheu, Mathew, Mathian, Mathias,
Mathieson, Mathieu, Matro, Mats, Matt,
Matteus, Matthaeus, Matthaios, Matthaus,
Matthäus, Mattheus, Matthews, Mattmias,
Matty, Matvey, Matyas, Mayhew

MATTY (Hebrew) a familiar form of
Matthew.
Mattie

MATUS (Czech) a form of Mathias.

MATVEY (Russian) a form of Matthew.
Matviy, Matviyko, Matyash, Motka, Motya

MATYAS (Polish) a form of Matthew.
Mátyás

MAULI (Hawaiian) a form of Maurice.

MAURICE (Latin) dark skinned; moor;
marshland. See also Seymour.
*Mauli, Maur, Maurance, Maureo, Mauricio,
Maurids, Mauriece, Maurikas, Maurin,
Maurino, Maurise, Mauritz, Maurius,
Maurizio, Mauro, Maurrel, Maurtel, Maury,
Maurycy, Meurig, Moore, Morice, Moritz,
Morrel, Morrice, Morrie, Morrill, Morris*

MAURICIO (Spanish) a form of
Maurice.
Mauriccio, Mauriceo, Maurico, Maurisio

MAURITZ (German) a form of Maurice.

MAURIZIO (Italian) a form of Maurice.

MAURO (Latin) a short form of
Maurice.
Maur, Maurio

MAURY (Latin) a familiar form of
Maurice.
Maurey, Maurie, Morrie

MAVERICK (American) independent.
Maverik, Maveryke, Mavric, Mavrick

MAWULI (Ewe) there is a God.

MAX (Latin) a short form of
Maximilian, Maxwell.
*Mac, Mack, Maks, Maxe, Maxx, Maxy,
Miksa*

MAXFIELD (English) Mack's field.

MAXI (Czech, Hungarian, Spanish) a
familiar form of Maximilian, Máximo.
Makszi, Maxey, Maxie, Maxis, Maxy

MAXIM (Russian) a form of Maxime.

MAXIME (French) most excellent.
Maxim, Maxyme

MAXIMILIAN (Latin) greatest.
*Mac, Mack, Maixim, Maksim, Maksym,
Max, Maxamillion, Maxemilian,
Maxemilion, Maxi, Maximalian, Maximili,
Maximilia, Maximiliano, Maximilianus,
Maximilien, Maximillian, Máximo,
Maximos, Maxmilian, Maxmillion, Maxon,
Maxymilian, Maxymillian, Mayhew, Miksa*

MAXIMILIANO (Italian) a form of
Maximilian.
Massimiliano, Maximiano, Maximino

MAXIMILLIAN (Latin) an alternate
form of Maximilian.
*Maximillan, Maximillano, Maximillien,
Maximillion, Maxmillian, Maxximillian,
Maxximillion*

MÁXIMO (Spanish) a form of
Maximilian.
*Massimo, Maxi, Maximiano, Maximiliano,
Maximino, Máximo*

MAXIMOS (Greek) a form of
Maximilian.

MAXWELL (English) great spring.
Max, Maxwel, Maxwill, Maxxwell, Maxy

MAXY (English) a familiar form of Max,
Maxwell.
Maxi

MAYER (Hebrew) an alternate form of
Meir. (Latin) an alternate form of
Magnus, Major.
Mahyar, Mayeer, Mayor, Mayur

MAYES (English) field.
Mayo, Mays

MAYHEW (English) a form of Matthew.

MAYNARD (English) powerful; brave.
See also Meinhard.
May, Mayne, Maynhard, Maynor, Ménard

MAYO (Irish) yew-tree plain. (English)
an alternate form of Mayes.
Geography: a county in Ireland.

MAYON (Hindi) god. Religion: ancient name for the Hindu god Krishna.

MAYONGA (Luganda) lake sailor.

MAZI (Ibo) sir.
Mazzi

MAZIN (Arabic) proper.
Mazen, Mazinn, Mazzin

MBITA (Swahili) born on a cold night.

MBWANA (Swahili) master.

MCGEORGE (Scottish) son of George.
MacGeorge

MCKADE (Scottish) son of Kade.
Mccade

MCKAY (Scottish) son of Kay.
Mackay, MacKay, Mckae, Mckai, McKay

MCKENZIE (Irish) an alternate form of Mackenzie.
Mccenzie, Mckennzie, Mckensey, Mckensie, Mckenson, Mckensson, Mckenzi, Mckenzy, Mckinzie

MCKINLEY (Irish) an alternate form of Mackinnley.
Mckinely, Mckinnely, Mckinnlee, Mckinnley, McKinnley

MEAD (English) meadow.
Meade, Meed

MEDGAR (German) a form of Edgar.

MEDWIN (German) faithful friend.

MEHETABEL (Hebrew) who God benefits.

MEHRDAD (Persian) gift of the sun.

MEHTAR (Sanskrit) prince.
Mehta

MEINHARD (German) strong, firm. See also Maynard.
Meinhardt, Meinke, Meino, Mendar

MEINRAD (German) strong counsel.

MEIR (Hebrew) one who brightens, shines; enlightener. History: a leading second-century scholar.
Mayer, Meyer, Muki, Myer

MEKA (Hawaiian) eyes.

MEL (English, Irish) a familiar form of Melvin.

MELBOURNE (English) mill stream.
Melborn, Melburn, Melby, Milborn, Milbourn, Milbourne, Milburn, Millburn, Millburne

MELCHIOR (Hebrew) king.
Meilseoir, Melchor, Melker, Melkior

MELDON (English) mill hill.
Melden

MELRONE (Irish) servant of Saint Ruadhan.

MELVERN (Native American) great chief.

MELVILLE (French) mill town. Literature: Herman Melville was a well-known nineteenth-century American writer.
Milville

MELVIN (Irish) armored chief. (English) mill friend; council friend. See also Vinny.
Malvin, Mel, Melvino, Melvon, Melvyn, Melwin, Melwyn, Melwynn

MENACHEM (Hebrew) comforter.
Menahem, Nachman

MENASSAH (Hebrew) cause to forget.
Menashe, Menashi, Menashia, Menashiah, Menashya, Manasseh

MENDEL (English) repairman.
Mendeley, Mendell, Mendie, Mendy

MENGESHA (Ethiopian) kingdom.

MENICO (Spanish) a short form of Domenico.

MENSAH (Ewe) third son.

MENZ (German) a short form of Clement.

MERCER (English) storekeeper.
Merce

MERED (Hebrew) revolter.

MEREDITH (Welsh) guardian from the sea.
Meredyth, Merideth, Meridith, Merry

MERION (Welsh) from Merion, England.
Merrion

MERLE (French) a short form of Merlin, Merrill.
Meryl

MERLIN (English) falcon. Literature: the wizard in King Arthur's court.
Marlon, Merle, Merlen, Merlinn, Merlyn, Merlynn

MERRICK (English) ruler of the sea.
Merek, Meric, Merick, Merik, Merric, Merrik, Meryk, Meyrick, Myrucj

MERRILL (Irish) bright sea. (French) famous.
Meril, Merill, Merle, Merrel, Merrell, Merril, Meryl

MERRITT (Latin, Irish) valuable; deserving.
Merit, Meritt, Merrett

MERTON (English) sea town.
Murton

MERV (Irish) a short form of Mervin.

MERVILLE (French) sea village.

MERVIN (Irish) a form of Marvin.

Merv, Mervyn, Mervynn, Merwin, Merwinn, Merwyn, Murvin, Murvyn, Myrvyn, Myrvynn, Myrwyn

MESHACH (Hebrew) artist. Bible: one of Daniel's three friends who were rescued from a fiery furnace by an angel.

MESUT (Turkish) happy.

METIKLA (Moquelumnan) reaching a hand under water to catch a fish.

METTE (Greek, Danish) pearl.
Almeta, Mete

MEURIG (Welsh) a form of Maurice.

MEYER (Hebrew) an alternate form of Meir. (German) farmer.
Mayer, Meier, Myer

MHINA (Swahili) delightful.

MICAH (Hebrew) an alternate form of Michael. Bible: a Hebrew prophet.
Mic, Micaiah, Michiah, Mika, Mikah, Myca, Mycah

MICHA (Hebrew) a short form of Michael.
Mica, Micha, Michah

MICHAEL (Hebrew) who is like God? See also Micah, Miguel, Mika, Miles.
Machael, Machas, Mahail, Maichail, Maikal, Makael, Makal, Makel, Makell, Makis, Meikel, Mekal, Mekhail, Mhichael, Micael, Micah, Micahel, Mical, Micha, Michaele, Michaell, Michail, Michak, Michal, Michale, Michalek, Michalel, Michau, Micheal, Micheil, Michel, Michele, Michelet, Michiel, Micho, Michoel, Mick, Mickael, Mickey, Mihail, Mihalje, Mihkel, Mika, Mikael, Mikáele, Mikal, Mike, Mikeal, Mikel, Mikelis, Mikell, Mikhail, Mikkel, Mikko, Miksa, Milko, Miquel, Misael, Misi, Miska, Mitchell, Mychael, Mychajlo, Mychal, Mykal, Mykhas

MICHAIL (Russian) a form of Michael.
Mihas, Mikail, Mikale, Misha

MICHAL (Polish) a form of Michael.
Michak, Michalek, Michall

MICHEAL (Irish) a form of Michael.

MICHEL (French) a form of Michael.
Michaud, Miche, Michee, Michell, Michelle, Michon

MICHELANGELO (Italian) a combination of Michael + Angelo. Art: Michelangelo Buonarroti was one of the greatest Italian Renaissance painters.
Michelange, Miguelangelo

MICHELE (Italian) a form of Michael.

MICHIO (Japanese) man with the strength of three thousand.

MICK (English) a short form of Michael, Mickey.
Mickerson

MICKAEL (English) a form of Michael.
Mickaele, Mickal, Mickale, Mickeal, Mickel, Mickell, Mickelle, Mickle

MICKENZIE (Irish) an alternate form of Mackenzie.
Mickenze, Mickenzy, Mikenzie

MICKEY (Irish) a familiar form of Michael.
Mick, Micki, Mickie, Micky, Miki, Mique

MICU (Hungarian) a form of Nick.

MIGUEL (Portuguese, Spanish) a form of Michael.
Migeel, Migel, Miguelly, Migui

MIGUELANGEL (Spanish) a combination of Miguel + Angel.

MIHAIL (Greek, Bulgarian, Romanian) a form of Michael.
Mihailo, Mihal, Mihalis, Mikail

MIKA (Hebrew) an alternate form of Micah. (Russian) a familiar form of Michael. (Ponca) raccoon.
Miika, Mikah

MIKAEL (Swedish) a form of Michael.
Mikaeel, Mikaele

MIKÁELE (Hawaiian) a form of Michael.
Mikele

MIKAL (Hebrew) an alternate form of Michael.
Mekal, Mikahl, Mikale

MIKASI (Omaha) coyote.

MIKE (Hebrew) a short form of Michael.
Mikey, Myk

MIKEAL (Irish) a form of Michael.

MIKEL (Basque) a form of Michael.
Mekel, Mikele, Mekell, Mikell, Mikelle

MIKELIS (Latvian) a form of Michael.
Mikus, Milkins

MIKHAIL (Greek, Russian) a form of Michael.
Mekhail, Mihály, Mikhael, Mikhale, Mikhalis, Mikhalka, Mikhall, Mikhel, Mikhial, Mikhos

MIKI (Japanese) tree.
Mikio

MIKKEL (Norwegian) a form of Michael.
Mikkael, Mikle

MIKKO (Finnish) a form of Michael.
Mikk, Mikka, Mikkohl, Mikkol, Miko, Mikol

MIKOLAJ (Polish) a form of Nicholas.
Mikolai

MIKOLAS (Greek) an alternate form of Nicholas.
Miklós, Milek

MIKSA (Hungarian) a form of Max.
Miks

MILAN (Italian) northerner. Geography: a city in northern Italy.
Milaan, Milano, Milen, Millan, Millen, Mylan, Mylen, Mylon, Mylynn

MILAP (Native American) giving.

MILBOROUGH (English) middle borough.
Milbrough

MILEK (Polish) a familiar form of Nicholas.

MILES (Greek) millstone. (Latin) soldier. (German) merciful. (English) a short form of Michael.
Milas, Milles, Milo, Milson, Myles

MILFORD (English) mill by the ford.

MILILANI (Hawaiian) heavenly caress.

MILKO (Czech) a form of Michael. (German) a familiar form of Emil.
Milkins

MILLARD (Latin) caretaker of the mill.
Mill, Millar, Miller, Millward, Milward, Myller

MILLER (English) miller, grain grinder.
Mellar, Millard, Millen

MILLS (English) mills.

MILO (German) an alternate form of Miles. A familiar form of Emil.
Millo, Mylo

MILOS (Greek, Slavic) pleasant.

MILOSLAV (Czech) lover of glory.
Milda

MILT (English) a short form of Milton.

MILTON (English) mill town.
Milt, Miltie, Milty, Mylton

MIMIS (Greek) a familiar form of Demetrius.

MIN (Burmese) king.
Mina

MINCHO (Spanish) a form of Benjamin.

MINEL (Spanish) a form of Manuel.

MINER (English) miner.

MINGAN (Native American) gray wolf.

MINGO (Spanish) a short form of Domingo.

MINH (Vietnamese) bright.
Minhao, Minhduc, Minhkhan, Minhtong, Minhy

MINKAH (Akan) just, fair.

MINOR (Latin) junior; younger.
Mynor

MINORU (Japanese) fruitful.

MIQUE (Spanish) a form of Mickey.
Mequel, Mequelin, Miquel

MIRON (Polish) peace.

MIROSLAV (Czech) peace; glory.
Mirek, Miroslaw, Miroslawy

MIRWAIS (Afghani) noble ruler. History: a famous king who lived in 900 A.D.

MISAEL (Hebrew) an alternate form of Michael.
Mischael, Mishael, Missael

MISHA (Russian) a short form of Michail.
Misa, Mischa, Mishael, Mishal, Mishe, Mishenka, Mishka

MISKA (Hungarian) a form of Michael.
Misi, Misik, Misko, Miso

MISTER (English) mister.
Mistur

MISU (Moquelumnan) rippling water.

MITCH (English) a short form of Mitchell.

MITCHEL (English) an alternate form of Mitchell.
Mitchael, Mitchal, Mitcheal, Mitchele, Mitchil, Mytchel

MITCHELL (English) a form of Michael.
Mitch, Mitchall, Mitchel, Mitchelle, Mitchem, Mytch, Mytchell

MITSOS (Greek) a familiar form of Demetrius.

MODESTO (Latin) modest.

MOE (English) a short form of Moses.
Mo

MOGENS (Dutch) powerful.

MOHAMAD (Arabic) an alternate form of Muhammad.
Mohamid

MOHAMED (Arabic) an alternate form of Muhammad.
Mohamd, Mohameed

MOHAMET (Arabic) an alternate form of Muhammad.
Mahomet, Mehemet, Mehmet

MOHAMMAD (Arabic) an alternate form of Muhammad.
Mahammad, Mohammadi, Mohammd, Mohammid, Mohanad, Mohmad

MOHAMMED (Arabic) an alternate form of Muhammad.
Mahammed, Mahomet, Mohammad, Mohaned, Mouhamed, Muhammad

MOHAMUD (Arabic) an alternate form of Muhammad.
Mohammud, Mohamoud

MOHAN (Hindi) delightful. Religion: another name for the Hindu god Krishna.

MOISES (Portuguese, Spanish) a form of Moses.
Moices, Moise, Moisés, Moisey, Moisis

MOISHE (Yiddish) a form of Moses.
Moshe

MOJAG (Native American) crying baby.

MOLIMO (Moquelumnan) bear going under shady trees.

MOMUSO (Moquelumnan) yellow jackets crowded in their nests for the winter.

MONA (Moquelumnan) gathering jimsonweed seed.

MONAHAN (Irish) monk.
Monaghan, Monoghan

MONGO (Yoruba) famous.

MONROE (Irish) Geography: the mouth of the Roe River.
Monro, Munro, Munroe

MONTAGUE (French) pointed mountain.
Montagne, Montagu, Monte

MONTANA (Spanish) mountain. Geography: a U.S. state. Culture: name popularized by football player Joe Montana.
Montaine, Montanna

MONTARO (Japanese) big boy.
Montario, Monterio, Montero

MONTE (Spanish) a short form of Montgomery.
Montae, Montaé, Montay, Montea, Montee, Monti, Montoya, Monty

MONTEL (American) a form of Montreal.
Montele, Montell, Montelle

MONTEZ (Spanish) dweller in the mountains.
Monteiz, Monteze, Montezz, Montisze

MONTGOMERY (English) rich man's mountain.
Monte, Montgomerie, Monty

MONTRE (French) show.
Montra, Montrae, Montray, Montraz, Montres, Montrey, Montrez, Montreze

MONTREAL (French) royal mountain. Geography: a city in Quebec.
Montel, Monterial, Monterrell, Montrail, Montrale, Montrall, Montreall, Montrell, Montrial

MONTRELL (French) an alternate form of Montreal.
Montral, Montrel, Montrele, Montrelle

MONTSHO (Tswana) black.

MONTY (English) a familiar form of Montgomery.

MOORE (French) dark; moor; marshland. See also Maurice.
Moor, Mooro, More

MORDECAI (Hebrew) martial, warlike. Mythology: Marduk was the Babylonian god of war.
Mord, Mordachai, Mordechai, Mordie, Mordy, Mort

MORDRED (Latin) painful. Literature: the nephew of King Arthur.
Modred

MOREL (French) an edible mushroom.
Morrel

MORELAND (English) moor; marshland.
Moorland, Morland

MORELL (French) dark; from Morocco.
Moor, Moore, Morelle, Morelli, Morill, Morrell, Morrill, Murrel, Murrell

MOREY (Greek) a familiar form of Moris. (Latin) an alternate form of Morrie.
Morrey, Morry

MORGAN (Scottish) sea warrior.
Morgen, Morghan, Morgin, Morgon, Morgun, Morgunn, Morgwn, Morgyn, Morrgan

MORIO (Japanese) forest.

MORIS (Greek) son of the dark one. (English) an alternate form of Morris.
Morey, Morisz, Moriz

MORITZ (German) a form of Maurice, Morris.
Morisz

MORLEY (English) meadow by the moor.
Moorley, Moorly, Morlee, Morleigh, Morlon, Morly, Morlyn, Morrley

MORRIE (Latin) a familiar form of Maurice, Morse.
Maury, Morey, Mori, Morie, Morry, Mory, Morye

MORRIS (Latin) dark skinned; moor; marshland. (English) a form of Maurice.
Moris, Moriss, Moritz, Morrese, Morrise, Morriss, Morry, Moss

MORSE (English) son of Maurice.
Morresse, Morrie, Morrison, Morrisson

MORT (French, English) a short form of Morten, Mortimer, Morton.
Morte, Mortey, Mortie, Mortty, Morty

MORTEN (Norwegian) a form of Martin.
Mort

MORTIMER (French) still water.
Mort, Mortymer

MORTON (English) town near the moor.
Mort

MORVEN (Scottish) mariner.
Morvien, Morvin

MOSE (Hebrew) a short form of Moses.

MOSES (Hebrew) drawn out of the water. (Egyptian) son, child. Bible: the Hebrew leader who brought the Ten Commandments down from Mount Sinai.
Moe, Moise, Moïse, Moisei, Moises, Moishe, Mose, Mosese, Moshe, Mosiah, Mosie, Moss, Mosses, Mosya, Mosze, Moszek, Mousa, Moyses, Moze

MOSHE (Hebrew, Polish) an alternate form of Moses.
Mosheh

MOSI (Swahili) first-born.

MOSS (Irish) a short form of Maurice, Morris. (English) a short form of Moses.

MOSWEN (African) light in color.

MOTEGA (Native American) new arrow.

MOUHAMED (Arabic) an alternate form of Muhammad.
Mouhamad, Mouhamadou, Mouhammed, Mouhamoin

MOUSA (Arabic) a form of Moses.
Moussa

MOZE (Lithuanian) a form of Moses.
Mozes, Mózes

MPASA (Ngoni) mat.

MPOSI (Nyakusa) blacksmith.

MPOZA (Luganda) tax collector.

MSRAH (Akan) sixth-born.

MTIMA (Ngoni) heart.

MUATA (Moquelumnan) yellow jackets in their nest.

MUGAMBA (Runyoro) talks too much.

MUGISA (Rutooro) lucky.
Mugisha, Mukisa

MUHAMMAD (Arabic) praised. History: the founder of the Islamic religion. See also Ahmad, Hamid, Yasin.
Mahmoud, Mahmúd, Mohamad, Mohamed, Mohamet, Mohamud, Mohammed, Mouhamed, Muhamad, Muhamed, Muhamet, Muhammadali, Muhammed

MUHANNAD (Arabic) sword.
Muhanad

MUHSIN (Arabic) beneficent; charitable.

MUHTADI (Arabic) rightly guided.

MUIR (Scottish) moor; marshland.

MUJAHID (Arabic) fighter in the way of Allah.

MUKASA (Luganda) God's chief administrator.

MUKHTAR (Arabic) chosen.
Mukhtaar

MUKUL (Sanskrit) bud, blossom; soul.

MULOGO (Musoga) wizard.

MUNDAN (Rhodesian) garden.

MUNDO (Spanish) a short form of Edmundo.

MUNDY (Irish) from Reamonn, Ireland.

MUNGO (Scottish) amiable.

MUN-HEE (Korean) literate; shiny.

MUNIR (Arabic) brilliant; shining.

MUNNY (Cambodian) wise.

MURACO (Native American) white moon.

MURALI (Hindi) god. Religion: another name for the Hindu god Krishna.

MURAT (Turkish) wish come true.

MURDOCK (Scottish) wealthy sailor.
Murdo, Murdoch, Murtagh

MURPHY (Irish) sea-warrior.
Murfey, Murfy

MURRAY (Scottish) sailor.
Macmurray, Moray, Murrey, Murry

MURTAGH (Irish) a form of Murdock.
Murtaugh

MUSA (Swahili) child.

MUSÁD (Arabic) untied camel.

MUSOKE (Rukonjo) born while a
rainbow was in the sky.

MUSTAFA (Arabic) chosen; royal.
*Mostafa, Mostaffa, Moustafa, Mustafaa,
Mustafah, Mustafe, Mustaffa, Mustafo,
Mustapha, Mustoffa, Mustofo*

MUSTAPHA (Arabic) an alternate
form of Mustafa.
Mostapha, Moustapha

MUTI (Arabic) obedient.

MWAKA (Luganda) born on New Year's
Eve.

MWAMBA (Nyakusa) strong.

MWANJE (Luganda) leopard.

MWINYI (Swahili) king.

MWITA (Swahili) summoner.

MYCHAJLO (Latvian) a form of
Michael.
Mykhaltso, Mykhas

MYCHAL (American) a form of
Michael.
Mychall, Mychalo, Mycheal

MYER (English) a form of Meir.
Myers, Myur

MYKAL, Mykel (American) a form of
Michael.
Mykael, Mikele, Mykell

MYLES (Latin) soldier. (German) an
alternate form of Miles.
Myels, Mylez, Mylles, Mylz

MYNOR (Latin) an alternate form of
Minor.

MYO (Burmese) city.

MYRON (Greek) fragrant ointment.
*Mehran, Mehrayan, My, Myran, Myrone,
Ron*

MYUNG-DAE (Korean) right; great.

MZUZI (Swahili) inventive.

N

NAAMAN (Hebrew) pleasant.

NABIHA (Arabic) intelligent.

NABIL (Arabic) noble.
Nabeel, Nabiel

NACHMAN (Hebrew) a short form of
Menachem.
Nachum, Nahum

NADA (Arabic) generous.

NADAV (Hebrew) generous; noble.
Nadiv

NADIDAH (Arabic) equal to anyone
else.

NADIM (Arabic) friend.
Nadeem

NADIR (Afghani, Arabic) dear, rare.
Nader

NADISU (Hindi) beautiful river.

NAEEM (Arabic) benevolent.
Naem, Naim, Naiym, Nieem

NAFTALI (Hebrew) wreath.
Naftalie

NAGID (Hebrew) ruler, prince.

NAHELE (Hawaiian) forest.

NAHMA (Native American) sturgeon.

NAILAH (Arabic) successful.

NAIRN (Scottish) river with alder trees.
Nairne

NAJEE (Arabic) an alternate form of
Naji.
Najae, Najée, Najei, Najiee

NAJI (Arabic) safe.
Najee, Najih

NAJÍB (Arabic) born to nobility.
Najib, Nejeeb

NAJJI (Muganda) second child.

NAKIA (Arabic) pure.
Nakai, Nakee, Nakeia, Naki, Nakiah, Nakii

NAKOS (Arapaho) sage, wise.

NALDO (Spanish) a familiar form
of Reginald.

NALREN (Dene) thawed out.

NAM (Vietnamese) scrape off.

NAMAKA (Hawaiian) eyes.

NAMID (Chippewa) star dancer.

NAMIR (Hebrew) leopard.
Namer

NANDIN (Hindi) god; destroyer.
Religion: another name for the Hindu
god Shiva.
Nandan

NANDO (German) a familiar form of
Ferdinand.
Nandor

NANGILA (Abaluhya) born while
parents traveled.

NANGWAYA (Mwera) don't mess
with me.

NANSEN (Swedish) son of Nancy.

NANTAI (Navajo) chief.

NANTAN (Apache) spokesman.

NAOKO (Japanese) straight, honest.

NAPAYSHNI (Lakota) he does not flee;
courageous.

NAPIER (Spanish) new city.
Neper

NAPOLEON (Greek) lion of the
woodland. (Italian) from Naples, Italy.
History: Napoleon Bonaparte was a
famous nineteenth-century French
emperor.
*Leon, Nap, Napolean, Napoléon, Napoleone,
Nappie, Nappy*

NAQUAN (American) a combination
of the prefix Na + Quan.
Naqawn, Naquain, Naquen, Naquon

NARAIN (Hindi) protector. Religion:
another name for the Hindu god
Vishnu.
Narayan

NARCISSE (French) a form of
Narcissus.
Narcis, Narciso, Narkis, Narkissos

NARCISSUS (Greek) daffodil.
Mythology: the youth who fell in
love with his own reflection.
Narcisse

NARD (Persian) chess player.

NARDO (German) strong, hardy.
(Spanish) a short form of Bernardo.

NARVE (Dutch) healthy, strong.

NASHASHUK (Fox, Sauk) loud
thunder.

NASHOBA (Choctaw) wolf.

NASIM (Persian) breeze, fresh air.
Naseem, Nassim

NASSER (Arabic) victorious.
Naseer, Naser, Nasier, Nasir, Nasr, Nassir,
Nassor

NAT (English) a short form of Nathan,
Nathaniel.
Natt, Natty

NATAL (Spanish) a form of Noël.
Natale, Natalie, Natalino, Natalio, Nataly

NATAN (Hebrew, Hungarian, Polish,
Russian, Spanish) God has given.
Naten

NATANAEL (Hebrew) an alternate
form of Nathaniel.
Natanel, Nataniel

NATE (Hebrew) a short form of Nathan,
Nathaniel.

NATESH (Hindi) destroyer. Religion:
another name for the Hindu god Shiva.

NATHAN (Hebrew) a short form of
Nathaniel. Bible: an Old Testament
prophet who saved Solomon's
kingdom.
Naethan, Nat, Nate, Nathann, Nathean,
Nathen, Nathian, Nathin, Nathon, Nathyn,
Natthan, Naythan, Nethan

NATHANAEL (Hebrew) an alternate
form of Nathaniel.
Nathanae, Nathanal, Nathaneal, Nathaneil,
Nathanel, Nathaneol

NATHANIAL (Hebrew) an alternate
form of Nathaniel.
Nathanyal, Nathanual

NATHANIE (Hebrew) a familiar form
of Nathaniel.
Nathania, Nathanni

NATHANIEL (Hebrew) gift of God.
Bible: one of the Twelve Apostles.
Nat, Natanael, Nate, Nathan, Nathanael,
Nathanial, Nathanie, Nathanielle, Nathanil,
Nathanile, Nathanuel, Nathanyel, Nathanyl,
Natheal, Nathel, Nathinel, Nethaniel,
Thaniel

NATHEN (Hebrew) an alternate form of
Nathan.

NAV (Gypsy) name.

NAVARRO (Spanish) plains.
Navarre

NAVDEEP (Sikh) new light.
Navdip

NAVIN (Hindi) new, novel.
Naveen, Naven

NAWAT (Native American) left-
handed.

NAWKAW (Winnebago) wood.

NAYATI (Native American) wrestler.

NAYLAND (English) island dweller.

NAZARETH (Hebrew) born in
Nazareth, Israel.
Nazaire, Nazaret, Nazarie, Nazario,
Nazerene, Nazerine

NAZIH (Arabic) pure, chaste.
Nazeeh, Nazeem, Nazeer, Nazieh, Nazim,
Nazir, Nazz

NDALE (Ngoni) trick.

NEAL (Irish) an alternate form of Neil.
Neale, Neall, Nealle, Nealon, Nealy

NECI (Latin) a familiar form of Ignatius.

NECTARIOS (Greek) saint. Religion: a recent saint in the Greek Orthodox church.

NED (English) a familiar form of Edward, Edwin.
Neddie, Neddym, Nedrick

NEHEMIAH (Hebrew) compassion of Jehovah. Bible: a Hebrew prophet.
Nahemiah, Nechemya, Nehemias, Nehemie, Nehemyah, Nehimiah, Nehmia, Nehmiah, Nemo, Neyamia

NEHRU (Hindi) canal.

NEIL (Irish) champion.
Neal, Neel, Neihl, Neile, Neill, Neille, Nels, Niall, Niele, Niels, Nigel, Nil, Niles, Nilo, Nils, Nyle

NEKA (Native American) wild goose.

NELEK (Polish) a form of Cornelius.

NELLIE (English) a familiar form of Cornelius, Cornell, Nelson.
Nell, Nelly

NELIUS (Latin) a short form of Cornelius.

NELO (Spanish) a form of Daniel.
Nello, Nilo

NELS (Scandinavian) a form of Neil, Nelson.
Nelse, Nelson, Nils

NELSON (English) son of Neil.
Nealson, Neilsen, Neilson, Nellie, Nels, Nelsen, Nilson, Nilsson

NEMESIO (Spanish) just.
Nemi

NEMO (Greek) glen, glade. (Hebrew) a short form of Nehemiah.

NEN (Egyptian) ancient waters.

NEPTUNE (Latin) sea ruler. Mythology: the Roman god of the sea.

NERO (Latin, Spanish) stern.
Neron, Nerone, Nerron

NESBIT (English) nose-shaped bend in a river.
Naisbit, Naisbitt, Nesbitt, Nisbet, Nisbett

NESTOR (Greek) traveler; wise.
Nester

NETHANIEL (Hebrew) an alternate form of Nathaniel.
Netanel, Netania, Netaniah, Netaniel, Netanya, Nethanel, Nethanial, Nethaniel, Nethanyal, Nethanyel

NETO (Spanish) a short form of Ernesto.

NEVADA (Spanish) covered in snow. Geography: a U.S. state.
Navada, Nevade

NEVAN (Irish) holy.
Nevean

NEVILLE (French) new town.
Nev, Nevil, Nevile, Nevill, Nevyle

NEVIN (Irish) worshiper of the saint. (English) middle; herb.
Nefen, Nev, Nevan, Neven, Nevins, Nevyn, Niven

NEWBOLD (English) new tree.

NEWELL (English) new hall.
Newall, Newel, Newyle

NEWLAND (English) new land.
Newlan

NEWLIN (Welsh) new lake.
Newlyn

NEWMAN (English) newcomer.
Neiman, Neimann, Neimon, Neuman, Numan, Numen

NEWTON (English) new town.
Newt

NGAI (Vietnamese) herb.

NGHIA (Vietnamese) forever.

NGOZI (Ibo) blessing.

NGU (Vietnamese) sleep.
Nguyen

NHEAN (Cambodian) self-knowledge.

NIALL (Irish) an alternate form of Neil. History: Niall of the Nine Hostages was a famous Irish ruler who founded the clan O'Neill.
Nial, Nialle

NIBAL (Arabic) arrows.
Nibel

NIBAW (Native American) standing tall.

NICABAR (Gypsy) stealthly.

NICHO (Spanish) a form of Dennis.

NICHOLAS (Greek) victorious people. Religion: the patron saint of children. See also Caelan, Claus, Cola, Colar, Cole, Colin, Colson, Klaus, Lasse, Mikolaj, Mikolas, Milek.
Niccolas, Nichalas, Nichelas, Nichele, Nichlas, Nichlos, Nichola, Nicholaas, Nicholaes, Nicholase, Nicholaus, Nichole, Nicholias, Nicholl, Nichollas, Nicholos, Nichols, Nicholus, Nick, Nickalus, Nicklaus, Nickolas, Nicky, Niclas, Niclasse, Nico, Nicola, Nicolai, Nicolas, Nicoles, Nicolis, Nicoll, Nicolo, Nikhil, Niki, Nikili, Nikita, Nikko, Niklas, Niko, Nikolai, Nikolas, Nikolaus, Nikolos, Nils, Nioclás, Niocol, Nycholas

NICHOLAUS (Greek) an alternate form of Nicholas.
Nichalaus, Nichalous, Nichaolas, Nichlaus, Nichloas, Nichlous, Nicholaos, Nicholous

NICHOLS, Nicholson (English) son of Nicholas.
Nicholes, Nicholis, Nicolls, Nickelson, Nickoles

NICK (English) a short form of Dominic, Nicholas. See also Micu.
Nic, Nik

NICKALUS (Greek) an alternate form of Nicholas.
Nickalas, Nickalis, Nickalos, Nickelas, Nickelus

NICKLAUS, Nicklas (Greek) an alternate form of Nicholas.
Nickalaus, Nickalous, Nickelous, Nicklauss, Nicklos, Nicklous, Nicklus, Nickolau, Nickolaus, Nicolaus, Niklaus, Nikolaus

NICKOLAS (Greek) an alternate form of Nicholas.
Nickolaos, Nickolis, Nickolos, Nickolus, Nickolys, Nickoulas

NICKY (Greek) a familiar form of Nicholas.
Nickey, Nicki, Nickie, Niki, Nikki

NICO (Greek) a short form of Nicholas.
Nicco

NICODEMUS (Greek) conqueror of the people.
Nicodem, Nicodemius, Nikodem, Nikodema, Nikodemious, Nikodim

NICOLA (Italian) a form of Nicholas. See also Cola.
Nicolá, Nikolah

NICOLAI (Norwegian, Russian) a form of Nicholas.
Nicholai, Nickolai, Nicolaj, Nicolau, Nicolay, Nicoly, Nikalai

NICOLAS (Italian) a form of Nicholas.
Nico, Nicolaas, Nicolás, Nicolaus, Nicoles, Nicolis, Nicolus

NICOLO (Italian) a form of Nicholas.
Niccolo, Niccolò, Nicol, Nicolao, Nicollo

NIELS (Danish) a form of Neil.
Niel, Nielsen, Nielson, Niles, Nils

NIEN (Vietnamese) year.

NIGAN (Native American) ahead.
Nigen

NIGEL (Latin) dark night.
Niegel, Nigal, Nigale, Nigele, Nigell, Nigiel,
Nigil, Nigle, Nijel, Nye, Nygel, Nyigel, Nyjil

NIKA (Yoruba) ferocious.

NIKE (Greek) victorious.
Nikka

NIKI (Hungarian) a familiar form of
Nicholas.
Nikia, Nikiah, Nikki, Nikkie, Nykei, Nykey

NIKITA (Russian) a form of Nicholas.
Nakita, Nakitas, Nikula

NIKITI (Native American) round and
smooth like an abalone shell.

NIKKO, Niko (Hungarian) forms of
Nicholas.
Nikoe, Nyko

NIKLAS (Latvian, Swedish) a form
of Nicholas.
Niklaas, Niklaus

NIKOLA (Greek) a short form of Nicholas.
Nikolao, Nikolay, Nykola

NIKOLAI (Estonian, Russian) a form of
Nicholas.
Kolya, Nikolais, Nikolaj, Nikolajs, Nikolay,
Nikoli, Nikolia, Nikula, Nikulas

NIKOLAS (Greek) an alternate form on
Nicholas.
Nicanor, Nikalas, Nikalis, Nikalus, Nikholas,
Nikolaas, Nikolaos, Nikolis, Nikolos, Nikos,
Nilos, Nykolas, Nykolus

NIKOLAUS (Greek) an alternate
form of Nicholas.
Nikalous, Nikolaos

NIKOLOS (Greek) an alternate form
of Nicholas. See also Kolya.
Niklos, Nikolaos, Nikolò, Nikolous, Nikolus,
Nikos, Nilos

NIL (Russian) a form of Neil.
Nilya

NILA (Hindi) blue.

NILES (English) son of Neil.
Nilesh, Nyles

NILO (Finnish) a form of Neil.

NILS (Swedish) a short form of Nicholas.

NIMROD (Hebrew) rebel. Bible: a
great-grandson of Noah.

NIÑO (Spanish) young child.

NIRAN (Tai) eternal.

NISHAN (Armenian) cross, sign, mark.
Nishon

NISSAN (Hebrew) sign, omen; miracle.
Nisan, Nissim, Nissin, Nisson

NITIS (Native American) friend.
Netis

NIXON (English) son of Nick.
Nixan, Nixson

NIZAM (Arabic) leader.

NKUNDA (Runyankore) loves those
who hate him.

N'NAMDI (Ibo) his father's name lives
on.

NOACH (Hebrew) an alternate form of
Noah.

NOAH (Hebrew) peaceful, restful. Bible:
the patriarch who built the ark to
survive the Great Flood.
Noach, Noak, Noe, Noé, Noi

NOAM (Hebrew) sweet; friend.

NOBLE (Latin) born to nobility.
Nobe, Nobie, Noby

NODIN (Native American) wind.
Knoton, Noton

NOE (Czech, French) a form of Noah.

NOÉ (Hebrew, Spanish) quiet, peaceful. See also Noah.

NOËL (French) day of Christ's birth. See also Natal.
Noel, Noél, Noell, Nole, Noli, Nowel, Nowell

NOHEA (Hawaiian) handsome.
Noha, Nohe

NOKONYU (Native American) katydid's nose.
Noko, Nokoni

NOLAN (Irish) famous; noble.
Noland, Nolande, Nolane, Nolen, Nolin, Nollan, Nolyn

NOLLIE (Latin, Scandinavian) a familiar form of Oliver.
Noll, Nolly

NORBERT (Scandinavian) brilliant hero.
Bert, Norberto, Norbie, Norby

NORBERTO (Spanish) a form of Norbert.

NORMAN (French) norseman. History: a name for the Scandinavians who conquered Normandy in the tenth century, and who later conquered England in 1066.
Norm, Normand, Normen, Normie, Normy

NORRIS (French) northerner. (English) Norman's horse.
Norice, Norie, Noris, Norreys, Norrie, Norry, Norrys

NORTHCLIFF (English) northern cliff.
Northcliffe, Northclyff, Northclyffe

NORTHROP (English) north farm.
North, Northup

NORTON (English) northern town.

NORVILLE (French, English) northern town.
Norval, Norvel, Norvell, Norvil, Norvill, Norvylle

NORVIN (English) northern friend.
Norvyn, Norwin, Norwinn, Norwyn, Norwynn

NORWARD (English) protector of the north.
Norwerd

NORWOOD (English) northern woods.

NOTAKU (Moquelumnan) growing bear.

NOWLES (English) a short form of Knowles.

NSOAH (Akan) seventh-born.

NUMA (Arabic) pleasant.

NUMAIR (Arabic) panther.

NUNCIO (Italian) messenger.
Nunzi, Nunzio

NURI (Hebrew, Arabic) my fire.
Nery, Noori, Nur, Nuris, Nurism, Nury

NURIEL (Hebrew, Arabic) fire of the Lord.
Nuria, Nuriah, Nuriya

NURU (Swahili) born in daylight.

NUSAIR (Arabic) bird of prey.

NWA (Nigerian) son.

NWAKE (Nigerian) born on market day.

NYE (English) a familiar form of Aneurin, Nigel.

NYLE (Irish) an alternate form of Neil. (English) island.
Nyal, Nyll

O

OAKES (English) oak trees.
Oak, Oakie, Oaks, Ochs

OAKLEY (English) oak-tree field.
Oak, Oakes, Oakie, Oaklee, Oakleigh, Oakly, Oaks

OALO (Spanish) a form of Paul.

OBA (Yoruba) king.

OBADELE (Yoruba) king arrives at the house.

OBADIAH (Hebrew) servant of God.
Obadias, Obed, Obediah, Obie, Ovadiach, Ovadiah, Ovadya

OBED (English) a short form of Obadiah.

OBERON (German) noble; bearlike. Literature: the king of the fairies in the Shakespearean play *A Midsummer Night's Dream*. See also Auberon, Aubrey.
Oberen, Oberron, Oeberon

OBERT (German) wealthy; bright.

OBIE (English) a familiar form of Obadiah.
Obbie, Obe, Obey, Obi, Oby

OCAN (Luo) hard times.

OCTAVIO (Latin) eighth. See also Tavey, Tavian.
Octave, Octavia, Octavian, Octaviano, Octavien, Octavious, Octavius, Octavo, Octavous, Octavus, Ottavio

OCTAVIOUS, Octavius (Latin) alternate forms of Octavio.
Octavaius, Octaveous, Octaveus, Octavias, Octaviaus, Octavis, Octavous, Octavus

ODAKOTA (Lakota) friendly.
Oda

ODD (Norwegian) point.
Oddvar

ODE (Benin) born along the road. (Irish, English) a short form of Odell.
Odey, Odie, Ody

ODED (Hebrew) encouraging.

ODELL (Greek) ode, melody. (Irish) otter. (English) forested hill.
Dell, Odall, Ode

ODIN (Scandinavian) ruler. Mythology: the chief Norse god.
Oden

ODION (Benin) first of twins.

ODO (Norwegian) a form of Otto.

ODOLF (German) prosperous wolf.
Odolff

ODOM (Ghanian) oak tree.

ODON (Hungarian) wealthy protector.
Odi

ODRAN (Irish) pale green.
Odhrán, Oran, Oren, Orin, Orran, Orren, Orrin

ODYSSEUS (Greek) wrathful. Literature: the hero of Homer's epic *The Odyssey*.

OFER (Hebrew) young deer.

OG (Aramaic) king. Bible: the king of Basham.

OGALEESHA (Lakota) red shirt.

OGBAY (Ethiopian) don't take him from me.

OGBONNA (Ibo) image of his father.
Ogbonnia

OGDEN (English) oak valley. Literature: Ogden Nash was a twentieth-century American writer.
Ogdan, Ogdon

OGIMA (Chippewa) chief.

OGUN (Nigerian) Mythology: the god of war.
Ogunkeye, Ogunsanwo, Ogunsheye

OHANKO (Native American) restless.

OHANNES (Turkish) a form of John.

OHANZEE (Lakota) comforting shadow.

OHIN (African) chief.
Ohan

OHITEKAH (Lakota) brave.

OISTIN (Irish) a form of Austin.
Osten, Ostyn, Ostynn

OJ (American) a combination of the initials O. + J.
O.J., Ojay

OJO (Yoruba) difficult delivery.

OKAPI (Swahili) giraffe-like animal with a long neck.

OKE (Hawaiian) a form of Oscar.

OKECHUKU (Ibo) God's gift.

OKEKE (Ibo) born on market day.
Okorie

OKIE (American) from Oklahoma.
Okee, Okey

OKO (Ga) older twin. (Yoruba) god of war.

OKORIE (Ibo) an alternate form of Okeke.

OKPARA (Ibo) first son.

OKUTH (Luo) born in a rain shower.

OLA (Yoruba) wealthy, rich.

OLAF (Scandinavian) ancestor. History: a patron saint and king of Norway.
Olaff, Olafur, Olav, Ole, Olef, Olof, Oluf

OLAJUWON (Yoruba) wealth and honor are God's gifts.
Olajawon, Olajawun, Olajowuan, Olajuan, Olajuanne, Olajuawon, Olajuwa, Olajuwan, Olaujawon, Oljuwoun

OLAMINA (Yoruba) this is my wealth.

OLATUNJI (Yoruba) honor reawakens.

OLAV (Scandinavian) an alternate form of Olaf.
Ola, Olave, Olavus, Ole, Olen, Olin, Olle, Olov, Olyn

OLE (Scandinavian) a familiar form of Olaf, Olav.
Olay, Oleh, Olle

OLEG (Latvian, Russian) holy.
Olezka

OLEKSANDR (Russian) a form of Alexander.
Olek, Olesandr, Olesko

OLÉS (Polish) a familiar form of Alexander.

OLIN (English) holly.
Olen, Olney, Olyn

OLINDO (Italian) from Olinthos, Italy.

OLIVER (Latin) olive tree. (Scandinavian) kind; affectionate.
Nollie, Oilibhéar, Oliverio, Oliverios, Olivero, Olivier, Oliviero, Oliwa, Ollie, Olliver, Ollivor, Olvan

OLIVIER (French) a form of Oliver.

OLIWA (Hawaiian) a form of Oliver.

OLLIE (English) a familiar form of Oliver.
Olie, Olle, Olley, Olly

OLO (Spanish) a short form of Orlando, Rolando.

OLUBAYO (Yoruba) highest joy.

OLUFEMI (Yoruba) wealth and honor favors me.

OLUJIMI (Yoruba) God gave me this.

OLUSHOLA (Yoruba) God has blessed me.

OMAR (Arabic) highest; follower of the Prophet. (Hebrew) reverent.
Omair, Omari, Omarr, Omer, Umar

OMARI (Swahili) a form of Omar.
Omare, Omaree, Omarey

OMER (Arabic) an alternate form of Omar.
Omeer, Omero

OMOLARA (Benin) child born at the right time.

ON (Burmese) coconut. (Chinese) peace.

ONAN (Turkish) prosperous.

ONAONA (Hawaiian) pleasant fragrance.

ONDRO (Czech) a form of Andrew.
Ondra, Ondre, Ondrea, Ondrey

O'NEIL (Irish) son of Neil.
Oneal, O'neal, Oneil, O'neill, Onel, Oniel, Onil

ONKAR (Hindi) pure being. Religion: another name for the Hindu god Shiva.

ONOFRIO (German) an alternate form of Humphrey.
Oinfre, Onfre, Onfrio, Onofre, Onofredo

ONSLOW (English) enthusiast's hill.
Ounslow

ONUFRY (Polish) a form of Humphrey.

ONUR (Turkish) honor.

OPHIR (Hebrew) faithful. Bible: an Old Testament character.

OPIO (Ateso) first of twin boys.

ORAL (Latin) verbal, speaker.

ORAN (Irish) green.
Odhran, Odran, Ora, Orane, Orran

ORATIO (Latin) an alternate form of Horatio.
Orazio

ORBÁN (Hungarian) born in the city.

ORDELL (Latin) beginning.
Orde

OREN (Hebrew) pine tree. (Irish) light skinned, white.
Oran, Orin, Oris, Orono, Orren, Orrin

ORESTES (Greek) mountain man. Mythology: the son of the Greek leader Agamemnon.
Aresty, Oreste

ORI (Hebrew) my light.
Oree, Orie, Orri, Ory

ORIEN (Latin) visitor from the east.
Orian, Orie, Orin, Oris, Oron, Orono, Orrin, Oryan

ORION (Greek) son of fire. Mythology: a hunter who became a constellation. See also Zorion.

ORJI (Ibo) mighty tree.

ORLANDO (German) famous throughout the land. (Spanish) a form of Roland.
Lando, Olando, Olo, Orlan, Orland, Orlanda, Orlandas, Orlandes, Orlandis, Orlandos, Orlandus, Orlo, Orlondo, Orlondon

ORLEANS (Latin) golden.
Orlean, Orlin

ORMAN (German) mariner, seaman. (Scandinavian) serpent, worm.
Ormand

ORMOND (English) bear mountain; spear protector.
Ormande, Ormon, Ormonde

ORO (Spanish) golden.

ORONO (Latin) a form of Oren.
Oron

ORRICK (English) old oak tree.
Orric

ORRIN (English) river. Geography: a river in England.
Orin, Oryn, Orynn

ORRIS (Latin) an alternate form of Horatio.
Oris, Orriss

ORRY (Latin) from the Orient.
Oarrie, Orrey, Orrie

ORSINO (Italian) a form of Orson.

ORSON (Latin) bearlike.
Orscino, Orsen, Orsin, Orsini, Orsino, Son, Sonny, Urson

ORTON (English) shore town.

ORTZI (Basque) sky.

ORUNJAN (Yoruba) born under the midday sun.

ORVAL (English) an alternate form of Orville.
Orvel

ORVILLE (French) golden village. History: Orville Wright and his brother Wilbur were the first men to fly an airplane.
Orv, Orval, Orvell, Orvie, Orvil

ORVIN (English) spear friend.
Orwin, Owynn

OSAHAR (Benin) God hears.

OSAYABA (Benin) God forgives.

OSAZE (Benin) whom God likes.

OSBERT (English) divine; bright.

OSBORN (Scandinavian) divine bear. (English) warrior of God.
Osbern, Osbon, Osborne, Osbourn, Osbourne, Osburn, Osburne, Oz, Ozzie

OSCAR (Scandinavian) divine spearman.
Oke, Oskar, Osker, Oszkar

OSEI (Fante) noble.
Osee

OSGOOD (English) divinely good.

O'SHEA (Irish) son of Shea.
Oshae, Oshai, Oshane, O'Shane, Oshaun, Oshay, Oshaye, Oshe, Oshea, Osheon

OSIP (Russian, Ukrainian) a form of Joseph, Yosef. See also Osya.

OSKAR (Scandinavian) an alternate form of Oscar.
Osker, Ozker

OSMAN (Turkish) ruler. (English) servant of God.
Osmanek, Osmen, Osmin, Otthmor, Ottmar

OSMAR (English) divine; wonderful.

OSMOND (English) divine protector.
Osmand, Osmonde, Osmont, Osmund, Osmunde, Osmundo

OSRIC (English) divine ruler.
Osrick

OSTIN (Latin) an alternate form of Austin.
Ostan, Osten, Ostyn

OSVALDO (Spanish) a form of Oswald.
Osbaldo, Osbalto, Osvald, Osvalda

OSWALD (English) God's power; God's crest. See also Waldo.
Osvaldo, Oswaldo, Oswall, Oswell, Oswold, Oz, Ozzie

OSWALDO (Spanish) a form of Oswald.

OSWIN (English) divine friend.
Osvin, Oswinn, Oswyn, Oswynn

OSYA (Russian) a familiar form of Osip.

OTA (Czech) prosperous.
Otik

OTADAN (Native American) plentiful.

OTAKTAY (Lakota) kills many; strikes many.

OTEK (Polish) a form of Otto.

OTELLO (Italian) a form of Othello.

OTEM (Luo) born away from home.

OTHELLO (Spanish) a form of Otto. Literature: the title character in the Shakespearean tragedy *Othello*.
Otello

OTHMAN (German) wealthy.
Ottoman

OTIS (Greek) keen of hearing. (German) son of Otto.
Oates, Odis, Otes, Otess, Otez, Otise, Ottis, Otys

OTTAH (Nigerian) thin baby.

OTTAR (Norwegian) point warrior; fright warrior.

OTTMAR (Turkish) an alternate form of Osman. History: the founder of the Ottoman Empire.
Otomars, Ottomar

OTTO (German) rich.

Odo, Otek, Otello, Otfried, Othello, Otho, Othon, Otik, Otilio, Otman, Oto, Otón, Otton, Ottone

OTTOKAR (German) happy warrior.
Otokars, Ottocar

OTU (Native American) collecting seashells in a basket.

OURAY (Ute) arrow. Astrology: born under the sign of Sagittarius.

OVED (Hebrew) worshiper, follower.

OWEN (Irish) born to nobility; young warrior. (Welsh) a form of Evan.
Owain, Owens, Owin, Uaine

OWNEY (Irish) elderly.
Oney

OXFORD (English) place where oxen cross the river.
Ford

OYA (Moquelumnan) speaking of the jacksnipe.

OYSTEIN (Norwegian) rock of happiness.
Ostein, Osten, Ostin, Øystein

OZ (Hebrew) a short form of Osborn, Oswald.

OZTURK (Turkish) pure; genuine Turk.

OZZIE (English) a familiar form of Osborn, Oswald.
Ossie, Ossy, Ozee, Ozi, Ozzi, Ozzy

P

PAAVO (Finnish) a form of Paul.
Paaveli

PABLO (Spanish) a form of Paul.
Pable, Paublo

PACE (English) a form of Pascal.
Payce

PACIFICO (Filipino) peaceful.

PACO (Italian) pack. (Spanish) a familiar form of Francisco. (Native American) bald eagle. See also Quico.
Pacorro, Panchito, Pancho, Paquito

PADDY (Irish) a familiar form of Padraic, Patrick.
Paddey, Paddi, Paddie

PADEN (English) an altenate form of Patton.

PADGET (English) a form of Page.
Padgett, Paget, Pagett

PADRAIC (Irish) a form of Patrick.
Paddrick, Paddy, Padhraig, Padrai, Pádraig, Padraigh, Padreic, Padriac, Padric, Padron, Padruig

PAGE (French) youthful assistant.
Padget, Paggio, Paige, Payge

PAIGE (English) a form of Page.

PAKELIKA (Hawaiian) a form of Patrick.

PAKI (African) witness.

PAL (Swedish) a form of Paul.

PÁL (Hungarian) a form of Paul.
Pali, Palika

PALAINA (Hawaiian) a form of Brian.

PALANI (Hawaiian) a form of Frank.

PALASH (Hindi) flowery tree.

PALBEN (Basque) blond.

PALLADIN (Native American) fighter.
Pallaton, Palleten

PALMER (English) palm-bearing pilgrim.
Pallmer, Palmar

PALTI (Hebrew) God liberates.
Palti-el

PANAS (Russian) immortal.

PANAYIOTIS (Greek) an alternate form of Peter.
Panagiotis, Panajotis, Panayioti, Panayoti, Panayotis

PANCHO (Spanish) a familiar form of Francisco, Frank.
Panchito

PANOS (Greek) an alternate form of Peter.
Petros

PAOLO (Italian) a form of Paul.

PAQUITO (Spanish) a familiar form of Paco.

PARAMESH (Hindi) greatest. Religion: another name for the Hindu god Shiva.

PARDEEP (Sikh) mystic light.
Pardip

PARIS (Greek) lover. Geography: the capital of France. Mythology: the prince of Troy who started the Trojan War by abducting Helen.
Paras, Paree, Pares, Parese, Parie, Parris, Parys

PARK (Chinese) cypress tree. (English) a short form of Parker.
Parke, Parkes, Parkey, Parks

PARKER (English) park keeper.
Park

PARKIN (English) little Peter.
Perkin

PARLAN (Scottish) a form of Bartholomew. See also Parthalán.

PARNELL (French) little Peter. History: Charles Stewart Parnell was a famous Irish politician.
Nell, Parle, Parnel, Parrnell, Pernell

PARR (English) cattle enclosure, barn.

PARRISH (English) church district.
Parish, Parrie, Parrisch, Parrysh

PARRY (Welsh) son of Harry.
Parrey, Parrie, Pary

PARTH (Irish) a short form of
Parthalán.
Partha, Parthey

PARTHALÁN (Irish) plow-man.
See also Bartholomew.
Parlan, Parth

PARTHENIOS (Greek) virgin. Religion:
a Greek Orthodox saint.

PASCAL (French) born on Easter or
Passover.
*Pace, Pascale, Pascalle, Paschal, Paschalis,
Pascoe, Pascow, Pascual, Pasquale*

PASCUAL (Spanish) a form of Pascal.
Pascul

PASHA (Russian) a form of Paul.
Pashenka, Pashka

PASQUALE (Italian) a form of Pascal.
Pascuale, Pasqual, Pasquali, Pasquel

PASTOR (Latin) spiritual leader.

PAT (English) a short form of Patrick.
(Native American) fish.
Pattie, Patty

PATAKUSU (Moquelumnan) ant biting
a person.

PATAMON (Native American) raging.

PATEK (Polish) a form of Patrick.
Patick

PATRIC (Latin) an alternate form of
Patrick.

PATRICE (French) a form of Patrick.

PATRICIO (Spanish) a form of Patrick.
Patricius, Patrizio

PATRICK (Latin) nobleman. Religion:
the patron saint of Ireland. See also
Fitzpatrick, Ticho.
*Paddy, Padraic, Pakelika, Pat, Patek, Patric,
Patrice, Patricio, Patrickk, Patrik, Patrique,
Patrizius, Patryk, Pats, Patsy, Pattrick*

PATRIN (Gypsy) leaf trail.

PATRYK (Latin) an alternate form
of Patrick.
Patryck

PATTERSON (Irish) son of Pat.
Patteson

PATTIN (Gypsy) leaf.

PATTON (English) warrior's town.
*Paden, Paten, Patin, Paton, Patten, Pattin,
Patty, Payton, Peyton*

PATWIN (Native American) man.

PATXI (Basque, Teutonic) free.

PAUL (Latin) small. Bible: Saul, later
renamed Paul, was the first to bring
the teachings of Christ to the Gentiles.
*Oalo, Paavo, Pablo, Pal, Pál, Pall, Paolo,
Pasha, Pasko, Pauli, Paulia, Paulin, Paulino,
Paulis, Paulo, Pauls, Paulus, Pavel, Pavlos,
Pawel, Pol, Poul*

PAULI (Latin) a familiar form of Paul.
Pauley, Paulie, Pauly

PAULIN (German, Polish) a form of
Paul.

PAULINO (Spanish) a form of Paul.

PAULO (Portuguese, Swedish,
Hawaiian) a form of Paul.

PAVEL (Russian) a form of Paul.
*Paavel, Pasha, Pavils, Pavlik, Pavlo,
Pavlusha, Pavlushenka, Pawl*

PAVIT (Hindi) pious, pure.

PAWEL (Polish) a form of Paul.
Pawelek, Pawl

PAX (Latin) peaceful.
Paz

PAXTON (Latin) peaceful town.
Packston, Pax, Paxon, Paxten, Paxtun

PAYAT (Native American) he is on his way.
Pay, Payatt

PAYDEN (English) an alternate form of Payton.
Paydon

PAYNE (Latin) man from the country.
Paine, Paynn

PAYTAH (Lakota) fire.
Pay, Payta

PAYTON (English) an alternate form of Patton.
Paiton, Pate, Payden, Peaton, Peighton, Peyton

PAZ (Spanish) a form of Pax.

PEARCE (English) an alternate form of Pierce.
Pears, Pearse

PEARSON (English) son of Peter. See also Pierson.
Pearsson, Pehrson, Peirson, Peterson

PEDER (Scandinavian) a form of Peter.
Peadar, Pedey

PEDRO (Spanish) a form of Peter.
Pedrin, Pedrín, Petronio

PEERS (English) a form of Peter.
Peerus, Piers

PEETER (Estonian) a form of Peter.
Peet

PEIRCE (English) a form of Peter.
Peirs

PEKELO (Hawaiian) a form of Peter.
Pekka

PELEKE (Hawaiian) a form of Frederick.

PELHAM (English) tannery town.

PELÍ (Latin, Basque) happy.

PELL (English) parchment.
Pall

PELLO (Greek, Basque) stone.
Peru, Piarres

PELTON (English) town by a pool.

PEMBROKE (Welsh) headland. (French) wine dealer. (English) broken fence.
Pembrook

PENIAMINA (Hawaiian) a form of Benjamin.
Peni

PENLEY (English) enclosed meadow.

PENN (Latin) pen, quill. (German) a short form of Penrod. (English) enclosure.
Pen, Penna, Penney, Pennie, Penny

PENROD (German) famous commander.
Penn, Pennrod, Rod

PEPA (Czech) a familiar form of Joseph.
Pepek, Pepik

PEPE (Spanish) a familiar form of José.
Pepillo, Pepito, Pequin, Pipo

PEPIN (German) determined; petitioner. History: Pepin the short, an eighth-century king of the Franks, was the father of Charlemagne.
Pepi, Peppie, Peppy

PEPPE (Italian) a familiar form of Joseph.
Peppi, Peppo, Pino

PER (Swedish) a form of Peter.

PERBEN (Greek, Danish) stone.

PERCIVAL (French) pierce the valley; pierce the veil of religion mystery. Literature: a name invented by Chrétien de Troyes for the knight-hero of his epic about the Holy Grail.
Parsafal, Parsefal, Parsifal, Parzival, Perc, Perce, Perceval, Percevall, Percivall, Percy, Peredur, Purcell

PERCY (French) a familiar form of Percival.
Pearcey, Pearcy, Percey, Percie, Piercey, Piercy

PEREGRINE (Latin) traveler; pilgrim; falcon.
Peregrin, Peregryne, Perine, Perry

PERICLES (Greek) just leader. History: an Athenian statesman and general.

PERICO (Spanish) a form of Peter.
Pequin, Perequin

PERINE (Latin) a short form of Peregrine.
Perino, Perion, Perrin, Perryn

PERKIN (English) little Peter.
Perka, Perkins, Perkyn, Perrin

PERNELL (French) an alternate form of Parnell.
Perren, Perrnall

PERRY (English) a familiar form of Peregrine, Peter.
Parry, Perrie, Perrye

PERTH (Scottish) thornbush thicket. Geography: a county in Scotland; a city in Australia.

PERVIS (Latin) passage.
Pervez

PESACH (Hebrew) spared. Religion: another name for the Jewish holiday Passover.
Pessach

PETAR (Greek) an alternate form of Peter.

PETE (English) a short form of Peter.
Peat, Peet, Petey, Peti, Petie, Piet, Pit

PETER (Greek, Latin) small rock. Bible: Simon, renamed Peter, was the leader of the Twelve Apostles. See also Boutros, Ferris, Takis.
Panayiotos, Panos, Peadair, Peder, Pedro, Peers, Peeter, Peirce, Pekelo, Per, Perico, Perion, Perkin, Perry, Petar, Pete, Péter, Peterke, Peterus, Petr, Petras, Petros, Petru, Petruno, Petter, Peyo, Piaras, Pierce, Piero, Pierre, Pieter, Pietrek, Pietro, Piotr, Piter, Piti, Pjeter, Pyotr

PETERSON (English) son of Peter.
Peteris, Petersen

PETIRI (Shona) where we are.
Petri

PETR (Bulgarian) a form of Peter.

PETRAS (Lithuanian) a form of Peter.
Petra, Petrelis

PETROS (Greek) an alternate form of Peter.
Petro

PETRU (Romanian) a form of Peter.
Petrukas, Petrus, Petruso

PETTER (Norwegian) a form of Peter.

PEVERELL (French) piper.
Peverall, Peverel, Peveril

PEYO (Spanish) a form of Peter.

PEYTON (English) an alternate form of Patton, Payton.
Peyt, Peyten, Peython, Peytonn

PHARAOH (Latin) ruler. History: a title for the ancient rulers of Egypt.
Faroh, Pharo, Pharoah, Pharoh

PHELAN (Irish) wolf.

PHELIPE (Spanish) a form of Philip.

PHELIX (Latin) an alternate form of Felix.

PHELPS (English) son of Phillip.

PHIL (Greek) a short form of Philip, Phillip.
Fil, Phill

PHILANDER (Greek) lover of mankind.

PHILBERT (English) an alternate form of Filbert.
Philibert, Phillbert

PHILEMON (Greek) kiss.
Phila, Philamina, Phileman, Philémon, Philmon

PHILIP (Greek) lover of horses. Bible: one of the Twelve Apostles. See also Felipe, Felippo, Filip, Fillipp, Filya, Fischel, Flip.
Phelps, Phelipe, Phil, Philipp, Philippe, Philippo, Phillip, Phillipos, Phillp, Philly, Philp, Phylip, Piers, Pilib, Pilipo, Pippo

PHILIPP (German) a form of Philip.
Phillipp

PHILIPPE (French) a form of Philip.
Philipe, Phillepe, Phillipe, Phillippe, Phillippee, Phyllipe

PHILLIP (Greek) an alternate form of Philip.
Phil, Phillipos, Phillipp, Phillips, Philly, Phyllip

PHILLIPOS (Greek) an alternate form of Phillip.

PHILLY (American) a familiar form of Philip, Phillip.
Phillie

PHILO (Greek) love.

PHINEAN (Irish) an alternate form of Finian.
Phinian

PHINEAS (English) a form of Pinchas.
Fineas, Phinehas, Phinny

PHIRUN (Cambodian) rain.

PHOENIX (Latin) phoenix, a legendary bird.
Phenix, Pheonix, Phynix

PHUOK (Vietnamese) good.
Phuoc

PIAS (Gypsy) fun.

PICKFORD (English) ford at the peak.

PICKWORTH (English) woodcutter's estate.

PIERCE (English) a form of Peter.
Pearce, Peerce, Peers, Peirce, Piercy, Piers

PIERO (Italian) a form of Peter.
Pero, Pierro

PIERRE (French) a form of Peter.
Peirre, Piere, Pierrot

PIERRE-LUC (French) a combination of Pierre + Luc.
Piere Luc

PIERS (English) a form of Philip.

PIERSON (English) son of Peter. See also Pearson.
Pierrson, Piersen, Piersson, Piersun

PIETER (Dutch) a form of Peter.
Pietr

PIETRO (Italian) a form of Peter.

PILAR (Spanish) pillar.

PILI (Swahili) second born.

PILIPO (Hawaiian) a form of Philip.

PILLAN (Native American) supreme essence.
Pilan

PIN (Vietnamese) faithful boy.

PINCHAS (Hebrew) oracle. (Egyptian) dark skinned.
Phineas, Pincas, Pinchos, Pincus, Pinkas, Pinkus, Pinky

PINKY (American) a familiar form of Pinchas.
Pink

PINO (Italian) a form of Joseph.

PIÑON (Tupi-Guarani) Mythology: the hunter who became the constellation Orion.

PIO (Latin) pious.

PIOTR (Bulgarian) a form of Peter.
Piotrek

PIPPIN (German) father.

PIRAN (Irish) prayer. Religion: the patron saint of miners.
Peran, Pieran

PIRRO (Greek, Spanish) flaming hair.

PISTA (Hungarian) a familiar form of István.
Pisti

PITI (Spanish) a form of Peter.

PITIN (Spanish) a form of Felix.
Pito

PITNEY (English) island of the strong-willed man.
Pittney

PITT (English) pit, ditch.

PLACIDO (Spanish) serene.
Placide, Placidus, Placyd, Placydo

PLATO (Greek) broad shouldered. History: a famous Greek philosopher.
Platon

PLATT (French) flat land.
Platte

POL (Swedish) a form of Paul.
Pól, Pola, Poul

POLDI (German) a familiar form of Leopold.
Poldo

POLLARD (German) close-cropped head.
Poll, Pollerd, Pollyrd

POLLOCK (English) a form of Pollux.
Pollack, Polloch

POLLUX (Greek) crown. Astronomy: one of the twins in the Gemini constellation.
Pollock

POLO (Greek) a short form of Apollo. (Tibetan) brave wanderer. Culture: a game played on horseback. History: Marco Polo was a Venetian explorer who traveled throughout Asia in the thirteenth and fourteenth centuries.

POMEROY (French) apple orchard.
Pommeray, Pommeroy

PONCE (Spanish) fifth. History: Juan Ponce de León of Spain searched for the fountain of youth in Florida.

PONY (Scottish) small horse.
Poni

PORFIRIO (Greek, Spanish) purple stone.
Porphirios, Prophyrios

PORTER (Latin) gatekeeper.
Port, Portie, Porty

POSHITA (Sanskrit) cherished.

PO SIN (Chinese) grand-father elephant.

POUL (Danish) a form of Paul.
Poulos, Poulus

POV (Gypsy) earth.

POWA (Native American) wealthy.

POWELL (English) alert.
Powel

PRAMAD (Hindi) rejoicing.

PRAVAT (Tai) history.

PREM (Hindi) love.

PRENTICE (English) apprentice.
Prent, Prentis, Prentiss, Printes, Printiss

PRESCOTT (English) priest's cottage.
See also Scott.
Prescot, Prestcot, Prestcott

PRESLEY (English) priest's meadow.
Presleigh, Presly, Presslee, Pressley, Prestley, Priestley, Priestly

PRESTON (English) priest's estate.
Prestan, Presten, Prestin, Prestyn

PREWITT (French) brave little one.
Preuet, Prewet, Prewett, Prewit, Pruit, Pruitt

PRICE (Welsh) son of the ardent one.
Brice, Bryce, Pryce

PRICHA (Tai) clever.

PRIMO (Italian) first; premier quality.
Preemo, Premo

PRINCE (Latin) chief; prince.
Prence, Prinz, Prinze

PRINCETON (English) princely town.
Prenston, Princeston, Princton

PROCTOR (Latin) official, administrator.
Prockter, Procter

PROKOPIOS (Greek) declared leader.

PROSPER (Latin) fortunate.
Prospero, Próspero

PRYOR (Latin) head of the monastery; prior.
Prior, Pry

PUMEET (Sanskrit) pure.

PURDY (Hindi) recluse.

PURVIS (French, English) providing food.
Pervis, Purves, Purviss

PUTNAM (English) dweller by the pond.
Putnem

PYOTR (Russian) a form of Peter.
Petenka, Petinka, Petrusha, Petya, Pyatr

Q

QABIL (Arabic) able.

QADIM (Arabic) ancient.

QADIR (Arabic) powerful.
Qaadir, Qadeer, Quaadir, Quadeer, Quadir

QAMAR (Arabic) moon.
Quamar, Quamir

QASIM (Arabic) divider.
Quasim

QIMAT (Hindi) valuable.

QUAASHIE (Ewe) born on Sunday.

QUADARIUS (American) a combination of Quan + Darius.
Quadara, Quadarious, Quadaris, Quandarious, Quandarius, Quandarrius, Qudarius, Qudaruis

QUADE (Latin) fourth.
Quadell, Quaden, Quadon, Quadre, Quadrie, Quadrine, Quadrion, Quaid, Quayd, Quayde, Qwade

QUAMAINE (American) a combination of Quan + Jermaine.

Quamaine (cont.)
Quamain, Quaman, Quamane, Quamayne,
Quarmaine

QUAN (Comanche) a short form of
Quanah.

QUANAH (Comanche) fragrant.
Quan

QUANDRE (American) a combination
of Quan + Andre.
Quandrae, Quandré

QUANT (Greek) means 'how much?'
Quanta, Quantae, Quantai, Quantas,
Quantay, Quante, Quantea, Quantey,
Quantez, Quantu

QUANTAVIUS (American) a
combination of Quan + Octavius.
Quantavian, Quantavin, Quantavion,
Quantavious, Quantavis, Quantavous,
Quatavious, Quatavius

QUASHAWN (American) a
combination of Quan + Shawn.
Quasean, Quashaan, Quashan, Quashaun,
Quashaunn, Quashon, Quashone, Quashun,
Queshan, Queshon, Qweshawn, Qyshawn

QUDAMAH (Arabic) courage.

QUENBY (Scandinavian) an alternate
form of Quimby.

QUENNELL (French) small oak.
Quenell, Quennel

QUENTEN (Latin) an alternate form of
Quentin.
Quienten

QUENTIN (Latin) fifth. (English)
Queen's town.
Qeuntin, Quantin, Quent, Quentan,
Quenten, Quentine, Quenton, Quentyn,
Quentynn, Quientin, Quinten, Quintin,
Quinton, Qwentin

QUENTON (Latin) an alternate form
of Quentin.
Quienton

QUICO (Spanish) a familiar form of
many names.
Paco

QUIGLEY (Irish) maternal side.
Quigly

QUILLAN (Irish) cub.
Quill, Quillen, Quillin, Quillon

QUIMBY (Scandinavian) woman's
estate.
Quenby, Quinby

QUINCY (French) fifth son's estate.
Quenci, Quency, Quince, Quincee, Quincey,
Quinci, Quinn, Quinncy, Quinnsy, Quinsey,
Quinzy

QUINDARIUS (American) a
combination of Quinn + Darius.
Quindarious, Quindarrius, Quinderious,
Quinderus, Quindrius

QUINLAN (Irish) strong; well shaped.
Quindlen, Quinlen, Quinlin, Quinn,
Quinnlan, Quinnlin

QUINN (Irish) a short form of Quincy,
Quinlan, Quinton.
Quin

QUINTAVIUS (American) a
combination of Quinn + Octavius.
Quintavious, Quintavis, Quintavus,
Quintayvious

QUINTEN (Latin) an alternate form of
Quentin.
Quinnten

QUINTIN (Latin) an alternate form
of Quentin.
Quinntin, Quintine, Quintyn

QUINTON (Latin) an alternate form of
Quentin.
Quinn, Quinneton, Quinnton, Quint,
Quintan, Quintann, Quintin, Quintion,
Quintus, Quitin, Quito, Quiton, Qunton,
Qwinton

QUIQUI (Spanish) a familiar form of Enrique.
Quinto, Quiquin

QUITIN (Latin) a short form of Quinton.
Quiten, Quito, Quiton

QUITO (Spanish) a short form of Quinton.

QUON (Chinese) bright.

R

RAANAN (Hebrew) fresh; luxuriant.

RABI (Arabic) breeze.
Rabbi, Rabee, Rabeeh, Rabiah, Rabie, Rabih

RACE (English) race.
Racel, Rayce

RACHAM (Hebrew) compassionate.
Rachaman, Rachamim, Rachim, Rachman, Rachmiel, Rachum, Raham, Rahamim

RAD (English) advisor. (Slavic) happy.
Raad, Radd, Raddie, Raddy, Rade, Radee, Radell, Radey, Radi

RADBERT (English) brilliant advisor.

RADBURN (English) red brook; brook with reeds.
Radborn, Radborne, Radbourn, Radbourne, Radburne

RADCLIFF (English) red cliff; cliff with reeds.
Radcliffe, Radclyffe

RADFORD (English) red ford; ford with reeds.

RADLEY (English) red meadow; meadow of reeds.
Radlea, Radlee, Radleigh, Radly

RADMAN (Slavic) joyful.
Radmen, Radusha

RADNOR (English) red shore; shore with reeds.

RADOMIL (Slavic) happy peace.

RADOSLAW (Polish) happy glory.
Radik, Rado, Radzmir, Slawek

RAEKWON (American) an alternate form of Raquan.
Raekwan, Raikwan, Rakwane, Rakwon

RAEQUAN (American) an alternate form of Raquan.
Raequon, Raeqwon, Raiquan, Raiquen, Raiqoun

RAESHAWN (American) an alternate form of Rashawn.
Raesean, Raeshaun, Raeshon, Raeshun

RAFAEL (Spanish) a form of Raphael. See also Falito.
Rafaelle, Rafaello, Rafaelo, Rafal, Rafeal, Rafeé, Rafel, Rafello, Raffael, Raffaelo, Raffeal, Raffel, Raffiel, Rafiel

RAFAELE (Italian) a form of Raphael.
Raffaele

RAFAL (Polish) a form of Raphael.

RAFE (English) a short form of Rafferty, Ralph.
Raff

RAFER (Irish) a short form of Rafferty.
Raffer

RAFFERTY (Irish) rich, prosperous.
Rafe, Rafer, Raferty, Raffarty, Raffer

RAFI (Hebrew) a familiar form of Raphael. (Arabic) exalted.
Raffe, Raffee, Raffi, Raffy, Rafi

RAFIQ (Arabic) friend.
Raafiq, Rafeeq, Rafic, Rafique

RAGHIB (Arabic) desirous.
Raquib

RAGHNALL (Irish) wise power.

RAGNAR (Norwegian) powerful army.
Ragnor, Rainer, Rainier, Ranieri, Rayner, Raynor, Reinhold

RAGO (Hausa) ram.

RAHEEM (Punjabi) compassionate God.
Rakeem

RAHIM (Arabic) merciful.
Raaheim, Rahaeim, Raheam, Raheim, Rahiem, Rahiim, Rahime, Rahium, Rakim

RAHMAN (Arabic) compassionate.
Rahmatt, Rahmet

RAHUL (Arabic) traveler.

RAÍD (Arabic) leader.

RAIDEN (Japanese) Mythology: the thunder god.
Raidan, Rayden

RAIMONDO (Italian) a form of Raymond.
Raymondo, Reimundo

RAIMUND (German) a form of Raymond.
Rajmund

RAIMUNDO (Portuguese, Spanish) a form of Raymond.
Mundo, Raimon, Raimond, Raimonds, Raymundo

RAINE (English) lord; wise.
Rain, Raines, Rayne

RAINER (German) counselor.
Rainar, Rainey, Rainier, Rainor, Raynier, Reinier

RAINEY (German) a familiar form of Rainer.
Raine, Rainee, Rainie, Rainney, Rainy, Reiny

RAINI (Tupi-Guarani) Religion: the Native American god who created the world.

RAISHAWN (American) an alternate form of Rashawn.
Raishon, Raishun

RAJABU (Swahili) born in the seventh month of the Islamic calendar.

RAJAH (Hindi) prince, chief.
Raj, Raja, Rajaah, Rajae, Rajahe, Rajan, Raje, Rajeh, Raji

RAJAK (Hindi) cleansing.

RAJAN (Hindi) an alternate form of Rajah.
Rajaahn, Rajain, Rajen, Rajin

RAKEEM (Punjabi) an alternate form of Raheem.
Rakeeme, Rakeim, Rakem

RAKIM (Arabic) an alternate form of Rahim.
Rakiim

RAKIN (Arabic) respectable.
Rakeen

RAKTIM (Hindi) bright red.

RALEIGH (English) an alternate form of Rawleigh.
Ralegh

RALPH (English) wolf counselor.
Radolphus, Rafe, Ralf, Ralpheal, Ralphel, Ralphie, Ralston, Raoul, Raul, Rolf

RALPHIE (English) a familiar form of Ralph.
Ralphy

RALSTON (English) Ralph's settlement.

RAM (Hindi) god; godlike. Religion: another name for the Hindu god Shiva. (English) male sheep.
Rami, Ramie, Ramy

RAMADAN (Arabic) ninth month of
the Arabic year.
Rama

RAMANAN (Hindi) god; godlike.
Religion: another name for the Hindu
god Shiva.
Raman, Ramandeep, Ramanjit, Ramanjot

RAMI (Spanish) a short form of Ramiro.
Rame, Ramee, Ramey, Ramih

RAMIRO (Portuguese, Spanish)
supreme judge.
*Ramario, Rameer, Rameir, Ramere,
Rameriz, Ramero, Rami, Ramires, Ramirez,
Ramos*

RAMÓN (Spanish) a form of Raymond.
Ramon, Remon, Remone, Romone

RAMONE (Dutch) a form of Raymond.
*Raemon, Raemonn, Ramond, Ramonte,
Remone*

RAMSDEN (English) valley of rams.

RAMSEY (English) ram's island.
*Ram, Ramsay, Ramsee, Ramsie, Ramsy,
Ramzee, Ramzey, Ramzi, Ramzy*

RANCE (English) a short form of
Laurence, Ransom. (American) a
familiar form of Laurence.
*Rancel, Rancell, Rances, Rancey, Rancie,
Rancy, Ransel, Ransell*

RAND (English) shield; warrior.
Randy

RANDAL (English) an alternate form of
Randall.
Randahl, Randale, Randel, Randl, Randle

RANDALL (English) an alternate form
of Randolph.
Randal, Randell, Randy, Randyll

RANDOLPH (English) shield-wolf.
*Randall, Randol, Randolf, Randolfo,
Randolpho, Randy, Ranolph*

RANDY (English) a familiar form of
Rand, Randall, Randolph.
*Randdy, Randee, Randey, Randi, Randie,
Ranndy*

RANGER (French) forest keeper.
Rainger, Range

RANGLE (American) cowboy.
Rangler, Wrangle

RANGSEY (Cambodian) seven kinds
of colors.

RANI (Hebrew) my song; my joy.
Ranen, Ranie, Ranon, Roni

RANIERI (Italian) a form of Ragnar.
Raneir, Ranier, Rannier

RANJAN (Hindi) delighted; gladdened.

RANKIN (English) small shield.
Randkin

RANSFORD (English) raven's ford.

RANSLEY (English) raven's field.

RANSOM (Latin) redeemer. (English)
son of the shield.
Rance, Ransome, Ranson

RAOUL (French) a form of Ralph,
Rudolph.
Raol, Raul, Raúl, Reuel

RAPHAEL (Hebrew) God has healed.
Bible: one of the archangels. Art: a
prominent painter of the Italian
Renaissance. See also Falito, Rafi.
*Rafael, Rafaele, Rafal, Rafel, Raphaél,
Raphale, Raphaello, Rapheal, Raphel,
Raphello, Raphiel, Ray, Rephael*

RAPHEAL (Hebrew) an alternate form
of Raphael.
Rafel, Raphiel

RAPIER (French) blade-sharp.

RAQUAN (American) a combination of the prefix Ra + Quan.
Raaquan, Rackwon, Racquan, Raekwon, Raequan, Rahquan, Raquané, Raquon, Raquwan, Raquwn, Raquwon, Raqwan, Raqwann

RASHAAD (Arabic) an alternate form of Rashad.

RASHAAN (American) an alternate form of Rashawn.
Rasaan, Rashan, Rashann

RASHAD (Arabic) wise counselor.
Raashad, Rachad, Rachard, Raeshad, Raishard, Rashaad, Rashadd, Rashade, Rashaud, Rasheed, Rashid, Rashod, Reshad, Rhashad, Rishad, Roshad

RASHARD (American) a form of Richard.
Rasharrd

RASHAUD (Arabic) an alternate form of Rashad.
Rachaud, Rashaude

RASHAUN (American) an alternate form of Rashawn.

RASHAWN (American) a combination of the prefix Ra + Shawn.
Raashawn, Raashen, Raeshawn, Rahshawn, Raishawn, Rasaun, Rasawn, Rashaan, Rashaun, Rashaw, Rashon, Rashun, Raushan, Raushawn, Rhashan, Rhashaun, Rhashawn

RASHEAN (American) a combination of the prefix Ra + Sean.
Rahsaan, Rahsean, Rahseen, Rasean, Rashane, Rasheen, Rashien, Rashiena

RASHEED (Arabic) an alternate form of Rashad.
Rashead, Rashed, Rasheid, Rhasheed

RASHID (Arabic) an alternate form of Rashad.
Rasheyd, Rashida, Rashidah, Rashied, Rashieda, Raushaid

RASHIDA (Swahili) righteous.

RASHIDI (Swahili) wise counselor.

RASHOD (Arabic) an alternate form of Rashad.
Rashoda, Rashodd, Rashoud, Rayshod, Rhashod

RASHON (American) an alternate form of Rashawn.
Rashion, Rashone, Rashonn, Rashuan, Rashun, Rashunn

RASMUS (Greek, Danish) a short form of Erasmus.

RAUL (French) a form of Ralph.

RAULAS (Lithuanian) a form of Laurence.

RAULO (Lithuanian) a form of Laurence.
Raulas

RAVEN (English) a short form of Ravenel.
Ravan, Ravean, Raveen, Ravin, Ravine, Ravon, Ravyn, Reven, Rhaven

RAVENEL (English) raven.
Raven, Ravenell, Revenel

RAVI (Hindi) sun. Religion: another name for the Hindu sun god Surya.
Ravee, Ravijot

RAVID (Hebrew) an alternate form of Arvid.

RAVIV (Hebrew) rain, dew.

RAVON (English) an alternate form of Raven.
Raveon, Ravion, Ravone, Ravonn, Ravonne, Rayvon, Revon

RAWDON (English) rough hill.

RAWLEIGH (English) deer meadow.
Raleigh, Rawle, Rawley, Rawling, Rawly, Rawylyn

RAWLINS (French) a form of Roland.
Rawlings, Rawlinson, Rawson

RAY (French) kingly, royal. (English) a
short form of Rayburn, Raymond.
See also Lei.
Rae, Raye

RAYAN (Irish) an alternate form
of Ryan.
Rayaun

RAYBURN (English) deer brook.
*Burney, Raeborn, Raeborne, Raebourn, Ray,
Raybourn, Raybourne, Rayburne*

RAYCE (English) an alternate form of
Race.

RAYDEN (Japanese) an alternate form
of Raiden.
Raidin, Raydun, Rayedon

RAYHAN (Arabic) favored by God.
Rayhaan

RAYI (Hebrew) my friend, my
companion.

RAYMON (English) an alternate form of
Raymond.
*Rayman, Raymann, Raymen, Raymone,
Raymun, Reamonn*

RAYMOND (English) mighty; wise
protector. See also Aymon.
*Radmond, Raemond, Raimondo, Raimund,
Raimundo, Ramón, Ramond, Ramonde,
Ramone, Ray, Raymand, Rayment, Raymon,
Raymont, Raymund, Raymunde,
Raymundo, Redmond, Reymond, Reymundo*

RAYMUNDO (Spanish) a form of
Raymond.
*Raemondo, Raimondo, Raimundo,
Raymondo*

RAYNALDO (Spanish) an alternate
form of Renaldo, Reynold.
Raynal, Raynald, Raynold

RAYNARD (French) an alternate form
of Renard, Reynard.
Raynarde

RAYNE (English) an alternate form
of Raine.
Raynee, Rayno

RAYNOR (Scandinavian) a form of
Ragnar.
*Rainer, Rainor, Ranier, Ranieri, Raynar,
Rayner*

RAYSHAWN (American) a
combination of Ray + Shawn.
*Raysean, Rayshaan, Rayshan, Rayshaun,
Raysheen, Rayshon, Rayshone, Rayshonn,
Rayshun, Rayshunn*

RAYSHOD (American) a form of
Rashad.
Raychard, Rayshad, Rayshard, Rayshaud

RAYVON (American) a form of Ravon.
*Rayvan, Rayvaun, Rayven, Rayvone,
Reyven, Reyvon*

RAZI (Aramaic) my secret.
Raz, Raziel, Raziq

READ (English) an alternate form of
Reed, Reid.
Raed, Raede, Raeed, Reaad, Reade

READING (English) son of the red
wanderer. Geography: a city in
Pennsylvania.
Redding, Reeding, Reiding

REAGAN (Irish) little king. History:
Ronald Wilson Reagan was the
fortieth U.S. president.
*Raegan, Reagen, Reaghan, Reegan, Reegen,
Regan, Reigan, Reighan, Reign, Rheagan*

REBEL (American) rebel.
Reb

RED (American) red, redhead.
Redd

REDA (Arabic) satisfied.
Ridha

REDFORD (English) red river crossing.
Ford, Radford, Reaford, Red, Redd

REDLEY (English) red meadow;
meadow with reeds.
Radley, Redlea, Redleigh, Redly

REDMOND (German) protecting
counselor. (English) an alternate form
of Raymond.
Radmond, Radmund, Reddin, Redmund

REDPATH (English) red path.

REECE (Welsh) enthusiastic; stream.
*Reace, Rece, Reese, Reice, Reyes, Rhys, Rice,
Ryese*

REED (English) an alternate form of
Reid.
Raeed, Read, Reyde, Rheed

REESE (Welsh) an alternate form
of Reece.
*Rease, Rees, Reis, Reise, Reiss, Rhys, Riese,
Riess*

REEVE (English) steward.
Reave, Reaves, Reeves

REG (English) a short form of Reginald.

REGAN (Irish) an alternate form of
Reagan.
Regen

REGGIE (English) a familiar form
of Reginald.
Regi, Regie

REGINAL (English) a form of Reginald.
Reginale, Reginel

REGINALD (English) king's advisor. An
alternate form of Reynold. See also
Naldo.
*Reg, Reggie, Regginald, Reggis, Reginal,
Reginaldo, Reginalt, Reginauld, Reginault,
Reginold, Reginuld, Regnauld, Ronald*

REGIS (Latin) regal.

REHEMA (Kiswahili) second-born.

REI (Japanese) rule, law.

REID (English) redhead.
Read, Reed, Reide, Reyd, Ried

REIDAR (Norwegian) nest warrior.

REILLY (Irish) an alternate form of
Riley.
Reiley, Reilley, Reily, Rielly

REINALDO (Spanish) a form
of Reynold.

REINHART (German) a form of
Reynard.
*Rainart, Rainhard, Rainhardt, Rainhart,
Reinart, Reinhard, Reinhardt, Renke*

REINHOLD (Swedish) a form of Ragnar.
Reinold

REKU (Finnish) a form of Richard.

REMI, Rémi (French) alternate forms of
Remy.
Remie, Remmie

REMINGTON (English) raven estate.
Rem, Reminton, Tony

REMUS (Latin) speedy, quick.
Mythology: Remus and his twin
brother Romulus founded Rome.

REMY (French) from Rheims, France.
Ramey, Remee, Remi, Rémi, Remmy

RENALDO (Spanish) a form of
Reynold.
Raynaldo, Reynaldo, Rinaldo

RENARD (French) an alternate form of
Reynard.
Ranard, Raynard, Reinard, Rennard

RENARDO (Italian) a form of Reynard.

RENATO (Italian) reborn.

RENAUD (French) a form of Reynard, Reynold.
Renauld, Renauldo, Renault, Renould

RENDOR (Hungarian) policeman.

RENÉ (French) reborn.
Renat, Renato, Renatus, Renault, Renay, Renee, Renny

RENFRED (English) lasting peace.

RENFREW (Welsh) raven woods.

RENJIRO (Japanese) virtuous.

RENNY (Irish) small but strong. (French) a familiar form of René.
Ren, Renn, Renne, Rennie

RENO (American) gambler. Geography: a gambling town in Nevada.
Renos, Rino

RENSHAW (English) raven woods.
Renishaw

RENTON (English) settlement of the roe deer.

RENZO (Latin) a familiar form of Laurence. (Italian) a short form of Lorenzo.
Renz, Renzy, Renzzo

RESHAD (American) a form of Rashad.
Reshade, Reshard, Resharrd, Reshaud, Reshawd, Reshead, Reshod

RESHAWN (American) a combination of the prefix Re + Shawn.
Reshaun, Reshaw, Reshon, Reshun

RESHEAN (American) a combination of the prefix Re + Sean.
Resean, Reshae, Reshane, Reshay, Reshayne, Reshea, Resheen, Reshey

REUBEN (Hebrew) behold a son.
Reuban, Reubin, Reuven, Rheuben, Rhuben, Rube, Ruben, Rubey, Rubin, Ruby, Rueben

REUVEN (Hebrew) an alternate form of Reuben.
Reuvin, Rouvin, Ruvim

REX (Latin) king.
Rexx

REXFORD (English) king's ford.

REXTON (English) king's town.

REY (Spanish) a short form of Reynaldo, Reynard, Reynold.

REYES (English) an alternate form of Reece.
Reyce

REYHAN (Arabic) favored by God.
Reyham

REYMOND (English) an alternate form of Raymond.
Reymon. Reymound, Reymund

REYMUNDO (Spanish) a form of Raymond.
Reimond, Reimonde, Reimundo, Reymon

REYNALDO (Spanish) a form of Reynold.
Renaldo, Rey, Reynauldo

REYNARD (French) wise; bold, courageous.
Raynard, Reinhard, Reinhardt, Reinhart, Renard, Renardo, Renaud, Rennard, Rey, Reynardo, Reynaud

REYNOLD (English) king's advisor. See also Reginald.
Rainault, Rainhold, Ranald, Raynald, Raynaldo, Reinald, Reinaldo, Reinaldos, Reinhart, Reinhold, Reinold, Reinwald, Renald, Renaldi, Renaldo, Renaud, Renauld, Rennold, Renold, Rey, Reynald, Reynaldo, Reynaldos, Reynol, Reynolds, Rinaldo, Ronald

RÉZ (Hungarian) copper; redhead.
Rezsö

RHETT (Welsh) an alternate form of Rhys. Literature: Rhett Butler was the hero of Margaret Mitchell's novel *Gone with the Wind*.
Rhet

RHODES (Greek) where roses grow. Geography: an island off the coast of Greece.
Rhoads, Rhodas, Rodas

RHYAN (Irish) an alternate form of Rian.
Rhian

RHYS (Welsh) an alternate form of Reece, Reese.
Rhett, Rhyce, Rhyse, Rice

RIAN (Irish) little king.
Rhyan

RIC (Italian, Spanish) a short form of Rico.
Ricca, Ricci, Ricco

RICARDO (Portuguese, Spanish) a form of Richard.
Racardo, Recard, Ricaldo, Ricard, Ricardoe, Ricardos, Riccardo, Riccarrdo, Ricciardo, Richardo

RICE (Welsh) an alternate form of Reece. (English) rich, noble.
Ryce

RICH (English) a short form of Richard.
Ritch

RICHARD (English) rich and powerful ruler. See also Aric, Dick, Juku, Likeke.
Rashard, Reku, Ricardo, Rich, Richar, Richards, Richardson, Richart, Richaud, Richer, Richerd, Richie, Richird, Richshard, Rick, Rickard, Rickert, Rickey, Ricky, Rico, Rihardos, Rihards, Rikard, Riocard, Riócard, Risa, Risardas, Rishard, Ristéard, Ritchard, Rostik, Rye, Rysio, Ryszard

RICHART (German) rich and powerful ruler. The original form of Richard.

RICHIE (English) a familiar form of Richard.
Richey, Richi, Richy, Rishi, Ritchie

RICHMAN (English) powerful.

RICHMOND (German) powerful protector.
Richmon, Richmound

RICK (German, English) a short form of Cedric, Frederick, Richard.
Ric, Ricke, Rickey, Ricks, Ricky, Rik, Riki, Rykk

RICKARD (Swedish) a form of Richard.

RICKER (English) powerful army.

RICKEY (English) a familiar form of Richard, Rick, Riqui.

RICKIE (English) an alternate form of Ricky.
Rickee, Ricki

RICKWARD (English) mighty guardian.
Rickwerd, Rickwood

RICKY (English) a familiar form of Richard, Rick.
Ricci, Rickie, Riczi, Riki, Rikki, Rikky, Riqui

RICO (Spanish) a familiar form of Richard. (Italian) a short form of Enrico.
Ric, Ricco

RIDA (Arabic) favor.

RIDDOCK (Irish) smooth field.
Riddick

RIDER (English) horseman.
Ridder, Ryder

RIDGE (English) ridge of a cliff.
Ridgy, Rig, Rigg

RIDGELEY (English) meadow near the ridge.
Ridgeleigh, Ridglea, Ridglee, Ridgleigh, Ridgley

RIDGEWAY (English) path along the ridge.

RIDLEY (English) meadow of reeds.
Rhidley, Riddley, Ridlea, Ridleigh, Ridly

RIEL (Spanish) a short form of Gabriel.

RIGBY (English) ruler's valley.

RIGEL (Arabic) foot. Astronomy: one of the stars in the Orion constellation.

RIGG (English) ridge.
Rigo

RIGOBERTO (German) splendid; wealthy.
Rigobert

RIKARD (Scandinavian) a form of Richard.
Rikárd

RIKI (Estonian) a form of Rick.
Rikkey, Rikki, Riks, Riky

RILEY (Irish) valiant.
Reilly, Rhiley, Rhylee, Rhyley, Rieley, Rielly, Riely, Rilee, Rilley, Rily, Rilye, Rylee, Ryley

RINALDO (Italian) a form of Reynold.
Rinald, Rinaldi

RING (English) ring.
Ringo

RINGO (Japanese) apple. (English) a familiar form of Ring.

RIO (Spanish) river. Geography: Rio de Janeiro is a seaport in Brazil.

RIORDAN (Irish) bard, royal poet.
Rearden, Reardin, Reardon

RIP (Dutch) ripe, full-grown. (English) a short form of Ripley.
Ripp

RIPLEY (English) meadow near the river.
Rip, Ripleigh, Ripply

RIQUI (Spanish) a form of Rickey.

RISHAD (American) a form of Rashad.
Rishaad

RISHAWN (American) a combination of the prefix Ri + Shawn.
Rishan, Rishaun, Rishon, Rishone

RISHI (Hindi) sage.

RISLEY (English) meadow with shrubs.
Rislea, Rislee, Risleigh, Risly, Wrisley

RISTO (Finnish) a short form of Christopher.

RISTON (English) settlement near the shrubs.
Wriston

RITCHARD (English) an alternate form of Richard.
Ritcherd, Ritchyrd, Ritshard, Ritsherd

RITCHIE (English) an alternate form of Richie.
Ritchy

RITHISAK (Cambodian) powerful.

RITTER (German) knight; chivalrous.
Rittner

RIVER (English) river; river bank.
Rivers, Riviera, Rivor

RIYAD (Arabic) gardens.
Riad, Riyaad, Riyadh, Riyaz, Riyod

ROALD (Norwegian) famous ruler.

ROAN (English) a short form of Rowan.
Rhoan

ROAR (Norwegian) praised warrior.
Roary

ROARKE (Irish) famous ruler.
Roark, Rorke, Rourke, Ruark

ROB (English) a short form of Robert.
Robb, Robe

ROBBIE (English) a familiar form of
Robert.
Robie, Robbi

ROBBY (English) a familiar form
of Robert.
Rhobbie, Robbey, Robhy, Roby

ROBERT (English) famous brilliance.
See also Bobek, Dob, Lopaka.
*Bob, Bobby, Rab, Rabbie, Raby, Riobard,
Riobart, Rob, Robars, Robart, Robbie, Robby,
Rober, Roberd, Robers, Roberte, Roberto,
Roberts, Robin, Robinson, Roibeárd,
Rosertas, Rubert, Ruberto, Rudbert, Rupert*

ROBERTO (Portuguese, Spanish) a form
of Robert.

ROBERTS, Robertson (English) son of
Robert.
*Roberson, Robertson, Robeson, Robinson,
Robson*

ROBIN (English) a short form of Robert.
*Robben, Robbin, Robbins, Robbyn, Roben,
Robinet, Robinn, Robins, Robyn, Roibín*

ROBINSON (English) son of Robert. An
alternate form of Roberts, Robertson.
*Robbinson, Robens, Robenson, Robson,
Robynson*

ROBYN (English) an alternate form
of Robin.

ROCCO (Italian) rock.
Rocca, Rocio, Rocko, Rocky, Roko, Roque

ROCHESTER (English) rocky fortress.
Chester, Chet

ROCK (English) a short form of
Rockwell.
Roch, Rocky

ROCKFORD (English) rocky ford.

ROCKLAND (English) rocky land.

ROCKLEDGE (English) rocky ledge.

ROCKLEY (English) rocky field.
Rockle

ROCKWELL (English) rocky spring.
Art: Norman Rockwell was a well-
known twentieth-century American
illustrator.
Rock

ROCKY (American) a familiar form of
Rocco, Rock.
Rockey, Rockie

ROD (English) a short form of Penrod,
Roderick, Rodney.
Rodd

RODAS (Greek, Spanish) an alternate
form of Rhodes.

RODDY (English) a familiar form of
Roderick.
Roddie, Rody

RODEN (English) red valley.
Rodin

RODERICH (German) an alternate
form of Roderick.

RODERICK (German) famous ruler.
See also Broderick.
*Rhoderick, Rod, Rodderick, Roddy, Roderic,
Roderich, Roderigo, Roderik, Roderrick,
Roderyck, Rodgrick, Rodrick, Rodricki,
Rodrigo, Rodrigue, Rodrugue, Roodney, Rory,
Rurik, Ruy*

RODGER (German) an alternate form
of Roger.
Rodge, Rodgy

RODMAN (German) famous man, hero.
Rodmond

RODNEY (English) island clearing.
*Rhodney, Rod, Rodnee, Rodnei, Rodni,
Rodnie, Rodnne, Rodny*

RODOLFO (Spanish) a form of
Rudolph.
Rodolpho, Rodulfo

RODRICK (German) an alternate form of Roderick.
Roddrick, Rodric, Rodrich, Rodrik, Rodrique, Rodryck, Rodryk

RODRIGO (Italian, Spanish) a form of Roderick.

RODRIGUEZ (Spanish) son of Rodrigo.
Roddrigues, Rodrigues, Rodriquez

RODRIK (German) famous ruler.

RODRIQUEZ (Spanish) an alternate form of Rodriguez.
Rodrigquez, Rodriques, Rodriquiez

ROE (English) roe deer.
Row, Rowe

ROGAN (Irish) redhead.
Rogein, Rogen

ROGELIO (Spanish) famous warrior.
Rojelio

ROGER (German) famous spearman. See also Lokela.
Rodger, Rog, Rogelio, Rogerick, Rogerio, Rogers, Rogiero, Rojelio, Rüdiger, Ruggerio, Rutger

ROGERIO (Portuguese, Spanish) a form of Roger.
Rogerios

ROHAN (Hindi) sandalwood.

ROHIN (Hindi) upward path.

ROHIT (Hindi) big and beautiful fish.

ROI (French) an alternate form of Roy.

ROJA (Spanish) red.
Rojay

ROLAND (German) famous throughout the land.
Loránd, Orlando, Rawlins, Rolan, Rolanda, Rolando, Rolek, Rolland, Rolle, Rollie, Rollin, Rollo, Rowe, Rowland, Ruland

ROLANDO (Portuguese, Spanish) a form of Roland.
Lando, Olo, Roldan, Roldán, Rolondo

ROLF (German) a form of Ralph. A short form of Rudolph.
Rolfe, Rolle, Rolph, Rolphe

ROLLE (Swedish) a familiar form of Roland, Rolf.

ROLLIE (English) a familiar form of Roland.
Roley, Rolle, Rolli, Rolly

ROLLIN (English) a form of Roland.
Rolin, Rollins

ROLLO (English) a familiar form of Roland.
Rolla, Rolo

ROLON (Spanish) famous wolf.

ROMAIN (French) a form of Roman.
Romaine, Romane, Romanne

ROMAN (Latin) from Rome, Italy.
Roma, Romain, Romann, Romanos, Romman, Romochka, Romy

ROMANOS (Greek) a form of Roman.
Romano

ROMARIO (Italian) a form of Romeo.
Romar, Romarius, Romaro, Romarrio

ROMEL (Latin) a short form of Romulus.
Romele, Romell, Romello, Rommel

ROMELLO (Italian) an alternate form of Romel.
Romelo, Rommello

ROMEO (Italian) pilgrim to Rome; Roman. Literature: the title character of the Shakespearean play *Romeo and Juliet*.
Romario, Roméo, Romero

ROMERO (Latin) an alternate form of Romeo.
Romario, Romeiro, Romer, Romere, Romerio, Romeris, Romeryo

ROMNEY (Welsh) winding river.
Romoney

ROMULUS (Latin) citizen of Rome. Mythology: Romulus and his twin brother Remus founded Rome.
Romel, Romolo, Romono, Romulo

ROMY (Italian) a familiar form Roman.
Rommie, Rommy

RON (Hebrew) a short form of Aaron, Ronald.
Ronn

RONALD (Scottish) a form of Reginald.
Ranald, Ron, Ronal, Ronaldo, Ronnald, Ronney, Ronnie, Ronnold, Ronoldo

RONALDO (Portuguese) a form of Ronald.

RÓNÁN (Irish) seal.
Renan, Ronan, Ronat

RONDEL (French) short poem.
Rondal, Rondale, Rondall, Rondeal, Rondell, Rondey, Rondie, Rondrell, Rondy, Ronel

RONEL (American) a form of Rondel.
Ronell, Ronelle, Ronnel, Ronnell, Ronyell

RONI (Hebrew) my song; my joy.
Rani, Roneet, Roney, Ronit, Ronli, Rony

RONNIE (Scottish) a familiar form of Ronald.
Roni, Ronie, Ronnie, Ronny

RONNY (Scottish) an alternate form of Ronnie.
Ronney

RONSON (Scottish) son of Ronald.
Ronaldson

RONTÉ (American) a combination of Ron + the suffix -te.
Rontae, Rontay, Ronte, Rontez

ROONEY (Irish) redhead.

ROOSEVELT (Dutch) rose field. History: Theodore and Franklin D. Roosevelt were the twenty-sixth and thirty-second U.S. presidents, respectively.
Roosvelt, Rosevelt

ROPER (English) rope maker.

RORY (German) a familiar form of Roderick. (Irish) red king.
Rorey, Rori, Rorrie, Rorry

ROSALIO (Spanish) rose.
Rosalino

ROSARIO (Portuguese) rosary.

ROSCOE (Scandinavian) deer forest.
Rosco

ROSHAD (American) a form of Rashad.
Roshard

ROSHEAN (American) a combination of the prefix Ro + Sean.
Roshain, Roshan, Roshane, Roshaun, Roshawn, Roshay, Rosheen, Roshene

ROSITO (Filipino) rose.

ROSS (Latin) rose. (Scottish) peninsula. (French) red.
Rosse, Rossell, Rossi, Rossie, Rossy

ROSSWELL (English) springtime of roses.
Rosvel

ROSTISLAV (Czech) growing glory.
Rosta, Rostya

ROSWALD (English) field of roses.
Ross, Roswell

ROTH (German) redhead.

ROTHWELL (Scandinavian) red spring.

ROVER (English) traveler.

ROWAN (English) tree with red berries.
Roan, Rowe, Rowen, Rowney, Rowyn

ROWELL (English) roe deer well.

ROWLAND (German) an alternate
form of Roland. (English) rough land.
Rowlando, Rowlands, Rowlandson

ROWLEY (English) rough meadow.
Rowlea, Rowlee, Rowleigh, Rowly

ROWSON (English) son of the redhead.

ROXBURY (English) rook's town or
fortress.
Roxburghe

ROY (French) king. A short form of
Royal, Royce. See also Conroy, Delroy,
Fitzroy, Leroy, Loe.
Rey, Roi, Roye, Ruy

ROYAL (French) kingly, royal.
Roy, Royale, Royall, Royell

ROYCE (English) son of Roy.
Roice, Roy, Royz

ROYDEN (English) rye hill.
Royd, Roydan

RUBEN (Hebrew) an alternate form of
Reuben.
Ruban, Rube, Rubean, Rubens, Rubin, Ruby

RUBERT (Czech) a form of Robert.

RUBY (Hebrew) a familiar form
of Reuben, Ruben.

RUDD (English) a short form of
Rudyard.

RUDA (Czech) a form of Rudolph.
Rude, Rudek

RUDI (Spanish) a familiar form of
Rudolph.
Ruedi

RUDO (Shona) love.

RUDOLF (German) an alternate form
of Rudolph.
Rodolf, Rodolfo, Rudolfo

RUDOLPH (German) famous wolf.
See also Dolf.
*Raoul, Rezsó, Rodolfo, Rodolph, Rodolphe,
Rolf, Ruda, Rudek, Rudi, Rudolf, Rudolpho,
Rudolphus, Rudy*

RUDOLPHO (Italian) a form of
Rudolph.

RUDY (English) a familiar form
of Rudolph.
Roody, Ruddy, Ruddie, Rudey, Rudi, Rudie

RUDYARD (English) red enclosure.
Rudd

RUEBEN (Hebrew) an alternate form
of Reuben.
Rueban, Ruebin

RUFF (French) redhead.

RUFIN (Polish) redhead.
Rufino

RUFORD (English) red ford; ford with
reeds.
Rufford

RUFUS (Latin) redhead.
*Rayfus, Rufe, Ruffis, Ruffus, Rufino, Rufo,
Rufous*

RUGBY (English) rook fortress. History:
a famous British school after which
the sport of rugby was named.

RUGGERIO (Italian) a form of Roger.
Rogero, Ruggero, Ruggiero

RUHAKANA (Rukiga) argumentative.

RULAND (German) an alternate form
of Roland.
Rulan, Rulon, Rulondo

RUMFORD (English) wide river crossing.

RUNAKO (Shona) handsome.

RUNE (German, Swedish) secret.

RUNROT (Tai) prosperous.

RUPERT (German) a form of Robert.
Ruperth, Ruperto, Ruprecht

RUPERTO (Italian) a form of Rupert.

RUPRECHT (German) an alternate form of Rupert.

RUSH (French) redhead. (English) a short form of Russell.
Rushi

RUSHFORD (English) ford with rushes.

RUSK (Spanish) twisted bread.

RUSKIN (French) redhead.
Rush, Russ

RUSS (French) a short form of Russell.

RUSSEL (French) an alternate form of Russell.

RUSSELL (French) redhead; fox colored. See also Lukela.
Roussell, Rush, Russ, Russel, Russelle, Rusty

RUSTY (French) a familiar form of Russell.
Ruste, Rusten, Rustie, Rustin, Ruston, Rustyn

RUTGER (Scandinavian) a form of Roger.
Ruttger

RUTHERFORD (English) cattle ford.
Rutherfurd

RUTLAND (Scandinavian) red land.

RUTLEDGE (English) red ledge.

RUTLEY (English) red meadow.

RUY (Spanish) a short form of Roderick.
Rui

RYAN (Irish) little king.
Rayan, Rhyan, Rhyne, Ryane, Ryann, Ryen, Ryian, Ryiann, Ryin, Ryne, Ryon, Ryuan, Ryun, Ryyan

RYCROFT (English) rye field.
Ryecroft

RYDER (English) an alternate form of Rider.
Rydder, Rye

RYE (English) a short form of Ryder. A grain used in cereal and whiskey. (Gypsy) gentleman.
Ry.

RYEN (Irish) an alternate form of Ryan.
Ryein, Ryien

RYERSON (English) son of Rider, Ryder.

RYESE (English) an alternate form of Reece.
Reyse, Ryez, Ryse

RYKER (American) a surname used as a first name.
Riker, Ryk

RYLAN (English) land where rye is grown.
Ryland, Rylean, Rylen, Rylin, Rylon, Rylyn, Rylynn

RYLAND (English) an alternate form of Rylan.
Ryeland, Rylund

RYLE (English) rye hill.
Ryal, Ryel

RYLEE (Irish) an alternate form of Riley.
Ryeleigh, Ryleigh, Rylie, Rillie

RYLEY (Irish) an alternate form of Riley.
Ryely

RYMAN (English) rye seller.

RYNE (Irish) an alternate form of Ryan.
Rynn

RYON (Irish) an alternate form of Ryan.

S

SABASTIAN (Greek) an alternate form
of Sebastian.
*Sabastain, Sabastiano, Sabastien, Sabastin,
Sabastion, Sabaston, Sabbastiun, Sabestian*

SABER (French) sword.
Sabir, Sabre

SABIN (Basque) ancient tribe of central
Italy.
Saban, Saben, Sabian, Sabien, Sabino

SABITI (Rutooro) born on Sunday.

SABOLA (Ngoni) pepper.

SABURO (Japanese) third-born son.

SACHA (Russian) an alternate form of
Sasha.
Sascha

SACHAR (Russian) a form of Zachary.

SADDAM (Arabic) powerful ruler.

SADIKI (Swahili) faithful.
Saadiq, Sadeek, Sadek, Sadik, Sadiq, Sadique

SADLER (English) saddle maker.
Saddler

SAFARI (Swahili) born while traveling.
Safa, Safarian

SAFFORD (English) willow-river
crossing.

SAGE (English) wise. Botany: an herb
with healing powers.
Sagen, Sager, Saige, Saje

SAHALE (Native American) falcon.
Sael, Sahal, Sahel, Sahil

SAHEN (Hindi) above.
Sahan

SAHIL (Native American) an alternate
form of Sahale.
Saheel, Sahel

SAHIR (Hindi) friend.

SA'ID (Arabic) happy.
*Sa'ad, Saaid, Saed, Sa'eed, Saeed, Sahid,
Saide, Sa'ied, Saied, Saiyed, Saiyeed, Sajid,
Sajjid, Sayed, Sayeed, Sayid, Seyed, Shahid*

SAJAG (Hindi) watchful.

SAKA (Swahili) hunter.

SAKERI (Danish) a form of Zachary.
Sakarai, Sakari

SAKIMA (Native American) king.

SAKURUTA (Pawnee) coming sun.

SAL (Italian) a short form of Salvatore.

SALAM (Arabic) lamb.
Salaam

SALAMON (Spanish) a form of
Solomon.
Saloman, Salomón

SALAUN (French) a form of Solomon.

SÁLIH (Arabic) right, good.
Saleeh, Saleh, Salehe

SALIM (Swahili) peaceful.

SALÍM (Arabic) peaceful, safe.
Saleem, Salem, Saliym, Salman

SALMALIN (Hindi) taloned.

SALMAN (Czech) a form of Salím,
Solomon.
Salmaan, Salmaine, Salmon

SALOMON (Hebrew) an alternate form of Solomon.
Salomone

SALTON (English) manor town; willow town.

SALVADOR (Spanish) savior.
Salvadore

SALVATORE (Italian) savior. See also Xavier.
Sal, Salbatore, Sallie, Sally, Salvator, Salvattore, Salvidor, Sauveur

SAM (Hebrew) a short form of Samuel.
Samm, Sammy, Sem, Shem, Shmuel

SAMBO (American) a familiar form of Samuel.
Sambou

SAMEER (Arabic) an alternate form of Samír.

SAMI, Samy (Hebrew) alternate forms of Sammy.
Sameeh, Sameh, Samie, Samih, Sammi

SAMÍR (Arabic) entertaining companion.
Sameer

SAMMAN (Arabic) grocer.
Saman, Sammon

SAMMY (Hebrew) a familiar form of Samuel.
Saamy, Samey, Sami, Sammee, Sammey, Sammie, Samy

SAMO (Czech) a form of Samuel.
Samho, Samko

SAMSON (Hebrew) like the sun. Bible: a strong man betrayed by Delilah.
Sampson, Sansao, Sansom, Sansón, Shem, Shimshon

SAMUAL (Hebrew) an alternate form of Samuel.
Samuael, Samuail

SAMUEL (Hebrew) heard God; asked of God. Bible: a famous Old Testament prophet and judge. See also Kamuela, Zamiel, Zanvil.
Sam, Samael, Samaru, Samauel, Samaul, Sambo, Sameul, Samiel, Sammail, Sammel, Sammuel, Sammy, Samo, Samouel, Samu, Samual, Samuele, Samuelis, Samuell, Samuello, Samuil, Samuka, Samule, Samuru, Samvel, Sanko, Saumel, Schmuel, Shem, Shmuel, Simão, Simuel, Somhairle, Zamuel

SAMUELE (Italian) a form of Samuel.
Samulle

SAMURU (Japanese) a form of Samuel.

SANAT (Hindi) ancient.

SANBORN (English) sandy brook.
Sanborne, Sanbourn, Sanbourne, Sanburn, Sanburne, Sandborn, Sandbourne

SANCHEZ (Latin) an alternate form of Sancho.
Sanchaz, Sancheze

SANCHO (Latin) sanctified; sincere. Literature: Sancho Panza was Don Quixote's faithful companion.
Sanchez, Sauncho

SANDEEP (Punjabi) enlightened.
Sandip

SANDER (English) a short form of Alexander, Lysander.
Sandor, Sándor, Saunder

SANDERS (English) son of Sander.
Sanderson, Saunders, Saunderson

SÁNDOR (Hungarian) a short form of Alexander.
Sanyi

SANDRO (Greek, Italian) a short form of Alexander.
Sandero, Sandor, Sandre, Saundro, Shandro

SANDY (English) a familiar form of Alexander.
Sande, Sandey, Sandi, Sandie

SANFORD (English) sandy river crossing.
Sandford

SANI (Hindi) Saturn. (Navajo) old.

SANJAY (American) a combination of Sanford + Jay.
Sanjaya, Sanje, Sanjey, Sanjo

SANJIV (Hindi) long lived.
Sanjeev

SANKAR (Hindi) god. Religion: another name for the Hindu god Shiva.

SANSÓN (Spanish) a form of Samson.
Sanson, Sansone, Sansun

SANTANA (Spanish) History: Antonio Santa Ana was a revolutionary general and president of Mexico.
Santanna

SANTIAGO (Spanish) a form of James.

SANTINO (Spanish) an alternate form of Santonio.
Santion

SANTO (Italian, Spanish) holy.
Santos

SANTON (English) sandy town.

SANTONIO (Spanish) Geography: a short form of San Antonio, a town in Texas.
Santino, Santon, Santoni

SANTOS (Spanish) saint.
Santo

SANTOSH (Hindi) satisfied.

SANYU (Luganda) happy.

SAQR (Arabic) falcon.

SAQUAN (American) a combination of the predix Sa + Quan.
Saquané, Saquin, Saquon, Saqwan, Saqwone

SARAD (Hindi) born in the autumn.

SARGENT (French) army officer.
Sargant, Sarge, Sarjant, Sergeant, Sergent, Serjeant

SARITO (Spanish) a form of Caesar.
Sarit

SARIYAH (Arabic) clouds at night.

SARNGIN (Hindi) archer; protector.

SAROJIN (Hindi) like a lotus.
Sarojun

SASHA (Russian) a short form of Alexander.
Sacha, Sash, Sashenka, Sashka, Sashok, Sausha

SASSON (Hebrew) joyful.
Sason

SATCHEL (French) small bag.
Satch

SATORDI (French) Saturn.
Satori

SAUL (Hebrew) asked for, borrowed. Bible: in the Old Testament, a king of Israel and the father of Jonathan; in the New Testament, Saint Paul's original name was Saul.
Saül, Shaul, Sol, Solly

SAVERIO (Italian) a form of Xavier.

SAVILLE (French) willow town.
Savelle, Savil, Savile, Savill, Savylle, Seville, Siville

SAVON (American) a masculine form of Savannah. (Spanish) a treeless plain.
Savan, Savaughn, Saveion, Saveon, Savhon, Saviahn, Savian, Savino, Savion, Savo, Savone, Sayvon, Sayvone

SAW (Burmese) early.

SAWYER (English) wood worker.
Sawyere

SAX (English) a short form of Saxon.
Saxe

SAXON (English) swordsman. History: the Roman name for Germanic people who fought with short swords.
Sax, Saxen, Saxsin, Saxxon

SAYER (Welsh) carpenter.
Say, Saye, Sayers, Sayr, Sayre, Sayres

SAYYID (Arabic) master.
Sayed, Sayid, Sayyad, Sayyed

SCANLON (Irish) little trapper.
Scanlan, Scanlen

SCHAFER (German) shepherd.
Schaefer, Schaffer, Schiffer, Shaffar, Shäffer

SCHMIDT (German) blacksmith.
Schmid, Schmit, Schmitt, Schmydt

SCHNEIDER (German) tailor.
Schnieder, Snider, Snyder

SCHÖN (German) handsome.
Schoen, Schönn, Shon

SCHUYLER (Dutch) sheltering.
Schuylar, Schyler, Scoy, Scy, Skuyler, Sky, Skylar, Skyler, Skylor

SCHYLER (Dutch) an alternate form of Schuyler.
Schylar, Schylre, Schylur

SCORPIO (Latin) dangerous, deadly. Astronomy: a southern constellation between Libra and Sagittarius resembling a scorpion. Astrology: the eighth sign of the zodiac.
Scorpeo

SCOTT (English) from Scotland. A familiar form of Prescott.
Scot, Scottie, Scotto, Scotty

SCOTTIE (English) a familiar form of Scott.
Scotie, Scotti

SCOTTY (English) a familiar form of Scott.
Scottey

SCOVILLE (French) Scott's town.

SCULLY (Irish) town crier.

SEABERT (English) shining sea.
Seabright, Sebert, Seibert

SEABROOK (English) brook near the sea.

SEAMUS (Irish) a form of James.
Seamas, Seumas, Shamus

SEAN (Hebrew) God is gracious. (Irish) a form of John.
Seaghan, Séan, Seán, Seanán, Seane, Seann, Shaan, Shaine, Shane, Shaun, Shawn, Shayne, Shon, Siôn

SEARLAS (Irish, French) a form of Charles.
Séarlas, Searles, Searlus

SEARLE (English) armor.

SEASAR (Latin) an alternate form of Caesar.
Seasare, Seazar, Sesar, Sesear, Sezar

SEATON (English) town near the sea.
Seeton, Seton

SEBASTIAN (Greek) venerable. (Latin) revered.
Bastian, Sabastian, Sabastien, Sebashtian, Sebastain, Sebastiane, Sebastiano, Sebastien, Sébastien, Sebastin, Sebastine, Sebastion, Sebbie, Sebestyén, Sebo, Sepasetiano

SEBASTIEN, Sébastien (French) forms of Sebastian.
Sebasten, Sebastyen

SEBASTION (Greek) an alternate form of Sebastian.

SEDGELY (English) sword meadow.
Sedgeley, Sedgly

SEDRIC (Irish) a form of Cedric.
Seddrick, Sederick, Sedrick, Sedrik, Sedriq

SEELEY (English) blessed.
Sealey, Seely, Selig

SEF (Egyptian) yesterday. Literature: an Egyption lion god in *The Book of the Dead.*

SEFTON (English) village of rushes.

SEFU (Swahili) sword.

SEGER (English) sea spear; sea warrior.
Seager, Seeger, Segar

SEGUN (Yoruba) conqueror.

SEGUNDO (Spanish) second.

SEIBERT (English) bright sea.
Seabert, Sebert

SEIF (Arabic) religion's sword.

SEIFERT (German) an alternate form of Siegfried.

SEIN (Basque) innocent.

SEKAYE (Shona) laughter.

SELBY (English) village by the mansion.
Selbey, Shelby

SELDON (English) willow tree valley.
Selden, Sellden

SELIG (German) a form of Seeley.
Seligman, Seligmann, Zelig

SELWYN (English) friend from the palace.
Selvin, Selwin, Selwinn, Selwynn, Selwynne, Wyn

SEMANDA (Luganda) cow clan.

SEMER (Ethiopian) a form of George.
Semere, Semier

SEMON (Greek) a form of Simon.
Semion

SEMPALA (Luganda) born in prosperous times.

SEN (Japanese) wood fairy.
Senh

SENER (Turkish) bringer of joy.

SENIOR (French) lord.

SENNETT (French) elderly.
Sennet

SENON (Spanish) living.

SENWE (African) dry as a grain stalk.

SEPP (German) a form of Joseph.
Seppi

SEPTIMUS (Latin) seventh.

SERAFINO (Portuguese) a form of Seraphim.

SERAPHIM (Hebrew) fiery, burning. Bible: the fiery angels who guard the throne of God.
Saraf, Saraph, Serafim, Serafin, Serafino, Seraphimus, Seraphin

SERENO (Latin) calm, tranquil.

SERGE (Latin) attendant.
Seargeoh, Serg, Sergei, Sergio, Sergios, Sergius, Sergiusz, Serguel, Sirgio, Sirgios

SERGEI (Russian) a form of Serge.
Sergey, Sergeyuk, Serghey, Sergi, Sergie, Sergo, Sergunya, Serhiy, Serhiyko, Serjiro, Serzh

SERGIO (Italian) a form of Serge.
Serginio, Serigo, Serjio

SERVANDO (Spanish) to serve.
Servan, Servio

SETH (Hebrew) appointed. Bible: the third son of Adam.
Set, Sethan, Sethe, Shet

SETIMBA (Luganda) river dweller. Geography: a river in Uganda.

SEUMAS (Scottish) a form of James.
Seaumus

SEVERIANO (Italian) a form of Séverin.

SÉVERIN (French) severe.
Seve, Sevé, Severan, Severian, Severiano, Severo, Sevien, Sevrin, Sevryn

SEVERN (English) boundary. Geography: a river in southern England.
Sevearn, Sevren, Sevrnn

SEVILEN (Turkish) beloved.

SEWARD (English) sea guardian.
Sewerd, Siward

SEWATI (Moquelumnan) curved bear claws.

SEXTON (English) church offical, sexton.

SEXTUS (Latin) sixth.
Sixtus

SEYMOUR (French) prayer. Religion: name honoring Saint Maur. See also Maurice.
Seamor, Seamore, Seamour, See

SHABOUH (Armenian) king, noble. History: a Persian king.

SHAD (Punjabi) happy-go-lucky.
Shadd

SHADI (Arabic) singer.
Shadde, Shaddi, Shaddy, Shade, Shadee, Shadeed, Shadey, Shadie, Shady, Shydee, Shydi

SHADRACH (Babylonian) god; godlike. Religion: another name for Aku, the sun god. Bible: one of Daniel's three companions in captivity.
Shad, Shadrack, Shadrick, Sheddrach, Shedrach, Shedrick

SHADWELL (English) shed by a well.

SHAH (Persian) king. History: a title for rulers of Iran.

SHAHEEM (American) a combination of Shah + Raheem.
Shaheim, Shahiem, Shahm

SHAHID (Arabic) an alternate form of Sa'id.
Shahed, Shaheed

SHAI (Hebrew) a short form of Yeshaya.
Shaie

SHAIMING (Chinese) life; sunshine.

SHAINE (Irish) an alternate form of Sean.
Shain

SHAKA (Zulu) founder, first. History: Shaka Zulu was the founder of the Zulu empire.

SHAKEEL (Arabic) an alternate form of Shaquille.
Shakeil, Shakel, Shakell, Shakiel, Shakil, Shakille, Shakyle

SHAKIR (Arabic) thankful.
Shaakir, Shakeer, Shakeir, Shakur

SHAKUR (Arabic) an alternate form of Shakir.
Shakuur

SHALOM (Hebrew) peace.
Shalum, Shlomo, Sholem, Sholom

SHALYA (Hindi) throne.

SHAMAN (Sanskrit) holy man, mystic, medicine man.

Shamaine, Shamaun, Shamin, Shamine,
Shammon, Shamon, Shamone

SHAMAR (Hebrew) an alternate form
of Shamir.
Shamaar, Shamare, Shamari

SHAMIR (Hebrew) precious stone.
Bible: a hard, precious stone used to
build Solomon's temple.
Shahmeer, Shahmir, Shamar, Shameer,
Shamyr

SHAMUS (Irish) an alternate form
of Seamus. (American) slang for
detective.
Shamas, Shames, Shamos, Shemus

SHAN (Irish) an alternate form of
Shane.
Shann, Shanne

SHANAHAN (Irish) wise, clever.

SHANDY (English) rambunctious.
Shandey, Shandie

SHANE (Irish) an alternate form of
Sean.
Shan, Shayn, Shayne

SHANGOBUNNI (Yoruba) gift from
Shango.

SHANLEY (Irish) small; ancient.
Shaneley, Shannley

SHANNON (Irish) small and wise.
Shanan, Shannan, Shannen, Shannin,
Shannone, Shanon

SHANTAE (French) an alternate form
of Chante.
Shant, Shanta, Shantai, Shante, Shantell,
Shantelle, Shanti, Shantia, Shantie,
Shanton, Shanty

SHAP (English) an alternate form of
Shep.

SHAQUAN (American) a combination
of the prefix Sha + Quan.

Shaqaun, Shaquand, Shaquane, Shaquann,
Shaquaunn, Shaquawn, Shaquen, Shaquian,
Shaquin, Shaqwan

SHAQUELL (American) a form of
Shaquille.
Shaqueal, Shaqueil, Shaquel, Shaquelle,
Shaquiel, Shaquiell, Shaquielle

SHAQUILLE (Arabic) handsome.
Shakeel, Shaquell, Shaquil, Shaquile,
Shaquill, Shaqul

SHAQUON (American) a combination
of the prefix Sha + Quon.
Shaikwon, Shaqon, Shaquoin, Shaquoné

SHARAD (Pakistani) autumn.
Sharod

SHARÍF (Arabic) honest; noble.
Shareef, Sharef, Shareff, Shareif, Sharief,
Sharife, Shariff, Shariyf, Sharrif, Sharyif

SHAROD (Pakistani) an alternate form
of Sharad.
Sharrod

SHARRON (Hebrew) flat area, plain.
Bible: the area from Mount Carmel
south to Jaffa, covered with oak trees.
Sharon, Sharone, Sharonn, Sharonne

SHATTUCK (English) little shad fish.

SHAUN (Irish) an alternate form of
Sean.
Shaughan, Shaughn, Shaugn, Shauna,
Shaunahan, Shaune, Shaunn, Shaunne

SHAVAR (Hebrew) comet.
Shavit

SHAVON (American) a combination of
the prefix Sha + Yvon.
Shauvan, Shauvon, Shavan, Shavaughn,
Shaven, Shavin, Shavone, Shawan, Shawon,
Shawun

SHAW (English) grove.

SHAWN (Irish) an alternate form of Sean.
Shawen, Shawne, Shawnee, Shawnn, Shawon

SHAWNTA (American) a combination of Shawn + suffixes beginning with a 't.'
Shawntae, Shawntel, Shawnti

SHAY (Irish) an alternate form of Shea.
Shae, Shai, Shaya, Shaye, Shey

SHAYAN (Cheyenne) an alternate form of Cheyenne.
Shayaan, Shayann, Shayon

SHAYNE (Hebrew) an alternate form of Sean.
Shayn, Shaynne, Shean

SHEA (Irish) courteous.
Shay

SHEDRICK (Babylonian) an alternate form of Shadrach.
Shadriq, Shederick, Shedric, Shedrique

SHEEHAN (Irish) little; peaceful.
Shean

SHEFFIELD (English) crooked field.
Field, Shef, Sheff, Sheffie, Sheffy

SHEL (English) a short form of Shelby, Sheldon, Shelton.

SHELBY (English) ledge estate.
Shel, Shelbe, Shelbey, Shelbie, Shell, Shellby, Shelley, Shelly

SHELDON (English) farm on the ledge.
Shel, Sheldan, Shelden, Sheldin, Sheldyn, Shell, Shelley, Shelly, Shelton

SHELLEY (English) a familiar form of Shelby, Sheldon, Shelton. Literature: Percy Bysshe Shelly was a British poet.
Shell, Shelly

SHELTON (English) town on a ledge.
Shel, Shelley, Shelten

SHEM (Hebrew) name; reputation. (English) a short form of Samuel. Bible: Noah's oldest son.

SHEN (Egyptian) sacred amulet. (Chinese) meditation.

SHEP (English) a short form of Shepherd.
Shap, Ship, Shipp

SHEPHERD (English) shepherd.
Shep, Shepard, Shephard, Shepp, Sheppard, Shepperd

SHEPLEY (English) sheep meadow.
Sheplea, Sheplee, Shepply, Shipley

SHERBORN (English) clear brook.
Sherborne, Sherbourn, Sherburn, Sherburne

SHERIDAN (Irish) wild.
Dan, Sheredan, Sheriden, Sheridon, Sherridan

SHERILL (English) shire on a hill.
Sheril, Sherril, Sherrill

SHERLOCK (English) light haired. Literature: Sherlock Holmes was Sir Arthur Conan Doyle's famous British detective character.
Sherlocke, Shurlock, Shurlocke

SHERMAN (English) sheep shearer; resident of a shire.
Scherman, Schermann, Sherm, Shermain, Shermaine, Shermann, Shermie, Shermon, Shermy

SHERROD (English) clearer of the land.
Sherod, Sherrad, Sherrard, Sherrodd

SHERWIN (English) swift runner, one who cuts the wind.
Sherveen, Shervin, Sherwan, Sherwind, Sherwinn, Sherwyn, Sherwynd, Sherwynne, Win

SHERWOOD (English) bright forest.
Sherwoode, Shurwood, Woody

SHIHAB (Arabic) blaze.

SHÌLÍN (Chinese) intellectual.
Shilan

SHILOH (Hebrew) God's gift.
Shi, Shile, Shiley, Shilo, Shiloe, Shy, Shyle, Shylo, Shyloh

SHIMON (Hebrew) an alternate form of Simon.
Shymon

SHIMSHON (Hebrew) an alternate form of Samson.
Shimson

SHING (Chinese) victory.
Shingae, Shingo

SHIPTON (English) sheep village; ship village.

SHIQUAN (American) a combination of the prefix Shi + Quan.
Shiquane, Shiquann, Shiquawn, Shiquoin, Shiqwan

SHIRO (Japanese) fourth-born son.

SHIVA (Hindi) life and death. Religion: the most common name for the god of destruction and reproduction.
Shiv, Shivan, Siva

SHLOMO (Hebrew) an alternate form of Solomon.
Shelmu, Shelomo, Shelomoh, Shlomi, Shlomot

SHMUEL (Hebrew) an alternate form of Samuel.
Shem, Shemuel, Shmelke, Shmiel, Shmulka

SHNEUR (Yiddish) senior.
Shneiur

SHON (German) an alternate form of Schön. (American) a form of Sean.
Shoan, Shoen, Shondae, Shondale, Shondel, Shone, Shonn, Shonntay, Shontae, Shontarious, Shouan, Shoun

SHUNNAR (Arabic) pheasant.

SI (Hebrew) a short form of Silas, Simon.
Sy

SID (French) a short form of Sidney.
Cyd, Siddie, Siddy, Sidey, Syd

SIDDEL (English) wide valley.
Siddell

SIDDHARTHA (Hindi) History: the original name of Buddha, an Indian mystic and founder of Buddhism.
Sida, Siddartha, Siddhaarth, Siddhart, Siddharth, Sidh, Sidharth, Sidhartha, Sidhdharth

SIDNEY (French) from Saint Denis, France.
Cydney, Sid, Sidnee, Sidny, Sidon, Sidonio, Sydney, Sydny

SIDONIO (Spanish) a form of Sidney.

SIDWELL (English) wide stream.

SIEGFRIED (German) victorious peace. Literature: a dragon-slaying hero. See also Zigfrid, Ziggy.
Seifert, Seifried, Siegfred, Siffre, Sig, Sigfrid, Sigfried, Sigfroi, Sigfryd, Siggy, Sigifredo, Sigvard, Singefrid, Sygfried, Szygfrid

SIERRA (Irish) black. (Spanish) saw toothed. Geography: a range of mountains with a sawtooth appearance.
Siera

SIG (German) a short form of Siegfried, Sigmund.

SIGIFREDO (German) an alternate form of Siegfried.
Sigefriedo, Sigfrido, Siguefredo

SIGGY (German) a familiar form of Siegfried, Sigmund.

SIGMUND (German) victorious protector. See also Ziggy, Zsigmond, Zygmunt.
Siegmund, Sig, Siggy, Sigismond, Sigismondo, Sigismund, Sigismundo, Sigismundus, Sigmond, Sigsmond, Szygmond

SIGURD (German, Scandinavian) victorious guardian.
Sigord, Sjure, Syver

SIGWALD (German) victorious leader.

SILAS (Latin) a short form of Silvan.
Si, Sias, Sylas

SILVAN (Latin) forest dweller.
Silas, Silvain, Silvano, Silvaon, Silvie, Silvio, Sylvain, Sylvan, Sylvanus, Sylvio

SILVANO (Italian) a form of Silvan.
Silvanos, Silvanus, Silvino

SILVESTER (Latin) an alternate form of Sylvester.
Silvestr, Silvestre, Silvestro, Silvy

SILVESTRO (Italian) a form of Sylvester.

SILVIO (Italian) a form of Silvan.

SIMÃO (Portuguese) a form of Samuel.

SIMBA (Swahili) lion. (Yao) a short form of Lisimba.
Sim

SIMCHA (Hebrew) joyful.
Simmy

SIMEON (French) a form of Simon.
Simione, Simone

SIMMS (Hebrew) son of Simon.
Simm, Sims

SIMMY (Hebrew) a familiar form of Simcha, Simon.
Simmey, Simmi, Simmie, Symmy

SIMON (Hebrew) he heard. Bible: in the Old Testament, the second son of Jacob and Leah; in the New Testament, one of the Twelve Disciples. See also Symington, Ximenes.
Saimon, Samien, Semon, Shimon, Si, Sim, Simao, Simen, Simeon, Simion, Simm, Simmon, Simmonds, Simmons, Simms, Simmy, Simonas, Simone, Simson, Simyon, Síomón, Symon, Szymon

SIMPSON (Hebrew) son of Simon.
Simonson, Simson

SINCLAIR (French) prayer. Religion: name honoring Saint Clair.
Sinclare, Synclair

SINGH (Hindi) lion.
Sing

SINJON (English) saint, holy man. Religion: name honoring Saint John.
Sinjin, Sinjun, Sjohn, Syngen, Synjen, Synjon

SIPATU (Moquelumnan) pulled out.

SIPHO (Zulu) present.

SIRAJ (Arabic) lamp, light.

SISEAL (Irish) a form of Cecil.

SISI (Fante) born on Sunday.

SIVA (Hindi) an alternate form of Shiva.
Siv

SIVAN (Hebrew) ninth month of the Jewish year.

SIWATU (Swahili) born during a time of conflict.
Siwazuri

SIWILI (Native American) long fox's tail.

SKAH (Lakota) white.
Skai

SKEE (Scandinavian) projectile.
Ski, Skie

SKEETER (English) swift.
Skeat, Skeet, Skeets

SKELLY (Irish) storyteller.
Shell, Skelley, Skellie

SKELTON (Dutch) shell town.

SKERRY (Scandinavian) stony island.

SKIP (Scandinavian) a short form of Skipper.

SKIPPER (Scandinavian) shipmaster.
Skip, Skipp, Skippie, Skipton

SKIRIKI (Pawnee) coyote.

SKULE (Norwegian) hidden.

SKYE (Dutch) a short form of Skylar, Skyler, Skylor.
Sky

SKYLAR (Dutch) an alternate form of Schuyler.
Skilar, Skkylar, Skye, Skyelar, Skylaar, Skylare, Skylarr, Skylayr

SKYLER (Dutch) an alternate form of Schuyler.
Skieler, Skiler, Skye, Skyeler, Skylee, Skyller

SKYLOR (Dutch) an alternate form of Schuyler.
Skye, Skyelor, Skyloer, Skylore, Skylour, Skylur, Skylyr

SLADE (English) child of the valley.
Slaide, Slayde

SLANE (Czech) salty.
Slan

SLATER (English) roof slater.
Slader, Slate, Slayter

SLAVA (Russian) a short form of Stanislav, Vladislav, Vyacheslav.
Slavik, Slavoshka

SLAWEK (Polish) a short form of Radoslaw.

SLEVIN (Irish) mountaineer.
Slaven, Slavin, Slawin

SLOAN (Irish) warrior.
Sloane, Slone

SMEDLEY (English) flat meadow.
Smedleigh, Smedly

SMITH (English) blacksmith.
Schmidt, Smid, Smidt, Smitt, Smitty, Smyth, Smythe

SNOWDEN (English) snowy hill.
Snowdon

SOCRATES (Greek) wise, learned. History: a famous ancient Greek philosopher.
Socratis, Sokrates, Sokratis

SOFIAN (Arabic) devoted.

SOHRAB (Persian) ancient hero.

SOJA (Yoruba) soldier.

SOL (Hebrew) a short form of Saul, Solomon.
Soll, Sollie, Solly

SOLLY (Hebrew) a familiar form of Saul, Solomon.
Sollie, Zollie, Zolly

SOLOMON (Hebrew) peaceful. Bible: a king of Israel famous for his wisdom. See also Zalman.
Salamen, Salamon, Salamun, Salaun, Salman, Salomo, Salomon, Selim, Shelomah, Shlomo, Sol, Solamh, Solaman, Solly, Solmon, Soloman, Solomonas, Sulaiman

SOLON (Greek) wise. History: a sixth-century Athenian lawmaker noted for his wisdom.

SOMERSET (English) place of the summer settlers. Literature: William Somerset Maugham was a well-known British writer.
Sommerset, Sumerset, Summerset

SOMERVILLE (English) summer town.
Somerton, Summerton, Summerville

SON (Vietnamese) mountain. (Native American) star. (English) son, boy. A short form of Madison, Orson.
Sonny

SONGAN (Native American) strong.
Song

SONNY (English) a familiar form of Grayson, Madison, Orson, Son.
Soni, Sonnie, Sony

SONO (Akan) elephant.

SÖREN (Danish) thunder; war. Mythology: Thor was the Norse god of thunder and war.
Sorren

SORREL (French) reddish brown.
Sorel, Sorell, Sorrell

SOROUSH (Persian) happy.

SOTERIOS (Greek) savior.
Soteris, Sotero

SOUTHWELL (English) south well.

SOVANN (Cambodian) gold.

SOWANDE (Yoruba) wise healer sought me out.

SPALDING (English) divided field.
Spaulding

SPANGLER (German) tinsmith.
Spengler

SPARK (English) happy.
Sparke, Sparkie, Sparky

SPEAR (English) spear carrier.
Speare, Spears, Speer, Speers, Spiers

SPEEDY (English) quick; successful.
Speed

SPENCE (English) a short form of Spencer.
Spense

SPENCER (English) dispenser of provisions.
Spence, Spencre, Spenser

SPENSER (English) an alternate form of Spencer. Literature: Edmund Spenser was the British poet who wrote *The Faerie Queene*.
Spanser, Spense

SPIKE (English) ear of grain; long nail.
Spyke

SPIRO (Greek) round basket; breath.
Spiridion, Spiridon, Spiros, Spyridon, Spyros

SPOOR (English) spur maker.
Spoors

SPROULE (English) energetic.
Sprowle

SPURGEON (English) shrub.

SPYROS (Greek) an alternate form of Spiro.

SQUIRE (English) knight's assistant; large landholder.

STACEY, Stacy (English) familiar forms of Eustace.
Stace, Stacee

STAFFORD (English) riverbank landing.
Staffard, Stafforde, Staford

STAMFORD (English) an alternate form of Stanford.

STAMOS (Greek) an alternate form of Stephen.
Stamatis, Stamatos

STAN (Latin, English) a short form of Stanley.

STANBURY (English) stone fortification.
Stanberry, Stanbery, Stanburghe, Stansbury

STANCIO (Spanish) a form of Constantine.
Stancy

STANCLIFF (English) stony cliff.
Stanclife, Stancliffe

STANDISH (English) stony parkland. History: Miles Standish was a prominent pilgrim in colonial America.

STANE (Slavic) a short form of Stanislaus.

STANFIELD (English) stony field.
Stansfield

STANFORD (English) rocky ford.
Sandy, Stamford, Stan, Standford, Stanfield

STANISLAUS (Latin) stand of glory. See also Lao, Tano.
Slavik, Stana, Standa, Stane, Stanislao, Stanislas, Stanislau, Stanislav, Stanislus, Stannes, Stano, Stasik, Stasio

STANISLAV (Slavic) a form of Stanislaus. See also Slava.
Stanislaw

STANLEY (English) stony meadow.
Stan, Stanely, Stanlea, Stanlee, Stanleigh, Stanly

STANMORE (English) stony lake.

STANNARD (English) hard as stone.

STANTON (English) stony farm.
Stan, Stanten, Staunton

STANWAY (English) stony road.

STANWICK (English) stony village.
Stanwicke, Stanwyck

STANWOOD (English) stony woods.

STARBUCK (English) challenger of fate. Literature: a character in Herman Melville's novel *Moby Dick*.

STARK (German) strong, vigorous.
Starke, Stärke, Starkie

STARLING (English) bird.
Sterling

STARR (English) star.
Star, Staret, Starlight, Starlon, Starwin

STASIK (Russian) a familiar form of Stanislaus.
Stas, Stash, Stashka, Stashko, Stasiek

STASIO (Polish) a form of Stanislaus.
Stas, Stasiek, Stasiu, Staska, Stasko

STAVROS (Greek) an alternate form of Stephen.

STEADMAN (English) owner of a farmstead.
Steadmann, Stedman, Stedmen, Steed

STEEL (English) like steel.
Steele

STEEN (German, Danish) stone.
Steenn, Stein

STEEVE (Greek) a short form of Steeven.

STEEVEN (Greek) an alternate form of Steven.
Steaven, Steavin, Steavon, Steevan, Steeve, Steevn

STEFAN (German, Polish, Swedish) a form of Stephen.
Steafan, Steafeán, Stefaan, Stefane, Stefanson, Stefaun, Stefawn, Steffan

STEFANO (Italian) an alternate form of Stephen.
Stefanos, Steffano

STEFANOS (Greek) a form of Stephen.
Stefans, Stefos, Stephano, Stephanos

STEFEN (Norwegian) a form of Stephen.
Steffen, Steffin, Stefin

STEFFAN (Swedish) an alternate form of Stefan.
Staffan

STEFON (Polish) a form of Stephon.
Staffon, Steffon, Steffone, Stefone, Stefonne

STEIN (German) an alternate form of Steen.
Steine, Steiner

STEINAR (Norwegian) rock warrior.

STEPAN (Russian) a form of Stephen.
Stepa, Stepane, Stepanya, Stepka, Stipan

STEPH (English) a short form of Stephen.

STEPHAN (Greek) an alternate form of Stephen.
Stepfan, Stephanas, Stephano, Stephanos, Stephanus, Stephaun

STÉPHANE (French) a form of Stephen.
Stefane, Stepháne, Stephanne

STEPHEN (Greek) crowned. See also Estéban, Estebe, Estevan, Estevao, Étienne, István, Szczepan, Tapani, Teb, Teppo, Tiennot.
Stamos, Stavros, Stefan, Stefano, Stefanos, Stefen, Stenya, Stepan, Stepanos, Steph, Stephan, Stephanas, Stéphane, Stephens, Stephenson, Stephfan, Stephin, Stephon, Stepven, Steve, Steven, Stevie

STEPHON (Greek) an alternate form of Stephen.
Stefon, Stepfon, Stepfone, Stephfon, Stephion, Stephone, Stephonne

STERLING (English) valuable; silver penny. An alternate form of Starling.
Sterlen, Sterlin, Stirling

STERN (German) star.

STERNE (English) austere.
Stearn, Stearne, Stearns

STETSON (Danish) stepson.
Steston, Steton, Stetsen, Stetzon

STEVAN (Greek) an alternate form of Steven.
Stevano, Stevanoe, Stevaughn, Stevean

STEVE (Greek) a short form of Stephen, Steven.
Steave, Stevie, Stevy

STEVEN (Greek) crowned. An alternate form of Stephen.
Steeven, Steiven, Stevan, Steve, Stevens, Stevie, Stevin, Stevon, Stiven

STEVENS (Greek) son of Steven.
Stevenson, Stevinson

STEVIE (English) a familiar form of Stephen, Steven.
Stevey, Stevy

STEVIN, Stevon (Greek) alternate forms of Steven.
Stevieon, Stevion, Stevyn

STEWART (English) an alternate form of Stuart.
Steward, Stu

STIAN (Norwegian) quick on his feet.

STIG (Swedish) mount.

STIGGUR (Gypsy) gate.

STILLMAN (English) quiet.
Stillmann, Stillmon

STING (English) spike of grain.

STOCKMAN (English) tree-stump remover.

STOCKTON (English) tree-stump town.

STOCKWELL (English) tree-stump well.

STODDARD (English) horse keeper.

STOFFEL (German) a short form of Christopher.

STOKER (English) furnace tender.
Stoke, Stokes, Stroker

STONE (English) stone.
Stoen, Stoner, Stoney, Stonie, Stonie, Stoniy, Stony

STORM (English) tempest, storm.
Storme, Stormey, Stormi, Stormmie, Stormy

STORR (Norwegian) great.
Story

STOVER (English) stove tender.

STOWE (English) hidden, packed away.

STRAHAN (Irish) minstrel.
Strachan

STRATFORD (English) bridge over the river. Literature: Stratford-upon-Avon was Shakespeare's birthplace.
Stradford

STRATTON (Scottish) river valley town.
Straten, Straton

STREPHON (Greek) one who turns. Literature: a character in Gilbert and Sullivan's play *Iolanthe*.

STROM (Greek) bed, mattress. (German) stream.

STRONG (English) powerful.

STROUD (English) thicket.

STRUTHERS (Irish) brook.

STU (English) a short form of Stewart, Stuart.
Stew

STUART (English) caretaker, steward. History: the Scottish and English royal dynasty.
Stewart, Stu, Stuarrt

STUDS (English) rounded nail heads; shirt ornaments; male horses used for breeding. History: Studs Terkel, a famous American radio journalist.
Stud, Studd

STYLES (English) stairs put over a wall to help cross it.
Stiles, Style, Stylz

SUBHI (Arabic) early morning.

SUCK CHIN (Korean) unshakable rock.

SUDI (Swahili) lucky.
Su'ud

SUED (Arabic) master, chief.
Suede

SUFFIELD (English) southern field.

SUGDEN (English) valley of sows.

SUHAIL (Arabic) gentle.
Sohail, Sohayl, Souhail, Suhael, Sujal

SUHUBA (Swahili) friend.

SUKRU (Turkish) grateful.

SULAIMAN (Arabic) a form of Solomon.
Sulaman, Sulay, Sulaymaan, Sulayman, Suleiman, Suleman, Suleyman, Sulieman, Sulman, Sulomon, Sulyman

SULLIVAN (Irish) black eyed.
Sullavan, Sullevan, Sully

SULLY (Irish) a familiar form of Sullivan. (French) stain, tarnish. (English) south meadow.
Sulleigh, Sulley

SULTAN (Swahili) ruler.
Sultaan

SUM (Tai) appropriate.

SUMMIT (English) peak, top.
Sumeet, Sumit, Summet, Summitt

SUMNER (English) church officer, summoner.
Summer

SUNDEEP (Punjabi) light; enlightened.
Sundip

SUNNY (English) sunny, sunshine.
Sun, Sunni

SUNREEP (Hindi) pure.
Sunrip

SUTCLIFF (English) southern cliff.
Sutcliffe

SUTHERLAND (Scandinavian) southern land.
Southerland, Sutherlan

SUTTON (English) southern town.

SVEN (Scandinavian) youth.
Svein, Svend, Svenn, Swen, Swenson

SWAGGART (English) one who sways and staggers.
Swaggert

SWAIN (English) herdsman; knight's attendant.
Swaine, Swane, Swanson, Swayne

SWALEY (English) winding stream.
Swail, Swailey, Swale, Swales

SWEENEY (Irish) small hero.
Sweeny

SWINBOURNE (English) stream used by swine.
Swinborn, Swinborne, Swinburn, Swinburne, Swinbyrn, Swynborn

SWINDEL (English) valley of the swine.
Swindell

SWINFEN (English) swine's mud.

SWINFORD (English) swine's crossing.
Swynford

SWINTON (English) swine town.

SY (Latin) a short form of Sylas, Symon.
Si

SYDNEY (French) an alternate form of Sidney.
Syd, Sydne, Sydnee, Syndey

SYED (Arabic) happy.
Syeed, Syid

SYING (Chinese) star.

SYLAS (Latin) an alternate form of Silas.
Sy, Syles, Sylus

SYLVAIN (French) a form of Silvan, Sylvester.
Sylvan, Sylvian

SYLVESTER (Latin) forest dweller.
Silvester, Silvestro, Sly, Syl, Sylvain, Sylverster, Sylvestre

SYMINGTON (English) Simon's town, Simon's estate.

SYMON (Greek) a form of Simon.
Sy, Syman, Symeon, Symion, Symms, Symon, Symone

SZCZEPAN (Polish) a form of Stephen.

SZYGFRID (Hungarian) a form of Siegfried.
Szigfrid

SZYMON (Polish) a form of Simon.

T

TAAVETI (Finnish) a form of David.
Taavi, Taavo

TAB (German) shining, brilliant. (English) drummer.
Tabb, Tabbie, Tabby

TABARI (Arabic) he remembers. History: a Muslim historian.
Tabahri, Tabares, Tabarious, Tabarius, Tabarus, Tabur

TABIB (Turkish) physician.
Tabeeb

TABO (Spanish) a short form of Gustave.

TABOR (Persian) drummer. (Hungarian) encampment.
Tabber, Taber, Taboras, Taibor, Tayber, Taybor, Taver

TAD (Greek, Latin) a short form of Thaddeus. (Welsh) father.
Tadd, Taddy, Tade, Tadek, Tadey

TADAN (Native American) plentiful.
Taden

TADARIUS (American) a combination of the prefix Ta + Darius.
Tadar, Tadarious, Tadaris, Tadarrius

TADDEO (Italian) a form of Thaddeus.
Tadeo

TADDEUS (Greek, Latin) an alternate form of Thaddeus.
Taddeous, Taddeusz, Taddius, Tadeas, Tades, Tadeusz, Tadio, Tadious

TADI (Omaha) wind.

TADZI (Carrier) loon.

TADZIO (Polish, Spanish) a form of Thaddeus.
Taddeusz

TAFFY (Welsh) a form of David. (English) a familiar form of Taft.

TAFT (English) river.
Taffy, Tafton

TAGE (Danish) day.
Tag

TAGGART (Irish) son of the priest.
Tagart, Taggert

TAHÍR (Arabic) innocent, pure.
Taheer

TAI (Vietnamese) weather; prosperous; talented.

TAIMA (Native American) born during a storm.

TAISHAWN (American) a combination of Tai + Shawn.
Taisen, Taishaun, Taishon

TAIT (Scandinavian) an alternate form of Tate.
Taite, Taitt

TAIWAN (Chinese) island; island dweller. Geography: a country off the coast of mainland China.
Taewon, Tahwan, Taivon, Taiwain, Tawain, Tawan, Tawann, Tawaun, Tawon, Taywan, Tywan

TAIWO (Yoruba) first-born of twins.

TAJ (Urdu) crown.
Taje, Tajee, Tajeh, Tajh, Taji

TAJO (Spanish) day.
Taio

TAJUAN (American) a combination of the prefix Ta + Juan.
Taijuan, Taijun, Taijuon, Tájuan, Tajwan, Taquan, Tyjuan

TAKEO (Japanese) strong as bamboo.
Takeyo

TAKIS (Greek) a familiar form of Peter.
Takias, Takius

TAKODA (Lakota) friend to everyone.

TAL (Hebrew) dew; rain.
Tali, Talia, Talley, Talor, Talya

TALBERT (German) bright valley.

TALBOT (French) boot maker.
Talbott, Tallbot, Tallbott, Tallie, Tally

TALCOTT (English) cottage near the lake.

TALE (Tswana) green.

TALEN (English) an alternate form of Talon.
Talin, Tallen

TALIB (Arabic) seeker.

TALIESIN (Welsh) radiant brow.
Tallas, Tallis

TALIKI (Hausa) fellow.

TALLI (Lenape) legendary hero.

TALMADGE (English) lake between two towns.
Talmage

TALMAI (Aramaic) mound; furrow. Bible: a king of Geshur and father-in-law of King David.
Telem

TALMAN (Aramaic) injured; oppressed.
Talmon

TALON (French, English) claw, nail.
Taelon, Taelyn, Talen, Tallin, Tallon, Talyn

TALOR (English) a form of Tal. An alternate form of Taylor.
Taelor, Taelur

TAM (Hebrew) honest. (English) a short form of Thomas. (Vietnamese) number eight.
Tama, Tamas, Tamás, Tameas, Tamlane, Tammany, Tammas, Tammen, Tammy

TAMAN (Slavic) dark, black.
Tama, Tamann, Tamin, Tamon, Tamone

TAMAR (Hebrew) date; palm tree.
Tamarie, Tamario, Tamarr, Timur

TAMBO (Swahili) vigorous.

TAMIR (Arabic) tall as a palm tree.
Tameer

TAMMY (English) a familiar form of Thomas.
Tammie

TAMSON (Scandinavian) son of Thomas.
Tamsen

TAN (Burmese) million. (Vietnamese) new.
Than

TANEK (Greek) immortal. See also Atek.

TANELI (Finnish) God is my judge.
Taneil, Tanell, Tanella

TANER (English) an alternate form of Tanner.
Tanar

TANGUY (French) warrior.

TANI (Japanese) valley.

TANMAY (Sanskrit) engrossed.

TANNER (English) leather worker, tanner.
Tan, Taner, Tanery, Tann, Tannar, Tannir, Tannor, Tanny

TANNIN (English) tan-colored, dark.
Tanin, Tannen, Tannon, Tanyen, Tanyon

TANNY (English) a familiar form of Tanner.
Tana, Tannee, Tanney, Tannie, Tany

TANO (Spanish) camp glory. (Russian) a short form of Stanislaus. (Ghanian) Geography: a river in Ghana.
Tanno

TANTON (English) town by the still river.

TAPAN (Sanskrit) sun; summer.

TAPANI (Finnish) a form of Stephen.
Tapamn, Teppo

TÄPKO (Kiowa) antelope.

TAQUAN (American) a combination of the prefix Ta + Quan.
Taquann, Taquawn, Taquon, Taqwan

TARAK (Sanskrit) star; protector.

TARAN (Sanskrit) heaven.
Tarran

TAREK (Arabic) an alternate form of Táriq.
Tareek, Tareke

TARELL (German) an alternate form of Terrell.
Tarelle, Tarrel, Tarrell, Taryl

TAREN (American) an alternate form of Taron.
Tarren, Tarrin

TARIF (Arabic) uncommon.
Tareef

TARIK (Arabic) an alternate form of Táriq.
Taric, Tarick, Tariek, Tarikh, Tarrick, Tarrik, Taryk

TÁRIQ (Arabic) conqueror. History: Tarik was the Muslim general who conquered Spain.
Tareck, Tarek, Tarik, Tarique, Tarreq, Tereik

TARLETON (English) Thor's settlement.
Tarlton

TARO (Japanese) first-born male.

TARON (American) a combination of Tad + Ron.
Taeron, Tahron, Taren, Tarone, Tarrion, Tarron, Taryn

TARRANT (Welsh) thunder.
Terrant

TARUN (Sanskrit) young, youth.
Taran

TARVER (English) tower; hill; leader.
Terver

TARYN (American) an alternate form of Taron.
Tarryn, Taryon

TAS (Gypsy) bird's nest.

TASHAWN (American) a combination of the prefix Ta + Shawn.
Tashaan, Tashan, Tashaun, Tashon, Tashun

TASS (Hungarian) ancient mythology name.

TASUNKE (Dakota) horse.

TATE (Scandinavian, English) cheerful. (Native American) long-winded talker.
Tait, Tayte

TATIUS (Latin) king, ruler. History: a Sabine king.
Tatianus, Tazio, Titus

TATUM (English) cheerful.

TAU (Tswana) lion.

TAUNO (Finnish) a form of Donald.

TAUREAN (Latin) strong; forceful. Astrology: born under the sign of Taurus.
Tauraun, Taurein, Taurin, Taurion, Taurone, Taurus

TAURUS (Latin) an alternate form of Taurean.
Taurice, Tauris

TAVARES (Aramaic) an alternate form of Tavor.
Tarvarres, Tavarres, Taveress

TAVARIS (Aramaic) an alternate form of Tavor.

Tavaris (cont.)
Tarvaris, Tavar, Tavaras, Tavari, Tavarian, Tavarious, Tavarius, Tavarous, Tavarri, Tavarris, Tavars, Tavarse, Tavarus, Tevaris, Tevarius, Tevarus

TAVEY (Latin) a familiar form of Octavio.

TAVI (Aramaic) good.

TAVIAN (Latin) a short form of Octavio.
Taveon, Taviann, Tavien, Tavieon, Tavin, Tavio, Tavion, Tavionne, Tavon, Tayvon

TAVISH (Scottish) a form of Thomas.
Tav, Tavi, Tavis

TAVO (Slavic) a short form of Gustave.

TAVON (American) a form of Tavian.
Tavonn, Tavonne, Tavonni

TAVOR (Aramaic) misfortune.
Tarvoris, Tavares, Tavaris, Tavores, Tavorious, Tavoris, Tavorise, Tavorres, Tavorris, Tavuris

TAWNO (Gypsy) little one.
Tawn

TAYIB (Hindi) good; delicate.

TAYLER (English) an alternate form of Taylor.
Tailer, Taylar, Tayller, Teyler

TAYLOR (English) tailor.
Tailor, Talor, Tayler, Tayllor, Taylour, Taylr, Teylor

TAYSHAWN (American) a combination of Taylor + Shawn.
Taysean, Tayshan, Tayshun, Tayson

TAYVON (American) a form of Tavian.
Tayvan, Tayvaughn, Tayven, Tayveon, Tayvin, Tayvohn, Taywon

TAZ (Arabic) shallow ornamental cup.
Tazz

TAZIO (Italian) a form of Tatius.

TEAGAN (Irish) an alternate form of Teague.
Teagen, Teagun, Teegan

TEAGUE (Irish) bard, poet.
Teag, Teagan, Teage, Teak, Tegan, Teige

TEARENCE (Latin) an alternate form of Terrence.
Tearance, Tearnce, Tearrance

TEARLACH (Scottish) a form of Charles.

TEARLE (English) stern, severe.

TEASDALE (English) river dweller. Geography: a river in England.

TEB (Spanish) a short form of Stephen.

TED (English) a short form of Edward, Edwin, Theodore.
Tedd, Tedek, Tedik, Tedson

TEDDY (English) a familiar form of Edward, Theodore.
Teddey, Teddie, Tedy

TEDMUND (English) protector of the land.
Tedman, Tedmond

TEDORIK (Polish) a form of Theodore.
Teodoor, Teodor, Teodorek

TEDRICK (American) a combination of Ted + Rick.
Teddrick, Tederick, Tedric

TEETONKA (Lakota) big lodge.

TEFERE (Ethiopian) seed.

TEGAN (Irish) an alternate form of Teague.
Teghan, Teigan, Tiegan

TEJ (Sanskrit) light; lustrous.

TEJAS (Sanskrit) sharp.

TEKLE (Ethiopian) plant.

TELEK (Polish) a form of Telford.

TELEM (Hebrew) mound; furrow.
Talmai, Tel

TELFORD (French) iron cutter.
Telek, Telfer, Telfor, Telfour

TELLER (English) storyteller.
Tell, Telly

TELLY (Greek) a familiar form of Teller, Theodore.

TELMO (English) tiller, cultivator.

TELUTCI (Moquelumnan) bear making dust as it runs.

TELVIN (American) a combination of the prefix Te + Melvin.
Tellvin, Telvan

TEM (Gypsy) country.

TEMAN (Hebrew) on the right side; southward.

TEMBO (Swahili) elephant.

TEMPEST (French) storm.

TEMPLE (Latin) sanctuary.

TEMPLETON (English) town near the temple.
Temp, Templeten

TENNANT (English) tenant, renter.
Tenant, Tennent

TENNESSEE (Cherokee) mighty warrior. Geography: a state in the American south.
Tennessee, Tennesy, Tennysee

TENNYSON (English) an alternate form of Dennison.
Tenney, Tenneyson, Tennie, Tennis, Tennison, Tenny, Tenson

TEO (Vietnamese) a form of Tom.

TEOBALDO (Italian, Spanish) a form of Theobald.

TEODORO (Italian, Spanish) a form of Theodore.
Teodore, Teodorico

TEPPO (French) a familiar form of Stephen.

TEQUAN (American) a combination of the prefix Te + Quan.
Tequinn, Tequon

TERANCE (Latin) an alternate form of Terrence.
Terriance

TERELL (German) an alternate form of Terrell.
Tarell, Tereall, Terel, Terelle, Tyrel

TEREMUN (Tiv) father's acceptance.

TERENCE (Latin) an alternate form of Terrence.
Teren, Teryn

TERENCIO (Spanish) a form of Terrence.

TERRAN (Latin) a short form of Terrance.
Teran, Teren, Terran, Terren

TERRANCE (Latin) an alternate form of Terrence.
Tarrance, Terran

TERRELL (German) thunder ruler.
Terell, Terrail, Terral, Terrale, Terrall, Terreal, Terrel, Terrelle, Terrill, Terryal, Terryel, Tirel, Tirrel, Tirrell, Turrell, Tyrel, Tyrell

TERRENCE (Latin) smooth.
Tarrance, Tearence, Terance, Terence, Terencio, Terrance, Terren, Terrin, Terry, Torrence, Tyreese

TERRICK (American) a combination of the prefix Te + Derrick.
Teric, Terick, Terik, Teriq, Terric, Terrik, Tirek, Tirik

TERRILL (German) an alternate form of Terrell.
Teriel, Teriell, Terril, Terryl, Terryll, Teryll, Teryl, Tyrill

TERRIN (Latin) a short form of Terrence.
Terin, Terrien, Terryn, Teryn, Tiren

TERRIS (Latin) son of Terry.

TERRON (American) a form of Tyrone.
Tereon, Terion, Terione, Teron, Terone, Terrion, Terrione, Terriyon, Terrone, Terronn, Terryon, Tiron

TERRY (English) a familiar form of Terrence. See also Keli.
Tarry, Terrey, Terri, Terrie, Tery

TERTIUS (Latin) third.

TESHAWN (American) a combination of the prefix Te + Shawn.
Tesean, Teshaun, Teshon

TEVA (Hebrew) nature.

TEVAN (American) an alternate form of Tevin.
Tevaughan, Tevaughn, Teven, Tevvan

TEVEL (Yiddish) a form of David.

TEVIN (American) a combination of the prefix Te + Kevin.
Teavin, Teivon, Tevan, Tevien, Tevinn, Tevon, Tevvin, Tevyn

TEVIS (Scottish) a form of Thomas.
Tevish

TEVON (American) an alternate form of Tevin.
Tevion, Tevohn, Tevone, Tevonne, Tevoun, Teyvon

TEWDOR (German) a form of Theodore.

TEX (American) from Texas.
Tejas

THABIT (Arabic) firm, strong.

THAD (Greek, Latin) a short form of Thaddeus.
Thadd, Thade, Thadee, Thady

THADDEUS (Greek) courageous. (Latin) praiser. Bible: one of the Twelve Apostles. See also Fadey.
Tad, Taddeo, Taddeus, Thaddis, Thadeaus, Tadzio, Thad, Thaddaeus, Thaddaus, Thaddeau, Thaddeaus, Thaddeo, Thaddeous, Thaddiaus, Thaddius, Thadeaou, Thadeous, Thadeus, Thadieus, Thadious, Thadius, Thadus

THADY (Irish) praise.
Thaddy

THAI (Vietnamese) many, multiple.

THAMAN (Hindi) god; godlike. Religion: another name for the Hindu god Shiva.

THAN (Burma) million.
Tan, Thanh

THANE (English) attendant warrior.
Thain, Thaine, Thayne

THANG (Vietnamese) victorious.

THANH (Vietnamese) finished.

THANIEL (Hebrew) a short form of Nathaniel.

THANOS (Greek) nobleman; bear-man.
Athanasios, Thanasis

THATCHER (English) roof thatcher, repairer of roofs.
Thacher, Thatch, Thaxter

THAW (English) melting ice.

THAYER (French) nation's army.
Thay

THEL (English) upper story.

THENGA (Yao) bring him.

THEO (English) a short form of
Theodore.

THEOBALD (German) people's prince.
See also Dietbald.
*Teobaldo, Thebault, Theòbault, Thibault,
Tibalt, Tibold, Tiebold, Tiebout, Toiboid,
Tybald, Tybalt, Tybault*

THEODORE (Greek) gift of God.
See also Feodor, Fyodor.
*Téadóir, Teador, Ted, Teddy, Tedor, Tedorek,
Tedorik, Telly, Teodomiro, Teodoro, Teodus,
Teos, Tewdor, Theo, Theodor, Theódor,
Theodors, Theodorus, Theodosios, Theodrekr,
Tivadar, Todor, Tolek, Tudor*

THEODORIC (German) ruler of the
people. See also Dedrick, Derek, Dirk.
Teodorico, Thedric, Thedrick, Thierry, Till

THEOPHILUS (Greek) loved by God.
Teofil, Théophile, Theophlous, Theopolis

THERON (Greek) hunter.
*Theran, Theren, Thereon, Therin, Therion,
Therrin, Therron, Theryn, Theryon*

THIAN (Vietnamese) smooth.
Thien

THIBAULT (French) a form of
Theobald.
Thibaud, Thibaut

THIERRY (French) a form of Theodoric.
Theirry, Theory

THOM (English) a short form of
Thomas.
Thomy

THOMA (German) a form of Thomas.

THOMAS (Greek, Aramaic) twin. Bible:
one of the Twelve Apostles. See also
Chuma, Foma, Maslin.

*Tam, Tammy, Tavish, Tevis, Thom, Thoma,
Thomason, Thomaz, Thomeson, Thomison,
Thommas, Thompson, Thomson, Tom, Toma,
Tomas, Tomás, Tomasso, Tomcy, Tomey,
Tomey, Tomi, Tommy, Toomas*

THOMPSON (English) son of Thomas.
Thomason, Thomison, Thomsen, Thomson

THOR (Scandinavian) thunder.
Mythology: the Norse god of thunder
and war.
Thorin, Tor, Tyrus

THORALD (Scandinavian) Thor's
follower.
Terrell, Terrill, Thorold, Torald

THORBERT (Scandinavian) Thor's
brightness.
Torbert

THORBJORN (Scandinavian) Thor's
bear.
Thorburn, Thurborn, Thurburn

THORGOOD (English) Thor is good.

THORLEIF (Scandinavian) Thor's
beloved.
Thorlief

THORLEY (English) Thor's meadow.
Thorlea, Thorlee, Thorleigh, Thorly, Torley

THORNDIKE (English) thorny
embankment.
Thorn, Thorndyck, Thorndyke, Thorne

THORNE (English) a short form of
names beginning with 'Thorn.'
Thorn, Thornie, Thorny

THORNLEY (English) thorny meadow.
*Thorley, Thorne, Thornlea, Thornleigh,
Thornly*

THORNTON (English) thorny town.
Thorne

THORPE (English) village.
Thorp

THORWALD (Scandinavian) Thor's forest.
Thorvald

THUC (Vietnamese) aware.

THURLOW (English) Thor's hill.
Thurlo

THURMOND (English) defended by Thor.
Thormond, Thurmund

THURSTON (Scandinavian) Thor's stone.
Thorstein, Thorstein, Thorsten, Thurstain, Thurstan, Thursten, Torsten, Torston

TIAGO (Spanish) a form of Jacob.

TIBERIO (Italian) from the Tibor River region.
Tiberias, Tiberious, Tiberiu, Tiberius, Tibius, Tyberious, Tyberius, Tyberrius

TIBOR (Hungarian) holy place.
Tiburcio

TICHAWANNA (Shona) we shall see.

TICHO (Spanish) a short form of Patrick.

TIELER (English) an alternate form of Tyler.
Tielar, Tielor, Tielyr

TIENNOT (French) a form of Stephen.
Tien

TIERNAN (Irish) lord.

TIERNEY (Irish) lordly.
Tiarnach, Tiernan

TIGE (English) a short form of Tiger.
Ti, Tig, Tighe, Ty, Tyg, Tyge, Tygh, Tyghe

TIGER (American) tiger; powerful and energetic.
Tige, Tigger, Tyger

TIIMU (Moquelumnan) caterpiller coming out of the ground.

TILDEN (English) tilled valley.
Tildon

TIKTU (Moquelumnan) bird digging up potatoes.

TILFORD (English) prosperous ford.

TILL (German) a short form of Theodoric.
Thilo, Til, Tillman, Tilman, Tillmann, Tilson

TILTON (English) prosperous town.

TIM (Greek) a short form of Timothy.
Timmie, Timmy

TIMIN (Arabic) born near the sea. Mythology: sea serpent.

TIMMOTHY (Greek) an alternate form of Timothy.
Timmathy, Timmithy, Timmoty, Timmthy

TIMMY (Greek) a familiar form of Timothy.
Timmie

TIMO (Finnish) a form of Timothy.
Timio

TIMOFEY (Russian) a form of Timothy.
Timofei, Timofej, Timofeo

TIMON (Greek) honorable. History: a famous Greek philosopher.

TIMOTEO (Portuguese, Spanish) a form of Timothy.

TIMOTHY (Greek) honoring God. See also Kimokeo.
Tadhg, Taidgh, Tiege, Tim, Tima, Timithy, Timka, Timkin, Timmothy, Timmy, Timo, Timofey, Timok, Timon, Timontheo, Timonthy, Timót, Timote, Timotei, Timoteo, Timoteus, Timothé, Timothée, Timotheo, Timotheos, Timotheus, Timothey, Timothie, Timthie, Tiomóid, Tisha, Tomothy, Tymon, Tymothy

TIMUR (Hebrew) an alternate form of Tamar. (Russian) conqueror.
Timour

TIN (Vietnamese) thinker.

TINO (Greek) a short form of Augustine. (Spanish) venerable, majestic. (Italian) small. A familiar form of Antonio.
Tion

TINSLEY (English) fortified field.

TIQUAN (American) a combination of the prefix Ti + Quan.
Tiquawn, Tiquine, Tiquon, Tiquwan, Tiqwan

TISHA (Russian) a form of Timothy.
Tishka

TISHAWN (American) a combination of the prefix Ti + Shawn.
Tishaan, Tishaun, Tishean, Tishon, Tishun

TITO (Italian) a form of Titus.
Titas, Titis, Titos

TITUS (Greek) giant. (Latin) hero. Bible: a recipient of one of Paul's New Testament letters.
Tite, Titek, Tito, Tytus

TIVON (Hebrew) nature lover.

TJ (American) a combination of the initials T. + J.
Teejay, Tj, T.J., T Jae, Tjayda

TOBAL (Spanish) a short form of Christopher.
Tabalito

TOBAR (Gypsy) road.

TOBI (Yoruba) great.

TOBIAS (Hebrew) God is good.
Tobia, Tobiah, Tobiás, Tobiath, Tobin, Tobit, Toby, Tobyas, Tuvya

TOBIN (Hebrew) an alternate form of Tobias.
Toben, Tobian, Tobyn, Tovin

TOBY (Hebrew) a familiar form of Tobias.
Tobbie, Tobby, Tobe, Tobee, Tobey, Tobie

TODD (English) fox.
Tod, Toddie, Toddy

TODOR (Basque, Russian) a form of Theodore.
Teodor, Todar, Todas, Todos

TOFT (English) small farm.

TOHON (Native American) cougar.

TOKALA (Dakota) fox.

TOLAND (English) owner of taxed land.
Tolan

TOLBERT (English) bright tax collector.

TOLLER (English) tax collector.

TOM (English) a short form of Tomas, Thomas.
Teo, Thom, Tommey, Tommie, Tommy

TOMA (Romanian) a form of Thomas.
Tomah

TOMAS (German) a form of Thomas.
Tom, Tomaisin, Tomaz, Tomcio, Tome, Tomek, Tomelis, Tomico, Tomik, Tomislaw, Tommas, Tomo, Tomson

TOMÁS (Irish, Spanish) a form of Thomas.
Tomas, Tómas, Tomasz

TOMASSO (Italian) a form of Thomas.
Tomaso, Tommaso

TOMBE (Kakwa) northerners. Geography: a village in northern Uganda.

TOMEY (Irish) a familiar form of Thomas.
Tome, Tomi, Tomie, Tomy

TOMI (Japanese) rich. (Hungarian) a form of Thomas.

TOMLIN (English) little Tom.
Tomkin, Tomlinson

TOMMIE (Hebrew) an alternate form of Tommy.
Tommi

TOMMY (Hebrew) a familiar form of Thomas.
Tommie, Tomy

TONDA (Czech) a form of Tony.
Tonek

TONG (Vietnamese) fragrant.

TONI (Greek, German, Slavic) a form of Tony.
Tonee, Tonie, Tonio, Tonis, Tonnie

TONIO (Portuguese) a form of Tony. (Italian) a short form of Antonio.
Tono, Tonyo

TONY (Greek) flourishing. (Latin) praiseworthy. (English) a short form of Anthony. A familiar form of Remington.
Tonda, Tonek, Toney, Toni, Tonik, Tonio, Tonny

TOOANTUH (Cherokee) spring frog.

TOOMAS (Estonian) a form of Thomas.
Toomis, Tuomas, Tuomo

TOPHER (Greek) a short form of Christopher, Kristopher.
Tofer, Tophor

TOPO (Spanish) gopher.

TOPPER (English) hill.

TOR (Norwegian) thunder. (Tiv) royalty, king.
Thor

TORIAN (Irish) an alternate form of Torin.
Toran, Torean, Toriano, Toriaun, Torien, Torrian, Torrien, Torryan

TORIN (Irish) chief.
Thorfin, Thorstein, Torian, Torion, Torrin, Toryn

TORKEL (Swedish) Thor's cauldron.

TORMEY (Irish) thunder spirit.
Tormé, Tormee

TORMOD (Scottish) north.

TORN (Irish) a short form of Torrence.
Toran

TORQUIL (Danish) Thor's kettle.
Torkel

TORR (English) tower.
Tory

TORRANCE (Irish) an alternate form of Torrence.
Torance

TORREN (Irish) a short form of Torrence.
Torehn, Toren

TORRENCE (Latin) an alternate form of Terrence. (Irish) knolls.
Tawrence, Toreence, Torence, Torenze, Torey, Torin, Torn, Torr, Torrance, Torren, Torreon, Torrin, Torry, Tory, Torynce, Tuarence, Turance

TORREY (English) an alternate form of Tory.
Toreey, Torie, Torre, Torri, Torrie, Torry

TORU (Japanese) sea.

TORY (English) familiar form of Torr, Torrence.
Torey, Tori, Torrey

TOSHI-SHITA (Japanese) junior.

TOVI (Hebrew) good.
Tov

TOWNLEY (English) town meadow.
Townlea, Townlee, Townleigh, Townlie,
Townly

TOWNSEND (English) town's end.
Town, Townes, Towney, Townie, Townsen,
Townshend, Towny

TRACE (Irish) an alternate form of Tracy.
Trayce

TRACEY (Irish) an alternate form of Tracy.
Traci

TRACY (Greek) harvester. (Latin)
courageous. (Irish) battler.
Trace, Tracey, Tracie, Treacy

TRADER (English) well-trodden path;
skilled worker.

TRAE (English) an alternate form of Trey.
Trai, Traie, Tre, Trea

TRAHERN (Welsh) strong as iron.
Traherne, Tray

TRAMAINE (Scottish) an alternate
form of Tremaine, Tremayne.
Tramain, Traman, Tramane, Tramayne,
Traymain, Traymon

TRAQUAN (American) a combination
of Travis + Quan.
Traequan, Traqon, Traquon, Traqwan,
Traqwaun, Trayquan, Trayquane, Trayqwon

TRASHAWN (American) a
combination of Travis + Shawn.
Trasen, Trashaun, Trasean, Trashon,
Trashone, Trashun, Trayshaun, Trayshawn

TRAUGOTT (German) God's truth.

TRAVARIS (French) an alternate form
of Travers.
Travares, Travaress, Travarious, Travarius,
Travarous, Travarus, Travauris, Traveress,
Traverez, Traverus, Travoris, Travorus

TRAVELL (English) traveller.
Travail, Travale, Travel, Travelis, Travelle,
Trevel, Trevell, Trevelle

TRAVEN (American) an alternate form
of Trevon.
Travin, Travine, Trayven

TRAVERS (French) crossroads.
Travaris, Traver, Travis

TRAVION (American) an alternate
form of Trevon.
Traveon, Travian, Travien, Travione,
Travioun

TRAVIS (English) a form of Travers.
Travais, Travees, Traves, Traveus, Travious,
Traviss, Travius, Travous, Travus, Travys,
Trayvis, Trevais, Trevis

TRAVON (American) an alternate form
of Trevon.
Traevon, Traivon, Travone, Travonn,
Travonne

TRAY (English) an alternate form of
Trey.
Traye

TRAYTON (English) town full of trees.
Trayten

TRAYVON (American) a combination
of Tray + Von.
Trayveon, Trayvin, Trayvion, Trayvond,
Trayvone, Trayvonne, Trayvyon

TREAVON (American) an alternate
form of Trevon.
Treavan, Treavin, Treavion

TREDWAY (English) well-worn road.
Treadway

TREMAINE, Tremayne (Scottish)
house of stone.
Tramaine, Tremain, Tremane, Treymaine,
Trimaine

TRENT (Latin) torrent, rapid stream. (French) thirty. Geography: a city in northern Italy.
Trente, Trentino, Trento, Trentonio

TRENTON (Latin) town by the rapid stream. Geography: a city in New Jersey.
Trendon, Trendun, Trenten, Trentin, Trentton, Trentyn, Trinten, Trintin, Trinton

TREQUAN (American) a combination of Trey + Quan.
Trequanne, Trequaun, Trequian, Trequon, Treqwon, Treyquane

TRESHAWN (American) a combination of Trey + Shawn.
Treshaun, Treshon, Treshun, Treysean, Treyshawn, Treyshon

TRESTON (Welsh) an alternate form of Tristan.
Trestan, Trestin, Trestton, Trestyn

TREV (Irish, Welsh) a short form of Trevor.

TREVAUGHN (American) a combination of Trey + Vaughn.
Trevaughan, Trevaugn, Trevaun, Trevaune, Trevaunn, Treyvaughn

TREVELYAN (English) Elian's homestead.

TREVIN (American) an alternate form of Trevon.
Trevian, Trevien, Trevine, Trevinne, Trevyn, Treyvin

TREVION (American) an alternate form of Trevon.
Trevione, Trevionne, Trevyon, Treyveon, Treyvion

TREVIS (English) an alternate form of Travis.
Treves, Trevez, Treveze, Trevius

TREVON (American) a combination of Trey + Von.
Traven, Travion, Travon, Tre, Treavon, Trévan, Treveyon, Trevin, Trevion, Trevohn, Trevoine, Trévon, Trevone, Trevonn, Trevonne, Treyvon

TREVOR (Irish) prudent. (Welsh) homestead.
Travor, Treavor, Trebor, Trefor, Trev, Trevar, Trevares, Trevarious, Trevaris, Trevarius, Trevaros, Trevarus, Trever, Trevore, Trevores, Trevoris, Trevorus, Trevour, Trevyr, Treyvor

TREY (English) three; third.
Trae, Trai, Tray, Treye, Tri, Trie

TREYVON (American) an alternate form of Trevon.
Treyvan, Treyven, Treyvenn, Treyvone, Treyvonn, Treyvun

TRIGG (Scandinavian) trusty.

TRINI (Latin) a short form of Trinity.

TRINITY (Latin) holy trinity.
Trenedy, Trini, Trinidy

TRIP, Tripp (English) traveler.

TRISTAN (Welsh) bold. Literature: a knight in the Arthurian legends who fell in love with his uncle's wife.
Treston, Tris, Trisan, Tristain, Tristano, Tristen, Tristian, Tristin, Triston, Tristyn, Trystan

TRISTANO (Italian) a form of Tristan.

TRISTEN (Welsh) an alternate form of Tristan.
Trisden, Trissten

TRISTIN (Welsh) an alternate form of Tristan.
Tristian, Tristinn

TRISTON (Welsh) an alternate form of Tristan.

TRISTRAM (Welsh) sorrowful. Literature: the title character in Laurence Sterne's eighteenth-century novel *Tristram Shandy*.
Tristam

TRISTYN (Welsh) an alternate form of Tristan.
Tristynne

TROT (English) trickling stream.

TROWBRIDGE (English) bridge by the tree.

TROY (Irish) foot soldier. (French) curly haired. (English) water. See also Koi.
Troi, Troye, Troyton

TRUE (English) faithful, loyal.
Tru

TRUESDALE (English) faithful one's homestead.

TRUITT (English) little and honest.
Truett

TRUMAN (English) honest. History: Harry S Truman was the thirty-third U.S. president.
Trueman, Trumain, Trumaine, Trumann

TRUMBLE (English) strong; bold.
Trumball, Trumbell, Trumbull

TRUSTIN (English) trustworthy.
Trustan, Trusten, Truston

TRYGVE (Norwegian) brave victor.

TRYSTAN (Welsh) an alternate form of Tristan.
Tryistan, Trysten, Trystian, Trystin, Trystn, Tryston, Trystyn

TSALANI (Ngoni) good-bye.

TSE (Ewe) younger of twins.

TU (Vietnamese) tree.

TUACO (Ghanian) eleventh-born.

TUAN (Vietnamese) goes smoothly.

TUCKER (English) fuller, tucker of cloth.
Tuck, Tuckie, Tucky, Tuckyr

TUDOR (Welsh) a form of Theodore. History: an English dynasty.
Todor

TUG (Scandinavian) draw, pull.
Tugg

TUKETU (Moquelumnan) bear making dust as it runs.

TUKULI (Moquelumnan) caterpillar crawling down a tree.

TULIO (Italian, Spanish) lively.
Tullio

TULLIS (Latin) title, rank.
Tullius, Tullos, Tully

TULLY (Latin) a familiar form of Tullis. (Irish) at peace with God.
Tull, Tulley, Tullie, Tullio

TUMAINI (Mwera) hope.

TUMU (Moquelumnan) deer thinking about eating wild onions.

TUNG (Vietnamese) stately, dignified. (Chinese) everyone.

TUNGAR (Sanskrit) high; lofty.

TUPI (Moquelumnan) pulled up.

TUPPER (English) ram raiser.

TURI (Spanish) a short form of Arthur.
Ture

TURK (English) from Turkey.

TURNER (Latin) lathe worker; woodworker.

TURPIN (Scandinavian) Finn named after Thor.

TUT (Arabic) strong and courageous.
History: a short form of Tutankhamen,
an Egyptian pharoah.
Tutt

TUTU (Spanish) a familiar form of
Justin.

TUVYA (Hebrew) an alternate form
of Tobias.
Tevya, Tuvia, Tuviah

TUWILE (Mwera) death is inevitable.

TUYEN (Vietnamese) angel.

TWAIN (English) divided in two.
Literature: Mark Twain (whose real
name was Samuel Clemens) was one of
the most prominent nineteenth-century
American writers.
*Tawine, Twaine, Twan, Twane, Tway, Twayn,
Twayne*

TWIA (Fante) born after twins.

TWITCHELL (English) narrow passage.
Twytchell

TWYFORD (English) double river
crossing.

TXOMIN (Basque) like the Lord.

TY (English) a short form of Tyler,
Tyrone, Tyrus.
Tye

TYEE (Native American) chief.

TYGER (English) a form of Tiger.
Tige, Tyg, Tygar

TYLAR (English) an alternate form of
Tyler.
Tyelar, Tylarr

TYLER (English) tile maker.
*Tieler, Tiler, Ty, Tyel, Tyeler, Tyelor, Tyhler,
Tylar, Tyle, Tylee, Tylere, Tyller, Tylor, Tylyr*

TYLOR (English) an alternate form of
Tyler.
Tylour

TYMON (Polish) a form of Timothy.
*Tymain, Tymaine, Tymane, Tymeik, Tymek,
Tymen*

TYMOTHY (English) a form of Timothy.
*Tymithy, Tymmothy, Tymoteusz, Tymothee,
Timothi*

TYNAN (Irish) dark.
Ty

TYNEK (Czech) a form of Martin.
Tynko

TYQUAN (American) a combination
of Ty + Quan.
*Tykwan, Tykwane, Tykwon, Tyquaan,
Tyquane, Tyquann, Tyquine, Tyquinn,
Tyquon, Tyquone, Tyquwon, Tyqwan*

TYRAN (American) a form of Tyrone.
Tyraine, Tyrane

TYREE (Scottish) island dweller.
Geography: Tiree is an island off the
west coast of Scotland.
Tyra, Tyrae, Tyrai, Tyray, Tyre, Tyrea, Tyrée

TYREESE (American) a form of
Terrence.
*Tyreas, Tyrease, Tyrece, Tyreece, Tyreice,
Tyres, Tyrese, Tyresse, Tyrez, Tyreze, Tyrice,
Tyriece, Tyriese*

TYREL, Tyrell (American) forms of
Terrell.
Tyrelle, Tyrrel, Tyrrell

TYRICK (American) a combination
of Ty + Rick.
*Tyreck, Tyreek, Tyreik, Tyrek, Tyreke, Tyric,
Tyriek, Tyrik, Tyriq, Tyrique*

TYRIN (American) a form of Tyrone.
Tyrinn, Tyrion, Tyrrin, Tyryn

TYRON (American) a form of Tyrone.
Tyrohn, Tyronn, Tyronna, Tyronne

TYRONE (Greek) sovereign. (Irish) land of Owen.
Tayron, Tayrone, Teirone, Terron, Ty, Tyerone, Tyhrone, Tyran, Tyrin, Tyron, Tyroney, Tyronne, Tyroon, Tyroun

TYRUS (English) a form of Thor.
Ty, Tyruss, Tyryss

TYSHAWN (American) a combination of Ty + Shawn.
Tyshan, Tyshaun, Tyshauwn, Tyshian, Tyshinn, Tyshion, Tyshon, Tyshone, Tyshonne, Tyshun, Tyshunn, Tyshyn

TYSON (French) son of Ty.
Tison, Tiszon, Tyce, Tycen, Tyesn, Tyeson, Tysen, Tysie, Tysin, Tysne, Tysone

TYTUS (Polish) a form of Titus.
Tyus

TYVON (American) a combination of Ty + Von.
Tyvan, Tyvin, Tyvinn, Tyvone, Tyvonne

TYWAN (Chinese) an alternate form of Taiwan.
Tywain, Tywaine, Tywane, Tywann, Tywaun, Tywen, Tywon, Tywone, Tywonne

TZADOK (Hebrew) righteous.
Tzadik, Zadok

TZION (Hebrew) sign from God.
Zion

TZURIEL (Hebrew) God is my rock.
Tzuriya

TZVI (Hebrew) deer.
Tzevi, Zevi

U

UAINE (Irish) a form of Owen.

UBADAH (Arabic) serves God.

UBAID (Arabic) faithful.

UBERTO (Italian) a form of Hubert.

UCHE (Ibo) thought.

UDAY (Sanskrit) to rise.

UDELL (English) yew-tree valley.
Dell, Eudel, Udale, Udall, Yudell

UDIT (Sanskrit) grown; shining.

UDO (Japanese) ginseng plant. (German) a short form of Udolf.

UDOLF (English) prosperous wolf.
Udo, Udolfo, Udolph

UGO (Italian) an alternate form of Hugh, Hugo.

UGUTZ (Basque) a form of John. Religion: name honoring John the Baptist.

UILLIAM (Irish) a form of William.
Uileog, Uilleam, Ulick

UINSEANN (Irish) a form of Vincent.

UISTEAN (Irish) intelligent.
Uisdean

UJA (Sanskrit) growing.

UKU (Hawaiian) flea, insect; skilled ukulele player.

ULAN (African) first-born twin.

ULBRECHT (German) an alternate form of Albert.

ULF (German) wolf.

ULFRED (German) peaceful wolf.

ULGER (German) warring wolf.

ULISES (Latin) an alternate form of Ulysses.
Ulishes, Ulisse, Ulisses

ULLOCK (German) sporting wolf.

ULMER (English) famous wolf.
Ullmar, Ulmar

ULMO (German) from Ulm, Germany.

ULRIC (German) an alternate form
of Ulrich.
Ullric

ULRICH (German) wolf ruler; ruler of
all. See also Alaric.
Uli, Ull, Ulric, Ulrick, Ulrik, Ulrike, Ulu, Ulz,
Uwe

ULTMAN (Hindi) god; godlike. Religion:
another name for the Hindu god Shiva.

ULYSES (Latin) an alternate form of
Ulysses.
Ulysee, Ulysees

ULYSSES (Latin) wrathful. A form
of Odysseus.
Eulises, Ulick, Ulises, Ulyses, Ulysse, Ulyssees,
Ulysses, Ulyssius

UMANG (Sanskrit) enthusiastic.
Umanga

UMAR (Arabic) an alternate form of
Omar.
Umair, Umarr, Umayr, Umer

UMBERTO (Italian) a form of Humbert.
Uberto

UMI (Yao) life.

UMIT (Turkish) hope.

UNAI (Basque) shepherd.
Una

UNER (Turkish) famous.

UNIKA (Lomwe) brighten.

UNIQUE (Latin) only, unique.
Uneek, Unek, Unikque, Uniqué, Unyque

UNWIN (English) nonfriend.
Unwinn, Unwyn

UPSHAW (English) upper wooded area.

UPTON (English) upper town.

UPWOOD (English) upper forest.

URBAN (Latin) city dweller; courteous.
Urbain, Urbaine, Urbane, Urbano, Urbanus,
Urvan, Urvane

URBANE (English) a form of Urban.

URBANO (Italian) a form of Urban.

URI (Hebrew) a short form of Uriah.
Urie

URIAH (Hebrew) my light. Bible: the
husband of Bathsheba and a captain
in David's army. See also Yuri.
Uri, Uria, Urias, Urijah

URIAN (Greek) heaven.
Urihaan

URIEL (Hebrew) God is my light.
Urie

URSON (French) a form of Orson.
Ursan, Ursus

URTZI (Basque) sky.

USAMAH (Arabic) like a lion.
Usama

USENI (Yao) tell me.
Usene, Usenet

USI (Yao) smoke.

USTIN (Russian) a form of Justin.

UTATCI (Moquelumnan) bear
scratching itself.

UTHMAN (Arabic) companion of the
Prophet.
Usman, Uthmaan

UTTAM (Sanskrit) best.

UWE (German) a familiar form of Ulrich.

UZI (Hebrew) my strength.
Uzzia

UZIEL (Hebrew) God is my strength; mighty force.
Uzie, Uzziah, Uzziel

UZOMA (Nigerian) born during a journey.

UZUMATI (Moquelumnan) grizzly bear.

V

VACHEL (French) small cow.
Vache, Vachell

VACLAV (Czech) wreath of glory.
Vasek

VADIN (Hindi) speaker.
Vaden

VAIL (English) valley.
Vaile, Vaill, Vale, Valle

VAL (Latin) a short form of Valentin.

VALBORG (Swedish) mighty mountain.

VALDEMAR (Swedish) famous ruler.

VALENTIN (Latin) strong; healthy.
Val, Valencio, Valenté, Valentijn, Valentine, Valentino, Valenton, Valentyn, Velentino

VALENTINO (Italian) a form of Valentin.

VALERIAN (Latin) strong; healthy.
Valeriano, Valerii, Valerio, Valeryn

VALERII (Russian) a form of Valerian.
Valera, Valerie, Valerij, Valerik, Valeriy, Valery

VALFRID (Swedish) strong peace.

VALIN (Hindi) an alternate form of Balin. Mythology: a tyrannical monkey king.

VALLIS (French) from Wales, England.
Valis

VALTER (Lithuanian, Swedish) a form of Walter.
Valters, Valther, Valtr, Vanda

VAN (Dutch) a short form of Vandyke.
Vander, Vane, Vann, Vanno

VANCE (English) thresher.

VANDA (Lithuanian) a form of Walter.
Vander

VANDYKE (Dutch) dyke.
Van

VANYA (Russian) a familiar form of Ivan.
Vanechka, Vanek, Vanja, Vanka, Vanusha, Wanya

VARDON (French) green knoll.
Vardaan, Varden, Verdan, Verdon, Verdun

VARIAN (Latin) variable.

VARICK (German) protecting ruler.
Varak, Varek, Warrick

VARTAN (Armenian) rose producer; rose giver.

VARUN (Hindi) rain god.
Varron

VASANT (Sanskrit) spring.
Vasanth

VASHAWN (American) a combination of the prefix Va + Shawn.
Vashae, Vashan, Vashann, Vashaun, Vashawnn, Vashon, Vashun, Vishon

VASILIS (Greek) an alternate form of Basil.

Vasilis (cont.)
Vas, Vasaya, Vaselios, Vashon, Vasil, Vasile, Vasileior, Vasileios, Vasilios, Vasilius, Vasilos, Vasilus, Vasily, Vassilios, Vasylko, Vasyltso, Vazul

VASILY (Russian) a form of Vasilis.
Vasilek, Vasili, Vasilii, Vasilije, Vasilik, Vasiliy, Vassili, Vassilij, Vasya, Vasyenka

VASIN (Hindi) ruler, lord.

VASU (Sanskrit) wealth.

VASYL (German, Slavic) a form of William.
Vasos, Vassily, Vassos, Vasya, Vasyuta, VaVaska, Wassily

VAUGHN (Welsh) small.
Vaughan, Vaughen, Vaun, Vaune, Von, Voughn

VEASNA (Cambodian) lucky.

VED (Sanskrit) sacred knowledge.

VEDIE (Latin) sight.

VEER (Sanskrit) brave.

VEGARD (Norwegian) sanctuary; protection.

VELVEL (Yiddish) wolf.

VENCEL (Hungarian) a short form of Wenceslaus.
Venci, Vencie

VENEDICTOS (Greek) a form of Benedict.
Venedict, Venediktos, Venka, Venya

VENIAMIN (Bulgarian) a form of Benjamin.
Venyamin, Verniamin

VENKAT (Hindi) god; godlike. Religion: another name for the Hindu god Shiva.

VENYA (Russian) a familiar form of Benedict.
Venedict, Venka

VERE (Latin, French) true.

VERED (Hebrew) rose.

VERGIL (Latin) an alternate form of Virgil.
Verge

VERN (Latin) a short form of Vernon.
Verna, Vernal, Verne, Verneal, Vernel, Vernell, Vernelle, Vernial, Vernine, Vernis, Vernol

VERNADOS (German) courage of the bear.

VERNER (German) defending army.
Varner

VERNEY (French) alder grove.
Vernie

VERNON (Latin) springlike; youthful.
Vern, Varnan, Vernen, Verney, Vernin

VERRILL (German) masculine. (French) loyal.
Verill, Verrall, Verrell, Verroll, Veryl

VIAN (English) full of life. A masculine short form of Vivian.

VIC (Latin) a short form of Victor.
Vick, Vicken, Vickenson

VICENTE (Spanish) a form of Vincent.
Vicent, Visente

VICENZO (Italian) a form of Vincent.

VICTOIR (French) a form of Victor.

VICTOR (Latin) victor, conqueror.
Vic, Victa, Victer, Victoir, Victoriano, Victorien, Victorin, Victorio, Viktor, Vitin, Vittorio, Vitya, Wikoli, Wiktor, Witek

VICTORIO (Spanish) a form of Victor.
Victorino

VIDAL (Spanish) a form of Vitas.
Vida, Vidale, Vidall, Videll

VIDAR (Norwegian) tree warrior.

VIDOR (Hungarian) cheerful.

VIDUR (Hindi) wise.

VIHO (Cheyenne) chief.

VIJAY (Hindi) victorious. Religion: another name for the Hindu god Shiva.

VIKAS (Hindi) growing.
Vikash, Vikesh

VIKRAM (Hindi) valorous.
Vikrum

VIKRANT (Hindi) powerful.
Vikran

VIKTOR (German, Hungarian, Russian) a form of Victor.
Viktoras, Viktors

VILHELM (German) a form of William.
Vilhelms, Vilho, Vilis, Viljo, Villem

VILI (Hungarian) a short form of William.
Villy, Vilmos

VILIAM (Czech) a form of William.
Vila, Vilek, Vilém, Viliami, Viliamu, Vilko, Vilous

VILJO (Finnish) a form of William.

VILLE (Swedish) a short form of William.

VIMAL (Hindi) pure.

VIN (Latin) a short form of Vincent.
Vinn

VINAY (Hindi) polite.

VINCE (English) a short form of Vincent.
Vence, Vint

VINCENT (Latin) victor, conqueror. See also Binkentios, Binky.
Uinseann, Vencent, Vicente, Vicenzo, Vikent, Vikenti, Vikesha, Vin, Vince,
Vincence, Vincens, Vincente, Vincentius, Vincents, Vincenty, Vincenzo, Vinci, Vincien, Vincient, Vinciente, Vincint, Vinny, Vinsent, Vinsint, Wincent

VINCENTE (Spanish) a form of Vincent.
Vencente

VINCENZO (Italian) a form of Vincent.
Vincenz, Vincenza, Vincenzio, Vinchenzo, Vinzenz

VINCI (Hungarian, Italian) a familiar form of Vincent.
Vinci, Vinco, Vincze

VINNY (English) a familiar form of Calvin, Melvin, Vincent.
Vinnee, Vinney, Vinni, Vinnie

VINOD (Hindi) happy, joyful.
Vinodh, Vinood

VINSON (English) son of Vincent.
Vinnis

VIPUL (Hindi) plentiful.

VIRAJ (Hindi) resplendent.

VIRAT (Hindi) very big.

VIRGIL (Latin) rod bearer, staff bearer. Literature: a Roman poet best known for his epic *Aenid*.
Vergil, Virge, Virgial, Virgie, Virgilio

VIRGILIO (Spanish) a form of Virgil.
Virjilio

VIROTE (Tai) strong, powerful.

VISHAL (Hindi) huge; great.
Vishaal

VISHNU (Hindi) protector.

VITAS (Latin) alive, vital.
Vidal, Vitus

VITO (Latin) a short form of Vittorio.
Veit, Vidal, Vital, Vitale, Vitalis, Vitas, Vitin, Vitis, Vitus, Vitya, Vytas

VITTORIO (Italian) a form of Victor.
Vito, Vitor, Vitorio, Vittore, Vittorios

VITYA (Russian) a form of Victor.
Vitenka, Vitka

VIVEK (Hindi) wisdom.
Vivekinan

VLADIMIR (Russian) famous prince.
See also Dima, Waldemar, Walter.
*Bladimir, Vimka, Vlad, Vladamir, Vladik,
Vladimar, Vladimeer, Vladimer, Vladimere,
Vladimire, Vladimyr, Vladjimir, Vladka,
Vladko, Vladlen, Vladmir, Volodimir,
Volodya, Volya, Vova, Wladimir*

VLADISLAV (Slavic) glorious ruler.
See also Slava.
*Vladik, Vladya, Vlas, Vlasislava,
Vyacheslav, Wladislav*

VLAS (Russian) a short form of
Vladislav.

VOLKER (German) people's guard.
Folke

VOLNEY (German) national spirit.

VON (German) a short form of many
German names.

VOVA (Russian) a form of Walter.
Vovka

VUAI (Swahili) savior.

VYACHESLAV (Russian) a form of
Vladislav. See also Slava.

WABAN (Chippewa) white.
Wabon

WADE (English) ford; river crossing.
*Wad, Wadesworth, Wadi, Wadie, Waed,
Waid, Waide, Wayde, Waydell, Whaid*

WADLEY (English) ford meadow.
Wadleigh, Wadly

WADSWORTH (English) village near
the ford.
Waddsworth

WAGNER (German) wagoner, wagon
maker. Music: Richard Wagner was
a famous German composer.
Waggoner

WAHID (Arabic) single; exclusively
unequaled.
Waheed

WAHKAN (Lakota) sacred.

WAHKOOWAH (Lakota) charging.

WAIN (English) a short form of
Wainwright. An alternate form of
Wayne.

WAINWRIGHT (English) wagon
maker.
*Wain, Wainright, Wayne, Wayneright,
Waynewright, Waynright, Wright*

WAITE (English) watchman.
Waitman, Waiton, Waits, Wayte

WAKEFIELD (English) wet field.
Field, Wake

WAKELY (English) wet meadow.

WAKEMAN (English) watchman.
Wake

WAKIZA (Native American)
determined warrior.

WALCOTT (English) cottage by the
wall.
Wallcot, Wallcott, Wolcott

WALDEMAR (German) powerful;
famous. See also Vladimir.
Valdemar, Waldermar, Waldo

WALDEN (English) wooded valley. Literature: Henry David Thoreau made Walden Pond famous with his book *Walden*.
Waldi, Waldo, Waldon, Welti

WALDO (German) a familiar form of Oswald, Waldemar, Walden.
Wald, Waldy

WALDRON (English) ruler.

WALEED (Arabic) newborn.
Waled, Walid

WALERIAN (Polish) strong; brave.

WALES (English) from Wales, England.
Wael, Wail, Wali, Walie, Waly

WALFORD (English) Welshman's ford.

WALFRED (German) peaceful ruler.
Walfredo, Walfried

WALI (Arabic) all-governing.

WALKER (English) cloth walker; cloth cleaner.
Wallie, Wally

WALLACE (English) from Wales.
Wallach, Wallas, Wallie, Wallis, Wally, Walsh, Welsh

WALLACH (German) a form of Wallace.
Wallache

WALLER (German) powerful. (English) wall maker.

WALLY (English) a familiar form of Walter.
Walli, Wallie

WALMOND (German) mighty ruler.

WALSH (English) an alternate form of Wallace.
Welch, Welsh

WALT (English) a short form of Walter, Walton.
Waltey, Waltli, Walty

WALTER (German) army ruler, general. (English) woodsman. See also Gautier, Gualberto, Gualtiero, Gutierre, Ladislav, Vladimir.
Valter, Vanda, Vova, Walder, Wally, Walt, Waltli, Walther, Waltr, Wat, Waterio, Watkins, Watson, Wualter

WALTHER (German) an alternate form of Walter.

WALTON (English) walled town.
Walt

WALTR (Czech) a form of Walter.

WALWORTH (English) fenced-in farm.

WALWYN (English) Welsh friend.
Walwin, Walwinn, Walwynn, Walwynne, Welwyn

WAMBLEE (Lakota) eagle.

WANG (Chinese) hope; wish.

WANIKIYA (Lakota) savior.

WANYA (Russian) an alternate form of Vanya.
Wanyai

WAPI (Native American) lucky.

WARBURTON (English) fortified town.

WARD (English) watchman, guardian.
Warde, Warden, Worden

WARDELL (English) watchman's hill.

WARDLEY (English) watchman's meadow.
Wardlea, Wardleigh

WARE (English) wary, cautious.

WARFIELD (English) field near the weir; fishtrap.

WARFORD (English) ford near the weir; fishtrap.

WARLEY (English) meadow near the weir; fishtrap.

WARNER (German) armed defender. (French) park keeper.
Werner

WARREN (German) general; warden; rabbit hutch.
Ware, Waring, Warrenson, Warrin, Warriner, Worrin

WARTON (English) town near the weir; fishtrap.

WARWICK (English) buildings near the weir; fishtrap.
Warick, Warrick

WASHBURN (English) overflowing river.

WASHINGTON (English) town near water. History: George Washington was the first U.S. president.
Wash

WASILI (Russian) a form of Basil.
Wasyl

WASIM (Arabic) graceful; good looking.
Waseem, Wasseem, Wassim

WATENDE (Nyakyusa) there will be revenge.

WATERIO (Spanish) a form of Walter.
Gualtiero

WATFORD (English) wattle ford; dam made of twigs and sticks.

WATKINS (English) son of Walter.
Watkin

WATSON (English) son of Walter.
Wathson, Whatson

WAVERLY (English) quaking aspen-tree meadow.
Waverlee, Waverley

WAYLAND (English) an alternate form of Waylon.
Weiland, Weyland

WAYLON (English) land by the road.
Wallen, Walon, Way, Waylan, Wayland, Waylen, Waylin, Weylin

WAYMAN (English) road man; traveler.
Waymon

WAYNE (English) wagon maker. A short form of Wainwright.
Wain, Wanye, Wayn, Waynell, Waynne, Wene, Whayne

WAZIR (Arabic) minister.

WEBB (English) weaver.
Web, Weeb

WEBER (German) weaver.
Webber, Webner

WEBLEY (English) weaver's meadow.
Webbley, Webbly, Webly

WEBSTER (English) weaver.

WEDDEL (English) valley near the ford.

WEI-QUO (Chinese) ruler of the country.
Wei

WELBORNE (English) spring-fed stream.
Welborn, Welbourne, Welburn, Wellborn, Wellborne, Wellbourn, Wellburn

WELBY (German) farm near the well.
Welbey, Welbie, Wellbey, Wellby

WELDON (English) hill near the well.
Weldan

WELFEL (Yiddish) a form of William.
Welvel

WELFORD (English) ford near the well.

WELLS (English) springs.
Welles

WELSH (English) an alternate form of Wallace, Walsh.
Welch

WELTON (English) town near the well.

WEMILAT (Native American) all give to him.

WEMILO (Native American) all speak to him.

WEN (Gypsy) born in winter.

WENCESLAUS (Slavic) wreath of honor. Music: 'Good King Wenceslaus' is a popular Christmas carol.
Vencel, Wenceslao, Wenceslas, Wenzel, Wenzell, Wiencyslaw

WENDELL (German) wanderer. (English) good dale, good valley.
Wandale, Wendall, Wendel, Wendle, Wendy

WENE (Hawaiian) a form of Wayne.

WENFORD (English) white ford.
Wynford

WENTWORTH (English) pale man's settlement.

WENUTU (Native American) clear sky.

WERNER (English) a form of Warner.
Wernhar, Wernher

WES (English) a short form of Wesley.
Wess

WESH (Gypsy) woods.

WESLEY (English) western meadow.
Wes, Weseley, Wesle, Weslee, Wesleyan, Weslie, Wesly, Wessley, Westleigh, Westley, Wezley

WEST (English) west.

WESTBROOK (English) western brook.
Brook, West, Westbrooke

WESTBY (English) western farmstead.

WESTCOTT (English) western cottage.
Wescot, Wescott, Westcot

WESTLEY (English) an alternate form of Wesley.
Westlee, Westly

WESTON (English) western town.
West, Westen, Westin

WETHERBY (English) wether-sheep farm.
Weatherbey, Weatherbie, Weatherby, Wetherbey, Wetherbie

WETHERELL (English) wether-sheep corner.

WETHERLY (English) wether-sheep meadow.

WEYLIN (English) an alternate form of Waylon.
Weylan, Weylyn

WHALLEY (English) woods near a hill.
Whaley

WHARTON (English) town on the bank of a lake.
Warton

WHEATLEY (English) wheat field.
Whatley, Wheatlea, Wheatleigh, Wheatly

WHEATON (English) wheat town.

WHEELER (English) wheel maker; wagon driver.

WHISTLER (English) whistler, piper.

WHIT (English) a short form of Whitman, Whitney.
Whitt, Whyt, Whyte, Wit, Witt

WHITBY (English) white house.

WHITCOMB (English) white valley.
Whitcombe, Whitcumb

WHITELAW (English) small hill.
Whitlaw

WHITEY (English) white skinned; white haired.

WHITFIELD (English) white field.

WHITFORD (English) white ford.

WHITLEY (English) white meadow.
Whitlea, Whitlee, Whitleigh

WHITMAN (English) white- haired man.
Whit

WHITMORE (English) white moor.
Whitmoor, Whittemore, Witmore, Wittemore

WHITNEY (English) white island; white water.
Whit, Whittney, Widney, Widny

WHITTAKER (English) white field.
Whitacker, Whitaker, Whitmaker

WICASA (Dakota) man.

WICENT (Polish) a form of Vincent.
Wicek, Wicus

WICHADO (Native American) willing.

WICKHAM (English) village enclosure.
Wick

WICKLEY (English) village meadow.
Wilcley

WID (English) wide.

WIES (German) renowned warrior.

WIKOLI (Hawaiian) a form of Victor.

WIKTOR (Polish) a form of Victor.

WILANU (Moquelumnan) pouring water on flour.

WILBERT (German) brilliant; resolute.
Wilberto, Wilburt

WILBUR (English) wall fortification; bright willows.
Wilber, Wilburn, Wilburt, Willbur, Wilver

WILDER (English) wilderness, wild.
Wylder

WILDON (English) wooded hill.
Wilden, Willdon

WILE (Hawaiian) a form of Willie.

WILEY (English) willow meadow; Will's meadow.
Whiley, Wildy, Willey, Wylie

WILFORD (English) willow-tree ford.
Wilferd

WILFRED (German) determined peacemaker.
Wilferd, Wilfredo, Wilfrid, Wilfride, Wilfried, Wilfryd, Will, Willfred, Willfried, Willie, Willy

WILFREDO (Spanish) a form of Wilfred.
Fredo, Wifredo, Wilfrido, Willfredo

WILHELM (German) determined guardian. The original form of William.
Wilhelmus, Willem

WILIAMA (Hawaiian) a form of William.
Pila, Wile

WILKIE (English) a familiar form of Wilkins.
Wikie, Wilke

WILKINS (English) William's kin.
Wilkens, Wilkes, Wilkie, Wilkin, Wilks, Willkes, Willkins

WILKINSON (English) son of little William.
Wilkenson, Willkinson

WILL (English) a short form of William.
Wil, Wilm, Wim

WILLARD (German) determined and brave.
Williard

WILLEM (German) a form of William.
Willim

WILLIAM (English) determined guardian. See also Gilamu, Guglielmo, Guilherme, Guillaume, Guillermo, Gwilym, Liam, Uilliam, Wilhelm.
Bill, Billy, Vasyl, Vilhelm, Vili, Viliam, Viljo, Ville, Villiam, Welfel, Wilek, Wiliam, Wiliama, Wiliame, Wiliame, Will, Willaim, Willam, Willeam, Willem, Williams, Willie, Willil, Willis, Willium, Williw, Willyam, Wim

WILLIAMS (German) son of William.
Wilams, Willaims, Williamson, Wuliams

WILLIE (German) a familiar form of William.
Wile, Wille, Willi, Willia, Willy

WILLIS (German) son of Willie.
Willice, Wills, Willus, Wyllis

WILLOUGHBY (English) willow farm.
Willoughbey, Willoughbie

WILLS (English) son of Will.

WILLY (German) an alternate form of Willie.
Willey, Wily

WILMER (German) determined and famous.
Willimar, Willmer, Wilm, Wilmar, Wylmar, Wylmer

WILMOT (Teutonic) resolute spirit.
Willmont, Willmot, Wilm, Wilmont

WILNY (Native American) eagle singing while flying.

WILSON (English) son of Will.
Wilkinson, Willson, Wilsen, Wolson

WILT (English) a short form of Wilton.

WILTON (English) farm by the spring.
Will, Wilt

WILU (Moquelumnan) chicken hawk squawking.

WIN (Cambodian) bright. (English) a short form of Winston and names ending in 'win.'
Winn, Winnie, Winny

WINCENT (Polish) a form of Vincent.
Wicek, Wicenty, Wicus, Wince, Wincenty

WINCHELL (English) bend in the road; bend in the land.

WINDSOR (English) riverbank with a winch. History: the surname of the British royal family.
Wincer, Winsor, Wyndsor

WINFIELD (English) friendly field.
Field, Winfred, Winfrey, Winifield, Winnfield, Wynfield, Wynnfield

WINFRIED (German) friend of peace.

WING (Chinese) glory.
Wing-Chiu, Wing-Kit

WINGATE (English) winding gate.

WINGI (Native American) willing.

WINSLOW (English) friend's hill.

WINSTON (English) friendly town; victory town.
Win, Winsten, Winstin, Winstonn, Winton, Wynstan, Wynston

WINTER (English) born in winter.
Winterford, Wynter

WINTHROP (English) victory at the crossroads.

WINTON (English) an alternate form of Winston.
Wynten, Wynton

WINWARD (English) friend's guardian; friend's forest.

WIT (Polish) life. (English) an alternate form of Whit. (Flemish) a short form of DeWitt.
Witt, Wittie, Witty

WITEK (Polish) a form of Victor.

WITHA (Arabic) handsome.

WITTER (English) wise warrior.

WITTON (English) wise man's estate.

WLADISLAV (Polish) a form of Vladislav.
Wladislaw

WOLCOTT (English) cottage in the woods.

WOLF (German, English) a short form of Wolfe, Wolfgang.
Wolff, Wolfie, Wolfy

WOLFE (English) wolf.
Wolf, Woolf

WOLFGANG (German) wolf quarrel. Music: Wolfgang Amadeus Mozart was a famous eighteenth-century Austrian composer.
Wolf, Wolfegang, Wolfgans

WOOD (English) a short form of Elwood, Garwood, Woodrow.
Woody

WOODFIELD (English) forest meadow.

WOODFORD (English) ford through the forest.

WOODROW (English) passage in the woods. History: Thomas Woodrow Wilson was the twenty-eighth U.S. president.
Wood, Woodman, Woodroe, Woody

WOODRUFF (English) forest ranger.

WOODSON (English) son of Wood.
Woods, Woodsen

WOODWARD (English) forest warden.
Woodard

WOODVILLE (English) town at the edge of the woods.

WOODY (American) a familiar form of Elwood, Garwood, Woodrow.
Wooddy, Woodie

WOOLSEY (English) victorious wolf.

WORCESTER (English) forest army camp.

WORDSWORTH (English) wolf-guardian's farm. Literature: William Wordsworth was a famous English poet.
Worth

WORIE (Ibo) born on market day.

WORTH (English) a short form of Woodsworth.
Worthey, Worthington, Worthy

WORTON (English) farm town.

WOUTER (German) powerful warrior.

WRANGLE (American) an alternate form of Rangle.
Wrangler

WRAY (Scandinavian) corner property. (English) crooked.
Wreh

WREN (Welsh) chief, ruler. (English) wren.

WRIGHT (English) a short form of Wainwright.

WRISLEY (English) an alternate form of Risley.
Wrisee, Wrislie, Wrisly

WRISTON (English) an alternate form of Riston.
Wryston

WULITON (Native American) will do well.

WUNAND (Native American) God is good.

WUYI (Moquelumnan) turkey vulture flying.

WYATT (French) little warrior.
Wiatt, Wyat, Wyatte, Wye, Wyeth, Wyett, Wyitt, Wytt

WYBERT (English) battle-bright.

WYBORN (Scandinavian) war bear.

WYCK (Scandinavian) village.

WYCLIFF (English) white cliff; village near the cliff.
Wyckliffe, Wycliffe

WYLIE (English) charming.
Wiley, Wye, Wyley, Wyllie, Wyly

WYMAN (English) fighter, warrior.

WYMER (English) famous in battle.

WYN (Welsh) light skinned, white. (English) friend. A short form of Selwyn.
Win, Wyne, Wynn, Wynne

WYNDHAM (Scottish) village near the winding road.
Windham, Wynndham

WYNONO (Native American) first-born son.

WYTHE (English) willow tree.

X

XABAT (Basque) savior.

XAIVER (Basque) an alternate form of Xavier.
Xajavier, Xzaiver

XAN (Greek) a short form of Alexander.
Xane

XANDER (Greek) a short form of Alexander.
Xande, Xzander

XANTHUS (Latin) golden haired.
Xanthos

XARLES (Basque) a form of Charles.

XAVIER (Arabic) bright. (Basque) owner of the new house. See also Exavier, Javier, Salvatore, Saverio.
Xabier, Xaiver, Xavaeir, Xaver, Xavian, Xaviar, Xavior, Xavon, Xavyer, Xever, Xizavier, Xxavier, Xzavier, Zavier

XENOPHON (Greek) strange voice.
Xeno, Zennie

XENOS (Greek) stranger; guest.
Zenos

XERXES (Persian) ruler. History: a name used by many Persian emperors.
Zerk

XIMENES (Spanish) a form of Simon.
Ximenez, Ximon, Ximun, Xymenes

XYLON (Greek) forest.

XZAVIER (Basque) an alternate form of Xavier.
Xzavaier, Xzaver, Xzavion, Xzavior, Xzvaier

Y

YADID (Hebrew) friend; beloved.
Yedid

YADON (Hebrew) he will judge.
Yadean, Yadin, Yadun

YAEL (Hebrew) an alternate form of Jael.

YAFEU (Ibo) bold.

YAGIL (Hebrew) he will rejoice.

YAGO (Spanish) a form of James.

YAHTO (Lakota) blue.

YAHYA (Arabic) living.
Yahye

YAIR (Hebrew) he will enlighten.
Yahir

YAKECEN (Dene) sky song.

YAKEZ (Carrier) heaven.

YAKOV (Russian) a form of Jacob.
Yaacob, Yaacov, Yaakov, Yachov, Yacoub, Yacov, Yakob, Yashko

YALE (German) productive. (English) old.

YAN, Yann (Russian) forms of John.
Yanichek, Yanick, Yanka, Yannick

YANA (Native American) bear.

YANCY (Native American) Englishman, Yankee.
Yan, Yance, Yancey, Yanci, Yansey, Yansy, Yantsey, Yauncey, Yauncy, Yency

YANICK, Yannick (Russian) familiar forms of Yan.
Yanic, Yanik, Yannic, Yannik, Yonic, Yonnik

YANKA (Russian) a familiar form of John.
Yanikm

YANNI (Greek) a form of John.
Ioannis, Yani, Yannakis, Yannis, Yanny, Yiannis, Yoni

YANTON (Hebrew) an alternate form of Johnathon, Jonathon.

YAO (Ewe) born on Thursday.

YAPHET (Hebrew) an alternate form of Japheth.
Yapheth, Yefat, Yephat

YARB (Gypsy) herb.

YARDAN (Arabic) king.

YARDEN (Hebrew) an alternate form of Jordan. Geography: another name for the Jordan River, which flows through Israel.

YARDLEY (English) enclosed meadow.
Lee, Yard, Yardlea, Yardlee, Yardleigh, Yardly

YAROM (Hebrew) he will raise up.
Yarum

YARON (Hebrew) he will sing; he will cry out.
Jaron, Yairon

YASASHIKU (Japanese) gentle; polite.

YASH (Hindi) victorious; glory.

YASHA (Russian) a form of Jacob, James.
Yascha, Yashka, Yashko

YASHWANT (Hindi) glorious.

YASIN (Arabic) prophet. Religion: another name for Muhammad.
Yasine, Yasseen, Yassin, Yassine, Yazen

YASIR (Afghani) humble; takes it easy. (Arabic) wealthy.

Yasar, Yaser, Yashar, Yasser

YASUO (Japanese) restful.

YATES (English) gates.
Yeats

YATIN (Hindi) ascetic.

YAVIN (Hebrew) he will understand.
Jabin

YAWO (Akan) born on Thursday.

YAZID (Arabic) his power will increase.
Yazeed, Yazide

YECHIEL (Hebrew) God lives.

YEDIDYA (Hebrew) an alternate form of Jedidiah. See also Didi.
Yadai, Yedidia, Yedidiah, Yido

YEGOR (Russian) a form of George. See also Egor, Igor.
Ygor

YEHOSHUA (Hebrew) an alternate form of Joshua.
Yeshua, Yeshuah, Yoshua, Y'shua, Yushua

YEHOYAKEM (Hebrew) an alternate form of Joachim, Joaquín.
Yakim, Yehayakim, Yokim, Yoyakim

YEHUDI (Hebrew) an alternate form of Judah.
Yechudi, Yechudit, Yehuda, Yehudah, Yehudit

YELUTCI (Moquelumnan) bear walking silently.

YEOMAN (English) attendant; retainer.
Yoeman, Youman

YEREMEY (Russian) a form of Jeremiah.
Yarema, Yaremka, Yeremy, Yerik

YERVANT (Armenian) king, ruler. History: an Armenian king.

YESHAYA (Hebrew) gift. See also Shai.

YESHURUN (Hebrew) right way.

YESKA (Russian) a form of Joseph.
Yesya

YESTIN (Welsh) just.

YEVGENYI (Russian) a form of Eugene.
Gena, Yevgeni, Yevgenij, Yevgeniy

YIGAL (Hebrew) he will redeem.
Yagel, Yigael

YIRMAYA (Hebrew) an alternate form of Jeremiah.
Yirmayahu

YISHAI (Hebrew) an alternate form of Jesse.

YISRAEL (Hebrew) an alternate form of Israel.
Yesarel, Yisroel

YITRO (Hebrew) an alternate form of Jethro.

YITZCHAK (Hebrew) an alternate form of Isaac. See also Itzak.
Yitzak, Yitzchok, Yitzhak

YNGVE (Swedish) ancestor; lord, master.

YO (Cambodian) honest.

YOAKIM (Slavic) a form of Jacob.
Yoackim

YOAN (German) an alternate form of Johan, Johann.
Yoann

YOAV (Hebrew) an alternate form of Joab.

YOCHANAN (Hebrew) an alternate form of John.
Yohanan

YOEL (Hebrew) an alternate form of Joel.

YOGESH (Hindi) ascetic. Religion: another name for the Hindu god Shiva.

YOHANCE (Hausa) a form of John.

YOHAN, Yohann (German) forms of Johan, Johann.
Yohane, Yohanes, Yohanne, Yohannes, Yohans, Yohn

YONAH (Hebrew) an alternate form of Jonah.
Yona, Yonas

YONATAN (Hebrew) an alternate form of Jonathan.
Yonathan, Yonathon, Yonaton, Yonattan

YONG (Chinese) courageous.
Yonge

YONG-SUN (Korean) dragon in the first position; courageous.

YONI (Greek) an alternate form of Yanni.
Yonis, Yonnas, Yonny, Yony

YOOFI (Akan) born on Friday.

YOOKU (Fante) born on Wednesday.

YORAM (Hebrew) high God.
Joram

YORGOS (Greek) an alternate form of George.
Yiorgos, Yorgo

YORK (English) boar estate; yew-tree estate.
Yorick, Yorke, Yorker, Yorkie, Yorrick

YORKOO (Fante) born on Thursday.

YOSEF (Hebrew) an alternate form of Joseph. See also Osip.
Yoceph, Yoosuf, Yoseff, Yoseph, Yosief, Yosif, Yosuf, Yosyf, Yousef, Yusif

YÓSHI (Japanese) adopted son.
Yoshiki, Yoshiuki

YOSHIYAHU (Hebrew) an alternate form of Josiah.
Yoshia, Yoshiah, Yoshiya, Yoshiyah, Yosiah

YOSKOLO (Moquelumnan) breaking off pinecones.

YOSU (Hebrew) an alternate form of Jesus.

YOTIMO (Moquelumnan) yellow jacket carrying food to its hive.

YOTTOKO (Native American) mud at the water's edge.

YOUNG (English) young.
Yung

YOUNG-JAE (Korean) pile of prosperity.

YOUNG-SOO (Korean) keeping the prosperity.

YOURI (Russian) an alternate form of Yuri.

YOUSEF (Yiddish) a form of Joseph.
Yousaf, Youseef, Yousef, Youseph, Yousif, Youssef, Yousseff, Yousuf

YOUSSEL (Yiddish) a familiar form of Joseph.
Yussel

YOV (Russian) a short form of Yoakim.

YOVANI (Slavic) an alternate form of Jovan.
Yovan, Yovanni, Yovanny, Yovany, Yovni

YOYI (Hebrew) a form of George.

YRJO (Finnish) a form of George.

YSIDRO (Greek) a short form of Isidore.

YU (Chinese) universe.
Yue

YUDELL (English) an alternate form of Udell.
Yudale, Yudel

YUKI (Japanese) snow.
Yukiko, Yukio, Yuuki

YUL (Mongolian) beyond the horizon.

YULE (English) born at Christmas.

YULI (Basque) youthful.

YUMA (Native American) son of a chief.

YUNUS (Turkish) a form of Jonah.

YURCEL (Turkish) sublime.

YURI (Russian, Ukrainian) a form of George. (Hebrew) a familiar form of Uriah.
Yehor, Youri, Yura, Yure, Yuric, Yurii, Yurij, Yurik, Yurko, Yurri, Yury, Yusha

YUSIF (Russian) a form of Joseph.
Yuseph, Yusof, Yussof, Yusup, Yuzef, Yuzep

YUSTYN (Russian) a form of Justin.
Yusts

YUSUF (Arabic, Swahili) a form of Joseph.
Yusef, Yusuff

YUTU (Moquelumnan) coyote out hunting.

YUVAL (Hebrew) rejoicing.

YVES (French) a form of Ivar, Ives.
Yvens, Yvon, Yyves

YVON (French) an alternate form of Ivar, Yves.
Ivon, Yuvon, Yvan, Yvonne

Z

ZAC (Hebrew) a short form of Zachariah, Zachary.
Zacc

ZACARIAS (Portuguese, Spanish) a form of Zachariah.
Zacaria, Zacariah

ZACARY (Hebrew) an alternate form of Zachary.
Zac, Zacaras, Zacari, Zacariah, Zacarias, Zacarie, Zacarious, Zacery, Zacory, Zacrye

ZACCARY (Hebrew) an alternate form of Zachary.
Zac, Zaccaeus, Zaccari, Zaccaria, Zaccariah, Zaccary, Zaccea, Zaccharie, Zacchary, Zacchery, Zaccury

ZACCHEUS (Hebrew) innocent, pure.
Zacceus, Zacchaeus, Zacchious

ZACH (Hebrew) a short form of Zachariah, Zachary.

ZACHARI (Hebrew) an alternate form of Zachary.
Zacheri

ZACHARIA (Hebrew) an alternate form of Zachary.
Zacharya

ZACHARIAH (Hebrew) God remembered.
Zac, Zacarias, Zacarius, Zacary, Zaccary, Zach, Zacharias, Zachary, Zacharyah, Zachory, Zachury, Zack, Zakaria, Zako, Zaquero, Zecharia, Zechariah, Zecharya, Zeggery, Zeke, Zhachory

ZACHARIAS (German) a form of Zachariah.
Zacarías, Zacharais, Zachariaus, Zacharius, Zackarias, Zakarias, Zecharias, Zekarias

ZACHARIE (Hebrew) an alternate
form of Zachary.
Zachare, Zacharee, Zachurie, Zecharie

ZACHARY (Hebrew) God remembered.
A familiar form of Zachariah. History:
Zachary Taylor was the twelfth U.S.
president. See also Sachar, Sakeri.
*Xachary, Zac, Zacary, Zaccary, Zach, Zacha,
Zachaery, Zachaios, Zacharay, Zacharey,
Zachari, Zacharia, Zacharias, Zacharie,
Zacharry, Zachaury, Zachery, Zachory,
Zachrey, Zachry, Zachuery, Zachury, Zack,
Zackary, Zackery, Zackory, Zakaria, Zakary,
Zakery, Zakkary, Zechary, Zechery, Zeke*

ZACHERY (Hebrew) an alternate form
of Zachary.
*Zacheray, Zacherey, Zacheria, Zacherias,
Zacheriah, Zacherie, Zacherius, Zackery*

ZACHORY (Hebrew) an alternate form
of Zachary.

ZACHRY (Hebrew) an alternate form of
Zachary.
Zachre, Zachrey, Zachri

ZACK (Hebrew) a short form of
Zachariah, Zachary.
Zach, Zak, Zaks

ZACKARY (Hebrew) an alternate form
of Zachary.
*Zack, Zackari, Zacharia, Zackare, Zackaree,
Zackariah, Zackarie, Zackery, Zackhary,
Zackie, Zackree, Zackrey, Zackry*

ZACKERY (Hebrew) an alternate form
of Zachery.
*Zackere, Zackeree, Zackerey, Zackeri,
Zackeria, Zackeriah, Zackerie, Zackerry*

ZACKORY (Hebrew) an alternate form
of Zachary.
*Zackoriah, Zackorie, Zacorey, Zacori,
Zacory, Zacry, Zakory*

ZADOK (Hebrew) a short form of
Tzadok.
Zaddik, Zadik, Zadoc, Zaydok

ZADORNIN (Basque) Saturn.

ZAFIR (Arabic) victorious.
Zafar, Zafeer, Zafer, Zaffar

ZAHID (Arabic) self-denying, ascetic.
Zaheed

ZAHIR (Arabic) shining, bright.
*Zahair, Zahar, Zaheer, Zahi, Zair, Zaire,
Zayyir*

ZAHUR (Swahili) flower.

ZAID (Arabic) increase, growth.
Zaied, Zaiid, Zayd

ZAIDE (Hebrew) older.

ZAIM (Arabic) brigadier general.

ZAIN (English) an alternate form of
Zane.
Zaine

ZAKARIA (Hebrew) an alternate form
of Zachariah.
*Zakaraiya, Zakareeya, Zakareeyah,
Zakariah, Zakariya, Zakeria, Zakeriah*

ZAKARIYYA (Arabic) prophet.
Religion: an Islamic prophet.

ZAKARY (Hebrew) an alternate form of
Zachery.
*Zak, Zakarai, Zakare, Zakaree, Zakari,
Zakarias, Zakarie, Zakarius, Zakariye, Zake,
Zakhar, Zaki, Zakir, Zakkai, Zako, Zakqary,
Zakree, Zakri, Zakris, Zakry*

ZAKERY (Hebrew) an alternate form of
Zachary.
Zakeri, Zakerie, Zakiry

ZAKI (Arabic) bright; pure. (Hausa) lion.
Zakee, Zakia, Zakie, Zakiy, Zakki

ZAKIA (Swahili) intelligent.

ZAKKARY (Hebrew) an alternate form
of Zachary.
Zakk, Zakkari, Zakkery, Zakkyre

ZAKO (Hungarian) a form of Zachariah.

ZALE (Greek) sea-strength.
Zayle

ZALMAI (Afghani) young.

ZALMAN (Yiddish) a form of Solomon.
Zaloman

ZAMIEL (German) a form of Samuel.
Zamal, Zamuel

ZAMIR (Hebrew) song; bird.
Zameer

ZAN (Italian) clown.
Zann, Zanni, Zannie, Zanny, Zhan

ZANDER (Greek) a short form of Alexander.
Zandore, Zandra, Zandrae, Zandy

ZANE (English) a form of John.
Zain, Zayne, Zhane

ZANIS (Latvian) an alternate form of Janis.
Zannis

ZANVIL (Hebrew) an alternate form of Samuel.
Zanwill

ZAQUAN (American) a combination of the prefix Za + Quan.
Zaquain, Zaquon, Zaqwan

ZAREB (African) protector.

ZARED (Hebrew) ambush.
Zaryd

ZAREK (Polish) may God protect the king.
Zarik, Zarrick, Zerek, Zerick, Zerric, Zerrick

ZAVIER (Arabic) an alternate form of Xavier.
Zavair, Zaverie, Zavery, Zavierre, Zavior, Zavyr, Zayvius, Zxavian

ZAYIT (Hebrew) olive.

ZAYNE (English) an alternate form of Zane.
Zayan, Zayin, Zayn

ZDENEK (Czech) follower of Saint Denis.

ZEB (Hebrew) a short form of Zebediah, Zebulon.
Zev

ZEBEDIAH (Hebrew) God's gift.
Zeb, Zebadia, Zebadiah, Zebedee, Zebedia, Zebidiah, Zedidiah

ZEBEDEE (Hebrew) a familiar form of Zebediah.
Zebadee

ZEBULON (Hebrew) exalted, honored; lofty house.
Zabulan, Zeb, Zebulan, Zebulen, Zebulin, Zebulun, Zebulyn, Zev, Zevulon, Zevulun, Zhebulen, Zubin

ZECHARIAH (Hebrew) an alternate form of Zachariah.
Zecharia, Zecharian, Zecheriah, Zechuriah, Zekariah, Zekarias, Zeke, Zekeria, Zekeriah, Zekerya

ZED (Hebrew) a short form of Zedekiah.

ZEDEKIAH (Hebrew) God is mighty and just.
Zed, Zedechiah, Zedekias, Zedikiah

ZEDIDIAH (Hebrew) an alternate form of Zebediah.

ZEEMAN (Dutch) seaman.

ZEÉV (Hebrew) wolf.
Zeévi, Zeff, Zif

ZEHEB (Turkish) gold.

ZEKE (Hebrew) a short form of Ezekiel, Zachariah, Zachary, Zechariah.

ZEKI (Turkish) clever, intelligent.
Zeky

ZELGAI (Afghani) heart.

ZELIG (Yiddish) a form of Selig.
Zeligman, Zelik

ZELIMIR (Slavic) wishes for peace.

ZEMAR (Afghani) lion.

ZEN (Japanese) religious. Religion: a form of Buddhism.

ZENDA (Czech) a form of Eugene.
Zhek

ZENO (Greek) cart; harness. History: a Greek philosopher.
Zenan, Zenas, Zenon, Zino, Zinon

ZEPHANIAH (Hebrew) treasured by God.
Zaph, Zaphania, Zeph, Zephan

ZEPHYR (Greek) west wind.
Zeferino, Zeffrey, Zephery, Zephire, Zephram, Zephran, Zephrin

ZERO (Arabic) empty, void.

ZEROUN (Armenian) wise and respected.

ZESHAWN (American) a combination of the prefix Ze + Shawn.
Zeshan, Zeshaun, Zeshon, Zishaan, Zishan, Zshawn

ZESIRO (Luganda) older of twins.

ZEUS (Greek) living. Mythology: chief god in the Greek pantheon who ruled from Mount Olympus.

ZEUSEF (Portuguese) a form of Joseph.

ZEV (Hebrew) a short form of Zebulon.

ZEVI (Hebrew) an alternate form of Tzvi.
Zhvie, Zhvy, Zvi

ZHEK (Russian) a short form of Evgeny.
Zhenechka, Zhenka, Zhenya

ZHÌXIN (Chinese) ambitious.
Zhi, Zhìhuán, Zhipeng, Zhi-yang, Zhìyuan

ZHUÀNG (Chinese) strong.

ZHORA (Russian) a form of George.
Zhorik, Zhorka, Zhorz, Zhurka

ZIA (Hebrew) trembling; moving.
Ziah

ZIGFRID (Latvian, Russian) a form of Siegfried.
Zegfrido, Zigfrids, Ziggy, Zygfryd, Zygi

ZIGGY (American) a familiar form of Siegfried, Sigmund.
Ziggie

ZIGOR (Basque) punishment.

ZILABA (Luganda) born while sick.
Zilabamuzale

ZIKOMO (Ngoni) thank you.

ZIMRA (Hebrew) song of praise.
Zemora, Zimrat, Zimri, Zimria, Zimriah, Zimriya

ZIMRAAN (Arabic) praise.

ZINAN (Japanese) second son.

ZINDEL (Yiddish) a form of Alexander.
Zindil, Zunde

ZION (Hebrew) sign, omen; excellent. Bible: name used to refer to the land of Israel and to the Hebrew people.
Tzion, Zyon

ZISKIND (Yiddish) sweet child.

ZIV (Hebrew) shining brightly. (Slavic) a short form of Ziven.

ZIVEN (Slavic) vigorous, lively.
Zev, Ziv, Zivka, Zivon

ZIYAD (Arabic) increase.
Zayd, Ziyaad

ZLATAN (Czech) gold.
Zlatek, Zlatko

ZOHAR (Hebrew) bright light.
Zohair

ZOLLIE, Zolly (Hebrew) alternate forms of Solly.
Zoilo

ZOLTÁN (Hungarian) life.

ZORBA (Greek) live each day.

ZORION (Basque) a form of Orion.
Zoran, Zoren, Zorian, Zoron, Zorrine, Zorrion

ZORYA (Slavic) star; dawn.

ZOTIKOS (Greek) saintly, holy. Religion: a recent saint in the Greek Orthodox church.

ZOTOM (Kiowa) a biter.

ZSIGMOND (Hungarian) a form of Sigmund.
Ziggy, Zigmund, Zsiga

ZUBERI (Swahili) strong.

ZUBIN (Hebrew) a short form of Zebulon.
Zubeen

ZUHAYR (Arabic) brilliant, shining.
Zyhair, Zuheer

ZUKA (Shona) sixpence.

ZURIEL (Hebrew) God is my rock.

ZYGMUNT (Polish) a form of Sigmund.

NOTES

NOTES

NOTES

NOTES